Mometrix

TEST PREPARATION

MW01445484

TExES

Special Education EC-12 (161)

Secrets Study Guide

Exam Review and TExES Practice Test for the Texas Examinations of Educator Standards

Written and edited by Mometrix Test Prep

Printed in the United States of America

This paper meets the requirements of ANSI/NISO Z39.48-1992 (Permanence of Paper).

Paperback
ISBN 13: 978-1-5167-4731-3
ISBN 10: 1-5167-4731-3

DEAR FUTURE EXAM SUCCESS STORY

First of all, **THANK YOU** for purchasing Mometrix study materials!

Second, congratulations! You are one of the few determined test-takers who are committed to doing whatever it takes to excel on your exam. **You have come to the right place.** We developed these study materials with one goal in mind: to deliver you the information you need in a format that's concise and easy to use.

In addition to optimizing your guide for the content of the test, we've outlined our recommended steps for breaking down the preparation process into small, attainable goals so you can make sure you stay on track.

We've also analyzed the entire test-taking process, identifying the most common pitfalls and showing how you can overcome them and be ready for any curveball the test throws you.

Standardized testing is one of the biggest obstacles on your road to success, which only increases the importance of doing well in the high-pressure, high-stakes environment of test day. Your results on this test could have a significant impact on your future, and this guide provides the information and practical advice to help you achieve your full potential on test day.

Your success is our success

We would love to hear from you! If you would like to share the story of your exam success or if you have any questions or comments in regard to our products, please contact us at **800-673-8175** or **support@mometrix.com**.

Thanks again for your business and we wish you continued success!

Sincerely,
The Mometrix Test Preparation Team

Need more help? Check out our flashcards at:
http://MometrixFlashcards.com/TExES

TABLE OF CONTENTS

Introduction

Thank you for purchasing this resource! You have made the choice to prepare yourself for a test that could have a huge impact on your future, and this guide is designed to help you be fully ready for test day. Obviously, it's important to have a solid understanding of the test material, but you also need to be prepared for the unique environment and stressors of the test, so that you can perform to the best of your abilities.

For this purpose, the first section that appears in this guide is the **Secret Keys**. We've devoted countless hours to meticulously researching what works and what doesn't, and we've boiled down our findings to the five most impactful steps you can take to improve your performance on the test. We start at the beginning with study planning and move through the preparation process, all the way to the testing strategies that will help you get the most out of what you know when you're finally sitting in front of the test.

We recommend that you start preparing for your test as far in advance as possible. However, if you've bought this guide as a last-minute study resource and only have a few days before your test, we recommend that you skip over the first two Secret Keys since they address a long-term study plan.

If you struggle with **test anxiety**, we strongly encourage you to check out our recommendations for how you can overcome it. Test anxiety is a formidable foe, but it can be beaten, and we want to make sure you have the tools you need to defeat it.

Secret Key #1 – Plan Big, Study Small

There's a lot riding on your performance. If you want to ace this test, you're going to need to keep your skills sharp and the material fresh in your mind. You need a plan that lets you review everything you need to know while still fitting in your schedule. We'll break this strategy down into three categories.

Information Organization

Start with the information you already have: the official test outline. From this, you can make a complete list of all the concepts you need to cover before the test. Organize these concepts into groups that can be studied together, and create a list of any related vocabulary you need to learn so you can brush up on any difficult terms. You'll want to keep this vocabulary list handy once you actually start studying since you may need to add to it along the way.

Time Management

Once you have your set of study concepts, decide how to spread them out over the time you have left before the test. Break your study plan into small, clear goals so you have a manageable task for each day and know exactly what you're doing. Then just focus on one small step at a time. When you manage your time this way, you don't need to spend hours at a time studying. Studying a small block of content for a short period each day helps you retain information better and avoid stressing over how much you have left to do. You can relax knowing that you have a plan to cover everything in time. In order for this strategy to be effective though, you have to start studying early and stick to your schedule. Avoid the exhaustion and futility that comes from last-minute cramming!

Study Environment

The environment you study in has a big impact on your learning. Studying in a coffee shop, while probably more enjoyable, is not likely to be as fruitful as studying in a quiet room. It's important to keep distractions to a minimum. You're only planning to study for a short block of time, so make the most of it. Don't pause to check your phone or get up to find a snack. It's also important to **avoid multitasking**. Research has consistently shown that multitasking will make your studying dramatically less effective. Your study area should also be comfortable and well-lit so you don't have the distraction of straining your eyes or sitting on an uncomfortable chair.

The time of day you study is also important. You want to be rested and alert. Don't wait until just before bedtime. Study when you'll be most likely to comprehend and remember. Even better, if you know what time of day your test will be, set that time aside for study. That way your brain will be used to working on that subject at that specific time and you'll have a better chance of recalling information.

Finally, it can be helpful to team up with others who are studying for the same test. Your actual studying should be done in as isolated an environment as possible, but the work of organizing the information and setting up the study plan can be divided up. In between study sessions, you can discuss with your teammates the concepts that you're all studying and quiz each other on the details. Just be sure that your teammates are as serious about the test as you are. If you find that your study time is being replaced with social time, you might need to find a new team.

Secret Key #2 – Make Your Studying Count

You're devoting a lot of time and effort to preparing for this test, so you want to be absolutely certain it will pay off. This means doing more than just reading the content and hoping you can remember it on test day. It's important to make every minute of study count. There are two main areas you can focus on to make your studying count.

Retention

It doesn't matter how much time you study if you can't remember the material. You need to make sure you are retaining the concepts. To check your retention of the information you're learning, try recalling it at later times with minimal prompting. Try carrying around flashcards and glance at one or two from time to time or ask a friend who's also studying for the test to quiz you.

To enhance your retention, look for ways to put the information into practice so that you can apply it rather than simply recalling it. If you're using the information in practical ways, it will be much easier to remember. Similarly, it helps to solidify a concept in your mind if you're not only reading it to yourself but also explaining it to someone else. Ask a friend to let you teach them about a concept you're a little shaky on (or speak aloud to an imaginary audience if necessary). As you try to summarize, define, give examples, and answer your friend's questions, you'll understand the concepts better and they will stay with you longer. Finally, step back for a big picture view and ask yourself how each piece of information fits with the whole subject. When you link the different concepts together and see them working together as a whole, it's easier to remember the individual components.

Finally, practice showing your work on any multi-step problems, even if you're just studying. Writing out each step you take to solve a problem will help solidify the process in your mind, and you'll be more likely to remember it during the test.

Modality

Modality simply refers to the means or method by which you study. Choosing a study modality that fits your own individual learning style is crucial. No two people learn best in exactly the same way, so it's important to know your strengths and use them to your advantage.

For example, if you learn best by visualization, focus on visualizing a concept in your mind and draw an image or a diagram. Try color-coding your notes, illustrating them, or creating symbols that will trigger your mind to recall a learned concept. If you learn best by hearing or discussing information, find a study partner who learns the same way or read aloud to yourself. Think about how to put the information in your own words. Imagine that you are giving a lecture on the topic and record yourself so you can listen to it later.

For any learning style, flashcards can be helpful. Organize the information so you can take advantage of spare moments to review. Underline key words or phrases. Use different colors for different categories. Mnemonic devices (such as creating a short list in which every item starts with the same letter) can also help with retention. Find what works best for you and use it to store the information in your mind most effectively and easily.

Secret Key #3 – Practice the Right Way

Your success on test day depends not only on how many hours you put into preparing, but also on whether you prepared the right way. It's good to check along the way to see if your studying is paying off. One of the most effective ways to do this is by taking practice tests to evaluate your progress. Practice tests are useful because they show exactly where you need to improve. Every time you take a practice test, pay special attention to these three groups of questions:

- The questions you got wrong
- The questions you had to guess on, even if you guessed right
- The questions you found difficult or slow to work through

This will show you exactly what your weak areas are, and where you need to devote more study time. Ask yourself why each of these questions gave you trouble. Was it because you didn't understand the material? Was it because you didn't remember the vocabulary? Do you need more repetitions on this type of question to build speed and confidence? Dig into those questions and figure out how you can strengthen your weak areas as you go back to review the material.

Additionally, many practice tests have a section explaining the answer choices. It can be tempting to read the explanation and think that you now have a good understanding of the concept. However, an explanation likely only covers part of the question's broader context. Even if the explanation makes perfect sense, **go back and investigate** every concept related to the question until you're positive you have a thorough understanding.

As you go along, keep in mind that the practice test is just that: practice. Memorizing these questions and answers will not be very helpful on the actual test because it is unlikely to have any of the same exact questions. If you only know the right answers to the sample questions, you won't be prepared for the real thing. **Study the concepts** until you understand them fully, and then you'll be able to answer any question that shows up on the test.

It's important to wait on the practice tests until you're ready. If you take a test on your first day of study, you may be overwhelmed by the amount of material covered and how much you need to learn. Work up to it gradually.

On test day, you'll need to be prepared for answering questions, managing your time, and using the test-taking strategies you've learned. It's a lot to balance, like a mental marathon that will have a big impact on your future. Like training for a marathon, you'll need to start slowly and work your way up. When test day arrives, you'll be ready.

Start with the strategies you've read in the first two Secret Keys—plan your course and study in the way that works best for you. If you have time, consider using multiple study resources to get different approaches to the same concepts. It can be helpful to see difficult concepts from more than one angle. Then find a good source for practice tests. Many times, the test website will suggest potential study resources or provide sample tests.

Practice Test Strategy

If you're able to find at least three practice tests, we recommend this strategy:

Untimed and Open-Book Practice

Take the first test with no time constraints and with your notes and study guide handy. Take your time and focus on applying the strategies you've learned.

Timed and Open-Book Practice

Take the second practice test open-book as well, but set a timer and practice pacing yourself to finish in time.

Timed and Closed-Book Practice

Take any other practice tests as if it were test day. Set a timer and put away your study materials. Sit at a table or desk in a quiet room, imagine yourself at the testing center, and answer questions as quickly and accurately as possible.

Keep repeating timed and closed-book tests on a regular basis until you run out of practice tests or it's time for the actual test. Your mind will be ready for the schedule and stress of test day, and you'll be able to focus on recalling the material you've learned.

Secret Key #4 – Pace Yourself

Once you're fully prepared for the material on the test, your biggest challenge on test day will be managing your time. Just knowing that the clock is ticking can make you panic even if you have plenty of time left. Work on pacing yourself so you can build confidence against the time constraints of the exam. Pacing is a difficult skill to master, especially in a high-pressure environment, so **practice is vital**.

Set time expectations for your pace based on how much time is available. For example, if a section has 60 questions and the time limit is 30 minutes, you know you have to average 30 seconds or less per question in order to answer them all. Although 30 seconds is the hard limit, set 25 seconds per question as your goal, so you reserve extra time to spend on harder questions. When you budget extra time for the harder questions, you no longer have any reason to stress when those questions take longer to answer.

Don't let this time expectation distract you from working through the test at a calm, steady pace, but keep it in mind so you don't spend too much time on any one question. Recognize that taking extra time on one question you don't understand may keep you from answering two that you do understand later in the test. If your time limit for a question is up and you're still not sure of the answer, mark it and move on, and come back to it later if the time and the test format allow. If the testing format doesn't allow you to return to earlier questions, just make an educated guess; then put it out of your mind and move on.

On the easier questions, be careful not to rush. It may seem wise to hurry through them so you have more time for the challenging ones, but it's not worth missing one if you know the concept and just didn't take the time to read the question fully. Work efficiently but make sure you understand the question and have looked at all of the answer choices, since more than one may seem right at first.

Even if you're paying attention to the time, you may find yourself a little behind at some point. You should speed up to get back on track, but do so wisely. Don't panic; just take a few seconds less on each question until you're caught up. Don't guess without thinking, but do look through the answer choices and eliminate any you know are wrong. If you can get down to two choices, it is often worthwhile to guess from those. Once you've chosen an answer, move on and don't dwell on any that you skipped or had to hurry through. If a question was taking too long, chances are it was one of the harder ones, so you weren't as likely to get it right anyway.

On the other hand, if you find yourself getting ahead of schedule, it may be beneficial to slow down a little. The more quickly you work, the more likely you are to make a careless mistake that will affect your score. You've budgeted time for each question, so don't be afraid to spend that time. Practice an efficient but careful pace to get the most out of the time you have.

Secret Key #5 – Have a Plan for Guessing

When you're taking the test, you may find yourself stuck on a question. Some of the answer choices seem better than others, but you don't see the one answer choice that is obviously correct. What do you do?

The scenario described above is very common, yet most test takers have not effectively prepared for it. Developing and practicing a plan for guessing may be one of the single most effective uses of your time as you get ready for the exam.

In developing your plan for guessing, there are three questions to address:

- When should you start the guessing process?
- How should you narrow down the choices?
- Which answer should you choose?

When to Start the Guessing Process

Unless your plan for guessing is to select C every time (which, despite its merits, is not what we recommend), you need to leave yourself enough time to apply your answer elimination strategies. Since you have a limited amount of time for each question, that means that if you're going to give yourself the best shot at guessing correctly, you have to decide quickly whether or not you will guess.

Of course, the best-case scenario is that you don't have to guess at all, so first, see if you can answer the question based on your knowledge of the subject and basic reasoning skills. Focus on the key words in the question and try to jog your memory of related topics. Give yourself a chance to bring the knowledge to mind, but once you realize that you don't have (or you can't access) the knowledge you need to answer the question, it's time to start the guessing process.

It's almost always better to start the guessing process too early than too late. It only takes a few seconds to remember something and answer the question from knowledge. Carefully eliminating wrong answer choices takes longer. Plus, going through the process of eliminating answer choices can actually help jog your memory.

Summary: Start the guessing process as soon as you decide that you can't answer the question based on your knowledge.

How to Narrow Down the Choices

The next chapter in this book (**Test-Taking Strategies**) includes a wide range of strategies for how to approach questions and how to look for answer choices to eliminate. You will definitely want to read those carefully, practice them, and figure out which ones work best for you. Here though, we're going to address a mindset rather than a particular strategy.

Your odds of guessing an answer correctly depend on how many options you are choosing from.

Number of options left	5	4	3	2	1
Odds of guessing correctly	20%	25%	33%	50%	100%

You can see from this chart just how valuable it is to be able to eliminate incorrect answers and make an educated guess, but there are two things that many test takers do that cause them to miss out on the benefits of guessing:

- Accidentally eliminating the correct answer
- Selecting an answer based on an impression

We'll look at the first one here, and the second one in the next section.

To avoid accidentally eliminating the correct answer, we recommend a thought exercise called **the $5 challenge**. In this challenge, you only eliminate an answer choice from contention if you are willing to bet $5 on it being wrong. Why $5? Five dollars is a small but not insignificant amount of money. It's an amount you could afford to lose but wouldn't want to throw away. And while losing $5 once might not hurt too much, doing it twenty times will set you back $100. In the same way, each small decision you make—eliminating a choice here, guessing on a question there—won't by itself impact your score very much, but when you put them all together, they can make a big difference. By holding each answer choice elimination decision to a higher standard, you can reduce the risk of accidentally eliminating the correct answer.

The $5 challenge can also be applied in a positive sense: If you are willing to bet $5 that an answer choice *is* correct, go ahead and mark it as correct.

Summary: Only eliminate an answer choice if you are willing to bet $5 that it is wrong.

Which Answer to Choose

You're taking the test. You've run into a hard question and decided you'll have to guess. You've eliminated all the answer choices you're willing to bet $5 on. Now you have to pick an answer. Why do we even need to talk about this? Why can't you just pick whichever one you feel like when the time comes?

The answer to these questions is that if you don't come into the test with a plan, you'll rely on your impression to select an answer choice, and if you do that, you risk falling into a trap. The test writers know that everyone who takes their test will be guessing on some of the questions, so they intentionally write wrong answer choices to seem plausible. You still have to pick an answer though, and if the wrong answer choices are designed to look right, how can you ever be sure that you're not falling for their trap? The best solution we've found to this dilemma is to take the decision out of your hands entirely. Here is the process we recommend:

Once you've eliminated any choices that you are confident (willing to bet $5) are wrong, select the first remaining choice as your answer.

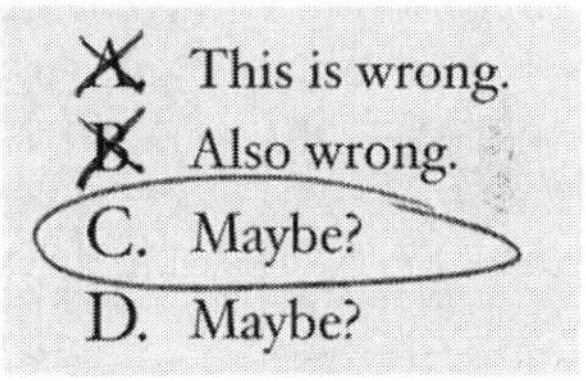

Whether you choose to select the first remaining choice, the second, or the last, the important thing is that you use some preselected standard. Using this approach guarantees that you will not be enticed into selecting an answer choice that looks right, because you are not basing your decision on how the answer choices look.

This is not meant to make you question your knowledge. Instead, it is to help you recognize the difference between your knowledge and your impressions. There's a huge difference between thinking an answer is right because of what you know, and thinking an answer is right because it looks or sounds like it should be right.

Summary: To ensure that your selection is appropriately random, make a predetermined selection from among all answer choices you have not eliminated.

Test-Taking Strategies

This section contains a list of test-taking strategies that you may find helpful as you work through the test. By taking what you know and applying logical thought, you can maximize your chances of answering any question correctly!

It is very important to realize that every question is different and every person is different: no single strategy will work on every question, and no single strategy will work for every person. That's why we've included all of them here, so you can try them out and determine which ones work best for different types of questions and which ones work best for you.

Question Strategies

✓ Read Carefully

Read the question and the answer choices carefully. Don't miss the question because you misread the terms. You have plenty of time to read each question thoroughly and make sure you understand what is being asked. Yet a happy medium must be attained, so don't waste too much time. You must read carefully and efficiently.

✓ Contextual Clues

Look for contextual clues. If the question includes a word you are not familiar with, look at the immediate context for some indication of what the word might mean. Contextual clues can often give you all the information you need to decipher the meaning of an unfamiliar word. Even if you can't determine the meaning, you may be able to narrow down the possibilities enough to make a solid guess at the answer to the question.

✓ Prefixes

If you're having trouble with a word in the question or answer choices, try dissecting it. Take advantage of every clue that the word might include. Prefixes can be a huge help. Usually, they allow you to determine a basic meaning. *Pre-* means before, *post-* means after, *pro-* is positive, *de-* is negative. From prefixes, you can get an idea of the general meaning of the word and try to put it into context.

✓ Hedge Words

Watch out for critical hedge words, such as *likely*, *may*, *can*, *sometimes*, *often*, *almost*, *mostly*, *usually*, *generally*, *rarely*, and *sometimes*. Question writers insert these hedge phrases to cover every possibility. Often an answer choice will be wrong simply because it leaves no room for exception. Be on guard for answer choices that have definitive words such as *exactly* and *always*.

✓ Switchback Words

Stay alert for *switchbacks*. These are the words and phrases frequently used to alert you to shifts in thought. The most common switchback words are *but*, *although*, and *however*. Others include *nevertheless, on the other hand, even though, while, in spite of, despite*, and *regardless of*. Switchback words are important to catch because they can change the direction of the question or an answer choice.

✓ Face Value

When in doubt, use common sense. Accept the situation in the problem at face value. Don't read too much into it. These problems will not require you to make wild assumptions. If you have to go beyond creativity and warp time or space in order to have an answer choice fit the question, then you should move on and consider the other answer choices. These are normal problems rooted in reality. The applicable relationship or explanation may not be readily apparent, but it is there for you to figure out. Use your common sense to interpret anything that isn't clear.

Answer Choice Strategies

✓ Answer Selection

The most thorough way to pick an answer choice is to identify and eliminate wrong answers until only one is left, then confirm it is the correct answer. Sometimes an answer choice may immediately seem right, but be careful. The test writers will usually put more than one reasonable answer choice on each question, so take a second to read all of them and make sure that the other choices are not equally obvious. As long as you have time left, it is better to read every answer choice than to pick the first one that looks right without checking the others.

✓ Answer Choice Families

An answer choice family consists of two (in rare cases, three) answer choices that are very similar in construction and cannot all be true at the same time. If you see two answer choices that are direct opposites or parallels, one of them is usually the correct answer. For instance, if one answer choice says that quantity *x* increases and another either says that quantity *x* decreases (opposite) or says that quantity *y* increases (parallel), then those answer choices would fall into the same family. An answer choice that doesn't match the construction of the answer choice family is more likely to be incorrect. Most questions will not have answer choice families, but when they do appear, you should be prepared to recognize them.

✓ Eliminate Answers

Eliminate answer choices as soon as you realize they are wrong, but make sure you consider all possibilities. If you are eliminating answer choices and realize that the last one you are left with is also wrong, don't panic. Start over and consider each choice again. There may be something you missed the first time that you will realize on the second pass.

✓ Avoid Fact Traps

Don't be distracted by an answer choice that is factually true but doesn't answer the question. You are looking for the choice that answers the question. Stay focused on what the question is asking for so you don't accidentally pick an answer that is true but incorrect. Always go back to the question and make sure the answer choice you've selected actually answers the question and is not merely a true statement.

✓ Extreme Statements

In general, you should avoid answers that put forth extreme actions as standard practice or proclaim controversial ideas as established fact. An answer choice that states the "process should be used in certain situations, if..." is much more likely to be correct than one that states the "process should be discontinued completely." The first is a calm rational statement and doesn't even make a definitive, uncompromising stance, using a hedge word *if* to provide wiggle room, whereas the second choice is far more extreme.

⊘ BENCHMARK

As you read through the answer choices and you come across one that seems to answer the question well, mentally select that answer choice. This is not your final answer, but it's the one that will help you evaluate the other answer choices. The one that you selected is your benchmark or standard for judging each of the other answer choices. Every other answer choice must be compared to your benchmark. That choice is correct until proven otherwise by another answer choice beating it. If you find a better answer, then that one becomes your new benchmark. Once you've decided that no other choice answers the question as well as your benchmark, you have your final answer.

⊘ PREDICT THE ANSWER

Before you even start looking at the answer choices, it is often best to try to predict the answer. When you come up with the answer on your own, it is easier to avoid distractions and traps because you will know exactly what to look for. The right answer choice is unlikely to be word-for-word what you came up with, but it should be a close match. Even if you are confident that you have the right answer, you should still take the time to read each option before moving on.

General Strategies

⊘ TOUGH QUESTIONS

If you are stumped on a problem or it appears too hard or too difficult, don't waste time. Move on! Remember though, if you can quickly check for obviously incorrect answer choices, your chances of guessing correctly are greatly improved. Before you completely give up, at least try to knock out a couple of possible answers. Eliminate what you can and then guess at the remaining answer choices before moving on.

⊘ CHECK YOUR WORK

Since you will probably not know every term listed and the answer to every question, it is important that you get credit for the ones that you do know. Don't miss any questions through careless mistakes. If at all possible, try to take a second to look back over your answer selection and make sure you've selected the correct answer choice and haven't made a costly careless mistake (such as marking an answer choice that you didn't mean to mark). This quick double check should more than pay for itself in caught mistakes for the time it costs.

⊘ PACE YOURSELF

It's easy to be overwhelmed when you're looking at a page full of questions; your mind is confused and full of random thoughts, and the clock is ticking down faster than you would like. Calm down and maintain the pace that you have set for yourself. Especially as you get down to the last few minutes of the test, don't let the small numbers on the clock make you panic. As long as you are on track by monitoring your pace, you are guaranteed to have time for each question.

⊘ DON'T RUSH

It is very easy to make errors when you are in a hurry. Maintaining a fast pace in answering questions is pointless if it makes you miss questions that you would have gotten right otherwise. Test writers like to include distracting information and wrong answers that seem right. Taking a little extra time to avoid careless mistakes can make all the difference in your test score. Find a pace that allows you to be confident in the answers that you select.

✓ KEEP MOVING

Panicking will not help you pass the test, so do your best to stay calm and keep moving. Taking deep breaths and going through the answer elimination steps you practiced can help to break through a stress barrier and keep your pace.

Final Notes

The combination of a solid foundation of content knowledge and the confidence that comes from practicing your plan for applying that knowledge is the key to maximizing your performance on test day. As your foundation of content knowledge is built up and strengthened, you'll find that the strategies included in this chapter become more and more effective in helping you quickly sift through the distractions and traps of the test to isolate the correct answer.

Now that you're preparing to move forward into the test content chapters of this book, be sure to keep your goal in mind. As you read, think about how you will be able to apply this information on the test. If you've already seen sample questions for the test and you have an idea of the question format and style, try to come up with questions of your own that you can answer based on what you're reading. This will give you valuable practice applying your knowledge in the same ways you can expect to on test day.

Good luck and good studying!

Understanding Individuals with Disabilities and Evaluating Their Needs

Developmental Processes

Cognitive, Social, and Emotional Development

Piaget's Four Stages of Cognitive Development

Jean Piaget's **four stages of cognitive development** are sensorimotor, preoperational, concrete operational, and formal operational. Each of these stages is a spectrum in which a child starts at one end and as they mature, begin to think about ideas in new and more-complex ways. During the **sensorimotor stage** (birth to 18 months), newborn infants have a very limited awareness of the physical world around them. As they grow, they begin to interact with their environments before developing object permanence at 7 to 9 months. Another important milestone that develops during this stage is early language development. During the **preoperational stage** (18-24 months to age 7), infants grow into young children and their language becomes more meaningful. They develop memory and imagination but cannot yet grasp complex concepts such as cause and effect or larger conceptualizations of time. The **concrete operational stage** (ages 7 to 12) is characterized by concrete reasoning. Children in this stage become more aware of the world around them and are less egocentric. They cannot yet think abstractly, but are still tied to concrete concepts. During the **formal operational stage** (adolescence to adulthood), adolescents are able to engage in abstract thinking. They are now able to formulate hypotheses and demonstrate logical thought and deductive reasoning.

Erikson's Psychosocial Stages of Human Development

Erik Erikson separated the stages of human development and behavior into eight approximate age groups. Erikson described these stages as points in life in which a person encounters various psychosocial crises and, depending on how they handled the crisis, emerge with particular developmental outcomes. For instance, the first stage posits the conflict between an infant trusting or mistrusting that they will be cared for. Erikson suggests that if an infant is well cared for, the infant should learn to generally have hope and trust that they will be cared for, and this lays a foundation for the next stage. Similarly, a child who has not been adequately cared for may learn to generally distrust that his or her needs will be met. Finally, the conclusion to the stage is not binary, but is on a spectrum. Healthy development means learning a balance between trust and mistrust and not to wholly trust or distrust. As children age, they build upon each previous stage. Growth and pace of development are unique to each individual and the timelines and outcomes vary from person to person.

Stage	Conflict	Age Range	Outcome
Stage 1	Trust vs. Mistrust	Birth to 18 months	Hope
Stage 2	Autonomy vs. Shame and Doubt	18 months to 3 years	Will
Stage 3	Initiative vs. Guilt	3 to 5 years	Purpose
Stage 4	Industry vs. Inferiority	6 to 11 years	Confidence
Stage 5	Identity vs. Confusion	12 to 18 years	Fidelity
Stage 6	Intimacy vs. Isolation	18 to 40 years	Love
Stage 7	Generativity vs. Stagnation	40 to 65 years	Care
Stage 8	Integrity vs. Despair	65 years to death	Wisdom

Social Cognitive Theory

Albert Bandura's social cognitive theory (SCT) describes the processes of social learning, in which individuals learn to perform behaviors by observing and interacting with others. The foundational concept for SCT is **observational learning,** which is based on the idea that a person learns behaviors by observing other people who are **modeling** a behavior, as well as the result that the model achieves. One simple example of observational learning is that children learn to hold utensils by watching adults hold the utensils. Bandura's theory focuses on the active and social nature of learning. Bandura's theory distinguishes itself from other cognitivist models in that it describes not only how individuals learns from their own experiences, but that an individual learns from observing other individuals and their responses. For instance, a boy may be unwilling and afraid to swim at the beach until he sees another person having a good time swimming. The boy is socially considering the consequences of going in the water, even though he has not yet experienced it himself.

Steps of Social Cognitive Theory

According to social cognitive theory, for observational learning to take place, an individual needs to work through four processes to effectively learn a behavior.

- **Attention** - the individual needs to be paying **attention** to the behavior and social environment.
- **Retention** – the individual needs to **retain** or remember information sufficiently to be able to imitate or practice it later.
- **Reproduction** – the individual needs to try to **perform** the behavior and practice it.
- **Motivation** – the individual must **want** to perform the behavior.

If one of these four processes breaks down, an individual will not be able to learn a behavior. For instance, if an individual doesn't pay attention, he won't be able to retain the necessary information to make an attempt at reproduction. Sometimes the behavior cannot be imitated because of limitations, such as physical skills or lack of equipment. For instance, an infant may be able to pay attention to, remember, and be motivated by walking, but may not have the physical prowess to attempt walking yet. Finally, if an individual is insufficiently motivated, they won't want to pay attention to or even attempt the behavior. Furthermore, an individual may not only be lacking in positive motivation, but may be adversely motivated by fear or other negative motivations.

Reciprocal Determinism

Bandura's social cognitive theory (SCT) was heavily linked to another of his theories known as reciprocal determinism. The theory of **reciprocal determinism** states that behavior, personal factors, and the social environment are all linked and influence one another. This model is built on the classical debate of the relationship of nature and nurture in psychology, whether personality is innate or learned. Bandura's reciprocal determinism theory describes all social situations as being made up of these three types of factors and describes how they may affect each other.

- **Personal factors** – the individual's *intrinsic* characteristics, such as personality, beliefs, cognitive factors, and physical attributes.
- **Environmental factors** – the external and *extrinsic* factors in a social situation, such as the physical environment or the number of people present.
- **Behavioral factors** – the individual's actions and inactions within a social situation.

Bandura's point in describing the link between these three types of factors is that they heavily and actively affect one another and can have either a positive or negative impact on learning situations.

In considering the impact of any one of these three factors, it is necessary to consider the impact it has on the other two.

Bandura's Box Experiment

Personal Factors Affect Behaviors	A child doesn't like going to school, so they act out in class.
Behaviors Affect the Environment	The teachers create a more restrictive environment in response to negative behaviors.
Environment Affect Personal Factors	The restrictive environment teaches the child (and perhaps others) to dislike going to school.

Social and Emotional Skill Expectations and Milestones of Toddlers and Preschoolers

Toddlers **18 months to 2 years old** typically begin to demonstrate their **independence** and show an increasing interest in **communication**. Toddlers exhibit temper tantrums and an increase in defiant behavior. Children in this age group begin to **imitate** the actions of familiar adults and engage in pretend play. They also demonstrate an interest in playing with other children but engage in **side-by-side play** (parallel play) instead of cooperative play. Preschoolers ages **3 and 4** continue to demonstrate independence and build on their communication skills. They may also demonstrate temper tantrums and defiant behavior. Preschoolers are able to verbalize a wider range of **emotions**, especially when they do not get what they want or have trouble communicating what they want. They begin to engage with their peers in **cooperative play** and start to play independently. Preschoolers are still interested in and engage in pretend play. At this age, they begin to recognize adults' moods or feelings. They begin to exhibit moments of helpfulness and kindness.

Social and Emotional Skill Expectations and Milestones of Grade Schoolers

Children typically enter kindergarten at ages **5 to 6**. They begin to exert their **independence** and test **boundaries** at home and school. They show a preference for playing with kids their own ages and sometimes their own genders. Their conversational language grows as they interact with other students. At ages **7 to 8**, children start to become aware of what others might think of them. They may be more sensitive to **interpersonal relationships** with their peers. They can aptly express their feelings but get frustrated when they do not have the right words. At ages **9 to 10**, children begin getting selective with their **peer friendships**. They may prefer a few close friends over getting along with everyone. They begin to demonstrate more **independence** and start attempting to develop their own **identities**. Children in this age group are able to communicate their feelings but can still get frustrated. They demonstrate a wide range of emotions in adult and peer interactions.

Effect of Environmental Factors on Social-Emotional Development

A person's **environment** has a large impact on social-emotional development. Factors that impact a child's social-emotional development include:

- Family relationships and environment
- Play-based learning
- A nurturing environment
- Exposure to good verbal skills

Children who grow up with strong, solid family relationships in stable environments tend to develop appropriate **social-emotional skills**. Children who experience family or environmental stress and trauma, such as divorce or constant fighting, may demonstrate deficits in their social-emotional growth. **Play-based learning** fosters important skills and brain development when children observe adults demonstrating acceptable social behavior. In positive, nurturing environments, children learn by watching adults interacting appropriately with one another. They learn skills that foster social and emotional well-being. The first sounds infants hear are voices. Children first grasp a sense of spoken language in their home environments. Caregivers that consistently speak to their children help them develop **strong verbal skills**, which are helpful in developing and maintaining social connections.

Physical and Motor Development

Physical Stages of Gross Motor Development in Children

Gross motor skills are motor skills required for large movements and movements of the body as a whole. Gross motor skills begin developing in **infancy** as children learn to crawl and walk. At ages **two to three**, children transition from toddling to walking, and then learn to jump, run, hop, throw, catch, and push themselves in riding toys with their feet. Children ages **three to four** become skilled at stair climbing. They also jump higher and develop better upper body mobility. Additionally, they develop the ability to ride a small bike or tricycle and kick large balls accurately. At ages **four to five**, children can go up and down stairs with ease. They also develop running mobility skills and speed and have more control when riding bikes or tricycles. Children ages **five to six** fine-tune previously learned gross motor skills. They are more adept at physical play skills, such as those needed to play on jungle gyms or swings independently. Children in this age range may demonstrate interest in organized sports and other physical activities. Children develop and refine their gross motor skills as they grow. A **delay** in a gross motor skill does not always indicate a disability. However, some disabilities are characterized by specific delays in gross motor skills. Parents and educators should be familiar with **gross motor skill milestones** in order to pinpoint any significant delays in students.

Fine Motor Abilities of Children

Fine motor skills are skills focused on smaller movements, usually involving the hands and fingers. Children ages **two to three** begin to make things using their hands, such as block towers. They can scribble with writing utensils and manipulate clay. They demonstrate conceptual knowledge of basic puzzles, fitting appropriate pieces into their correct locations. At this age, children begin to demonstrate a right- or left-hand dominance. Adjusting fasteners, such as buttons and snaps, independently dressing and undressing, and cutting paper with scissors are fine motor milestones for children ages **three to four**. These children also fine-tune their use of eating utensils and can use larger writing tools, maintaining a specific grip instead of a grasp. Children ages **four to five** refine their artistic skills as they become more confident in hand dominance and drawing. Children ages **five to seven** begin to demonstrate fine motor abilities such as writing letters and numbers and creating shapes. They use utensils and writing tools with greater ease. Children in this age range can complete self-care tasks, such as teeth brushing, independently. A child with a **fine motor delay** would demonstrate a significant deficit in one or more fine motor skills at one or more stages of development.

Disabilities Under IDEA

Types of Disabilities

Medical disabilities include problems related to diseases, illnesses, trauma, and genetic conditions. **Physical disabilities** include problems related to fine and gross motor skills and can include sensory input or sensory perception disorders. Medical and physical disabilities often manifest with other disabilities, such as **learning disabilities**. Medical disabilities that affect educational performance usually fall under the IDEA's "other health impairment" or "traumatic brain injury" categories. Students with physical disabilities, such as cerebral palsy, can be eligible for special education under the IDEA's "orthopedic impairment" category. However, for either medical or physical disabilities to qualify, they must **adversely affect educational performance**. For example, a student with cerebral palsy would not be eligible for special education or an IEP if the disability does not affect educational performance. The student would receive accommodations and modifications under a 504 plan.

Low-Incidence Disabilities and High-Incidence Disabilities

Low-incidence disabilities account for up to 20% of all students' disabilities. Students with low-incidence disabilities have sometimes received assistance for their disabilities starting from an early age. **Low-incidence disabilities** include intellectual disabilities, multiple disabilities, hearing impairments, orthopedic impairments, other health impairments, visual impairments, certain autism spectrum conditions, deaf-blindness, traumatic brain injury, and significant developmental delays. **High-incidence disabilities** account for up to 80% of all students' disabilities. While students with high-incidence disabilities present with academic, social, communication, or behavioral problems they can often be held to the same standards as their regular education peers. Children with high-incidence disabilities may perform at the same capacities as their similar-aged peers but have deficits in reading, math, writing, handwriting, or maintaining attention. High-incidence disabilities include speech and language impairments, learning disabilities, attention deficit hyperactivity disorder, emotional disorders, mild intellectual disabilities, certain autism spectrum conditions, and cognitive delays.

Interventions for Students with Physical Disabilities

A physical disability refers to any disability that limits **gross mobility** and prevents **normal body movement**. For example, muscular dystrophy is a physical disability that weakens muscles over time. Students with physical disabilities require early interventions and should begin to receive them before grade school. When students with physical disabilities enter grade school, they may receive interventions and related services if they qualify for special education and receive **individualized education programs (IEPs)** or **504 plans**. When physical disabilities do not affect the students' academic success, they may be put on 504 plans to receive appropriate related services, accommodations, or modifications. When physical disabilities are present with other disabilities or the physical disabilities affect academic performance, students may be put on IEPs and receive appropriate related services, accommodations, and modifications. Teachers, intervention specialists, physiotherapists, occupational therapists, and speech language pathologists work as a team in implementing appropriate accommodations, modifications, and related services to assist students with physical disabilities.

Accommodations and Modifications

Students **with speech, language, visual,** or **hearing impairments** (including **deafness**) that adversely affect their educational performance receive **accommodations**, modifications, and related services specific to their disabilities. Students with these impairments may be educated alongside peers and provided with related services outside of the general education classroom. Accommodations, modifications, and related services are provided based on the severity of the disability.

An **orthopedic impairment (OI)** severely hinders mobility or motor activity. Accommodations, modifications, and related services in the classroom environment may be appropriate for students with OI. Students with **intellectual disabilities (ID)**, such as Down syndrome, often need supports in place for communication, self-care, and social skills. The educational implications of a **traumatic**

brain injury (TBI) are unique to the individual and are therefore treated on a case-by-case basis. Students with **multiple disabilities (MD)** have needs that cannot be met in any one program. Sometimes their needs are so great that they must be educated in partial inclusion or self-contained settings.

Disability Categories in the Individuals with Disabilities Education Act (IDEA)

- **Specific Learning Disabilities (SLD)** is the umbrella term for children who struggle with issues in their abilities to read, write, speak, listen, reason, or do math.
- **Other Health Impairment (OHI)** is another umbrella term for a disability that limits a child's strength, energy, or alertness.
- **Autism Spectrum Disorder (ASD)** is a disability that mostly affects a child's social and communication skills, and sometimes behavior.
- **Emotional Disturbance (ED)** is a disability category for a number of mental disorders.
- **Speech or Language Impairment** covers children with language impairments.
- **Visual Impairment or Blindness** is a disability category for children with visual impairments that significantly impair their abilities to learn.
- **Deafness** is the category for students who cannot hear even with a hearing aid.
- **Hearing Impairment** describes hearing loss that is not a pervasive as deafness. This is distinguished from deafness categorically as the types of interventions needed are very different.
- **Deaf-Blindness** cover children diagnosed with both deafness and blindness.
- Those with **Orthopedic Impairments** have impairments to their bodies that interfere with the performance of daily living skills.
- An **Intellectual Disability** is the diagnosis for children with below-average intellectual abilities or intelligence quotients (IQ).
- **Traumatic Brain Injury (TBI)** covers children who have suffered from TBIs.
- **Multiple Disabilities** as a category means a child has more than one disability defined by IDEA and requires educational interventions that go beyond standard interventions for one category.

Review Video: Understanding Learning Disability Needs of Students
Visit mometrix.com/academy and enter code: 662775

Specific Learning Disability

Early Indications of a Specific Learning Disability

Early indications of SLDs can include medical history, problems with speech acquisition, problems with socialization, academic delays, and behavioral delays. Delays in certain milestones may indicate learning disabilities, but these delays may also be due to other causes. Premature birth, serious childhood illnesses, frequent ear infections, and sleep disorders are **medical factors** that can influence the development of learning disabilities. Children that develop SLDs may demonstrate early delays in **speech**. Late speech development, pronunciation problems, and stuttering may indicate SLDs, but they may also be issues that are unrelated to SLDs and can be addressed by individualized speech instruction. Students with SLDs may also have problems adjusting **socially** and may demonstrate social skills that are not age appropriate. Depending on when the children enter academic settings, they may demonstrate academic delays compared to similar-aged peers. These delays are usually determined using formal and informal assessments in educational settings. **Behaviors** such as hyperactivity or difficulty following directions may also indicate a child has an

SLD. However, these indicators do not definitely mean that a child has a learning disability, and some of the indicators overlap with characteristics of other disabilities.

Instructional Strategies for Teaching Students with Specific Learning Disabilities

While there is no one strategy that works effectively with all students with specific learning disabilities, there are some strategies that tend to produce **positive outcomes** for these students. Direct instruction, learning strategy instruction, and a multi-sensory approach are three large-scale interventions that can be used to promote student learning. **Direct instruction** is teacher-driven instruction that targets specific skills; this is sometimes delivered in resource rooms. **Learning strategy instruction** is a method for teaching students with disabilities different tools and techniques useful for learning new content or skills. This includes techniques like chunking the content, sequencing tasks, and small group instruction. A **multi-sensory approach** ensures that students are receiving and interacting with new information and skills using more than one sense at a time. This approach is helpful for students with learning disabilities because it targets many different ways of learning.

Dyslexia and Dysgraphia Disorders

Students with dyslexia are eligible for special education under the specific learning disability category in the Individuals with Disabilities Education Act if their educational performance is significantly impacted by their disabilities. **Dyslexia** is a permanent condition that makes it difficult for people to read. This affects reading accuracy, fluency, and comprehension. Dyslexia also generalizes to difficulties in the content areas of writing, mathematics, and spelling. Children who have dyslexia often have difficulties with **phonemic awareness skills** and **decoding**. It is not a disability that affects vision or the way people see letters. Dyslexia may coexist with other conditions such as **dysgraphia**, which is a disorder that causes issues with written expression. With dysgraphia, children often struggle with holding pencils and writing letters accurately. It is difficult for students with dysgraphia to distinguish shapes, use correct letter spacing, read maps, copy text, understand spelling rules, and more.

Sensory Processing Disorders

A person with a deficit in the brain's ability to interpret sensory information has a sensory processing disorder (**SPD**). In people without SPD, their brain receptors can interpret sensory input and then they demonstrate appropriate reactions. In people with SPD, their sensory input is blocked from brain receptors, resulting in abnormal reactions. Previously known as a sensory integration disorder, SPD is not a disability specifically defined or eligible under the Individuals with Disabilities Education Act (IDEA). However, many students with disabilities defined by the IDEA, like autism, also experience some sort of sensory processing disorder. Students with SPD may display **oversensitive or under-sensitive responses** to their environments, stimuli, and senses. They may not understand physical boundaries, such as where their bodies are in space, and may bump into things and demonstrate clumsiness. These students may get upset easily, throw tantrums, demonstrate high anxiety, and not handle changes well.

Other Health Impairments

Qualifications to Be Eligible for Special Education Under the Category of OHI

The category of other health impairment (**OHI**) under the Individuals with Disabilities Education Act (IDEA) indicates that a child has **limited strength, vitality, or alertness**. This includes hyper-alertness or hypo-alertness to environmental stimuli. In order to be eligible for special education under this category according to the IDEA, the disability must **adversely affect educational performance**. It must also be due to **chronic or acute health problems**, such as attention deficit disorder (ADD), attention deficit hyperactivity disorder (ADHD), diabetes, epilepsy, heart conditions, hemophilia, lead poisoning, leukemia, nephritis, rheumatic fever, sickle cell anemia, or Tourette's syndrome. Since the OHI category encompasses a number of different disabilities, teachers and parents must rely on a student's individualized education program to ensure that individual academic needs are met and appropriate accommodations and modifications are provided.

Educational Implications for Students with ADHD or ADD

The Individuals with Disabilities Education Act (IDEA) does **not** recognize attention deficit hyperactivity disorder (ADHD) or attention deficit disorder (ADD) in any of its 13 major disability categories. Students may be diagnosed with ADHD or ADD by a physician, but this diagnosis is not enough to qualify them for **special education services**. When ADHD or ADD are present with an IDEA-recognized disability, the student qualifies for special education services under that disability. A student whose ability to learn is affected by ADHD or ADD can receive services with a 504 plan in place. **Section 504 of the Rehabilitation Act of 1973** requires that any child whose disability affects a major life activity receive appropriate **accommodations** and **modifications** in the learning environment. Parents who think a child's ADHD or ADD adversely affects educational functioning may request a formal evaluation to be performed by the school. If the child is found to qualify for special education services, they then receive services under the IDEA's **other health impairment** category.

ADHD and ADD

Children with **attention deficit hyperactivity disorder (ADHD)** may demonstrate hyperactivity, inattention, and impulsivity. However, they may demonstrate hyperactivity and inattention only or hyperactivity and impulsivity only. Children with **attention deficit disorder (ADD)** demonstrate inattention and impulsivity but not hyperactivity. Students with either ADHD or ADD may have difficulties with attention span, following instructions, and concentrating to the point that their educational performance is affected. Since ADD and ADHD symptoms are common among children, their presence does not necessarily indicate that a child has ADD or ADHD. ADD and ADHD are not caused by certain environmental factors, such as diet or watching too much television. Symptoms may be exacerbated by these factors, but the causes can be heredity, chemical imbalances, issues with brain functions, environmental toxins, or prenatal trauma, such as the mother smoking or drinking during pregnancy.

Autism Spectrum Disorder

Autism is a **spectrum disorder**, which means the characteristics associated with the disability vary depending on the student. However, there are common repetitive and patterned behaviors associated with communication and social interactions for this population of students. Students with autism may demonstrate delayed or different speech patterns, the inability to understand body language or facial expressions, and the inability to exhibit appropriate speech patterns, body language, or facial expressions. In a classroom environment, students with autism may demonstrate **repetitive behaviors** that are distracting, such as hand flapping or making vocalizations. Some students with autism demonstrate **preoccupation** with doing activities, tasks, or routines in certain ways. This preoccupation can lead to difficulties when the students are asked to make changes to activities, tasks, or routines. Furthermore, some students with autism prefer to **participate** in a limited range of activities and may get upset when asked to participate in activities outside of their self-perceived ranges. This preference for a limited range of activities may even translate into repetitive behaviors or obsessive and fanatic focus on particular topics. Extreme interest in one topic can lead to disruptions when students with autism are asked to speak or write about different topics.

Concurrent Autism Spectrum Disorder and Other Learning Disabilities

Misinformation about autism spectrum disorder (ASD) and its relation to other learning disabilities runs rampant within school communication and needs clarification to prevent harmful stereotyping of students. ASD, as a spectrum disorder, means that the way it presents varies widely and does not always affect students in the same ways. Autism spectrum disorder is frequently confused with intellectual disabilities (ID), which is when an individual has a low IQ; however, students with ASD can have IQs ranging from significantly delayed to above average or gifted. ASD is also distinctive in that it largely involves difficulties with social understanding and communication, as well as fixations on repetitive routines and behaviors. It is important for an educational professional to understand the difference between ASD and other types of disabilities that commonly co-occur or which have overlapping symptoms. For instance, students with learning disabilities and students with ASD may both have challenges with reading nonverbal cues, staying organized, and expressing themselves, but that does not mean that they have the same underlying conditions or needs. The professional educational community must be aware and cautious when describing various disabilities to prevent the spread of misinformation and harmful stereotyping.

Early Signs of a Child Having ASD

Early signs of **autism spectrum disorder (ASD)** include impairments or delays in social interactions and communication, repetitive behaviors, limited interests, and abnormal eating habits. Students with ASD typically do not interact in conversations in the same ways as similar-aged peers without ASD. They may demonstrate inability to engage in pretend play and may pretend they don't hear when being spoken to. Hand flapping, vocal sounds, or compulsive interactions with objects are repetitive behaviors sometimes demonstrated by students with ASD. They may only demonstrate interest in talking about one topic or interacting with one object. They may also demonstrate self-injurious behavior or sleep problems, in addition to having a limited diet of preferred foods. **Early intervention** is key for these students in order to address and improve functioning. These students may also benefit from **applied behavior analysis** to target specific behaviors and require speech and language therapy, occupational therapy, social skills instruction, or other services geared toward improving intellectual functioning.

Characteristics of Social Skill Delays in Students with ASD

Autism spectrum disorder (ASD) is a disability that can affect a student's social, communication, and behavioral abilities. **Social skill delays and deficits** are common for students with ASD. Social skill delays go hand in hand with **communication limitations** for students with ASD. This includes conversational focus on one or two narrow topics or ideas, making it difficult for them to hold two-way conversations about things that do not interest them. Some students with ASD engage in repetitive language or echolalia or rely on standard phrases to communicate with others. Their **speech and language skills** may be delayed compared to their similar-aged peers. This may also impact their abilities to engage in effective conversations. The **nonverbal skills** of students with ASD may also be misinterpreted, such as avoiding eye contact while speaking or being spoken to.

Early Communication and Social Skill Delays in Students with ASD

Students with delays in communication development often need and receive some type of assistance or instruction with communication and social skills. Early intervention for these students is key, as communication difficulties may be a symptom **of autism spectrum disorder (ASD)**. For students with ASD, the need for communication and social skills instruction varies depending on the individual student. Key characteristics of **early communication difficulties** for a student with ASD include not responding to his or her name, not pointing at objects of interest, avoiding eye contact, not engaging in pretend play, delayed speech or language skills, or repeating words or phrases. Children with ASD may also exhibit overreaction or underreaction to environmental stimuli. Key characteristics of **early social skill difficulties** for a student with ASD may include preferring to play alone, trouble understanding personal feelings or the feelings of others, not sharing interests with others, and difficulty with personal space boundaries. Infants with ASD may not respond to their names and demonstrate reduced babbling and reduced interest in people. Toddlers with ASD may demonstrate decreased interest in social interactions, difficulty with pretend play, and a preference for playing alone.

Socratic Method for Students with ASD

With the Socratic method of teaching, students are **guided** by their teachers in their own educational discovery learning processes. This involves students intrinsically seeking knowledge or answers to problems. This method can be helpful for facilitating and enhancing the **social and emotional abilities** of students with disabilities, particularly autism spectrum disorder (ASD). The Socratic method requires **dialogue** in order to successfully facilitate the teacher/student guided learning process. This is beneficial for students with ASD, who generally struggle with appropriate communication and social skills. This method emphasizes **information seeking and communication skills** by engaging students in class discussions, assignment sharing, and group work. Communication for information-seeking purposes is often a deficit of students with ASD. Sharing of ideas is a concept that develops naturally in guided learning and often requires flexibility in the thought process, another skill that students with ASD struggle with. These skills can be taught to and reinforced in students with and without disabilities in order to develop skills essential to lifelong learning processes.

Emotional Disturbances

A diagnosis of an emotional disturbance (**ED**) can also be referred to as a **behavioral disorder** or **mental illness**. Causes of emotional disturbances are generally unclear. However, heredity, brain disorders, and diet are some factors that influence the development of emotional disturbances. The emotional disturbance category includes psychological disorders, such as anxiety disorders, bipolar disorder, eating disorders, and obsessive-compulsive disorder. Children who have emotional disturbances that affect their educational performance are eligible for **special education** under IDEA. Indicators of emotional disturbances include hyperactivity, aggression, withdrawal, immaturity, and academic difficulties. While many children demonstrate these indicators throughout their development, a strong indicator of an emotional disturbance is a **prolonged demonstration** of these behaviors.

Issues Students with Emotional Disturbances Experience in the Instructional Setting

Students with the diagnosis of emotional disturbance as defined by the IDEA require **emotional and behavioral support** in the classroom. Students with ED may also require **specialized academic instruction** in addition to behavioral and emotional support. The amount of support given varies according to the needs of individual students. These students also need **scaffolded instruction** in social skills, self-awareness, self-esteem, and self-control. Students with ED often exhibit behaviors that impede their learning or the learning of others. **Positive behavioral interventions and supports (PBIS)** is a preventative instructional strategy that focuses on promoting positive behaviors in students. With PBIS, teachers or other professionals make changes to students' environments in order to decrease problem behaviors. PBIS involves collecting information on a problem behavior, identifying positive interventions to support the student before behaviors escalate, and implementing supports to decrease targeted negative behaviors. Supports can be implemented schoolwide or in the classroom. However, for students with ED, **classroom supports** are more effective because they can be individualized.

Speech and Language Impairments

Speech and language impairments, sometimes referred to as **communication disorders**, are disabilities recognized by the Individuals with Disabilities Education Act. Students diagnosed with communication disorders are eligible for special education if they qualify for services. Early indicators of communication disorders include but are not limited to:

- Not smiling or interacting with others
- Lack of babbling or cooing in infants
- Lack of age-appropriate comprehension skills
- Speech that is not easily understood
- Issues with age-appropriate syntax development
- Issues with age-appropriate social skills
- Deficits in reading and writing skills
- Beginning or ending words with incorrect sounds
- Hearing loss
- Stuttering

These indicators may also be linked to other disabilities, such as hearing impairments or autism spectrum disorder. Although prolonged demonstration of these indicators may suggest communication disorders, some children demonstrate delays and then self-correct over time.

Facilitating Learning for Students with Speech or Language Impairments

In order to teach students with speech or language impairments, also referred to as **communication disorders**, teachers and other professionals can use the **strategies** listed below:

- Use visuals and concrete examples to help students with communication disorders take in new information. Link the visuals with spoken words or phrases.
- Use visuals or photographs to introduce or reinforce vocabulary.
- Use repetition of spoken words to introduce or reinforce vocabulary.
- Model conversational and social skills, which helps students with communication disorders become familiar with word pronunciation.
- Speak at a slower rate when necessary, especially when presenting new information.
- Consistently check for understanding.
- Be aware that communication issues may sometimes result in other issues, such as behavioral or social skill issues.
- Pair actions and motions with words to emphasize meaning, especially for students with receptive language disorders.

Receptive Language Disorders

Children with receptive language disorders often demonstrate appropriate expressive language skills and hear and read at age-appropriate levels. However, they may seem like they are not paying attention or engaging in activities, or they may appear to have difficulties following or understanding directions. They may refrain from asking questions or interrupt frequently during activities, especially during read-aloud activities. It may appear as if they are not listening, but children with receptive language disorders have difficulty perceiving **meaning** from what they hear. Children with this disorder may consistently leave tasks incomplete unless the tasks are broken down into smaller steps. This is due to issues with processing directions, especially **verbal directions**. Children with receptive language disorders may not respond appropriately or at all to questions from peers or adults. Answers to comprehension questions, especially when texts are read aloud, may be off topic or incorrect. Children with receptive language disorders have trouble gathering and connecting meaning to what they hear. A receptive language disorder is not exclusively a learning disability. However, children who have receptive disorders may have learning disabilities.

Visual Impairment or Blindness

Visual impairments range from low vision to blindness. The Individuals with Disabilities Education Act defines a **visual impairment** as an impairment in vision that is great enough to affect a child's educational performance. **Blindness** is defined as a visual acuity of 20/200 or less in the dominant eye. Some people diagnosed with blindness still have minimal sight. Early indicators of a visual impairment or blindness in children include:

- Holding things close to the eyes or face
- Experiencing fatigue after looking at things closely
- Having misaligned eyes
- Squinting
- Tilting the head or covering one eye to see things up close or far away
- Demonstrating clumsiness
- Appearing to see better during the day

Students with visual impairments benefit the most from early interventions, especially when the impairments are present with other disabilities. Appropriate interventions vary based on students' needs and whether or not they have other disabilities. Modifications, such as magnified text, Braille, auditory support, and text-tracking software, can help level the learning plane for these students.

Deafness, Hearing Impairment, and Deaf-Blindness

Deafness, hearing impairment, and deaf-blindness are each considered their own categories under IDEA, as the types and levels of intervention vary widely between them. **Deafness** is defined as a complete or nearly-complete loss of hearing, to the degree that a hearing aid cannot help. Deaf students often need specialized interventions to help with safety and with communication, such as through communication aids, assistive devices, and sign language. **Hearing impairments** consist of all qualifying degrees of hearing loss that are not severe enough to qualify as deafness. Interventions may include communication aids and training, as well as hearing aids. **Deaf-blindness** is restricted to students who are both deaf and blind concurrently. Deaf-blind students usually require considerable help with communication and daily living skills.

Effect of Hearing Loss on Language Development

Hearing language is part of learning language. Children with **hearing loss** miss out on sounds associated with language, and this can affect their listening, speaking, reading, social skills, and overall school success. Hearing loss can sometimes lead to delayed speech and language, learning disabilities in school, insecurities, and issues with socialization and making friends. Children with hearing loss may:

- Have trouble learning abstract vocabulary like *since* and *before*
- Omit article words in sentences like *a* and *an*
- Fall behind in core components of learning and development without early interventions
- Have difficulty speaking in and understanding sentences
- Speak in shorter sentences
- Have difficulty including word endings like *-ing* and *-s*
- Have issues speaking clearly because they cannot accurately hear sounds

- Omit quiet sounds like *p, sh,* or *f*
- Be unable to hear what their own voices sound like

Children with hearing loss are more likely to fall behind in school due to their hearing deficits. They can easily fall behind without support from interventions, teachers, and their families. Early **hearing testing** is essential to ensure that interventions, such as sign language, can be introduced to promote school and life success for children with hearing loss.

Orthopedic Impairment

Qualifications to Receive Special Education for Orthopedic Impairment

Students who qualify to receive special education under the Individuals with Disabilities Education Act orthopedic impairment (**OI**) category have an orthopedic impairment that adversely affects educational performance. This includes children with congenital anomalies, impairments caused by disease, or impairments from other causes, such as cerebral palsy or amputations. An orthopedic impairment alone does not qualify a student for special education and an IEP. Once a student's educational performance is proven to be affected by the orthopedic impairment, the student becomes eligible for special education and placed on an IEP. The **IEP** determines the student's least restrictive environment, individualized goals for academic skills or adaptive behavior, and any appropriate accommodations or modifications. Students with orthopedic impairments whose educational performance is not affected may receive accommodations and modifications on **504 plans**, if appropriate. Strategies for instruction should be determined and implemented on a case-by-case basis, as the orthopedic impairment category covers a broad range of disabilities.

Intellectual Disabilities

Determining If a Child May Have an Intellectual Disability

Intellectual disability is primarily diagnosed when a child under 18 years old scores lower than 70 on an IQ test. Individuals may also be diagnosed with intellectual disabilities when they have an IQ under 75 with a concurrent disability that also impairs their functional skills, such as spastic quadriplegia which severely impairs movement. Students diagnosed with intellectual disabilities (**ID**) demonstrate deficits in academic skills, abstract thinking, problem solving, language development, new skill acquisition, and retaining information. Students with intellectual disabilities often do not adequately meet developmental or social milestones. They demonstrate **deficits in functioning** with one or more basic living skills. Students with intellectual disabilities struggle conceptually and may have difficulties with time and money concepts, short-term memory, time management, pre-academic skills, planning, and strategizing. Students with ID demonstrate poor social judgment and decision-making skills because they have trouble understanding social cues and rules. They may grasp concrete social concepts before abstract ones and significantly later than their similar-aged, regular education peers. These students also tend to struggle with self-care skills, household tasks, and completing tasks that may be easy for similar-aged peers.

Determining Severity of Intellectual Disabilities

There are four levels of intellectual disabilities: mild, moderate, severe, and profound. Specific factors are used to determine whether a disability is mild, severe, and profound. Intellectual levels are measured using cognitive- and research-based assessments. An **intellectual disability (ID)** is defined as significant cognitive deficits to intellectual functioning, such as reasoning, problem solving, abstract thinking, and comprehension. A **mild intellectual disability** is the most common type of intellectual disability. People with mild to moderate ID can generally participate in independent living activities and learn practical life skills and adaptive behaviors. People diagnosed with **severe intellectual disabilities** demonstrate major developmental delays. They struggle with simple routines and self-care skills. Additionally, they often understand speech but have trouble with expressive communication. People with **profound ID** cannot live independently, and they depend heavily on care from other people and resources. They are likely to have concurrent congenital disorders that affect their intellectual functioning.

Educational Implications for Students with Intellectual Disabilities

According to the Individuals with Disabilities Education Act, students who are eligible for special education under the category of **intellectual disability** have significantly lower intellectual abilities, along with adaptive behavior deficits. Previously, intellectual disability was referred to as "mental retardation" in the IDEA. In 2010, President Obama signed **Rosa's Law**, which changed the term to "intellectual disability." The definition of the disability category remained unchanged. Educational implications of a diagnosis of an intellectual disability differ depending on students' needs as determined by their individualized education programs (IEPs). Students with intellectual disabilities often display **limitations to mental functioning** in areas like communication, self-care, and social skills (adaptive behavior). In many cases, these skills must be addressed in the educational environments in addition to any academic skill deficits. Learning adaptive behaviors and academic skills takes longer for students with intellectual disabilities. Their special education placements depend upon what environments are least restrictive. This depends on the individual student and is determined in the IEP.

Promoting a Positive Educational Performance for Students with Intellectual Disabilities

Students with intellectual disabilities often present with skill levels that are far below those of similar-aged peers. Because of deficits in academic, behavioral, and social skills, these students require **specialized instruction**, which varies depending on the needs of each individual student. An effective strategy for promoting a positive educational performance is to collect observations and data on the academic, behavioral, and social skill levels of the individual student. Teachers usually work with professionals in related services, like speech language pathologists, to address needs and implement educational interventions that work for this population of students. These students can benefit from **communication interventions** focused on interactions they may have with adults and peers. Students may benefit from augmentative and alternative communication (AAC) devices, visual activity schedules and other visual supports, and computer-based instruction when learning communication and social skills. Students with ID may also require **behavioral interventions** to teach appropriate behaviors or decrease negative behaviors. They may also benefit from increased **peer interactions** through structured social groups in order to promote appropriate communication skills.

Multiple Disabilities

Components of the Multiple Disability Eligibility Category According to the IDEA

The multiple disabilities category according to the IDEA applies to students who have two or more disabilities occurring simultaneously. The multiple disability category does not include deaf-blindness, which has its own category under the IDEA. Students with **multiple disabilities** present with such **severe educational needs** that they cannot be accommodated in special education settings that address only one disability. Placement in special education programs is determined by students' **least restrictive environments** as defined in their **individualized education programs**. Students with multiple disabilities often present with communication deficits, mobility challenges, and deficits in adaptive behavior and need one-on-one instruction or assistance when performing daily activities.

Educational Responses for Students with Disabilities

Role of Cultural Competence in Schools and Special Education

Cultural competence, the awareness and appreciation of cultural differences, helps avoid **cultural and linguistic bias**. Schools that demonstrate **cultural competence** have an appreciation of families and their unique backgrounds. Cultural competence is important because it assists with incorporating knowledge and appreciation of other cultures into daily practices and teaching. This helps increase the quality and effectiveness of how students with unique cultural and linguistic backgrounds are provided with services. It also helps produce better outcomes for these students. In special education, being culturally competent means being aware of cultural and linguistic differences, especially when considering children for the identification process. Adapting to the **diversity and cultural contexts** of the surrounding communities allows teachers to better understand flags for referrals. Teachers that continually assess their awareness of the cultures and diversity of the communities where they teach demonstrate cultural competence. In order for schools and teachers to be described as culturally competent, they should have a process for recognizing diversity.

Cultural and Linguistic Differences vs. Learning Difficulties

Many schools are enriched with cultural diversity. It is important for special educators to identify if a suspected learning disability may instead be a **cultural or linguistic difference**. Teachers and schools must increase awareness of cultural and linguistic differences in order to avoid overidentification of certain populations as having learning difficulties. Some ways a child's behavior may represent cultural or linguistic differences are demonstrated in the **interactions** between teachers and students. In some cultures, children are asked to make eye contact to ensure they are listening, whereas in other cultures, children are taught to look down or away when being spoken to by an adult. Certain facial expressions and behaviors may be interpreted differently by students because of their cultural backgrounds. Additionally, teaching methods that are comfortable and effective for some students may be ineffective for others due to differing cultural backgrounds. Cultural values and characteristics may vary between teachers and students and contribute to the students' school performance. It is important for teachers to be **self-aware** and constantly **assess** whether ineffective teaching methods are due to learning difficulties or cultural and linguistic diversity.

Strategies for Teaching ELLs and Students with Disabilities

English language learners (ELLs) are often at risk of being unnecessarily referred for special education services. This is frequently a result of **inadequate planning** for the needs of English language learners rather than skill deficits. To ensure that the needs of ELLs are met and discrimination is avoided, educators can implement strategies for **targeting their learning processes**. Strategies similar to those utilized in inclusive special education settings, such as using visuals to supplement instruction, are helpful. This type of nonlinguistic representation helps convey meaning to ELLs. Working in groups with peers helps students with disabilities and ELLs demonstrate communication and social skills while working toward common goals. Allowing students to write and speak in their first languages until they feel comfortable speaking in English is a scaffolding strategy that can also be implemented. Sentence frames that demonstrate familiar sentence formats help all students to practice speaking and writing in structured, formal ways.

Teaching Appropriate Communication Skills to ELLs with Disabilities

Students with disabilities who are also English language learners (ELLs) have the additional challenge of **language barriers** affecting their access to learning. These barriers, combined with the disabilities, can make instruction for these students challenging. For ELL students with disabilities, it is important for teachers to rely on **appropriate instructional strategies** in order to determine what is affecting the students' access to information. Strategies for teaching ELLs are similar to those for teaching nonverbal students. Pairing **visuals** with words helps students make concrete connections between the written words and the pictures. Consistently seeing the words paired with the visuals increases the likelihood of the students beginning to interpret word meanings. Using sign language or other gestures is another way teachers can facilitate word meaning. When used consistently, students make connections between the visual word meanings and the written words. Teachers can also provide opportunities for ELLs to access language by having all students in the classroom communicate in a **consistent manner**. The goal of this instructional strategy is for peers to model appropriate verbal communication as it applies to different classroom situations.

The Roles and Rights Families have in the Education of Children with Disabilities

Under the IDEA, parents and legal guardians of children with disabilities have **procedural safeguards** that protect their rights. The safeguards also provide parents and legal guardians with the means to resolve any disputes with school systems. **Parents and legal guardians** may underestimate their importance to individualized education program (IEP) teams. However, they are important members of IEP teams and integral parts of the decision-making processes for their children's educational journeys. Parents and legal guardians often work more closely with their children than other adults. Therefore, as part of IEP teams, they serve as **advocates** and can often provide insight regarding the children's backgrounds, educational and developmental histories, strengths, and weaknesses. Parents and legal guardians are also important decision makers in transition meetings, when students with disabilities move from one level of school to another. Their input in transition meetings helps ensure that appropriate services and supports are in place at the next levels of school so that students can succeed.

Educational Implications of a Diagnosis of SLD, OHI, ASD, and ED

Students with a **specific learning disability (SLD)** may struggle with instruction in general education classrooms and require specific instruction fine-tuned to their individual needs. Their annual IEP goals may target specific skills that are not age appropriate but are appropriate to their unique learning needs. Students with **other health impairments (OHI)** can include those with ADHD, diabetes, HIV/AIDS, heart conditions, and more. Students with OHI receive accommodations for their unique health or educational needs on a case-by-case basis. Students with **autism spectrum disorder (ASD)** may rely on the use of visuals or other ways to express feelings or communicate. Students with ASD may not respond to everyday conversations or classroom situations the same ways their peers do. They require supports to learn how to express their needs within the general education classroom. Students with **emotional disturbances (ED)** exhibit an inability to learn that is not due to intellectual, sensory, or health problems. Students with ED also exhibit an inability to form and maintain appropriate relationships with peers and adults, demonstrate inappropriate behaviors, and may exhibit depression or general unhappiness.

Effect of Emotional and Psychological Needs on Students with Disabilities

When a child is diagnosed with a disability, educators often primarily focus on the educational implications. However, students with disabilities also have **emotional needs** associated with their disabilities. These needs vary by student and disability. Generally, students with disabilities struggle emotionally. Symptoms may include low self-esteem, anxiety, acting out, reduced intrinsic motivation, and physical effects, like headaches. Educators, parents, and other professionals can manage the emotional needs of students with disabilities by talking with them about the disability diagnoses and educational implications. Educators can increase their **awareness** of how students might be feeling about the diagnoses and identify situations that may cause anxiety or acting out.

Educators can also help by praising students consistently, even for small actions, which can help with confidence. Parents, educators, and other professionals can also work together to ensure that the students receive instruction in the most appropriate educational environments for their disabilities.

Classroom Strategies Promoting Social-Emotional Development and Growth

Classroom environments should emanate **positivity** and **growth**. Classrooms that promote **social-emotional development and growth** provide security for students and create environments where learning takes place. Teachers can promote social-emotional development and growth by creating predictable classroom routines with visual reminders, keeping classrooms free of dangerous objects and materials, and arranging for learning to take place in large and small groups. They can also rotate activities and materials to keep students engaged, provide appropriate materials for learning centers, and create opportunities for children to engage socially. Teachers can act as nurturing adults by encouraging social interactions and problem solving, modeling appropriate language and social skills, encouraging and validating children's thoughts and feelings, and using clear signals to indicate transitions between activities. Teachers should build community environments in their classrooms, build appropriate relationships with students by getting to know their strengths and weaknesses, and demonstrate good conflict resolution and problem-solving abilities.

Gardner's Theory of Multiple Intelligences

Howard Gardner developed the theory of multiple intelligences, which outlines seven different ways he believes people can learn. Gardner's theory was based on the idea that everyone understands the world through different intelligences and that **individual intelligence strengths** are what make people different. The multiple intelligences are described below.

- **Visual-spatial thinkers** think about things visually. They are very aware of their environments. They are good at activities like completing puzzles, drawing, and reading maps. They learn best through the use of visuals, such as graphs and diagrams.
- **Bodily-kinesthetic thinkers** learn best with a hands-on approach. They process information by doing. They learn best through physical activities.
- **Musical thinkers** are sensitive to music, sound, and rhythm in their environments. They learn best when lesson concepts are turned into musical features like lyrics and songs.
- **Interpersonal thinkers** like to learn by interacting with others. They find learning easy in group environments like seminars and lecture halls.
- **Intrapersonal thinkers** are independent learners. They learn best using introspection.
- **Linguistic thinkers** are efficient and use words to express themselves. They are auditory learners who enjoy reading, word games, and making up stories.
- **Logical-mathematical thinkers** learn best through patterns in and relationships between ideas. They think conceptually and reasonably.
- **Naturalistic thinkers** learn through interaction and exploration of the natural environments and tend to be well in tune with their environments.

Cognitive Behavioral Theory

The cognitive behavioral theory states that people form their own negative or positive concepts that affect their behaviors. The cognitive behavioral theory involves a **cognitive triad** of thoughts and behaviors. This triad refers to thoughts about the **self**, the **world and environment**, and the **future**. In times of stress, people's thoughts can become distressed or dysfunctional. Sometimes cognitive behavioral therapy, based on the cognitive behavioral theory model, is used to help people address and manage their thoughts. This process involves people examining their thoughts more closely in order to bring them back to more realistic, grounded ways of thinking. People's thoughts and perceptions can often affect their lives negatively and lead to unhealthy emotions and behaviors. **Cognitive behavioral therapy** helps people to adjust their thinking, learn ways to access healthy thoughts, and learn behaviors incompatible with unhealthy or unsafe behaviors.

Importance of Adaptive Behavior Skills Instruction for Students with Disabilities

Adaptive behavior skills refer to age-appropriate behaviors that people need to live independently and function in daily life. **Adaptive behavior skills** include self-care, following rules, managing money, making friends, and more. For students with disabilities, especially severely limiting disabilities, adaptive behavior skills may need to be included in daily instruction. Adaptive behavior skills can be separated into conceptual skills, social skills, and practical life skills. **Conceptual skills** include academic concepts, such as reading, math, money, time, and communication skills. **Social skills** instruction focuses on teaching students to get along with others, communicate appropriately, and maintain appropriate behavior inside and outside the school environment. **Practical life skills** are skills needed to perform the daily living tasks, such as bathing, eating, sitting and standing, and using the bathroom. Adaptive behavior assessments are useful in assessing what adaptive behavior skills need to be addressed for each student. These assessments are usually conducted using observations and questionnaires completed by parents, teachers, or students.

Chapter Quiz

1. Which of the following updated the term *mental retardation* to *intellectual disability*?

a. Sean's Law
b. Amy's Law
c. Mary's Law
d. Rosa's Law

2. Blindness is defined as a visual acuity of less than or equal to:

a. 20/200
b. 20/20
c. 2/20
d. 2/200

3. Low-incidence disabilities can account for up to which percentage of all students' disabilities?

a. 20%
b. 30%
c. 40%
d. 50%

4. Which of the following is NOT considered an adaptive behavior skill category?

a. Environmental
b. Social
c. Conceptual
d. Practical life

5. During which age range do children typically become skilled at stair climbing?

a. 2-3
b. 3-4
c. 4-5
d. 5-6

6. During which age range do children typically begin showing right- or left-hand dominance?

a. 1-2
b. 2-3
c. 3-4
d. 4-5

7. The IDEA recognizes how many major disability categories?

a. 10
b. 11
c. 12
d. 13

8. Which of the following is NOT a term used to describe an intensity level of intellectual disability?

a. Mild
b. Profound
c. Major
d. Severe

9. Bandura's social cognitive learning theory includes how many stages of observational learning?

a. Three
b. Four
c. Five
d. Six

10. Which of the following is the method of teaching where students are guided by their teachers in their own learning process?

a. Hippocratic
b. Aristotelian
c. Euclidean
d. Socratic

11. Which of the following is NOT part of the cognitive triad of cognitive behavioral theory?

a. Self
b. World
c. Past
d. Future

12. At what age do children typically begin to become aware of what others might think of them?

a. 5-6
b. 7-8
c. 9-10
d. 10-11

Chapter Quiz Answer Key

1. D: According to the Individuals with Disabilities Education Act (IDEA), students who are eligible for special education under the category of "intellectual disability" have significantly lower intellectual abilities, along with adaptive behavior deficits. Previously, intellectual disability was referred to as *mental retardation*. In 2010, President Obama signed Rosa's Law, which changed the term to *intellectual disability*. The definition of the disability category remained unchanged.

2. A: Visual impairment ranges from low vision to blindness. The Individuals with Disabilities Education Act defines a visual impairment as an impairment in vision that is great enough to affect a child's educational performance. Blindness is defined as a visual acuity of 20/200 or less in the dominant eye.

3. A: Low-incidence disabilities account for up to 20% of all students' disabilities. Students with low-incidence disabilities have sometimes received assistance for their disabilities starting from an early age. This group includes students with intellectual disabilities and significant developmental delays. Low-incidence disabilities can include intellectual disabilities, multiple disabilities, hearing impairments, orthopedic impairments, other health impairments, visual impairments, autism, deaf-blindness, traumatic brain injury, and developmental delays.

4. A: Adaptive behavior skills include self-care skills, following rules, managing money, making friends, and more. For students with disabilities, especially severely limiting disabilities, adaptive behavior skills may need to be included in daily instruction. Adaptive behavior skills can be separated into conceptual skills, social skills, and practical life skills. Conceptual skills include academic concepts, such as reading, math, money, time, and communication skills. Social skills instruction focuses on teaching students to get along with others, communicate appropriately, and maintain appropriate behavior inside and outside the school environment. Practical life skills are skills needed to perform the tasks of daily living.

5. B: Gross motor skills are larger motor skills that require movement of the body as a whole. Gross motor skills begin developing in infancy as children learn to crawl and walk. At ages two to three, children transition from toddling to walking, then learn to jump, run, hop, throw, catch, and push themselves in riding toys with their feet. Children ages three to four become skilled at stair climbing. They also jump higher and develop better upper-body mobility. Additionally, they develop the ability to ride a small bike or tricycle and kick large balls accurately. At ages four to five, children can go up and down stairs with ease. They also develop running mobility skills and speed and have more control when riding bikes or tricycles. Children ages five to six fine-tune previously learned gross motor skills. They are more adept at physical play skills, such as those needed to play on jungle gyms or swings independently.

6. B: Fine motor skills are skills focused on smaller movements, usually involving the hands and fingers. Children ages two to three begin to make things, such as block towers, using their hands. They can scribble with writing utensils and manipulate playdough. They demonstrate conceptual knowledge of basic puzzles, fitting appropriate pieces into their correct locations. At this age, children begin to demonstrate a right- or left-hand dominance. Adjusting fasteners, such as buttons and snaps, independently dressing and undressing, and cutting paper with scissors are fine-motor milestones for children ages three to four. These children also fine-tune their eating skills and use larger writing tools, maintaining a specific grip instead of a grasp. Children ages four to five improve their fine motor skills. Their artistic skills become more refined as they become more confident in hand dominance and drawing. Children ages five to seven begin to demonstrate fine motor abilities such as writing letters and numbers and creating shapes.

7. D: The Individuals with Disabilities Education Act (IDEA) does not recognize attention deficit hyperactivity disorder (ADHD) or attention deficit disorder (ADD) in any of its 13 major disability categories. Students may be diagnosed with ADHD or ADD only by a physician, but this diagnosis is not enough to qualify the student for special education services.

8. C: There are three levels of intellectual disabilities: severe, profound, and mild.

9. B: Albert Bandura's social cognitive learning theory features four stages or processes of observational learning: attention, retention, production, and motivation. Observational learning is based on the idea that a person modifies behavior after being provided with a model for the behavior. Not to be confused with exact imitation of behavior, observational learning occurs when a behavior is witnessed, then demonstrated later as a result of witnessing the behavior.

10. D: With the Socratic method of teaching, students are guided by their teachers in their own educational discovery learning processes. This involves students internally seeking knowledge or answers to problems. This method can be helpful for facilitating and enhancing the social and emotional abilities of students with disabilities, particularly autism spectrum disorder (ASD).

11. C: The cognitive behavioral theory states that people form their own negative or positive concepts that affect their behaviors. The cognitive behavioral theory involves a cognitive triad of human thoughts and behaviors. This triad refers to human thoughts about the self, the world and environment, and the future.

12. B: Children typically enter kindergarten at ages 5-6. They begin to exert their independence and test boundaries at home and school. They show a preference for playing with kids their own ages and sometimes their own genders. Their conversational language grows as they interact with other students. At ages 7-8, children start to become aware of what others might think of them. They may be more sensitive to interpersonal relationships with their peers. They can aptly express their feelings but get frustrated when they do not have the right words.

Social and Functional Living Skills

Targeting and Implementing Social Skills Instruction

Developing good social skills is essential for lifelong success, and people with disabilities often struggle with these skills. Addressing social skill behavior is most effective when specific **social skill needs** are identified, and **social skills instruction** is implemented as a collaborative effort between parents and teachers.

Evaluating **developmental milestones** is helpful in targeting social skills that need to be addressed and taught. If a child with a disability is not demonstrating a milestone, such as back and forth communication, the skill can be evaluated to determine if it should be taught. However, meeting milestones is not a reliable way to measure a student's social skill ability, as some children naturally progress more slowly. **Social skill deficits** may be acquisition deficits, performance deficits, or fluency deficits. A student with an **acquisition deficit** demonstrates an absence of a skill or behavior. A student with a **performance deficit** does not implement a social skill consistently. A student with a **fluency deficit** needs assistance with demonstrating a social skill effectively or fluently. Once a student's social skill need is identified, teachers, parents, and other professionals can collaborate to address it by establishing a routine or a behavior contract or implementing applied behavior analysis.

Purposes and Benefits of Social Skills Groups

Social skills groups are useful for helping students with social skill deficits learn and practice appropriate skills with their peers. Social skills groups are primarily composed of similarly aged peers with and without disabilities. An adult leads these groups and teaches students skills needed for making friends, succeeding in school and life, and sometimes obtaining and maintaining a job. Other professionals, such as school psychologists or speech language pathologists, may also lead social skills groups. Social skills groups work by facilitating **conversation** and focusing on **skill deficits**. These groups can help students learn to read facial cues, appropriately greet others, begin conversations, respond appropriately, maintain conversations, engage in turn-taking, and request help when needed.

Receiving Special Education Services in the Least Restrictive Environment

The Individuals with Disabilities Education Act (IDEA) requires a free and appropriate public education (FAPE) to be provided in a student's **least restrictive environment (LRE)**. This means that a student with a disability who qualifies for special education should be educated in a free, appropriate, and public setting and be placed in an instructional setting that meets the LRE principle. The IDEA states that LRE means students with disabilities should participate in the general education classroom "to the maximum extent appropriate." **Mainstreaming** and **inclusion** are ways for students with disabilities to participate in general education classrooms while receiving appropriate accommodations, modifications, interventions, and related services. The amount of time students spend in an LRE suitable for their individual needs is stated in their Individualized Education Program (IEP). The accommodations, modifications, interventions, and related services the student should receive are also outlined in the IEP. Students who need special education services for more than 50% of the day may be placed in other instructional settings that meet their LRE needs, such as resource rooms or self-contained classrooms.

Continuum of Special Education Services

The IDEA mandates that school systems educate students with disabilities with students who do not have disabilities to the maximum extent that is appropriate. The IDEA also mandates that schools not take students out of regular education classes unless the classes are not benefiting the students. Supplementary aids and support services must be in place before students can be considered for removal. Schools must offer a **continuum of special education services** that range from restrictive to least restrictive. In a typical continuum of services, regular education classrooms offer the **least restrictive access** to students with disabilities. Next on the continuum are resource rooms, followed by special classes that target specific deficits. Special schools, homebound services, hospitals, and institutions are the most restrictive education environments. The number of students at each stage of the continuum decreases as restriction increases. Fewer students benefit more from being educated in hospitals or institutions than in resource rooms.

Evidence-Based Methods for Promoting Self-Determination

Students with disabilities often need to be taught **self-determination** and **self-advocacy** skills. These skills may not come easily to students with specific disorders, like ASD. Self-determination involves a comprehensive understanding of one's own **strengths and limitations**. Self-determined people are **goal-oriented** and intrinsically motivated to **improve themselves**. Teachers can facilitate the development of these skills in a number of ways, starting in early elementary school. In early elementary school, teachers can promote self-determination by teaching choice-making skills and providing clear consequences for choices. Teachers can also promote problem-solving and self-management skills, like having students evaluate their own work. At the middle school and junior high school level, students can be taught to evaluate and analyze their choices. They can also learn academic and personal goal-setting skills and decision-making skills. At the high school level, teachers can promote decision-making skills, involvement in educational planning (e.g., students attending their IEP meetings), and strategies like self-instruction, self-monitoring, and self-evaluation. Throughout the education process, teachers should establish and maintain high standards for learning, focus on students' strengths, and create positive learning environments that promote choice and problem-solving skills.

Teaching Self-Awareness Skills

Students engage in private self-awareness and public self-awareness. Some students with disabilities have the additional challenge of needing instruction in **self-awareness skills**. Special educators and other professionals can facilitate the instruction of self-awareness skills by teaching students to be **aware** of their thoughts, feelings, and actions; to recognize that other people have needs and feelings; and to recognize how their behaviors **affect other people**. Students can be taught self-awareness by identifying their own strengths and weaknesses and learning to self-monitor errors in assignments. They can also be taught to identify what materials or steps are needed to complete tasks and to advocate for accommodations or strategies that work for them. Special educators or other professionals should frequently talk with students about their performance and encourage them to discuss their mistakes without criticism.

Importance of Learning Self-Advocacy Skills

Self-advocacy is an important skill to learn for people entering adulthood. For students with disabilities, **self-advocacy skills** are especially important for success in **post-secondary environments**. Teaching and learning self-advocacy skills should begin when students enter grade school and be reinforced in the upper grade levels. Students with disabilities who have the potential to enter post-secondary education or employment fields need to learn self-advocacy skills in order to **communicate** how their disabilities may affect their education or job performance and their need for supports and possible accommodations. Students with disabilities who graduate or age out of their IEPs do not receive the **educational supports** they received at the grade school level. It is essential for students to advocate for themselves in the absence of teachers or caregivers advocating for them, especially when students independently enter post-secondary employment, training, or educational environments. Many colleges, universities, communities, and workplaces offer services to students with disabilities, but it is up to the students to advocate for themselves and seek them out.

Teaching Functional Living Skills

Also known as life skills, functional living skills are that students need to live independently. Ideally, students leave high school having gained functional skills. For students with special needs, **functional living skills instruction** may be needed to gain independent living skills. Students with developmental or cognitive disabilities sometimes need to acquire basic living skills, such as self-feeding or toileting. **Applied behavior analysis** is a process by which these skills can be identified, modeled, and taught. Students must also learn functional math and language arts skills, such as managing money and reading bus schedules. Students may also participate in **community-based instruction** to learn skills while completing independent living tasks in the community. These skills include grocery shopping, reading restaurant menus, and riding public transportation. **Social skills instruction** is also important for these students, as learning appropriate social interactions is necessary to function with community members.

Chapter Quiz

1. When a student demonstrates an absence of a skill or behavior, it is called a(n):

a. Performance deficit
b. Fluency deficit
c. Acquisition deficit
d. Knowledge deficit

2. Which of the following is NOT an activity that could be used for community-based instruction?

a. Grocery shopping
b. Reading restaurant menus
c. Walk in a park
d. Riding public transportation

Chapter Quiz Answer Key

1. C: Social skill deficits may be acquisition deficits, performance deficits, or fluency deficits. Acquisition deficits occur when a student demonstrates an absence of a skill or behavior. Performance deficits occur when a student does not implement a social skill consistently. A fluency deficit means a student needs assistance with demonstrating a social skill effectively or fluently. Once the student's social skill need is identified, teachers, parents, and other professionals can collaborate to incorporate an established routine or behavior contract or to implement applied behavior analysis.

2. C: Students may also participate in community-based instruction to learn skills while completing independent living tasks in the community. These skills include grocery shopping, reading restaurant menus, and riding public transportation. Social skills instruction is also important for these students, as learning appropriate social interactions is necessary to function with community members.

Assessment

Types of Developmental Assessments

Developmental assessments measure the development of infants, toddlers, and preschoolers. These **norm-referenced tests** measure fine and gross motor skills; communication and language; and social, cognitive, and self-help milestones that young children should achieve at certain ages. When a child is suspected of having a **developmental delay**, a developmental assessment is useful in identifying the child's strengths and weaknesses. These assessments map out the **progress** of a child compared to the progress of similar-aged children. Developmental assessments are also useful in identifying if the delay is significant or can be overcome with time. These assessments can be used to determine what **educational placement** is most appropriate for a child with a developmental delay. Developmental assessments are administered via observations and questionnaires. Parents, legal guardians, caregivers, and instructors who are most familiar with the child provide the most insight on developmental strengths and weaknesses.

Screening Tests for Identifying Students Who Need Special Education

When determining if a child needs special education, **screening tests** are the first step. The Individuals with Disabilities Education Act (IDEA) offers guidance for schools to implement screening tests. Districts and schools often have school-wide processes in place for screening students for **special education**. Screening tests can also be used to identify students who are falling behind in class. The advantage of screening tests is that they are easily administered. They require few materials and little time and planning in order to administer. Additionally, they can be used to quickly assess students' strengths and weaknesses, they do not have to be administered one on one, and they can be used class wide. Screening tests can be as simple as paper-and-pencil quizzes assessing what students know. They are used for measuring visual acuity, auditory skills, physical health, development, basic academic skills, behavioral problems, risk of behavioral problems, language skills, and verbal and nonverbal intelligence.

Individual Intelligence Tests vs. Individual Academic Achievement Tests

Intelligence tests measure a student's capacity for abstract thinking, mental reasoning, judgment, and decision-making. These **norm-referenced tests** help determine a student's **overall intelligence**, which correlates with **potential academic performance**. Intelligence tests can be used to determine if a student's deficits are due to intellectual disabilities or related to specific learning disabilities or emotional disorders. They can also measure verbal skills, motor performance, and visual reasoning. Intelligence tests are also known as **intelligence quotient tests (IQ tests)**. IQ tests should be administered by trained professionals to ensure the tests are administered accurately. Unlike intelligence tests, individual academic achievement tests measure a student's strengths and weaknesses in individual skills. They are also norm referenced and used to determine if a student needs **special education services**. Results from individual academic tests help determine areas of concern or possible deficits for an individual student. Unlike intelligence tests, individual academic tests can be administered by teachers.

Adaptive Behavior Scale Assessments

Adaptive behavior scales are useful for diagnosing a student with an **intellectual disability** that affects the development or progression of adaptive behavior. They are used in preschools and for determining eligibility for **special education** in grade schools. They are also used in planning the **curriculum** for students with intellectual disabilities. Adaptive behavior scales are standardized but not always norm referenced because of difficulties comparing expectations for some adaptive and maladaptive skills exhibited by similar-aged peers. In terms of curriculum planning, these assessments can determine the type and quantity of assistance a student may need. Adaptive behavior scale assessments identify a student's level of **independence**. Adaptive behavior scales can be used to determine **skill abilities** associated with daily living, community functioning, social skills, communication, motor functions, and basic academic skills. Teachers and other professionals can administer adaptive behavior scales to students with intellectual disabilities to determine starting points for improving their adaptive behavior deficits.

Curriculum-Based Measurement of Student Academic Progress

Curriculum-based measurement (**CBM**) is a way for teachers to track how students are **progressing** in mathematics, language arts, social studies, science, and other skills. It is also useful for communicating progress to parents or legal guardians. CBM results can determine whether or not current **instructional strategies** are effective for particular students. In the same respect, CBM can determine if students are meeting the **standards** laid out in their IEP goals. If CBM results shows that instructional strategies are not effective or goals are not being met, teachers should change instructional strategies. CBM can be revisited to determine whether or not the newly implemented strategies are effective. Progress can sometimes be charted to present a visual for how a student is progressing in a particular content area or with a specific skill.

Woodcock-Johnson Achievement Tests

High-Incidence Disabilities

Woodcock-Johnson achievement tests can be used as diagnostic tools for identifying children with **high-incidence disabilities**. The Woodcock-Johnson Tests of Achievement and the Woodcock-Johnson Tests of Cognitive Abilities are comprehensively useful for assessing children's:

- Intellectual abilities
- Cognitive abilities
- Aptitude
- Oral language
- Academic achievements

These norm-referenced tests are valuable in understanding children's strengths and weaknesses and how they compare to cohorts of normally progressing, similar-aged peers. For example, **Woodcock-Johnson achievement tests (WJ tests)** are useful in identifying children with language disorders because children with language disorders typically score lower on the listening comprehension and fluid reasoning test sections. The WJ tests are useful diagnostic tools for identifying children with attention deficit hyperactivity disorder (ADHD) as well. While children with ADHD may perform similarly to children with learning disabilities, their key deficits are in the cognitive efficiency, processing speed, academic fluency, short-term memory, and long-term retrieval test sections.

Learning Disabilities in Reading and Mathematics

The Woodcock-Johnson achievement tests (WJ tests) include a test of **achievement** and a test of **cognitive abilities**. Together, these assessments are useful in the diagnostic process of identifying a student with a **disability**. Additionally, they are helpful for identifying specific **deficits** in a student's reading or math skills. WJ tests are norm-referenced and compare the results of a child's performance to that of a cohort of children of similar age and average intellectual abilities. These assessments provide information about **reading disorders**, such as dyslexia, because they measure phonological awareness, rapid automatized naming, processing speed, and working memory. WJ tests report on a child's cognitive functioning in these test areas. These assessments also provide useful information for students with learning deficits in **mathematics**. Performance on the math calculation skills and math reasoning test sections provides information on specific deficits in general comprehension, fluid reasoning, and processing speed. Deficits in these areas are correlated to learning disabilities in mathematics.

The Weschler Intelligence Scale

The Weschler Intelligence Scale is an assessment that measures the cognitive abilities of children and adults. The **Weschler Intelligence Scale for Children (WISC)** measures a child's **verbal intelligence** (including comprehension and vocabulary) and **performance intelligence** (including reasoning and picture completion). The WISC is an intelligence quotient test that is useful for helping diagnose a student with a **cognitive disability**. A score below 100 indicates below-average intelligence. WISC results are useful tools for evaluating a student with a disability. Tests results can be used to measure and report on a student's general intelligence and provide insight into the student's cognitive abilities in order to determine an appropriate educational pathway. Results can be reported in a student's evaluation team report and individualized education program (IEP) in order to justify special education services or have a starting point for IEP goals. WISC results are especially important in an evaluation team report, and are generally completed at least once every three years, because they contribute to describing the **overall performance profile** of a student with a disability.

Kaufman Assessment Battery for Children

The Kaufman Assessment Battery for Children (**K-ABC**) is a unique standardized test because it is used to evaluate preschoolers, minority groups, and children with learning disabilities. The K-ABC can be used to assess children ages 2–18 and is meant to be used with children who are nonverbal, bilingual, or English speaking. However, it is especially useful in assessing the abilities of students who are **nonverbal**. The K-ABC can be used to help determine students' educational placements and assist with their educational planning. This assessment has four components that measure students' abilities, which are described below:

- The **sequential processing scale** assesses short-term memory and problem-solving skills when putting things in sequential order.
- The **simultaneous processing scale** assesses problem-solving skills for completing multiple processes simultaneously, such as identifying objects and reproducing design shapes using manipulatives.
- The **achievement component** measures expressive vocabulary, mathematics skills, and reading and decoding skills.
- The **mental processing component** assesses the abilities a student demonstrates on the sequential and simultaneous processing scales.

The K-ABC is also unique because it includes a **nonverbal scale** that can be administered to children with hearing or speech impairments and children who do not speak English.

Vineland Adaptive Behavior Scales

The Vineland Adaptive Behavior Scales (**VABS**) assesses the personal and social skills of children and adults. **Adaptive behavior** refers to the skills needed for day-to-day activities and independent living. Children with disabilities sometimes have deficits in adaptive behavior, and the VABS is useful for planning their **educational pathways**. It is an especially useful tool for developing **transition plans and goals** for students of appropriate ages on IEPs. The VABS is a process that involves people who know the students best, like parents and teachers. The teacher version and parent version of this assessment can be delivered via interview or survey. The parent version focuses on a student's adaptive behavior at home, while the teacher version focuses on adaptive behavior in the school setting. Version III of the VABS assesses four **domains**: communication, activities of daily living, social relationships, and motor skills. A student's parents or caregivers fill out a form pertaining to home life and a teacher fills out a form pertaining to school settings. The comprehensive score from both the teacher and parent version are used to report abilities in the four domains.

Types of Cognitive Assessments

Cognitive tests assess the **cognitive functioning abilities** of children and adults. They are useful tools for diagnosing or identifying children with disabilities who are eligible for **special education services** under the Individuals with Disabilities Education Act. Examples of cognitive tests used in diagnosing or identifying children with disabilities include aptitude tests and intelligence quotient (IQ) tests. There are also cognitive assessments that measure verbal reasoning, numerical reasoning, abstract reasoning, spatial ability, verbal ability, and more. Children's cognitive abilities are related to how quickly they **process** information. Assessment results can be good measurements of how quickly children may learn new information or tasks. Cognitive assessments provide specific information about children's cognitive functioning by providing measurements of their intelligence, attention, concentration, processing speed, language and communication, visual-spatial abilities, and short- and long-term memory capabilities. Results can also be used on a child's evaluation team report or to develop goals for an IEP.

Prenatal, Perinatal, and Neonatal Disabilities

Prenatal, perinatal, and neonatal risk factors can be genetic or environmental. These risk factors put infants at risk for developing **intellectual disabilities** that affect their day-to-day lives. An intellectual disability (**ID**) is a disability that significantly limits a child's overall cognitive abilities. **Prenatal** risk factors include genetic syndromes (e.g., Down syndrome), brain malformation, maternal diseases, and environmental influences. Drugs, alcohol, or poison exposure can all affect an unborn child. **Perinatal** (during delivery) risk factors include labor and delivery trauma or anoxia at birth. **Neonatal** (post-birth) risk factors include hypoxic ischemic brain injury, traumatic brain injury, infections, seizure disorders, and toxic metabolic syndromes. Early screening and applicable assessments are tools used to identify young children with intellectual disabilities and can assist with providing special education services under the Individuals with Disabilities Education Act. These tools can also help assess the severity of deficits and the need for special services, such as occupational therapy.

Advantages and Disadvantages of Curriculum-Based Assessments

Curriculum-based assessments (**CBAs**) determine if students are making adequate progress through the curriculum. They can be administered by a teacher, special educator, or school psychologist. CBAs have advantages over norm-referenced assessments, like developmental assessments, because they are not used to compare performance between students. Other types of assessments measure a student's cumulative abilities across multiple skills instead of assessing individual skills. CBAs measure student progress in more **individualized** ways. They are especially useful for measuring IEP goal progress. Since CBAs are **teacher-created assessments**, they provide opportunities to assess students informally and formally on IEP goals. For example, a teacher may verbally quiz a student on ten addition problems to determine if the student is making progress on math IEP goals. CBAs are also used in the "response to intervention" process to identify students with special needs by measuring the effectiveness of interventions provided to them.

Advantages and Disadvantages of Using Formal Assessments

Formal assessments measure whether students are learning what they are supposed to be learning. Formal assessments help teachers determine what their students know. They typically measure how students are **performing** compared to their similar-aged peers. Examples of formal assessments include quizzes, tests, standardized tests, achievement tests, aptitude tests, and norm-referenced tests.

Formal assessments have the same set of expectations for all students and are graded using the same criteria. However, students with disabilities do not always learn or retain content in the same ways as their similar-aged peers. The use of **universal criteria** to assess what students have learned is one disadvantage of formal assessments for students with disabilities. An advantage of formal assessments is that they allow teachers to collect **baseline data** on students' educational performance by comparing their performance to age- or grade-based performance criteria. Additionally, students with disabilities can receive **accommodations and modifications** when taking these types of assessments. Accommodations and modifications are implemented based on needs specific to each student. The goal is to level the playing field for these students on formal assessments, like standardized state tests.

Advantages and Disadvantages of Using Informal Assessments

Informal assessments can provide teachers with a lot of information about students' educational **strengths and weaknesses**. Informal assessments are also used to guide teachers' daily instruction by providing constant and immediate **feedback** about students' learning processes. Examples of informal assessments include observations and rating scales, checks of daily work, homework, group projects, checklists, and rubrics.

Informal assessments offer some advantages. They are often easy to implement and allow teachers to gather useful data. Informal assessments may be naturally less stressful for students because they often do not realize they are being tested. When test stress factors are removed, results from informal assessments may provide more accurate reflections of students' **abilities**.

Disadvantages of informal assessments include **hidden bias** or **stereotypes** held by the person administering the assessment. Teachers implementing informal assessments must be conscious of and avoid bias in order to receive accurate information about students' educational performance.

Formative Assessments

Formative assessments are any assessment that takes place in the **middle of a unit of instruction**. The goals of formative assessments are to help teachers understand where a student is in their progress toward **mastering** the current unit's content and to provide the students with **ongoing feedback** throughout the unit. The advantage of relying heavily on formative assessments in instruction is that it allows the teacher to continuously **check for comprehension** and adjust instruction as needed to ensure that the whole class is adequately prepared to proceed at the end of the unit. Formative assessments are often a mixture of formal and informal assessments. Formal formative assessments often include classwork, homework, and quizzes. Examples of informal formative assessments include simple comprehension checks during instruction, class-wide discussions of the current topic, and exit slips, which are written questions posed by teachers at the end of class, which helps the teacher quickly review which students are struggling with the concepts.

Summative Assessments

Summative assessments are assessments given at the end of an instructional unit, with the purpose of testing whether the students comprehend the sum of the materials within the unit. A unit might be defined as a 6-week period on a topic or could be defined as the semester or whole year in a class. Summative assessments tend to be formal and take the form of tests, projects, or portfolios.

The main distinction is that summative assessments are not given to help inform future instruction on the topic. Instead, they measure the mastery of learning standards.

Summative assessments use standards or benchmarks to measure student success at certain **checkpoints** during the learning process. They are almost always high stakes, heavily weighted, and should always be formally graded. Information from summative assessments can be used to report on student progress. Teachers can use a variety of summative assessments to determine where students are in the learning process. These types of assessments also play a role in identifying benchmarked progress and the educational needs of students with disabilities.

These types of assessments often feature a narrower range of question types, such as multiple choice, short answer, and essay questions to help with systematic grading. Examples of summative assessments include state tests, end-of-unit or chapter tests, end-of-semester exams, and assessments that formally measure student mastery of topics against a established benchmarks.

Review Video: Formative and Summative Assessments
Visit mometrix.com/academy and enter code: 804991

Alternate Assessments

Students with and without disabilities are typically expected to take the same standardized tests, sometimes with accommodations and modifications. Some students with disabilities take **alternate assessments**, which are forms of the standardized tests that other students take. Students that participate in alternate assessments are unable to participate in state standardized tests even with accommodations. Less than 1% of students in public school districts participate in alternate assessments. They are mostly intended for students with **intellectual disabilities** or **severe cognitive delays**. Alternate assessments are based on **alternate achievement standards (AAS)**, which are modified versions of state achievement standards. Alternate assessments are a way for students' progress to be assessed with standards that are more appropriate for their skills. For example, a state standard for math may not be appropriate for a student with an intellectual disability. Instead, the student may have the alternate standard of demonstrating the ability to count money to make a purchase. Teachers, parents, and students work collaboratively to demonstrate that the achievement standards are met.

Role of Formal Assessments in the Education of a Student with Disabilities

Formal assessments measure how well a student has mastered learning material and are useful in detecting if a student is **falling behind** in general or at the end of a unit. Formal test results can be used to compare the performance of a student with disabilities against other students of similar demographics. **Developmental assessments** are norm-referenced tests that are designed to assess the development of young children. Developmental assessments are used to identify the strengths and weaknesses of a child suspected of having a disability. **Intelligence tests** are another type of norm-referenced test that can determine a student's potential to learn academic skills. Intelligence tests, sometimes called IQ tests, also indicate a student's specific level of intelligence. This is helpful in knowing if a student's learning problems are associated with sub-average intellectual abilities or other factors, such as an emotional disturbance. A student with an emotional disturbance or specific learning disability would have an average or above-average intelligence score, whereas a student with intellectual disabilities would have a sub-average score. **Curriculum-based assessments** are also helpful in determining where, specifically, a student needs the most help within a content area.

Interest Inventories

Interest inventories are tools for measuring people's interests or preferences in activities. They are useful for gathering information about a student's likes and dislikes. In special education, interest inventories are sometimes used to help develop the **transition portion** of an IEP. A student's interests as determined by an interest inventory can be used to drive the entire IEP. For an older student with a driving interest in mind, interest inventories can also be reflected in the annual IEP goals. Interest inventories can come in the form of observations, ability tests, or self-reported inventories. They can also work as age-appropriate **transition assessments** used in the transition statement section of the IEP. An advantage of interest inventories is that they help students get to know their own strengths and interests. They are also useful in guiding students with disabilities into thinking about post-secondary careers, education, or independent living.

Role of Informal Assessments in the Education of a Student with Disabilities

Informal assessments are a little more flexible for teachers, particularly in the ways they can be administered in the classroom. In special education, informal assessments play an important role in **adjusting instruction** to meet the specific needs of a student. Using informal assessment outcomes to drive instruction helps ensure that academic or behavioral student needs are met. Informal assessments are also helpful in adjusting instruction to meet **specific goals or objectives** on a student's IEP. Checklists, running records, observations, and work samples are all informal assessments from which data for IEP goals can be collected. **Checklists** can include behaviors or academic skills the student is meant to achieve. **Running records** help provide insight into student behavior over time by focusing on a sequence of events. **Work samples** are helpful in providing a concrete snapshot of a student's academic capabilities.

Chapter Quiz

1. A score of less than ________ on the Wechsler Intelligence Scale for Children (WISC) denotes below-average intelligence.

a. 50
b. 75
c. 100
d. 150

2. The Kaufman Assessment Battery for Children (K-ABC) is especially useful for assessing:

a. Children with high-incidence disabilities
b. Nonverbal children
c. Bilingual children
d. Preschoolers

3. How many components does the Kaufman Assessment Battery for Children (K-ABC) have?

a. Three
b. Four
c. Five
d. Six

4. Which of the following is NOT one of the domains assessed by Version II of the Vineland Adaptive Behavior Scale (VABS)?

a. Communication
b. Social skills
c. Daily living skills
d. Visual-spatial skills

5. Which of the following is perinatal?

a. Brain malformation
b. Hypoxic ischemic injury
c. Genetic syndromes
d. Labor and delivery trauma

Chapter Quiz Answer Key

1. C: The Wechsler Intelligence Scale for Children (WISC) measures a child's verbal intelligence (including comprehension and vocabulary) and performance intelligence (including reasoning and picture completion). The WISC is an intelligence quotient test that is useful for helping to diagnose a student with a cognitive disability. A score below 100 indicates below-average intelligence.

2. B: The K-ABC can be used to assess children ages 2 to 18 and is meant to be used with children who are nonverbal, bilingual, or English speaking. However, it is especially useful in assessing the abilities of students who are nonverbal.

3. B: The K-ABC can be used to help determine students' educational placements and assist with their educational planning. This assessment has four components that measure students' abilities:

- The sequential processing scale assesses short-term memory and problem-solving skills when putting things in sequential order.
- The simultaneous processing scale assesses problem-solving skills for completing multiple processes simultaneously, such as identifying objects and reproducing design shapes using manipulatives.
- The achievement component measures expressive vocabulary, mathematics skills, and reading and decoding skills.
- The mental processing component assesses the abilities a student demonstrates on the sequential and simultaneous processing scales.

4. D: Using the VABS is a process that involves people who know the students best, like parents and/or teachers. The teacher version and parent version of this assessment can be conducted via interview or survey. The parent version focuses on a student's adaptive behavior at home, while the teacher version focuses on adaptive behavior in the school setting. Version II of the VABS assesses four domains: communication, daily living skills, socialization, and social skills. A student's comprehensive score from both the teacher and parent version are used to report abilities in the four domains.

5. D: Prenatal (pre-birth) risks include genetic syndromes (e.g., Down syndrome), brain malformation, maternal diseases, and environmental influences. Drugs, alcohol, or poison exposure can all affect an unborn child. Perinatal (during delivery) risks include labor and delivery trauma or anoxia at birth. Neonatal (post-birth) risks include hypoxic ischemic injury (brain injury), traumatic brain injury, infections, seizure disorders, and toxic metabolic syndromes.

Individualized Programs and Modifications

Developing and Writing Measurable IEP Goals

According to the Individuals with Disabilities Education Act (IDEA), students eligible for special education receive individualized education program (IEP) goals, which must contain specific **components**. Components of a **measurable IEP goal** include condition, performance, criteria, assessment, and standard. Measurable goals also include how skill mastery will be **assessed**, such as through observations or work samples. In the provided example below, the criteria is clearly measurable, as Jacob will either succeed or fail at multiple trials, and the ratio of successes to numbers of attempts should be recorded and dated throughout the IEP year to show his progress. Goals should also be **standards-based** whenever possible and may be required.

For example, an IEP goal may state, "By the end of this IEP, Jacob will use appropriate skills to communicate his needs in 4/5 trials."

- **Condition** refers to when, where, and how the disability will be addressed. "By the end of this IEP" is the condition of the goal.
- **Performance** is what the student is expected to accomplish during the condition of the goal. In this case, that is "Jacob will use appropriate skills to communicate his needs."
- The last part of the goal stating "in 4/5 trials" is the **criteria** that outlines how well the goal will be performed.

Determining the Placement of a Student with a Disability

With every student, the ideal goal is placement in the **general education classroom** as much as possible while still meeting the student's educational needs and ensuring a successful educational experience. The IDEA does not require that students be placed in the regular education classroom, but it does require that students be placed in their **least restrictive environment (LRE)** as defined by the student's IEP team. Ultimately, the IEP team determines what **environment** best suits the student based on the student's specific needs. The IEP team is responsible for determining what educational environment would provide the student with the maximum appropriate educational benefit. While justification for removing a student from the regular education classroom is common and appropriate, as occurs when a student is placed in a resource room, the IEP team must explain the reasoning in the student's IEP. **Justification** must specifically state why the student cannot be educated with accommodations and services in the regular education classroom during any part of the school day. Justification for removal cannot be the perceived instructional limitations of the regular education teacher or concerns over extra instructional time needed to educate a student with a disability.

Roles and Responsibilities of the Special Education Instructor in a Full or Partial Inclusion Setting vs. a Self-Contained Classroom

Students with mild to moderate disabilities are often placed in **inclusion** or **partial inclusion classrooms**. The responsibilities of the special educator include assisting and collaborating with the general education teacher to create a curriculum with **modifications** that meets the learning styles and needs of the students with disabilities. The special educator may circulate during lessons or classwork to help students when needed and provide modifications to the general education curriculum to best meet the individual needs of each student.

The role of a special educator in a **self-contained classroom** is much different. Students in a self-contained classroom typically have disabilities that significantly limit their ability to receive quality education in inclusion or partial inclusion settings. Students with moderate disabilities in self-contained classrooms receive **modified instruction** with accommodations. The special educator is usually assisted by teaching assistants or paraprofessionals who help the educator meet the needs of individual students.

Special educators in inclusion, partial inclusion, and self-contained classrooms share some similar **responsibilities**. These responsibilities include monitoring IEP data on annual goals for each student, giving standardized pre-tests and post-tests, facilitating parent-teacher conferences, completing annual IEP reviews, and developing curriculum.

Specially Designed Instruction

Specially designed instruction (**SDI**) in special education refers to specialized teaching given to students in a co-taught inclusion classroom. While a teacher teaches the class, the special education teacher provides specialized instruction in parallel to a student to help clarify the information. This is distinctive from adaptation and modification, as the content and its medium do not change for SDI. While the general education class engages in instruction, a special education teacher provides SDI to meet the specific needs of learners who may not be successful learning in the same ways as their similar-aged peers. The main purpose of SDI is to provide a student with access to the general education setting without substantially changing the content as it is aligned with state standards.

Universal Design for Learning

Universal design for learning (UDL) is a flexible approach to learning that keeps students' individual needs in mind. Teachers that utilize **UDL** offer different ways for students to access material and engage in content. This approach is helpful for many students but particularly those with learning and attention issues. The **principles of UDL** all center on varying instruction and assessment to appeal to the needs of students who think in various ways.

Principles of the Universal Design for Learning	
Multiple means of *representation*	*Instructional content* should be demonstrated in various ways so that students may learn in a mode that is effective for them.
Multiple means of *expression*	*Assessment* should be administered in a variety of ways to adequately allow students to demonstrate their knowledge. This includes quizzes, homework, presentations, classwork, etc.
Multiple means of *engagement*	Instruction should include a variety of *motivational factors* that help to interest and challenge students in exciting ways.

Role of Local Education Agency Representatives in IEP Meetings

A local education agency (**LEA**) representative is a member of the IEP team who is trained in special education curriculum, general education curriculum, and community resources. In many cases, a school building leader or principal may fulfil the role of LEA representative. An LEA rep must be a licensed professional who knows the student and is familiar with the IEP process. The role of LEA representatives in IEP meetings is to make sure the information presented is compliant with the IDEA standards. LEA representatives are also responsible for ensuring that the school district is **compliant** with procedural components of IDEA and that eligible students are receiving free and appropriate public educations (FAPEs). This role is necessary on the IEP team because whereas the whole IEP team should have the students' best interests in mind, they may not understand the doctrines of IDEA law and be able to consider compliance. As a result, they must act as the primary advocate for effective implementation of the IEP.

Involvement of Students with IEPs in the Transition Process in High School

Most states require **transition statements** to be made when students reach age 14 during the IEP year. Federal law requires students 16 years of age or older to have transition statements; post-secondary goals for independent living, employment, and education; and summaries of performance that include the results of the most recent transition assessments. Per federal law, students of transition age must be invited to their **IEP meetings**. It is important for students on IEPs to **participate** in the transition process because it helps them figure out what they want to do after they graduate from high school. Participation in the process gets them thinking about living independently, post-secondary education options, and employment options. Students usually have opportunities to participate in formal and informal assessments like interest inventories that help them define their interests. Transition goals for independent living, employment, and education should be based on the results of these assessments and any other interests the students have expressed. The students participate in the **implementation** of the transition goals by completing activities associated with their indicated interests.

Student Support Teams

A **student support team (SST)** is a team made up of parents and educational professionals who work to support students in the general education classroom who are struggling with academics, disciplines, health problems, or any other anticipated or actual problem that does not qualify the student for an special education or supports from an IEP. In this support team model, a group of educators works to identify and provide early intervention services for any student exhibiting academic or behavioral problems. The purpose of this kind of SST is to offer different supports, such as monitoring student progress, developing intervention plans, and referring students for intervention services. While the primary goal of this kind of SST is to provide support for students **struggling with school**, it can also shift focus to supporting students at risk of **dropping out of school**. Another primary objective of an SST is to identify students who are likely to have disabilities or who may need 504 plans to succeed in school and to recommend them for referrals so they are not left without necessary supports.

Amendments to an Individualized Education Program

A student's individualized education program (**IEP**) is in effect for one year. Academic goals, objectives, benchmarks, transition goals, and any accommodations and modifications are to be in place for the student for the duration of the IEP. An **amendment** to the IEP can be made when a change is needed before the year is over. An amendment is an agreement between the student, parents or legal guardians, and the IEP team. IEP meetings for amendments can be requested at any time. IEP amendments can be requested if a student is not making adequate progress toward the goals, if the goals become inappropriate in some way for the student, or when the student has met all IEP goals and requires new ones. If new information about the student becomes available, the IEP can be amended. Students, parents, and other team members may also request amendment meetings if they think that other accommodations and modifications are needed or should be removed.

How the Needs of Students with IEPs Are Met in the School Environment

IEPs communicate what **services** are to be provided for children with disabilities in the school setting, the children's **present levels of performance (PLOPs)**, and how their disabilities affect **academic performance**. IEPs also specify **annual goals** appropriate to the students' specific needs and any accommodations or modifications that need to be provided. Schools and teachers working with students with disabilities have the responsibility to implement these IEP components when working with the students. Additionally, schools and teachers working with students with disabilities must ensure that the students' individualized annual goals are met within a year of the students' IEP effective dates. It is up to the IEP teams to determine what classroom settings would most benefit the students while also appropriately meeting their IEP goals with the fewest barriers. Special educators must determine how data is collected, and then obtain and record data on how the students are meeting their IEP goals. Special educators are responsible for providing intervention services based on the data results. They must also ensure that any accommodations or modifications listed on the IEPs are implemented in both general education and self-contained classrooms.

Accommodation vs. Modification in IEPs

Formal accommodations, adaptations, and modifications for a student with a disability are listed on the individualized education program. **Accommodations** change *how* a student learns the material, while an **adaptation** or **modification** changes *what* a student is taught or expected to learn.

- **Accommodations** are changes to the instruction or assessment that do *not* alter the curricular requirements. For instance, a student with accommodations may be allowed to answer a test orally instead of writing the answers or might be given pre-structured notes to help organize thoughts during instruction. These types of changes do not fundamentally change the information taught or the requirements for passing.
- **Adaptations** or **Modifications** are changes to the instruction or assessment that do fundamentally change the curricular requirements, but which enable a student with a disability to participate. Examples of adaptations include substitution of activities for related materials, exemption from answering particular types of questions on assessments, and removing or reducing time limits when taking tests.

For state standardized tests, accommodations like extra time and frequent breaks can be provided. Students that need modifications to state tests may complete alternate assessments that may not cover the same material as the standard exams.

Creating a SMART Annual Goal in an IEP

A good IEP goal describes how far the student is expected to **progress** toward the goal by the next IEP. Since IEPs should be revised once a year, a good annual IEP goal should describe what the student is capable of doing in a one-year timeframe. Creating **SMART** IEP goals can help the student determine realistic expectations of what can be achieved in a year. SMART IEP goals are specific, measurable, attainable, relevant, and time-bound. Goals are **specific** when they list the targeted result in the skill or subject area. Goals should also be specific to the student's needs. Goals that are **measurable** state the way a student's progress will be measured. Measurable goals list how accurately a student should meet the goal. **Attainable** goals are realistic for the student to achieve in one year. **Relevant** goals outline what a student needs to do to accomplish the goal. For example, a SMART goal may state, "During the school week, Robert will use his device to communicate greetings 80% of the time in 4/5 trials." **Time-bound** goals include a timeframe for the student to achieve the goal. They also list when and how often progress will be measured.

Role of an Initial Evaluation Assessment in Qualifying a Student for Special Education

When a student is determined to need special education, it means the student has a disability or disabilities adversely affecting educational performance. It may also mean the student's needs cannot be addressed in the general education classroom with or without accommodations and that **specially designed instruction (SDI)** is required. An **initial evaluation** of the student is required for special education eligibility. The evaluation is comprehensive and includes existing data collected on the student and additional assessments needed to determine eligibility. Individual school districts decide what assessments should be completed for the student's initial evaluation. Each district is responsible for and should provide assessments that measure functional, developmental, and academic information. The student's parents or legal guardians are responsible for providing outside information relevant to the student's education, such as medical needs assessed outside of the school district by qualified providers.

Purpose of an IEP

The purpose of an individualized education program (IEP) is to guide the learning of a student with a **disability** in the educational environment. An IEP is a written statement for a student eligible for **special education**. An initial IEP is **implemented** once the child has been evaluated and determined to be in need of special education. After the initial IEP, **IEP meetings** are conducted annually (or more) in order to update the plan to meet the needs of the student. IEPs are created, reviewed, and revised according to individual state and federal laws. These plans include the amount of time the student will spend in the special education classroom based on the level of need. They also include any related services the student might need (such as speech-language therapy) as well as academic and behavioral goals for the year. As the student learns and changes, performance levels and goals change as well. A student's present levels of performance are included and updated yearly, as are the academic and behavioral goals.

Members of an Individualized Education Program Team

IEPs are updated **annually** following the initial IEP. IEP team members meet at least once a year to discuss a student's progress and make changes to the IEP. The required members of a student's IEP team include the student's parents or legal guardians, one of the student's general education teachers, the special education teacher, a school representative, an individual who can interpret the instructional implications of evaluation results, and if appropriate, the student. Anyone else who has knowledge or expertise about the student may also attend. **Parents and legal guardians** contribute unique expertise about the student, typically having the benefit of knowing the child well. **General education teachers** can speak to how the student is performing in the general education classroom. The **special education teacher** can report on progress made toward academic and behavioral goals and present levels of performance. A **school representative** must be qualified to provide or supervise specially designed instruction, be knowledgeable of the general education curriculum, and be knowledgeable about school resources. The **individual who can interpret evaluation results** can be an existing team member or someone else who is qualified to report on evaluation results. **Advocates**, such as counselors or therapists who see the student outside the school day, can also attend the meeting to speak on the student's behalf.

Legal Rights of Parents or Legal Guardians

IEP meetings occur annually for each student. However, it is a **parent or legal guardian's right** to request a meeting at any point during the school year. The student's school is responsible for identifying and evaluating the child; developing, reviewing, or revising the IEP; and determining what placement setting best suits the needs of the student. It is within the parent or legal guardian's rights to have **input** in all processes related to the student. Under the Individuals with Disabilities Education Act (IDEA), parents have the right to participate in IEP meetings, have an independent evaluation in addition to the one the school provides, give or deny consent for the IEP, contest a school's decision, and obtain private education paid for by the public school. In specific circumstances, if the student is determined to need services that the public school cannot provide, the public school district may need to pay for the student's tuition at a private school where the student's needs can be met.

Collaborative Consultation between Educational Professionals

Collaborative consultation refers to the special educator or other professional providing advice to the general education teacher about a student on an IEP. Special educators and other IEP team members, such as school psychologists and related service professionals, serve as the **experts** and have knowledge about how individual students learn and behave. This is especially important when students with IEPs are included in the general education classroom. Special educators and general education teachers must work collaboratively to ensure that students are reaching their potential in the general education setting. Examples of **collaborative consultation** include the special educator serving as a consultant to the general education teacher by providing advice on a student's IEP, accommodations, modifications, and IEP goal tracking. Another way the special educator or other professional can assist the general educator is by providing skill and strategy instruction to students on IEPs outside the general education classroom. The idea behind this method is for students to generalize these skills and strategies to the general education classroom.

Public School Responsibilities to Parents and Legal Guardians of Students on IEPs

The school must invite the parents or legal guardians to any **IEP meetings** and provide advance notice of the meetings. Each meeting notice is required to include the purpose of the meeting, its time and location, and who will attend. The location of the meeting is likely the student's school, but legally it must be held at a mutually agreed-upon place and time. If the parent or legal guardian cannot attend the IEP meeting, the school must ensure participation in another way, such as video or telephone conference. The meeting can be conducted without the parent or legal guardian if the school district cannot get the parent or legal guardian to attend. A parent or legal guardian can request a meeting, and the school can refuse or deny the request. If denied, the school must provide a **prior written notice** explaining their refusal. A prior written notice is a document outlining important school district decisions about a student on an IEP.

Environmental Modifications for Students with Disabilities in the Classroom

Students with disabilities may need environmental modifications in order to be successful in their classrooms, homes, and communities. **Environmental modifications** are adaptations that allow people with disabilities to maneuver through their environments with as little resistance as possible. They allow for more **independent living experiences**, especially for those with limited mobility. Environmental modifications ensure the health, safety, and welfare of the people who need them. Examples of environmental modifications in the home, community, or school include ramps, hydraulic lifts, widened doorways and hallways, automatic doors, handrails, and grab bars. Roll-in showers, water faucet controls, worktable or work surface adaptations, and cabinet and shelving adaptations are also environmental modifications that can be provided if necessary. Other adaptations include heating and cooling adaptations and electrical adaptations to accommodate devices or equipment. Environmental modifications in the home are typically provided by qualified agencies or providers. The Americans with Disabilities Act ensures that environmental modifications are provided in the **community** to help avoid discrimination against people with disabilities.

Chapter Quiz

1. Which of the following components of a measurable IEP goal refers to when, where, and how the disability will be addressed?

a. Condition
b. Performance
c. Criteria
d. Assessment

2. Which of the following is NOT a main principle of Universal Design for Learning (UDL)?

a. Communication
b. Representation
c. Action and expression
d. Engagement

3. Which of the following information about a local education agency (LEA) representative is FALSE?

a. An LEA member is also known as a district representative.
b. An LEA member is not required to have a license, but he or she must be familiar with the IEP process, and—when part of an IEP meeting—must know the student involved.
c. An LEA member is responsible for ensuring that the school district is compliant with procedural components of the IDEA.
d. An LEA member is a member of the school district where any special education meetings take place.

4. Which of the following is an example of a modification?

a. A student with a reading difficulty is able to listen to the text being read.
b. A student receives a shorter reading assignment than other students.
c. A student is given extra time to complete a test.
d. A student is given frequent breaks during a longer assignment.

Chapter Quiz Answer Key

1. A: Components of a measurable IEP goal include condition, performance, criteria, assessment, and standard. Condition refers to when, where, and how the disability will be addressed. For example, an iEP goal may state, "By the end of this IEP, Jacob will use appropriate skills to communicate his needs in 4/5 trials." "By the end of this IEP" is the condition of the goal.

2. A: The three main principles of UDL are representation, action and expression, and engagement. Through these principles, UDL ensures multiple means of representation, multiple ways for students to interact with the material, and multiple ways to motivate students.

3. B: Local education agency (LEA) representatives are knowledgeable about special education curricula, general education curricula, and community resources. An LEA member is also known as a district representative. An LEA member is a member of the school district where any special education meetings take place. In an Individualized Education Program (IEP) meeting, LEAs are members of the school district that referred the student for special education services. LEAs contribute their knowledge during the IEP meeting. An LEA member must be a licensed professional who knows the student and is familiar with the IEP process. The role of LEA members in IEP meetings is to make sure the information presented is compliant with the Individuals with Disabilities Education Act (IDEA) standards. LEAs are also responsible for ensuring that the school district is compliant with procedural components of the IDEA and that eligible students are receiving free and appropriate public educations (FAPEs).

4. B: Accommodations change *how* a student learns the material, while a modification changes *what* a student is taught or expected to learn. In classroom instruction, accommodations level the playing field for students with disabilities by helping them learn the same material and have the same expectations as their classmates. For example, a student with a reading difficulty might receive the accommodation of being able to listen to the text being read. Modifications are for students who are academically far behind their peers. An example of a classroom instructional modification would be a student receiving a shorter reading assignment or an assignment catered to the student's reading level.

Promoting Student Learning and Development

Promoting Student Learning and Development

Teaching Strategies and Accommodations for Students with Working Memory Deficits

Working memory is critical for remembering letters and numbers, listening to short instructions, reading and understanding content, completing homework independently, and understanding social cues. When **working memory skills** are absent or slow to develop, learning may be difficult. This may get worse for children over time. As they fail to develop or retain working memory capabilities, their overall **cognitive abilities** begin to suffer. Working memory deficits vary among people with disabilities, but accommodations can make up for missing or underdeveloped skills. Educators can implement **strategies** like reducing the children's workload; being aware of when children might be reaching memory overload; and providing visual cues, positive feedback, testing alternatives, and extra time. **Accommodations** in an IEP for a student with working memory deficits might include frequent breaks, small group instruction, and extended time for tests and assignments.

Classroom Accommodations That Allow Students with Disabilities to Be Successful

Accommodations are flexible classroom tools because they can be used to provide **interventions** without time or location boundaries. They remove **barriers** to learning for students with disabilities, and they change how students learn. Accommodations do not change what students are learning or expected to know. Classroom accommodations may be outlined in students' IEPs and 504 plans or simply provided as needed by special educators or general educators. Accommodations are put into place to ensure that students with disabilities are accessing the learning process with the fewest barriers, putting them on the same levels as their peers without disabilities. **Presentation accommodations** include allowing students to listen to oral instructions, providing written lists of instructions, and allowing students to use readers to assist with comprehension. **Response accommodations** include allowing students to provide oral responses, capture responses via audio recording, and use spelling dictionaries or spell-checkers when writing. **Accommodations to setting** include special seating (wherever the students learn best), use of sensory tools, and special lighting.

Effect of Home Life Factors on Learning and Development

Students' home lives are interconnected with their school lives. **Home life factors**, especially negative ones, are difficult for students to avoid generalizing to the school environment. **Home stressors** can often develop into dysfunction at school. Factors that affect the learning and development of students with disabilities include academic, environmental, intellectual, language, medical, perceptual, and psychological factors. **Academic factors** include developmental delays in core content areas, lack of basic skills, and apparent inconsistency of learning in certain stages of development. **Environmental factors** occur when children are exposed to home life trauma, such as divorce, drug abuse, alcoholism, parental fighting, or family illness. **Intellectual factors** include limited intellectual abilities or unnoticed gifted abilities. **Language factors** include issues with language barriers or language acquisition, such as aphasia, bilingualism, expressive language disorder, and pragmatic language disorder. **Medical factors** include attention-deficit/hyperactivity disorder, muscular problems, and hearing problems. **Perceptual factors** include any factors that affect or slow down students' processing of information. **Psychological factors** include depression, anxiety, and conduct disorders.

Social Skill Deficits That Occur in Students with Disabilities

Social skills generally develop alongside language development and emotional development, as they are a major component of communication and awareness. Social skills need to be taught to some students with disabilities, such as students with autism. **Social skills instruction** involves the teaching of basic communication skills, empathy and rapport skills, interpersonal skills, problem-solving skills, and accountability. **Basic communication skills** include listening, following directions, and taking turns in conversations. **Emotional communication skills** include demonstrating empathy and building rapport with others. **Interpersonal skills** include sharing, joining activities, and participating in turn taking. **Problem-solving skills** include asking for help, apologizing to others, making decisions, and accepting consequences. **Accountability** includes following through on promises and accepting criticism appropriately. These are skills that do not come naturally to students with social skill deficits.

Obtaining Accommodations in the Classroom Setting

When parents or legal guardians of children with disabilities believe that **accommodations** may help their children, they can arrange to speak with teachers about informal supports. **Informal supports** are strategies teachers can put into place to assist students with their learning processes. These changes do not require paperwork and can be implemented during classroom instruction. Teachers can experiment with informal supports to determine what will be most helpful for removing the barriers to learning students might be experiencing. If it is determined that students need bigger changes to how they learn, **formal evaluations** can take place. Students who do not already have IEPs or 504 plans may be evaluated to collect data on their needs. For students with IEPs or 504 plans, accommodations can be included the next time these plans are updated. The IEPs or 504 plans can also be **amended** if the need for the accommodations is immediate, such as if they need to be put in place before standardized testing time. **Data** supporting the need for the accommodations must be provided and listed in the comprehensive initial evaluations and all versions of IEPs and 504 plans.

Informal Supports vs. Formal Accommodations

Informal supports are generally easier to implement in the classroom setting. They do not necessarily have to be implemented only for students with IEPs or students with disabilities. Students who have not been evaluated for special education services can receive **informal supports** to ensure classroom success. Teachers may use informal supports to help students who are struggling with the ways they are learning. They may demonstrate that the students are able to learn with the accommodations in place. Informal supports are often the first step to indicating that students are in need of **special education services**. **Formal accommodations** are put in place when students become eligible for IEPs or 504 plans. Formal supports are written into the IEPs or 504 plans and then required by law to be provided. Examples of informal supports include frequent breaks, special seating, quiet areas for test taking or studying, teacher cues, and help with basic organizational skills. These informal supports may eventually turn into formal supports if students become eligible for special education services.

Inclusion Classroom Setting

The principle of **least restrictive environment (LRE)** is a right guaranteed under the Individuals with Disabilities Education Act (IDEA) to protect a student from unnecessary restriction or seclusion from the general population. IDEA does not expressly define an LRE for each specific disability, so it is the responsibility of the IEP team of professionals, including the student's parent or legal guardian, to determine the best **LRE setting** possible for an individual student. **Mainstreaming** or **inclusion** is the practice of keeping students with disabilities in the general education setting for the entire school day. The students may receive supports and services like aides, assistive technology, accommodations, and modifications that are appropriate for their individual needs. These supports and services are intended to help students with disabilities gain access to the general education curriculum with the fewest possible barriers. The principle of LRE also sits on a spectrum and allows for variable inclusion or separation throughout parts of the day depending on a student's particular needs. As this is a student right, any more restrictive setting must be **justified by necessity** in students' IEPs and cannot be determined by convenience or financial considerations of the school or staff.

Self-Contained Classroom Setting

According to the Individuals with Disabilities Education Act, LRE standards require students to spend as much time as possible with their non-disabled peers in the **general education setting**. This means students should receive general education "to the maximum extent appropriate," and special classes, special schools, or removal from the general education classroom should only be considered when students' needs are greater than what can be provided by supplementary aids and services. A **self-contained classroom setting** can be a separate class within a school or a separate school for students with disabilities whose needs are greater than what can be offered in the general education classroom even with educational supports. These settings may provide specialized instruction and support for students with similar needs. Placement in self-contained classrooms must be justified in students' IEPs.

Partial Mainstream/Inclusion Classroom Setting

It is generally up to the individualized education program team of professionals and the parent or legal guardian to determine the LRE that best suits the needs of a student. In a **partial mainstream/inclusion classroom setting**, a student spends part of the day in the **general education classroom** and part the day in a separate, **special education classroom**. This type of LRE is appropriate when a student's needs are greater than what can be provided in the general education classroom even with educational supports or services in place. For example, a student with severe deficits in mathematical skills may receive math instruction in a separate classroom or receive one-on-one or small group instruction. Placement in partial mainstream/inclusion classrooms must be justified in students' IEPs.

Specialized Education Settings

School districts sometimes offer specialized education settings for students with disabilities, such as **special preschools**. Preschools for children with disabilities typically focus on children aged 3–5 years. They are important resources for teaching early learning, communication, and social skills that are essential for children with disabilities. In **life skills settings**, students with disabilities can receive specialized instruction in academic, social, behavioral, and daily-living skills. **Social behavior skills settings** are sometimes called "applied behavior skills settings" or "behavior skills settings." In this setting, the primary focus is on social and decision-making skills. **Transition settings** are available for students making the transition from high school to life after high school. Students with IEPs can stay in high school until the age of 21 or 22, depending on the calendar month they turn 22. Transition settings assist students with work experiences, post-secondary education experiences, and independent living skills.

Parents and Legal Guardians Ensuring Accommodations Are Being Provided

Accommodations are changes to the ways children with disabilities learn, not changes to what the children are learning. While parents and legal guardians may only receive **formal updates** on how accommodations are being provided or helping the students during specified reporting times (unless students' IEPs or 504 plans specifically state otherwise), they can ask for **reports** on goal progress or accommodations for their students at any time. Parents and legal guardians can ensure that accommodations are successfully implemented by using the progress reports and asking the right questions. Parents and legal guardians can ensure that accommodations are being provided in a number of ways. They can **advocate** for their students by making sure the accommodations are being implemented on a regular basis. Parents and legal guardians also have the right to ask if their students are using the accommodations on a **regular basis**. If they are being used on a regular basis, parents and legal guardians can explore additional options that might help their students. Parents and legal guardians can work with special education teachers and the IEP teams to ensure that their students' accommodations are being received and are effective.

Evaluating, Modifying, and Adapting the Classroom Setting Using the UDL

The **universal design for learning (UDL)** is a framework that encourages teachers to design their instruction and assessment in ways that allow for **multiple means** for the student to learn and express their knowledge. The UDL model is most successful when the teacher prepares a classroom setting that encourages the success of students with and without disabilities. Knowledge of the **characteristics** of students with different disabilities, as well as the unique **learning needs** of these students, enables the teacher to address these needs in the classroom setting. Setting clear short- and long-term goals for students is one way to meet the UDL standards. A traditional classroom may offer one assignment for all students to complete, but a UDL-compliant classroom may offer **different assignments** or **different ways** for students to complete assignments. UDL-compliant classrooms often offer **flexible workspaces** for students to complete their classwork and may offer quiet spaces for individual work or group tables for group work. UDL-compliant teachers recognize that students access information differently and provide different ways for students to gain **access** to the information, such as through audio text or physical models to work with. The universal design for learning assumes students learn in a variety of ways, even if those ways have not been clearly identified; it follows that all instruction and assessment can be improved by making it more varied and accessible.

Modifying Classroom Curriculum and Materials for UDL

Curriculum

In order for a **universal design for learning (UDL) model classroom** to be successful, the teacher must evaluate, modify, and adapt the **curriculum** and **materials** to best suit the needs of the individual students. UDL contrasts with a one-size-fits-all concept of curriculum planning, where lesson plans are developed and implemented strictly based on how teachers expect students to learn. Instead, a successful UDL model addresses the many **specific needs** of the students. These needs vary depending on the unique abilities each classroom of students presents. UDL-compliant teachers can evaluate the success of lessons by checking for comprehension throughout lessons instead of only upon lesson completion. Evaluation methods used informally can provide a lot of information about whether students are grasping the concepts. Teachers use the results of the evaluations to modify and adapt classroom instruction to meet the needs of the students. Other means for diversifying the materials include using multiple assignment completion options and use of varied means of accessing the materials, such as both written, digital, and audio forms of a text. These means of instruction can take place simultaneously. For instance, a UDL-compliant teacher may choose to pair audio output and text for all students during a reading assignment in order to target students with listening or comprehension difficulties.

Principles of the Universal Design for Learning Model

The UDL model contains three principles that aim to level the playing field for all learners. **Principle I** of the universal design for learning model primarily focuses on what **representation or version** of information is being taught. This principle aims to target an audience of diverse learners. By providing multiple ways for students to approach content, teachers can ensure that the unique needs of all learners in their classrooms are met. **Principle II** examines how people learn. This principle focuses on the concept that students learn best when provided with **multiple ways** to demonstrate what they have learned. In Principle II compliant classrooms, students are given more than one option for expressing themselves. **Principle III** focuses on providing multiple ways for students to engage in the learning process. Principle III compliant teachers provide options for keeping content **interesting and relevant** to all types of learners. Effective UDL-model classrooms provide multiple ways to present content, engage in learning, and express what was learned.

Collaborative Teaching in an Inclusion Classroom

If determined by an individualized education program, a student with a disability may participate in an **inclusive setting**. In some classrooms, students participate in **co-taught settings**. In this **collaborative teaching environment**, the general educator and special educator work together to meet the goals of the students with disabilities in the regular education classroom. Students in this setting are all taught to the same educational standards. However, accommodations and modifications may be implemented for students with disabilities. In a successful collaborative teaching model, the special educator and general educator may cooperatively implement the accommodations and modifications for these students. A two-teacher setting also gives students more opportunities to receive individualized instruction, work in small groups, or receive one-on-one attention. Collaborative teaching in the co-taught setting can facilitate differentiated instruction, help teachers follow the universal design for learning framework, and provide individualized learning opportunities.

Implementing Modifications and Accommodations in an Inclusion Classroom

General educators can work with special educators to create an effective **co-teaching model**. In an effective co-teaching model, both general educators and special educators are guided by the **universal design for learning framework**. This helps ensure that the needs of the diverse group of learners are being met. Students' individualized education programs expressly document any required modifications, such as reduced work. In a co-teaching model, student modifications are communicated to the **general educator**. The **special educator** can work with the general educator to provide the modifications in an inclusive classroom setting. Students' IEPs also expressly document any required **accommodations**. These accommodations may or may not be used in an inclusive setting, depending on the relevancy of the accommodation. For example, the accommodation of using a calculator would be utilized in a math class but not a social studies class. In addition to expressly written accommodations, special educators and general educators can work together in an inclusive setting to provide appropriate accommodations during the learning process. These accommodations may be part of informal assessments used to adjust instruction.

Role of Paraeducators

Paraeducators, sometimes referred to as aides or paraprofessionals, are part of students' education teams. **Paraeducators** work under the supervision of special educators or principals and are key contributors to the learning process for certain students. Their primary role, especially if their positions are funded by the Individuals with Disabilities Education Act, is to provide **educational**

support for students. The use of paraeducators is noted in students' IEPs. Paraeducators can facilitate the learning process for students by removing learning barriers, keeping track of goal progress, and organizing goal-tracking activities. Paraeducators cannot introduce new concepts or take over the role of teachers. Paraeducators cannot make changes to what students are learning unless specific modifications are listed in students' IEPs. They cannot provide accommodations unless the accommodations are appropriate for what is written in students' IEPs. Paraeducators may also be instructed by supervising teachers or principals to facilitate and monitor accommodations or modifications for students and reinforce learned concepts.

Fostering the Communication Development of Students with ASD

Students with **autism spectrum disorder (ASD)** vary in their need for communication and social skill assistance and instruction. Some students with ASD may demonstrate slight to extreme delays in language; difficulty sustaining conversations; and the inability to understand body language, tone of voice, and facial expressions. Since ASD is a **spectrum disorder**, there typically is no single instructional strategy or technique that works for all students with the disorder. Some **evidence-based strategies** are effective for teaching appropriate communication skills to students with ASD. **Applied behavior analysis (ABA)** is an evidence-based strategy that involves providing an intervention and analyzing its effectiveness for a student with ASD. **Discrete trial training (DTT)** is a teaching strategy that is more structured than ABA. It focuses on teaching and reinforcing skills in smaller increments. **Pivotal response treatment (PRT)** is an ABA-derived approach that focuses more on meaningful reinforcement when generally positive behaviors occur. Where ABA targets very specific tasks, PRT targets behaviors categorically or more generally. Furthermore, instead of using an unrelated, supplemented reward system, such as giving candy for completing a task, the rewards used should be related to the desired behavior. For instance, suppose a targeted goal is to have the individual work on politely asking for things generally. The PRT-based reward involved might be something more related like giving the individual the toy or desired object as a reward for asking for it.

Managing Distractions That May Affect Learning and Development

Managing distractions is a part of good teaching practices. Special educators demonstrate good **classroom management strategies** when they do the following:

- Create positive learning environments by getting to know students' individual emotional, intellectual, social, and physical needs
- Remove or accommodate environmental triggers specific to students
- Remove or accommodate behavioral triggers
- Encourage students to help with classroom jobs and small tasks
- Create lesson plans with anticipated behaviors in mind
- Attempt verbal de-escalation first when behavioral issues arise
- Set clear, consistent rules
- Set and follow through with consequences for breaking the rules
- Take time to get to know students and their triggers
- Create seating arrangements that minimize distractions, such as placing distractable students closer to the teacher
- Teach social, thinking, test-taking, problem-solving, and self-regulation skills alongside academic content
- Use visual aids in lessons
- Utilize peer-instruction opportunities

- Provide opportunities for breaks
- Incorporate computer-based programs, which can hold the attention of students with disabilities like autism

Strategies for Planning, Implementing, and Facilitating Intrinsic Motivation

Intrinsic motivation is a person's inner drive to engage in an activity or behavior. Students with special needs often struggle with intrinsic motivation as a skill. This requires special educators and other professionals to promote and teach intrinsic motivation to students. Teachers can **promote intrinsic motivation** by giving students opportunities to demonstrate **achievement**. This can be done by challenging students with intellectual risks and helping them focus on difficult classwork or tasks. Teachers can build upon students' strengths by providing daily opportunities in the classroom for students to demonstrate their **strengths** instead of focusing on their weaknesses. Offering choices throughout the day provides students with ownership of their decision-making and communicates that they have choices in the classroom environment. Teachers should allow students to **fail without criticism** and should promote self-reflection in order to build students' confidence. Teachers should promote self-management and organizational skills like instructing students on how to **break down tasks**.

Instructional Methods for Teaching Students with Social Skill Deficits

Students with social skill deficits may or may not require explicit social skills instruction. These deficits can be addressed in inclusive settings. **Social skills instruction** can be delivered to entire classes or individual students, depending on the needs of the students. Also, **one-on-one** or **small group social skills instruction** can be delivered by professionals like speech-language pathologists. In both settings, it is important to model appropriate manners, hold students responsible for their actions, and have clear and concise rules and consequences. This creates educational environments that are both predictable and safe. Social situations that produce undesired outcomes can be remediated by **role-playing** the situations and teaching students positive responses. **Social stories** are another way to foster social skills growth. Often, these social stories demonstrate appropriate responses to specific social situations. The goal is for the students to generalize learned concepts to their school and home environments.

Promoting Learning and Development

Educators that practice effective strategies for **promoting learning and development** create successful learning environments and help struggling learners. Teachers should take the time to know the **strengths and weaknesses** of individual students in order to plan and implement instructional matches, including a curriculum that challenges students without frustrating them. **Scaffolding** is a strategy that breaks larger concepts into smaller chunks. This process helps students learn new concepts and apply prior knowledge. Instruction should be broken up into step-by-step strategies in order to allow students to follow those steps or remediate certain concepts. **Modeling and demonstrating** tasks or concepts are useful for teaching problem-solving abilities. Students mastering new content should receive consistent, positive **feedback** for their achievements. Additionally, students should be given opportunities to **talk through their processes** with peers or in teacher-led groups when learning new concepts.

Selecting a Developmentally Appropriate Curriculum

Choosing a developmentally appropriate curriculum is challenging for educators. Special educators have the additional challenge of finding a curriculum that meets the needs of the **individual students with disabilities**. The end result is not usually a one-size-fits-all curriculum because that goes against the intentions of IEPs designed to meet the needs of students with special needs. Instead, special educators often pick and choose curriculum components that best meet the needs of differing abilities in the classroom. When selecting an appropriate curriculum, special educators should consider the following:

- Standards and goals that are appropriate to the needs of the students
- Best practices that have been found effective for students
- Curricula that are engaging and challenging
- Instruction and activities that are multi-modal
- IEP goals
- Real-world experiences
- Different ways of learning that help teachers understand students' learning processes
- Collaboration with co-teachers to deliver appropriate instruction

In some special education settings, the curriculum is already chosen. In these settings, teachers can collaborate with co-teachers to find ways to provide instruction that meets standards and the individual needs of the students.

Accessibility Components of a Picture Exchange Communication System

A Picture Exchange Communication System (**PECS**) is a communication system for people with little or no **communicative abilities**. This system is a way for the students to access their environments using **picture symbols** to communicate meaning, wants, and needs. For example, a child may point to a picture symbol to request a book. A PECS is a way for students with communication disorders to develop their **verbal communication** without actually speaking. It reduces frustration and problem behaviors by providing students with an avenue to express what they want to say. It is commonly used for students with autism spectrum disorder in the form of augmentative communication devices. It can also be used for students with other impairments whose communicative abilities are affected. PECS focuses on **functional communication skills** and can be practiced in home, school, and community environments.

Using Visual Supports to Facilitate Instruction and Self-Monitoring Strategies

Many students learn best when provided with instruction and activities that appeal to multiple senses. A **multi-modal approach** is especially important for students with developmental disabilities, who may need supports that match their individual ways of learning. **Visual supports** are concrete representations of information used to convey meaning. Teachers can use visual supports to help students with developmental disabilities understand what is being taught and communicated to them. Visual supports can help students with understanding classroom rules, making decisions, communicating with others, staying organized, and reducing frustrations. **Visual schedules** show students visual representations of their daily schedules. This assists with transitions between activities, which can sometimes be difficult for students with disabilities. Visuals can be used to help students share information about themselves or their school days with their peers and parents. Visual supports can also be used with checklists to help facilitate independence. For example, behavior checklists can be used to help students monitor their own behaviors.

Using Instructional Methods to Address Independent Living Skills

When applicable, goals for independent living skills are included in the **transition section** of students' IEPs. However, **independent living skills education** should begin well before students reach high school, regardless of whether these skills are addressed in their IEP goals. **Functional skills instruction** is necessary to teach students skills needed to gain independence. Instructional methods used to address independent living skills for students with disabilities include making life skills instruction part of the daily curriculum. An appropriate **task analysis** can be used to determine what skills need to be taught. **Functional academic skills**, especially in the areas of math and language arts, should also be included in the curriculum. Telling time, balancing a checkbook, and recognizing signs and symbols are just some examples of basic skills that students can generalize outside of the classroom environment. The goal of **community-based instruction** is to help students develop skills needed to succeed in the community, such as skills needed when riding a bus or shopping. This type of instruction may be harder to implement than basic social skills training, which should be part of the daily curriculum.

Chapter Quiz

1. Which of the following is NOT a likely accommodation for a child with working memory deficits?

a. Avoiding breaks
b. Offering small-group instruction
c. Allowing extended time for tests and assignments
d. Providing visual cues

2. The Universal Design for Learning model contains how many principles?

a. Five
b. Four
c. Three
d. Two

3. Which of the following is FALSE concerning paraeducators?

a. They cannot introduce new concepts.
b. They cannot remove learning barriers.
c. They cannot make changes to what students are learning, unless specific modifications are listed in the students' IEPs.
d. They cannot provide accommodations unless the accommodations are appropriate for what is written in the students' IEPs.

4. Which of the following evidence-based strategies targets progress in areas of development, rather than focusing on decreasing specific behaviors, in children with ASD?

a. Applied behavior analysis
b. Discrete trial training
c. Universal Design for Learning model
d. Pivotal response treatment

5. Which of the following is NOT a way for teachers to promote intrinsic motivation?

a. Allowing students to fail without criticism
b. Instructing students on how to break down tasks
c. Minimizing challenging classwork or tasks
d. Giving students opportunities to demonstrate their strengths

6. A PECS might be used with a student with ASD. PECS stands for:

a. Picture Exchange Communication System
b. Parent-Educator Communication System
c. Physical Education Curriculum Standard
d. Public Educator Communication Strategy

Chapter Quiz Answer Key

1. A: Accommodations in an Individualized Education Program for a student with working memory deficits might include frequent breaks, small-group instruction, and extended time for tests and assignments.

2. C: The UDL model contains three principles that aim to level the playing field for all learners. Principle I of the UDL model focuses on what representation or version of information is being taught. This principle aims to target an audience of diverse learners. By providing multiple ways for students to approach content, teachers can ensure that the unique needs of all learners in their classrooms are met. Principle II examines the "how" of learning. This principle focuses on the concept that students learn best when provided multiple ways to demonstrate what they have learned. In Principle II-compliant classrooms, students are given more than one option for expressing themselves. Principle III maintains a focus on providing multiple ways for students to engage in the learning process. Principle III-compliant teachers provide options for keeping content interesting and relevant to all types of learners.

3. B: Paraeducators can facilitate the learning process for students by removing learning barriers, keeping track of goal progress, or organizing goal-tracking activities. Paraeducators cannot introduce new concepts or take over the role of highly qualified teachers. Paraeducators cannot make changes to what students are learning, unless specific modifications are listed in the students' IEPs. They cannot provide accommodations unless the accommodations are appropriate for what is written in the students' IEPs. The paraeducators may also be instructed by supervising teachers or principals to facilitate and monitor accommodations or modifications for students and reinforce learned concepts.

4. D: Since ASD is a spectrum disorder, there typically is no single instructional strategy or technique that works for all students with the disorder. Some evidence-based strategies are effective for teaching appropriate communication skills to students with ASD. Applied behavior analysis (ABA) is an evidence-based strategy that involves providing an intervention and analyzing its effectiveness for a student with ASD. Discrete trial training (DTT) is a teaching strategy that is more structured than ABA. It focuses on teaching and reinforcing skills in smaller increments. Pivotal response treatment (PRT) is an ABA-derived approach that focuses more on meaningful reinforcement when general behaviors occur. PRT targets progress in areas of development rather than focusing on decreasing specific behaviors.

5. C: Teachers can promote intrinsic motivation by giving students opportunities to demonstrate achievement. This can be done by challenging students with intellectual risks and helping them focus on challenging classwork or tasks. Teachers should also build upon students' strengths by providing daily opportunities in the classroom for students to demonstrate their strengths instead of focusing on their weaknesses. Offering choices throughout the day provides students with ownership of their decision-making and communicates that they have choices in the classroom environment. Teachers should also allow students to fail without criticism and instead promote self-reflection in order to build students' confidence. Teachers should also instruct students on how to break down tasks, and should promote other self-management skills and organizational skills.

6. A: A Picture Exchange Communication System (PECS) is a communication system for people with little or no communicative abilities. This system is a way for students to access their environments. PECS is a way for people with limited communicative abilities to use picture symbols to communicate meaning, wants, and needs.

Planning and Delivering Instruction

Teaching Strategies for Students Learning at Different Educational Levels

Learning styles of students differ, regardless of whether or not the students have disabilities. When addressing groups of students in inclusion settings, it is important for teachers to organize and implement teaching strategies that address learning at **different educational levels**. Students generally fall into one or more learning modes. Some are visual learners, some are auditory learners, some are kinesthetic or tactile learners, and some learn best using a combination of these approaches. Teachers can address students' educational levels by creating lessons that allow learning to take place visually, auditorily, and kinesthetically. **Visual learners** prefer information that has been visually organized, such as in graphic organizers or diagrams. **Auditory learners** prefer information presented in spoken words. Lessons that target auditory learners provide opportunities for students to engage in conversations and question material. **Kinesthetic learners** prefer a hands-on approach to learning. These learners prefer to try out new tasks and learn as they go. Lessons that include opportunities for these three types of learning to occur can successfully target different educational levels.

Components of a Differentiated Curriculum

Differentiated instruction is different from individualized instruction. It targets the strengths of students and can work well in both special education and general education settings. **Differentiated instruction** is also useful for targeting the needs of students with **learning and attention deficits**. With differentiated instruction, teachers adjust their instructional processes to meet the needs of the individual students. Teaching strategies and classroom management skills are based largely on each particular class of students instead of on methods that may have been successful in the past. Teachers can differentiate content, classroom activities, student projects, and the learning environments. For example, students may be encouraged to choose topics of personal interest to focus on for projects. Students are held to the same standards but have many choices in terms of project topics. **Differentiated content** provides access to a variety of resources to encourage student choice over what and how they learn. **Differentiated learning environments** are flexible to meet the ever-changing needs of the students.

Differentiated Instruction

Differentiated instruction is effective in general education settings, team-teaching settings, and special education settings because it targets the **strengths** of students. Differentiated instruction is used to target the different ways that students learn instead of taking a one-size-fits-all approach. Differentiated instruction is used in lieu of individualized instruction because it uses a variety of instructional approaches and allows students access to a variety of materials to help them access the curriculum. **Effective differentiated instruction** includes small group work, reciprocal learning, and continual assessment.

Small group work allows for the individual learning styles and needs of students to be addressed. In small groups, students receive instruction by rotating through groups. Group work should be used sparingly or be well-regulated to ensure that all of the students in the group is learning for themselves and contributing to group work sufficiently. Groups may be shuffled or have assigned roles within the group to ensure a good division of labor. In **reciprocal learning**, students play the role of the teacher, instructing the class by sharing what they know and asking content questions of their peers. Teachers who practice **continual assessment** can determine if their differentiated instructional methods are effective or if they need to be changed. Assessments can determine what needs to be changed in order for students to participate in effective classroom environments.

Teaching Communication to Students Who Are Nonverbal

Nonverbal students have extra challenges in addition to learning content. These students may need extra instruction in academic areas as well as specialized instruction in the area of communication skills. Students with **nonverbal disabilities** may also need social skills instruction, struggle with abstract concepts, and dislike changes to their routines. Teachers can **facilitate learning** for nonverbal students by making changes to their classroom environments, by teaching strategies for comprehending concepts, and by providing materials to accommodate their needs. Teachers can also provide accommodations or modifications to classwork and tests to make the content accessible to nonverbal students. Using visuals to represent actions, words, or concepts is a helpful instructional strategy for teaching nonverbal students, especially when teaching new material. Additionally, teachers can assist nonverbal students by taking measures to prevent undesirable behaviors from occurring.

Co-Teaching Models

Co-teaching models are utilized in collaborative, inclusive teaching settings that include students with and without disabilities. General educators teach alongside special educators and hold all students to the same educational standards. In the **one teach/one support model**, one instructor teaches a lesson while the other instructor supports students who have questions or need assistance. A **parallel teaching model** involves a class being split into two groups, with one instructor teaching each group. The **alternative teaching model** may be appropriate in situations where it is necessary to instruct small groups of students. In this model, one instructor teaches a large group of students while the other provides instruction to a smaller group of students. In **station teaching**, students are split into small groups and work in several teaching centers while both instructors provide support. Teachers participating in **team teaching** collaboratively plan and implement lesson content, facilitate classroom discussions, and manage discipline. Successful co-teaching uses all of these models as appropriate to meet the needs of diverse groups of learners in the inclusive classroom setting.

Intervention Strategies for the Instruction of Students with Multiple Disabilities

Working with students with multiple disabilities can be challenging. However, strategies used in other special education settings can be implemented to promote the success of students with multiple disabilities. Effective strategies include the following:

- Setting **long-term goals**, which may last for a few years depending on how long students are in the same classrooms
- Working **collaboratively** with team members, like paraprofessionals and related services professionals, to ensure that they carry out students' educational objectives consistently
- Developing and maintaining **group goals** that the adults and students in the classrooms can strive to achieve together
- Working with students and paraprofessionals and consulting paraprofessionals frequently for **feedback**
- Demonstrating **patience** when waiting for students to respond or complete tasks
- Learning about how students **communicate**, which may involve gestures, a Picture Exchange Communication System, or other methods
- Driving instruction and education goals based on how students **learn best**
- Considering how students will **respond** when designing lessons, including accounting for response time during instruction

Remedial Instruction vs. Special Education

Though the terms are sometimes used interchangeably, remedial instruction does not always equal special education. The difference between remedial instruction and special education has a lot to do with the intellectual levels of the students. In **remedial instruction**, a student has average or better-than-average intellectual abilities but may struggle with **skills** in one or more content areas. Remedial instruction provides one-on-one instruction to students who are falling behind. Remedial programs are often mainstreamed into general education classrooms to address the varying learning abilities of students. Remedial instruction can be delivered by general education teachers. **Special education** programs address the needs of students who may have lower intellectual abilities that require individualized instruction. Students in special education have **disabilities** specified by the Individuals with Disabilities Education Act and use individualized education programs. Unlike remedial instruction, special education requires qualified and credentialed special educators to decide how to best provide interventions in classroom settings for students with disabilities.

Teaching Social Interactions to Students Who Are Nonverbal

Students who are nonverbal may have access to **communication systems** implemented by trained professionals. Teachers, caretakers, and other professionals work with the students to use the communication systems effectively. The goal of a communication system is to teach a nonverbal student how to "talk" and engage in **age-appropriate social skills**. In order for nonverbal students to learn appropriate social interactions, they must spend time learning communication skills, just as they learn academic content. Communication skills can be taught in isolation or as part of students' daily activities. Giving nonverbal students opportunities to foster communication skills in **familiar environments** makes it easier for them to learn appropriate social interactions. Teachers, caregivers, and other professionals must demonstrate how to use communication systems to engage in conversations, make requests, and answer questions. Most importantly, nonverbal students must be instructed to **access** their "words" (communication systems) at all times throughout the school and home environments.

Remedial Instruction vs. Compensatory Approaches to Intervention

Compensatory interventions can be offered in the form of programs or services that help students with special needs or students who are at risk. The compensatory approach is different from remedial instruction because remedial instruction involves the breaking of concepts or tasks into smaller chunks and reteaching information. The **remedial approach** focuses on repetition and developing or reinforcing certain skills. The **compensatory approach** is implemented when a remedial approach is not working. It focuses on building upon students' strengths and working with or around their weaknesses. Tools such as audiobooks, text-to-speech software, speech recognition software, and other types of assistive technology are compensatory accommodations that help provide a free and appropriate education for students with disabilities who might otherwise continue to demonstrate skill deficits without these tools. Compensatory approaches and remedial instruction can and should be delivered at the same time to help ensure that students with disabilities are meeting their potential.

Levels of Bloom's Taxonomy of Learning Domains

Bloom's taxonomy of learning domains is a tool that can be used for instructional planning, curriculum planning, and assessment. It is used to promote and elicit higher levels of thinking instead of relying on rote memorization. Bloom's taxonomy can enhance instructional experiences for students by helping them to extend their **thinking skills**. This taxonomy is a useful tool for teachers wanting to improve students' thinking abilities. The taxonomy includes a list of **cognitive**

skills ranked from lower-order thinking to higher-order thinking. **Remembering** is the lowest level on the taxonomy. This involves simply remembering or recalling information. **Comprehending** is the next level, which involves thinking about and understanding information. When students demonstrate **application**, the next level, they show that they can use information and apply it to real-life interactions. In the **analyzing** level, students are able to categorize, compare, and contrast information. Students demonstrate the second-to-last level, **evaluating**, by making decisions and demonstrating judgment. **Creating** is the last level, which involves using prior knowledge and generalizing it to new concepts.

Mapping

Concept maps are visual organizers that help students with understanding and comprehension. They are generally easy to create and implement. Concept maps should be used before approaching new learning concepts. The purpose of a concept map is to help students organize new information and make connections between other content, thoughts, and ideas. Concept maps can be constructed as part of **teacher-led instruction**, which is a strategy that may be beneficial for students in lower grades. They can also be constructed independently or in small groups and then discussed as a class, which is a strategy more beneficial for students in higher grades. Concept mapping starts with **identifying major concepts** from reading selections or texts. Then the major ideas are sorted into **categories**, which can be adjusted as the process continues. Arrows or other visuals can be used to demonstrate how the ideas are connected. The last integral part of the concept mapping process is the **sharing piece**, when students reflect and talk about the processes and concept maps.

Culturally Responsive Teaching and Instruction

Culturally responsive teaching (**CRT**) involves teachers implementing instruction in a variety of culturally diverse ways in order to target all students. CRT teachers respect their own cultures and the cultures of others by taking the applicable cultures into consideration during planning and instruction. CRT instruction is student centered, considers students' unique abilities and strengths, and helps build and maintain student confidence in their specific cultures. CRT instruction is about reflecting cultural pride, learning styles, and tools. Successful CRT instruction allows all students to **engage** more and **comprehend** content that applies to them. Games created to address learning objectives require attention and processing and can teach skills that emphasize use of cultural tools to solve problems. Social learning helps students become responsible for their own learning processes and develop cultural competence, which is the set of skills needed to recognize, learn about, and communicate respectfully with and about other cultures. Benefits of CRT include establishing inclusive classroom environments, encouraging individual development and decision-making, assisting with overall comprehension, and putting a greater emphasis on the value of learning.

Voice Recognition Software

Voice recognition software and communication software can assist students who struggle with speaking or communicating. **Voice recognition software** allows people to speak commands into microphones to interact with the computer instead of using a keyboard. This feature helps create a **least restrictive environment** for a student with a disability because it removes the sometimes challenging aspect of using a keyboard while working on a computer. Voice recognition software allows users to carry out actions such as opening documents, saving documents, and moving the cursor. It also allows users to "write" sentences and paragraphs by speaking into the microphones in word processing programs. In order for voice recognition software to be effective, the user must learn to dictate words distinctly into a microphone. This ensures that the correct word is heard and dictated by the voice-to-text software. Some programs collect information and familiarize themselves with people's particular voice qualities. Over time, the systems adapt to people's voices and become more efficient.

Effectively Instructing Students Using Assistive Technology

Assistive technology (**AT**) refers to tools that are effective for teaching students with learning disabilities, as they address a number of potential special needs. The purpose of AT is to level the playing field for students with **learning disabilities**, particularly when they are participating in general education classrooms. AT can address learning difficulties in math, listening, organization, memory, reading, and writing. **AT for listening** can assist students who have difficulties processing language. For example, a personal listening device can help a student hear a teacher's voice more clearly. **AT for organization and memory** can help students with self-management tasks, such as keeping assignment calendars or retrieving information using hand-held devices. **AT for reading** often includes text-to-speech devices that assist with students' reading fluency, decoding, comprehension, and other skill deficits. **AT for writing** assists students who struggle with handwriting or writing development. Some AT writing devices help with actual handwriting, while others assist with spelling, punctuation, grammar, word usage, or text organization.

Types of Assistive Technology Tools

Assistive technology (AT) tools can be physical objects and devices or online resources that assist students with disabilities in their learning. The purpose of AT tools is to provide students with disabilities **equal access to the curriculum** by accommodating their individual needs to promote positive outcomes. **Personal listening devices (PLDs)**, sometimes called FM systems, are devices that clarify teachers' words. With a PLD, a teacher speaks into a small microphone and the words transmit clearly into a student's headphone or earpiece. **Sound field systems** amplify teachers' voices to eliminate sound issues in classroom environments. **Noise-cancelling headphones** are useful for students who need to work independently and limit distractions or behavioral triggers. **Audio recorders** allow students to record lectures or lessons and refer to the recordings later at their own pace. Some note-taking applications will transcribe audio into written words. Captioning is available to pair visual words with spoken words. **Text-to-speech (TTS) software** lets students see and hear words at the same time. TTS and audiobook technology can help students with fluency, decoding, and comprehension skills.

Instructing Nonverbal Students on the Use of Augmentative and Alternative Communication Systems

Students with communication disorders may require the use of augmentative or alternative communication systems. Communication systems are used to help the students effectively demonstrate **expressive and receptive language** and engage in **social skills**. Teaching appropriate communication skills is a collaborative effort between the students' caretakers, teachers, and other professionals. Typically, **speech services** are written into students' IEPs and the services are delivered by **speech language pathologists (SLPs)**. Depending on the requirements in the IEPs, the SLPs may work one on one with students or work with the teachers to incorporate speech and language skills throughout students' school days. In order for communication systems to work for nonverbal students, measures must be taken to ensure that the particular systems are appropriate for what the students need. It is important for the caretakers, teachers, other professionals, and even classmates to model using the devices so the students can learn how to "talk" appropriately. Students must also have constant access to the systems and receive consistent opportunities to communicate with the systems at home and at school.

Use of Visual Representation Systems with Students with Autism

Assistive technology (AT) helps increase learning opportunities for students with autism by eliminating barriers to learning. AT can help improve students' expressive communication skills, attention skills, motivation skills, academic skills, and more. **Visual representation systems** in the form of objects, photographs, drawings, or written words provide concrete representations of words for students with autism. Visual representations, such as simple pictures paired with words, can be used to create visual schedules for students with autism. Photographs can be used to help students learn vocabulary words and the names of people and places. Written words should be paired with the visual representations in order to create links between the concrete objects and the actual words. The goal is for students to eventually recognize the words without the pictures. Visual representation systems can also help facilitate easier transitions between activities or places, which can be difficult for students with autism.

Benefits of Vocational Education

Students with disabilities often participate in vocational education in order to gain **independent living skills**. Often, schools and communities offer services that provide vocational training for people with disabilities. These programs offer students **job-specific skills training** and opportunities to earn certifications, diplomas, or certificates. They often involve **hands-on learning experiences** focused on building skills specific to certain occupations. These programs are beneficial to students with disabilities who may struggle with grasping abstract concepts learned in typical classroom environments. Hands-on training in vocational programs can be a meaningful way for students with disabilities to both learn academic concepts and gain living skills needed to function in post-graduate life. Vocational education opportunities offer alternatives for students with disabilities who might otherwise drop out of high school. These programs also serve as a viable option for younger students to work towards, as most vocational education programs are offered to students in upper grade levels.

Supporting Classroom Transitions

Transitioning to life after high school can be a difficult process, particularly for students with disabilities. It is important for teachers to facilitate and support these **transitions** before students exit their special education programs. **Structured learning environments** that include independent workstations and learning centers provide opportunities for independent learning to occur. **Independent workstations** give students chances to practice previously introduced concepts or perform previously introduced tasks. **Learning centers** provide small group settings where new skills can be taught. Students can also rotate through different learning centers that offer art lessons, focus on academic skills, or provide breaks or leisure activities. **Classroom layout** also plays an important role. Teachers should plan their classroom layouts based on individual student needs in order to create comfortable, predictable environments for students with disabilities. **Visual schedules** help students transition between centers by providing them with concrete schedule references.

Vocational Skills Needed to Be Successful in Work Environments

Informal vocational training often begins before students even get to high school. Teachers include informal vocational training skills in their classrooms by teaching academic and communication skills. **Academic skills** can both spark and strengthen students' career interests and provide learning platforms to build upon. **Communication skills**, like giving and following instructions and processing information, generalize to work environments. **Social and interpersonal skills**, like problem-solving abilities and participating in phone conversations, are important for performance in workplaces. Students need to learn important **vocational and**

occupational skills required by most jobs, such as interacting appropriately with coworkers and keeping track of worked hours. Students also need formal or informal training in completing resumes, cover letters, and tax forms. Training may also include interview practice and job search guidance.

Resources to Promote Successful Transitions to Life after High School

In some states, **statements of transition** should be included in individualized education programs at age 14 for students with disabilities. In most states, the Individuals with Disabilities Education Act mandates that transition plans be put in place for students with IEPs at age 16 and every year thereafter. Some schools and communities have programs and resources available to facilitate students' successful transitions to life after high school. Throughout the transition process, it is important that students and their caregivers participate in any decision-making processes. **Vocational education courses**, sometimes called career and technical education (CTE) courses, offer academic course alternatives. The courses usually specialize in specific trades or occupations. They can serve to spark or maintain students' interests in vocational fields. Some schools offer **post-secondary enrollment options (PSEO)**, where students can participate in college courses, earning both high school and college credits. **Career assessments**, including interest inventories and formal and informal vocational assessments, serve to gauge students' career interests. These can be worked into students' transitional goals in their IEPs and should be conducted frequently, as students' interests change.

Components of a Transition Plan

Transition plans are flexible, but formal plans that help a student identify his or her goals for after school and act as a roadmap to help the support team advocate for the student's future. They generally include post-secondary goals and expected transition services. The four goal areas are vocational training, post-secondary education, employment, and independent living. **Transition goals** must be results oriented and measurable. Goals can be general, but the transition activities need to be quantified to reflect what the student can complete in the IEP year. It is common for interests to change from year to year; therefore, goals and plans may change as well. **Transition services** are determined once the goals are established. Transition services include types of instruction the student will receive in school, related services, community experiences, career or college counseling, and help with adaptive behavior skills. Goals and transition services must be reviewed and updated each year. Academic goals in the IEP can also support transition goals. For example, math goals can focus on money management skills as part of a transition plan.

Factors That Influence Successful Transitions to Post-Secondary Life

Parents or legal guardians, teachers, school professionals, community members, and students themselves can all contribute to successful transitions to post-secondary life. Key **factors** that help students successfully transition include the following:

- Participation in standards-based education
- Work preparation and career-based learning experiences
- Leadership skills
- Access to and experience with community services, such as mental health and transportation services
- Family involvement and support

Standards-based education ensures that students receive consistent and clear expectations with a curriculum that is aligned to the universal design for learning standards. Exposure to work preparation and career-based learning experiences ensures that students receive opportunities to discover potential career interests or hobbies. Connections and experiences with community activities provide students with essential post-secondary independent living skills. Family involvement and support ensure that students have advocates for their needs and interests. Families can also help students connect with school and community-based supports that facilitate their career interests.

Including Measurable and Challenging Objectives in Lesson Plans

No matter what types of goals are being designed, they can benefit from following a systematic checklist to make sure the goals are set up for success. Objective, well-defined goals are much easier and rewarding to accomplish than undefined or obscure goals. **SMART** is a mnemonic system that can be used as a framework for many types of instructional planning. SMART goals vary slightly between different forms of the model, but are generally made up of the following elements:

- **Specific** – Goals must be well-targeted and not overly generalized.
- **Measurable** – Goals must be measurable or testable to determine whether progress has been made.
- **Achievable** – Goals must be realistic to meet and not overly difficult.
- **Relevant** – Goals must be motivating and pertinent to the individual.
- **Timely or Time-bound** – Goals must have a specific timeframe.

Teachers can use SMART objectives to build a framework for effectively executing the lesson plans. The components of a SMART goal may also correspond to the **five "W" and one "H" questions** to help ground the goal into something that is concrete and attainable:

- **Specific**
    - **What** is the specific thing I want to accomplish?
- **Measurable** and **Achievable**
    - **Who** do I need help from or **who** is involved?
    - **How** can I accomplish this goal?
- **Relevant**
    - **Why** is this goal important?
- **Timely**
    - **When** will I be able to accomplish this goal and what is the timeline for my goal?

Chapter Quiz

1. Which of the following co-teaching models involves a class being split into two groups, with one instructor teaching each group?

a. One teach/one support
b. Parallel teaching
c. Alternative teaching
d. Team-teaching

2. Which of the following is NOT an intervention strategy for the instruction of students with multiple disabilities?

a. Working collaboratively with team members
b. Implementing multiple restrictions to limit disruption
c. Demonstrating patience
d. Developing and maintaining group goals

3. Which of the following is NOT a feature of effective differentiated instruction?

a. Targeting individual strengths rather than taking a one-size-fits-all approach
b. Large-group work
c. Reciprocal learning
d. Continual assessment

4. Which of the following is FALSE concerning remedial instruction and special education?

a. In remedial instruction, a student has average or better-than-average intellectual abilities but may struggle with skills in one or more content areas.
b. Remedial programs are often mainstreamed into general education classrooms to address the varying learning abilities of classroom students.
c. The difference between remedial instruction and special education has little to do with the intellectual levels of the students.
d. Special education requires qualified and credentialed special educators.

5. What is the lowest level of Bloom's taxonomy?

a. Remembering
b. Comprehending
c. Applying
d. Evaluating

6. TTS is a form of assistive technology. TTS stands for:

a. Type-text script
b. Text-training system
c. Tools Teaching Speech
d. Text-to-speech

Chapter Quiz Answer Key

1. B: In co-teaching, general educators teach alongside special educators and hold all students to the same educational standards. In successful co-teaching settings, the various co-teaching models are used fluidly. In the one teach/one support model, one instructor teaches a lesson while the other instructor supports students who have questions or need assistance. The parallel teaching model involves splitting a class into two groups, with one instructor teaching each group. The alternative teaching model may be appropriate in situations where it is necessary to instruct small groups of students. In this model, one instructor teaches a large group of students while the other instructs a smaller group of students. In station teaching, students are split into small groups and work in several teaching centers while both instructors provide support. Teachers participating in team-teaching collaboratively plan and implement lesson content, facilitate classroom discussions, and manage discipline. These models all take place in the inclusive classroom setting and are intended to meet the needs of diverse groups of learners.

2. B: Working with students with multiple disabilities can be challenging. However, strategies used in other special education settings can be implemented to promote the success of students with multiple disabilities. Effective strategies include:

- Setting long-term goals, which may last for a few years depending on how long students are in the same classrooms
- Working collaboratively with team members, like paraprofessionals and related services professionals, to ensure that the students' educational objectives are carried out consistently by all adults
- Developing and maintaining group goals that the adults and students in the classrooms can strive to achieve together
- Working with students and paraprofessionals and consulting paraprofessionals frequently for feedback
- Demonstrating patience when waiting for children to respond or complete tasks
- Learning about how students communicate, which may involve gestures, a Picture Exchange Communication System, or other methods
- Driving instructional and educational goals based on how students learn best
- Considering how students will respond when designing lessons, which includes accounting for response time during instruction

3. B: Differentiated instruction is effective in general education settings, team-teaching settings, and special education settings because it targets the strengths of classroom students. Differentiated instruction is used to target the different ways that students learn instead of taking a one-size-fits-all approach. Differentiated instruction is used in lieu of individualized instruction because it uses a variety of instructional approaches and allows students access to a variety of materials to help them access the curriculum. Effective differentiated instruction includes small-group work, reciprocal learning, and continual assessment.

4. C: Though the terms are sometimes used interchangeably, remedial instruction does not always equal special education. The difference between remedial instruction and special education has a lot to do with the intellectual levels of the students. In remedial instruction, a student has average or better-than-average intellectual abilities but may struggle with skills in one or more content areas. When schools or teachers offer remedial instructional programs or opportunities in the classroom, they offer one-on-one instruction to students who are falling behind. Remedial programs are often mainstreamed into general education classrooms to address the varying learning abilities of classroom students. Remedial instruction can be delivered by general education teachers. Special education programs address the needs of students who may have lower intellectual abilities that require individualized instruction. Students in special education have disabilities specified by the Individuals with Disabilities Education Act and use Individualized Education Programs. Unlike remedial instruction, special education requires qualified and credentialed special educators to decide how to best provide interventions in classroom settings for students with disabilities.

5. A: The taxonomy includes a list of cognitive skills ranked from lower-order thinking to higher-order thinking. Remembering is the lowest level on the taxonomy. This involves simply recalling information. Comprehending, the next level, involves thinking about and understanding information. When students demonstrate application, the next level, they show that they can use information and apply it to real-life interactions. In the analyzing level, students are able to categorize, compare, and contrast information. Students demonstrate the second-to-last level, evaluating, by making decisions and demonstrating judgement. Creating, the last level, involves using prior knowledge and generalizing it to new concepts.

6. D: Text-to-speech (TTS) software lets students see and hear words at the same time. TTS and audiobook technology can help students with fluency, decoding, and comprehension skills.

Planning and Managing the Learning Environment

Characteristics of Effective Structured Learning Environments

A structured learning environment is an important component of good **classroom management**. Teachers that create environments that are conducive for teaching and learning create environments where students feel safe. In **effective structured learning environments**, teachers create solid relationships with students by getting to know them and their interests. Often, this information can be used to implement learning activities based on students' interests. Another way to promote effective structured learning environments is to consistently follow implemented rules and maintain **consistency** in procedures in order to communicate what to expect to students. Transitioning students appropriately between activities increases time spent learning. Additionally, teachers that spend time designing effective lesson plans that anticipate student behaviors create solid environments for their students. Teachers can also establish good learning environments by promoting target behaviors. This means promoting standards of behavior and clear consequences for breaking rules. Students that have clear expectations learn in effective structured learning environments.

Curriculum and Assignment Modifications in the Classroom for Students with Disabilities

Modifications are changes to what students are taught or expected to learn. Students with disabilities can receive **curriculum modifications** as determined by their specific needs and as written out in their Individualized Education Programs. Curriculum modifications allow students to learn material that is different from what their general education peers learn. For example, students with classroom modifications may receive assignments with fewer math problems or with reading samples appropriate for their reading levels. Students with curriculum modifications may receive different grading tiers than their peers. The ways teachers grade their assignments may be different from how the teachers grade their peers' assignments. Students may also be excused from particular projects or given project guidelines that are different and better suited to their individual needs. **Assignment modifications** include completing fewer or different homework problems than peers, writing shorter papers, answering fewer questions on classwork and tests, and creating alternate projects or assignments.

Purpose of Non-Traditional Classroom Seating Arrangements

Seating arrangements are part of good classroom management strategies, especially for students with disabilities. Special education settings and inclusion settings often require flexibility with instruction and versatility with **seating arrangements**. The traditional setting includes rows of desks facing the area where the teacher conducts instruction. More **student-centered arrangements** include a horseshoe seating arrangement, a group pod arrangement, or a paired arrangement. A **horseshoe seating arrangement** is conducive to student-centered instruction because it allows the students to face each other and the instructor to move around the classroom easily. This setup facilitates classroom discussions and encourages interactions between instructors and students and among peers. The **group pod** or **paired-pod arrangement** is useful for student-centered instruction like small group work. This arrangement is also helpful when students need to rotate through lesson stages or work in small groups on projects. Effective teachers do not use one seating arrangement for the entire year. Best practices indicate that seating arrangements should change and be tied to the intent of lesson objectives.

Determining the Special Education Setting Placement

Special education setting placement is determined in a student's Individualized Education Program (IEP), as specified by the Individuals with Disabilities Education Act (IDEA). IDEA requires that students be placed in **general education classrooms** to the maximum extent possible. Students should be placed in environments that are most appropriate for them, known as the **least restrictive environment**. If students can be educated in general education classrooms (**inclusion**) when provided with appropriate accommodations, they can be placed in general education classrooms. When students with disabilities need modifications to curriculum that are significantly below grade level or different than their peers, the students may be placed in **resource rooms** for remedial instruction. However, the students may also participate in the general education curriculum with modified work that meets their current abilities. For example, a student who struggles in math can use a calculator accommodation in the inclusion setting. A student whose math skills are two grade levels below the skills of same-aged peers may be placed in an inclusion setting with modifications or receive instruction in a resource room.

Function of a Multidisciplinary Team-Teaching Model

The three disciplinary team models include a multidisciplinary team, an interdisciplinary team, and a transdisciplinary team. The **multidisciplinary team** is usually composed of the special educator, general education teacher, parents, paraprofessionals, principal, and school psychologist. As a whole, this team presents a comprehensive group of expertise, qualifications, and skills. In the multidisciplinary team model, these professionals do not collaborate, but instead work alongside each other to pursue a **common goal** for the individual student with special needs. The multidisciplinary team model is effective for evaluating a student for referral for special education, completing pre-referral testing, and completing an Individualized Education Program or Evaluation Team Report. Sometimes this team is referred to as the child study team or student support team. In this model, professionals usually pull out students to work with them individually. Parents and legal guardians are a part of this process. Professionals working with the student should openly communicate their processes and the results of any evaluations or informal observations.

Interdisciplinary Team Model

An interdisciplinary team model features the **general education teacher** providing all curriculum and accommodations for a student with an Individualized Education Program. In this model, the special educator and other professionals relevant to the education of the student collaborate to ensure that the curriculum meets the needs of the student and the accommodations are appropriate. This model is not a team-teaching model. Advantages of this model include the collaboration of all IEP team members towards a common goal and the student's needs being addressed by one teacher instead of several different teachers or professionals. The disadvantages of this model include difficulties with collaboration between professionals and issues with delivering related services to students who need them. Related service provision sometimes includes one-on-one instruction, which requires the student to be pulled out for a certain amount of time during general education instruction. This model may also not be appropriate for students with intense needs, as they often require **individualized education** in order to meet IEP goals. They may also require specific accommodations and modifications not suitable for the general education classroom.

Transdisciplinary Team-Teaching Model

In this model, professionals working with the student work together collaboratively to ensure the individual needs of the student are met. The **special educator** may teach in the general education classroom, delivering instruction to both students with and without disabilities. This model features a team-teaching experience for classroom students, where the special educator and general educator may take turns teaching. The presence of the special educator in the general education setting means the special educator can offer advice for **accommodating** the students with special needs in the classroom. Additionally, this model provides opportunities for teachers and other professionals to communicate consistently about students' progress, share ideas, and work collaboratively to solve any issues that arise. The effectiveness of this model relies heavily on the collaboration of the special educator and the general educator addressing the major features of this team-teaching model.

Advantages and Disadvantages of Team-Teaching Models

Students with and without disabilities present a variety of **learning abilities** in the general education classroom. One advantage of team-teaching models in this setting is being able to target the unique abilities, learning methods, and skills that each student brings to the classroom. Another advantage is effective classroom management. In an **effective team-teaching model**, one teacher provides the instruction, while the other practices classroom management skills to minimize disruptions and promote a safe learning environment. This model encourages class participation, facilitates group activities, and provides multiple means of engagement for learning content. One disadvantage is there may be an offset between the teachers sharing a class. When one teacher is not open to multiple methods of delivering instruction, the team-teaching approach is ineffective. Planning and making group decisions regarding curriculum can be time consuming and stressful in a team-teaching environment.

Lifting Guidelines for Students Who Require Physical Lifting

Teachers and paraprofessionals may encounter students with physical disabilities who require **assisted transfers**. In some circumstances, students must be **lift-assisted** from their wheelchairs in order to participate in physical therapy or floor activities. While this practice is more common in low-incidence classrooms and not always a job requirement, it is important to know school guidelines for **lifting techniques** to keep staff and students safe. Knowing school guidelines for lifting can also help prevent back injuries from occurring. Physical therapists working with the students should be consulted before attempting student lifts. They are trained professionals who know specific procedures for lifting students in order to keep the students and staff members safe. Every school district has policies for lift-assisted student transfers. Each student should be evaluated to determine if a one-person lift or two-person lift is needed. Two-person lifts are for heavier students, and some school districts do not allow two-person lifts for safety reasons.

How Cooperative Learning Works

Cooperative learning is an interpersonal group learning process where students learn concepts by working together in **small groups**. Cooperative learning involves collaboration among small groups to achieve common goals. With **formal cooperative learning**, an instructor oversees the learning of lesson material or completion of assignments for students in these small groups. With **informal cooperative learning**, the instructor supervises group activities by keeping students cognitively active but does not guide instruction or assignments. For example, a teacher might use a class period to show a movie but provide a list of questions for students to complete during the movie. In the special education classroom, cooperative learning is helpful when students need specific skills targeted or remediated. It is also helpful for separating students who are learning different content at different levels. For example, a cooperative learning activity may involve multiple groups of students with differing levels of mathematic abilities. Group work also promotes development of interpersonal skills as students interact with one another.

Benefit of Multiple Modality Instruction and Activities

The purpose of multiple modality instruction is to engage students by offering different ways to learn the same material. **Multiple modality teaching** also addresses students' unique learning styles. Learning modalities are generally separated into four categories: **visual** (seeing), **auditory** (hearing), **kinesthetic** (moving), and **tactile** (touch) modalities. This way of teaching targets students who may have deficits in one or more modalities. It is also helpful for students who struggle in one or more of the learning categories. If a student struggles with understanding content that is presented visually, a lesson that includes auditory, kinesthetic, and tactile components may engage learning. Additionally, presenting lesson material and activities in a multi-modal approach helps improve student memory and retention by solidifying concepts through multiple means of engagement. This approach is also useful for students with **attention disorders** who may struggle in environments where one mode of teaching is used. The multiple modality approach ensures that activities, such as kinesthetic or tactile activities, keep more than one sense involved with the learning process.

Components of a Successful Team-Teaching Model

A successful team-teaching model is one where the teachers involved set clear, effective, specific **goals** for performance. These goals must demonstrate clarity. All team-teaching members must be clear on the components of the goals and their potential outcomes. Clear goals allow team members and students to know what they are working towards as a classroom. Goals should be specific and measurable. **Goal criteria** should be qualified in percentages or quantities. This provides hard evidence for how effectively the team-teaching classroom is meeting the goals. Challenging goals set high expectations for what the team needs to work towards. Challenging goals ensure that team members and classroom students are working to achieve goals right outside their ability levels. Goals that are too challenging can be frustrating for all team members and students. A successful team-teaching model also reflects **commitment** from team members and any other professionals involved in the classroom.

Classroom Timing, Schedule, and Organization Accommodations

Timing, schedule, and organizational accommodations change the ways students with disabilities have access to classrooms with the fewest barriers to learning. Students who need these accommodations receive them as written statements in their Individualized Education Programs, 504 Plans, or as teachers see fit during classroom time. **Timing accommodations** allow students more time to complete tasks or tests and/or process instructions. They also allow students to access frequent breaks during assignments or tests. **Schedule accommodations** include taking tests in chunks over periods of time or several days, taking test sections in different orders, and/or taking tests during specific times of day. **Organizational skill accommodations** include assistance with time management, marking texts with highlighters, maintaining daily assignment or work schedules, and/or receiving study skills instruction. When accommodations are written in a student's IEP, the student has access to them for state standardized tests. When and how accommodations are put into place is left to the discretion of the teacher unless specifically written in the student's IEP or 504 Plan.

Creating Inclusive Learning Environments That Address Unique Needs

Effective inclusive environments abide by the **Universal Design for Learning framework**. Special educators and general educators can work together to create learning environments that are accessible to the unique needs of students with language or physical needs. This can be done by providing **multiple ways** for students to access lesson concepts, express learned concepts, and engage in the learning process. For students with language barriers, signs, symbols, pictures, and learning concepts may have different meanings than they do for students without language barriers. Keeping this in mind, teachers can address UDL guidelines for students with **language barriers** by providing diverse ways to activate prior knowledge, emphasizing key learning elements, and using visuals to guide the learning process. For students with **physical barriers**, teachers can level the learning process by making their physical classroom environments accessible and providing different ways for students to express what they have learned. In general, teachers abiding by UDL framework would have these supports in place in order to ensure that the needs of diverse learners are met.

Fostering Positive and Inclusive Learning Environments Addressing Students with Learning or Cognitive Needs

Whether in the general education classroom or special education classroom, the Universal Design for Learning model should foster **positive and inclusive learning environments**. General education and special education teachers can take measures to ensure the UDL concept is implemented to address the unique needs of students with **cognitive or behavioral needs**. Since each student presents different needs, a one-size-fits-all approach to learning is not suitable or UDL compliant for these students. Special educators and general educators should openly communicate about the unique learning needs of the students with learning or cognitive needs. General strategies include receiving regular **input from special educators** on how to best meet the needs of the students in the classroom. This includes sharing information with any **paraprofessionals and aides** regarding how to assist the students in the general education classroom. UDL base strategies include the general educators providing multiple means by which students can complete the assignments. Students with cognitive disabilities may also benefit from the use of concrete examples and instruction, especially when addressing abstract concepts.

Fostering Positive and Inclusive Learning Environments Addressing Students with Behavioral Needs

The **Universal Design for Learning (UDL) concepts** can be implemented to reduce challenging behavior in the classroom. They can also be used to help students with behavioral needs find success in the general education classroom. **Lack of student engagement** is compatible with the presentation of **challenging behaviors**. When UDL concepts are demonstrated appropriately, engagement can improve. Providing **multiple means of representation** is one UDL strategy for improving engagement and challenging behavior. This means the classroom teacher provides multiple ways of presenting the teaching material in order to engage as many students as possible. Teachers that provide multiple means of representation look to activate prior knowledge and help students make sense of the current content. UDL compliant strategies also include providing **multiple means of expression**. Teachers applying UDL principles recognize that differentiating activities and assignments addresses a variety of abilities and learning styles. UDL compliant teachers should also provide **multiple means of engagement**. Successful engagement in learning can often offset challenging behaviors by helping students focus on lesson material. Offering both challenging and simplistic work options and making engaging, solid connections to past and/or future lesson content can minimize the possibility of problems arising in the classroom.

Chapter Quiz

1. Horseshoe, group-pod, and paired-pod arrangements are all forms of:

a. Curriculum modifications
b. Assignment modifications
c. Student-centered classroom management
d. Teacher-centered classroom management

2. Which team-teaching model does NOT collaborate?

a. Intradisciplinary
b. Interdisciplinary
c. Multidisciplinary
d. Transdisciplinary

3. Learning modalities are generally separated into how many categories?

a. Three
b. Four
c. Five
d. Six

4. Who should be contacted before attempting student lifts?

a. Parent/guardian
b. Doctor
c. Paraprofessional
d. Physical therapist

Chapter Quiz Answer Key

1. C: Seating arrangements are part of good classroom management strategies, especially for students with disabilities. Special education settings and inclusion settings often require flexibility with instruction and versatility with seating arrangements. The traditional setting includes rows of desks facing the area where the teacher conducts instruction. More student-centered arrangements include a horseshoe seating arrangement, a group-pod arrangement, or a paired arrangement. A horseshoe seating arrangement is conducive to student-centered instruction because it allows the students to face each other, and allows the instructor to move around the classroom easily. This setup facilitates classroom discussions and encourages interactions between instructors and students and among peers. The group-pod and paired-pod arrangements are useful for student-centered instruction like small-group work. These arrangements are also helpful when students need to rotate through lesson stages or work in small groups on projects.

2. C: The multidisciplinary team is usually composed of the special educator, general education teacher, parents, paraprofessionals, principal, and school psychologist. As a whole, this team presents a comprehensive set of expertise, qualifications, and skills. In the multidisciplinary team model, these professionals do not collaborate, but instead work alongside each other to pursue a common goal for the individual student with special needs.

3. B: Learning modalities are generally separated into four categories: visual (seeing), auditory (hearing), kinesthetic (moving), and tactile (touch) modalities. Implementing multiple modalities in teaching helps students who may have deficits in one or more modalities. It is also helpful for students who struggle in one or more of the learning categories.

4. D: Teachers and paraprofessionals may encounter students with physical disabilities who require assisted transfers. In some circumstances, students must be lift-assisted from their wheelchairs in order to participate in physical therapy or floor activities. While this practice is more common in low-incidence classrooms and not always a job requirement, it is important to know school guidelines for lifting techniques to keep staff and students safe. Knowing school guidelines for lifting can also help prevent back injuries. Physical therapists working with the students should be consulted before attempting student lifts. They are trained professionals who know specific procedures for lifting students in order to keep the students and staff members safe. Every school district has policies for lift-assisted student transfers.

Promoting Student Achievement in English Language Arts and Reading

English Language Arts Pedagogy

Classroom Materials That Support Literacy Across the Curriculum

In a classroom that supports literacy, the teacher should provide **labels** combining words and pictures on all objects. This continually stimulates students to associate written language with the objects and concepts it represents. Especially to support disabled students, teachers should use their particular interests and needs as a guide for labeling things. Printed directions, signs, calendars, and schedules are materials that students should use regularly in the classroom. These help students realize how language is used in everyday life. When the class is studying a certain topic, theme, or book, the teacher and students can work together to redesign the classroom using printed and written materials that reflect that topic, theme, or book. This enables students to fully experience and "live" the lesson rather than just observing it. All of the materials must be adapted for any students' special needs. For instance, in a class including blind/visually impaired students, labels, signs and other print materials can incorporate Braille words and textured surfaces.

Addressing Diverse Student Abilities and Needs

Teachers must consider the **diversity** among the skills and needs of their students as they design their classroom learning environments. The teachers should **individualize** the setting and their instruction so that every student is represented. Individualization and instructional differentiation should not only address disabled students' needs; they should also regularly provide suitable opportunities for these students to participate on an ongoing basis in activities that involve literacy and integrate it into all content areas. According to research, a salient need of students with diverse literacy backgrounds is that they often have trouble connecting new information to their existing knowledge. This ability is a critical component of learning. When teachers plan and organize their classrooms to offer literacy activities that are accessible to disabled students—and that immerse them in literacy experiences and give them opportunities to connect new with old information, and spoken with printed language—these students can then access the general education curriculum.

Activities for Students with Disabilities to Develop Literacy Skills and Participate in General Curriculum

To participate in the general curriculum, students with disabilities need to understand the **alphabetic principle**, i.e. that printed language represents spoken language; connect print with speech; and be able to relate new information to their prior knowledge. Teachers can support these developments by designing classrooms as literacy-rich settings, immersing special-needs and other students in **accessible literacy activities** across all content areas. For example, students can interact with alphabet-letter magnets, cookie-cutters, and stamps; concrete manipulatives allow students not developmentally ready for exclusively abstract thought to understand concepts using real objects. Discussing daily schedules requires students to read and comprehend printed language, and then use spoken language to demonstrate and apply their understanding. Playing letter/word games like Bingo, Pictionary, Boggle, and Scrabble gives practice with creating and manipulating language, enhancing recognition and cognitive flexibility. Providing photos of peers, teachers, staff, and classroom activities and having students label them helps students connect written language with familiar, meaningful images. Daily communication notebooks help students further integrate literacy into their school days.

Implications of Cultural and Linguistic Differences Regarding Literacy Development

Educational research shows that the **cultural values** of families and/or communities influence children's literacy development, and also that culture is a significant factor to understanding children's home literacy environments. Researchers have also found that cultural purposes, perspectives, and contexts affect how students with disabilities in particular interact with the literacy environments they encounter. They say children's preparation levels entering formal education reflect their families' and communities' values and beliefs about literacy. Cultural attitudes about literacy then influence how schools deliver instruction and literacy experiences. Teachers must assess culturally diverse students' interactions with the environment, and design literacy-rich classrooms, with students' diverse backgrounds in mind. Students learning English (ELL/ESL) enter school either not knowing English or just learning it, lacking exposure to specific vocabulary and literature. Literacy-rich classrooms help them participate in regular curriculum. Teacher should read aloud often to these students, include print in their native language in classrooms, permit mistakes during student attempts to use English, encourage students to reread books repeatedly. and plan activities entailing language use.

Drawbacks of Whole-Class and Small-Group Reading, and Flexible Grouping Model

A major disadvantage of **whole-class reading** is that students who read above the average class level go unchallenged and can become bored, while students reading below average level are lost. Yet the **small-group method** intended to remedy this also has the drawback that, as traditionally implemented, most time is used for skill instruction, leaving far too little time for students to actually read the text. One solution is a **flexible grouping model**, e.g., Grouping Without Tracking (Paratore, 1990). This model uses a "sandwich" structure: teachers give students shared-reading processes at the beginning and end of the lesson, but provide differentiated instruction to two groups in the middle as they read the text. Teachers give indirect guidance to students who can read more independently, and more direct support to struggling readers. Teachers reunite the groups to lead them in a final discussion. Students with reading difficulties gain reading proficiency and comprehension from direct teacher support, enabling them to contribute better to the whole-class discussion, so all share this experience equally.

Jigsaw Approach to Shared Reading

Students reading below grade level may be able to access and comprehend some texts or portions of them, but have difficulty with harder parts/texts—for example, informational texts with more challenging subject matter and specialized vocabulary. When a text intended for the whole class contains such challenging material, one solution the teacher can use is a **jigsaw approach**. The teacher selects various portions of the text that are less difficult and assigns them to students reading below grade level. Whereas such texts overall might present struggles for these students, they find the easier portions more manageable when they tackle only these parts, as selected and assigned by the teacher, in small groups of students with comparable reading levels. The teacher makes each small student group responsible for comprehension of their assigned portion of text. Then the teacher brings the class back together, having each group report what they read, understood, and learned. The whole class then collaborates to help each other make connections among the learning each group reported.

Using Themes to Connect Texts

Any inclusive classroom will contain students who read at various age/grade levels. As a result, some books used as core texts are going to present difficulties for some of the students, who read below grade level and/or lack background knowledge and vocabulary of the subject. One way a teacher can facilitate all students' comprehension of such texts is to provide **supplementary texts** that allow readers at different levels easier access—texts on the same subject or theme as the more difficult core text. Teachers have students read these more accessible texts independently during small-group reading periods. This makes it easier for students with less reading proficiency to learn the core vocabulary and build their background knowledge. Thus, they are more prepared to tackle the more difficult core text during whole-class shared reading periods. With such preparation, less proficient readers are more likely to become engaged and active participants in the shared reading of a difficult text in the whole-group setting.

Assigning Students to Small Groups for Guided Reading Exercises

Expert educators and researchers recommend that when teachers divide classes into small student groups for **guided reading**, they should not be overly concerned with assigning students to exact reading levels. Rather, though they will want to group students whose literacy development is similar and who read around a similar level, they should give more attention to organizing groups according to the students' *areas of need*. For example, a teacher might identify students who share in common a need for help with noticing changes in setting, other students who share difficulties with recognizing and differentiating characters, some students who demonstrate problems with following and/or reproducing events they read in a text in the correct chronological sequence, some students who have trouble identifying and/or articulating the main idea in a text portion, etc. The teacher can create a group of students sharing one of these challenges, announce to the class what this group's focus is, and then invite other students to join this group by choice if they experience the same need.

Helping Teachers Provide More Equitable Learning Opportunities Using Word Counts

Books designed for lower reading levels typically contain fewer words, both per page and overall. Yet students who are reading below their grade levels require not fewer reading opportunities, but more, to practice and improve their reading skills. For example, within one class of second-grade students, the teacher might have one group using a text with over 80 words on just the first page, while another group uses a text with a total of 80 words in the entire book. This difference shows that the teacher will need to use several texts within certain groups to give them equal amounts of reading material and practice as readers of denser/longer texts during group reading times. Teachers can look at the backs of the books they assign during guided reading sessions, and maintain simple logs of their **word counts**. Comparing these word counts among groups can help teachers to equalize the numbers of words that each student group actually works with during small-group guided reading periods.

Connecting Text Sets for Small-Group Guided Reading Across Different Reading Difficulty Levels

When teachers select textbooks to teach a unit/lesson on a certain topic, they often compile **text sets**—groups of books all related to the same topic/theme. Because classes usually include students reading at different levels, teachers also often gather books at different reading levels for text sets. When collecting books representing multiple reading levels, the teacher can also intentionally organize the text set so all books are connected. For example, the books might share similar content; similar language, style, and vocabulary words; or similar layouts. Selecting books sharing such a commonality at different reading levels makes it easier for students to draw useful connections between easier and harder texts. It also facilitates students' flexibility in working across multiple reading levels, which builds their skills and confidence for faster progress. Additionally, to prepare some students to read books that teachers felt would prove too difficult otherwise, they can use easier texts with similar themes/language/formats to establish contexts for the harder ones.

Enhancing Students' Independent Reading Through the Reading Material Provided

In addition to whole-class and small-group reading exercises, students need some time reading **texts of their own choice**, which they can easily read with little or no support, to attain comfort, fluency, and confidence. To ensure more opportunities for practice, with equal time for all students, teachers should provide text sets at multiple reading levels for each content area. Experts suggest 70% of books should be easily accessible, and, in addition to classroom libraries, using rolling carts lets book collections travel among classrooms. Multiple reading levels let more advanced readers peruse a harder text, while less advanced readers read several easier texts; this equalizes the time and words they have for practicing. Because critics find some leveled readers lack variety in gender/race/class/other sociocultural aspects of characters, teachers should build diverse book collections representing all students. Teachers can inform their selections via student interest surveys and familiarity with students' individual identities, personalities, and special interests. Knowing individual students can help match them to texts as effectively as leveled book lists.

Engaging Students in Reading

Experts find excessive attention to **leveling** as a way of matching texts to students can be restrictive, undermining high-quality instruction that balances the needs of the reader with the demands of the text. Teachers must consider that assigning certain texts will cause students to disengage from reading and avoid it rather than engage in it. In the real world, people read many different kinds of materials. Therefore, a teacher has better chances of finding texts that engage students, and that motivate them to read and allow them to perceive themselves as readers, by mindfully selecting **varied text genres** with **varied difficulty**. In classrooms incorporating various student reading levels, this can be the best method to procure classroom acceptability of accessible texts. Teachers can also use **individualized instructional formats**, such as Readers Workshop (Atwell, 1998), which balance issues of difficulty, choice, and engagement; develop reader communities affording more reading experiences with authenticity, meaning, and enjoyment; and form stronger, positive teacher-student relationships via individualized consultations. Teachers should also incorporate **accessible alternative texts** for independent activities.

Alternative Reading and Writing Forms to Help Students Attain Greater Progress in Reading

When students read and write outside of school, they choose many alternative forms of reading and writing. To engage these students while they are in school, teachers should think about adding such **alternative materials** to their own instructional programs. For example, teachers might incorporate such media as graphic novels, magazines, newspapers, plays, anthologies of poetry, e-books and other digital/online content, and texts that students have written themselves. Educational experts advise that just because it can be harder to determine the reading levels of such alternative text formats, teachers should not shy away from using them. Because they represent examples of text that people (including students) read in real life, they provide not only excellent practice for students' present and future reading of real-world materials, but also motivation to read and meaningful experiences in reading. Another boon of using these authentic, alternative texts is that they frequently incorporate multiple reading levels, so that nearly every student can read some portions of them.

Viewing Skills

Viewing skills can be sharpened by having students look at a single image, such as a work of art or a cartoon, and simply asking students what they **see**. The teacher can ask what is happening in the image, and then elicit the details that clue the students in to what is happening. Of course, there may be more than one thing happening. The teacher should also question the students about the message of the image, its purpose, its point of view, and its intended audience. The teacher should ask for first impressions, and then provide some background or additional information to see if it changes the way students look at or interpret the image. The conclusion of the lesson should include questions about what students learned from the exercise about the topic, themselves, and others.

Benefits

Students are exposed to multiple **images** every day. It is important for them to be able to effectively **interpret** these images. They should be able to make sense of images and the spoken and print language that often accompany them. Learning can be enhanced with images because they allow for quicker connections to prior knowledge than verbal information. Visuals in the classroom can also be motivational, can support verbal information, and can express main points, sometimes resulting in instant recognition.

Some of the common types of images that students see every day include: bulletin boards, computer graphics, diagrams, drawings, illustrations, maps, photographs, posters, book covers, advertisements, websites, multimedia presentations, puppet shows, television, videos, print cartoons, models, paintings, animation, drama or dance performances, films, and online newscasts and magazines.

Activities to Strengthen Skills

Activities at school that can be used to strengthen the **viewing skills** of students of varying ages include:

- **Picture book discussions** – Students can develop an appreciation of visual text and the language that goes with it through guided discussions of picture books that focus on the style and color of the images and other details that might capture a child's attention.
- **Gallery walks** – Students can walk around a room or hallway viewing the posted works of other students and hear presentations about the works. They can also view a display prepared by the teacher. Students are expected to take notes as they walk around, have discussions, and perhaps do a follow-up report.
- **Puppet theater and drama presentations** – Students can learn about plots, dialogue, situations, characters, and the craft of performance from viewing puppet or drama presentations, which also stimulate oral communication and strengthen listening skills. Discussions or written responses should follow performances to check for detail acquisition.

Classroom Viewing Center

A **classroom viewing center** should contain magazines, CD-ROMs, books, videos, and individual pictures (photographs or drawings). Students should have a **viewing guide** that explains expectations related to the viewing center (before, during, and after using the center). For younger students, the teacher can ask questions that guide them through the viewing rather than expecting them to read the guidelines and write responses.

- **Before** viewing, students should think about what they already know about the subject and what they want to learn from the viewing.
- **During** the viewing, students should make notes about whatever interests them or is new to them.
- **After** viewing, students could discuss or individually write down what they found to be the most interesting idea or striking image and explain why it caught their attention.

Types of Questions to Ask If Viewing Is a Narrative

A teacher should make students responsible for gaining information or insight from the **viewing**. Setting expectations increases student attention and critical thinking. As with any viewing, the students should consider what they already know about the topic and what they hope to gain by watching the narrative before viewing it. During the viewing, the students should take notes (perhaps to answer questions provided by the teacher).

After the viewing, students should be able to answer the following questions:

- What was the time period and setting of the story?
- Who were the main characters?
- How effective was the acting?
- What was the problem or goal in the story?
- How was the problem solved or the goal achieved?
- How would you summarize the story?
- What did you learn from the story?
- What did you like or dislike about the story or its presentation?
- Would you recommend this viewing to others?
- How would you rate it?

Difficulties Related to Learning by Listening

It is difficult to learn just by listening because the instruction is presented only in spoken form. Therefore, unless students take notes, there is nothing for them to review. However, an active listener will anticipate finding a **message** in an oral presentation and will listen for it, **interpreting** tone and gestures as the presentation progresses. In group discussions, students are often too busy figuring out what they will say when it is their turn to talk to concentrate on what others are saying. Therefore, they don't learn from others, but instead come away knowing only what they already knew. Students should be required to respond directly to the previous speaker before launching into their own comments. This practice will force students to listen to each other and learn that their own responses will be better because of what can be added by listening to others.

Graphic Organizers

The purpose of **graphic organizers** is to help students classify ideas and communicate more efficiently and effectively. Graphic organizers are visual outlines or templates that help students grasp key concepts and master subject matter by simplifying them down to basic points. They also help guide students through processes related to any subject area or task. Examples of processes include brainstorming, problem solving, decision making, research and project planning, and studying. Examples of graphic organizers include:

- **Reading** – These can include beginning, middle, and end graphs or event maps.
- **Science** – These can include charts that show what animals need or how to classify living things.
- **Math** – These can include horizontal bar graphs or time lines.
- **Language arts** – These can include alphabet organizers or charts showing the components of the five-paragraph essay.
- **General** – These can include KWL charts or weekly planners.

Speaking Skills Children in Elementary/Intermediate School Should Have

Children of elementary/intermediate school age should be able to:

- Speak at an appropriate volume, tone, and pace that is understandable and appropriate to the audience
- Pronounce most words accurately
- Use complete sentences
- Make eye contact
- Use appropriate gestures with speech
- Exhibit an awareness of audience and adjust content to fit the audience (adjust word choices and style to be appropriate for peers or adults)
- Ask relevant questions
- Respond appropriately when asked questions about information or an opinion, possibly also being able to provide reasons for opinions
- Speak in turn, not interrupt, and include others in conversations
- Provide a summary or report orally
- Participate in small and large group discussions and debates
- Read orally before an audience
- Conduct short interviews
- Provide directions and explanations orally, including explanations of class lessons

Viewing Skills Elementary/Intermediate School Children Should Have

Children of elementary school age should be developing or have attained the ability to understand the importance of **media** in people's lives. They should understand that television, radio, films, and the Internet have a role in everyday life. They should also be able to use media themselves (printing out material from the Internet or making an audio or video tape, for example). They should also be aware that the purpose of advertising is to sell. Children of intermediate school age should be developing or have attained the ability to **obtain and compare information** from newspapers, television, and the Internet. They should also be able to judge its **reliability and accuracy** to some extent. Children of this age should be able to tell the difference between fictional and non-fictional materials in media. They should also be able to use a variety of media, visuals, and sounds to make a presentation.

Listening Skills Children Should Develop Through Their Elementary/Intermediate School Years

Through the elementary/intermediate school years, children should develop the following listening skills:

- Follow oral instructions consistently
- Actively listen to peers and teachers
- Avoid creating distracting behavior or being distracted by the behavior of others most of the time
- Respond to listening activities and exhibit the ability to discuss, illustrate, or write about the activity and show knowledge of the content and quality of the listening activity
- Respond to listening activities and exhibit the ability to identify themes, similarities, differences, ideas, forms, and styles of activities
- Respond to a persuasive speaker and exhibit the ability to analyze and evaluate the credibility of the speaker and form an opinion describing whether they agree or disagree with the point made
- Demonstrate appropriate social behavior while part of an audience

Stages of Writing

The **three stages of writing** are drawing, dictating, and writing. During the **drawing stage**, young learners use scribbles or pictures to convey their message. When asked to "read" their drawing, children in the drawing stage will use their picture to tell a story, as if they were mimicking a book being read to them. In the **dictation stage**, learners will tell their thoughts to a literate person, who will in turn write the words for the child. During this stage, the student is aware that the written words on the page represent their thoughts and can sometimes recognize the beginning sounds of the words they are saying, including some sight words. In the third and final stage, the **writing stage**, students are able to write their own thoughts in a way that can be recognized by others. Both beginning and ending sounds are represented in the words, along with some vowels. Students in this stage also understand spacing between words and the idea of creating complete sentences.

Norm-Referenced and Criterion-Referenced Assessments

Norm-referenced assessments are used to gauge a student's success by comparing his or her score to a theoretical "average" score achieved by students of the same age or grade level. With a norm-referenced assessment, a student's achievement is decided based on how much better or worse that student scored in comparison to his or her peers. In contrast, **criterion-referenced assessments** are scored based on each student's individual ability to show mastery of specific learning standards. Students are deemed successful if they are able to achieve mastery of concepts that are appropriate for their age or grade level, regardless of how their peers perform.

IRI

The **Informal Reading Inventory (IRI)**, also known as the **Qualitative Reading Inventory (QRI)** is a survey used to assess the instructional needs of individual readers. The IRI is used to determine a reader's grade-level reading, fluency, comprehension, vocabulary, oral reading accuracy, word recognition, word meaning, and reading strategies. The IRI is an ongoing assessment that should be administered several times a year starting from first grade through twelfth grade. Teachers should use the outcomes of these assessments to determine appropriate reading material for individual students and to identify and implement specific needs and strategies for individual learners or groups of learners.

Universal Screening Assessments, Diagnostic Assessments, and Progress Monitoring

Universal screening assessments are brief surveys given to all students at the beginning of each school year, which are used to determine the mastery of critical skills and concepts. These screenings should be repeated approximately three times a year to ensure that students are performing at age-appropriate levels. **Diagnostic assessments** are used to help educators make sense of universal screening assessment scores. Based on diagnostics, teachers can identify the specific educational gaps of individual students and use that information to modify and differentiate instruction. **Progress monitoring** is used to determine if the educational interventions and strategies put in place (based on the diagnostic testing) are actually working. Struggling students are often monitored more closely to ensure that educational gaps are being filled at an appropriate and sufficient rate.

Formal and Informal Assessments

Formal assessments, which include norm-based assessments, criterion-based assessments, intelligence tests, and diagnostic assessments are data driven. These types of assessments are used to determine a student's overall achievement and can be used to compare each student's abilities to his or her peers. Formal assessments are often shared with students and stakeholders to determine whether or not a student is performing at an appropriate level for his or her age or grade level. **Informal assessments**, which include running records, cloze tests, reading inventories, portfolios, and so on are not data driven. Instead, informal assessments use performance-driven tasks to guide instruction and provide informal ratings about each student's individual progress. During these assessments, each student's performance is used to monitor his or her progress and guide future instruction, often in preparation for a formal assessment.

Evaluating Appropriateness of Assessment Instrument or Practice

The two main factors that must be considered when evaluating the appropriateness of assessment instruction and practices are curriculum alignment and cultural bias. **Curriculum alignment** is the act of teaching students the concepts that they will eventually be tested on. To reach proficiency on the standards outlined by state or district mandates, teachers must continuously teach and assess the standards. Avoiding **cultural bias** ensures that all students are given access to all relevant lessons, instruction, and materials. Furthermore, avoiding cultural bias ensures that all students are given a fair opportunity to succeed on any given assessment. This includes accommodating students of certain subgroups with assessment modifications, such as additional testing time, taking the test in his or her native language, and creating types of assessments that are accessible and achievable for students of all backgrounds.

Example Evaluation of Scoring Method

A teacher is assessing a student's ability to identify the main idea of a text. The student correctly identifies the main idea but includes several spelling errors in her written response. The teacher lowers the student's grade, taking points off for misspellings. In this example, the teacher's scoring method is **inappropriate** for the concept being assessed. Although misspellings should be addressed and remedied, the question was designed to assess the student's ability to identify the main idea of the passage. It was not intended to assess the spelling abilities of the student. By lowering the student's score based on misspellings, the teacher is insinuating that the student is unable to correctly identify the main idea of a passage, which is not the case. When assessing a specific skill, it is important that teachers score students based on their ability to complete isolated skills for data to accurately drive future instruction.

Penmanship

Penmanship is a word used to describe a person's *handwriting*. The three main characteristics of penmanship are letter formation, size, and spacing. When teaching penmanship, teachers should start by helping students to correctly form each letter, using arrows to dictate the order and direction in which parts of each letter should be written. Once students have mastered each letter, teachers should focus on letter size or proportion. For example, smaller letters (like c, e, and n) should be half the size of larger letters (such as k, l, or t). Finally, proper spacing should be taught, both between letters and words. Once spacing between words has been mastered, students should begin to work on including punctuation and appropriate spacing between sentences.

Importance of Listening and Speaking Strategies

Both listening and speaking strategies are important skills for students in all areas of education. To achieve the highest success, students should be taught how to effectively **speak** and exchange dialogue in large- and small-group settings. In addition, students should be encouraged to question, retell, or reenact the words of others. Equally important, students must learn to actively **listen** and visualize the words of others so that they are able to understand the purpose of what someone else is saying. To check for listening, students should be encouraged to summarize what they have heard and complete graphic organizers outlining important concepts or facts. When given ample opportunity to both speak and listen, students are more likely to excel across all content areas.

Developing Listening and Speaking Skills with Dramatic Play

Dramatic play is a type of play in which students are assigned specific roles and encouraged to act those roles out. In dramatic play, students are typically assigned a character but not a script. They are encouraged to take on the feelings and actions of the character they have been assigned and act as that character would act. Dramatic play is an excellent strategy for developing speaking skills as students must clearly identify and express the feelings of their characters. They must speak clearly and loudly enough so that the other actors and the audience can hear what they are saying. In addition, students must actively listen to what the other students in the play are saying to appropriately respond to the actions and words of the other characters in an effort to further develop the story line.

Chapter Quiz

1 A teacher selects various portions of a text that are less difficult and assigns them to students reading below grade level. This describes which of the following?

a. Undercut approach
b. Scaffold method
c. Jigsaw approach
d. Chain method

2. How many stages of writing are there?

a. Five
b. Four
c. Three
d. Two

3. Which of the following is NOT considered a formal assessment?

a. Intelligence tests
b. Criterion-based assessments
c. Norm-based assessments
d. Cloze tests

4. Experts suggest which percentage of books should be easily accesible?

a. 50 percent
b. 60 percent
c. 70 percent
d. 80 percent

Chapter Quiz Answer Key

1 C: Students reading below grade level may be able to access and comprehend some texts (or portions of them), but may struggle with more difficult material, such as informational texts with more challenging subject matter and specialized vocabulary. When a text intended for the whole class contains such challenging material, one solution the teacher can use is a jigsaw approach. The teacher selects various portions of the text that are less difficult and assigns them to students reading below grade level. Whereas such texts overall might present struggles for these students, they find the easier portions more manageable when they tackle only these parts, as selected and assigned by the teacher, in small groups of students with comparable reading levels. The teacher makes each small student group responsible for comprehension of their assigned portion of text. Then the teacher brings the class back together, having each group report what they read, understood, and learned. The whole class then collaborates to help each other make connections among the learning each group reported.

2. C: The three stages of writing are drawing, dictating, and writing. During the drawing stage, young learners use scribbles or pictures to convey their message.

3. D: Informal assessments are not driven by data. Instead, they use performance-driven tasks to guide instruction and provide informal ratings about each student's individual progress. Informal assessments include running records, cloze tests, reading inventories, and portfolios, among others.

4. C: Experts suggest 70 percent of books should be easily accessible. This includes not only classroom libraries but also rolling carts that let book collections travel among classrooms. Multiple reading levels let more advanced readers peruse a harder text, while less advanced readers read easier texts, equalizing the time and words the students have for practicing.

Parts of Speech

The Eight Parts of Speech

Nouns

When you talk about a person, place, thing, or idea, you are talking about a **noun**. The two main types of nouns are **common** and **proper** nouns. Also, nouns can be abstract (i.e., general) or concrete (i.e., specific).

Common Nouns

Common nouns are generic names for people, places, and things. Common nouns are not usually capitalized.

Examples of common nouns:

People: boy, girl, worker, manager

Places: school, bank, library, home

Things: dog, cat, truck, car

Review Video: What is a Noun?
Visit mometrix.com/academy and enter code: 344028

Proper Nouns

Proper nouns name specific people, places, or things. All proper nouns are capitalized.

Examples of proper nouns:

People: Abraham Lincoln, George Washington, Martin Luther King, Jr.

Places: Los Angeles, California; New York; Asia

Things: Statue of Liberty, Earth, Lincoln Memorial

Note: When referring to the planet that we live on, capitalize *Earth*. When referring to the dirt, rocks, or land, lowercase *earth*.

General and Specific Nouns

General nouns are the names of conditions or ideas. **Specific nouns** name people, places, and things that are understood by using your senses.

General nouns:

Condition: beauty, strength

Idea: truth, peace

Specific nouns:

People: baby, friend, father

Places: town, park, city hall

Things: rainbow, cough, apple, silk, gasoline

Collective Nouns

Collective nouns are the names for a group of people, places, or things that may act as a whole. The following are examples of collective nouns: *class, company, dozen, group, herd, team,* and *public.* Collective nouns usually require an article, which denotes the noun as being a single unit. For instance, a choir is a group of singers. Even though there are many singers in a choir, the word choir is grammatically treated as a single unit. If we refer to the members of the group, and not the group itself, it is no longer a collective noun.

Incorrect: The *choir are* going to compete nationally this year.

Correct: The *choir is* going to compete nationally this year.

Incorrect: The *members* of the choir *is* competing nationally this year.

Correct: The *members* of the choir *are* competing nationally this year.

Pronouns

Pronouns are words that are used to stand in for nouns. A pronoun may be classified as personal, intensive, relative, interrogative, demonstrative, indefinite, and reciprocal.

Personal: *Nominative* is the case for nouns and pronouns that are the subject of a sentence. *Objective* is the case for nouns and pronouns that are an object in a sentence. *Possessive* is the case for nouns and pronouns that show possession or ownership.

Singular

	Nominative	Objective	Possessive
First Person	I	me	my, mine
Second Person	you	you	your, yours
Third Person	he, she, it	him, her, it	his, her, hers, its

Plural

	Nominative	Objective	Possessive
First Person	we	us	our, ours
Second Person	you	you	your, yours
Third Person	they	them	their, theirs

Intensive: I myself, you yourself, he himself, she herself, the (thing) itself, we ourselves, you yourselves, they themselves

Relative: which, who, whom, whose

Interrogative: what, which, who, whom, whose

Demonstrative: this, that, these, those

Indefinite: all, any, each, everyone, either/neither, one, some, several

Reciprocal: each other, one another

Review Video: Nouns and Pronouns
Visit mometrix.com/academy and enter code: 312073

Verbs

If you want to write a sentence, then you need a verb. Without a verb, you have no sentence. The verb of a sentence indicates action or being. In other words, the verb shows something's action or state of being or the action that has been done to something.

Transitive and Intransitive Verbs

A **transitive verb** is a verb whose action (e.g., drive, run, jump) indicates a receiver (e.g., car, dog, kangaroo). **Intransitive verbs** do not indicate a receiver of an action. In other words, the action of the verb does not point to a subject or object.

Transitive: He plays the piano. | The piano was played by him.

Intransitive: He plays. | John plays well.

A dictionary will tell you whether a verb is transitive or intransitive. Some verbs can be transitive and intransitive.

Action Verbs and Linking Verbs

Action verbs show what the subject is doing. In other words, an action verb shows action. Unlike most types of words, a single action verb, in the right context, can be an entire sentence. **Linking verbs** link the subject of a sentence to a noun or pronoun, or they link a subject with an adjective. You always need a verb if you want a complete sentence. However, linking verbs on their own cannot be a complete sentence.

Common linking verbs include *appear, be, become, feel, grow, look, seem, smell, sound,* and *taste.* However, any verb that shows a condition and connects to a noun, pronoun, or adjective that describes the subject of a sentence is a linking verb.

Action: He sings. | Run! | Go! | I talk with him every day. | She reads.

Linking:

Incorrect: I am.

Correct: I am John. | The roses smell lovely. | I feel tired.

Note: Some verbs are followed by words that look like prepositions, but they are a part of the verb and a part of the verb's meaning. These are known as phrasal verbs, and examples include *call off, look up*, and *drop off.*

Review Video: Action Verbs and Linking Verbs
Visit mometrix.com/academy and enter code: 743142

VOICE

Transitive verbs come in active or passive **voice**. If something does an action or is acted upon, then you will know whether a verb is active or passive. When the subject of the sentence is doing the action, the verb is in **active voice**. When the subject is acted upon, the verb is in **passive voice**.

Active: Jon drew the picture. (The subject *Jon* is doing the action of *drawing a picture.*)

Passive: The picture is drawn by Jon. (The subject *picture* is receiving the action from Jon.)

VERB TENSES

A verb **tense** shows the different form of a verb to point to the time of an action. The present and past tense are indicated by the verb's form. An action in the present, *I talk,* can change form for the past: *I talked.* However, for the other tenses, an auxiliary (i.e., helping) verb is needed to show the change in form. These helping verbs include *am, are, is* | *have, has, had* | *was, were, will* (or *shall*).

Present: I talk	Present perfect: I have talked
Past: I talked	Past perfect: I had talked
Future: I will talk	Future perfect: I will have talked

Present: The action happens at the current time.

Example: He *walks* to the store every morning.

To show that something is happening right now, use the progressive present tense: I *am walking*.

Past: The action happened in the past.

Example: He *walked* to the store an hour ago.

Future: The action is going to happen later.

Example: I *will walk* to the store tomorrow.

Present perfect: The action started in the past and continues into the present or took place previously at an unspecified time.

Example: I *have walked* to the store three times today.

Past perfect: The second action happened in the past. The first action came before the second.

Example: Before I walked to the store (Action 2), I *had walked* to the library (Action 1).

Future perfect: An action that uses the past and the future. In other words, the action is complete before a future moment.

Example: When she comes for the supplies (future moment), I *will have walked* to the store (action completed before the future moment).

Review Video: Present Perfect, Past Perfect, and Future Perfect Verb Tenses
Visit mometrix.com/academy and enter code: 269472

Conjugating Verbs

When you need to change the form of a verb, you are **conjugating** a verb. The key forms of a verb are singular, present tense (dream); singular, past tense (dreamed); and the past participle (have dreamed). Note: the past participle needs a helping verb to make a verb tense. For example, I *have dreamed* of this day. The following tables demonstrate some of the different ways to conjugate a verb:

Singular

Tense	First Person	Second Person	Third Person
Present	I dream	You dream	He, she, it dreams
Past	I dreamed	You dreamed	He, she, it dreamed
Past Participle	I have dreamed	You have dreamed	He, she, it has dreamed

Plural

Tense	First Person	Second Person	Third Person
Present	We dream	You dream	They dream
Past	We dreamed	You dreamed	They dreamed
Past Participle	We have dreamed	You have dreamed	They have dreamed

Mood

There are three **moods** in English: the indicative, the imperative, and the subjunctive.

The **indicative mood** is used for facts, opinions, and questions.

Fact: You can do this.

Opinion: I think that you can do this.

Question: Do you know that you can do this?

The **imperative** is used for orders or requests.

Order: You are going to do this!

Request: Will you do this for me?

The **subjunctive mood** is for wishes and statements that go against fact.

Wish: I wish that I were famous.

Statement against fact: If I were you, I would do this. (This goes against fact because I am not you. You have the chance to do this, and I do not have the chance.)

ADJECTIVES

An **adjective** is a word that is used to modify a noun or pronoun. An adjective answers a question: *Which one? What kind?* or *How many?* Usually, adjectives come before the words that they modify, but they may also come after a linking verb.

Which one? The *third* suit is my favorite.

What kind? This suit is *navy blue*.

How many? I am going to buy *four* pairs of socks to match the suit.

Review Video: Descriptive Text
Visit mometrix.com/academy and enter code: 174903

ARTICLES

Articles are adjectives that are used to distinguish nouns as definite or indefinite. **Definite** nouns are preceded by the article *the* and indicate a specific person, place, thing, or idea. **Indefinite** nouns are preceded by *a* or *an* and do not indicate a specific person, place, thing, or idea. *A*, *an*, and *the* are the only articles. Note: *An* comes before words that start with a vowel sound. For example, "Are you going to get an **u**mbrella?"

Definite: I lost *the* bottle that belongs to me.

Indefinite: Does anyone have *a* bottle to share?

Review Video: Function of Articles
Visit mometrix.com/academy and enter code: 449383

COMPARISON WITH ADJECTIVES

Some adjectives are relative and other adjectives are absolute. Adjectives that are **relative** can show the comparison between things. **Absolute** adjectives can also show comparison, but they do so in a different way. Let's say that you are reading two books. You think that one book is perfect, and the other book is not exactly perfect. It is not possible for one book to be more perfect than the other. Either you think that the book is perfect, or you think that the book is imperfect. In this case, perfect and imperfect are absolute adjectives.

Relative adjectives will show the different **degrees** of something or someone to something else or someone else. The three degrees of adjectives include positive, comparative, and superlative.

The **positive** degree is the normal form of an adjective.

Example: This work is *difficult*. | She is *smart*.

The **comparative** degree compares one person or thing to another person or thing.

Example: This work is *more difficult* than your work. | She is *smarter* than me.

The **superlative** degree compares more than two people or things.

Example: This is the *most difficult* work of my life. | She is the *smartest* lady in school.

Review Video: What is an Adjective?
Visit mometrix.com/academy and enter code: 470154

Adverbs

An **adverb** is a word that is used to **modify** a verb, adjective, or another adverb. Usually, adverbs answer one of these questions: *When? Where? How?* and *Why?* The negatives *not* and *never* are considered adverbs. Adverbs that modify adjectives or other adverbs **strengthen** or **weaken** the words that they modify.

Examples:

He walks *quickly* through the crowd.

The water flows *smoothly* on the rocks.

Note: Adverbs are usually indicated by the morpheme *-ly*, which has been added to the root word. For instance, *quick* can be made into an adverb by adding *-ly* to construct *quickly*. Some words that end in *-ly* do not follow this rule and can behave as other parts of speech. Examples of adjectives ending in *-ly* include: *early, friendly, holy, lonely, silly*, and *ugly*. To know if a word that ends in *-ly* is an adjective or adverb, check your dictionary. Also, while many adverbs end in *-ly*, you need to remember that not all adverbs end in *-ly*.

Examples:

He is *never* angry.

You are *too* irresponsible to travel alone.

Review Video: What is an Adverb?
Visit mometrix.com/academy and enter code: 713951

Review Video: Adverbs that Modify Adjectives
Visit mometrix.com/academy and enter code: 122570

Comparison with Adverbs

The rules for comparing adverbs are the same as the rules for adjectives.

The **positive** degree is the standard form of an adverb.

Example: He arrives *soon*. | She speaks *softly* to her friends.

The **comparative** degree compares one person or thing to another person or thing.

Example: He arrives *sooner* than Sarah. | She speaks *more softly* than him.

The **superlative** degree compares more than two people or things.

Example: He arrives *soonest* of the group. | She speaks the *most softly* of any of her friends.

Prepositions

A **preposition** is a word placed before a noun or pronoun that shows the relationship between an object and another word in the sentence.

Common prepositions:

about	before	during	on	under
after	beneath	for	over	until
against	between	from	past	up
among	beyond	in	through	with
around	by	of	to	within
at	down	off	toward	without

Examples:

The napkin is *in* the drawer.

The Earth rotates *around* the Sun.

The needle is *beneath* the haystack.

Can you find "me" *among* the words?

Review Video: Prepositions
Visit mometrix.com/academy and enter code: 946763

Conjunctions

Conjunctions join words, phrases, or clauses and they show the connection between the joined pieces. **Coordinating conjunctions** connect equal parts of sentences. **Correlative conjunctions** show the connection between pairs. **Subordinating conjunctions** join subordinate (i.e., dependent) clauses with independent clauses.

Coordinating Conjunctions

The **coordinating conjunctions** include: *and, but, yet, or, nor, for,* and *so*

Examples:

The rock was small, *but* it was heavy.

She drove in the night, *and* he drove in the day.

Correlative Conjunctions

The **correlative conjunctions** are: *either...or* | *neither...nor* | *not only...but also*

Examples:

Either you are coming *or* you are staying.

He *not only* ran three miles *but also* swam 200 yards.

Review Video: Coordinating and Correlative Conjunctions
Visit mometrix.com/academy and enter code: 390329

Review Video: Adverb Equal Comparisons
Visit mometrix.com/academy and enter code: 231291

Subordinating Conjunctions

Common **subordinating conjunctions** include:

after	since	whenever
although	so that	where
because	unless	wherever
before	until	whether
in order that	when	while

Examples:

I am hungry *because* I did not eat breakfast.

He went home *when* everyone left.

Review Video: Subordinating Conjunctions
Visit mometrix.com/academy and enter code: 958913

Interjections

Interjections are words of exclamation (i.e., audible expression of great feeling) that are used alone or as a part of a sentence. Often, they are used at the beginning of a sentence for an introduction. Sometimes, they can be used in the middle of a sentence to show a change in thought or attitude.

Common Interjections: Hey! | Oh, | Ouch! | Please! | Wow!

Chapter Quiz

1. Which of the following is NOT considered a type of mood?

a. Indicative
b. Imperative
c. Subjunctive
d. Conjunctive

2. How many different degrees of relative adjectives are there?

a. Two
b. Three
c. Four
d. Five

3. In general, adverbs may modify all of the following, EXCEPT:

a. Another adverb.
b. Adjectives.
c. Proper nouns.
d. Verbs.

Chapter Quiz Answer Key

1. D: There are three moods in English: the indicative, the imperative, and the subjunctive.

2. B: Relative adjectives will show the different degrees of something or someone to something else or someone else. The three degrees of adjectives include positive, comparative, and superlative.

3. C: An adverb is a word that is used to modify a verb, adjective, or another adverb. Usually, adverbs answer one of the questions: *When? Where? How?* and *Why?* The negatives *not* and *never* are considered adverbs. Adverbs that modify adjectives or other adverbs strengthen or weaken the words that they modify.

Agreement and Sentence Structure

Subjects and Predicates

Subjects

The **subject** of a sentence names who or what the sentence is about. The subject may be directly stated in a sentence, or the subject may be the implied *you*. The **complete subject** includes the simple subject and all of its modifiers. To find the complete subject, ask *Who* or *What* and insert the verb to complete the question. The answer, including any modifiers (adjectives, prepositional phrases, etc.), is the complete subject. To find the **simple subject**, remove all of the modifiers in the complete subject. Being able to locate the subject of a sentence helps with many problems, such as those involving sentence fragments and subject-verb agreement.

Examples:

The small, red car is the one that he wants for Christmas.
(simple subject: car; complete subject: The small, red car)

The young artist is coming over for dinner.
(simple subject: artist; complete subject: The young artist)

Review Video: Subjects in English
Visit mometrix.com/academy and enter code: 444771

In **imperative** sentences, the verb's subject is understood (e.g., [You] Run to the store), but is not actually present in the sentence. Normally, the subject comes before the verb. However, the subject comes after the verb in sentences that begin with *There are* or *There was*.

Direct:

John knows the way to the park.	Who knows the way to the park?	John
The cookies need ten more minutes.	What needs ten minutes?	The cookies
By five o'clock, Bill will need to leave.	Who needs to leave?	Bill
There are five letters on the table for him.	What is on the table?	Five letters
There were coffee and doughnuts in the house.	What was in the house?	Coffee and doughnuts

Implied:

Go to the post office for me.	Who is going to the post office?	You
Come and sit with me, please?	Who needs to come and sit?	You

Predicates

In a sentence, you always have a predicate and a subject. The subject tells what the sentence is about, and the **predicate** explains or describes the subject.

Think about the sentence *He sings*. In this sentence, we have a subject (He) and a predicate (sings). This is all that is needed for a sentence to be complete. Most sentences contain more information, but if this is all the information that you are given, then you have a complete sentence.

Now, let's look at another sentence: *John and Jane sing on Tuesday nights at the dance hall.*

subject: John and Jane | predicate: sing on Tuesday nights at the dance hall.

John and Jane sing on Tuesday nights at the dance hall.

SUBJECT-VERB AGREEMENT

Verbs **agree** with their subjects in number. In other words, singular subjects need singular verbs. Plural subjects need plural verbs. **Singular** is for **one** person, place, or thing. **Plural** is for **more than one** person, place, or thing. Subjects and verbs must also share the same point of view, as in first, second, or third person. The present tense ending *-s* is used on a verb if its subject is third person singular; otherwise, the verb's ending is not modified.

Review Video: Subject-Verb Agreement
Visit mometrix.com/academy and enter code: 479190

NUMBER AGREEMENT EXAMPLES:

singular subject: Dan | singular verb: calls

Single Subject and Verb: Dan calls home.

Dan is one person. So, the singular verb *calls* is needed.

plural subject: Dan and Bob | plural verb: call

Plural Subject and Verb: Dan and Bob call home.

More than one person needs the plural verb *call*.

PERSON AGREEMENT EXAMPLES:

First Person: I *am* walking.

Second Person: You *are* walking.

Third Person: He *is* walking.

COMPLICATIONS WITH SUBJECT-VERB AGREEMENT

WORDS BETWEEN SUBJECT AND VERB

Words that come between the simple subject and the verb have no bearing on subject-verb agreement.

Examples:

singular subject: joy | singular verb: returns

The joy of my life returns home tonight.

The phrase *of my life* does not influence the verb *returns*.

singular subject / singular verb

The question that still remains unanswered is "Who are you?"

Don't let the phrase "*that still remains…*" trouble you. The subject *question* goes with *is.*

Compound Subjects

A compound subject is formed when two or more nouns joined by *and*, *or*, or *nor* jointly act as the subject of the sentence.

Joined by And

When a compound subject is joined by *and*, it is treated as a plural subject and requires a plural verb.

Examples:

plural subject / plural verb

You and Jon are invited to come to my house.

plural subject / plural verb

The pencil and paper belong to me.

Joined by Or/Nor

For a compound subject joined by *or* or *nor*, the verb must agree in number with the part of the subject that is closest to the verb (italicized in the examples below).

Examples:

subject / verb

Today or tomorrow is the day.

subject / verb

Stan or Phil wants to read the book.

subject / verb

Neither the pen nor the book is on the desk.

subject / verb

Either the blanket or pillows arrive this afternoon.

Indefinite Pronouns as Subject

An indefinite pronoun is a pronoun that does not refer to a specific noun. Different indefinite pronouns may only function as a singular noun, only function as a plural noun, or change depending on how they are used.

Always Singular

Pronouns such as *each*, *either*, *everybody*, *anybody*, *somebody*, and *nobody* are always singular.

Examples:

> Each (singular subject) of the runners has (singular verb) a different bib number.
>
> Is (singular verb) either (singular subject) of you ready for the game?

Note: The words *each* and *either* can also be used as adjectives (e.g., *each* person is unique). When one of these adjectives modifies the subject of a sentence, it is always a singular subject.

> Everybody (singular subject) grows (singular verb) a day older every day.
>
> Anybody (singular subject) is (singular verb) welcome to bring a tent.

Always Plural

Pronouns such as *both*, *several*, and *many* are always plural.

Examples:

> Both (plural subject) of the siblings were (plural verb) too tired to argue.
>
> Many (plural subject) have tried (plural verb), but none have succeeded.

Depend on Context

Pronouns such as *some*, *any*, *all*, *none*, *more*, and *most* can be either singular or plural depending on what they are representing in the context of the sentence.

Examples:

> All (singular subject) of my dog's food was (singular verb) still there in his bowl.
>
> By the end of the night, all (plural subject) of my guests were (plural verb) already excited about coming to my next party.

Other Cases Involving Plural or Irregular Form

Some nouns are **singular in meaning but plural in form**: news, mathematics, physics, and economics.

> The *news is* coming on now.
>
> *Mathematics is* my favorite class.

Some nouns are plural in form and meaning, and have **no singular equivalent**: scissors and pants.

> Do these *pants come* with a shirt?
>
> The *scissors are* for my project.

Mathematical operations are **irregular** in their construction, but are normally considered to be **singular in meaning**.

> *One plus one is* two.
>
> *Three times three is* nine.

Note: Look to your **dictionary** for help when you aren't sure whether a noun with a plural form has a singular or plural meaning.

Complements

A complement is a noun, pronoun, or adjective that is used to give more information about the subject or verb in the sentence.

Direct Objects

A direct object is a noun or pronoun that takes or receives the **action** of a verb. (Remember: a complete sentence does not need a direct object, so not all sentences will have them. A sentence needs only a subject and a verb.) When you are looking for a direct object, find the verb and ask *who* or *what*.

Examples:

> I took *the blanket.*
>
> Jane read *books.*

Indirect Objects

An indirect object is a word or group of words that show how an action had an **influence** on someone or something. If there is an indirect object in a sentence, then you always have a direct object in the sentence. When you are looking for the indirect object, find the verb and ask *to/for whom or what.*

Examples:

We taught $\overbrace{\text{the old dog}}^{\text{indirect object}}$ $\overbrace{\text{a new trick}}^{\text{direct object}}$.

I gave $\overbrace{\text{them}}^{\text{indirect object}}$ $\overbrace{\text{a math lesson}}^{\text{direct object}}$.

Review Video: Direct and Indirect Objects
Visit mometrix.com/academy and enter code: 817385

Predicate Nominatives and Predicate Adjectives

As we looked at previously, verbs may be classified as either action verbs or linking verbs. A linking verb is so named because it links the subject to words in the predicate that describe or define the subject. These words are called predicate nominatives (if nouns or pronouns) or predicate adjectives (if adjectives).

Examples:

My $\overbrace{\text{father}}^{\text{subject}}$ is a $\overbrace{\text{lawyer}}^{\text{predicate nominative}}$.

Your $\overbrace{\text{mother}}^{\text{subject}}$ is $\overbrace{\text{patient}}^{\text{predicate adjective}}$.

Pronoun Usage

The **antecedent** is the noun that has been replaced by a pronoun. A pronoun and its antecedent **agree** when they have the same number (singular or plural) and gender (male, female, or neutral).

Examples:

Singular agreement: $\overbrace{\text{John}}^{\text{antecedent}}$ came into town, and $\overbrace{\text{he}}^{\text{pronoun}}$ played for us.

Plural agreement: $\overbrace{\text{John and Rick}}^{\text{antecedent}}$ came into town, and $\overbrace{\text{they}}^{\text{pronoun}}$ played for us.

To determine which is the correct pronoun to use in a compound subject or object, try each pronoun **alone** in place of the compound in the sentence. Your knowledge of pronouns will tell you which one is correct.

Example:

Bob and (I, me) will be going.

Test: (1) *I will be going* or (2) *Me will be going*. The second choice cannot be correct because *me* cannot be used as the subject of a sentence. Instead, *me* is used as an object.

Answer: Bob and I will be going.

When a pronoun is used with a noun immediately following (as in "we boys"), try the sentence **without the added noun**.

Example:

(We/Us) boys played football last year.

Test: (1) *We played football last ye*ar or (2) *Us played football last year*. Again, the second choice cannot be correct because *us* cannot be used as a subject of a sentence. Instead, *us* is used as an object.

Answer: We boys played football last year.

Review Video: Pronoun Usage
Visit mometrix.com/academy and enter code: 666500

Review Video: What is Pronoun-Antecedent Agreement?
Visit mometrix.com/academy and enter code: 919704

A pronoun should point clearly to the **antecedent**. Here is how a pronoun reference can be unhelpful if it is puzzling or not directly stated.

Unhelpful: Ron and Jim (antecedent) went to the store, and he (pronoun) bought soda.

Who bought soda? Ron or Jim?

Helpful: Jim (antecedent) went to the store, and he (pronoun) bought soda.

The sentence is clear. Jim bought the soda.

Some pronouns change their form by their placement in a sentence. A pronoun that is a **subject** in a sentence comes in the **subjective case**. Pronouns that serve as **objects** appear in the **objective case**. Finally, the pronouns that are used as **possessives** appear in the **possessive case**.

Examples:

Subjective case: *He* is coming to the show.

The pronoun *He* is the subject of the sentence.

Objective case: Josh drove *him* to the airport.

The pronoun *him* is the object of the sentence.

Possessive case: The flowers are *mine.*

The pronoun *mine* shows ownership of the flowers.

The word *who* is a subjective-case pronoun that can be used as a **subject**. The word *whom* is an objective-case pronoun that can be used as an **object**. The words *who* and *whom* are common in subordinate clauses or in questions.

Examples:

He knows who (subject) wants (verb) to come.

He knows the man whom (object) we want (verb) at the party.

Clauses

A clause is a group of words that contains both a subject and a predicate (verb). There are two types of clauses: independent and dependent. An **independent clause** contains a complete thought, while a **dependent (or subordinate) clause** does not. A dependent clause includes a subject and a verb, and may also contain objects or complements, but it cannot stand as a complete thought without being joined to an independent clause. Dependent clauses function within sentences as adjectives, adverbs, or nouns.

Example:

I am running (independent clause) because I want to stay in shape. (dependent clause)

The clause *I am running* is an independent clause: it has a subject and a verb, and it gives a complete thought. The clause *because I want to stay in shape* is a dependent clause: it has a subject and a verb, but it does not express a complete thought. It adds detail to the independent clause to which it is attached.

Review Video: What is a Clause?
Visit mometrix.com/academy and enter code: 940170

Review Video: Independent and Dependent Clauses
Visit mometrix.com/academy and enter code: 556903

Types of Dependent Clauses

Adjective Clauses

An **adjective clause** is a dependent clause that modifies a noun or a pronoun. Adjective clauses begin with a relative pronoun (*who, whose, whom, which,* and *that*) or a relative adverb (*where, when,* and *why*).

Also, adjective clauses come after the noun that the clause needs to explain or rename. This is done to have a clear connection to the independent clause.

Examples:

I learned the reason (independent clause) why I won the award. (adjective clause)

This is the place (independent clause) where I started my first job. (adjective clause)

An adjective clause can be an essential or nonessential clause. An essential clause is very important to the sentence. **Essential clauses** explain or define a person or thing. **Nonessential clauses** give more information about a person or thing but are not necessary to define them. Nonessential clauses are set off with commas while essential clauses are not.

Examples:

A person who works hard at first can often rest later in life. (essential clause: who works hard at first)

Neil Armstrong, who walked on the moon, is my hero. (nonessential clause: who walked on the moon)

Review Video: Adjective Clauses and Phrases
Visit mometrix.com/academy and enter code: 520888

Adverb Clauses

An **adverb clause** is a dependent clause that modifies a verb, adjective, or adverb. In sentences with multiple dependent clauses, adverb clauses are usually placed immediately before or after the independent clause. An adverb clause is introduced with words such as *after, although, as, before, because, if, since, so, unless, when, where*, and *while*.

Examples:

When you walked outside, I called the manager. (adverb clause: When you walked outside)

I will go with you unless you want to stay. (adverb clause: unless you want to stay)

Noun Clauses

A **noun clause** is a dependent clause that can be used as a subject, object, or complement. Noun clauses begin with words such as *how, that, what, whether, which, who,* and *why*. These words can also come with an adjective clause. Unless the noun clause is being used as the subject of the sentence, it should come after the verb of the independent clause.

Examples:

The real mystery is how you avoided serious injury. (noun clause: how you avoided serious injury)

What you learn from each other depends on your honesty with others. (noun clause: What you learn from each other)

Subordination

When two related ideas are not of equal importance, the ideal way to combine them is to make the more important idea an independent clause and the less important idea a dependent or subordinate clause. This is called **subordination**.

Example:

> **Separate ideas**: The team had a perfect regular season. The team lost the championship.
>
> **Subordinated**: Despite having a perfect regular season, *the team lost the championship.*

Phrases

A phrase is a group of words that functions as a single part of speech, usually a noun, adjective, or adverb. A **phrase** is not a complete thought, but it adds detail or explanation to a sentence, or renames something within the sentence.

Prepositional Phrases

One of the most common types of phrases is the prepositional phrase. A **prepositional phrase** begins with a preposition and ends with a noun or pronoun that is the object of the preposition. Normally, the prepositional phrase functions as an **adjective** or an **adverb** within the sentence.

Examples:

> prepositional phrase
>
> The picnic is on the blanket.
>
> prepositional phrase
>
> I am sick with a fever today.
>
> prepositional phrase
>
> Among the many flowers, John found a four-leaf clover.

Verbal Phrases

A **verbal** is a word or phrase that is formed from a verb but does not function as a verb. Depending on its particular form, it may be used as a noun, adjective, or adverb. A verbal does **not** replace a verb in a sentence.

Examples:

> verb
>
> Correct: Walk a mile daily.
>
> This is a complete sentence with the implied subject *you*.
>
> verbal
>
> Incorrect: To walk a mile.
>
> This is not a sentence since there is no functional verb.

There are three types of verbal: **participles**, **gerunds**, and **infinitives**. Each type of verbal has a corresponding **phrase** that consists of the verbal itself along with any complements or modifiers.

Participles

A **participle** is a type of verbal that always functions as an adjective. The present participle always ends with *-ing*. Past participles end with *-d, -ed, -n,* or *-t*.

Examples: dance (verb) | dancing (present participle) | danced (past participle)

Participial phrases most often come right before or right after the noun or pronoun that they modify.

Examples:

Shipwrecked on an island (participial phrase), the boys started to fish for food.

Having been seated for five hours (participial phrase), we got out of the car to stretch our legs.

Praised for their work (participial phrase), the group accepted the first-place trophy.

Gerunds

A **gerund** is a type of verbal that always functions as a **noun**. Like present participles, gerunds always end with *-ing*, but they can be easily distinguished from one another by the part of speech they represent (participles always function as adjectives). Since a gerund or gerund phrase always functions as a noun, it can be used as the subject of a sentence, the predicate nominative, or the object of a verb or preposition.

Examples:

We want to be known for teaching (gerund) the poor (teaching the poor: object of preposition).

Coaching (gerund) this team (Coaching this team: subject) is the best job of my life.

We like practicing (gerund) our songs (practicing our songs: object of verb) in the basement.

Infinitives

An **infinitive** is a type of verbal that can function as a noun, an adjective, or an adverb. An infinitive is made of the word *to* and the basic form of the verb. As with all other types of verbal phrases, an infinitive phrase includes the verbal itself and all of its complements or modifiers.

Examples:

infinitive: To join; noun: To join the team

To join the team is my goal in life.

infinitive: to eat; adjective: to eat for the night

The animals have enough food to eat for the night.

infinitive: to exercise; adverb: to exercise their muscles

People lift weights to exercise their muscles.

> **Review Video: Gerunds, Infinitives, and Participles**
> Visit mometrix.com/academy and enter code: 634263

Appositive Phrases

An **appositive** is a word or phrase that is used to explain or rename nouns or pronouns. Noun phrases, gerund phrases, and infinitive phrases can all be used as appositives.

Examples:

appositive: hunters at heart

Terriers, hunters at heart, have been dressed up to look like lap dogs.

The noun phrase *hunters at heart* renames the noun *terriers*.

appositive: to save and invest his money

His plan, to save and invest his money, was proven as a safe approach.

The infinitive phrase explains what the plan is.

Appositive phrases can be **essential** or **nonessential**. An appositive phrase is essential if the person, place, or thing being described or renamed is too general for its meaning to be understood without the appositive.

Examples:

essential: George Washington and Thomas Jefferson

Two of America's Founding Fathers, George Washington and Thomas Jefferson, served as presidents.

nonessential: two Founding Fathers

George Washington and Thomas Jefferson, two Founding Fathers, served as presidents.

Absolute Phrases

An absolute phrase is a phrase that consists of **a noun followed by a participle**. An absolute phrase provides **context** to what is being described in the sentence, but it does not modify or explain any particular word; it is essentially independent.

Examples:

The alarm ringing, he pushed the snooze button. (noun: The alarm; participle: ringing; absolute phrase: The alarm ringing)

The music paused, she continued to dance through the crowd. (noun: The music; participle: paused; absolute phrase: The music paused)

Parallelism

When multiple items or ideas are presented in a sentence in series, such as in a list, the items or ideas must be stated in grammatically equivalent ways. In other words, if one idea is stated in gerund form, the second cannot be stated in infinitive form. For example, to write, *I enjoy reading and to study* would be incorrect. An infinitive and a gerund are not equivalent. Instead, you should write *I enjoy reading and studying*. In lists of more than two, all items must be parallel.

Example:

Incorrect: He stopped at the office, grocery store, and the pharmacy before heading home.

The first and third items in the list of places include the article *the*, so the second item needs it as well.

Correct: He stopped at the office, *the* grocery store, and the pharmacy before heading home.

Example:

Incorrect: While vacationing in Europe, she went biking, skiing, and climbed mountains.

The first and second items in the list are gerunds, so the third item must be as well.

Correct: While vacationing in Europe, she went biking, skiing, and *mountain climbing*.

Review Video: Parallel Sentence Construction
Visit mometrix.com/academy and enter code: 831988

Sentence Purpose

There are four types of sentences: declarative, imperative, interrogative, and exclamatory.

A **declarative** sentence states a fact and ends with a period.

The football game starts at seven o'clock.

An **imperative** sentence tells someone to do something and generally ends with a period. An urgent command might end with an exclamation point instead.

Don't forget to buy your ticket.

An **interrogative** sentence asks a question and ends with a question mark.

Are you going to the game on Friday?

An **exclamatory** sentence shows strong emotion and ends with an exclamation point.

I can't believe we won the game!

Review Video: Functions of a Sentence
Visit mometrix.com/academy and enter code: 475974

Sentence Structure

Sentences are classified by structure based on the type and number of clauses present. The four classifications of sentence structure are the following:

Simple: A simple sentence has one independent clause with no dependent clauses. A simple sentence may have **compound elements** (i.e., compound subject or verb).

Examples:

single subject | single verb
Judy watered the lawn.

compound subject | single verb
Judy and Alan watered the lawn.

single subject | compound verb | compound verb
Judy watered the lawn and pulled weeds.

compound subject | compound verb | compound verb
Judy and Alan watered the lawn and pulled weeds.

Compound: A compound sentence has two or more independent clauses with no dependent clauses. Usually, the independent clauses are joined with a comma and a coordinating conjunction or with a semicolon.

Examples:

independent clause | independent clause
The time has come, and we are ready.

independent clause | independent clause
I woke up at dawn; the sun was just coming up.

Complex: A complex sentence has one independent clause and at least one dependent clause.

Examples:

dependent clause | independent clause
Although he had the flu, Harry went to work.

independent clause | dependent clause
Marcia got married, after she finished college.

Compound-Complex: A compound-complex sentence has at least two independent clauses and at least one dependent clause.

Examples:

independent clause | dependent clause | independent clause

John is my friend who went to India, and he brought back souvenirs.

independent clause | independent clause | dependent clause

You may not realize this, but we heard the music that you played last night.

Review Video: Sentence Structure
Visit mometrix.com/academy and enter code: 700478

Sentence variety is important to consider when writing an essay or speech. A variety of sentence lengths and types creates rhythm, makes a passage more engaging, and gives writers an opportunity to demonstrate their writing style. Writing that uses the same length or type of sentence without variation can be boring or difficult to read. To evaluate a passage for effective sentence variety, it is helpful to note whether the passage contains diverse sentence structures and lengths. It is also important to pay attention to the way each sentence starts and avoid beginning with the same words or phrases.

Sentence Fragments

Recall that a group of words must contain at least one **independent clause** in order to be considered a sentence. If it doesn't contain even one independent clause, it is called a **sentence fragment**.

The appropriate process for **repairing** a sentence fragment depends on what type of fragment it is. If the fragment is a dependent clause, it can sometimes be as simple as removing a subordinating word (e.g., when, because, if) from the beginning of the fragment. Alternatively, a dependent clause can be incorporated into a closely related neighboring sentence. If the fragment is missing some required part, like a subject or a verb, the fix might be as simple as adding the missing part.

Examples:

Fragment: Because he wanted to sail the Mediterranean.

Removed subordinating word: He wanted to sail the Mediterranean.

Combined with another sentence: Because he wanted to sail the Mediterranean, he booked a Greek island cruise.

Run-on Sentences

Run-on sentences consist of multiple independent clauses that have not been joined together properly. Run-on sentences can be corrected in several different ways:

Join clauses properly: This can be done with a comma and coordinating conjunction, with a semicolon, or with a colon or dash if the second clause is explaining something in the first.

Example:

Incorrect: I went on the trip, we visited lots of castles.

Corrected: I went on the trip, and we visited lots of castles.

Split into separate sentences: This correction is most effective when the independent clauses are very long or when they are not closely related.

Example:

Incorrect: The drive to New York takes ten hours, my uncle lives in Boston.

Corrected: The drive to New York takes ten hours. My uncle lives in Boston.

Make one clause dependent: This is the easiest way to make the sentence correct and more interesting at the same time. It's often as simple as adding a subordinating word between the two clauses or before the first clause.

Example:

Incorrect: I finally made it to the store and I bought some eggs.

Corrected: When I finally made it to the store, I bought some eggs.

Reduce to one clause with a compound verb: If both clauses have the same subject, remove the subject from the second clause, and you now have just one clause with a compound verb.

Example:

Incorrect: The drive to New York takes ten hours, it makes me very tired.

Corrected: The drive to New York takes ten hours and makes me very tired.

Note: While these are the simplest ways to correct a run-on sentence, often the best way is to completely reorganize the thoughts in the sentence and rewrite it.

Review Video: Fragments and Run-on Sentences
Visit mometrix.com/academy and enter code: 541989

DANGLING AND MISPLACED MODIFIERS

DANGLING MODIFIERS

A dangling modifier is a dependent clause or verbal phrase that does not have a clear logical connection to a word in the sentence.

Example:

dangling modifier

Incorrect: Reading each magazine article, the stories caught my attention.

The word *stories* cannot be modified by *Reading each magazine article*. People can read, but stories cannot read. Therefore, the subject of the sentence must be a person.

dependent clause

Corrected: Reading each magazine article, I was entertained by the stories.

Example:

dangling modifier

Incorrect: Ever since childhood, my grandparents have visited me for Christmas.

The speaker in this sentence can't have been visited by her grandparents when *they* were children, since she wouldn't have been born yet. Either the modifier should be clarified or the sentence should be rearranged to specify whose childhood is being referenced.

dependent clause

Clarified: Ever since I was a child, my grandparents have visited for Christmas.

dependent clause

Rearranged: I have enjoyed my grandparents visiting for Christmas, ever since childhood.

MISPLACED MODIFIERS

Because modifiers are grammatically versatile, they can be put in many different places within the structure of a sentence. The danger of this versatility is that a modifier can accidentally be placed where it is modifying the wrong word or where it is not clear which word it is modifying.

Example:

modifier

Incorrect: She read the book to a crowd that was filled with beautiful pictures.

The book was filled with beautiful pictures, not the crowd.

modifier

Corrected: She read the book that was filled with beautiful pictures to a crowd.

Example:

Ambiguous: Derek saw a bus nearly hit a man on his way to work. (modifier: on his way to work)

Was Derek on his way to work or was the other man?

Derek: On his way to work, Derek saw a bus nearly hit a man. (modifier: On his way to work)

The other man: Derek saw a bus nearly hit a man who was on his way to work. (modifier: who was on his way to work)

Split Infinitives

A split infinitive occurs when a modifying word comes between the word *to* and the verb that pairs with *to*.

Example: To *clearly* explain vs. *To explain* clearly | To *softly* sing vs. *To sing* softly

Though considered improper by some, split infinitives may provide better clarity and simplicity in some cases than the alternatives. As such, avoiding them should not be considered a universal rule.

Double Negatives

Standard English allows **two negatives** only when a **positive** meaning is intended. For example, *The team was not displeased with their performance.* Double negatives to emphasize negation are not used in standard English.

Negative modifiers (e.g., never, no, and not) should not be paired with other negative modifiers or negative words (e.g., none, nobody, nothing, or neither). The modifiers *hardly, barely*, and *scarcely* are also considered negatives in standard English, so they should not be used with other negatives.

CHAPTER QUIZ

1. Which of the following is an imperative statement?

a. John knows the way to the park.
b. There are five letters on the table for him.
c. Go to the post office for me.
d. The cookies need to cook for a few more minutes.

2. Which of the following is NOT a word used to combine nouns to make a compound subject?

a. Or
b. Nor
c. And
d. Also

3. Which of the following is always singular?

a. Each
b. Both
c. Several
d. Many

4. Identify the indirect object of the following sentence: "We taught the old dog a new trick."

a. We
b. Taught
c. The old dog
d. A new trick

5. Identify the infinitive of the following sentence: "The animals have enough food to eat for the night."

a. The animals
b. Have enough food
c. To eat
d. For the night

6. How many types of sentences are there?

a. Three
b. Four
c. Five
d. Six

7. Which of the following sentences correctly expresses the idea of parallelism?

a. He stopped at the office, grocery store, and the pharmacy before heading home.
b. While vacationing in Europe, she went biking, skiing, and climbed mountains.
c. The crowd jumped and cheered, roared and hollered, and whistled as the game concluded.
d. The flurry of blows left him staggered, discombobulated, and overwhelmed before falling.

8. Identify the phrase, "The music paused," in the following sample sentence:

"The music paused, she continued to dance through the crowd."

a. Subordinate phrase
b. Essential appositive
c. Nonessential appositive
d. Absolute phrase

Chapter Quiz Answer Key

1. C: In an imperative sentence, the verb's subject is understood without actually appearing or being named in the sentence itself. For example, in the imperative sentence, "Run to the store," the subject is the person being told to run.

2. D: A compound subject is formed when two or more nouns joined by *and*, *or*, or *nor* jointly act as the subject of the sentence.

3. A: Pronouns such as *each*, *either*, *everybody*, *anybody*, *somebody*, and *nobody* are always singular.

4. C: An indirect object is a word or group of words that show how an action had an influence on someone or something. If there is an indirect object in a sentence, then there will always be a direct object in the sentence. When looking for the indirect object, find the verb and ask *to, for whom*, or *what.*

indirect object (the old dog) — direct object (a new trick)

We taught the old dog a new trick.

5. C: An infinitive is a type of verbal that can function as a noun, an adjective, or an adverb. An infinitive is made of the word *to* and the basic form of the verb. As with all other types of verbal phrases, an infinitive phrase includes the verbal itself and all of its complements or modifiers.

infinitive (to eat)

The animals have enough food to eat for the night.

adjective (to eat for the night)

6. B: There are four types of sentences: declarative, imperative, interrogative, and exclamatory.

7. D: When multiple items or ideas are presented in a sentence in series, such as in a list, the items or ideas must be stated in grammatically equivalent ways. In other words, if one idea is stated in gerund form, the second cannot be stated in infinitive form. For example, writing "I enjoy *reading* and *to study*" would be incorrect. An infinitive and a gerund are not equivalent. Instead, the sentence should be, "I enjoy *reading* and *studying*." In lists of more than two, all items must be parallel.

Example:

Incorrect: He stopped at the office, grocery store, and the pharmacy before heading home.

(The first and third items in the list of places include the article *the*, so the second item needs it as well.)

Correct: He stopped at the office, *the* grocery store, and the pharmacy before heading home.

8. D: An absolute phrase is a phrase that consists of a noun followed by a participle. An absolute phrase provides context to what is being described in the sentence, but it does not modify or explain any particular word; it is essentially independent.

noun participle

The music paused, she continued to dance through the crowd.

absolute phrase

Punctuation

End Punctuation

Periods

Use a period to end all sentences except direct questions and exclamations. Periods are also used for abbreviations.

Examples: 3 p.m. | 2 a.m. | Mr. Jones | Mrs. Stevens | Dr. Smith | Bill, Jr. | Pennsylvania Ave.

Note: An abbreviation is a shortened form of a word or phrase.

Question Marks

Question marks should be used following a **direct question**. A polite request can be followed by a period instead of a question mark.

Direct Question: What is for lunch today? | How are you? | Why is that the answer?

Polite Requests: Can you please send me the item tomorrow. | Will you please walk with me on the track.

Review Video: Question Marks
Visit mometrix.com/academy and enter code: 118471

Exclamation Marks

Exclamation marks are used after a word group or sentence that shows much feeling or has special importance. Exclamation marks should not be overused. They are saved for proper **exclamatory interjections**.

Example: We're going to the finals! | You have a beautiful car! | "That's crazy!" she yelled.

Review Video: Exclamation Points
Visit mometrix.com/academy and enter code: 199367

Commas

The comma is a punctuation mark that can help you understand connections in a sentence. Not every sentence needs a comma. However, if a sentence needs a comma, you need to put it in the right place. A comma in the wrong place (or an absent comma) will make a sentence's meaning unclear. These are some of the rules for commas:

Use Case	Example
Before a **coordinating conjunction** joining independent clauses	Bob caught three fish, and I caught two fish.
After an **introductory phrase**	After the final out, we went to a restaurant to celebrate.
After an **adverbial clause**	Studying the stars, I was awed by the beauty of the sky.
Between **items in a series**	I will bring the turkey, the pie, and the coffee.
For **interjections**	Wow, you know how to play this game.
After ***yes*** **and** ***no*** **responses**	No, I cannot come tomorrow.
Separate **nonessential modifiers**	John Frank, who coaches the team, was promoted today.
Separate **nonessential appositives**	Thomas Edison, an American inventor, was born in Ohio.
Separate **nouns of direct address**	You, John, are my only hope in this moment.
Separate **interrogative tags**	This is the last time, correct?
Separate **contrasts**	You are my friend, not my enemy.
Writing **dates**	July 4, 1776, is an important date to remember.
Writing **addresses**	He is meeting me at 456 Delaware Avenue, Washington, D.C., tomorrow morning.
Writing **geographical names**	Paris, France, is my favorite city.
Writing **titles**	John Smith, PhD, will be visiting your class today.
Separate **expressions like** ***he said***	"You can start," she said, "with an apology."

Also, you can use a comma **between coordinate adjectives** not joined with *and*. However, not all adjectives are coordinate (i.e., equal or parallel).

Incorrect: The kind, brown dog followed me home.

Correct: The kind, loyal dog followed me home.

There are two simple ways to know if your adjectives are coordinate. One, you can join the adjectives with *and*: *The kind and loyal dog*. Two, you can change the order of the adjectives: *The loyal, kind dog*.

Review Video: When to Use a Comma
Visit mometrix.com/academy and enter code: 786797

Semicolons

The semicolon is used to connect major sentence pieces of equal value. Some rules for semicolons include:

Use Case	Example
Between closely connected independent clauses **not connected with a coordinating conjunction**	You are right; we should go with your plan.
Between independent clauses **linked with a transitional word**	I think that we can agree on this; however, I am not sure about my friends.
Between items in a **series that has internal punctuation**	I have visited New York, New York; Augusta, Maine; and Baltimore, Maryland.

Review Video: How to Use Semicolons
Visit mometrix.com/academy and enter code: 370605

Colons

The colon is used to call attention to the words that follow it. A colon must come after a **complete independent clause**. The rules for colons are as follows:

Use Case	Example
After an independent clause to **make a list**	I want to learn many languages: Spanish, German, and Italian.
For **explanations**	There is one thing that stands out on your resume: responsibility.
To give a **quote**	He started with an idea: "We are able to do more than we imagine."
After the **greeting in a formal letter**	To Whom It May Concern:
Show **hours and minutes**	It is 3:14 p.m.
Separate a **title and subtitle**	The essay is titled "America: A Short Introduction to a Modern Country."

Review Video: Colons
Visit mometrix.com/academy and enter code: 868673

Parentheses

Parentheses are used for additional information. Also, they can be used to put labels for letters or numbers in a series. Parentheses should be not be used very often. If they are overused, parentheses can be a distraction instead of a help.

Examples:

Extra Information: The rattlesnake (see Image 2) is a dangerous snake of North and South America.

Series: Include in the email (1) your name, (2) your address, and (3) your question for the author.

Review Video: Parentheses
Visit mometrix.com/academy and enter code: 947743

Quotation Marks

Use quotation marks to close off **direct quotations** of a person's spoken or written words. Do not use quotation marks around indirect quotations. An indirect quotation gives someone's message without using the person's exact words. Use **single quotation marks** to close off a quotation inside a quotation.

Direct Quote: Nancy said, "I am waiting for Henry to arrive."

Indirect Quote: Henry said that he is going to be late to the meeting.

Quote inside a Quote: The teacher asked, "Has everyone read 'The Gift of the Magi'?"

Quotation marks should be used around the titles of **short works**: newspaper and magazine articles, poems, short stories, songs, television episodes, radio programs, and subdivisions of books or websites.

Examples:

"Rip Van Winkle" (short story by Washington Irving)

"O Captain! My Captain!" (poem by Walt Whitman)

Although it is not standard usage, quotation marks are sometimes used to highlight **irony** or the use of words to mean something other than their dictionary definition. This type of usage should be employed sparingly, if at all.

Examples:

The boss warned Frank that he was walking on "thin ice."	Frank is not walking on real ice. Instead, he is being warned to avoid mistakes.
The teacher thanked the young man for his "honesty."	The quotation marks around *honesty* show that the teacher does not believe the young man's explanation.

Review Video: Quotation Marks
Visit mometrix.com/academy and enter code: 884918

Periods and commas are put **inside** quotation marks. Colons and semicolons are put **outside** the quotation marks. Question marks and exclamation points are placed inside quotation marks when they are part of a quote. When the question or exclamation mark goes with the whole sentence, the mark is left outside of the quotation marks.

Examples:

Period and comma	We read "The Gift of the Magi," "The Skylight Room," and "The Cactus."
Semicolon	They watched "The Nutcracker"; then, they went home.
Exclamation mark that is a part of a quote	The crowd cheered, "Victory!"
Question mark that goes with the whole sentence	Is your favorite short story "The Tell-Tale Heart"?

Apostrophes

An apostrophe is used to show **possession** or the **deletion of letters in contractions**. An apostrophe is not needed with the possessive pronouns *his, hers, its, ours, theirs, whose*, and *yours*.

Singular Nouns: David's car | a book's theme | my brother's board game

Plural Nouns that end with -*s*: the scissors' handle | boys' basketball

Plural Nouns that end without -*s*: Men's department | the people's adventure

Review Video: When to Use an Apostrophe
Visit mometrix.com/academy and enter code: 213068

Review Video: Punctuation Errors in Possessive Pronouns
Visit mometrix.com/academy and enter code: 221438

Hyphens

Hyphens are used to **separate compound words**. Use hyphens in the following cases:

Use Case	Example
Compound numbers from 21 to 99 when written out in words	This team needs twenty-five points to win the game.
Written-out fractions that are used as adjectives	The recipe says that we need a three-fourths cup of butter.
Compound adjectives that come before a noun	The well-fed dog took a nap.
Unusual compound words that would be hard to read or easily confused with other words	This is the best anti-itch cream on the market.

Note: This is not a complete set of the rules for hyphens. A dictionary is the best tool for knowing if a compound word needs a hyphen.

Review Video: Hyphens
Visit mometrix.com/academy and enter code: 981632

Dashes

Dashes are used to show a **break** or a **change in thought** in a sentence or to act as parentheses in a sentence. When typing, use two hyphens to make a dash. Do not put a space before or after the dash. The following are the functions of dashes:

Use Case	Example
Set off parenthetical statements or an **appositive with internal punctuation**	The three trees—oak, pine, and magnolia—are coming on a truck tomorrow.
Show a **break or change in tone or thought**	The first question—how silly of me—does not have a correct answer.

Ellipsis Marks

The ellipsis mark has **three** periods (...) to show when **words have been removed** from a quotation. If a **full sentence or more** is removed from a quoted passage, you need to use **four** periods to show the removed text and the end punctuation mark. The ellipsis mark should not be used at the beginning of a quotation. The ellipsis mark should also not be used at the end of a quotation unless some words have been deleted from the end of the final sentence.

Example:

> "Then he picked up the groceries...paid for them...later he went home."

BRACKETS

There are two main reasons to use brackets:

Use Case	Example
Placing **parentheses inside of parentheses**	The hero of this story, Paul Revere (a silversmith and industrialist [see Ch. 4]), rode through towns of Massachusetts to warn of advancing British troops.
Adding **clarification or detail to a quotation** that is not part of the quotation	The father explained, "My children are planning to attend my alma mater [State University]."

Review Video: Brackets
Visit mometrix.com/academy and enter code: 727546

Chapter Quiz

1. Which of the following correctly implements the use of parentheses?

a. The rattlesnake (see Image 2) is a dangerous snake of North and South America.
b. The rattlesnake see (Image 2) is a dangerous snake of North and South America.
c. The rattlesnake see Image (2) is a dangerous snake of North and South America.
d. The rattlesnake (see Image) (2) is a dangerous snake of North and South America.

2. Which of the following correctly describes the placement of punctuation in reference to quotations?

a. Periods and commas are put outside quotation marks; colons and semicolons go inside.
b. Periods and colons are put outside quotation marks; commas and semicolons go inside.
c. Periods and commas are put inside quotation marks; colons and semicolons go outside.
d. Periods and colons are put inside quotation marks; commas and semicolons go outside.

3. Which of the following correctly implements the use of commas?

a. He is meeting me at, 456 Delaware Avenue, Washington, D.C., tomorrow morning.
b. He is meeting me at 456 Delaware Avenue, Washington, D.C., tomorrow morning.
c. He is meeting me at 456 Delaware Avenue Washington, D.C. tomorrow morning.
d. He is meeting me at 456 Delaware Avenue, Washington, D.C. tomorrow morning.

Chapter Quiz Answer Key

1. A: Parentheses are used for additional information. Also, they can be used to put labels for letters or numbers in a series. Parentheses should be not be used very often because their overuse can become a distraction.

2. C: Periods and commas are put inside quotation marks, while colons and semicolons are put outside quotation marks. Question marks and exclamation points are placed inside quotation marks when they are part of a quote. When the question mark or exclamation point is not part of a quoted section but instead part of an entire sentence, then it is left outside of the quotation marks.

3. B: These are some of the rules for commas:

Use Case	Example
Before a **coordinating conjunction** joining independent clauses	Bob caught three fish, and I caught two fish.
After an **introductory phrase**	After the final out, we went to a restaurant to celebrate.
After an **adverbial clause**	Studying the stars, I was awed by the beauty of the sky.
Between **items in a series**	I will bring the turkey, the pie, and the coffee.
For **interjections**	Wow, you know how to play this game.
After ***yes* and *no* responses**	No, I cannot come tomorrow.
Separate **nonessential modifiers**	John Frank, who coaches the team, was promoted today.
Separate **nonessential appositives**	Thomas Edison, an American inventor, was born in Ohio.
Separate **nouns of direct address**	You, John, are my only hope in this moment.
Separate **interrogative tags**	This is the last time, correct?
Separate **contrasts**	You are my friend, not my enemy.
Writing **dates**	July 4, 1776, is an important date to remember.
Writing **addresses**	He is meeting me at 456 Delaware Avenue, Washington, D.C., tomorrow morning.
Writing **geographical names**	Paris, France, is my favorite city.
Writing **titles**	John Smith, PhD, will be visiting your class today.
Separate **expressions like "he said"**	"You can start," she said, "with an apology."

Common Usage Mistakes

Word Confusion

Which, That, and Who

The words *which*, *that*, and *who* can act as **relative pronouns** to help clarify or describe a noun.

Which is used for things only.

Example: Andrew's car, *which is old and rusty,* broke down last week.

That is used for people or things. *That* is usually informal when used to describe people.

Example: Is this the only book *that Louis L'Amour wrote?*

Example: Is Louis L'Amour the author *that wrote Western novels?*

Who is used for people or for animals that have an identity or personality.

Example: Mozart was the composer *who wrote those operas.*

Example: John's dog, *who is called Max,* is large and fierce.

Homophones

Homophones are words that sound alike (or similar) but have different **spellings** and **definitions**. A homophone is a type of **homonym**, which is a pair or group of words that are pronounced or spelled the same, but do not mean the same thing.

To, Too, and Two

To can be an adverb or a preposition for showing direction, purpose, and relationship. See your dictionary for the many other ways to use *to* in a sentence.

Examples: I went to the store. | I want to go with you.

Too is an adverb that means *also, as well, very,* or *in excess.*

Examples: I can walk a mile too. | You have eaten too much.

Two is a number.

Example: You have two minutes left.

There, Their, and They're

There can be an adjective, adverb, or pronoun. Often, *there* is used to show a place or to start a sentence.

Examples: I went there yesterday. | There is something in his pocket.

Their is a pronoun that is used to show ownership.

Examples: He is their father. | This is their fourth apology this week.

They're is a contraction of *they are.*

Example: Did you know that they're in town?

Knew and New

Knew is the past tense of *know.*

Example: I knew the answer.

New is an adjective that means something is current, has not been used, or is modern.

Example: This is my new phone.

Then and Than

Then is an adverb that indicates sequence or order:

Example: I'm going to run to the library and then come home.

Than is special-purpose word used only for comparisons:

Example: Susie likes chips more than candy.

Its and It's

Its is a pronoun that shows ownership.

Example: The guitar is in its case.

It's is a contraction of *it is.*

Example: It's an honor and a privilege to meet you.

Note: The *h* in honor is silent, so *honor* starts with the vowel sound *o*, which must have the article *an*.

Your and You're

Your is a pronoun that shows ownership.

Example: This is your moment to shine.

You're is a contraction of *you are.*

Example: Yes, you're correct.

Saw and Seen

Saw is the past-tense form of *see.*

Example: I saw a turtle on my walk this morning.

Seen is the past participle of *see.*

Example: I have seen this movie before.

Affect and Effect

There are two main reasons that *affect* and *effect* are so often confused: 1) both words can be used as either a noun or a verb, and 2) unlike most homophones, their usage and meanings are closely related to each other. Here is a quick rundown of the four usage options:

Affect (n): feeling, emotion, or mood that is displayed

Example: The patient had a flat *affect*. (i.e., his face showed little or no emotion)

Affect (v): to alter, to change, to influence

Example: The sunshine *affects* the plant's growth.

Effect (n): a result, a consequence

Example: What *effect* will this weather have on our schedule?

Effect (v): to bring about, to cause to be

Example: These new rules will *effect* order in the office.

The noun form of *affect* is rarely used outside of technical medical descriptions, so if a noun form is needed on the test, you can safely select *effect*. The verb form of *effect* is not as rare as the noun form of *affect*, but it's still not all that likely to show up on your test. If you need a verb and you can't decide which to use based on the definitions, choosing *affect* is your best bet.

Homographs

Homographs are words that share the same spelling, but have different meanings and sometimes different pronunciations. To figure out which meaning is being used, you should be looking for context clues. The context clues give hints to the meaning of the word. For example, the word *spot* has many meanings. It can mean "a place" or "a stain or blot." In the sentence "After my lunch, I saw a spot on my shirt," the word *spot* means "a stain or blot." The context clues of "After my lunch" and "on my shirt" guide you to this decision. A homograph is another type of homonym.

Bank

(noun): an establishment where money is held for savings or lending

(verb): to collect or pile up

Content

(noun): the topics that will be addressed within a book

(adjective): pleased or satisfied

(verb): to make someone pleased or satisfied

Fine

(noun): an amount of money that acts a penalty for an offense

(adjective): very small or thin

(adverb): in an acceptable way

(verb): to make someone pay money as a punishment

Incense

(noun): a material that is burned in religious settings and makes a pleasant aroma

(verb): to frustrate or anger

LEAD

(noun): the first or highest position

(noun): a heavy metallic element

(verb): to direct a person or group of followers

(adjective): containing lead

OBJECT

(noun): a lifeless item that can be held and observed

(verb): to disagree

PRODUCE

(noun): fruits and vegetables

(verb): to make or create something

REFUSE

(noun): garbage or debris that has been thrown away

(verb): to not allow

SUBJECT

(noun): an area of study

(verb): to force or subdue

TEAR

(noun): a fluid secreted by the eyes

(verb): to separate or pull apart

Chapter Quiz

1. Which of the following correctly implements the word "affect"?

a. These new rules will affect order in the office.
b. What affect will this weather have on our schedule?
c. The patient had a flat affect during her examination.
d. His narcissism had a detrimental affect on everyone around him.

2. "Affect" and "effect" would be considered which of the following?

a. Homographs
b. Synonyms
c. Antonyms
d. Homophones

Chapter Quiz Answer Key

1. C: There are two main reasons that *affect* and *effect* are so often confused: 1) both words can be used as either a noun or a verb; and 2) unlike most homophones, their usage and meanings are closely related to each other. Here is a quick rundown of the four usage options:

Affect (n): feeling, emotion, or mood that is displayed

Example: The patient had a flat *affect* (i.e., his face showed little or no emotion).

Affect (v): to alter, to change, to influence

Example: The sunshine *affects* the plant's growth.

Effect (n): a result, a consequence

Example: What *effect* will this weather have on our schedule?

Effect (v): to bring about, to cause to be

Example: These new rules will *effect* order in the office.

The noun form of *affect* is rarely used outside of technical medical descriptions, so if a noun form is needed on the test, *effect* is a safe selection. The verb form of *effect* is not as rare as the noun form of *affect*, but it's still not likely to show up on a test. If a verb is needed and the definitions aren't enough of an indicator for which one to use, choosing *affect* is the safest option.

2. D: Homophones are words that sound alike (or similar) but have different spellings and definitions. A homophone is a type of homonym, which is a pair or group of words that are pronounced or spelled the same, but do not mean the same thing.

The Writing Process

Brainstorming

Brainstorming is a technique that is used to find a creative approach to a subject. This can be accomplished by simple **free-association** with a topic. For example, with paper and pen, write every thought that you have about the topic in a word or phrase. This is done without critical thinking. You should put everything that comes to your mind about the topic on your scratch paper. Then, you need to read the list over a few times. Next, look for patterns, repetitions, and clusters of ideas. This allows a variety of fresh ideas to come as you think about the topic.

Free Writing

Free writing is a more structured form of brainstorming. The method involves taking a limited amount of time (e.g., 2 to 3 minutes) to write everything that comes to mind about the topic in complete sentences. When time expires, review everything that has been written down. Many of your sentences may make little or no sense, but the insights and observations that can come from free writing make this method a valuable approach. Usually, free writing results in a fuller expression of ideas than brainstorming because thoughts and associations are written in complete sentences. However, both techniques can be used to complement each other.

Planning

Planning is the process of organizing a piece of writing before composing a draft. Planning can include creating an outline or a graphic organizer, such as a Venn diagram, a spider-map, or a flowchart. These methods should help the writer identify their topic, main ideas, and the general organization of the composition. Preliminary research can also take place during this stage. Planning helps writers organize all of their ideas and decide if they have enough material to begin their first draft. However, writers should remember that the decisions they make during this step will likely change later in the process, so their plan does not have to be perfect.

Drafting

Writers may then use their plan, outline, or graphic organizer to compose their first draft. They may write subsequent drafts to improve their writing. Writing multiple drafts can help writers consider different ways to communicate their ideas and address errors that may be difficult to correct without rewriting a section or the whole composition. Most writers will vary in how many drafts they choose to write, as there is no "right" number of drafts. Writing drafts also takes away the pressure to write perfectly on the first try, as writers can improve with each draft they write.

Revising, Editing, and Proofreading

Once a writer completes a draft, they can move on to the revising, editing, and proofreading steps to improve their draft. These steps begin with making broad changes that may apply to large sections of a composition and then making small, specific corrections. **Revising** is the first and broadest of these steps. Revising involves ensuring that the composition addresses an appropriate audience, includes all necessary material, maintains focus throughout, and is organized logically. Revising may occur after the first draft to ensure that the following drafts improve upon errors from the first draft. Some revision should occur between each draft to avoid repeating these errors. The **editing** phase of writing is narrower than the revising phase. Editing a composition should include steps such as improving transitions between paragraphs, ensuring each paragraph is on topic, and improving the flow of the text. The editing phase may also include correcting grammatical errors that cannot be fixed without significantly altering the text. **Proofreading** involves fixing misspelled words, typos, other grammatical errors, and any remaining surface-level flaws in the composition.

Recursive Writing Process

However you approach writing, you may find comfort in knowing that the revision process can occur in any order. The **recursive writing process** is not as difficult as the phrase may make it seem. Simply put, the recursive writing process means that you may need to revisit steps after completing other steps. It also implies that the steps are not required to take place in any certain order. Indeed, you may find that planning, drafting, and revising can all take place at about the same time. The writing process involves moving back and forth between planning, drafting, and revising, followed by more planning, more drafting, and more revising until the writing is satisfactory.

Review Video: Recursive Writing Process
Visit mometrix.com/academy and enter code: 951611

Technology in the Writing Process

Modern technology has yielded several tools that can be used to make the writing process more convenient and organized. Word processors and online tools, such as databases and plagiarism detectors, allow much of the writing process to be completed in one place, using one device.

Technology for Planning and Drafting

For the planning and drafting stages of the writing process, word processors are a helpful tool. These programs also feature formatting tools, allowing users to create their own planning tools or create digital outlines that can be easily converted into sentences, paragraphs, or an entire essay draft. Online databases and references also complement the planning process by providing convenient access to information and sources for research. Word processors also allow users to keep up with their work and update it more easily than if they wrote their work by hand. Online word processors often allow users to collaborate, making group assignments more convenient. These programs also allow users to include illustrations or other supplemental media in their compositions.

Technology for Revising, Editing, and Proofreading

Word processors also benefit the revising, editing, and proofreading stages of the writing process. Most of these programs indicate errors in spelling and grammar, allowing users to catch minor errors and correct them quickly. There are also websites designed to help writers by analyzing text for deeper errors, such as poor sentence structure, inappropriate complexity, lack of sentence variety, and style issues. These websites can help users fix errors they may not know to look for or may have simply missed. As writers finish these steps, they may benefit from checking their work for any plagiarism. There are several websites and programs that compare text to other documents and publications across the internet and detect any similarities within the text. These websites show the source of the similar information, so users know whether or not they referenced the source and unintentionally plagiarized its contents.

Technology for Publishing

Technology also makes managing written work more convenient. Digitally storing documents keeps everything in one place and is easy to reference. Digital storage also makes sharing work easier, as documents can be attached to an email or stored online. This also allows writers to publish their work easily, as they can electronically submit it to other publications or freely post it to a personal blog, profile, or website.

Chapter Quiz

1. Which of the following is a more structured form of brainstorming?

a. Free writing
b. Planning
c. Drafting
d. Proofreading

Chapter Quiz Answer Key

1. A: Free writing is a more structured form of brainstorming. The method involves taking a limited amount of time (e.g., two to three minutes) to write everything that comes to mind about the topic in complete sentences. When time expires, review everything that has been written down. Many of the sentences may make little or no sense, but the insights and observations that can come from free writing make this method a valuable approach. Usually, free writing results in a fuller expression of ideas than brainstorming because thoughts and associations are written in complete sentences. However, both techniques can be used to complement each other.

Outlining and Organizing Ideas

Main Ideas, Supporting Details, and Outlining a Topic

A writer often begins the first paragraph of a paper by stating the **main idea** or point, also known as the **topic sentence**. The rest of the paragraph supplies particular details that develop and support the main point. One way to visualize the relationship between the main point and supporting information is by considering a table: the tabletop is the main point, and each of the table's legs is a supporting detail or group of details. Both professional authors and students can benefit from planning their writing by first making an outline of the topic. Outlines facilitate quick identification of the main point and supporting details without having to wade through the additional language that will exist in the fully developed essay, article, or paper. Outlining can also help readers to analyze a piece of existing writing for the same reason. The outline first summarizes the main idea in one sentence. Then, below that, it summarizes the supporting details in a numbered list. Writing the paper then consists of filling in the outline with detail, writing a paragraph for each supporting point, and adding an introduction and conclusion.

Introduction

The purpose of the introduction is to capture the reader's attention and announce the essay's main idea. Normally, the introduction contains 50-80 words, or 3-5 sentences. An introduction can begin with an interesting quote, a question, or a strong opinion—something that will **engage** the reader's interest and prompt them to keep reading. If you are writing your essay to a specific prompt, your introduction should include a **restatement or summarization** of the prompt so that the reader will have some context for your essay. Finally, your introduction should briefly state your **thesis or main idea**: the primary thing you hope to communicate to the reader through your essay. Don't try to include all of the details and nuances of your thesis, or all of your reasons for it, in the introduction. That's what the rest of the essay is for!

Review Video: Introduction
Visit mometrix.com/academy and enter code: 961328

Thesis Statement

The thesis is the main idea of the essay. A temporary thesis, or working thesis, should be established early in the writing process because it will serve to keep the writer focused as ideas develop. This temporary thesis is subject to change as you continue to write.

The temporary thesis has two parts: a **topic** (i.e., the focus of your essay based on the prompt) and a **comment**. The comment makes an important point about the topic. A temporary thesis should be interesting and specific. Also, you need to limit the topic to a manageable scope. These three questions are useful tools to measure the effectiveness of any temporary thesis:

- Does the focus of my essay have enough interest to hold an audience?
- Is the focus of my essay specific enough to generate interest?
- Is the focus of my essay manageable for the time limit? Too broad? Too narrow?

The thesis should be a generalization rather than a fact because the thesis prepares readers for facts and details that support the thesis. The process of bringing the thesis into sharp focus may help in outlining major sections of the work. Once the thesis and introduction are complete, you can address the body of the work.

Review Video: Thesis Statements
Visit mometrix.com/academy and enter code: 691033

Supporting the Thesis

Throughout your essay, the thesis should be **explained clearly and supported** adequately by additional arguments. The thesis sentence needs to contain a clear statement of the purpose of your essay and a comment about the thesis. With the thesis statement, you have an opportunity to state what is noteworthy of this particular treatment of the prompt. Each sentence and paragraph should build on and support the thesis.

When you respond to the prompt, use parts of the passage to support your argument or defend your position. Using supporting evidence from the passage strengths your argument because readers can see your attention to the entire passage and your response to the details and facts within the passage. You can use facts, details, statistics, and direct quotations from the passage to uphold your position. Be sure to point out which information comes from the original passage and base your argument around that evidence.

Body

In an essay's introduction, the writer establishes the thesis and may indicate how the rest of the piece will be structured. In the body of the piece, the writer **elaborates** upon, **illustrates**, and **explains** the **thesis statement**. How writers arrange supporting details and their choices of paragraph types are development techniques. Writers may give examples of the concept introduced in the thesis statement. If the subject includes a cause-and-effect relationship, the author may explain its causality. A writer will explain or analyze the main idea of the piece throughout the body, often by presenting arguments for the veracity or credibility of the thesis statement. Writers may use development to define or clarify ambiguous terms. Paragraphs within the body may be organized using natural sequences, like space and time. Writers may employ **inductive reasoning**, using multiple details to establish a generalization or causal relationship, or **deductive reasoning**, proving a generalized hypothesis or proposition through a specific example or case.

Review Video: Drafting Body Paragraphs
Visit mometrix.com/academy and enter code: 724590

Paragraphs

After the introduction of a passage, a series of body paragraphs will carry a message through to the conclusion. Each paragraph should be **unified around a main point**. Normally, a good topic sentence summarizes the paragraph's main point. A topic sentence is a general sentence that gives an introduction to the paragraph.

The sentences that follow support the topic sentence. However, though it is usually the first sentence, the topic sentence can come as the final sentence to the paragraph if the earlier sentences give a clear explanation of the paragraph's topic. This allows the topic sentence to function as a concluding sentence. Overall, the paragraphs need to stay true to the main point. This means that any unnecessary sentences that do not advance the main point should be removed.

The main point of a paragraph requires adequate development (i.e., a substantial paragraph that covers the main point). A paragraph of two or three sentences does not cover a main point. This is especially true when the main point of the paragraph gives strong support to the argument of the thesis. An occasional short paragraph is fine as a transitional device. However, a well-developed argument will have paragraphs with more than a few sentences.

METHODS OF DEVELOPING PARAGRAPHS

Common methods of adding substance to paragraphs include examples, illustrations, analogies, and cause and effect.

- **Examples** are supporting details to the main idea of a paragraph or a passage. When authors write about something that their audience may not understand, they can provide an example to show their point. When authors write about something that is not easily accepted, they can give examples to prove their point.
- **Illustrations** are extended examples that require several sentences. Well-selected illustrations can be a great way for authors to develop a point that may not be familiar to their audience.
- **Analogies** make comparisons between items that appear to have nothing in common. Analogies are employed by writers to provoke fresh thoughts about a subject. These comparisons may be used to explain the unfamiliar, to clarify an abstract point, or to argue a point. Although analogies are effective literary devices, they should be used carefully in arguments. Two things may be alike in some respects but completely different in others.
- **Cause and effect** is an excellent device to explain the connection between an action or situation and a particular result. One way that authors can use cause and effect is to state the effect in the topic sentence of a paragraph and add the causes in the body of the paragraph. This method can give an author's paragraphs structure, which always strengthens writing.

TYPES OF PARAGRAPHS

A **paragraph of narration** tells a story or a part of a story. Normally, the sentences are arranged in chronological order (i.e., the order that the events happened). However, flashbacks (i.e., an anecdote from an earlier time) can be included.

A **descriptive paragraph** makes a verbal portrait of a person, place, or thing. When specific details are used that appeal to one or more of the senses (i.e., sight, sound, smell, taste, and touch), authors give readers a sense of being present in the moment.

A **process paragraph** is related to time order (i.e., First, you open the bottle. Second, you pour the liquid, etc.). Usually, this describes a process or teaches readers how to perform a process.

Comparing two things draws attention to their similarities and indicates a number of differences. When authors contrast, they focus only on differences. Both comparing and contrasting may be done point-by-point, noting both the similarities and differences of each point, or in sequential paragraphs, where you discuss all the similarities and then all the differences, or vice versa.

Breaking Text into Paragraphs

For most forms of writing, you will need to use multiple paragraphs. As such, determining when to start a new paragraph is very important. Reasons for starting a new paragraph include:

- To mark off the introduction and concluding paragraphs
- To signal a shift to a new idea or topic
- To indicate an important shift in time or place
- To explain a point in additional detail
- To highlight a comparison, contrast, or cause and effect relationship

Paragraph Length

Most readers find that their comfort level for a paragraph is between 100 and 200 words. Shorter paragraphs cause too much starting and stopping and give a choppy effect. Paragraphs that are too long often test the attention span of readers. Two notable exceptions to this rule exist. In scientific or scholarly papers, longer paragraphs suggest seriousness and depth. In journalistic writing, constraints are placed on paragraph size by the narrow columns in a newspaper format.

The first and last paragraphs of a text will usually be the introduction and conclusion. These special-purpose paragraphs are likely to be shorter than paragraphs in the body of the work. Paragraphs in the body of the essay follow the subject's outline (e.g., one paragraph per point in short essays and a group of paragraphs per point in longer works). Some ideas require more development than others, so it is good for a writer to remain flexible. A paragraph of excessive length may be divided, and shorter ones may be combined.

Coherent Paragraphs

A smooth flow of sentences and paragraphs without gaps, shifts, or bumps will lead to paragraph **coherence**. Ties between old and new information can be smoothed using several methods:

- **Linking ideas clearly**, from the topic sentence to the body of the paragraph, is essential for a smooth transition. The topic sentence states the main point, and this should be followed by specific details, examples, and illustrations that support the topic sentence. The support may be direct or indirect. In **indirect support**, the illustrations and examples may support a sentence that in turn supports the topic directly.
- The **repetition of key words** adds coherence to a paragraph. To avoid dull language, variations of the key words may be used.
- **Parallel structures** are often used within sentences to emphasize the similarity of ideas and connect sentences giving similar information.
- Maintaining a **consistent verb tense** throughout the paragraph helps. Shifting tenses affects the smooth flow of words and can disrupt the coherence of the paragraph.

Review Video: How to Write a Good Paragraph
Visit mometrix.com/academy and enter code: 682127

Sequence Words and Phrases

When a paragraph opens with the topic sentence, the second sentence may begin with a phrase like *first of all*, introducing the first supporting detail or example. The writer may introduce the second supporting item with words or phrases like *also*, *in addition*, and *besides*. The writer might introduce succeeding pieces of support with wording like, *another thing*, *moreover*, *furthermore*, or *not only that, but*. The writer may introduce the last piece of support with *lastly*, *finally*, or *last but not least*. Writers get off the point by presenting off-target items not supporting the main point. For example, a main point *my dog is not smart* is supported by the statement, *he's six years old and still doesn't answer to his name*. But *he cries when I leave for school* is not supportive, as it does not indicate lack of intelligence. Writers stay on point by presenting only supportive statements that are directly relevant to and illustrative of their main point.

Review Video: Sequence
Visit mometrix.com/academy and enter code: 489027

Transitions

Transitions between sentences and paragraphs guide readers from idea to idea and indicate relationships between sentences and paragraphs. Writers should be judicious in their use of transitions, inserting them sparingly. They should also be selected to fit the author's purpose—transitions can indicate time, comparison, and conclusion, among other purposes. Tone is also important to consider when using transitional phrases, varying the tone for different audiences. For example, in a scholarly essay, *in summary* would be preferable to the more informal *in short*.

When working with transitional words and phrases, writers usually find a natural flow that indicates when a transition is needed. In reading a draft of the text, it should become apparent where the flow is disrupted. At this point, the writer can add transitional elements during the revision process. Revising can also afford an opportunity to delete transitional devices that seem heavy handed or unnecessary.

Review Video: Transitions in Writing
Visit mometrix.com/academy and enter code: 233246

TYPES OF TRANSITIONAL WORDS

Time	Afterward, immediately, earlier, meanwhile, recently, lately, now, since, soon, when, then, until, before, etc.
Sequence	too, first, second, further, moreover, also, again, and, next, still, besides, finally
Comparison	similarly, in the same way, likewise, also, again, once more
Contrasting	but, although, despite, however, instead, nevertheless, on the one hand... on the other hand, regardless, yet, in contrast.
Cause and Effect	because, consequently, thus, therefore, then, to this end, since, so, as a result, if... then, accordingly
Examples	for example, for instance, such as, to illustrate, indeed, in fact, specifically
Place	near, far, here, there, to the left/right, next to, above, below, beyond, opposite, beside
Concession	granted that, naturally, of course, it may appear, although it is true that
Repetition, Summary, or Conclusion	as mentioned earlier, as noted, in other words, in short, on the whole, to summarize, therefore, as a result, to conclude, in conclusion
Addition	and, also, furthermore, moreover
Generalization	in broad terms, broadly speaking, in general

Review Video: Transitional Words and Phrases
Visit mometrix.com/academy and enter code: 197796

Review Video: What are Transition Words?
Visit mometrix.com/academy and enter code: 707563

Review Video: How to Effectively Connect Sentences
Visit mometrix.com/academy and enter code: 948325

CONCLUSION

Two important principles to consider when writing a conclusion are strength and closure. A strong conclusion gives the reader a sense that the author's main points are meaningful and important, and that the supporting facts and arguments are convincing, solid, and well developed. When a conclusion achieves closure, it gives the impression that the writer has stated all necessary information and points and completed the work, rather than simply stopping after a specified length. Some things to avoid when writing concluding paragraphs include:

- Introducing a completely new idea
- Beginning with obvious or unoriginal phrases like "In conclusion" or "To summarize"
- Apologizing for one's opinions or writing
- Repeating the thesis word for word rather than rephrasing it
- Believing that the conclusion must always summarize the piece

Review Video: Drafting Conclusions
Visit mometrix.com/academy and enter code: 209408

Chapter Quiz

1. Which of the following is considered the main idea of an essay?

a. Topic
b. Body
c. Theme
d. Thesis

2. Which of the following are supporting details to the main idea of a paragraph or a passage?

a. Analogies
b. Examples
c. Cause and effect
d. Transitions

3. Which of the following is NOT a transitional word or phrase in the concession category?

a. Granted that
b. Naturally
c. Broadly speaking
d. It may appear

Chapter Quiz Answer Key

1. D: The thesis is the main idea of an essay. A temporary thesis, or working thesis, should be established early in the writing process because it will serve to keep the writer focused as ideas develop. This temporary thesis is subject to change as writing continues. The thesis should be a generalization rather than a fact because the thesis prepares readers for facts and details that support the thesis. The process of bringing the thesis into sharp focus may help in outlining major sections of the work. Once the thesis and introduction are complete, the body of the work can be addressed.

2. B: Examples are supporting details to the main idea of a paragraph or a passage. When authors write about something that their audience may not understand or that is not easily accepted, they can provide an example to show their point.

3. C: Types of transitional words

Time	Afterward, immediately, earlier, meanwhile, recently, lately, now, since, soon, when, then, until, before, etc.
Sequence	Too, first, second, further, moreover, also, again, and, next, still, besides, finally
Comparison	Similarly, in the same way, likewise, also, again, once more
Contrasting	But, although, despite, however, instead, nevertheless, on the one hand... on the other hand, regardless, yet, in contrast.
Cause and effect	Because, consequently, thus, therefore, then, to this end, since, so, as a result, if... then, accordingly
Examples	For example, for instance, such as, to illustrate, indeed, in fact, specifically
Place	Near, far, here, there, to the left/right, next to, above, below, beyond, opposite, beside
Concession	Granted that, naturally, of course, it may appear, although it is true that
Repetition, summary, or conclusion	As mentioned earlier, as noted, in other words, in short, on the whole, to summarize, therefore, as a result, to conclude, in conclusion
Addition	And, also, furthermore, moreover
Generalization	In broad terms, broadly speaking, in general

Writing Style and Form

Writing Style and Linguistic Form

Linguistic form encodes the literal meanings of words and sentences. It comes from the phonological, morphological, syntactic, and semantic parts of a language. **Writing style** consists of different ways of encoding the meaning and indicating figurative and stylistic meanings. An author's writing style can also be referred to as his or her **voice**.

Writers' stylistic choices accomplish three basic effects on their audiences:

- They **communicate meanings** beyond linguistically dictated meanings,
- They communicate the **author's attitude**, such as persuasive or argumentative effects accomplished through style, and
- They communicate or **express feelings**.

Within style, component areas include:

- Narrative structure
- Viewpoint
- Focus
- Sound patterns
- Meter and rhythm
- Lexical and syntactic repetition and parallelism
- Writing genre
- Representational, realistic, and mimetic effects
- Representation of thought and speech
- Meta-representation (representing representation)
- Irony
- Metaphor and other indirect meanings
- Representation and use of historical and dialectal variations
- Gender-specific and other group-specific speech styles, both real and fictitious
- Analysis of the processes for inferring meaning from writing

Level of Formality

The relationship between writer and reader is important in choosing a **level of formality** as most writing requires some degree of formality. **Formal writing** is for addressing a superior in a school or work environment. Business letters, textbooks, and newspapers use a moderate to high level of formality. **Informal writing** is appropriate for private letters, personal emails, and business correspondence between close associates.

For your exam, you will want to be aware of informal and formal writing. One way that this can be accomplished is to watch for shifts in point of view in the essay. For example, unless writers are using a personal example, they will rarely refer to themselves (e.g., "*I* think that *my* point is very clear.") to avoid being informal when they need to be formal.

Also, be mindful of an author who addresses his or her audience **directly** in their writing (e.g., "Readers, *like you*, will understand this argument.") as this can be a sign of informal writing. Good writers understand the need to be consistent with their level of formality. Shifts in levels of formality or point of view can confuse readers and cause them to discount the message.

Clichés

Clichés are phrases that have been **overused** to the point that the phrase has no importance or has lost the original meaning. These phrases have no originality and add very little to a passage. Therefore, most writers will avoid the use of clichés. Another option is to make changes to a cliché so that it is not predictable and empty of meaning.

Examples:

> When life gives you lemons, make lemonade.
>
> Every cloud has a silver lining.

Jargon

Jargon is **specialized vocabulary** that is used among members of a certain trade or profession. Since jargon is understood by only a small audience, writers will use jargon in passages that will only be read by a specialized audience. For example, medical jargon should be used in a medical journal but not in a New York Times article. Jargon includes exaggerated language that tries to impress rather than inform. Sentences filled with jargon are not precise and are difficult to understand.

Examples:

> "He is going to *toenail* these frames for us." (Toenail is construction jargon for nailing at an angle.)
>
> "They brought in a *kip* of material today." (Kip refers to 1000 pounds in architecture and engineering.)

Slang

Slang is an **informal** and sometimes private language that is understood by some individuals. Slang terms have some usefulness, but they can have a small audience. So, most formal writing will not include this kind of language.

Examples:

> "Yes, the event was a blast!" (In this sentence, *blast* means that the event was a great experience.)
>
> "That attempt was an epic fail." (By *epic fail*, the speaker means that his or her attempt was not a success.)

Colloquialism

A colloquialism is a word or phrase that is found in informal writing. Unlike slang, **colloquial language** will be familiar to a greater range of people. However, colloquialisms are still considered inappropriate for formal writing. Colloquial language can include some slang, but these are limited to contractions for the most part.

Examples:

> "Can *y'all* come back another time?" (Y'all is a contraction of "you all.")
>
> "Will you stop him from building this *castle in the air*?" (A "castle in the air" is an improbable or unlikely event.)

Academic Language

In educational settings, students are often expected to use academic language in their schoolwork. Academic language is also commonly found in dissertations and theses, texts published by academic journals, and other forms of academic research. Academic language conventions may vary between fields, but general academic language is free of slang, regional terminology, and noticeable grammatical errors. Specific terms may also be used in academic language, and it is important to understand their proper usage. A writer's command of academic language impacts their ability to communicate in an academic or professional context. While it is acceptable to use colloquialisms, slang, improper grammar, or other forms of informal speech in social settings or at home, it is inappropriate to practice non-academic language in academic contexts.

Tone

Tone may be defined as the writer's **attitude** toward the topic, and to the audience. This attitude is reflected in the language used in the writing. The tone of a work should be **appropriate to the topic** and to the intended audience. While it may be fine to use slang or jargon in some pieces, other texts should not contain such terms. Tone can range from humorous to serious and any level in between. It may be more or less formal, depending on the purpose of the writing and its intended audience. All these nuances in tone can flavor the entire writing and should be kept in mind as the work evolves.

Word Selection

A writer's choice of words is a signature of their style. Careful thought about the use of words can improve a piece of writing. A passage can be an exciting piece to read when attention is given to the use of vivid or specific nouns rather than general ones.

Example:

> General: His kindness will never be forgotten.
>
> Specific: His thoughtful gifts and bear hugs will never be forgotten.

Attention should also be given to the kind of verbs that are used in sentences. Active verbs (e.g., run, swim) are about an action. Whenever possible, an **active verb should replace a linking verb** to provide clear examples for arguments and to strengthen a passage overall. When using an active verb, one should be sure that the verb is used in the active voice instead of the passive voice. Verbs are in the active voice when the subject is the one doing the action. A verb is in the passive voice when the subject is the recipient of an action.

Example:

> Passive: The winners were called to the stage by the judges.
>
> Active: The judges called the winners to the stage.

Conciseness

Conciseness is writing that communicates a message in the fewest words possible. Writing concisely is valuable because short, uncluttered messages allow the reader to understand the author's message more easily and efficiently. Planning is important in writing concise messages. If you have in mind what you need to write beforehand, it will be easier to make a message short and to the point. Do not state the obvious.

Revising is also important. After the message is written, make sure you have effective, pithy sentences that efficiently get your point across. When reviewing the information, imagine a conversation taking place, and concise writing will likely result.

Appropriate Kinds of Writing for Different Tasks, Purposes, and Audiences

When preparing to write a composition, consider the audience and purpose to choose the best type of writing. Three common types of writing are persuasive, expository, and narrative. **Persuasive**, or argumentative writing, is used to convince the audience to take action or agree with the author's claims. **Expository** writing is meant to inform the audience of the author's observations or research on a topic. **Narrative** writing is used to tell the audience a story and often allows more room for creativity. While task, purpose, and audience inform a writer's mode of writing, these factors also impact elements such as tone, vocabulary, and formality.

For example, students who are writing to persuade their parents to grant them some additional privilege, such as permission for a more independent activity, should use more sophisticated vocabulary and diction that sounds more mature and serious to appeal to the parental audience. However, students who are writing for younger children should use simpler vocabulary and sentence structure, as well as choose words that are more vivid and entertaining. They should treat their topics more lightly, and include humor when appropriate. Students who are writing for their classmates may use language that is more informal, as well as age-appropriate.

Review Video: Writing Purpose and Audience
Visit mometrix.com/academy and enter code: 146627

Chapter Quiz

1. Which of the following would NOT be considered formal writing?

a. Private letters
b. Business letters
c. Textbooks
d. Newspapers

2. Which of the following sentences contains a verb in the passive voice?

a. The judges called the winners to the stage for their awards.
b. Each applicant must fill out all of the forms required.
c. He raced through the copse of trees with the grace of a deer.
d. I was told that there would be food available at the party.

Chapter Quiz Answer Key

1. A: The relationship between writer and reader is important in choosing a level of formality because most writing requires some degree of formality. Formal writing is for addressing a superior in a school or work environment. Business letters, textbooks, and newspapers use a moderate to high level of formality. Informal writing is appropriate for private letters, personal emails, and business correspondence between close associates.

2. D: Attention should also be given to the kind of verbs that are used in sentences. Active verbs (e.g., run, swim) are about an action. Whenever possible, an active verb should replace a linking verb to provide clear examples for arguments and to strengthen a passage overall. When using an active verb, one should be sure that the verb is used in the active voice instead of the passive voice. Verbs are in the active voice when the subject is the one doing the action. A verb is in the passive voice when the subject is the recipient of an action.

Modes of Writing

Essays

Essays usually focus on one topic, subject, or goal. There are several types of essays, including informative, persuasive, and narrative. An essay's structure and level of formality depend on the type of essay and its goal. While narrative essays typically do not include outside sources, other types of essays often require some research and the integration of primary and secondary sources.

The basic format of an essay typically has three major parts: the introduction, the body, and the conclusion. The body is further divided into the writer's main points. Short and simple essays may have three main points, while essays covering broader ranges and going into more depth can have almost any number of main points, depending on length.

An essay's introduction should answer three questions:

1. What is the **subject** of the essay?

   If a student writes an essay about a book, the answer would include the title and author of the book and any additional information needed—such as the subject or argument of the book.

2. How does the essay **address** the subject?

   To answer this, the writer identifies the essay's organization by briefly summarizing main points and the evidence supporting them.

3. What will the essay **prove**?

   This is the thesis statement, usually the opening paragraph's last sentence, clearly stating the writer's message.

The body elaborates on all the main points related to the thesis, introducing one main point at a time, and includes supporting evidence with each main point. Each body paragraph should state the point in a topic sentence, which is usually the first sentence in the paragraph. The paragraph should then explain the point's meaning, support it with quotations or other evidence, and then explain how this point and the evidence are related to the thesis. The writer should then repeat this procedure in a new paragraph for each additional main point.

The conclusion reiterates the content of the introduction, including the thesis, to remind the reader of the essay's main argument or subject. The essay writer may also summarize the highlights of the argument or description contained in the body of the essay, following the same sequence originally used in the body. For example, a conclusion might look like: Point 1 + Point 2 + Point 3 = Thesis, or Point 1 → Point 2 → Point 3 → Thesis Proof. Good organization makes essays easier for writers to compose and provides a guide for readers to follow. Well-organized essays hold attention better and are more likely to get readers to accept their theses as valid.

Informative vs. Persuasive Writing

Informative writing, also called explanatory or expository writing, begins with the basis that something is true or factual, while **persuasive** writing strives to prove something that may or may not be true or factual. Whereas argumentative text is written to **persuade** readers to agree with the author's position, informative text merely **provides information and insight** to readers. Informative writing concentrates on **informing** readers about why or how something is as it is. This can include offering new information, explaining how a process works, and developing a concept for readers. To accomplish these objectives, the essay may name and distinguish various things within a category, provide definitions, provide details about the parts of something, explain a particular function or behavior, and give readers explanations for why a fact, object, event, or process exists or occurs.

NARRATIVE WRITING

Put simply, **narrative** writing tells a story. The most common examples of literary narratives are novels. Non-fictional biographies, autobiographies, memoirs, and histories are also narratives. Narratives should tell stories in such a way that the readers learn something or gain insight or understanding. Students can write more interesting narratives by describing events or experiences that were meaningful to them. Narratives should start with the story's actions or events, rather than long descriptions or introductions. Students should ensure that there is a point to each story by describing what they learned from the experience they narrate. To write an effective description, students should include sensory details, asking themselves what they saw, heard, felt or touched, smelled, and tasted during the experiences they describe. In narrative writing, the details should be **concrete** rather than **abstract**. Using concrete details enables readers to imagine everything that the writer describes.

Review Video: Narratives
Visit mometrix.com/academy and enter code: 280100

SENSORY DETAILS

Students need to use vivid descriptions when writing descriptive essays. Narratives should also include descriptions of characters, things, and events. Students should remember to describe not only the visual detail of what someone or something looks like, but details from other senses, as well. For example, they can contrast the feeling of a sea breeze to that of a mountain breeze, describe how they think something inedible would taste, and compare sounds they hear in the same location at different times of day and night. Readers have trouble visualizing images or imagining sensory impressions and feelings from abstract descriptions, so concrete descriptions make these more real.

CONCRETE VS. ABSTRACT DESCRIPTIONS IN NARRATIVE

Concrete language provides information that readers can grasp and may empathize with, while **abstract language**, which is more general, can leave readers feeling disconnected, empty, or even confused. "It was a lovely day" is abstract, but "The sun shone brightly, the sky was blue, the air felt warm, and a gentle breeze wafted across my skin" is concrete. "Ms. Couch was a good teacher" uses abstract language, giving only a general idea of the writer's opinion. But "Ms. Couch is excellent at helping us take our ideas and turn them into good essays and stories" uses concrete language, giving more specific examples of what makes Ms. Couch a good teacher. "I like writing poems but not essays" gives readers a general idea that the student prefers one genre over another, but not why. But when reading, "I like writing short poems with rhythm and rhyme, but I hate writing five-page essays that go on and on about the same ideas," readers understand that the student prefers the brevity, rhyme, and meter of short poetry over the length and redundancy of longer prose.

AUTOBIOGRAPHICAL NARRATIVES

Autobiographical narratives are narratives written by an author about an event or period in their life. Autobiographical narratives are written from one person's perspective, in first person, and often include the author's thoughts and feelings alongside their description of the event or period. Structure, style, or theme varies between different autobiographical narratives, since each narrative is personal and specific to its author and his or her experience.

Reflective Essay

A less common type of essay is the reflective essay. **Reflective essays** allow the author to reflect, or think back, on an experience and analyze what they recall. They should consider what they learned from the experience, what they could have done differently, what would have helped them during the experience, or anything else that they have realized from looking back on the experience. Reflection essays incorporate both objective reflection on one's own actions and subjective explanation of thoughts and feelings. These essays can be written for a number of experiences in a formal or informal context.

Journals and Diaries

A **journal** is a personal account of events, experiences, feelings, and thoughts. Many people write journals to express their feelings and thoughts or to help them process experiences they have had. Since journals are **private documents** not meant to be shared with others, writers may not be concerned with grammar, spelling, or other mechanics. However, authors may write journals that they expect or hope to publish someday; in this case, they not only express their thoughts and feelings and process their experiences, but they also attend to their craft in writing them. Some authors compose journals to record a particular time period or a series of related events, such as a cancer diagnosis, treatment, surviving the disease, and how these experiences have changed or affected them. Other experiences someone might include in a journal are recovering from addiction, journeys of spiritual exploration and discovery, time spent in another country, or anything else someone wants to personally document. Journaling can also be therapeutic, as some people use journals to work through feelings of grief over loss or to wrestle with big decisions.

Examples of Diaries in Literature

The Diary of a Young Girl by Dutch Jew Anne Frank (1947) contains her life-affirming, nonfictional diary entries from 1942-1944 while her family hid in an attic from World War II's genocidal Nazis. *Go Ask Alice* (1971) by Beatrice Sparks is a cautionary, fictional novel in the form of diary entries by Alice, an unhappy, rebellious teen who takes LSD, runs away from home and lives with hippies, and eventually returns home. Frank's writing reveals an intelligent, sensitive, insightful girl, raised by intellectual European parents—a girl who believes in the goodness of human nature despite surrounding atrocities. Alice, influenced by early 1970s counterculture, becomes less optimistic. However, similarities can be found between them: Frank dies in a Nazi concentration camp while the fictitious Alice dies from a drug overdose. Both young women are also unable to escape their surroundings. Additionally, adolescent searches for personal identity are evident in both books.

Review Video: Journals, Diaries, Letters, and Blogs
Visit mometrix.com/academy and enter code: 432845

Letters

Letters are messages written to other people. In addition to letters written between individuals, some writers compose letters to the editors of newspapers, magazines, and other publications, while some write "Open Letters" to be published and read by the general public. Open letters, while intended for everyone to read, may also identify a group of people or a single person whom the letter directly addresses. In everyday use, the most-used forms are business letters and personal or friendly letters. Both kinds share common elements: business or personal letterhead stationery; the writer's return address at the top; the addressee's address next; a salutation, such as "Dear [name]" or some similar opening greeting, followed by a colon in business letters or a comma in personal letters; the body of the letter, with paragraphs as indicated; and a closing, like "Sincerely/Cordially/Best regards/etc." or "Love," in intimate personal letters.

Early Letters

The Greek word for "letter" is *epistolē*, which became the English word "epistle." The earliest letters were called epistles, including the New Testament's epistles from the apostles to the Christians. In ancient Egypt, the writing curriculum in scribal schools included the epistolary genre. Epistolary novels frame a story in the form of letters. Examples of noteworthy epistolary novels include:

- *Pamela* (1740), by 18th-century English novelist Samuel Richardson
- *Shamela* (1741), Henry Fielding's satire of *Pamela* that mocked epistolary writing.
- *Lettres persanes* (1721) by French author Montesquieu
- *The Sorrows of Young Werther* (1774) by German author Johann Wolfgang von Goethe
- *The History of Emily Montague* (1769), the first Canadian novel, by Frances Brooke
- *Dracula* (1897) by Bram Stoker
- *Frankenstein* (1818) by Mary Shelley
- *The Color Purple* (1982) by Alice Walker

Blogs

The word "blog" is derived from "weblog" and refers to writing done exclusively on the internet. Readers of reputable newspapers expect quality content and layouts that enable easy reading. These expectations also apply to blogs. For example, readers can easily move visually from line to line when columns are narrow, while overly wide columns cause readers to lose their places. Blogs must also be posted with layouts enabling online readers to follow them easily. However, because the way people read on computer, tablet, and smartphone screens differs from how they read print on paper, formatting and writing blog content is more complex than writing newspaper articles. Two major principles are the bases for blog-writing rules: The first is while readers of print articles skim to estimate their length, online they must scroll down to scan; therefore, blog layouts need more subheadings, graphics, and other indications of what information follows. The second is onscreen reading can be harder on the eyes than reading printed paper, so legibility is crucial in blogs.

Rules and Rationales for Writing Blogs

1. Format all posts for smooth page layout and easy scanning.
2. Column width should not be too wide, as larger lines of text can be difficult to read
3. Headings and subheadings separate text visually, enable scanning or skimming, and encourage continued reading.
4. Bullet-pointed or numbered lists enable quick information location and scanning.
5. Punctuation is critical, so beginners should use shorter sentences until confident in their knowledge of punctuation rules.
6. Blog paragraphs should be far shorter—two to six sentences each—than paragraphs written on paper to enable "chunking" because reading onscreen is more difficult.
7. Sans-serif fonts are usually clearer than serif fonts, and larger font sizes are better.
8. Highlight important material and draw attention with **boldface**, but avoid overuse. Avoid hard-to-read *italics* and ALL CAPITALS.
9. Include enough blank spaces: overly busy blogs tire eyes and brains. Images not only break up text but also emphasize and enhance text and can attract initial reader attention.
10. Use background colors judiciously to avoid distracting the eye or making it difficult to read.
11. Be consistent throughout posts, since people read them in different orders.
12. Tell a story with a beginning, middle, and end.

Specialized Modes of Writing

Editorials

Editorials are articles in newspapers, magazines, and other serial publications. Editorials express an opinion or belief belonging to the majority of the publication's leadership. This opinion or belief generally refers to a specific issue, topic, or event. These articles are authored by a member, or a small number of members, of the publication's leadership and are often written to affect their readers, such as persuading them to adopt a stance or take a particular action.

Resumes

Resumes are brief, but formal, documents that outline an individual's experience in a certain area. Resumes are most often used for job applications. Such resumes will list the applicant's work experience, certification, and achievements or qualifications related to the position. Resumes should only include the most pertinent information. They should also use strategic formatting to highlight the applicant's most impressive experiences and achievements, to ensure the document can be read quickly and easily, and to eliminate both visual clutter and excessive negative space.

Reports

Reports summarize the results of research, new methodology, or other developments in an academic or professional context. Reports often include details about methodology and outside influences and factors. However, a report should focus primarily on the results of the research or development. Reports are objective and deliver information efficiently, sacrificing style for clear and effective communication.

Memoranda

A memorandum, also called a memo, is a formal method of communication used in professional settings. Memoranda are printed documents that include a heading listing the sender and their job title, the recipient and their job title, the date, and a specific subject line. Memoranda often include an introductory section explaining the reason and context for the memorandum. Next, a memorandum includes a section with details relevant to the topic. Finally, the memorandum will conclude with a paragraph that politely and clearly defines the sender's expectations of the recipient.

Chapter Quiz

1. The Greek word *epistolē* means:

a. Pistol.
b. Epistaxis.
c. Essay.
d. Letter.

2. What are the two major principles used to create an orderly blog?

a. The content must be interesting with various fonts and color combinations, and it should take less than 10 minutes to read in its entirety.
b. Blog layouts need more subheadings, graphics, and other indications of what information follows, and the content must be interesting with various fonts and color combinations.
c. Legibility is crucial because onscreen reading is hard on the eyes, and it should take less than 10 minutes to read in its entirety.
d. Blog layouts need more subheadings, graphics, and other indications of what information follows, and legibility is crucial because onscreen reading is hard on the eyes.

Chapter Quiz Answer Key

1. D: The Greek word for "letter" is *epistolē*, which became the English word "epistle." The earliest letters were called epistles, including the New Testament's epistles from the apostles to the Christians. In ancient Egypt, the writing curriculum in scribal schools included the epistolary genre. Epistolary novels frame a story in the form of letters.

2. D: There are two major principles that form the basis for blog-writing rules. The first is that while readers of print can skim articles to estimate their length, they must scroll down to scan something published online, meaning that blog layouts need more subheadings, graphics, and other indications of what information follows. The second principle is that onscreen reading can be harder on the eyes than reading printed paper, so legibility is crucial in blogs.

Prose

Common Forms of Prose Fiction

Historical, Picaresque, Gothic, and Psychological Fiction

Historical fiction is set in particular historical periods, including prehistoric and mythological. Examples include Walter Scott's *Rob Roy* and *Ivanhoe*; Leo Tolstoy's *War and Peace;* Robert Graves' *I, Claudius;* Mary Renault's *The King Must Die* and *The Bull from the Sea* (an historical novel using Greek mythology); Virginia Woolf's *Orlando* and *Between the Acts;* and John Dos Passos's *U.S.A* trilogy. **Picaresque** novels recount episodic adventures of a rogue protagonist or *pícaro,* like Miguel de Cervantes' *Don Quixote* or Henry Fielding's *Tom Jones.* **Gothic** novels originated as a reaction against 18th-century Enlightenment rationalism, featuring horror, mystery, superstition, madness, supernatural elements, and revenge. Early examples include Horace Walpole's *Castle of Otranto,* Matthew Gregory Lewis' *Monk*, Mary Shelley's *Frankenstein*, and Bram Stoker's *Dracula.* In America, Edgar Allan Poe wrote many Gothic works. Contemporary novelist Anne Rice has penned many Gothic novels under the pseudonym A. N. Roquelaure. **Psychological** novels, originating in 17th-century France, explore characters' motivations. Examples include Abbé Prévost's *Manon Lescaut;* George Eliot's novels; Fyodor Dostoyevsky's *Crime and Punishment;* Tolstoy's *Anna Karenina;* Gustave Flaubert's *Madame Bovary;* and the novels of Henry James, James Joyce, and Vladimir Nabokov.

Novels of Manners

Novels of manners are fictional stories that observe, explore, and analyze the social behaviors of a specific time and place. While deep psychological themes are more universal across different historical periods and countries, the manners of a particular society are shorter-lived and more varied; the **novel of manners** captures these societal details. Novels of manners can also be regarded as symbolically representing, in artistic form, certain established and secure social orders. Characteristics of novels of manners include descriptions of a society with defined behavioral codes; language that uses standardized, impersonal formulas; and inhibition of emotional expression, as contrasted with the strong emotions expressed in romantic or sentimental novels. Jane Austen's detailed descriptions of English society and characters struggling with the definitions and restrictions placed on them by society are excellent models of the novel of manners. In the 20th century, Evelyn Waugh's *Handful of Dust* is a novel of social manners, and his *Sword of Honour* trilogy contains novels of military manners. Another 20th-century example is *The Unbearable Bassington* by Saki (the pen name of writer H. H. Munro), focusing on Edwardian society.

Western-World Sentimental Novels

Sentimental love novels originated in the movement of Romanticism. Eighteenth-century examples of novels that emphasize the emotional aspect of love include Samuel Richardson's *Pamela* (1740) and Jean-Jacques Rousseau's *Nouvelle Héloïse* (1761). Also in the 18th century, Laurence Sterne's novel *Tristram Shandy* (1760-1767) is an example of a novel with elements of sentimentality. The Victorian era's rejection of emotionalism caused the term "sentimental" to have undesirable connotations. However, even non-sentimental novelists such as William Makepeace Thackeray and Charles Dickens incorporated sentimental elements in their writing. A 19th-century author of genuinely sentimental novels was Mrs. Henry Wood (e.g., *East Lynne,* 1861). In the 20th century, Erich Segal's sentimental novel *Love Story* (1970) was a popular bestseller.

Epistolary Novels

Epistolary novels are told in the form of letters written by their characters rather than in typical narrative form. Samuel Richardson, the best-known author of epistolary novels like *Pamela* (1740) and *Clarissa* (1748), widely influenced early Romantic epistolary novels throughout Europe that freely expressed emotions. Richardson, a printer, published technical manuals on letter-writing for young gentlewomen; his epistolary novels were fictional extensions of those nonfictional instructional books. Nineteenth-century English author Wilkie Collins' *The Moonstone* (1868) was a mystery written in epistolary form. By the 20th century, the format of well-composed written letters came to be regarded as artificial and outmoded. A 20th-century evolution of letters was tape-recording transcripts, such as in French playwright Samuel Beckett's drama *Krapp's Last Tape.* Though evoking modern alienation, Beckett still created a sense of fictional characters' direct communication without author intervention as Richardson had.

Pastoral Novels

Pastoral novels lyrically idealize country life as idyllic and utopian, akin to the Garden of Eden. *Daphnis and Chloe*, written by Greek novelist Longus around the second or third century, influenced Elizabethan pastoral romances like Thomas Lodge's *Rosalynde* (1590), which inspired Shakespeare's *As You Like It*, and Philip Sidney's *Arcadia* (1590). Jacques-Henri Bernardin de St. Pierre's French work *Paul et Virginie* (1787) demonstrated the early Romantic view of the innocence and goodness of nature. Though the style lost popularity by the 20th century, pastoral elements can still be seen in novels like *The Rainbow* (1915) and *Lady Chatterley's Lover* (1928), both by D. H. Lawrence. Growing realism transformed pastoral writing into less ideal and more dystopian, distasteful and ironic depictions of country life in George Eliot's and Thomas Hardy's novels. Saul Bellow's novel *Herzog* (1964) may demonstrate how urban ills highlight an alternative pastoral ideal. The pastoral style is commonly thought to be overly idealized and outdated today, as seen in Stella Gibbons' pastoral satire, Cold Comfort Farm (1932).

Bildungsroman

Bildungsroman is German for "education novel." This term is also used in English to describe "apprenticeship" novels focusing on coming-of-age stories, including youth's struggles and searches for things such as identity, spiritual understanding, or the meaning in life. Johann Wolfgang von Goethe's *Wilhelm Meisters Lehrjahre* (1796) is credited as the origin of this genre. Two of Charles Dickens' novels, *David Copperfield* (1850) and *Great Expectations* (1861), also fit this form. H. G. Wells wrote *bildungsromans* about questing for apprenticeships to address the complications of modern life in *Joan and Peter* (1918) and from a Utopian perspective in *The Dream* (1924). School *bildungsromans* include Thomas Hughes' *Tom Brown's School Days* (1857) and Alain-Fournier's *Le Grand Meaulnes* (1913). Many Hermann Hesse novels, including *Demian, Steppenwolf, Siddhartha, Magister Ludi,* and *Beneath the Wheel* are *bildungsromans* about a struggling, searching youth. Samuel Butler's *The Way of All Flesh* (1903) and James Joyce's *A Portrait of the Artist as a Young Man* (1916) are two modern examples. Variations include J. D. Salinger's *The Catcher in the Rye* (1951), set both within and beyond school, and William Golding's *Lord of the Flies* (1955), a novel not set in a school but one that is a coming-of-age story nonetheless.

Roman à Clef

Roman à clef, French for "novel with a key," refers to books that require a real-life frame of reference, or key, for full comprehension. In Geoffrey Chaucer's *Canterbury Tales,* the Nun's Priest's Tale contains details that confuse readers unaware of history about the Earl of Bolingbroke's involvement in an assassination plot. Other literary works fitting this form include John Dryden's political satirical poem "Absalom and Achitophel" (1681), Jonathan Swift's satire "A Tale of a Tub" (1704), and George Orwell's political allegory *Animal Farm* (1945), all of which cannot be understood completely without knowing their camouflaged historical contents. *Roman à clefs* disguise truths too dangerous for authors to state directly. Readers must know about the enemies of D. H. Lawrence and Aldous Huxley to appreciate their respective novels: *Aaron's Rod* (1922) and

Point Counter Point (1928). Marcel Proust's *Remembrance of Things Past (À la recherché du temps perdu,* 1871-1922) is informed by his social context. James Joyce's *Finnegans Wake* is an enormous *roman à clef* containing multitudinous personal references.

Review Video: Major Forms of Prose
Visit mometrix.com/academy and enter code: 565543

Other Common Types of Prose

- A **narrative** is any composition that tells a story. Narratives have characters, settings, and a structure. Narratives may be fiction or nonfiction stories and may follow a linear or nonlinear structure. The purpose of a narrative is generally to entertain, but nonfiction narratives can be informative, as well. Narratives also appear in a variety of structures and formats.
- **Biographies** are books written about another person's life. Biographies can be valuable historical resources. Though they provide a narrow view of the relevant time period and culture, their specificity can also provide a unique context for that period or culture. Biographies, especially those whose subject was a well-known and influential figure, can provide a more complete picture of the figure's life or contributions. Biographies can also serve as a source of inspiration or communicate a moral because of their focus on one person over an extended period of time.
- **Myths**, or stories from mythology, exist in most ancient cultures and continue to influence modern cultures. Mythology is so influential that it has even inspired numerous pieces of modern literature and media in popular culture. While popular culture most clearly references mythology from the Ancient Greek and Roman cultures, literature has been influenced by mythologies from around the entire world. Since mythology is so prevalent in ancient literature, it makes sense that universal themes and morals often appear in mythology and even drive some myths. This suggests connections between cultures through the stories they pass down.
- **Fables** are short, didactic stories that typically feature imaginary creatures or talking animals. The famous story "The Tortoise and the Hare" is a fable. Fables are still told and used today because of their universally understandable morals and characters, making them suitable for children's literature and media.
- **Fairy tales** are stories that involve fictional creatures or realistic characters with fantastical traits and abilities. Fairy tales often end happily and depict the victory of good over evil. The plots and characters in fairy tales are often far-fetched and whimsical.
- **Folk Tales** are stories that have withstood time and are usually popular in a particular region or culture. Folk tales often depict the clever success of a common person, though the story may, alternatively, end poorly for the protagonist. Folk tales are easily confused with fairytales because fairytales can be a type of folk tale.
- **Legends** are stories that typically focus on one character and highlight their victory over a particular enemy or obstacle. Legends often feature some facts or are inspired by true events, but are still understood to be either exaggerated or partially fictional. Heroes are often the protagonists of legends as they often save or protect others as they conquer enemies and obstacles.

- A **short story** is a fictional narrative that is shorter than a novel. However, there is not a definite page or word count that defines the short story category. Short stories tend to focus on one or few elements of a story in order to efficiently tell the story. Though they are often brief, short stories may still contain a moral or impact their readers.

> **Review Video: Myths, Fables, Legends, and Fairy Tales**
> Visit mometrix.com/academy and enter code: 347199

Common Genres in Prose

- The **mystery** genre includes stories with plots that follow a protagonist as they work to solve an unexplained situation, such as a murder, disappearance, or robbery. Protagonists of mysteries may be hired professionals or amateurs who solve the mystery despite their lack of experience and resources. Mysteries allow the reader to solve the case along with the protagonist, and often grant the reader an advantageous perspective, creating dramatic irony. The *Sherlock Holmes* novels by Sir Arthur Conan Doyle are examples of mystery novels.
- **Science fiction** is a genre that is based on the manipulation and exaggeration of real scientific discoveries and processes. These works are speculative and frequently depict a world where scientific discoveries and society have progressed beyond the point reached at the time of the work's creation. Works of science fiction often take place in a distant location or time, allowing for the dramatic advancements and conveniences they often depict. *Dune*, written by Frank Herbert, is an example of a science-fiction novel.
- The **fantasy** genre includes stories that feature imaginary creatures and supernatural abilities, but often take place in settings that resemble real places and cultures in history. Fantasy novels usually follow a gifted protagonist from humble beginnings as they embark on a quest, journey, or adventure and encounter mystical beings and personally challenging obstacles. Common themes in the fantasy genre include personal growth, good versus evil, and the value of the journey. J.R.R. Tolkien's *The Lord of the Rings* trilogy belongs to the fantasy genre.
- **Realistic fiction** describes fictional narratives that include events and characters that do not exist, but could appear in reality. Within the narrative, these characters and events may be depicted in real places. For example, Pip, the protagonist of Charles Dickens's *Great Expectations*, was not a real person, but the novel shows him living in London, England for much of his young adulthood. Realistic fiction contains no far-fetched or impossible elements and presents situations that can or do occur in real life. A contemporary example of realistic fiction is *Wonder* by R.J. Palacio.
- **Historical fiction** includes works that take place in the past and model their setting after real historical cultures, societies, and time periods. These works may include real historical figures and events, but they also may not. Works of historical fiction must be fully informed by the period and location they are set in, meaning both the major and minor details of the work must be historically compatible with the work's setting. Examples of historical fiction include Kathryn Stockett's *The Help* and Markus Zusak's *The Book Thief.*
- The phrase **literary nonfiction** describes nonfiction narratives that present true facts and events in a way that entertains readers and displays creativity. Literary nonfiction, also called creative nonfiction, may resemble fiction in its style and flow, but the truth of the events it describes sets it apart from fictional literature. Different types of books may be considered literary nonfiction, such as biographies, if they appear to employ creativity in their writing. An example of literary nonfiction is *The Immortal Life of Henrietta Lacks* by Rebecca Skloot.

Realism and Satire

Realism

Realism is a literary form with the goal of representing reality as faithfully as possible. Its genesis in Western literature was a reaction against the sentimentality and extreme emotionalism of the works written during the Romantic literary movement, which championed feelings and emotional expression. Realists focused in great detail on immediacy of time and place, on specific actions of their characters, and the justifiable consequences of those actions. Some techniques of **realism** include writing in vernacular (conversational language), using specific dialects, and placing an emphasis on character rather than plot. Realistic literature also often addresses ethical issues. Historically, realistic works have often concentrated on the middle classes of the authors' societies. Realists eschew treatments that are too dramatic or sensationalistic as exaggerations of the reality that they strive to portray as closely as they are able. Influenced by his own bleak past, Fyodor Dostoevsky wrote several novels, such as *Crime and Punishment* (1866) that shunned romantic ideals and sought to portray a stark reality. Henry James was a prominent writer of realism in novels such as *Daisy Miller* (1879). Samuel Clemens (Mark Twain) skillfully represented the language and culture of lower-class Mississippi in his novel *The Adventures of Huckleberry Finn* (1885).

Satire

Satire uses sarcasm, irony, and humor as social criticism to lampoon human folly. Unlike realism, which intends to depict reality as it exists without exaggeration, **satire** often involves creating situations or ideas that deliberately exaggerate reality to appear ridiculous to illuminate flawed behaviors. Ancient Roman satirists included Horace and Juvenal. Alexander Pope's poem "The Rape of the Lock" satirized the values of fashionable members of the 18th-century upper-middle class, which Pope found shallow and trivial. The theft of a lock of hair from a young woman is blown out of proportion: the poem's characters regard it as seriously as they would a rape. Irishman Jonathan Swift satirized British society, politics, and religion in works like "A Modest Proposal" and *Gulliver's Travels.* In "A Modest Proposal," Swift used essay form and mock-serious tone, satirically "proposing" cannibalism of babies and children as a solution to poverty and overpopulation. He satirized petty political disputes in *Gulliver's Travels.*

Chapter Quiz

1. Which novel is credited as the origin of the *bildungsroman*, or the "education novel" genre?

a. *Don Quixote*
b. *Herzog*
c. *Steppenwolf*
d. *Wilhelm Meisters Lehrjahre*

2. Which of the following is considered to be a *roman à clef*, or a "novel with a key"?

a. H. G. Wells' *The Dream* (1924)
b. Jacques-Henri Bernardin de St. Pierre's *Paul et Virginie* (1787)
c. George Orwell's *Animal Farm* (1945)
d. Jean-Jacques Rousseau's *Nouvelle Héloïse* (1761)

Chapter Quiz Answer Key

1. D: *Bildungsroman* is German for "education novel." This term is also used in English to describe so-called "apprenticeship" novels focusing on coming-of-age stories, including youth's struggles and searches for things such as identity, spiritual understanding, or the meaning in life. Johann Wolfgang von Goethe's *Wilhelm Meisters Lehrjahre* (1796) is credited as the origin of this genre. Two of Charles Dickens' novels, *David Copperfield* (1850) and *Great Expectations* (1861), also fit this form. H. G. Wells wrote *bildungsromans* about questing for apprenticeships to address the complications of modern life in *Joan and Peter* (1918) and from a Utopian perspective in *The Dream* (1924). School *bildungsromans* include Thomas Hughes' *Tom Brown's School Days* (1857) and Alain-Fournier's *Le Grand Meaulnes* (1913). Many Hermann Hesse novels, including *Demian, Steppenwolf, Siddhartha, Magister Ludi,* and *Beneath the Wheel* are *bildungsromans* about a struggling, searching youth. Samuel Butler's *The Way of All Flesh* (1903) and James Joyce's *A Portrait of the Artist as a Young Man* (1916) are two modern examples. Variations include J. D. Salinger's *The Catcher in the Rye* (1951), set both within and beyond school; and William Golding's *Lord of the Flies* (1955), a novel not set in a school but one that is a coming-of-age story nonetheless.

2. C: *Roman à clef* is French for "novel with a key." It refers to books that require a real-life frame of reference, or key, for full comprehension. In Geoffrey Chaucer's *Canterbury Tales,* the Nun's Priest's Tale contains details that confuse readers unaware of history about the Earl of Bolingbroke's involvement in an assassination plot. Other literary works fitting this form include John Dryden's political satirical poem "Absalom and Achitophel" (1681), Jonathan Swift's satire "A Tale of a Tub" (1704), and George Orwell's political allegory *Animal Farm* (1945), all of which cannot be understood completely without knowing their camouflaged historical contents. *Roman à clefs* disguise truths too dangerous for authors to state directly.

Poetry

Poetry Terminology

Unlike prose, which traditionally (except in forms like stream of consciousness) consists of complete sentences connected into paragraphs, poetry is written in **verses**. These may form complete sentences, clauses, or phrases. Poetry may be written with or without rhyme. It can be metered, following a particular rhythmic pattern such as iambic, dactylic, spondaic, trochaic, or **anapestic**, or may be without regular meter. The terms **iamb** and **trochee**, among others, identify stressed and unstressed syllables in each verse. Meter is also described by the number of beats or stressed syllables per verse: **dimeter** (2), **trimeter** (3), **tetrameter** (4), **pentameter** (5), and so forth. Using the symbol ᴗ to denote unstressed and / to denote stressed syllables, **iambic** = ᴗ/; **trochaic** = /ᴗ; **spondaic** =//; **dactylic** =/ᴗᴗ; **anapestic** =ᴗᴗ/. **Rhyme schemes** identify which lines rhyme, such as ABAB, ABCA, AABA, and so on. Poetry with neither rhyme nor meter is called **free verse**. Poems may be in free verse, metered but unrhymed, rhymed but without meter, or using both rhyme and meter. In English, the most common meter is iambic pentameter. Unrhymed iambic pentameter is called **blank verse**.

Review Video: Different Types of Rhyme
Visit mometrix.com/academy and enter code: 999342

Review Video: Evocative Words and Rhythm
Visit mometrix.com/academy and enter code: 894610

Major Forms of Poetry

From man's earliest days, he expressed himself with poetry. A large percentage of the surviving literature from ancient times is in **epic poetry**, utilized by Homer and other Greco-Roman poets. Epic poems typically recount heroic deeds and adventures, using stylized language and combining dramatic and lyrical conventions. **Epistolary poems**, poems that are written and read as letters, also developed in ancient times. In the fourteenth and fifteenth centuries, the **ballad** became a popular convention. Ballads often follow a rhyme scheme and meter and focus on subjects such as love, death, and religion. Many ballads tell stories, and several modern ballads are put to music. From these early conventions, numerous other poetic forms developed, such as **elegies**, **odes**, and **pastoral poems**. Elegies are mourning poems written in three parts: lament, praise of the deceased, and solace for loss. Odes evolved from songs to the typical poem of the Romantic time period, expressing strong feelings and contemplative thoughts. Pastoral poems idealize nature and country living. Poetry can also be used to make short, pithy statements. **Epigrams** (memorable rhymes with one or two lines) and **limericks** (two lines of iambic dimeter followed by two lines of iambic dimeter and another of iambic trimeter) are known for humor and wit.

Haiku

Haiku was originally a Japanese poetry form. In the 13th century, haiku was the opening phrase of renga, a 100-stanza oral poem. By the 16th century, haiku diverged into a separate short poem. When Western writers discovered haiku, the form became popular in English, as well as other languages. A haiku has 17 syllables, traditionally distributed across three lines as 5/7/5, with a pause after the first or second line. Haiku are syllabic and unrhymed. Haiku philosophy and technique are that brevity's compression forces writers to express images concisely, depict a moment in time, and evoke illumination and enlightenment. An example is 17th-century haiku master Matsuo Basho's classic: "An old silent pond... / A frog jumps into the pond, / splash! Silence again." Modern American poet Ezra Pound revealed the influence of haiku in his two-line poem "In a Station of the Metro." In this poem, line 1 has 12 syllables (combining the syllable count of the first two lines of a haiku) and line 2 has 7, but it still preserves haiku's philosophy and imagistic technique: "The apparition of these faces in the crowd; / Petals on a wet, black bough."

Sonnets

The sonnet traditionally has 14 lines of iambic pentameter, tightly organized around a theme. The Petrarchan sonnet, named for 14th-century Italian poet Petrarch, has an eight-line stanza, the octave, and a six-line stanza, the sestet. There is a change or turn, known as the volta, between the eighth and ninth verses, setting up the sestet's answer or summary. The rhyme scheme is ABBA/ABBA/CDECDE or CDCDCD. The English or Shakespearean sonnet has three quatrains and one couplet, with the rhyme scheme ABAB/CDCD/EFEF/GG. This format better suits English, which has fewer rhymes than Italian. The final couplet often contrasts sharply with the preceding quatrains, as in Shakespeare's sonnets—for example, Sonnet 130, "My mistress' eyes are nothing like the sun…And yet, by heaven, I think my love as rare / As any she belied with false compare." Variations on the sonnet form include Edmund Spenser's Spenserian sonnet in the 16th century, John Milton's Miltonic sonnet in the 17th century, and sonnet sequences. Sonnet sequences are seen in works such as John Donne's *La Corona* and Elizabeth Barrett Browning's *Sonnets from the Portuguese.*

Review Video: Structural Elements of Poetry
Visit mometrix.com/academy and enter code: 265216

Poetic Themes and Devices

Carpe Diem Tradition in Poetry

Carpe diem is Latin for "seize the day." A long poetic tradition, it advocates making the most of time because it passes swiftly and life is short. It is found in multiple languages, including Latin, Torquato Tasso's Italian, Pierre de Ronsard's French, and Edmund Spenser's English, and is often used in seduction to argue for indulging in earthly pleasures. Roman poet Horace's Ode 1.11 tells a younger woman, Leuconoe, to enjoy the present, not worrying about inevitable aging. Two Renaissance Metaphysical Poets, Andrew Marvell and Robert Herrick, treated *carpe diem* more as a call to action. In "To His Coy Mistress," Marvell points out that time is fleeting, arguing for love, and concluding that because they cannot stop time, they may as well defy it, getting the most out of the short time they have. In "To the Virgins, to Make Much of Time," Herrick advises young women to take advantage of their good fortune in being young by getting married before they become too old to attract men and have babies.

"To His Coy Mistress" begins, "Had we but world enough, and time, / This coyness, lady, were no crime." Using imagery, Andrew Marvell describes leisure they could enjoy if time were unlimited. Arguing for seduction, he continues famously, "But at my back I always hear/Time's winged chariot hurrying near; / And yonder all before us lie / Deserts of vast eternity." He depicts time as turning beauty to death and decay. Contradictory images in "amorous birds of prey" and "tear our pleasures with rough strife / Through the iron gates of life" overshadow romance with impending death, linking present pleasure with mortality and spiritual values with moral considerations. Marvell's concluding couplet summarizes *carpe diem*: "Thus, though we cannot make our sun / Stand still, yet we will make him run." "To the Virgins, to Make Much of Time" begins with the famous "Gather ye rosebuds while ye may." Rather than seduction to live for the present, Robert Herrick's experienced persona advises young women's future planning: "Old time is still a-flying / And this same flower that smiles today, / Tomorrow will be dying."

Effect of Structure on Meaning in Poetry

The way a poem is structured can affect its meaning. Different structural choices can change the way a reader understands a poem, so poets are careful to ensure that the form they use reflects the message they want to convey. The main structural elements in poetry include **lines** and **stanzas**. The number of lines within a stanza and the number of stanzas vary between different poems, but some poetic forms require a poem to have a certain number of lines and stanzas. Some of these forms also require each line to conform to a certain meter, or number and pattern of syllables. Many forms are associated with a certain topic or tone because of their meter. Poetic forms include sonnets, concrete poems, haiku, and villanelles. Another popular form of poetry is free verse, which is poetry that does not conform to a particular meter or rhyme scheme.

The arrangement of lines and stanzas determines the speed at which a poem is read. Long lines are generally read more quickly since the reader is often eager to reach the end of the line and does not have to stop to find the next word. Short lines cause the reader to briefly pause and look to the next line, so their reading is slowed. These effects often contribute to the meaning a reader gleans from a poem, so poets aim to make the line length compatible with the tone of their message.

For example, Edgar Allan Poe's poem "The Raven" is written with mostly long lines. The poem's speaker experiences troubling events and becomes paranoid throughout the poem, and he narrates his racing thoughts. Poe's use of long lines leads the reader to read each line quickly, allowing their reading experience to resemble the thoughts of the narrator:

> Deep into that darkness peering, long I stood there wondering, fearing,
> Doubting, dreaming dreams no mortal ever dared to dream before;
>   But the silence was unbroken, and the stillness gave no token,
>   And the only word there spoken was the whispered word, "Lenore?"
> This I whispered, and an echo murmured back the word, "Lenore!"—
>   Merely this and nothing more.

The poem's meter also contributes to its tone, but consider the same stanza written using shorter lines:

> Deep into that darkness peering,
> long I stood there wondering, fearing,
> Doubting, dreaming dreams no mortal
> ever dared to dream before;
>   But the silence was unbroken,
> and the stillness gave no token,
>   And the only word there spoken
> was the whispered word, "Lenore?"
> This I whispered, and an echo
> murmured back the word, "Lenore!"—
>   Merely this and nothing more.

Breaking the lines apart creates longer pauses and a slower, more suspenseful experience for the reader. While the tone of the poem is dark and suspense is appropriate, the longer lines allow Poe to emphasize and show the narrator's emotions. The narrator's emotions are more important to the poem's meaning than the creation of suspense, making longer lines more suitable in this case.

Concrete Poetry

A less common form of poetry is concrete poetry, also called shape poetry. **Concrete poems** are arranged so the full poem takes a shape that is relevant to the poem's message. For example, a concrete poem about the beach may be arranged to look like a palm tree. This contributes to a poem's meaning by influencing which aspect of the poem or message that the reader focuses on. In the beach poem example, the image of the palm tree leads the reader to focus on the poem's setting and visual imagery. The reader may also look for or anticipate the mention of a palm tree in the poem. This technique allows the poet to direct the reader's attention and emphasize a certain element of their work.

Free Verse

Free verse is a very common form of poetry. Because **free verse** poetry does not always incorporate meter or rhyme, it relies more heavily on punctuation and structure to influence the reader's experience and create emphasis. Free verse poetry makes strategic use of the length and number of both lines and stanzas. While meter and rhyme direct the flow and tone of other types of poems, poets of free verse pieces use the characteristics of lines and stanzas to establish flow and tone, instead.

Free verse also uses punctuation in each line to create flow and tone. The punctuation in each line directs the reader to pause after certain words, allowing the poet to emphasize specific ideas or images to clearly communicate their message. Similar to the effects of line length, the presence of punctuation at the end of a line can create pauses that affect a reader's pace. **End-stopped** lines, or lines with a punctuation mark at the end, create a pause that can contribute to the poem's flow or create emphasis. **Enjambed** lines, or lines that do not end with a punctuation mark, carry a sentence to the next line and create an effect similar to long lines. The use of enjambment can speed up a poem's flow and reflect an idea within the poem or contribute to tone.

Poetic Structure to Enhance Meaning

The opening stanza of Romantic English poet, artist and printmaker William Blake's famous poem "The Tyger" demonstrates how a poet can create tension by using line length and punctuation independently of one another: "Tyger! Tyger! burning bright / In the forests of the night, / What immortal hand or eye / Could frame thy fearful symmetry?" The first three lines of this stanza are **trochaic** (/◡), with "masculine" endings—that is, strongly stressed syllables at the ends of each of the lines. But Blake's punctuation contradicts this rhythmic regularity by not providing any divisions between the words "bright" and "In" or between "eye" and "Could." This irregular punctuation foreshadows how Blake disrupts the meter at the end of this first stanza by using a contrasting **dactyl** (/◡◡), with a "feminine" (unstressed) ending syllable in the last word, "symmetry." Thus, Blake uses structural contrasts to heighten the intrigue of his work.

In enjambment, one sentence or clause in a poem does not end at the end of its line or verse, but runs over into the next line or verse. Clause endings coinciding with line endings give readers a feeling of completion, but enjambment influences readers to hurry to the next line to finish and understand the sentence. In his blank-verse epic religious poem "Paradise Lost," John Milton wrote: "Anon out of the earth a fabric huge / Rose like an exhalation, with the sound / Of dulcet symphonies and voices sweet, / Built like a temple, where pilasters round / Were set, and Doric pillars overlaid / With golden architrave." Only the third line is end-stopped. Milton, describing the palace of Pandemonium bursting from Hell up through the ground, reinforced this idea through phrases and clauses bursting through the boundaries of the lines. A **caesura** is a pause in mid-verse. Milton's commas in the third and fourth lines signal caesuras. They interrupt flow, making the narration jerky to imply that Satan's glorious-seeming palace has a shaky and unsound foundation.

Couplets and Meter to Enhance Meaning in Poetry

When a poet uses a couplet—a stanza of two lines, rhymed or unrhymed—it can function as the answer to a question asked earlier in the poem, or the solution to a problem or riddle. Couplets can also enhance the establishment of a poem's mood, or clarify the development of a poem's theme. Another device to enhance thematic development is irony, which also communicates the poet's tone and draws the reader's attention to a point the poet is making. The use of meter gives a poem a rhythmic context, contributes to the poem's flow, makes it more appealing to the reader, can represent natural speech rhythms, and produces specific effects. For example, in "The Song of Hiawatha," Henry Wadsworth Longfellow uses trochaic (/ ᴗ) tetrameter (four beats per line) to evoke for readers the rhythms of Native American chanting: "*By* the *shores* of *Gitch*e *Gum*ee, / *By* the *shin*ing *Big*-Sea-*Wat*er / *Stood* the *wig*wam *of* No*ko*mis." (Italicized syllables are stressed; non-italicized syllables are unstressed.)

Reflection of Content Through Structure

Wallace Stevens' short yet profound poem "The Snow Man" is reductionist: the snow man is a figure without human biases or emotions. Stevens begins, "One must have a mind of winter," the criterion for realizing nature and life does not inherently possess subjective qualities; we only invest it with these. Things are not as we see them; they simply are. The entire poem is one long sentence of clauses connected by conjunctions and commas, and modified by relative clauses and phrases. The successive phrases lead readers continually to reconsider as they read. Stevens' construction of the poem mirrors the meaning he conveys. With a mind of winter, the snow man, Stevens concludes, "nothing himself, beholds nothing that is not there, and the nothing that is."

Contrast of Content and Structure

Robert Frost's poem "Stopping by Woods on a Snowy Evening" (1923) is deceptively short and simple, with only four stanzas, each of only four lines, and short and simple words. Reinforcing this is Frost's use of regular rhyme and meter. The rhythm is iambic tetrameter throughout; the rhyme scheme is AABA in the first three stanzas and AAAA in the fourth. In an additional internal subtlety, B ending "here" in the first stanza is rhymed with A endings "queer," "near," and "year" of the second; B ending "lake" in the second is rhymed in A endings "shake," "mistake," and "flake" of the third. The final stanza's AAAA endings reinforce the ultimate darker theme. Though the first three stanzas seem to describe quietly watching snow fill the woods, the last stanza evokes the seductive pull of mysterious death: "The woods are lovely, dark and deep," countered by the obligations of living life: "But I have promises to keep, / And miles to go before I sleep, / And miles to go before I sleep." The last line's repetition strengthens Frost's message that despite death's temptation, life's course must precede it.

Effects of Figurative Devices on Meaning in Poetry

Through exaggeration, **hyperbole** communicates the strength of a poet's or persona's feelings and enhances the mood of the poem. **Imagery** appeals to the reader's senses, creating vivid mental pictures, evoking reader emotions and responses, and helping to develop themes. **Irony** also aids thematic development by drawing the reader's attention to the poet's point and communicating the poem's tone. Thematic development is additionally supported by the comparisons of **metaphors** and **similes**, which emphasize similarities, enhance imagery, and affect readers' perceptions. The use of **mood** communicates the atmosphere of a poem, builds a sense of tension, and evokes the reader's emotions. **Onomatopoeia** appeals to the reader's auditory sense and enhances sound imagery even when the poem is visual (read silently) rather than auditory (read aloud). **Rhyme** connects and unites verses, gives the rhyming words emphasis, and makes poems more fluent. **Symbolism** communicates themes, develops imagery, evokes readers' emotions, and elicits a response from the reader.

Review Video: What is Sensory Language?
Visit mometrix.com/academy and enter code: 177314

Repetition to Enhance Meaning

A **villanelle** is a nineteen-line poem composed of five tercets and one quatrain. The defining characteristic is the repetition: two lines appear repeatedly throughout the poem. In Theodore Roethke's "The Waking," the two repeated lines are "I wake to sleep, and take my waking slow," and "I learn by going where I have to go." At first these sound paradoxical, but the meaning is gradually revealed through the poem. The repetition also fits with the theme of cycle: the paradoxes of waking to sleep, learning by going, and thinking by feeling represent a constant cycle through life. They also symbolize abandoning conscious rationalism to embrace spiritual vision. We wake from the vision to "Great Nature," and "take the lively air." "This shaking keeps me steady"—another paradox—juxtaposes and balances fear of mortality with ecstasy in embracing experience. The transcendent vision of all life's interrelationship demonstrates, "What falls away is always. And is near." Readers experience the poem holistically, like music, through Roethke's integration of theme, motion, and sound.

Sylvia Plath's villanelle "Mad Girl's Love Song" narrows the scope from universal to personal but keeps the theme of cycle. The two repeated lines, "I shut my eyes and all the world drops dead" and "(I think I made you up inside my head.)" reflect the existential viewpoint that nothing exists in any absolute reality outside of our own perceptions. In the first stanza, the middle line, "I lift my lids and all is born again," in its recreating the world, bridges between the repeated refrain statements—one of obliterating reality, the other of having constructed her lover's existence. Unlike other villanelles wherein key lines are subtly altered in their repetitions, Plath repeats these exactly each time. This reflects the young woman's love, constant throughout the poem as it neither fades nor progresses.

Chapter Quiz

1. Unrhymed iambic pentameter is also known as which of the following?

a. Anapestic verse
b. Sonnet
c. Free verse
d. Blank verse

2. Which of the following refers to a mid-verse pause that interrupts flow?

a. Caesura
b. Exeunt
c. Soliloquy
d. Enjambment

3. A villanelle is a nineteen-line poem that consists of which of the following?

a. Four tercets and two quatrains
b. Five tercets and one quatrain
c. Four couplets and four tercets
d. Five couplets and three tercets

Chapter Quiz Answer Key

1. D: Poems may be in free verse, metered but unrhymed, rhymed but without meter, or using both rhyme and meter. In English, the most common meter is iambic pentameter. Unrhymed iambic pentameter is called blank verse.

2. A: A caesura is a pause in mid-verse.

3. B: A villanelle is a 19-line poem composed of five tercets and one quatrain. The defining characteristic is the repetition: two lines appear repeatedly throughout the poem.

Drama

Early Development

English **drama** originally developed from religious ritual. Early Christians established traditions of presenting pageants or mystery plays, traveling on wagons and carts through the streets to depict Biblical events. Medieval tradition assigned responsibility for performing specific plays to the different guilds. In Middle English, "mystery" referred to craft, or trade, and religious ritual and truth. Historically, mystery plays were to be reproduced exactly the same every time they were performed, like religious rituals. However, some performers introduced individual interpretations of roles and even improvised. Thus, drama was born. Narrative detail and nuanced acting were evident in mystery cycles by the Middle Ages. As individualized performance evolved, plays on other subjects also developed. Middle English mystery plays that still exist include the York Cycle, Coventry Cycle, Chester Mystery Plays, N-Town Plays, and Towneley/Wakefield Plays. In recent times, these plays began to draw interest again, and several modern actors, such as Dame Judi Dench, began their careers with mystery plays.

Review Video: Dramas
Visit mometrix.com/academy and enter code: 216060

Defining Characteristics

In the Middle Ages, plays were commonly composed in **verse**. By the time of the Renaissance, Shakespeare and other dramatists wrote plays that mixed **prose**, **rhymed verse**, and **blank verse**. The traditions of costumes and masks were seen in ancient Greek drama, medieval mystery plays, and Renaissance drama. Conventions like **asides**, in which actors make comments directly to the audience unheard by other characters, and **soliloquies** were also common during Shakespeare's Elizabethan dramatic period. **Monologues** date back to ancient Greek drama. Elizabethan dialogue tended to use colloquial prose for lower-class characters' speech and stylized verse for upper-class characters. Another Elizabethan convention was the play-within-a-play, as in *Hamlet.* As drama moved toward realism, dialogue became less poetic and more conversational, as in most modern English-language plays. Contemporary drama, both onstage and onscreen, includes a convention of **breaking the fourth wall**, as actors directly face and address audiences.

Comedy

Today, most people equate the idea of **comedy** with something funny, and of **tragedy** with something sad. However, the ancient Greeks defined these differently. Comedy needed not be humorous or amusing; it needed only a happy ending. The classical definition of comedy, as included in Aristotle's works, is any work that tells the story of a sympathetic main character's rise in fortune. According to Aristotle, protagonists need not be heroic or exemplary, nor evil or worthless, but ordinary people of unremarkable morality. Comic figures who were sympathetic were usually of humble origins, proving their "natural nobility" through their actions as they were tested. Characters born into nobility were often satirized as self-important or pompous.

Shakespearean Comedy

William Shakespeare lived in England from 1564-1616. He was a poet and playwright of the Renaissance period in Western culture. He is generally considered the foremost dramatist in world literature and the greatest author to write in the English language. He wrote many poems, particularly sonnets, of which 154 survive today, and approximately 38 plays. Though his sonnets are greater in number and are very famous, he is best known for his plays, including comedies, tragedies, tragicomedies and historical plays. His play titles include: *All's Well That Ends Well, As You Like It, The Comedy of Errors, Love's Labour's Lost, Measure for Measure, The Merchant of Venice,*

The Merry Wives of Windsor, A Midsummer Night's Dream, Much Ado About Nothing, The Taming of the Shrew, The Tempest, Twelfth Night, The Two Gentlemen of Verona, The Winter's Tale, King John, Richard II, Henry IV, Henry V, Richard III, Romeo and Juliet, Coriolanus, Titus Andronicus, Julius Caesar, Macbeth, Hamlet, Troilus and Cressida, King Lear, Othello, Antony and Cleopatra, and *Cymbeline.* Some scholars have suggested that Christopher Marlowe wrote several of Shakespeare's works. While most scholars reject this theory, Shakespeare did pay homage to Marlowe, alluding to several of his characters, themes, or verbiage, as well as borrowing themes from several of his plays (e.g., Marlowe's *Jew of Malta* influenced Shakespeare's *Merchant of Venice*).

When Shakespeare was writing, during the Elizabethan period of the Renaissance, Aristotle's version of comedies was popular. While some of Shakespeare's comedies were humorous and others were not, all had happy endings. *A Comedy of Errors* is a farce. Based and expanding on a Classical Roman comedy, it is lighthearted and includes slapstick humor and mistaken identity. *Much Ado About Nothing* is a romantic comedy. It incorporates some more serious themes, including social mores, perceived infidelity, marriage's duality as both trap and ideal, honor and its loss, public shame, and deception, but also much witty dialogue and a happy ending.

DRAMATIC COMEDY

Three types of dramas classified as comedy include the farce, the romantic comedy, and the satirical comedy.

FARCE

The **farce** is a zany, goofy type of comedy that includes pratfalls and other forms of slapstick humor. The characters in a farce tend to be ridiculous or fantastical in nature. The plot also tends to contain highly improbable events, featuring complications and twists that continue throughout, and incredible coincidences that would likely never occur in reality. Mistaken identity, deceptions, and disguises are common devices used in farcical comedies. Shakespeare's play *The Comedy of Errors,* with its cases of accidental mistaken identity and slapstick, is an example of farce. Contemporary examples of farce include the Marx Brothers' movies, the Three Stooges movies and TV episodes, and the *Pink Panther* movie series.

ROMANTIC COMEDY

Romantic comedies are probably the most popular of the types of comedy, in both live theater performances and movies. They include not only humor and a happy ending, but also love. In the typical plot of a **romantic comedy**, two people well suited to one another are either brought together for the first time, or reconciled after being separated. They are usually both sympathetic characters and seem destined to be together, yet they are separated by some intervening complication, such as ex-lovers, interfering parents or friends, or differences in social class. The happy ending is achieved through the lovers overcoming all these obstacles. William Shakespeare's *Much Ado About Nothing*, Walt Disney's version of *Cinderella* (1950), and Broadway musical *Guys and Dolls* (1955) are example of romantic comedies. Many live-action movies are also examples of romantic comedies, such as *The Princess Bride* (1987), *Sleepless in Seattle* (1993), *You've Got Mail* (1998), and *Forget Paris* (1995).

SATIRICAL COMEDY AND BLACK COMEDY

Satires generally mock and lampoon human foolishness and vices. **Satirical comedies** fit the classical definition of comedy by depicting a main character's rise in fortune, but they also fit the definition of satire by making that main character either a fool, morally corrupt, or cynical in attitude. All or most of the other characters in the satirical comedy display similar foibles. These include gullible types, such as cuckolded spouses and dupes, and deceptive types, such as tricksters, con artists, criminals, hypocrites, and fortune seekers, who prey on the gullible. Some classical examples of satirical comedies include *The Birds* by ancient Greek comedic playwright Aristophanes, and *Volpone* by 17th-century poet and playwright Ben Jonson, who made the comedy of humors popular. When satirical comedy is extended to extremes, it becomes **black comedy**, wherein the comedic occurrences are grotesque or terrible.

Tragedy

The opposite of comedy is tragedy, portraying a hero's fall in fortune. While by classical definitions, tragedies could be sad, Aristotle went further, requiring that they depict suffering and pain to cause "terror and pity" in audiences. Additionally, he decreed that tragic heroes be basically good, admirable, or noble, and that their downfalls result from personal action, choice, or error, not by bad luck or accident.

Aristotle's Criteria for Tragedy

In his *Poetics,* Aristotle defined five critical terms relative to tragedy:

- ***Anagnorisis***: Meaning tragic insight or recognition, this is a moment of realization by a tragic hero or heroine that he or she has become enmeshed in a "web of fate."
- ***Hamartia***: This is often called a "tragic flaw," but is better described as a tragic error. *Hamartia* is an archery term meaning a shot missing the bull's eye, used here as a metaphor for a mistake—often a simple one—which results in catastrophe.
- ***Hubris***: While often called "pride," this is actually translated as "violent transgression," and signifies an arrogant overstepping of moral or cultural bounds—the sin of the tragic hero who over-presumes or over-aspires.
- ***Nemesis***: translated as "retribution," this represents the cosmic punishment or payback that the tragic hero ultimately receives for committing hubristic acts.
- ***Peripateia***: Literally "turning," this is a plot reversal consisting of a tragic hero's pivotal action, which changes his or her status from safe to endangered.

Hegel's Theory of Tragedy

Georg Wilhelm Friedrich Hegel (1770-1831) proposed a different theory of tragedy than Aristotle (384-322 BC), which was also very influential. Whereas Aristotle's criteria involved character and plot, Hegel defined tragedy as a dynamic conflict of opposite forces or rights. For example, if an individual believes in the moral philosophy of the conscientious objector (i.e., that fighting in wars is morally wrong) but is confronted with being drafted into military service, this conflict would fit Hegel's definition of a tragic plot premise. Hegel theorized that a tragedy must involve some circumstance in which two values, or two rights, are fatally at odds with one another and conflict directly. Hegel did not view this as good triumphing over evil, or evil winning out over good, but rather as one good fighting against another good unto death. He saw this conflict of two goods as truly tragic. In ancient Greek playwright Sophocles' tragedy *Antigone,* the main character experiences this tragic conflict between her public duties and her family and religious responsibilities.

Revenge Tragedy

Along with Aristotelian definitions of comedy and tragedy, ancient Greece was the origin of the **revenge tragedy**. This genre became highly popular in Renaissance England, and is still popular today in contemporary movies. In a revenge tragedy, the protagonist has suffered a serious wrong, such as the murder of a family member. However, the wrongdoer has not been punished. In contemporary plots, this often occurs when some legal technicality has interfered with the miscreant's conviction and sentencing, or when authorities are unable to locate and apprehend the criminal. The protagonist then faces the conflict of suffering this injustice, or exacting his or her own justice by seeking revenge. Greek revenge tragedies include *Agamemnon* and *Medea.* Playwright Thomas Kyd's *The Spanish Tragedy* (1582-1592) is credited with beginning the Elizabethan genre of revenge tragedies. Shakespearean revenge tragedies include *Hamlet* (1599-1602) and *Titus Andronicus* (1588-1593). A Jacobean example is Thomas Middleton's *The Revenger's Tragedy* (1606, 1607).

HAMLET'S "TRAGIC FLAW"

Despite virtually limitless interpretations, one way to view Hamlet's tragic error generally is as indecision. He suffers the classic revenge tragedy's conflict of whether to suffer with his knowledge of his mother's and uncle's assassination of his father, or to exact his own revenge and justice against Claudius, who has assumed the throne after his crime went unknown and unpunished. Hamlet's famous soliloquy, "To be or not to be" reflects this dilemma. Hamlet muses "Whether 'tis nobler in the mind to suffer the slings and arrows of outrageous fortune, / Or to take arms against a sea of troubles, / And by opposing end them?" Hamlet both longs for and fears death, as "the dread of something after death ... makes us rather bear those ills we have / Than fly to others that we know not ... Thus, conscience does make cowards of us all." For most of the play, Hamlet struggles with his responsibility to avenge his father, who was killed by Hamlet's uncle, Claudius. So, Hamlet's tragic error at first might be considered a lack of action. But he then makes several attempts at revenge, each of which end in worse tragedy, until his efforts are ended by the final tragedy—Hamlet's own death.

Chapter Quiz

1. How many critical terms relative to tragedy did Aristotle outline?

a. Five
b. Six
c. Seven
d. Eight

2. Who theorized that a tragedy must involve some circumstance in which two values, or two rights, are fatally at odds with one another and conflict directly?

a. Aristophanes
b. Hegel
c. Shakespeare
d. Marlowe

Chapter Quiz Answer Key

1. A: In his *Poetics,* Aristotle defined five critical terms relative to tragedy.

- Anagnorisis: A tragic insight or recognition; a moment of realization by a tragic hero or heroine that he or she has become enmeshed in a "web of fate."
- Hamartia: Often called a "tragic flaw," but better described as a tragic error. *Hamartia* is an archery term meaning a shot missing the bull's eye, used here as a metaphor for a mistake—often a simple one—that results in catastrophe.
- Hubris: Often equated with pride, *hubris* in this context is actually translated as "violent transgression" and signifies an arrogant overstepping of moral or cultural bounds—the sin of the tragic hero who over-presumes or over-aspires.
- Nemesis: Translated as "retribution," this represents the cosmic punishment or payback that the tragic hero ultimately receives for committing hubristic acts.
- Peripateia: Literally "turning," this is a plot reversal consisting of a tragic hero's pivotal action, which changes his or her status from safe to endangered.

2. B: Georg Wilhelm Friedrich Hegel (1770-1831) proposed a different theory of tragedy than Aristotle (384-322 BC), which was also very influential. Whereas Aristotle's criteria involved character and plot, Hegel defined tragedy as a dynamic conflict of opposite forces or rights. For example, if an individual believes in the moral philosophy of the conscientious objector (i.e., that fighting in wars is morally wrong) but is confronted with being drafted into military service, this conflict would fit Hegel's definition of a tragic plot premise. Hegel theorized that a tragedy must involve some circumstance in which two values (or two rights) are fatally at odds with one another and conflict directly. Hegel did not view this as good triumphing over evil, or evil winning out over good, but rather as one good fighting against another good unto death. He saw this conflict of two goods as truly tragic. In ancient Greek playwright Sophocles' tragedy *Antigone,* the main character experiences this tragic conflict between her public duties and her family and religious responsibilities.

Informational Texts

Text Features in Informational Texts

The **title of a text** gives readers some idea of its content. The **table of contents** is a list near the beginning of a text, showing the book's sections and chapters and their coinciding page numbers. This gives readers an overview of the whole text and helps them find specific chapters easily. An **appendix**, at the back of the book or document, includes important information that is not present in the main text. Also at the back, an **index** lists the book's important topics alphabetically with their page numbers to help readers find them easily. **Glossaries**, usually found at the backs of books, list technical terms alphabetically with their definitions to aid vocabulary learning and comprehension. Boldface print is used to emphasize certain words, often identifying words included in the text's glossary where readers can look up their definitions. **Headings** separate sections of text and show the topic of each. **Subheadings** divide subject headings into smaller, more specific categories to help readers organize information. **Footnotes**, at the bottom of the page, give readers more information, such as citations or links. **Bullet points** list items separately, making facts and ideas easier to see and understand. A **sidebar** is a box of information to one side of the main text giving additional information, often on a more focused or in-depth example of a topic.

Illustrations and **photographs** are pictures that visually emphasize important points in text. The captions below the illustrations explain what those images show. Charts and tables are visual forms of information that make something easier to understand quickly. Diagrams are drawings that show relationships or explain a process. Graphs visually show the relationships among multiple sets of information plotted along vertical and horizontal axes. Maps show geographical information visually to help readers understand the relative locations of places covered in the text. Timelines are visual graphics that show historical events in chronological order to help readers see their sequence.

> **Review Video: Informative Text**
> Visit mometrix.com/academy and enter code: 924964

Language Use

Literal and Figurative Language

As in fictional literature, informational text also uses both **literal language**, which means just what it says, and **figurative language**, which imparts more than literal meaning. For example, an informational text author might use a simile or direct comparison, such as writing that a racehorse "ran like the wind." Informational text authors also use metaphors or implied comparisons, such as "the cloud of the Great Depression." Imagery may also appear in informational texts to increase the reader's understanding of ideas and concepts discussed in the text.

Explicit and Implicit Information

When informational text states something explicitly, the reader is told by the author exactly what is meant, which can include the author's interpretation or perspective of events. For example, a professor writes, "I have seen students go into an absolute panic just because they weren't able to complete the exam in the time they were allotted." This explicitly tells the reader that the students were afraid, and by using the words "just because," the writer indicates their fear was exaggerated out of proportion relative to what happened. However, another professor writes, "I have had students come to me, their faces drained of all color, saying 'We weren't able to finish the exam.'" This is an example of implicit meaning: the second writer did not state explicitly that the students were panicked. Instead, he wrote a description of their faces being "drained of all color." From this description, the reader can infer that the students were so frightened that their faces paled.

Review Video: Explicit and Implicit Information
Visit mometrix.com/academy and enter code: 735771

TECHNICAL LANGUAGE

Technical language is more impersonal than literary and vernacular language. Passive voice makes the tone impersonal. For example, instead of writing, "We found this a central component of protein metabolism," scientists write, "This was found a central component of protein metabolism." While science professors have traditionally instructed students to avoid active voice because it leads to first-person ("I" and "we") usage, science editors today find passive voice dull and weak. Many journal articles combine both. Tone in technical science writing should be detached, concise, and professional. While one may normally write, "This chemical has to be available for proteins to be digested," professionals write technically, "The presence of this chemical is required for the enzyme to break the covalent bonds of proteins." The use of technical language appeals to both technical and non-technical audiences by displaying the author or speaker's understanding of the subject and suggesting their credibility regarding the message they are communicating.

TECHNICAL MATERIAL FOR NON-TECHNICAL READERS

Writing about **technical subjects** for **non-technical readers** differs from writing for colleagues because authors place more importance on delivering a critical message than on imparting the maximum technical content possible. Technical authors also must assume that non-technical audiences do not have the expertise to comprehend extremely scientific or technical messages, concepts, and terminology. They must resist the temptation to impress audiences with their scientific knowledge and expertise and remember that their primary purpose is to communicate a message that non-technical readers will understand, feel, and respond to. Non-technical and technical styles include similarities. Both should formally cite any references or other authors' work utilized in the text. Both must follow intellectual property and copyright regulations. This includes the author's protecting his or her own rights, or a public domain statement, as he or she chooses.

Review Video: Technical Passages
Visit mometrix.com/academy and enter code: 478923

NON-TECHNICAL AUDIENCES

Writers of technical or scientific material may need to write for many non-technical audiences. Some readers have no technical or scientific background, and those who do may not be in the same field as the authors. Government and corporate policymakers and budget managers need technical information they can understand for decision-making. Citizens affected by technology or science are a different audience. Non-governmental organizations can encompass many of the preceding groups. Elementary and secondary school programs also need non-technical language for presenting technical subject matter. Additionally, technical authors will need to use non-technical language when collecting consumer responses to surveys, presenting scientific or para-scientific material to the public, writing about the history of science, and writing about science and technology in developing countries.

USE OF EVERYDAY LANGUAGE

Authors of technical information sometimes must write using non-technical language that readers outside their disciplinary fields can comprehend. They should use not only non-technical terms, but also normal, everyday language to accommodate readers whose native language is different than the language the text is written in. For example, instead of writing that "eustatic changes like thermal expansion are causing hazardous conditions in the littoral zone," an author would do better to write that "a rising sea level is threatening the coast." When technical terms cannot be avoided, authors should also define or explain them using non-technical language. Although authors must cite references and acknowledge their use of others' work, they should avoid the kinds of references or citations that they would use in scientific journals—unless they reinforce author messages. They should not use endnotes, footnotes, or any other complicated referential techniques because non-technical journal publishers usually do not accept them. Including high-resolution illustrations, photos, maps, or satellite images and incorporating multimedia into digital publications will enhance non-technical writing about technical subjects. Technical authors may publish using non-technical language in e-journals, trade journals, specialty newsletters, and daily newspapers.

Making Inferences About Informational Text

With informational text, reader comprehension depends not only on recalling important statements and details, but also on reader inferences based on examples and details. Readers add information from the text to what they already know to draw inferences about the text. These inferences help the readers to fill in the information that the text does not explicitly state, enabling them to understand the text better. When reading a nonfictional autobiography or biography, for example, the most appropriate inferences might concern the events in the book, the actions of the subject of the autobiography or biography, and the message the author means to convey. When reading a nonfictional expository (informational) text, the reader would best draw inferences about problems and their solutions, and causes and their effects. When reading a nonfictional persuasive text, the reader will want to infer ideas supporting the author's message and intent.

Structures or Organizational Patterns in Informational Texts

Informational text can be **descriptive**, appealing to the five senses and answering the questions what, who, when, where, and why. Another method of structuring informational text is sequence and order. **Chronological** texts relate events in the sequence that they occurred, from start to finish, while how-to texts organize information into a series of instructions in the sequence in which the steps should be followed. **Comparison-contrast** structures of informational text describe various ideas to their readers by pointing out how things or ideas are similar and how they are different. **Cause and effect** structures of informational text describe events that occurred and identify the causes or reasons that those events occurred. **Problem and solution** structures of informational texts introduce and describe problems and offer one or more solutions for each problem described.

Determining an Informational Author's Purpose

Informational authors' purposes are why they write texts. Readers must determine authors' motivations and goals. Readers gain greater insight into a text by considering the author's motivation. This develops critical reading skills. Readers perceive writing as a person's voice, not simply printed words. Uncovering author motivations and purposes empowers readers to know what to expect from the text, read for relevant details, evaluate authors and their work critically, and respond effectively to the motivations and persuasions of the text. The main idea of a text is what the reader is supposed to understand from reading it; the purpose of the text is why the author has written it and what the author wants readers to do with its information. Authors state some purposes clearly, while other purposes may be unstated but equally significant. When stated purposes contradict other parts of a text, the author may have a hidden agenda. Readers can better evaluate a text's effectiveness, whether they agree or disagree with it, and why they agree or disagree through identifying unstated author purposes.

Identifying Author's Point of View or Purpose

In some informational texts, readers find it easy to identify the author's point of view and purpose, such as when the author explicitly states his or her position and reason for writing. But other texts are more difficult, either because of the content or because the authors give neutral or balanced viewpoints. This is particularly true in scientific texts, in which authors may state the purpose of their research in the report, but never state their point of view except by interpreting evidence or data.

To analyze text and identify point of view or purpose, readers should ask themselves the following four questions:

1. With what main point or idea does this author want to persuade readers to agree?
2. How does this author's word choice affect the way that readers consider this subject?
3. How do this author's choices of examples and facts affect the way that readers consider this subject?
4. What is it that this author wants to accomplish by writing this text?

Review Video: Understanding the Author's Intent
Visit mometrix.com/academy and enter code: 511819

Review Video: Author's Position
Visit mometrix.com/academy and enter code: 827954

Evaluating Arguments Made by Informational Text Writers

When evaluating an informational text, the first step is to identify the argument's conclusion. Then identify the author's premises that support the conclusion. Try to paraphrase premises for clarification and make the conclusion and premises fit. List all premises first, sequentially numbered, then finish with the conclusion. Identify any premises or assumptions not stated by the author but required for the stated premises to support the conclusion. Read word assumptions sympathetically, as the author might. Evaluate whether premises reasonably support the conclusion. For inductive reasoning, the reader should ask if the premises are true, if they support the conclusion, and if so, how strongly. For deductive reasoning, the reader should ask if the argument is valid or invalid. If all premises are true, then the argument is valid unless the conclusion can be false. If it can, then the argument is invalid. An invalid argument can be made valid through alterations such as the addition of needed premises.

Use of Rhetoric in Informational Texts

There are many ways authors can support their claims, arguments, beliefs, ideas, and reasons for writing in informational texts. For example, authors can appeal to readers' sense of **logic** by communicating their reasoning through a carefully sequenced series of logical steps to help "prove" the points made. Authors can appeal to readers' **emotions** by using descriptions and words that evoke feelings of sympathy, sadness, anger, righteous indignation, hope, happiness, or any other emotion to reinforce what they express and share with their audience. Authors may appeal to the **moral** or **ethical values** of readers by using words and descriptions that can convince readers that something is right or wrong. By relating personal anecdotes, authors can supply readers with more accessible, realistic examples of points they make, as well as appealing to their emotions. They can provide supporting evidence by reporting case studies. They can also illustrate their points by making analogies to which readers can better relate.

Chapter Quiz

1. Which of the following is the first step in evaluating an informational text?

a. Read word assumptions sympathetically
b. List all premises sequentially
c. Determine if the premises are true
d. Identify the argument's conclusion

2. Which of the following is NOT considered a type of appeal for an author to use?

a. Logic
b. Ethics
c. Emotions
d. Imagination

Chapter Quiz Answer Key

1. D: When evaluating an informational text, the first step is to identify the argument's conclusion. After that comes identifying the author's premises that support the conclusion. The reader should try to paraphrase premises for clarification and make the conclusion and premises fit. List all premises first, sequentially numbered, then finish with the conclusion. Identify any premises or assumptions not stated by the author but required for the stated premises to support the conclusion. Read word assumptions sympathetically, as the author might. Evaluate whether premises reasonably support the conclusion. For inductive reasoning, the reader should ask if the premises are true, if they support the conclusion, and how strong that support is. For deductive reasoning, the reader should ask if the argument is valid or invalid. If all premises are true, then the argument is valid unless the conclusion can be false. If it can, then the argument is invalid. An invalid argument can be made valid through alterations such as the addition of needed premises.

2. D: There are many ways authors can support their claims, arguments, beliefs, ideas, and reasons for writing in informational texts. For example, authors can appeal to readers' sense of logic by communicating their reasoning through a carefully sequenced series of logical steps to support their positions. Authors can appeal to readers' emotions by using descriptions and words that evoke feelings of sympathy, sadness, anger, righteous indignation, hope, happiness, or any other emotion to reinforce what they express and share with their audience. Authors may appeal to the moral or ethical values of readers by using words and descriptions that can convince readers that something is right or wrong. By relating personal anecdotes, authors can appeal to readers' emotions and supply them with more accessible, realistic examples of points they make. They can provide supporting evidence by reporting case studies. They can also illustrate their points by making analogies to which readers can better relate.

Persuasive Techniques

Persuasive Techniques

To **appeal using reason**, writers present logical arguments, such as using "If... then... because" statements. To **appeal to emotions**, authors may ask readers how they would feel about something or to put themselves in another's place, present their argument as one that will make the audience feel good, or tell readers how they should feel. To **appeal to character**, **morality**, or **ethics**, authors present their points to readers as the right or most moral choices. Authors cite expert opinions to show readers that someone very knowledgeable about the subject or viewpoint agrees with the author's claims. **Testimonials**, usually via anecdotes or quotations regarding the author's subject, help build the audience's trust in an author's message through positive support from ordinary people. **Bandwagon appeals** claim that everybody else agrees with the author's argument and persuade readers to conform and agree, also. Authors **appeal to greed** by presenting their choice as cheaper, free, or more valuable for less cost. They **appeal to laziness** by presenting their views as more convenient, easy, or relaxing. Authors also anticipate potential objections and argue against them before audiences think of them, thereby depicting those objections as weak.

Authors can use **comparisons** like analogies, similes, and metaphors to persuade audiences. For example, a writer might represent excessive expenses as "hemorrhaging" money, which the author's recommended solution will stop. Authors can use negative word connotations to make some choices unappealing to readers, and positive word connotations to make others more appealing. Using **humor** can relax readers and garner their agreement. However, writers must take care: ridiculing opponents can be a successful strategy for appealing to readers who already agree with the author, but can backfire by angering other readers. **Rhetorical questions** need no answer, but create effect that can force agreement, such as asking the question, "Wouldn't you rather be paid more than less?" **Generalizations** persuade readers by being impossible to disagree with. Writers can easily make generalizations that appear to support their viewpoints, like saying, "We all want peace, not war" regarding more specific political arguments. **Transfer** and **association** persuade by example: if advertisements show attractive actors enjoying their products, audiences imagine they will experience the same. **Repetition** can also sometimes effectively persuade audiences.

Review Video: Using Rhetorical Strategies for Persuasion
Visit mometrix.com/academy and enter code: 302658

Classical Author Appeals

In his *On Rhetoric,* ancient Greek philosopher Aristotle defined three basic types of appeal used in writing, which he called *pathos*, *ethos*, and *logos*. ***Pathos*** means suffering or experience and refers to appeals to the emotions (the English word *pathetic* comes from this root). Writing that is meant to entertain audiences, by making them either happy, as with comedy, or sad, as with tragedy, uses *pathos*. Aristotle's *Poetics* states that evoking the emotions of terror and pity is one of the criteria for writing tragedy. ***Ethos*** means character and connotes ideology (the English word *ethics* comes from this root). Writing that appeals to credibility, based on academic, professional, or personal merit, uses *ethos*. ***Logos*** means "I say" and refers to a plea, opinion, expectation, word or speech, account, opinion, or reason (the English word *logic* comes from this root.) Aristotle used it to mean persuasion that appeals to the audience through reasoning and logic to influence their opinions.

Critical Evaluation of Effectiveness of Persuasive Methods

First, readers should identify the author's **thesis**—what he or she argues for or against. They should consider the argument's content and the author's reason for presenting it. Does the author offer **solutions** to problems raised? If so, are they realistic? Note all central ideas and evidence supporting the author's thesis. Research any unfamiliar subjects or vocabulary. Readers should then outline or summarize the work in their own words. Identify which types of appeals the author uses. Readers should evaluate how well the author communicated meaning from the reader's perspective: Did they respond to emotional appeals with anger, concern, happiness, etc.? If so, why? Decide if the author's reasoning sufficed for changing the reader's mind. Determine whether the content and presentation were accurate, cohesive, and clear. Readers should also ask themselves whether they found the author believable or not, and why or why not.

Evaluating an Argument

Argumentative and persuasive passages take a stand on a debatable issue, seek to explore all sides of the issue, and find the best possible solution. Argumentative and persuasive passages should not be combative or abusive. The word *argument* may remind you of two or more people shouting at each other and walking away in anger. However, an argumentative or persuasive passage should be a calm and reasonable presentation of an author's ideas for others to consider. When an author writes reasonable arguments, his or her goal is not to win or have the last word. Instead, authors want to reveal current understanding of the question at hand and suggest a solution to a problem. The purpose of argument and persuasion in a free society is to reach the best solution.

Evidence

The term **text evidence** refers to information that supports a main point or minor points and can help lead the reader to a conclusion about the text's credibility. Information used as text evidence is precise, descriptive, and factual. A main point is often followed by supporting details that provide evidence to back up a claim. For example, a passage may include the claim that winter occurs during opposite months in the Northern and Southern hemispheres. Text evidence for this claim may include examples of countries where winter occurs in opposite months. Stating that the tilt of the Earth as it rotates around the sun causes winter to occur at different times in separate hemispheres is another example of text evidence. Text evidence can come from common knowledge, but it is also valuable to include text evidence from credible, relevant outside sources.

Review Video: Textual Evidence
Visit mometrix.com/academy and enter code: 486236

Evidence that supports the thesis and additional arguments needs to be provided. Most arguments must be supported by facts or statistics. A fact is something that is known with certainty, has been verified by several independent individuals, and can be proven to be true. In addition to facts, examples and illustrations can support an argument by adding an emotional component. With this component, you persuade readers in ways that facts and statistics cannot. The emotional component is effective when used alongside objective information that can be confirmed.

Credibility

The text used to support an argument can be the argument's downfall if the text is not credible. A text is **credible**, or believable, when its author is knowledgeable and objective, or unbiased. The author's motivations for writing the text play a critical role in determining the credibility of the text and must be evaluated when assessing that credibility. Reports written about the ozone layer by an environmental scientist and a hairdresser will have a different level of credibility.

Review Video: Author Credibility
Visit mometrix.com/academy and enter code: 827257

Appeal to Emotion

Sometimes, authors will appeal to the reader's emotion in an attempt to persuade or to distract the reader from the weakness of the argument. For instance, the author may try to inspire the pity of the reader by delivering a heart-rending story. An author also might use the bandwagon approach, in which he suggests that his opinion is correct because it is held by the majority. Some authors resort to name-calling, in which insults and harsh words are delivered to the opponent in an attempt to distract. In advertising, a common appeal is the celebrity testimonial, in which a famous person endorses a product. Of course, the fact that a famous person likes something should not really mean anything to the reader. These and other emotional appeals are usually evidence of poor reasoning and a weak argument.

Review Video: Emotional Language in Literature
Visit mometrix.com/academy and enter code: 759390

Counter Arguments

When authors give both sides to the argument, they build trust with their readers. As a reader, you should start with an undecided or neutral position. If an author presents only his or her side to the argument, then they are not exhibiting credibility and are weakening their argument.

Building common ground with readers can be effective for persuading neutral, skeptical, or opposed readers. Sharing values with undecided readers can allow people to switch positions without giving up what they feel is important. People who may oppose a position need to feel that they can change their minds without betraying who they are as a person. This appeal to having an open mind can be a powerful tool in arguing a position without antagonizing other views. Objections can be countered on a point-by-point basis or in a summary paragraph. Be mindful of how an author points out flaws in counter arguments. If they are unfair to the other side of the argument, then you should lose trust with the author.

Rhetorical Devices

- An **anecdote** is a brief story authors may relate to their argument, which can illustrate their points in a more real and relatable way.
- **Aphorisms** concisely state common beliefs and may rhyme. For example, Benjamin Franklin's "Early to bed and early to rise / Makes a man healthy, wealthy, and wise" is an aphorism.
- **Allusions** refer to literary or historical figures to impart symbolism to a thing or person and to create reader resonance. In John Steinbeck's *Of Mice and Men*, protagonist George's last name is Milton. This alludes to John Milton, who wrote *Paradise Lost*, and symbolizes George's eventual loss of his dream.
- **Satire** exaggerates, ridicules, or pokes fun at human flaws or ideas, as in the works of Jonathan Swift and Mark Twain.
- A **parody** is a form of satire that imitates another work to ridicule its topic or style.
- A **paradox** is a statement that is true despite appearing contradictory.
- **Hyperbole** is overstatement using exaggerated language.
- An **oxymoron** combines seeming contradictions, such as "deafening silence."
- **Analogies** compare two things that share common elements.
- **Similes** (stated comparisons using the words *like* or *as*) and **metaphors** (stated comparisons that do not use *like* or *as*) are considered forms of analogy.
- When using logic to reason with audiences, **syllogism** refers either to deductive reasoning or a deceptive, very sophisticated, or subtle argument.

- **Deductive reasoning** moves from general to specific, **inductive reasoning** from specific to general.
- **Diction** is author word choice that establishes tone and effect.
- **Understatement** achieves effects like contrast or irony by downplaying or describing something more subtly than warranted.
- **Chiasmus** uses parallel clauses, the second reversing the order of the first. Examples include T. S. Eliot's "Has the Church failed mankind, or has mankind failed the Church?" and John F. Kennedy's "Ask not what your country can do for you; ask what you can do for your country."
- **Anaphora** regularly repeats a word or phrase at the beginnings of consecutive clauses or phrases to add emphasis to an idea. A classic example of anaphora was Winston Churchill's emphasis of determination: "[W]e shall fight on the beaches, we shall fight on the landing grounds, we shall fight in the fields and in the streets, we shall fight in the hills; we shall never surrender..."

Chapter Quiz

1. Which of the following rhetorical devices exaggerates, ridicules, or pokes fun at human flaws or ideas?

a. Allusions
b. Satire
c. Parody
d. Hyperbole

2. An author arguing that his point is correct because everybody else already agrees with it is an example of which persuasive technique?

a. Appeal to laziness
b. Bandwagon appeal
c. Testimonials
d. Generalizations

Chapter Quiz Answer Key

1. B: Rhetorical devices:

- An anecdote is a brief story authors may relate to their argument, which can illustrate their points in a more real and relatable way.
- Aphorisms concisely state common beliefs and may rhyme. For example, Benjamin Franklin's "Early to bed and early to rise / Makes a man healthy, wealthy, and wise" is an aphorism.
- Allusions refer to literary or historical figures to impart symbolism to a thing or person and to create reader resonance. In John Steinbeck's *Of Mice and Men,* protagonist George's last name is Milton. This alludes to John Milton, who wrote *Paradise Lost*, and symbolizes George's eventual loss of his dream.
- Satire exaggerates, ridicules, or pokes fun at human flaws or ideas, as in the works of Jonathan Swift and Mark Twain.
- A parody is a form of satire that imitates another work to ridicule its topic or style.
- A paradox is a statement that is true despite appearing contradictory.
- Hyperbole is overstatement using exaggerated language.
- An oxymoron combines seeming contradictions, such as "deafening silence."
- Analogies compare two things that share common elements.
- Similes (stated comparisons using the words *like* or *as*) and metaphors (stated comparisons that do not use *like* or *as*) are considered forms of analogy.
- When using logic to reason with audiences, syllogism refers either to deductive reasoning or a deceptive, very sophisticated, or subtle argument.
- Deductive reasoning moves from general to specific, while inductive reasoning moves from specific to general.
- Diction is author word choice that establishes tone and effect.
- Understatement achieves effects like contrast or irony by downplaying or describing something more subtly than warranted.
- Chiasmus uses parallel clauses, with the second clause reversing the order of the first. Examples include T. S. Eliot's "Has the Church failed mankind, or has mankind failed the Church?" and John F. Kennedy's "Ask not what your country can do for you—ask what you can do for your country."

- Anaphora regularly repeats a word or phrase at the beginnings of consecutive clauses or phrases to add emphasis to an idea. A classic example of anaphora was Winston Churchill's emphasis of determination: "[W]e shall fight on the beaches, we shall fight on the landing grounds, we shall fight in the fields and in the streets, we shall fight in the hills; we shall never surrender..."

2. B: Bandwagon appeals claim that everybody else agrees with the author's argument and thus try to persuade readers to conform and agree as well.

Arguments and Logical Errors

Author's Argument in Argumentative Writing

In argumentative writing, the argument is a belief, position, or opinion that the author wants to convince readers to believe as well. For the first step, readers should identify the **issue**. Some issues are controversial, meaning people disagree about them. Gun control, foreign policy, and the death penalty are all controversial issues. The next step is to determine the **author's position** on the issue. That position or viewpoint constitutes the author's argument. Readers should then identify the **author's assumptions**: things he or she accepts, believes, or takes for granted without needing proof. Inaccurate or illogical assumptions produce flawed arguments and can mislead readers. Readers should identify what kinds of **supporting evidence** the author offers, such as research results, personal observations or experiences, case studies, facts, examples, expert testimony and opinions, and comparisons. Readers should decide how relevant this support is to the argument.

Review Video: Argumentative Writing
Visit mometrix.com/academy and enter code: 561544

Evaluating an Author's Argument

The first three reader steps to **evaluate an author's argument** are to identify the **author's assumptions**, identify the **supporting evidence**, and decide **whether the evidence is relevant**. For example, if an author is not an expert on a particular topic, then that author's personal experience or opinion might not be relevant. The fourth step is to assess the **author's objectivity**. For example, consider whether the author introduces clear, understandable supporting evidence and facts to support the argument. The fifth step is evaluating whether the author's **argument is complete**. When authors give sufficient support for their arguments and also anticipate and respond effectively to opposing arguments or objections to their points, their arguments are complete. However, some authors omit information that could detract from their arguments. If instead they stated this information and refuted it, it would strengthen their arguments. The sixth step in evaluating an author's argumentative writing is to assess whether the **argument is valid**. Providing clear, logical reasoning makes an author's argument valid. Readers should ask themselves whether the author's points follow a sequence that makes sense, and whether each point leads to the next. The seventh step is to determine whether the author's **argument is credible**, meaning that it is convincing and believable. Arguments that are not valid are not credible, so step seven depends on step six. Readers should be mindful of their own biases as they evaluate and should not expect authors to conclusively prove their arguments, but rather to provide effective support and reason.

Evaluating an Author's Method of Appeal

To evaluate the effectiveness of an appeal, it is important to consider the author's purpose for writing. Any appeals an author uses in their argument must be relevant to the argument's goal. For example, a writer that argues for the reclassification of Pluto, but primarily uses appeals to emotion, will not have an effective argument. This writer should focus on using appeals to logic and support their argument with provable facts. While most arguments should include appeals to logic, emotion, and credibility, some arguments only call for one or two of these types of appeal. Evidence can support an appeal, but the evidence must be relevant to truly strengthen the appeal's effectiveness. If the writer arguing for Pluto's reclassification uses the reasons for Jupiter's classification as evidence, their argument would be weak. This information may seem relevant because it is related to the classification of planets. However, this classification is highly dependent on the size of the celestial object, and Jupiter is significantly bigger than Pluto. This use of evidence is illogical and does not support the appeal. Even when appropriate evidence and appeals are used, appeals and arguments lose their effectiveness when they create logical fallacies.

Opinions, Facts, and Fallacies

Critical thinking skills are mastered through understanding various types of writing and the different purposes of authors can have for writing different passages. Every author writes for a purpose. When you understand their purpose and how they accomplish their goal, you will be able to analyze their writing and determine whether or not you agree with their conclusions.

Readers must always be aware of the difference between fact and opinion. A **fact** can be subjected to analysis and proven to be true. An **opinion**, on the other hand, is the author's personal thoughts or feelings and may not be altered by research or evidence. If the author writes that the distance from New York City to Boston is about two hundred miles, then he or she is stating a fact. If the author writes that New York City is too crowded, then he or she is giving an opinion because there is no objective standard for overpopulation. Opinions are often supported by facts. For instance, an author might use a comparison between the population density of New York City and that of other major American cities as evidence of an overcrowded population. An opinion supported by facts tends to be more convincing. On the other hand, when authors support their opinions with other opinions, readers should employ critical thinking and approach the argument with skepticism.

Review Video: Fact or Opinion
Visit mometrix.com/academy and enter code: 870899

Reliable Sources

When you have an argumentative passage, you need to be sure that facts are presented to the reader from **reliable sources**. An opinion is what the author thinks about a given topic. An opinion is not common knowledge or proven by expert sources, instead the information is the personal beliefs and thoughts of the author. To distinguish between fact and opinion, a reader needs to consider the type of source that is presenting information, the information that backs-up a claim, and the author's motivation to have a certain point-of-view on a given topic. For example, if a panel of scientists has conducted multiple studies on the effectiveness of taking a certain vitamin, then the results are more likely to be factual than those of a company that is selling a vitamin and simply claims that taking the vitamin can produce positive effects. The company is motivated to sell their product, and the scientists are using the scientific method to prove a theory. Remember, if you find sentences that contain phrases such as "I think...", then the statement is an opinion.

Biases

In their attempts to persuade, writers often make mistakes in their thought processes and writing choices. These processes and choices are important to understand so you can make an informed decision about the author's credibility. Every author has a point of view, but authors demonstrate a **bias** when they ignore reasonable counterarguments or distort opposing viewpoints. A bias is evident whenever the author's claims are presented in a way that is unfair or inaccurate. Bias can be intentional or unintentional, but readers should be skeptical of the author's argument in either case. Remember that a biased author may still be correct. However, the author will be correct in spite of, not because of, his or her bias.

A **stereotype** is a bias applied specifically to a group of people or a place. Stereotyping is considered to be particularly abhorrent because it promotes negative, misleading generalizations about people. Readers should be very cautious of authors who use stereotypes in their writing. These faulty assumptions typically reveal the author's ignorance and lack of curiosity.

Review Video: Bias and Stereotype
Visit mometrix.com/academy and enter code: 644829

Chapter Quiz

1. Which of the following is NOT one of the first three steps of evaluating an author's argument?

a. Identify the author's assumptions
b. Identify the supporting evidence
c. Evaluate if the author's argument is complete
d. Decide if the supporting evidence is relevant

Chapter Quiz Answer Key

1. C: The first three reader steps to evaluate an author's argument are to identify the author's assumptions, identify the supporting evidence, and decide whether the evidence is relevant. For example, if an author is not an expert on a particular topic, then that author's personal experience or opinion might not be relevant. The fourth step is to assess the author's objectivity. For example, consider whether the author introduces clear, understandable supporting evidence and facts to support the argument. The fifth step is evaluating whether the author's argument is complete. When authors give sufficient support for their arguments and also anticipate and respond effectively to opposing arguments or objections to their points, their arguments are complete. However, some authors omit information that could detract from their arguments. If instead they stated this information and refuted it, it would likely strengthen their arguments. The sixth step in evaluating an author's argumentative writing is to assess whether the argument is valid. Providing clear, logical reasoning makes an author's argument valid. Readers should ask themselves whether the author's points follow a sequence that makes sense, and whether each point leads to the next. The seventh step is to determine whether the author's argument is credible, meaning that it is convincing and believable. Arguments that are not valid are not credible, so step seven depends on step six. Readers should be mindful of their own biases as they evaluate and should not expect authors to conclusively prove their arguments, but rather to provide effective support and reason.

Vocabulary and Word Relationships

Synonyms and Antonyms

When you understand how words relate to each other, you will discover more in a passage. This is explained by understanding **synonyms** (e.g., words that mean the same thing) and **antonyms** (e.g., words that mean the opposite of one another). As an example, *dry* and *arid* are synonyms, and *dry* and *wet* are antonyms.

There are many pairs of words in English that can be considered synonyms, despite having slightly different definitions. For instance, the words *friendly* and *collegial* can both be used to describe a warm interpersonal relationship, and one would be correct to call them synonyms. However, *collegial* (kin to *colleague*) is often used in reference to professional or academic relationships, and *friendly* has no such connotation.

If the difference between the two words is too great, then they should not be called synonyms. *Hot* and *warm* are not synonyms because their meanings are too distinct. A good way to determine whether two words are synonyms is to substitute one word for the other word and verify that the meaning of the sentence has not changed. Substituting *warm* for *hot* in a sentence would convey a different meaning. Although warm and hot may seem close in meaning, warm generally means that the temperature is moderate, and hot generally means that the temperature is excessively high.

Antonyms are words with opposite meanings. *Light* and *dark*, *up* and *down*, *right* and *left*, *good* and *bad*: these are all sets of antonyms. Be careful to distinguish between antonyms and pairs of words that are simply different. *Black* and *gray*, for instance, are not antonyms because gray is not the opposite of black. *Black* and *white*, on the other hand, are antonyms.

Not every word has an antonym. For instance, many nouns do not. What would be the antonym of *chair*? During your exam, the questions related to antonyms are more likely to concern adjectives. You will recall that adjectives are words that describe a noun. Some common adjectives include *purple*, *fast*, *skinny*, and *sweet*. From those four adjectives, *purple* is the item that lacks a group of obvious antonyms.

Review Video: What Are Synonyms and Antonyms?
Visit mometrix.com/academy and enter code: 105612

Affixes

Affixes in the English language are morphemes that are added to words to create related but different words. Derivational affixes form new words based on and related to the original words. For example, the affix *–ness* added to the end of the adjective *happy* forms the noun *happiness.* Inflectional affixes form different grammatical versions of words. For example, the plural affix *–s* changes the singular noun *book* to the plural noun *books*, and the past tense affix *–ed* changes the present tense verb *look* to the past tense *looked.* Prefixes are affixes placed in front of words. For example, *heat* means to make hot; *preheat* means to heat in advance. Suffixes are affixes placed at the ends of words. The *happiness* example above contains the suffix *–ness.* Circumfixes add parts both before and after words, such as how *light* becomes *enlighten* with the prefix *en-* and the suffix *–en.* Interfixes create compound words via central affixes: *speed* and *meter* become *speedometer* via the interfix *–o–*.

Review Video: Affixes
Visit mometrix.com/academy and enter code: 782422

Word Roots, Prefixes, and Suffixes to Help Determine Meanings of Words

Many English words were formed from combining multiple sources. For example, the Latin *habēre* means "to have," and the prefixes *in-* and *im-* mean a lack or prevention of something, as in *insufficient* and *imperfect.* Latin combined *in-* with *habēre* to form *inhibēre,* whose past participle was *inhibitus.* This is the origin of the English word *inhibit,* meaning to prevent from having. Hence by knowing the meanings of both the prefix and the root, one can decipher the word meaning. In Greek, the root *enkephalo-* refers to the brain. Many medical terms are based on this root, such as encephalitis and hydrocephalus. Understanding the prefix and suffix meanings (*-itis* means inflammation; *hydro-* means water) allows a person to deduce that encephalitis refers to brain inflammation and hydrocephalus refers to water (or other fluid) in the brain.

Review Video: Determining Word Meanings
Visit mometrix.com/academy and enter code: 894894

Review Video: Root Words in English
Visit mometrix.com/academy and enter code: 896380

Prefixes

While knowing prefix meanings helps ESL and beginning readers learn new words, other readers take for granted the meanings of known words. However, prefix knowledge will also benefit them for determining meanings or definitions of unfamiliar words. For example, native English speakers and readers familiar with recipes know what *preheat* means. Knowing that *pre-* means in advance can also inform them that *presume* means to assume in advance, that *prejudice* means advance judgment, and that this understanding can be applied to many other words beginning with *pre-.* Knowing that the prefix *dis-* indicates opposition informs the meanings of words like *disbar, disagree, disestablish,* and many more. Knowing *dys-* means bad, impaired, abnormal, or difficult informs *dyslogistic, dysfunctional, dysphagia,* and *dysplasia.*

Suffixes

In English, certain suffixes generally indicate both that a word is a noun, and that the noun represents a state of being or quality. For example, *-ness* is commonly used to change an adjective into its noun form, as with *happy* and *happiness, nice* and *niceness,* and so on. The suffix *–tion* is commonly used to transform a verb into its noun form, as with *converse* and *conversation or move* and *motion.* Thus, if readers are unfamiliar with the second form of a word, knowing the meaning of the transforming suffix can help them determine meaning.

Prefixes for Numbers

Prefix	Definition	Examples
bi-	two	bisect, biennial
mono-	one, single	monogamy, monologue
poly-	many	polymorphous, polygamous
semi-	half, partly	semicircle, semicolon
uni-	one	uniform, unity

Prefixes for Time, Direction, and Space

Prefix	Definition	Examples
a-	in, on, of, up, to	abed, afoot
ab-	from, away, off	abdicate, abjure
ad-	to, toward	advance, adventure
ante-	before, previous	antecedent, antedate
anti-	against, opposing	antipathy, antidote
cata-	down, away, thoroughly	catastrophe, cataclysm
circum-	around	circumspect, circumference
com-	with, together, very	commotion, complicate
contra-	against, opposing	contradict, contravene
de-	from	depart
dia-	through, across, apart	diameter, diagnose
dis-	away, off, down, not	dissent, disappear
epi-	upon	epilogue
ex-	out	extract, excerpt
hypo-	under, beneath	hypodermic, hypothesis
inter-	among, between	intercede, interrupt
intra-	within	intramural, intrastate
ob-	against, opposing	objection
per-	through	perceive, permit
peri-	around	periscope, perimeter
post-	after, following	postpone, postscript
pre-	before, previous	prevent, preclude
pro-	forward, in place of	propel, pronoun
retro-	back, backward	retrospect, retrograde
sub-	under, beneath	subjugate, substitute
super-	above, extra	supersede, supernumerary
trans-	across, beyond, over	transact, transport
ultra-	beyond, excessively	ultramodern, ultrasonic

Negative Prefixes

Prefix	Definition	Examples
a-	without, lacking	atheist, agnostic
in-	not, opposing	incapable, ineligible
non-	not	nonentity, nonsense
un-	not, reverse of	unhappy, unlock

EXTRA PREFIXES

Prefix	Definition	Examples
for-	away, off, from	forget, forswear
fore-	previous	foretell, forefathers
homo-	same, equal	homogenized, homonym
hyper-	excessive, over	hypercritical, hypertension
in-	in, into	intrude, invade
mal-	bad, poorly, not	malfunction, malpractice
mis-	bad, poorly, not	misspell, misfire
neo-	new	Neolithic, neoconservative
omni-	all, everywhere	omniscient, omnivore
ortho-	right, straight	orthogonal, orthodox
over-	above	overbearing, oversight
pan-	all, entire	panorama, pandemonium
para-	beside, beyond	parallel, paradox
re-	backward, again	revoke, recur
sym-	with, together	sympathy, symphony

Below is a list of common suffixes and their meanings:

ADJECTIVE SUFFIXES

Suffix	Definition	Examples
-able (-ible)	capable of being	toler*able*, ed*ible*
-esque	in the style of, like	picturesque, grotesque
-ful	filled with, marked by	thankful, zestful
-ific	make, cause	terrific, beatific
-ish	suggesting, like	churlish, childish
-less	lacking, without	hopeless, countless
-ous	marked by, given to	religious, riotous

Noun Suffixes

Suffix	Definition	Examples
-acy	state, condition	accuracy, privacy
-ance	act, condition, fact	acceptance, vigilance
-ard	one that does excessively	drunkard, sluggard
-ation	action, state, result	occupation, starvation
-dom	state, rank, condition	serfdom, wisdom
-er (-or)	office, action	teach*er*, elevat*or*, hon*or*
-ess	feminine	waitress, duchess
-hood	state, condition	manhood, statehood
-ion	action, result, state	union, fusion
-ism	act, manner, doctrine	barbarism, socialism
-ist	worker, follower	monopolist, socialist
-ity (-ty)	state, quality, condition	acid*ity*, civil*ity*, twen*ty*
-ment	result, action	Refreshment
-ness	quality, state	greatness, tallness
-ship	position	internship, statesmanship
-sion (-tion)	state, result	revi*sion*, expedi*tion*
-th	act, state, quality	warmth, width
-tude	quality, state, result	magnitude, fortitude

Verb Suffixes

Suffix	Definition	Examples
-ate	having, showing	separate, desolate
-en	cause to be, become	deepen, strengthen
-fy	make, cause to have	glorify, fortify
-ize	cause to be, treat with	sterilize, mechanize

Denotative vs. Connotative Meaning

The **denotative** meaning of a word is the literal meaning. The **connotative** meaning goes beyond the denotative meaning to include the emotional reaction that a word may invoke. The connotative meaning often takes the denotative meaning a step further due to associations the reader makes with the denotative meaning. Readers can differentiate between the denotative and connotative meanings by first recognizing how authors use each meaning. Most non-fiction, for example, is fact-based and authors do not use flowery, figurative language. The reader can assume that the writer is using the denotative meaning of words. In fiction, the author may use the connotative meaning. Readers can determine whether the author is using the denotative or connotative meaning of a word by implementing context clues.

Review Video: Connotation and Denotation
Visit mometrix.com/academy and enter code: 310092

Nuances of Word Meaning Relative to Connotation, Denotation, Diction, and Usage

A word's denotation is simply its objective dictionary definition. However, its connotation refers to the subjective associations, often emotional, that specific words evoke in listeners and readers. Two or more words can have the same dictionary meaning, but very different connotations. Writers use diction (word choice) to convey various nuances of thought and emotion by selecting synonyms for other words that best communicate the associations they want to trigger for readers. For example, a car engine is naturally greasy; in this sense, "greasy" is a neutral term. But when a person's smile, appearance, or clothing is described as "greasy," it has a negative connotation. Some words have even gained additional or different meanings over time. For example, *awful* used to be used to describe things that evoked a sense of awe. When *awful* is separated into its root word, awe, and suffix, -ful, it can be understood to mean "full of awe." However, the word is now commonly used to describe things that evoke repulsion, terror, or another intense, negative reaction.

Review Video: Word Usage in Sentences
Visit mometrix.com/academy and enter code: 197863

Context Clues

Readers of all levels will encounter words that they have either never seen or have encountered only on a limited basis. The best way to define a word in **context** is to look for nearby words that can assist in revealing the meaning of the word. For instance, unfamiliar nouns are often accompanied by examples that provide a definition. Consider the following sentence: *Dave arrived at the party in hilarious garb: a leopard-print shirt, buckskin trousers, and bright green sneakers.* If a reader was unfamiliar with the meaning of garb, he or she could read the examples (i.e., a leopard-print shirt, buckskin trousers, and high heels) and quickly determine that the word means *clothing*. Examples will not always be this obvious. Consider this sentence: *Parsley, lemon, and flowers were just a few of the items he used as garnishes.* Here, the word *garnishes* is exemplified by parsley, lemon, and flowers. Readers who have eaten in a variety of restaurants will probably be able to identify a garnish as something used to decorate a plate.

Review Video: Context Clues
Visit mometrix.com/academy and enter code: 613660

Using Contrast in Context Clues

In addition to looking at the context of a passage, readers can use contrast to define an unfamiliar word in context. In many sentences, the author will not describe the unfamiliar word directly; instead, he or she will describe the opposite of the unfamiliar word. Thus, you are provided with some information that will bring you closer to defining the word. Consider the following example: *Despite his intelligence, Hector's low brow and bad posture made him look obtuse.* The author writes that Hector's appearance does not convey intelligence. Therefore, *obtuse* must mean unintelligent. Here is another example: *Despite the horrible weather, we were beatific about our trip to Alaska*. The word *despite* indicates that the speaker's feelings were at odds with the weather. Since the weather is described as *horrible*, then *beatific* must mean something positive.

Substitution to Find Meaning

In some cases, there will be very few contextual clues to help a reader define the meaning of an unfamiliar word. When this happens, one strategy that readers may employ is **substitution**. A good reader will brainstorm some possible synonyms for the given word, and he or she will substitute these words into the sentence. If the sentence and the surrounding passage continue to make sense, then the substitution has revealed at least some information about the unfamiliar word. Consider the sentence: *Frank's admonition rang in her ears as she climbed the mountain.* A reader unfamiliar with *admonition* might come up with some substitutions like *vow, promise, advice, complaint*, or *compliment*. All of these words make general sense of the sentence, though their meanings are diverse. However, this process has suggested that an admonition is some sort of message. The substitution strategy is rarely able to pinpoint a precise definition, but this process can be effective as a last resort.

Occasionally, you will be able to define an unfamiliar word by looking at the descriptive words in the context. Consider the following sentence: *Fred dragged the recalcitrant boy kicking and screaming up the stairs.* The words *dragged*, *kicking*, and *screaming* all suggest that the boy does not want to go up the stairs. The reader may assume that *recalcitrant* means something like unwilling or protesting. In this example, an unfamiliar adjective was identified.

Additionally, using description to define an unfamiliar noun is a common practice compared to unfamiliar adjectives, as in this sentence: *Don's wrinkled frown and constantly shaking fist identified him as a curmudgeon of the first order.* Don is described as having a *wrinkled frown and constantly shaking fist*, suggesting that a *curmudgeon* must be a grumpy person. Contrasts do not always provide detailed information about the unfamiliar word, but they at least give the reader some clues.

Words with Multiple Meanings

When a word has more than one meaning, readers can have difficulty determining how the word is being used in a given sentence. For instance, the verb *cleave*, can mean either *join* or *separate*. When readers come upon this word, they will have to select the definition that makes the most sense. Consider the following sentence: *Hermione's knife cleaved the bread cleanly.* Since a knife cannot join bread together, the word must indicate separation. A slightly more difficult example would be the sentence: *The birds cleaved to one another as they flew from the oak tree.* Immediately, the presence of the words *to one another* should suggest that in this sentence *cleave* is being used to mean *join*. Discovering the intent of a word with multiple meanings requires the same tricks as defining an unknown word: look for contextual clues and evaluate the substituted words.

Context Clues to Help Determine Meanings of Words

If readers simply bypass unknown words, they can reach unclear conclusions about what they read. However, looking for the definition of every unfamiliar word in the dictionary can slow their reading progress. Moreover, the dictionary may list multiple definitions for a word, so readers must search the word's context for meaning. Hence context is important to new vocabulary regardless of reader methods. Four types of context clues are examples, definitions, descriptive words, and opposites. Authors may use a certain word, and then follow it with several different examples of what it describes. Sometimes authors actually supply a definition of a word they use, which is especially true in informational and technical texts. Authors may use descriptive words that elaborate upon a vocabulary word they just used. Authors may also use opposites with negation that help define meaning.

Examples and Definitions

An author may use a word and then give examples that illustrate its meaning. Consider this text: "Teachers who do not know how to use sign language can help students who are deaf or hard of hearing understand certain instructions by using gestures instead, like pointing their fingers to indicate which direction to look or go; holding up a hand, palm outward, to indicate stopping; holding the hands flat, palms up, curling a finger toward oneself in a beckoning motion to indicate 'come here'; or curling all fingers toward oneself repeatedly to indicate 'come on', 'more', or 'continue.'" The author of this text has used the word "gestures" and then followed it with examples, so a reader unfamiliar with the word could deduce from the examples that "gestures" means "hand motions." Readers can find examples by looking for signal words "for example," "for instance," "like," "such as," and "e.g."

While readers sometimes have to look for definitions of unfamiliar words in a dictionary or do some work to determine a word's meaning from its surrounding context, at other times an author may make it easier for readers by defining certain words. For example, an author may write, "The company did not have sufficient capital, that is, available money, to continue operations." The author defined "capital" as "available money," and heralded the definition with the phrase "that is." Another way that authors supply word definitions is with appositives. Rather than being introduced by a signal phrase like "that is," "namely," or "meaning," an appositive comes after the vocabulary word it defines and is enclosed within two commas. For example, an author may write, "The Indians introduced the Pilgrims to pemmican, cakes they made of lean meat dried and mixed with fat, which proved greatly beneficial to keep settlers from starving while trapping." In this example, the appositive phrase following "pemmican" and preceding "which" defines the word "pemmican."

Descriptions

When readers encounter a word they do not recognize in a text, the author may expand on that word to illustrate it better. While the author may do this to make the prose more picturesque and vivid, the reader can also take advantage of this description to provide context clues to the meaning of the unfamiliar word. For example, an author may write, "The man sitting next to me on the airplane was obese. His shirt stretched across his vast expanse of flesh, strained almost to bursting." The descriptive second sentence elaborates on and helps to define the previous sentence's word "obese" to mean extremely fat. A reader unfamiliar with the word "repugnant" can decipher its meaning through an author's accompanying description: "The way the child grimaced and shuddered as he swallowed the medicine showed that its taste was particularly repugnant."

Opposites

Text authors sometimes introduce a contrasting or opposing idea before or after a concept they present. They may do this to emphasize or heighten the idea they present by contrasting it with something that is the reverse. However, readers can also use these context clues to understand familiar words. For example, an author may write, "Our conversation was not cheery. We sat and talked very solemnly about his experience and a number of similar events." The reader who is not familiar with the word "solemnly" can deduce by the author's preceding use of "not cheery" that "solemn" means the opposite of cheery or happy, so it must mean serious or sad. Or if someone writes, "Don't condemn his entire project because you couldn't find anything good to say about it," readers unfamiliar with "condemn" can understand from the sentence structure that it means the opposite of saying anything good, so it must mean reject, dismiss, or disapprove. "Entire" adds another context clue, meaning total or complete rejection.

Syntax to Determine Part of Speech and Meanings of Words

Syntax refers to sentence structure and word order. Suppose that a reader encounters an unfamiliar word when reading a text. To illustrate, consider an invented word like "splunch." If this word is used in a sentence like "Please splunch that ball to me," the reader can assume from syntactic context that "splunch" is a verb. We would not use a noun, adjective, adverb, or preposition with the object "that ball," and the prepositional phrase "to me" further indicates "splunch" represents an action. However, in the sentence, "Please hand that splunch to me," the reader can assume that "splunch" is a noun. Demonstrative adjectives like "that" modify nouns. Also, we hand someone some*thing*—a thing being a noun; we do not hand someone a verb, adjective, or adverb. Some sentences contain further clues. For example, from the sentence, "The princess wore the glittering splunch on her head," the reader can deduce that it is a crown, tiara, or something similar from the syntactic context, without knowing the word.

Syntax to Indicate Different Meanings of Similar Sentences

The syntax, or structure, of a sentence affords grammatical cues that aid readers in comprehending the meanings of words, phrases, and sentences in the texts that they read. Seemingly minor differences in how the words or phrases in a sentence are ordered can make major differences in meaning. For example, two sentences can use exactly the same words but have different meanings based on the word order:

- "The man with a broken arm sat in a chair."
- "The man sat in a chair with a broken arm."

While both sentences indicate that a man sat in a chair, differing syntax indicates whether the man's or chair's arm was broken.

Determining Meaning of Phrases and Paragraphs

Like unknown words, the meanings of phrases, paragraphs, and entire works can also be difficult to discern. Each of these can be better understood with added context. However, for larger groups of words, more context is needed. Unclear phrases are similar to unclear words, and the same methods can be used to understand their meaning. However, it is also important to consider how the individual words in the phrase work together. Paragraphs are a bit more complicated. Just as words must be compared to other words in a sentence, paragraphs must be compared to other paragraphs in a composition or a section.

Determining Meaning in Various Types of Compositions

To understand the meaning of an entire composition, the type of composition must be considered. **Expository writing** is generally organized so that each paragraph focuses on explaining one idea, or part of an idea, and its relevance. **Persuasive writing** uses paragraphs for different purposes to organize the parts of the argument. **Unclear paragraphs** must be read in the context of the paragraphs around them for their meaning to be fully understood. The meaning of full texts can also be unclear at times. The purpose of composition is also important for understanding the meaning of a text. To quickly understand the broad meaning of a text, look to the introductory and concluding paragraphs. Fictional texts are different. Some fictional works have implicit meanings, but some do not. The target audience must be considered for understanding texts that do have an implicit meaning, as most children's fiction will clearly state any lessons or morals. For other fiction, the application of literary theories and criticism may be helpful for understanding the text.

Additional Resources for Determining Word Meaning and Usage

While these strategies are useful for determining the meaning of unknown words and phrases, sometimes additional resources are needed to properly use the terms in different contexts. Some words have multiple definitions, and some words are inappropriate in particular contexts or modes of writing. The following tools are helpful for understanding all meanings and proper uses for words and phrases.

- **Dictionaries** provide the meaning of a multitude of words in a language. Many dictionaries include additional information about each word, such as its etymology, its synonyms, or variations of the word.
- **Glossaries** are similar to dictionaries, as they provide the meanings of a variety of terms. However, while dictionaries typically feature an extensive list of words and comprise an entire publication, glossaries are often included at the end of a text and only include terms and definitions that are relevant to the text they follow.

- **Spell Checkers** are used to detect spelling errors in typed text. Some spell checkers may also detect the misuse of plural or singular nouns, verb tenses, or capitalization. While spell checkers are a helpful tool, they are not always reliable or attuned to the author's intent, so it is important to review the spell checker's suggestions before accepting them.
- **Style Manuals** are guidelines on the preferred punctuation, format, and grammar usage according to different fields or organizations. For example, the Associated Press Stylebook is a style guide often used for media writing. The guidelines within a style guide are not always applicable across different contexts and usages, as the guidelines often cover grammatical or formatting situations that are not objectively correct or incorrect.

Chapter Quiz

1. Which of the following affixes refers to the *-o-* in "speedometer"?

a. Prefix
b. Suffix
c. Interfix
d. Circumfix

2. Adding the suffix *-ness* to a word typically does which of the following?

a. Changes a verb to a noun
b. Changes a verb to an adjective
c. Changes an adjective to a noun
d. Changes a noun to a verb

3. Which of the following is NOT considered a common adjective suffix?

a. *-acy*
b. *-able*
c. *-ish*
d. *-less*

4. Which of the following defines the noun suffix *-ation*?

a. Act, condition, fact
b. Action, state, result
c. Quality, state, result
d. State, rank, condition

Chapter Quiz Answer Key

1. C: Prefixes are affixes placed in front of words. For example, *heat* means to make hot, while *preheat* means to heat in advance. Suffixes are affixes placed at the ends of words. The *happiness* example above contains the suffix *-ness.* Circumfixes add parts both before and after words, such as how *light* becomes *enlighten* with the prefix *en-* and the suffix *-en.* Interfixes create compound words via central affixes: *speed* and *meter* become *speedometer* via the interfix *-o-*.

2. C: In English, certain suffixes generally indicate both that a word is a noun, and that the noun represents a state of being or quality. For example, *-ness* is commonly used to change an adjective into its noun form, as with *happy* and *happiness, kind* and *kindness,* and so on.

3. A: Adjective suffixes:

Suffix	Definition	Examples
-able (-ible)	capable of being	tolerable, edible
-esque	in the style of, like	picturesque, grotesque
-ful	filled with, marked by	thankful, zestful
-ific	make, cause	terrific, beatific
-ish	suggesting, like	churlish, childish
-less	lacking, without	hopeless, countless
-ous	marked by, given to	religious, riotous

4. B: Noun suffixes:

Suffix	Definition	Examples
-acy	state, condition	accuracy, privacy
-ance	act, condition, fact	acceptance, vigilance
-ard	one that does excessively	drunkard, sluggard
-ation	action, state, result	occupation, starvation
-dom	state, rank, condition	serfdom, wisdom
-er (-or)	office, action	teacher, elevator, honor
-ess	feminine	waitress, duchess
-hood	state, condition	manhood, statehood
-ion	action, result, state	union, fusion
-ism	act, manner, doctrine	barbarism, socialism
-ist	worker, follower	monopolist, socialist
-ity (-ty)	state, quality, condition	acidity, civility, twenty
-ment	result, action	refreshment
-ness	quality, state	greatness, tallness
-ship	position	internship, statesmanship
-sion (-tion)	state, result	revision, expedition
-th	act, state, quality	warmth, width
-tude	quality, state, result	magnitude, fortitude

Figurative Language

Literal and Figurative Meaning

When language is used **literally**, the words mean exactly what they say and nothing more. When language is used **figuratively**, the words mean something beyond their literal meaning. For example, "The weeping willow tree has long, trailing branches and leaves" is a literal description. But "The weeping willow tree looks as if it is bending over and crying" is a figurative description—specifically, a **simile** or stated comparison. Another figurative language form is **metaphor**, or an implied comparison. A good example is the metaphor of a city, state, or city-state as a ship, and its governance as sailing that ship. Ancient Greek lyrical poet Alcaeus is credited with first using this metaphor, and ancient Greek tragedian Aeschylus then used it in *Seven Against Thebes,* and then Plato used it in the *Republic.*

Figures of Speech

A **figure of speech** is a verbal expression whose meaning is figurative rather than literal. For example, the phrase "butterflies in the stomach" does not refer to actual butterflies in a person's stomach. It is a metaphor representing the fluttery feelings experienced when a person is nervous or excited—or when one "falls in love," which does not mean physically falling. "Hitting a sales target" does not mean physically hitting a target with arrows as in archery; it is a metaphor for meeting a sales quota. "Climbing the ladder of success" metaphorically likens advancing in one's career to ascending ladder rungs. Similes, such as "light as a feather" (meaning very light, not a feather's actual weight), and hyperbole, like "I'm starving/freezing/roasting," are also figures of speech. Figures of speech are often used and crafted for emphasis, freshness of expression, or clarity.

Review Video: Figures of Speech
Visit mometrix.com/academy and enter code: 111295

Figurative Language

Figurative language extends past the literal meanings of words. It offers readers new insight into the people, things, events, and subjects covered in a work of literature. Figurative language also enables readers to feel they are sharing the authors' experiences. It can stimulate the reader's senses, make comparisons that readers find intriguing or even startling, and enable readers to view the world in different ways. When looking for figurative language, it is important to consider the context of the sentence or situation. Phrases that appear out of place or make little sense when read literally are likely instances of figurative language. Once figurative language has been recognized, context is also important to determining the type of figurative language being used and its function. For example, when a comparison is being made, a metaphor or simile is likely being used. This means the comparison may emphasize or create irony through the things being compared. Seven specific types of figurative language include: alliteration, onomatopoeia, personification, imagery, similes, metaphors, and hyperbole.

Review Video: Figurative Language
Visit mometrix.com/academy and enter code: 584902

Alliteration and Onomatopoeia

Alliteration describes a series of words beginning with the same sounds. **Onomatopoeia** uses words imitating the sounds of things they name or describe. For example, in his poem "Come Down, O Maid," Alfred Tennyson writes of "The moan of doves in immemorial elms, / And murmuring of innumerable bees." The word "moan" sounds like some sounds doves make, "murmuring" represents the sounds of bees buzzing. Onomatopoeia also includes words that are simply meant to represent sounds, such as "meow," "kaboom," and "whoosh."

Review Video: Alliterations Are All Around
Visit mometrix.com/academy and enter code: 462837

PERSONIFICATION

Another type of figurative language is **personification**. This is describing a non-human thing, like an animal or an object, as if it were human. The general intent of personification is to describe things in a manner that will be comprehensible to readers. When an author states that a tree *groans* in the wind, he or she does not mean that the tree is emitting a low, pained sound from a mouth. Instead, the author means that the tree is making a noise similar to a human groan. Of course, this personification establishes a tone of sadness or suffering. A different tone would be established if the author said that the tree was *swaying* or *dancing*. Alfred Tennyson's poem "The Eagle" uses all of these types of figurative language: "He clasps the crag with crooked hands." Tennyson used alliteration, repeating /k/ and /kr/ sounds. These hard-sounding consonants reinforce the imagery, giving visual and tactile impressions of the eagle.

Review Video: Personification
Visit mometrix.com/academy and enter code: 260066

SIMILES AND METAPHORS

Similes are stated comparisons using "like" or "as." Similes can be used to stimulate readers' imaginations and appeal to their senses. Because a simile includes *like* or *as,* the device creates more space between the description and the thing being described than a metaphor does. If an author says that *a house was like a shoebox*, then the tone is different than the author saying that the house *was* a shoebox. Authors will choose between a metaphor and a simile depending on their intended tone.

Similes also help compare fictional characters to well-known objects or experiences, so the reader can better relate to them. William Wordsworth's poem about "Daffodils" begins, "I wandered lonely as a cloud." This simile compares his loneliness to that of a cloud. It is also personification, giving a cloud the human quality loneliness. In his novel *Lord Jim* (1900), Joseph Conrad writes in Chapter 33, "I would have given anything for the power to soothe her frail soul, tormenting itself in its invincible ignorance like a small bird beating about the cruel wires of a cage." Conrad uses the word "like" to compare the girl's soul to a small bird. His description of the bird beating at the cage shows the similar helplessness of the girl's soul to gain freedom.

Review Video: Similes
Visit mometrix.com/academy and enter code: 642949

A **metaphor** is a type of figurative language in which the writer equates something with another thing that is not particularly similar, instead of using *like* or *as*. For instance, *the bird was an arrow arcing through the sky*. In this sentence, the arrow is serving as a metaphor for the bird. The point of a metaphor is to encourage the reader to consider the item being described in a *different way*. Let's continue with this metaphor for a flying bird. You are asked to envision the bird's flight as being similar to the arc of an arrow. So, you imagine the flight to be swift and bending. Metaphors are a way for the author to describe an item *without being direct and obvious*. This literary device is a lyrical and suggestive way of providing information. Note that the reference for a metaphor will not always be mentioned explicitly by the author. Consider the following description of a forest in winter: *Swaying skeletons reached for the sky and groaned as the wind blew through them.* In this example, the author is using *skeletons* as a metaphor for leafless trees. This metaphor creates a spooky tone while inspiring the reader's imagination.

LITERARY EXAMPLES OF METAPHOR

A **metaphor** is an implied comparison, i.e., it compares something to something else without using "like", "as", or other comparative words. For example, in "The Tyger" (1794), William Blake writes, "Tyger Tyger, burning bright, / In the forests of the night." Blake compares the tiger to a flame not by saying it is like a fire, but by simply describing it as "burning." Henry Wadsworth Longfellow's poem "O Ship of State" (1850) uses an extended metaphor by referring consistently throughout the entire poem to the state, union, or republic as a seagoing vessel, referring to its keel, mast, sail, rope, anchors, and to its braving waves, rocks, gale, tempest, and "false lights on the shore." Within the extended metaphor, Wordsworth uses a specific metaphor: "the anchors of thy hope!"

TED HUGHES' ANIMAL METAPHORS

Ted Hughes frequently used animal metaphors in his poetry. In "The Thought Fox," a model of concise, structured beauty, Hughes characterizes the poet's creative process with succinct, striking imagery of an idea entering his head like a wild fox. Repeating "loneliness" in the first two stanzas emphasizes the poet's lonely work: "Something else is alive / Beside the clock's loneliness." He treats an idea's arrival as separate from himself. Three stanzas detail in vivid images a fox's approach from the outside winter forest at starless midnight—its nose, "Cold, delicately" touching twigs and leaves; "neat" paw prints in snow; "bold" body; brilliant green eyes; and self-contained, focused progress—"Till, with a sudden sharp hot stink of fox," he metaphorically depicts poetic inspiration as the fox's physical entry into "the dark hole of the head." Hughes ends by summarizing his vision of a poet as an interior, passive idea recipient, with the outside world unchanged: "The window is starless still; the clock ticks, / The page is printed."

Review Video: Metaphors in Writing
Visit mometrix.com/academy and enter code: 133295

HYPERBOLE

Hyperbole is excessive exaggeration used for humor or emphasis rather than for literal meaning. For example, in *To Kill a Mockingbird*, Harper Lee wrote, "People moved slowly then. There was no hurry, for there was nowhere to go, nothing to buy and no money to buy it with, nothing to see outside the boundaries of Maycomb County." This was not literally true; Lee exaggerates the scarcity of these things for emphasis. In "Old Times on the Mississippi," Mark Twain wrote, "I... could have hung my hat on my eyes, they stuck out so far." This is not literal, but makes his description vivid and funny. In his poem "As I Walked Out One Evening", W. H. Auden wrote, "I'll love you, dear, I'll love you / Till China and Africa meet, / And the river jumps over the mountain / And the salmon sing in the street." He used things not literally possible to emphasize the duration of his love.

Review Video: Hyperbole and Understatement
Visit mometrix.com/academy and enter code: 308470

LITERARY IRONY

In literature, irony demonstrates the opposite of what is said or done. The three types of irony are **verbal irony**, **situational irony**, and **dramatic irony**. Verbal irony uses words opposite to the meaning. Sarcasm may use verbal irony. One common example is describing something that is confusing as "clear as mud." For example, in his 1986 movie *Hannah and Her Sisters,* author, director, and actor Woody Allen says to his character's date, "I had a great evening; it was like the Nuremburg Trials." Notice these employ similes. In situational irony, what happens contrasts with what was expected. O. Henry's short story *The Gift of the Magi* uses situational irony: a husband and wife each sacrifice their most prized possession to buy each other a Christmas present. The irony is that she sells her long hair to buy him a watch fob, while he sells his heirloom pocket-watch to buy her the jeweled combs for her hair she had long wanted; in the end, neither of them can use their gifts. In dramatic irony, narrative informs audiences of more than its characters know. For example, in *Romeo and Juliet,* the audience is made aware that Juliet is only asleep, while Romeo believes her to be dead, which then leads to Romeo's death.

Review Video: What is the Definition of Irony?
Visit mometrix.com/academy and enter code: 374204

Idioms

Idioms create comparisons, and often take the form of similes or metaphors. Idioms are always phrases and are understood to have a meaning that is different from its individual words' literal meaning. For example, "break a leg" is a common idiom that is used to wish someone luck or tell them to perform well. Literally, the phrase "break a leg" means to injure a person's leg, but the phrase takes on a different meaning when used as an idiom. Another example is "call it a day," which means to temporarily stop working on a task, or find a stopping point, rather than literally referring to something as "a day." Many idioms are associated with a region or group. For example, an idiom commonly used in the American South is "'til the cows come home." This phrase is often used to indicate that something will take or may last for a very long time, but not that it will literally last until the cows return to where they reside.

Chapter Quiz

1. Who is credited with first using the metaphor of a city, state, or city-state as a ship?

a. Theseus
b. Aeschylus
c. Alcaeus
d. Plato

2. How many forms of irony are there?

a. Two
b. Three
c. Four
d. Five

Chapter Quiz Answer Key

1. C: Another figurative language form is metaphor, or an implied comparison. A good example is the metaphor of a city, state, or city-state as a ship, and its governance as sailing that ship. Ancient Greek lyrical poet Alcaeus is credited with first using this metaphor, followed by ancient Greek tragedian Aeschylus using it in *Seven Against Thebes,* and then Plato using it in the *Republic.*

2. B: In literature, irony demonstrates the opposite of what is said or done. The three types of irony are verbal irony, situational irony, and dramatic irony. Verbal irony uses words opposite to the meaning. Sarcasm may use verbal irony. One common example is describing something that is confusing as "clear as mud." In his 1986 movie *Hannah and Her Sisters,* author, director, and actor Woody Allen says to his character's date, "I had a great evening; it was like the Nuremburg Trials." Notice these employ similes. In situational irony, what happens contrasts with what was expected. O. Henry's short story *The Gift of the Magi* uses situational irony: a husband and wife each sacrifice their most prized possession to buy each other a Christmas present. The irony is that she sells her long hair to buy him a watch fob, while he sells his heirloom pocket-watch to buy her the jeweled combs for her hair she had long wanted; in the end, neither of them can use their gifts. In dramatic irony, narrative informs audiences of more than its characters know. For example, in *Romeo and Juliet,* the audience is made aware that Juliet is only asleep, while Romeo believes her to be dead, which then leads to Romeo's death.

Literary Elements

Literary Terminology

- In works of prose such as novels, a group of connected sentences covering one main topic is termed a **paragraph**.
- In works of poetry, a group of verses similarly connected is called a **stanza**.
- In drama, when early works used verse, these were also divided into stanzas or **couplets**.
- Drama evolved to use predominantly prose. Overall, whether prose or verse, the conversation in a play is called **dialogue**.
- Large sections of dialogue spoken by one actor are called **soliloquies** or **monologues**.
- Dialogue that informs audiences but is unheard by other characters is called an **aside**.
- Novels and plays share certain common elements, such as:
    - **Characters** - the people in the story.
    - **Plot** - the action of the story.
    - **Climax** - when action or dramatic tension reaches its highest point.
    - **Denouement** - the resolution following the climax.
- Sections dividing novels are called **chapters**, while sections of plays are called **acts**.
- Subsections of plays' acts are called **scenes**. Novel chapters usually do not have subsections. However, some novels do include groups of chapters that form different sections.

Literary Analysis

The best literary analysis shows special insight into at least one important aspect of a text. When analyzing literary texts, it can be difficult to find a starting place. Many texts can be analyzed several different ways, often leaving an overwhelming number of options for writers to consider. However, narrowing the focus to a particular element of literature can be helpful when preparing to analyze a text. Symbolism, themes, and motifs are common starting points for literary analysis. These three methods of analysis can lead to a holistic analysis of a text, since they involve elements that are often distributed throughout the text. However, not all texts feature these elements in a way that facilitates a strong analysis, if they are present at all. It is also common to focus on character or plot development for analysis. These elements are compatible with theme, symbolism, and allusion. Setting and imagery, figurative language, and any external contexts can also contribute to analysis or complement one of these other elements. The application of a critical, or literary, theory to a text can also provide a thorough and strong analysis.

Setting and Time Frame

A literary text has both a setting and time frame. A **setting** is the place in which the story as a whole is set. The **time frame** is the period in which the story is set. This may refer to the historical period the story takes place in or if the story takes place over a single day. Both setting and time frame are relevant to a text's meaning because they help the reader place the story in time and space. An author uses setting and time frame to anchor a text, create a mood, and enhance its meaning. This helps a reader understand why a character acts the way he does, or why certain events in the story are important. The setting impacts the **plot** and character **motivations**, while the time frame helps place the story in **chronological context**.

EXAMPLE

Read the following excerpt from The Adventures of Huckleberry Finn by Mark Twain and analyze the relevance of setting to the text's meaning:

> We said there warn't no home like a raft, after all. Other places do seem so cramped up and smothery, but a raft don't. You feel mighty free and easy and comfortable on a raft.

This excerpt from *The Adventures of Huckleberry Finn* by Mark Twain reveals information about the **setting** of the book. By understanding that the main character, Huckleberry Finn, lives on a raft, the reader can place the story on a river, in this case, the Mississippi River in the South before the Civil War. The information about the setting also gives the reader clues about the **character** of Huck Finn: he clearly values independence and freedom, and he likes the outdoors. The information about the setting in the quote helps the reader to better understand the rest of the text.

THEME

The **theme** of a passage is what the reader learns from the text or the passage. It is the lesson or **moral** contained in the passage. It also is a unifying idea that is used throughout the text; it can take the form of a common setting, idea, symbol, design, or recurring event. A passage can have two or more themes that convey its overall idea. The theme or themes of a passage are often based on **universal themes**. They can frequently be expressed using well-known sayings about life, society, or human nature, such as "Hard work pays off" or "Good triumphs over evil." Themes are not usually stated **explicitly**. The reader must figure them out by carefully reading the passage. Themes are often the reason why passages are written; they give a passage unity and meaning. Themes are created through **plot development**. The events of a story help shape the themes of a passage.

EXAMPLE

Explain why "Take care of what you care about" accurately describes the theme of the following excerpt.

> Luca collected baseball cards, but he wasn't very careful with them. He left them around the house. His dog liked to chew. One day, Luca and his friend Bart were looking at his collection. Then they went outside. When Luca got home, he saw his dog chewing on his cards. They were ruined.

This excerpt tells the story of a boy who is careless with his baseball cards and leaves them lying around. His dog ends up chewing them and ruining them. The lesson is that if you care about something, you need to take care of it. This is the theme, or point, of the story. Some stories have more than one theme, but this is not really true of this excerpt. The reader needs to figure out the theme based on what happens in the story. Sometimes, as in the case of fables, the theme is stated directly in the text. However, this is not usually the case.

Review Video: Themes in Literature
Visit mometrix.com/academy and enter code: 732074

PLOT AND STORY STRUCTURE

The **plot** includes the events that happen in a story and the order in which they are told to the reader. There are several types of plot structures, as stories can be told in many ways. The most common plot structure is the chronological plot, which presents the events to the reader in the same order they occur for the characters in the story. Chronological plots usually have five main parts, the **exposition**, **rising action**, the **climax**, **falling action**, and the **resolution**. This type of plot structure guides the reader through the story's events as the characters experience them and is the easiest structure to understand and identify. While this is the most common plot structure, many stories are nonlinear, which means the plot does not sequence events in the same order the characters experience them. Such stories might include elements like flashbacks that cause the story to be nonlinear.

Review Video: How to Make a Story Map
Visit mometrix.com/academy and enter code: 261719

Exposition

The **exposition** is at the beginning of the story and generally takes place before the rising action begins. The purpose of the exposition is to give the reader context for the story, which the author may do by introducing one or more characters, describing the setting or world, or explaining the events leading up to the point where the story begins. The exposition may still include events that contribute to the plot, but the **rising action** and main conflict of the story are not part of the exposition. Some narratives skip the exposition and begin the story with the beginning of the rising action, which causes the reader to learn the context as the story intensifies.

Conflict

A **conflict** is a problem to be solved. Literary plots typically include one conflict or more. Characters' attempts to resolve conflicts drive the narrative's forward movement. **Conflict resolution** is often the protagonist's primary occupation. Physical conflicts like exploring, wars, and escapes tend to make plots most suspenseful and exciting. Emotional, mental, or moral conflicts tend to make stories more personally gratifying or rewarding for many audiences. Conflicts can be external or internal. A major type of internal conflict is some inner personal battle, or **man versus self**. Major types of external conflicts include **man versus nature**, **man versus man**, and **man versus society**. Readers can identify conflicts in literary plots by identifying the protagonist and antagonist and asking why they conflict, what events develop the conflict, where the climax occurs, and how they identify with the characters.

Read the following paragraph and discuss the type of conflict present:

> Timothy was shocked out of sleep by the appearance of a bear just outside his tent. After panicking for a moment, he remembered some advice he had read in preparation for this trip: he should make noise so the bear would not be startled. As Timothy started to hum and sing, the bear wandered away.

There are three main types of conflict in literature: **man versus man**, **man versus nature**, and **man versus self**. This paragraph is an example of man versus nature. Timothy is in conflict with the bear. Even though no physical conflict like an attack exists, Timothy is pitted against the bear. Timothy uses his knowledge to "defeat" the bear and keep himself safe. The solution to the conflict is that Timothy makes noise, the bear wanders away, and Timothy is safe.

Review Video: Conflict
Visit mometrix.com/academy and enter code: 559550

Review Video: Determining Relationships in a Story
Visit mometrix.com/academy and enter code: 929925

Rising Action

The **rising action** is the part of the story where conflict **intensifies**. The rising action begins with an event that prompts the main conflict of the story. This may also be called the **inciting incident**. The main conflict generally occurs between the protagonist and an antagonist, but this is not the only type of conflict that may occur in a narrative. After this event, the protagonist works to resolve the main conflict by preparing for an altercation, pursuing a goal, fleeing an antagonist, or doing some other action that will end the conflict. The rising action is composed of several additional events that increase the story's tension. Most often, other developments will occur alongside the growth of the main conflict, such as character development or the development of minor conflicts. The rising action ends with the **climax**, which is the point of highest tension in the story.

Climax

The **climax** is the event in the narrative that marks the height of the story's conflict or tension. The event that takes place at the story's climax will end the rising action and bring about the results of the main conflict. If the conflict was between a good protagonist and an evil antagonist, the climax may be a final battle between the two characters. If the conflict is an adventurer looking for heavily guarded treasure, the climax may be the adventurer's encounter with the final obstacle that protects the treasure. The climax may be made of multiple scenes, but can usually be summarized as one event. Once the conflict and climax are complete, the **falling action** begins.

Falling Action

The **falling action** shows what happens in the story between the climax and the resolution. The falling action often composes a much smaller portion of the story than the rising action does. While the climax includes the end of the main conflict, the falling action may show the results of any minor conflicts in the story. For example, if the protagonist encountered a troll on the way to find some treasure, and the troll demanded the protagonist share the treasure after retrieving it, the falling action would include the protagonist returning to share the treasure with the troll. Similarly, any unexplained major events are usually made clear during the falling action. Once all significant elements of the story are resolved or addressed, the story's resolution will occur. The **resolution** is the end of the story, which shows the final result of the plot's events and shows what life is like for the main characters once they are no longer experiencing the story's conflicts.

Resolution

The way the conflict is **resolved** depends on the type of conflict. The plot of any book starts with the lead up to the conflict, then the conflict itself, and finally the solution, or **resolution**, to the conflict. In **man versus man** conflicts, the conflict is often resolved by two parties coming to some sort of agreement or by one party triumphing over the other party. In **man versus nature** conflicts, the conflict is often resolved by man coming to some realization about some aspect of nature. In **man versus self** conflicts, the conflict is often resolved by the character growing or coming to an understanding about part of himself.

Syntax and Word Choice

Authors use words and **syntax**, or sentence structure, to make their texts unique, convey their own writing style, and sometimes to make a point or emphasis. They know that word choice and syntax contribute to the reader's understanding of the text as well as to the tone and mood of a text.

Review Video: What is Syntax?
Visit mometrix.com/academy and enter code: 242280

Allusion

An allusion is an uncited but recognizable reference to something else. Authors use language to make allusions to places, events, artwork, and other books in order to make their own text richer. For example, an author may allude to a very important text in order to make his own text seem more important. Martin Luther King, Jr. started his "I Have a Dream" speech by saying "Five score years ago..." This is a clear allusion to President Abraham Lincoln's "Gettysburg Address" and served to remind people of the significance of the event. An author may allude to a place to ground his text or make a cultural reference to make readers feel included. There are many reasons that authors make allusions.

> **Review Video: Allusions**
> Visit mometrix.com/academy and enter code: 294065

Comic Relief

Comic relief is the use of comedy by an author to break up a dramatic or tragic scene and infuse it with a bit of **lightheartedness**. In William Shakespeare's *Hamlet*, two gravediggers digging the grave for Ophelia share a joke while they work. The death and burial of Ophelia are tragic moments that directly follow each other. Shakespeare uses an instance of comedy to break up the tragedy and give his audience a bit of a break from the tragic drama. Authors sometimes use comic relief so that their work will be less depressing; other times they use it to create irony or contrast between the darkness of the situation and the lightness of the joke. Often, authors will use comedy to parallel what is happening in the tragic scenes.

> **Review Video: What is Comic Relief?**
> Visit mometrix.com/academy and enter code: 779604

Mood and Tone

Mood is a story's atmosphere, or the feelings the reader gets from reading it. The way authors set the mood in writing is comparable to the way filmmakers use music to set the mood in movies. Instead of music, though, writers judiciously select descriptive words to evoke certain **moods**. The mood of a work may convey joy, anger, bitterness, hope, gloom, fear, apprehension, or any other emotion the author wants the reader to feel. In addition to vocabulary choices, authors also use figurative expressions, particular sentence structures, and choices of diction that project and reinforce the moods they want to create. Whereas mood is the reader's emotions evoked by reading what is written, **tone** is the emotions and attitudes of the writer that she or he expresses in the writing. Authors use the same literary techniques to establish tone as they do to establish mood. An author may use a humorous tone, an angry or sad tone, a sentimental or unsentimental tone, or something else entirely.

Mood and Tone in The Great Gatsby

To understand the difference between mood and tone, look at this excerpt from F. Scott Fitzgerald's *The Great Gatsby*. In this passage, Nick Caraway, the novel's narrator, is describing his affordable house, which sits in a neighborhood full of expensive mansions.

> "I lived at West Egg, the—well the less fashionable of the two, though this is a most superficial tag to express the bizarre and not a little sinister contrast between them. My house was at the very tip of the egg, only fifty yard from the Sound, and squeezed between two huge places that rented for twelve or fifteen thousand a season ... My own house was an eyesore, but it was a small eyesore, and it had been overlooked, so I had a view of the water,

a partial view of my neighbor's lawn, and the consoling proximity of millionaires—all for eighty dollars a month."

In this description, the mood created for the reader does not match the tone created through the narrator. The mood in this passage is one of dissatisfaction and inferiority. Nick compares his home to his neighbors', saying he lives in the "less fashionable" neighborhood and that his house is "overlooked," an "eyesore," and "squeezed between two huge" mansions. He also adds that his placement allows him the "consoling proximity of millionaires." A literal reading of these details leads the reader to have negative feelings toward Nick's house and his economic inferiority to his neighbors, creating the mood.

However, Fitzgerald also conveys an opposing attitude, or tone, through Nick's description. Nick calls the distinction between the neighborhoods "superficial," showing a suspicion of the value suggested by the neighborhoods' titles, properties, and residents. Nick also undermines his critique of his own home by calling it "a small eyesore" and claiming it has "been overlooked." However, he follows these statements with a description of his surroundings, claiming that he has "a view of the water" and can see some of his wealthy neighbor's property from his home, and a comparison between the properties' rent. While the mental image created for the reader depicts a small house shoved between looming mansions, the tone suggests that Nick enjoys these qualities about his home, or at least finds it charming. He acknowledges its shortcomings, but includes the benefits of his home's unassuming appearance.

Review Video: <u>Style, Tone, and Mood</u>
Visit mometrix.com/academy and enter code: 416961

Character Development

When depicting characters or figures in a written text, authors generally use actions, dialogue, and descriptions as characterization techniques. Characterization can occur in both fiction and nonfiction and is used to show a character or figure's personality, demeanor, and thoughts. This helps create a more engaging experience for the reader by providing a more concrete picture of a character or figure's tendencies and features. Characterizations also gives authors the opportunity to integrate elements such as dialects, activities, attire, and attitudes into their writing.

To understand the meaning of a story, it is vital to understand the characters as the author describes them. We can look for contradictions in what a character thinks, says, and does. We can notice whether the author's observations about a character differ from what other characters in the story say about that character. A character may be dynamic, meaning they change significantly during the story, or static, meaning they remain the same from beginning to end. Characters may be two-dimensional, not fully developed, or may be well developed with characteristics that stand out vividly. Characters may also symbolize universal properties. Additionally, readers can compare and contrast characters to analyze how each one developed.

A well-known example of character development can be found in Charles Dickens's *Great Expectations*. The novel's main character, Pip, is introduced as a young boy, and he is depicted as innocent, kind, and humble. However, as Pip grows up and is confronted with the social hierarchy of Victorian England, he becomes arrogant and rejects his loved ones in pursuit of his own social advancement. Once he achieves his social goals, he realizes the merits of his former lifestyle, and lives with the wisdom he gained in both environments and life stages. Dickens shows Pip's ever-changing character through his interactions with others and his inner thoughts, which evolve as his personal values and personality shift.

Review Video: Character Changes
Visit mometrix.com/academy and enter code: 408719

Dialogue

Effectively written dialogue serves at least one, but usually several, purposes. It advances the story and moves the plot, develops the characters, sheds light on the work's theme or meaning, and can, often subtly, account for the passage of time not otherwise indicated. It can alter the direction that the plot is taking, typically by introducing some new conflict or changing existing ones. **Dialogue** can establish a work's narrative voice and the characters' voices and set the tone of the story or of particular characters. When fictional characters display enlightenment or realization, dialogue can give readers an understanding of what those characters have discovered and how. Dialogue can illuminate the motivations and wishes of the story's characters. By using consistent thoughts and syntax, dialogue can support character development. Skillfully created, it can also represent real-life speech rhythms in written form. Via conflicts and ensuing action, dialogue also provides drama.

Dialogue in Fiction

In fictional works, effectively written dialogue does more than just break up or interrupt sections of narrative. While **dialogue** may supply exposition for readers, it must nonetheless be believable. Dialogue should be dynamic, not static, and it should not resemble regular prose. Authors should not use dialogue to write clever similes or metaphors, or to inject their own opinions. Nor should they use dialogue at all when narrative would be better. Most importantly, dialogue should not slow the plot movement. Dialogue must seem natural, which means careful construction of phrases rather than actually duplicating natural speech, which does not necessarily translate well to the written word. Finally, all dialogue must be pertinent to the story, rather than just added conversation.

Foreshadowing

Foreshadowing is a device authors use to give readers **hints** about events that will take place later in a story. Foreshadowing most often takes place through a character's dialogue or actions. Sometimes the character will know what is going to happen and will purposefully allude to future events. For example, consider a protagonist who is about to embark on a journey through the woods. Just before the protagonist begins the trip, another character says, "Be careful, you never know what could be out in those woods!" This alerts the reader that the woods may be dangerous and prompts the reader to expect something to attack the protagonist in the woods. This is an example of foreshadowing through warning. Alternatively, a character may unknowingly foreshadow later events. For example, consider a story where a brother and sister run through their house and knock over a vase and break it. The brother says, "Don't worry, we'll clean it up! Mom will never know!" However, the reader knows that their mother will most likely find out what they have done, so the reader expects the siblings to later get in trouble for running, breaking the vase, and hiding it from their mother.

Symbolism

Symbolism describes an author's use of a **symbol**, an element of the story that **represents** something else. Symbols can impact stories in many ways, including deepening the meaning of a story or its elements, comparing a story to another work, or foreshadowing later events in a story. Symbols can be objects, characters, colors, numbers, or anything else the author establishes as a symbol. Symbols can be clearly established through direct comparison or repetition, but they can also be established subtly or gradually over a large portion of the story. Another form of symbolism is **allusion**, which is when something in a story is used to prompt the reader to think about another work. Many well-known works use **Biblical allusions**, which are allusions to events or details in the Bible that inform a work or an element within it.

Point of View

Another element that impacts a text is the author's point of view. The **point of view** of a text is the perspective from which a passage is told. An author will always have a point of view about a story before he or she draws up a plot line. The author will know what events they want to take place, how they want the characters to interact, and how they want the story to resolve. An author will also have an opinion on the topic or series of events which is presented in the story that is based on their prior experience and beliefs.

The two main points of view that authors use, especially in a work of fiction, are first person and third person. If the narrator of the story is also the main character, or *protagonist*, the text is written in first-person point of view. In first person, the author writes from the perspective of *I*. Third-person point of view is probably the most common that authors use in their passages. Using third person, authors refer to each character by using *he* or *she*. In third-person omniscient, the narrator is not a character in the story and tells the story of all of the characters at the same time.

Review Video: Point of View
Visit mometrix.com/academy and enter code: 383336

First-Person Narration

First-person narratives let narrators express inner feelings and thoughts, especially when the narrator is the protagonist as Lemuel Gulliver is in Jonathan Swift's *Gulliver's Travels.* The narrator may be a close friend of the protagonist, like Dr. Watson in Sir Arthur Conan Doyle's *Sherlock Holmes.* Or, the narrator can be less involved with the main characters and plot, like Nick Carraway in F. Scott Fitzgerald's *The Great Gatsby.* When a narrator reports others' narratives, she or he is a "**frame narrator**," like the nameless narrator of Joseph Conrad's *Heart of Darkness* or Mr. Lockwood in Emily Brontë's *Wuthering Heights.* **First-person plural** is unusual but can be effective. Isaac Asimov's *I, Robot*, William Faulkner's *A Rose for Emily*, Maxim Gorky's *Twenty-Six Men and a Girl*, and Jeffrey Eugenides' *The Virgin Suicides* all use first-person plural narration. Author Kurt Vonnegut is the first-person narrator in his semi-autobiographical novel *Timequake.* Also unusual, but effective, is a **first-person omniscient** (rather than the more common third-person omniscient) narrator, like Death in Markus Zusak's *The Book Thief* and the ghost in Alice Sebold's *The Lovely Bones.*

Second-Person Narration

While **second-person** address is very commonplace in popular song lyrics, it is the least used form of narrative voice in literary works. Popular serial books of the 1980s like *Fighting Fantasy* or *Choose Your Own Adventure* employed second-person narratives. In some cases, a narrative combines both second-person and first-person voices, using the pronouns *you* and *I*. This can draw readers into the story, and it can also enable the authors to compare directly "your" and "my" feelings, thoughts, and actions. When the narrator is also a character in the story, as in Edgar Allan Poe's short story "The Tell-Tale Heart" or Jay McInerney's novel *Bright Lights, Big City,* the narrative is better defined as first-person despite it also addressing "you."

Third-Person Narration

Narration in the third person is the most prevalent type, as it allows authors the most flexibility. It is so common that readers simply assume without needing to be informed that the narrator is not a character in the story, or involved in its events. **Third-person singular** is used more frequently than **third-person plural**, though some authors have also effectively used plural. However, both singular and plural are most often included in stories according to which characters are being described. The third-person narrator may be either objective or subjective, and either omniscient or limited. **Objective third-person** narration does not include what the characters described are thinking or feeling, while **subjective third-person** narration does. The **third-person omniscient** narrator knows everything about all characters, including their thoughts and emotions, and all related places, times, and events. However, the **third-person limited** narrator may know everything about a particular character, but is limited to that character. In other words, the narrator cannot speak about anything that character does not know.

Alternating-Person Narration

Although authors more commonly write stories from one point of view, there are also instances wherein they alternate the narrative voice within the same book. For example, they may sometimes use an omniscient third-person narrator and a more intimate first-person narrator at other times. In J. K. Rowling's series of *Harry Potter* novels, she often writes in a third-person limited narrative, but sometimes changes to narration by characters other than the protagonist. George R. R. Martin's series *A Song of Ice and Fire* changes the point of view to coincide with divisions between chapters. The same technique is used by Erin Hunter (a pseudonym for several authors of the *Warriors, Seekers,* and *Survivors* book series). Authors using first-person narrative sometimes switch to third-person to describe significant action scenes, especially those where the narrator was absent or uninvolved, as Barbara Kingsolver does in her novel *The Poisonwood Bible.*

Historical and Social Context

Fiction that is heavily influenced by a historical or social context cannot be comprehended as the author intended if the reader does not keep this context in mind. Many important elements of the text will be influenced by any context, including symbols, allusions, settings, and plot events. These contexts, as well as the identity of the work's author, can help to inform the reader about the author's concerns and intended meanings. For example, George Orwell published his novel *1984* in the year 1949, soon after the end of World War II. At that time, following the defeat of the Nazis, the Cold War began between the Western Allied nations and the Eastern Soviet Communists. People were therefore concerned about the conflict between the freedoms afforded by Western democracies versus the oppression represented by Communism. Orwell had also previously fought in the Spanish Civil War against a Spanish regime that he and his fellows viewed as oppressive. From this information, readers can infer that Orwell was concerned about oppression by totalitarian governments. This informs *1984*'s story of Winston Smith's rebellion against the oppressive "Big Brother" government, of the fictional dictatorial state of Oceania, and his capture, torture, and ultimate conversion by that government. Some literary theories also seek to use historical and social contexts to reveal deeper meanings and implications in a text.

Textual Evidence

No literary analysis is complete without textual evidence. Summaries, paraphrases, and quotes are all forms of textual evidence, but direct quotes from the text are the most effective form of evidence. The best textual evidence is relevant, accurate, and clearly supports the writer's claim. This can include pieces of descriptions, dialogue, or exposition that shows the applicability of the analysis to the text. Analysis that is average, or sufficient, shows an understanding of the text; contains supporting textual evidence that is relevant and accurate, if not strong; and shows a specific and clear response. Analysis that partially meets criteria also shows understanding, but the textual evidence is generalized, incomplete, only partly relevant or accurate, or connected only weakly. Inadequate analysis is vague, too general, or incorrect. It may give irrelevant or incomplete textual evidence, or may simply summarize the plot rather than analyzing the work. It is important to incorporate textual evidence from the work being analyzed and any supplemental materials and to provide appropriate attribution for these sources.

Chapter Quiz

1. Which of the following is the least used form of narration used in literature?

a. First-person
b. Second-person
c. Third-person limited
d. Third-person omniscient

2. Which of the following lists the terms of chronological plots in order from first to last?

a. Exposition, rising action, climax, falling action, resolution
b. Rising action, exposition, falling action, climax, resolution
c. Rising action, exposition, climax, falling action, resolution
d. Resolution, exposition, climax, falling action, rising action

3. If a writer alludes to another piece of literature, that writer is doing which of the following?

a. Admiring it
b. Criticizing it
c. Defending its conclusions
d. Referencing it

Chapter Quiz Answer Key

1. B: While second-person address is very commonplace in popular song lyrics, it is the least used form of narrative voice in literary works. Popular serial books of the 1980s like *Fighting Fantasy* or *Choose Your Own Adventure* employed second-person narratives. In some cases, a narrative combines both second-person and first-person voices, using the pronouns *you* and *I*. This can draw readers into the story, and it can also enable the authors to compare directly "your" and "my" feelings, thoughts, and actions. When the narrator is also a character in the story, as in Edgar Allan Poe's short story "The Tell-Tale Heart" or Jay McInerney's novel *Bright Lights, Big City,* the narrative is better defined as first-person despite it also addressing "you."

2. A: The most common plot structure is the chronological plot, which presents the events to the reader in the same order they occur for the characters in the story. Chronological plots usually have five main parts: the exposition, rising action, the climax, falling action, and the resolution. This type of plot structure guides the reader through the story's events as the characters experience them and is the easiest structure to understand and identify.

3. D: An allusion is an uncited but recognizable reference to something else. Authors use language to make allusions to places, events, artwork, and other books in order to make their own text richer. For example, an author may allude to a very important text in order to make his own text seem more important.

Themes and Plots in Literature

Themes in Literature

When we read parables, their themes are the lessons they aim to teach. When we read fables, the moral of each story is its theme. When we read fictional works, the authors' perspectives regarding life and human behavior are their themes. Unlike in parables and fables, themes in literary fiction are usually not meant to preach or teach the readers a lesson. Hence, themes in fiction are not as explicit as they are in parables or fables. Instead, they are implicit, and the reader only infers them. By analyzing the fictional characters through thinking about their actions and behavior, understanding the setting of the story, and reflecting on how its plot develops, the reader comes to infer the main theme of the work. When writers succeed, they communicate with their readers such that common ground is established between author and audience. While a reader's individual experience may differ in its details from the author's written story, both may share universal underlying truths which allow author and audience to connect.

Determining Theme

In well-crafted literature, theme, structure, and plot are interdependent and inextricable: each element informs and reflects the others. The structure of a work is how it is organized. The theme is the central idea or meaning found in it. The plot is what happens in the story. Titles can also inform us of a work's theme. For instance, the title of Edgar Allan Poe's "The Tell-Tale Heart" informs readers of the story's theme of guilt before they even read about the repeated heartbeat the protagonist hears immediately before and constantly after committing and hiding a murder. Repetitive patterns of events or behaviors also give clues to themes. The same is true of symbols. For example, in F. Scott Fitzgerald's *The Great Gatsby,* for Jay Gatsby the green light at the end of the dock symbolizes Daisy Buchanan and his own dreams for the future. More generally, it is also understood as a symbol of the American Dream, and narrator Nick Carraway explicitly compares it to early settlers' sight of America rising from the ocean.

Thematic Development

Theme in The Great Gatsby

In *The Great Gatsby*, F. Scott Fitzgerald portrayed 1920s America as greedy, cynical, and rife with moral decay. Jay Gatsby's lavish weekly parties symbolize the reckless excesses of the Jazz Age. The growth of bootlegging and organized crime in reaction to Prohibition is symbolized by the character of Meyer Wolfsheim and by Gatsby's own ill-gotten wealth. Fitzgerald symbolized social divisions using geography. The "old money" aristocrats like the Buchanans lived on East Egg, while the "new money" bourgeois like Gatsby lived on West Egg. Fitzgerald also used weather, as many authors have, to reinforce narrative and emotional tones in the novel. Just as in *Romeo and Juliet*, where William Shakespeare set the confrontation of Tybalt and Mercutio and its deadly consequences on the hottest summer day under a burning sun, in *The Great Gatsby*, Fitzgerald did the same with Tom Wilson's deadly confrontation with Gatsby. Both works are ostensible love stories carrying socially critical themes about the destructiveness of pointless and misguided behaviors—family feuds in the former, pursuit of money in the latter.

Review Video: Thematic Development
Visit mometrix.com/academy and enter code: 576507

Theme in Les Misérables

In Victor Hugo's novel *Les Misérables*, the overall metamorphosis of protagonist Jean Valjean from a cynical ex-convict into a noble benefactor demonstrates Hugo's theme of the importance of love and compassion for others. Hugo also reflects this in more specific plot events. For example, Valjean's love for Cosette sustains him through many difficult periods and trying events. Hugo illustrates how love and compassion for others beget the same in them: Bishop Myriel's kindness to Valjean eventually inspires him to become honest. Years later, Valjean, as M. Madeleine, has rescued Fauchelevent from under a fallen carriage, Fauchelevent returns the compassionate act by giving Valjean sanctuary in the convent. M. Myriel's kindness also ultimately enables Valjean to rescue Cosette from the Thénardiers. Receiving Valjean's father-like love enables Cosette to fall in love with and marry Marius, and the love between Cosette and Marius enables the couple to forgive Valjean for his past crimes when they are revealed.

THEME IN "THE TELL-TALE HEART"

In one of his shortest stories, "The Tell-Tale Heart," Poe used economy of language to emphasize the murderer-narrator's obsessive focus on bare details like the victim's cataract-milky eye, the sound of a heartbeat, and insistence he is sane. The narrator begins by denying he is crazy, even citing his extreme agitation as proof of sanity. Contradiction is then extended: the narrator loves the old man, yet kills him. His motives are irrational—not greed or revenge, but to relieve the victim of his "evil eye." Because "eye" and "I" are homonyms, readers may infer that eye/I symbolizes the old man's identity, contradicting the killer's delusion that he can separate them. The narrator distances himself from the old man by perceiving his eye as separate, and dismembering his dead body. This backfires when he imagines the victim's heartbeat, which is really his own, just before he kills him and frequently afterward. Guilty and paranoid, he gives himself away. Poe predated Freud in exploring the paradox of killing those we love and the concept of projecting our own processes onto others.

THEME IN THE WORKS OF WILLIAM FAULKNER AND CHARLES DICKENS

William Faulkner contrasts the traditions of the antebellum South with the rapid changes of post-Civil War industrialization in his short story "A Rose for Emily." Living inside the isolated world of her house, Emily Grierson denies the reality of modern progress. Contradictorily, she is both a testament to time-honored history and a mysterious, eccentric, unfathomable burden. Faulkner portrays her with deathlike imagery even in life, comparing her to a drowned woman and referring to her skeleton. Emily symbolizes the Old South; as her social status is degraded, so is the antebellum social order. Like Miss Havisham in Charles Dickens' *Great Expectations,* Emily preserves her bridal bedroom, denying change and time's passage. Emily tries to control death through denial, shown in her necrophilia with her father's corpse and her killing of Homer Barron to stop him from leaving her, then also denying his death. Faulkner uses the motif of dust throughout to represent not only the decay of Emily, her house, and Old Southern traditions, but also how her secrets are obscured from others.

THEME IN MOBY-DICK

The great White Whale in *Moby-Dick* plays various roles to different characters. In Captain Ahab's obsessive, monomaniacal quest to kill it, the whale represents all evil, and Ahab believes it his duty and destiny to rid the world of it. Ishmael attempts through multiple scientific disciplines to understand the whale objectively, but fails—it is hidden underwater and mysterious to humans—reinforcing Melville's theme that humans can never know everything; here the whale represents the unknowable. Melville reverses white's usual connotation of purity in Ishmael's dread of white, associated with crashing waves, polar animals, albinos—all frightening and unnatural. White is often viewed as an absence of color, yet white light is the sum total of all colors in the spectrum. In the same way, white can signify both absence of meaning, and totality of meaning incomprehensible to humans. As a creature of nature, the whale also symbolizes how 19th-century white men's exploitative expansionistic actions were destroying the natural environment.

Theme in The Old Man and the Sea

Because of the old fisherman Santiago's struggle to capture a giant marlin, some people characterize Ernest Hemingway's *The Old Man and the Sea* as telling of man against nature. However, it can more properly be interpreted as telling of man's role as part of nature. Both man and fish are portrayed as brave, proud, and honorable. In Hemingway's world, all creatures, including humans, must either kill or be killed. Santiago reflects, "man can be destroyed but not defeated," following this principle in his life. As heroes are often created through their own deaths, Hemingway seems to believe that while being destroyed is inevitable, destruction enables living beings to transcend it by fighting bravely with honor and dignity. Hemingway echoes Romantic poet John Keats' contention that only immediately before death can we understand beauty as it is about to be destroyed. He also echoes ancient Greek and Roman myths and the Old Testament with the tragic flaw of overweening pride or overreaching. Like Icarus, Prometheus, and Adam and Eve, the old man "went out too far."

Universal Themes

The Old Testament book of Genesis, the Quran, and the Epic of Gilgamesh all contain flood stories. Versions differ somewhat, yet marketed similarities also exist. Genesis describes a worldwide flood, attributing it to God's decision that mankind, his creation, had become incontrovertibly wicked in spirit and must be destroyed for the world to start anew. The Quran describes the flood as regional, caused by Allah after sending Nuh (notice the similarity in name to Noah) as a messenger to his people to cease their evil. The Quran stipulates that Allah only destroys those who deny or ignore messages from his messengers. In the Gilgamesh poems Utnapishtim, like Noah, is instructed to build a ship to survive the flood. Both men also send out birds afterward as tests, using doves and a raven, though with different outcomes. Many historians and archeologists believe a Middle Eastern tidal wave was a real basis for these stories. However, their universal themes remain the same: the flood was seen as God's way of wiping out humans whose behavior had become ungodly.

Theme of Overreaching

A popular theme throughout literature is the human trait of **reaching too far** or **presuming too much**. In Greek mythology, Daedalus constructed wings of feathers and wax that men might fly like birds. He permitted his son Icarus to try them, but cautioned the boy not to fly too close to the sun. The impetuous youth (in what psychologist David Elkind later named adolescence's myth of invincibility) ignored this, flying too close to the sun. The wax melted, the wings disintegrated, and Icarus fell into the sea and perished. In the Old Testament, God warned Adam and Eve not to eat fruit from the tree of knowledge of good and evil. Because they ignored this command, they were banished from Eden's eternal perfection, condemning them to mortality and suffering. The Romans were themselves examples of overreaching in their conquest and assimilation of most of the then-known world and their ultimate demise. In Christopher Marlowe's *Dr. Faustus* and Johann Wolfgang von Goethe's *Faust,* the protagonist sells his soul to the Devil for unlimited knowledge and success, ultimately leading to his own tragic end.

Story Vs. Discourse

In terms of plot, "story" is the characters, places, and events originating in the author's mind, while "discourse" is how the author arranges and sequences events—which may be chronological or not. Story is imaginary; discourse is words on the page. Discourse allows a story to be told in different ways. One element of plot structure is relating events differently from the order in which they occurred. This is easily done with cause-and-effect; for example, in the sentence, "He died following a long illness," we know the illness preceded the death, but the death precedes the illness in words. In Kate Chopin's short story "The Story of an Hour" (1894), she tells some of the events out of chronological order, which has the effect of amplifying the surprise of the ending for the reader. Another element of plot structure is selection. Chopin omits some details, such as Mr. Mallard's trip home; this allows readers to be as surprised at his arrival as Mrs. Mallard is.

Plot and Meaning

Novelist E. M. Forster has made the distinction between story as relating a series of events, such as a king dying and then his queen dying, versus plot as establishing motivations for actions and causes for events, such as a king dying and then his queen dying from grief over his death. Thus, plot fulfills the function of helping readers understand cause-and-effect in events and underlying motivations in characters' actions, which in turn helps them understand life. This affects a work's meaning by supporting its ability to explain why things happen, why people do things, and ultimately the meaning of life. Some authors find that while story events convey meaning, they do not tell readers there is any one meaning in life or way of living, but rather are mental experiments with various meanings, enabling readers to explore. Hence stories may not necessarily be constructed to impose one definitive meaning, but rather to find some shape, direction, and meaning within otherwise random events.

Classic Analysis of Plot Structure

In *Poetics,* Aristotle defined plot as "the arrangement of the incidents." He meant not the story, but how it is structured for presentation. In tragedies, Aristotle found results driven by chains of cause and effect preferable to those driven by the protagonist's personality or character. He identified "unity of action" as necessary for a plot's wholeness, meaning its events must be internally connected, not episodic or relying on *deus ex machina* or other external intervention. A plot must have a beginning, middle, and end. Gustav Freytag adapted Aristotle's ideas into his Pyramid (1863). The beginning, today called the exposition, incentive, or inciting moment, emphasizes causes and de-emphasizes effects. Aristotle called the ensuing cause and effect *desis*, or tying up, today called complications which occur during the rising action. These culminate in a crisis or climax, Aristotle's *peripateia.* This occurs at the plot's middle, where cause and effect are both emphasized. The falling action, which Aristotle called the *lusis* or unraveling, is today called the dénouement. The resolution comes at the catastrophe, outcome, or end, when causes are emphasized and effects de-emphasized.

Review Video: Plot line Definition
Visit mometrix.com/academy and enter code: 944011

Analysis of Plot Structures Through Recurring Patterns

Authors of fiction select characters, places, and events from their imaginations and arrange them to create a story that will affect their readers. One way to analyze plot structure is to compare and contrast different events in a story. For example, in Kate Chopin's "The Story of an Hour," a very simple but key pattern of repetition is the husband's leaving and then returning. Such patterns fulfill the symmetrical aspect that Aristotle said was required of sound plot structure. In James Baldwin's short story, "Sonny's Blues," the narrator is Sonny's brother. In an encounter with one of Sonny's old friends early in the story, the brother initially disregards his communication. In a subsequent flashback, Baldwin informs us that this was the same way he had treated Sonny. In Nathaniel Hawthorne's "Young Goodman Brown," a pattern is created by the protagonist's recurrent efforts not to go farther into the wood. In Herman Melville's "Bartleby the Scrivener" and in William Faulkner's "Barn Burning," patterns are also created by repetition such as Bartleby's repeated refusals and the history of barn-burning episodes, respectively.

LITERARY THEORIES AND CRITICISM AND INTERPRETATION

Literary theory includes ideas that guide readers through the process of interpreting literature. Literary theory, as a subject, encompasses several specific, focused theories that lead readers to interpret or analyze literature through the context of the theory using the subjects and elements it involves. Some commonly used and discussed literary theories include **postcolonial theory**, **gender and feminist theory**, **structuralism**, **new historicism**, **reader-response theory**, and **sociological criticism**.

- **Postcolonial theory** involves the historical and geographical context of a work and leads readers to consider how colonization informs the plot, characters, setting, and other elements in the work.
- **Gender and feminist theory** invites readers to interpret a text by looking at its treatment of and suggestions about women and a culture's treatment of women. As with most literary theories, this information can be clearly stated or strongly implied in a work, but it may also be gleaned through looking closely at symbols, characters, and plot elements in a work.
- **Structuralism** uses the structure and organization of a work and the foundations of language to examine how and what a text conveys about the human experience and how those findings connect to common human experiences.
- **New historicism** heavily relies on the cultural and historical context of a work, including when it was written, where the author lives or lived, the culture and history of that location, and other works from the same culture. New historical readings seek to examine these details to expose the ideologies of the location and culture that influenced the work.
- **Reader-response theory** uses the individual reader's response to the text and experience while reading the text to examine the meaning of the reader's relationship with the text and what that relationship suggests about the reader or the factors impacting their experience.
- **Sociological criticism** considers the societies that are relevant to a text. The author's society and any reader's society are important to the text, as sociological criticism seeks to uncover what the text implies or reveals about those societies. This method of criticism can also involve studying the presentation of a society within the text and applying it to the author's society or their other writings.

Chapter Quiz

1. David Elkind's term "adolescence's myth of invincibility" is derived from which classical story?

a. The Epic of Gilgamesh
b. *Dr. Faustus*
c. Daedalus and Icarus
d. *Odyssey*

2. Which of the following is NOT a commonly used and discussed literary theory?

a. Gender and feminist theory
b. Sociological criticism
c. Precolonial theory
d. New historicism

Chapter Quiz Answer Key

1. C: A popular theme throughout literature is the human trait of reaching too far or presuming too much. In Greek mythology, Daedalus constructed wings from feathers and wax so that men might fly like birds. He permitted his son Icarus to try them, but cautioned the boy not to fly too close to the sun. The impetuous youth (in what psychologist David Elkind later named "adolescence's myth of invincibility") ignored this, flying too close to the sun. The wax melted, the wings disintegrated, and Icarus fell into the sea and perished.

2. C: Literary theory includes ideas that guide readers through the process of interpreting literature. As a subject, literary theory encompasses several specific, focused theories that lead readers to interpret or analyze literature through the context of the theory using the subjects and elements it involves. Some commonly used and discussed literary theories include postcolonial theory, gender and feminist theory, structuralism, new historicism, reader-response theory, and sociological criticism.

Reading Comprehension

Understanding a Passage

One of the most important skills in reading comprehension is the identification of **topics** and **main ideas**. There is a subtle difference between these two features. The topic is the subject of a text (i.e., what the text is all about). The main idea, on the other hand, is the most important point being made by the author. The topic is usually expressed in a few words at the most while the main idea often needs a full sentence to be completely defined. As an example, a short passage might be written on the topic of penguins, and the main idea could be written as *Penguins are different from other birds in many ways*. In most nonfiction writing, the topic and the main idea will be **stated directly** and often appear in a sentence at the very beginning or end of the text. When being tested on an understanding of the author's topic, you may be able to skim the passage for the general idea by reading only the first sentence of each paragraph. A body paragraph's first sentence is often—but not always—the main **topic sentence** which gives you a summary of the content in the paragraph.

However, there are cases in which the reader must figure out an **unstated** topic or main idea. In these instances, you must read every sentence of the text and try to come up with an overarching idea that is supported by each of those sentences.

Note: The main idea should not be confused with the thesis statement. While the main idea gives a brief, general summary of a text, the thesis statement provides a **specific perspective** on an issue that the author supports with evidence.

Review Video: Topics and Main Ideas
Visit mometrix.com/academy and enter code: 407801

Supporting details are smaller pieces of evidence that provide backing for the main point. In order to show that a main idea is correct or valid, an author must add details that prove their point. All texts contain details, but they are only classified as supporting details when they serve to reinforce some larger point. Supporting details are most commonly found in informative and persuasive texts. In some cases, they will be clearly indicated with terms like *for example* or *for instance*, or they will be enumerated with terms like *first*, *second*, and *last*. However, you need to be prepared for texts that do not contain those indicators. As a reader, you should consider whether the author's supporting details really back up his or her main point. Details can be factual and correct, yet they may not be **relevant** to the author's point. Conversely, details can be relevant, but be ineffective because they are based on opinion or assertions that cannot be proven.

Review Video: Supporting Details
Visit mometrix.com/academy and enter code: 396297

An example of a main idea is: *Giraffes live in the Serengeti of Africa*. A supporting detail about giraffes could be: *A giraffe in this region benefits from a long neck by reaching twigs and leaves on tall trees.* The main idea gives the general idea that the text is about giraffes. The supporting detail gives a specific fact about how the giraffes eat.

Organization of the Text

The way a text is organized can help readers understand the author's intent and his or her conclusions. There are various ways to organize a text, and each one has a purpose and use. Usually, authors will organize information logically in a passage so the reader can follow and locate the information within the text. However, since not all passages are written with the same logical structure, you need to be familiar with several different types of passage structure.

Review Video: Organizational Methods to Structure Text
Visit mometrix.com/academy and enter code: 606263

Review Video: Sequence of Events in a Story
Visit mometrix.com/academy and enter code: 807512

Chronological

When using **chronological** order, the author presents information in the order that it happened. For example, biographies are typically written in chronological order. The subject's birth and childhood are presented first, followed by their adult life, and lastly the events leading up to the person's death.

Cause and Effect

One of the most common text structures is **cause and effect**. A **cause** is an act or event that makes something happen, and an **effect** is the thing that happens as a result of the cause. A cause-and-effect relationship is not always explicit, but there are some terms in English that signal causes, such as *since*, *because*, and *due to*. Furthermore, terms that signal effects include *consequently, therefore, this leads to*. As an example, consider the sentence *Because the sky was clear, Ron did not bring an umbrella*. The cause is the clear sky, and the effect is that Ron did not bring an umbrella. However, readers may find that sometimes the cause-and-effect relationship will not be clearly noted. For instance, the sentence *He was late and missed the meeting* does not contain any signaling words, but the sentence still contains a cause (he was late) and an effect (he missed the meeting).

Review Video: Cause and Effect
Visit mometrix.com/academy and enter code: 868099

Multiple Effects

Be aware of the possibility for a single cause to have **multiple effects.** (e.g., *Single cause*: Because you left your homework on the table, your dog engulfed the assignment. *Multiple effects*: As a result, you receive a failing grade, your parents do not allow you to go out with your friends, you miss out on the new movie, and one of your classmates spoils it for you before you have another chance to watch it).

Multiple Causes

Also, there is the possibility for a single effect to have **multiple causes.** (e.g., *Single effect*: Alan has a fever. *Multiple causes*: An unexpected cold front came through the area, and Alan forgot to take his multi-vitamin to avoid getting sick.) Additionally, an effect can in turn be the cause of another effect, in what is known as a cause-and-effect chain. (e.g., As a result of her disdain for procrastination, Lynn prepared for her exam. This led to her passing her test with high marks. Hence, her resume was accepted and her application was approved.)

Cause and Effect in Persuasive Essays

Persuasive essays, in which an author tries to make a convincing argument and change the minds of readers, usually include cause-and-effect relationships. However, these relationships should not always be taken at face value. Frequently, an author will assume a cause or take an effect for granted. To read a persuasive essay effectively, readers need to judge the cause-and-effect relationships that the author is presenting. For instance, imagine an author wrote the following: *The* *parking deck has been unprofitable because people would prefer to ride their bikes.* The relationship is clear: the cause is that people prefer to ride their bikes, and the effect is that the parking deck has been unprofitable. However, readers should consider whether this argument is conclusive. Perhaps there are other reasons for the failure of the parking deck: a down economy, excessive fees, etc. Too often, authors present causal relationships as if they are fact rather than opinion. Readers should be on the alert for these dubious claims.

Problem-Solution

Some nonfiction texts are organized to **present a problem** followed by a solution. For this type of text, the problem is often explained before the solution is offered. In some cases, as when the problem is well known, the solution may be introduced briefly at the beginning. Other passages may focus on the solution, and the problem will be referenced only occasionally. Some texts will outline multiple solutions to a problem, leaving readers to choose among them. If the author has an interest or an allegiance to one solution, he or she may fail to mention or describe accurately some of the other solutions. Readers should be careful of the author's agenda when reading a problem-solution text. Only by understanding the author's perspective and interests can one develop a proper judgment of the proposed solution.

Compare and Contrast

Many texts follow the **compare-and-contrast** model in which the similarities and differences between two ideas or things are explored. Analysis of the similarities between ideas is called **comparison**. In an ideal comparison, the author places ideas or things in an equivalent structure, i.e., the author presents the ideas in the same way. If an author wants to show the similarities between cricket and baseball, then he or she may do so by summarizing the equipment and rules for each game. Be mindful of the similarities as they appear in the passage and take note of any differences that are mentioned. Often, these small differences will only reinforce the more general similarity.

Review Video: Compare and Contrast
Visit mometrix.com/academy and enter code: 798319

Thinking critically about ideas and conclusions can seem like a daunting task. One way to ease this task is to understand the basic elements of ideas and writing techniques. Looking at the ways different ideas relate to each other can be a good way for readers to begin their analysis. For instance, sometimes authors will write about two ideas that are in opposition to each other. Or, one author will provide his or her ideas on a topic, and another author may respond in opposition. The analysis of these opposing ideas is known as **contrast**. Contrast is often marred by the author's obvious partiality to one of the ideas. A discerning reader will be put off by an author who does not engage in a fair fight. In an analysis of opposing ideas, both ideas should be presented in clear and reasonable terms. If the author does prefer a side, you need to read carefully to determine the areas where the author shows or avoids this preference. In an analysis of opposing ideas, you should proceed through the passage by marking the major differences point by point with an eye that is looking for an explanation of each side's view. For instance, in an analysis of capitalism and communism, there is an importance in outlining each side's view on labor, markets, prices, personal responsibility, etc. Additionally, as you read through the passages, you should note whether the opposing views present each side in a similar manner.

Sequence

Readers must be able to identify a text's **sequence**, or the order in which things happen. Often, when the sequence is very important to the author, the text is indicated with signal words like *first,* *then*, *next*, and *last*. However, a sequence can be merely implied and must be noted by the reader. Consider the sentence *He walked through the garden and gave water and fertilizer to the plants.* Clearly, the man did not walk through the garden before he collected water and fertilizer for the plants. So, the implied sequence is that he first collected water, then he collected fertilizer, next he walked through the garden, and last he gave water or fertilizer as necessary to the plants. Texts do not always proceed in an orderly sequence from first to last. Sometimes they begin at the end and start over at the beginning. As a reader, you can enhance your understanding of the passage by taking brief notes to clarify the sequence.

Making Connections to Enhance Comprehension

Reading involves thinking. For good comprehension, readers make **text-to-self**, **text-to-text**, and **text-to-world connections**. Making connections helps readers understand text better and predict what might occur next based on what they already know, such as how characters in the story feel or what happened in another text. Text-to-self connections with the reader's life and experiences make literature more personally relevant and meaningful to readers. Readers can make connections before, during, and after reading—including whenever the text reminds them of something similar they have encountered in life or other texts. The genre, setting, characters, plot elements, literary structure and devices, and themes an author uses allow a reader to make connections to other works of literature or to people and events in their own lives. Venn diagrams and other graphic organizers help visualize connections. Readers can also make double-entry notes: key content, ideas, events, words, and quotations on one side, and the connections with these on the other.

Summarizing Literature to Support Comprehension

When reading literature, especially demanding works, **summarizing** helps readers identify important information and organize it in their minds. They can also identify themes, problems, and solutions, and can sequence the story. Readers can summarize before, during, and after they read. They should use their own words, as they do when describing a personal event or giving directions. Previewing a text's organization before reading by examining the book cover, table of contents, and illustrations also aids summarizing. Making notes of key words and ideas in a graphic organizer while reading can benefit readers in the same way. Graphic organizers are another useful method; readers skim the text to determine main ideas and then narrow the list with the aid of the organizer. Unimportant details should be omitted in summaries. Summaries can be organized using description, problem-solution, comparison-contrast, sequence, main ideas, or cause-and-effect.

Review Video: Summarizing Text
Visit mometrix.com/academy and enter code: 172903

Paraphrasing

Paraphrasing is another method that the reader can use to aid in comprehension. When paraphrasing, one puts what they have read into their own words by rephrasing what the author has written, or one "translates" all of what the author shared into their own words by including as many details as they can.

Chapter Quiz

1. All of the following are used for good comprehension, EXCEPT:

a. Text-to-self connections.
b. Text-to-others connections.
c. Text-to-text connections.
d. Text-to-world connections.

2. All of the following are terms in English that signal causes, EXCEPT:

a. Because.
b. Due to.
c. Since.
d. Therefore.

Chapter Quiz Answer Key

1. B: Reading involves thinking. For good comprehension, readers make text-to-self, text-to-text, and text-to-world connections. Making connections helps readers understand text better and predict what might occur next based on what they already know, such as how characters in the story feel or what happened in another text. Text-to-self connections with the reader's life and experiences make literature more personally relevant and meaningful to readers. Readers can make connections before, during, and after reading—including whenever the text reminds them of something similar they have encountered in life or other texts. The genre, setting, characters, plot elements, themes, and literary structure and devices an author uses allow a reader to make connections to other works of literature or to people and events in their own lives. Venn diagrams and other graphic organizers help visualize connections. Readers can also make double-entry notes: key content, ideas, events, words, and quotations on one side, and the connections with these on the other.

2. D: One of the most common text structures is cause and effect. A cause is an act or event that makes something happen, and an effect is the thing that happens as a result of the cause. A cause-and-effect relationship is not always explicit, but there are some terms in English that signal causes, such as *since*, *because*, and *due to*. Furthermore, terms that signal effects include *consequently, therefore,* and *this leads to*. As an example, consider the sentence, "Because the sky was clear, Ron did not bring an umbrella." The cause is the clear sky, and the effect is that Ron did not bring an umbrella. However, readers may find that sometimes the cause-and-effect relationship will not be clearly noted. For instance, the sentence, "He was late and missed the meeting," does not contain any signaling words, but the sentence still contains a cause ("he was late") and an effect ("he missed the meeting").

Making Predictions and Inferences

Making Predictions

When we read literature, **making predictions** about what will happen in the writing reinforces our purpose for reading and prepares us mentally. A **prediction** is a guess about what will happen next. Readers constantly make predictions based on what they have read and what they already know. We can make predictions before we begin reading and during our reading. Consider the following sentence: *Staring at the computer screen in shock, Kim blindly reached over for the brimming glass of water on the shelf to her side.* The sentence suggests that Kim is distracted, and that she is not looking at the glass that she is going to pick up. So, a reader might predict that Kim is going to knock over the glass. Of course, not every prediction will be accurate: perhaps Kim will pick the glass up cleanly. Nevertheless, the author has certainly created the expectation that the water might be spilled.

As we read on, we can test the accuracy of our predictions, revise them in light of additional reading, and confirm or refute our predictions. Predictions are always subject to revision as the reader acquires more information. A reader can make predictions by observing the title and illustrations; noting the structure, characters, and subject; drawing on existing knowledge relative to the subject; and asking "why" and "who" questions. Connecting reading to what we already know enables us to learn new information and construct meaning. For example, before third-graders read a book about Johnny Appleseed, they may start a KWL chart—a list of what they *Know*, what they *Want* to know or learn, and what they have *Learned* after reading. Activating existing background knowledge and thinking about the text before reading improves comprehension.

Review Video: Predictive Reading Visit mometrix.com/academy and enter code: 437248

Test-taking tip: To respond to questions requiring future predictions, your answers should be based on evidence of past or present behavior and events.

Evaluating Predictions

When making predictions, readers should be able to explain how they developed their prediction. One way readers can defend their thought process is by citing textual evidence. Textual evidence to evaluate reader predictions about literature includes specific synopses of the work, paraphrases of the work or parts of it, and direct quotations from the work. These references to the text must support the prediction by indicating, clearly or unclearly, what will happen later in the story. A text may provide these indications through literary devices such as foreshadowing. Foreshadowing is anything in a text that gives the reader a hint about what is to come by emphasizing the likelihood of an event or development. Foreshadowing can occur through descriptions, exposition, and dialogue. Foreshadowing in dialogue usually occurs when a character gives a warning or expresses a strong feeling that a certain event will occur. Foreshadowing can also occur through irony. However, unlike other forms of foreshadowing, the events that seem the most likely are the opposite of what actually happens. Instances of foreshadowing and irony can be summarized, paraphrased, or quoted to defend a reader's prediction.

Review Video: Textual Evidence for Predictions Visit mometrix.com/academy and enter code: 261070

Drawing Conclusions from Inferences

Inferences about literary text are logical conclusions that readers make based on their observations and previous knowledge. An inference is based on both what is found in a passage or a story and what is known from personal experience. For instance, a story may say that a character is frightened and can hear howling in the distance. Based on both what is in the text and personal knowledge, it is a logical conclusion that the character is frightened because he hears the sound of wolves. A good inference is supported by the information in a passage.

Implicit and Explicit Information

By inferring, readers construct meanings from text that are personally relevant. By combining their own schemas or concepts and their background information pertinent to the text with what they read, readers interpret it according to both what the author has conveyed and their own unique perspectives. Inferences are different from **explicit information**, which is clearly stated in a passage. Authors do not always explicitly spell out every meaning in what they write; many meanings are implicit. Through inference, readers can comprehend implied meanings in the text, and also derive personal significance from it, making the text meaningful and memorable to them. Inference is a natural process in everyday life. When readers infer, they can draw conclusions about what the author is saying, predict what may reasonably follow, amend these predictions as they continue to read, interpret the import of themes, and analyze the characters' feelings and motivations through their actions.

Example of Drawing Conclusions from Inferences

Read the excerpt and decide why Jana finally relaxed.

> Jana loved her job, but the work was very demanding. She had trouble relaxing. She called a friend, but she still thought about work. She ordered a pizza, but eating it did not help. Then, her kitten jumped on her lap and began to purr. Jana leaned back and began to hum a little tune. She felt better.

You can draw the conclusion that Jana relaxed because her kitten jumped on her lap. The kitten purred, and Jana leaned back and hummed a tune. Then she felt better. The excerpt does not explicitly say that this is the reason why she was able to relax. The text leaves the matter unclear, but the reader can infer or make a "best guess" that this is the reason she is relaxing. This is a logical conclusion based on the information in the passage. It is the best conclusion a reader can make based on the information he or she has read. Inferences are based on the information in a passage, but they are not directly stated in the passage.

Test-taking tip: While being tested on your ability to make correct inferences, you must look for **contextual clues**. An answer can be true, but not the best or most correct answer. The contextual clues will help you find the answer that is the **best answer** out of the given choices. Be careful in your reading to understand the context in which a phrase is stated. When asked for the implied meaning of a statement made in the passage, you should immediately locate the statement and read the **context** in which the statement was made. Also, look for an answer choice that has a similar phrase to the statement in question.

Review Video: Inference
Visit mometrix.com/academy and enter code: 379203

Review Video: How to Support a Conclusion
Visit mometrix.com/academy and enter code: 281653

Chapter Quiz

1. Which of the following describes logical conclusions that readers make based on their observations and previous knowledge?

a. Imperatives
b. Interrogatives
c. Inferences
d. Predictions

Chapter Quiz Answer Key

1. C: Inferences about literary text are logical conclusions that readers make based on their observations and previous knowledge. An inference is based on both what is found in a passage or a story and what is known from personal experience. For instance, a story may say that a character is frightened and can hear howling in the distance. Based on both what is in the text and personal knowledge, it is a logical conclusion that the character is frightened because they hear the sound of wolves. A good inference is supported by the information in a passage.

Interactions with Texts

Purposes for Writing

In order to be an effective reader, one must pay attention to the author's **position** and **purpose**. Even those texts that seem objective and impartial, like textbooks, have a position and bias. Readers need to take these positions into account when considering the author's message. When an author uses emotional language or clearly favors one side of an argument, his or her position is clear. However, the author's position may be evident not only in what he or she writes, but also in what he or she doesn't write. In a normal setting, a reader would want to review some other texts on the same topic in order to develop a view of the author's position. If this was not possible, then you would want to at least acquire some background about the author. However, since you are in the middle of an exam and the only source of information is the text, you should look for language and argumentation that seems to indicate a particular stance on the subject.

Review Video: Author's Position
Visit mometrix.com/academy and enter code: 827954

Usually, identifying the author's **purpose** is easier than identifying his or her position. In most cases, the author has no interest in hiding his or her purpose. A text that is meant to entertain, for instance, should be written to please the reader. Most narratives, or stories, are written to entertain, though they may also inform or persuade. Informative texts are easy to identify, while the most difficult purpose of a text to identify is persuasion because the author has an interest in making this purpose hard to detect. When a reader discovers that the author is trying to persuade, he or she should be skeptical of the argument. For this reason, persuasive texts often try to establish an entertaining tone and hope to amuse the reader into agreement. On the other hand, an informative tone may be implemented to create an appearance of authority and objectivity.

An author's purpose is evident often in the organization of the text (e.g., section headings in bold font points to an informative text). However, you may not have such organization available to you in your exam. Instead, if the author makes his or her main idea clear from the beginning, then the likely purpose of the text is to inform. If the author begins by making a claim and provides various arguments to support that claim, then the purpose is probably to persuade. If the author tells a story or wants to gain the reader's attention more than to push a particular point or deliver information, then his or her purpose is most likely to entertain. As a reader, you must judge authors on how well they accomplish their purpose. In other words, you need to consider the type of passage (e.g., technical, persuasive, etc.) that the author has written and if the author has followed the requirements of the passage type.

Making Logical Conclusions about a Passage

A reader should always be drawing conclusions from the text. Sometimes conclusions are **implied** from written information, and other times the information is **stated directly** within the passage. One should always aim to draw conclusions from information stated within a passage, rather than to draw them from mere implications. At times an author may provide some information and then describe a counterargument. Readers should be alert for direct statements that are subsequently rejected or weakened by the author. Furthermore, you should always read through the entire passage before drawing conclusions. Many readers are trained to expect the author's conclusions at either the beginning or the end of the passage, but many texts do not adhere to this format.

Drawing conclusions from information implied within a passage requires confidence on the part of the reader. **Implications** are things that the author does not state directly, but readers can assume based on what the author does say. Consider the following passage: *I stepped outside and opened my umbrella. By the time I got to work, the cuffs of my pants were soaked.* The author never states that it is raining, but this fact is clearly implied. Conclusions based on implication must be well supported by the text. In order to draw a solid conclusion, readers should have **multiple pieces of evidence**. If readers have only one piece, they must be assured that there is no other possible explanation than their conclusion. A good reader will be able to draw many conclusions from information implied by the text, which will be a great help on the exam.

DRAWING CONCLUSIONS

A common type of inference that a reader has to make is **drawing a conclusion**. The reader makes this conclusion based on the information provided within a text. Certain facts are included to help a reader come to a specific conclusion. For example, a story may open with a man trudging through the snow on a cold winter day, dragging a sled behind him. The reader can logically **infer** from the setting of the story that the man is wearing heavy winter clothes in order to stay warm. Information is implied based on the setting of a story, which is why **setting** is an important element of the text. If the same man in the example was trudging down a beach on a hot summer day, dragging a surf board behind him, the reader would assume that the man is not wearing heavy clothes. The reader makes inferences based on their own experiences and the information presented to them in the story.

Test-taking tip: When asked to identify a conclusion that may be drawn, look for critical "hedge" phrases, such as *likely*, *may*, *can*, and *will often*, among many others. When you are being tested on this knowledge, remember the question that writers insert into these hedge phrases to cover every possibility. Often an answer will be wrong simply because there is no room for exception. Extreme positive or negative answers (such as always or never) are usually not correct. When answering these questions, the reader **should not** use any outside knowledge that is not gathered directly or reasonably inferred from the passage. Correct answers can be derived straight from the passage.

EXAMPLE

Read the following sentence from *Little Women* by Louisa May Alcott and draw a conclusion based upon the information presented:

> *You know the reason Mother proposed not having any presents this Christmas was because it is going to be a hard winter for everyone; and she thinks we ought not to spend money for pleasure, when our men are suffering so in the army.*

Based on the information in the sentence, the reader can conclude, or **infer**, that the men are away at war while the women are still at home. The pronoun *our* gives a clue to the reader that the character is speaking about men she knows. In addition, the reader can assume that the character is speaking to a brother or sister, since the term "Mother" is used by the character while speaking to another person. The reader can also come to the conclusion that the characters celebrate Christmas, since it is mentioned in the **context** of the sentence. In the sentence, the mother is presented as an unselfish character who is opinionated and thinks about the wellbeing of other people.

Comparing Two Stories

When presented with two different stories, there will be **similarities** and **differences** between the two. A reader needs to make a list, or other graphic organizer, of the points presented in each story. Once the reader has written down the main point and supporting points for each story, the two sets of ideas can be compared. The reader can then present each idea and show how it is the same or different in the other story. This is called **comparing and contrasting ideas**.

The reader can compare ideas by stating, for example: "In Story 1, the author believes that humankind will one day land on Mars, whereas in Story 2, the author believes that Mars is too far away for humans to ever step foot on." Note that the two viewpoints are different in each story that the reader is comparing. A reader may state that: "Both stories discussed the likelihood of humankind landing on Mars." This statement shows how the viewpoint presented in both stories is based on the same topic, rather than how each viewpoint is different. The reader will complete a comparison of two stories with a conclusion.

Review Video: Comparing Two Stories
Visit mometrix.com/academy and enter code: 833765

Outlining a Passage

As an aid to drawing conclusions, **outlining** the information contained in the passage should be a familiar skill to readers. An effective outline will reveal the structure of the passage and will lead to solid conclusions. An effective outline will have a title that refers to the basic subject of the text, though the title does not need to restate the main idea. In most outlines, the main idea will be the first major section. Each major idea in the passage will be established as the head of a category. For instance, the most common outline format calls for the main ideas of the passage to be indicated with Roman numerals. In an effective outline of this kind, each of the main ideas will be represented by a Roman numeral and none of the Roman numerals will designate minor details or secondary ideas. Moreover, all supporting ideas and details should be placed in the appropriate place on the outline. An outline does not need to include every detail listed in the text, but it should feature all of those that are central to the argument or message. Each of these details should be listed under the corresponding main idea.

Review Video: Outlining
Visit mometrix.com/academy and enter code: 584445

Using Graphic Organizers

Ideas from a text can also be organized using **graphic organizers**. A graphic organizer is a way to simplify information and take key points from the text. A graphic organizer such as a timeline may have an event listed for a corresponding date on the timeline, while an outline may have an event listed under a key point that occurs in the text. Each reader needs to create the type of graphic organizer that works the best for him or her in terms of being able to recall information from a story. Examples include a spider-map, which takes a main idea from the story and places it in a bubble with supporting points branching off the main idea. An outline is useful for diagramming the main and supporting points of the entire story, and a Venn diagram compares and contrasts characteristics of two or more ideas.

Review Video: Graphic Organizers
Visit mometrix.com/academy and enter code: 665513

Summarizing

A helpful tool is the ability to **summarize** the information that you have read in a paragraph or passage format. This process is similar to creating an effective outline. First, a summary should accurately define the main idea of the passage, though the summary does not need to explain this main idea in exhaustive detail. The summary should continue by laying out the most important supporting details or arguments from the passage. All of the significant supporting details should be included, and none of the details included should be irrelevant or insignificant. Also, the summary should accurately report all of these details. Too often, the desire for brevity in a summary leads to the sacrifice of clarity or accuracy. Summaries are often difficult to read because they omit all of the graceful language, digressions, and asides that distinguish great writing. However, an effective summary should communicate the same overall message as the original text.

Evaluating a Passage

It is important to understand the logical conclusion of the ideas presented in an informational text. **Identifying a logical conclusion** can help you determine whether you agree with the writer or not. Coming to this conclusion is much like making an inference: the approach requires you to combine the information given by the text with what you already know and make a logical conclusion. If the author intended for the reader to draw a certain conclusion, then you can expect the author's argumentation and detail to be leading in that direction.

One way to approach the task of drawing conclusions is to make brief **notes** of all the points made by the author. When the notes are arranged on paper, they may clarify the logical conclusion. Another way to approach conclusions is to consider whether the reasoning of the author raises any pertinent questions. Sometimes you will be able to draw several conclusions from a passage. On occasion these will be conclusions that were never imagined by the author. Therefore, be aware that these conclusions must be **supported directly by the text**.

Evaluation of Summaries

A summary of a literary passage is a condensation in the reader's own words of the passage's main points. Several guidelines can be used in evaluating a summary. The summary should be complete yet concise. It should be accurate, balanced, fair, neutral, and objective, excluding the reader's own opinions or reactions. It should reflect in similar proportion how much each point summarized was covered in the original passage. Summary writers should include tags of attribution, like "Macaulay argues that" to reference the original author whose ideas are represented in the summary. Summary writers should not overuse quotations; they should only quote central concepts or phrases they cannot precisely convey in words other than those of the original author. Another aspect of evaluating a summary is considering whether it can stand alone as a coherent, unified composition. In addition, evaluation of a summary should include whether its writer has cited the original source of the passage they have summarized so that readers can find it.

Chapter Quiz

1. Which of the following is most important when drawing conclusions from a text?

a. The conclusions make sense to others.
b. The conclusions are supported directly by the text.
c. The conclusions agree with previous convictions.
d. The conclusions align with the author's purpose for writing the text.

2. All of the following are true about summaries, EXCEPT:

a. They should focus on the main point of the text rather than proportional to how much each point was covered in the passage.
b. They should be accurate, balanced, fair, neutral, and objective.
c. They should be complete and concise.
d. They should only quote central concepts or phrases that cannot be precisely conveyed in words other than those of the original author.

Chapter Quiz Answer Key

1. B: It is important to understand the logical conclusion of the ideas presented in an informational text. Identifying a logical conclusion can help readers determine whether they agree with the writer or not. Coming to this conclusion is much like making an inference: the approach requires readers to combine the information given by the text with what they already know and make a logical conclusion. If the author intended for the reader to draw a certain conclusion, then readers can expect the author's argumentation and detail to be leading in that direction. Sometimes a reader will be able to draw several conclusions from a passage. On occasion these will be conclusions that were never imagined by the author. Therefore, be aware that these conclusions must be supported directly by the text.

2. A: A summary of a literary passage is a condensation in the reader's own words of the passage's main points. Several guidelines can be used in evaluating a summary. The summary should be complete yet concise. It should be accurate, balanced, fair, neutral, and objective, excluding the reader's own opinions or reactions. It should reflect in similar proportion how much each point summarized was covered in the original passage. Summary writers should include tags of attribution, like "Macaulay argues that" to reference the original author whose ideas are represented in the summary. Summary writers should not overuse quotations, but only quote central concepts or phrases they cannot precisely convey in words other than those of the original author. Another aspect of evaluating a summary is considering whether it can stand alone as a coherent, unified composition. In addition, evaluation of a summary should include whether its writer has cited the original source of the passage they have summarized so that readers can find it.

Language and Dialect

Diversity and Situational Nature of Language

Language is a diverse tool that allows people to communicate. However, language is often impacted and molded by the culture that uses it. This can make it difficult to learn and use a new language, since not all native speakers of the language will use it or interpret it the same way. For example, English is spoken all over America, but Americans in various regions of the country speak using different **dialects**. Other differences in speech include **accents** and **rhythm of speech**. Language is also manipulated by situations. Some terms and phrases have multiple meanings. A word's meaning often depends on the **context** in which the word or phrase is used, meaning that non-native speakers must learn to interpret situations to understand messages.

Factors of Language and Communication

Influences on Language

While dialect and diction are heavily influenced by an individual's culture and the location and history of the place they live, other personal factors can also impact language. A person's ethnicity, religious beliefs or background, and gender can influence the way they use and understand language. **Ethnicity** impacts language by incorporating a group's communication norms into an individual's speech and behavior. These norms may affect a speaker's tone, volume, or pace. These factors may lead others outside of that group to misinterpret the speaker's message, depending on their understanding of how those factors are used in speech. A person's **religious beliefs** can also affect their use of language. Religious beliefs and practices may lead an individual to abstain from using certain terms and may change the context in which a speaker uses specific words, or change their understanding of the word's usage. Additionally, a person may use language differently depending on their gender. **Gender's** influence on communication varies by region and industry. A region or industry's treatment of gender roles often impacts language use among its members. This can lead members of one gender group to be more assertive or submissive or to use different terms and phrases.

Culture and Communication

Individuals from different countries and cultures communicate differently. Not only do many people speak different languages, but they also speak using different inflections, volumes, tones, and dialects. These factors can have a significant impact on communication, even if the communicators speak the same language. In different cultures, certain behaviors are associated with different meanings and implications. When communicators from different cultures have a conversation, these expectations and associations may lead to misunderstanding. For example, Americans are considered to be louder and more demonstrative than people from other countries. Someone from a country where people speak more quietly who is not aware of this characterization may perceive an American's volume or large gestures as an indication of anger, when in reality, the American speaker is calm. The American may similarly perceive the other person as sad or shy due to their quiet voice, when the speaker is actually happy and comfortable in the conversation. Awareness of these factors and effects promotes respect for others and helps speakers understand the reasons for differences in communication, rather than allowing these differences to create division or conflict.

Language vs. Dialect

Languages are distinct and structured forms of verbal communication. Languages have cohesive sets of rules and words that are shared between the majority of that language's users. The main identifier of a language is that members of one language group are incapable of communicating fluently with members of another language group. New languages are formed as different dialects grow further apart until the members of each dialect can no longer innately communicate with each other.

Dialects are subsets of languages that do not violate the rules of the language as a whole, but which vary from other dialects in vocabulary usage, grammar forms, pronunciation, and spelling. Two major groupings of dialects are American and British English. Most American English and British English speakers can communicate with relative ease with one another, though the pronunciation, vocabulary (torch vs. flashlight; trunk vs. boot), spelling (meter vs. metre; color vs. colour), and grammar (in American English, collective nouns are always considered singular, but can be singular or plural in British English).

DEVELOPMENT OF DIALECTS OVER TIME

Dialects are formed primarily through the influences of location and time, but can be the result of other elements of **social stratification** as well (economic, ethnic, religious, etc.). As one group of a language's speakers is separated from another, in British and American English speakers for example, the language develops in isolated locations at the same time, resulting in distinct dialects. Language changes continuously over time as new words and phrases are adopted and others are phased out. Eventually, these small changes result culminate into enough grammar and vocabulary changes that the speakers of the distinct dialects cannot easily communicate with one another. The dialects can then be recognized as distinct languages.

USE OF DIALECT IN MEDIA

Literary authors often use dialect when writing dialogue to illustrate the social and geographical backgrounds of specific characters, which supports character development. For example, in *The Adventures of Huckleberry Finn* (1885), Mark Twain's novel is written in the dialect of a young, uneducated, white, Southern character, opening with this sentence: "You don't know about me without you have read a book by the name of The Adventures of Tom Sawyer, but that ain't no matter." Twain uses a different and exaggerated dialect to represent the speech of the African-American slave Jim: "We's safe, Huck, we's safe! Jump up and crack yo' heels. Dat's de good ole Cairo at las', I jis knows it."

In *To Kill a Mockingbird,* author Harper Lee used dialect in the characters' dialogue to portray an uneducated boy in the American South: "Reckon I have. Almost died the first year I come to school and et them pecans—folks say he pizened 'em." Lee also uses many Southern regional expressions, such as "right stove up," "What in the sam holy hill?", "sit a spell," "fess" (meaning "confess"), "jim-dandy," and "hush your fussing." These contribute to Lee's characterization of the people she describes, who live in a small town in Alabama circa the 1930s. In *Wuthering Heights* (1847), Emily Bronte reproduces Britain's 18th–19th-century Yorkshire dialect in the speech of servant Joseph: "Running after t'lads, as usuald!... If I war yah, maister, I'd just slam t'boards i' their faces all on 'em, gentle and simple! Never a day ut yah're off, but yon cat o' Linton comes sneaking hither; and Miss Nelly, shoo's a fine lass!"

DIALECT VS. DICTION

When written as characters' dialogue in literary works, dialect represents the particular pronunciation, grammar, and figurative expressions used by certain groups of people based on their geographic region, social class, and cultural background. For example, when a character says, "There's gold up in them thar hills," the author is using dialect to add to the characterization of that individual. Diction is more related to individual characters than to groups of people. The way in which a specific character speaks, including his or her choice of words, manner of expressing himself or herself, and use of grammar all represent individual types of diction. For example, two characters in the same novel might describe the same action or event using different diction: One says "I'm heading uptown for the evening," and the other says "I'm going out for a night on the town." These convey the same literal meaning, but due to their variations in diction, the speakers are expressing themselves in slightly different ways.

Review Video: Dialogue, Paradox, and Dialect
Visit mometrix.com/academy and enter code: 684341

Influences on Regional Dialect

Linguistic researchers have identified regional variations in vocabulary choices, which have evolved because of differences in local climates and how they influence human behaviors. For example, in the Southern United States, the Linguistic Atlas of the Gulf States (LAGS) Project by Dr. Lee Pederson of Emory University discovered and documented that people living in the northern or Upland section of the Piedmont plateau region call the fungal infection commonly known as athlete's foot "toe itch," but people living in the southern or Lowland section call it "ground itch." The explanation for this difference is that in the north, temperatures are cooler and people wear shoes accordingly, so they associate the itching with the feet in their description, but in the south, temperatures are hotter and people often went barefoot, so they associated the itching with the ground that presumably transmitted the infection.

Using Dialect in Writing

Dialect is most appropriate for informal or creative writing. Using dialectal writing when communicating casually or informally, such as in a text message or a quick email to a peer, is acceptable. However, in academic and professional contexts, writing using indications of dialect is inappropriate and often unacceptable. If the audience includes individuals who have a higher rank than the author, or authority over the author, it is best not to write in a way that suggests a dialect.

Chapter Quiz

1. Dialect can be used in all of the following situations, EXCEPT:

a. Creative writing.
b. Text messages.
c. Emails to peers.
d. Professional contexts.

Chapter Quiz Answer Key

1. D: Dialect is most appropriate for informal or creative writing. Using dialectal writing when communicating casually or informally, such as in a text message or a quick email to a peer, is acceptable. However, in academic and professional contexts, writing using indications of dialect is inappropriate and often unacceptable. If the audience includes individuals who have a higher rank than the author, or authority over the author, then it is best not to write in a way that suggests a dialect.

World Literature

American Literary Periods

Dark Romantics

In American literature, a group of late Romantic writers are recognized as **Dark Romantics**. These authors' works may be associated with both the Romantic and Gothic movements. These works emphasize nature and emotion, aligning them with Romanticism, and include dark themes and tones, aligning them with Gothic literature. However, these works do not all feature the historically inspired characteristics of Gothic literature, and their morals or outcomes more closely resemble those of Romantic literature. The Dark Romantics include writers such as Edgar Allan Poe, Nathaniel Hawthorne, Emily Dickinson, and Herman Melville.

Transcendentalism

Transcendentalism was a smaller movement that occurred alongside the American Romantic movement. The **transcendentalists** shared the Romantic emphasis on emotion and also focused heavily on how a person experiences life through their senses. They extended these sentiments to suggest that through embracing one's senses, an individual could transcend, or experience a state of being above physical humanity. They also extended the Romantic emphasis on subjectivity through their praise of self-sufficiency, as exemplified through Ralph Waldo Emerson's *Self-Reliance*. Emerson was a prominent transcendentalist. His writings included an essay titled *Nature*, which explains a progression from the use of the senses to the achievement of transcendence. Transcendentalist literature includes several essays that discuss the value of the senses and emotions or the process of transcendence. Transcendentalists also wrote poetry that includes the frequent use of imagery, metaphors, and references to nature. These elements reflect the ideas of transcendentalism and create a resemblance to the alleged experience of transcendence. Ralph Waldo Emerson, Henry David Thoreau, and Walt Whitman were all prominent writers in this movement.

Colonial America

The **colonial era** in America was influenced by immigration from England to what is now New England. These immigrants were mainly Puritans who centered their society in New England on their religious beliefs, allowing those beliefs to inform all aspects of their lives. This is apparent in the literature of the time, as much of it includes essays and sermons that discuss religion or the way the Puritans believed one should live and conduct themselves. Colonial literature also includes many poems, and these works also discuss or reference religious ideas and themes. There was not much fiction written in Colonial America, as most of the literature was written to inform or persuade.

Romantic Period

The **American Romantic** movement is also known as the American Renaissance. This movement yielded several notable American writers and works that began characterizing American literature and differentiating it from British literature. This literature, written after the American Revolutionary War and until the end of the Civil War, praised individualism and featured an expression of national pride and patriotism. The transcendentalists' extreme ideas about self-sufficiency and subjectivity reiterated this individualism, and their recommendations about society and its structure furthered the separation of American literature from British literature. While this period shaped the definition of American literature, it is criticized for featuring a narrow view of

American politics and social issues at the time, as well as promoting a small group of similar writers.

Review Video: Authors in the Romantic Period
Visit mometrix.com/academy and enter code: 752719

Harlem Renaissance

The **Harlem Renaissance** took place in America during the 1920s and 1930s. The changing economy and opportunities led African Americans in the south to seek new lifestyles in other parts of America at the beginning of the 20th century. Many moved to Harlem, a small area in New York City. This group of African Americans yielded highly influential scholarly and artistic works, including poetry, fiction, music, and plays. The Harlem Renaissance marked an opportunity for these intellectuals and artists, who were largely ignored in the aftermath of the Civil War, to use their talents and express themselves through their works. While artists often featured personal expression in their works, the Harlem Renaissance was unique in its volume of culturally expressive works. This cultural expression and the movement's main ideas also contributed to the Civil Rights movement by promoting a spirit of unity among African Americans. The Harlem Renaissance eventually ended in the wake of the stock market crash in 1929. As the Great Depression began, financial support for the arts dwindled, making it difficult for many artists to succeed financially. Some members of the Harlem Renaissance who influenced American literature include Langston Hughes, Zora Neale Hurston, and Paul Robeson.

British Literary Periods

Neoclassical

The **British Neoclassical** period began in the middle of the 17th century and ended in the late 18th century. The latter part of the movement also took place alongside the Enlightenment, a period of scientific discovery and study that influenced many Western cultures. The Enlightenment's concern with intellectual pursuits and improvement increased discussions of introspection, or an individual's analysis of their own behavior, thoughts, and self. These ideas also affected society in England, as they contributed to a general attitude of complacency and a desire to ignore the past. The period saw a slightly increased acceptance of female writers, as their works were viewed as a method of self-reflection and improvement. The changes in British society allowed several new forms of literature to gain popularity and acceptance, usually for their introspective qualities. Essays, diaries, and letters all displayed the author's thoughts and experience, aligning them with the culture's values. Novels also gained popularity, as many were fictional diaries or epistolary novels. Journalism flourished during the Neoclassical period, leading to the creation of the newspaper. Literary criticism also gained popularity, though it was used to criticize an author and their style rather than examine or analyze the content of the work.

Victorian

The **Victorian Era** in England was influenced by a variety of events and ideas, many of which were influenced by the Victorians' economy. The Industrial Revolution in England changed the circumstances of work for the Victorians. The changing industries and lack of labor laws led to several problems and a wide division between Victorian social classes. These factors inspired and saturated much of Victorian literature. Many novels' plots and characters were heavily influenced by social and economic issues, and many poems referenced and criticized specific events that occurred during this period.

While the structure of Victorian society was a major influence on literature, there were other popular topics that appeared in literature. Topics like evolution, psychology, and colonization frequently appeared in Victorian literature, reflecting the concerns and interests of the Victorian culture. The Victorian society was also characterized by a strict moral code that supported the view of women as homemakers and criticized the idea of female writers. Not only did this affect the portrayal of women in literature, but it also led some female novelists, such as the Bronte sisters, to write under a pseudonym and present their works as having been written by a man. Victorian literature also popularized forms of literature, including the novel and the dramatic monologue, a poetic form developed by Robert Browning. Victorian writers include Charles Dickens, Oscar Wilde, Elizabeth Barrett Browning, Emily Bronte, Matthew Arnold, and Thomas Hardy.

World Literary Characteristics and Periods

While many other nations shared literary movements with America and England, there are numerous literary movements that are unique to other countries and cultures. Some of these literary movements can be understood as variations of movements like Romanticism or modernism, since they occurred at similar times and feature similar elements, but the political and cultural events of each country shaped their version of each movement. Most regions also have some type of mythology, and while different mythologies have similar characters and events, each region's mythology is unique and significant to the region's literature. Another common feature of world literature is colonialism. Many nations are former colonies of European countries, and the effects of colonization are present in modern literature from countries worldwide, making it a key feature of many regions' body of literature.

African Literature

Literature from some cultures was not recorded until the 19th century, causing any movements and trends to be informed by ideas told aloud. This is true of African literature, where stories and ideas were spoken and passed down through the generations. Early African poetry was often metaphorical, structured or written to form a paradox, and included a riddle or puzzling statement. Proverbs and didactic tales were also told frequently, reflecting the dominant religions in a given region and time period. These poems and stories also reflect the variety of languages spoken in Africa and the shifts in each language's usage. Early African literature, once people began writing it down, included stories and proverbs that had been passed down, translations of religious texts, and descriptions of the way of life in different African cultures or groups. These cultures and the events specific to each of them produce a unique body of literature that places emphasis on certain topics and ideas. For example, much of the modern literature written in South Africa discusses politics and issues of race, since the country's history is characterized by events and movements that revolved around these topics.

Asian Literature

Asian literature features writings from several different countries and languages and has spanned many centuries. Many popular forms of writing have come from Asia, such as the haiku. A couple of significant literary movements include The Hungry Generation in South Asia and the Misty Poets in China. The Hungry Generation is a literary movement involving literature written in the Bengali language, spoken mainly in West Bengal and Bangladesh. The literature is characterized by unique and innovative writing, which impacted the use of figurative language in the region. The Hungry Generation also discussed cultural issues, particularly colonization in the region, and many participants were arrested for their work. The Misty Poets in China were characterized by their expressive use of abstractions. Their name, Misty Poets, comes from their writings, which were difficult to interpret due to their use of abstract language and ambiguity. This movement was partly inspired by the Misty Poets' distaste for literary realism, though its influence is detectable within their poetry. Many of the Misty Poets were punished for their poetry, since the poetry of this movement was also politically critical.

Latin American Literature

Latin American literature has several literary movements, many of which occurred near the same time as American and British literary movements and share ideas and trends with their English counterparts. Despite these similarities, each of these movements is distinguishable as its own movement with unique impacts of Latin American literature. By the 17th century, written language was in use in Mexico, and Latin American literary trends and figures had been recognized. During the 18th century, Latin American literature featured a variety of ideas and themes within each form of literature. By the 19th century, literary themes were more unified throughout popular Latin American literature. In the early 19th century, Latin American literature embraced the Romantic movement as it came to an end in England and the United States. Several Latin American countries were also fighting for independence during this time, amplifying the Romantic idea of national pride and identity.

In the wake of the Romantic movement, Latin American literature introduced the unique *Modernismo* movement, which yielded a large volume of poetry and is characterized by the use of whimsical imagery and discussions of spiritual ideas. Following *Modernismo* was the *Vanguardia* movement, which was created to introduce diversity within Latin American literature after modernism permeated the literature of the time. *Vanguardia* involved writers taking risks in their writing and breaking the mold from typical Latin American literature. In the 20th century, *Estridentismo* followed the *Vanguardia* movement, marrying the *Vanguardia* movement with the European Avant-Garde movement. Other 20th century movements functioned similarly by adapting literary movements from other regions to suit the themes and trends in Latin American literature, reflect Latin American cultures, and set their literature apart from other cultures.

Chapter Quiz

1. Which of the following writers is NOT considered a Dark Romantic?

a. Edgar Allan Poe
b. Emily Dickinson
c. Herman Melville
d. Ralph Waldo Emerson

2. Langston Hughes, Zora Neale Hurston, and Paul Robeson were members of which literary movement?

a. British Neoclassical period
b. American Romantic movement
c. Harlem Renaissance
d. Hungry Generation

Chapter Quiz Answer Key

1. D: In American literature, a group of late Romantic writers are recognized as Dark Romantics. These authors' works may be associated with both the Romantic and Gothic movements. These works emphasize nature and emotion, aligning them with Romanticism—and include dark themes and tones, aligning them with Gothic literature. However, these works do not all feature the historically inspired characteristics of Gothic literature, and their morals or outcomes more closely resemble those of Romantic literature. The Dark Romantics include writers such as Edgar Allan Poe, Nathaniel Hawthorne, Emily Dickinson, and Herman Melville.

2. C: The Harlem Renaissance took place in America during the 1920s and 1930s. The changing economy and opportunities led African Americans in the south to seek new lifestyles in other parts of America at the beginning of the 20th century. Many moved to Harlem, a small area in New York City. This group of African Americans yielded highly influential scholarly and artistic works, including poetry, fiction, music, and plays. The Harlem Renaissance marked an opportunity for these intellectuals and artists, who were largely ignored in the aftermath of the Civil War, to use their talents and express themselves through their works. While artists often featured personal expression in their works, the Harlem Renaissance was unique in its volume of culturally expressive works. This cultural expression and the movement's main ideas also contributed to the Civil Rights movement by promoting a spirit of unity among African Americans. The Harlem Renaissance eventually ended in the wake of the stock market crash in 1929. As the Great Depression began, financial support for the arts dwindled, making it difficult for many artists to succeed financially. Some members of the Harlem Renaissance who influenced American literature include Langston Hughes, Zora Neale Hurston, and Paul Robeson.

Literary Periods and Movements

Old English

The English language developed over a long period of time through interactions between different groups in Europe, including the Romans, the Germans, and the Celtics. The Anglo-Saxons, a group that left what is now Germany and settled in England, further established the English language by using what is now called **Old English**. While Old English laid foundations for modern English, its usage fundamentally differs from the way English is used today. For example, Old English relied on inflections to create meaning, placing little importance on the order of the words in the sentence. Its use of verbs and tenses also differs from modern English grammar. The Anglo-Saxons also used kennings, or compound words that functioned as figurative language.

Old English, as a language influenced by several cultures, had dialects from its inception. Differences in usage also came from the division between secular and religious cultures. This division heavily influenced Old English literature, as most of the literature from the time is categorized according to the set of beliefs it reflects. Most of the influential literature of the time includes riddles, poems, or translations of religious texts. Surviving Old English poetry mainly discusses real heroes and battles or provides a narrative about a fictional hero. Many of these fictional poems are considered *lays*, or *lais*, which are narrative poems that are structured using couplets of lines containing eight syllables each. The translations were often of passages from the Christian Bible, adaptations of Biblical passages, or copies of Christian hymns. Old English persisted until the 12th century, where it was eventually replaced with Middle English. Influential literature from this period includes *Beowulf*, "The Wanderer," "The Wife's Lament," and "The Seafarer."

Middle English

Old English was replaced by **Middle English**, which was used from the 12th century to the 16th century. Old English was not governed by a consistent set of grammatical rules until the Norse people, their language, and its structure influenced the integration of grammar into English, leading to Middle English. Middle English relied less on inflections than Old English, instead creating variations by using affixes and synonyms. The development of grammar was further facilitated by the printing press, which made it easier for writers to comply with grammar rules since the printing of identical copies reduced variation between texts.

Old English's evolution into Middle English can be narrowed down to three stages: Early, Central, and Late Middle English. Early Middle English, though it showed a change in the language, maintained the writing style of Old English. Central Middle English is characterized by the development of dialects within written communication, which is partly due to scribes who translated texts or parts of texts using terms from their own dialect, rather than the source. Late Middle English includes numerous developments that created the foundation for Modern English. *The Canterbury Tales*, "Sir Gawain and the Green Knight," and "Le Morte d'Arthur" are all Middle English texts that are still read and studied today.

The Renaissance

The **Renaissance** swept through Europe and lasted for multiple centuries, bringing many developments in culture, the arts, education, and philosophy. The Renaissance in England did not begin until the late 15th century. Though ideas and cultures of the past, especially those of the ancient Greeks and Romans, inspired the Renaissance, the period saw innumerable developments in the English language and literature. The Renaissance was characterized by a focus on the humanities, allowing the arts, including literature, to flourish. At the time, drama was possibly the most popular form of literature, as the popularity of plays and theatrical performances greatly increased. Much of Renaissance literature is still studied today, maintaining its influence on Western literature. Poetry was also popular, and the period saw the development of new forms of poetry, such as the sonnet. Sonnets are often recognized according to one of four styles, each of which was popularized by a Renaissance writer. Lyrical poetry, which discusses emotions and is often written using first-person point of view, was also popular during the Renaissance.

In addition to new forms and literary trends, the Renaissance period also impacted English literature by facilitating discussion over the translation of the Bible. Education at the time often included instruction in Greek and Latin, allowing those with an education to read ancient texts in their original language. However, this instruction did not reach the majority of the public. The Protestant Reformation encouraged discussions about translating the Bible to make it accessible to more people. This suggestion was challenged by those who doubted the ability of the English language to fully reflect the original text. Eventually, the Bible was translated to English, and William Tyndale's partial translation became especially influential for later translations and the continuing development of the English language. Influential writers of the English Renaissance include William Shakespeare, John Donne, John Milton, Edmund Spenser, and Christopher Marlowe.

Gothic

The Gothic literary movement, beginning in the 18th century and persisting through the 19th century, took inspiration from the architecture and cultures of the Late Middle Ages in Europe. The Late Middle Ages saw the popularity of Gothic architecture, most prominently in places of worship. These structures inspired many of the settings in **Gothic literature**, as a large volume of Gothic literature takes place in an impressive location, such as a castle or ornate mansion. Gothic works also are often set in the past, long before the time the story was written. This aligns with prominent themes in Gothic literature, as several pieces are informed by an event that occurred before the story begins or a character who died before the plot's first event.

Another common characteristic of Gothic literature is its eerie, dark, suspenseful tone. Authors of Gothic literature often created this tone by setting their works in secluded and strange locations and incorporating intense, unsettling, or even supernatural events and scenarios into the plot. This tone is also created through the theme of death or mortality that often appears in Gothic literature. These characteristics support the aim of many Gothic writers to create fiction that evokes a certain emotion from the reader or shapes their reading experience. Well-known authors of Gothic literature include Horace Walpole, Ann Radcliffe, Edgar Allan Poe, and Nathaniel Hawthorne. While the Gothic literary movement took place in the 18th and 19th centuries, many works have been published in more recent centuries that have several characteristics of Gothic literature and may be included within the overall Gothic genre.

Naturalism

Naturalism was an active literary movement in the late 19th century, taking place alongside movements such as realism and modernism. **Naturalism**, like realism, rejected the emotional focus and sentimentality of Romanticism and provided a type of social commentary. However, the naturalist movement stretched the ideas of realism, promoting literature that authentically depicts the life of the common man and criticizing the influence of morality on such literature. Naturalist literature often includes characters who belong to a lower class and experience circumstances beyond their own control and takes place in urban settings. Prominent themes in naturalist literature include nature as an apathetic force, the influence of heredity, and life as something to be endured and survived. One of the most influential naturalist writers is French writer Emile Zola. Influential American Naturalists include Stephen Crane, Hamlin Garland, and Theodore Dreiser.

MODERNISM

The Modernist literary movement was largely influenced by industrialization, which heavily impacted both the Unites States and England, primarily in the 19th century. **Modernism** in literature was characterized by an attempt to turn away from the norms and traditions of literature and use new techniques and methods. Modernist literature was often written in first person and used literary devices and techniques to reveal problems within society. For the American modernists, these societal changes came from industrialization and the first World War, which effected the general view of human nature and reliability. In England, there were additional factors contributing to this shift. Modernism began during Queen Victoria's reign, which defined the period known as the Victorian Era. The Victorian society was characterized by a strict moral code that permeated England's society at the time. This moral code was incompatible with the Modernist's desire to turn away from tradition, but the changes that accompanied Victoria's death in 1901 enabled the Modernist movement to grow in England. American Modernist writers include Ezra Pound, William Carlos Williams, and Gertrude Stein. British Modernist writers include Matthew Arnold, William Butler Yeats, T. S. Eliot, and Joseph Conrad.

POSTMODERNISM

Postmodernism grew out of Modernism's reliance on science and universal assertions, but emphasized the individual's subjective perception of reality, as it is often more authentic to an individual's experience than a universally applied statement. Postmodernism asserts that since each person creates their own version of reality, fully and accurately defining reality is futile and impossible. Due to this skepticism, postmodern writers use many concrete details, rather than abstract details, because they can be objectively observed and are not left up to the individual. The postmodernist literary movement began around the 1960s. The literary movement included a variety of new genres and techniques, reflecting the postmodernist idea that things like art cannot be truly defined or simplified. Notable American writers of the postmodernist movement include Kurt Vonnegut, John Barth, and Thomas Pynchon. British postmodernist writers include John Fowles and Julian Barnes.

Chapter Quiz

1. Which of the following writers is included in the postmodernist movement?

a. Kurt Vonnegut
b. T. S. Eliot
c. Joseph Conrad
d. Stephen Crane

Chapter Quiz Answer Key

1. A: Postmodernism grew out of Modernism's reliance on science and universal assertions, but emphasized the individual's subjective perception of reality because it is often more authentic to an individual's experience than a universally applied statement. Postmodernism asserts that, because each person creates their own version of reality, fully and accurately defining reality is futile and impossible. Due to this skepticism, postmodern writers use many concrete details because, unlike abstract details, they can be objectively observed and are not left up to the individual. The postmodernist literary movement began around the 1960s. The literary movement included a variety of new genres and techniques, reflecting the postmodernist idea that things like art cannot be truly defined or simplified. Notable American writers of the postmodernist movement include Kurt Vonnegut, John Barth, and Thomas Pynchon. British postmodernist writers include John Fowles and Julian Barnes.

Public Speaking

Speeches

Speeches are written to be delivered in spoken language in public, to various groups of people, at formal or informal events. Some generic types include welcome speeches, thank-you speeches, keynote addresses, position papers, commemorative and dedication speeches, and farewell speeches. Speeches are commonly written in present tense and usually begin with an introduction greeting the audience. At official functions, specific audience members are named ("Chairperson [name]," "Principal [name], teachers, and students," etc.) and when audiences include a distinguished guest, he or she is often named as well. Then the speaker introduces him or herself by name, position, and department or organization as applicable. After the greeting, the speaker then introduces the topic and states the purpose of the speech. The body of the speech follows, similarly to the body of an essay, stating its main points, an explanation of each point, and supporting evidence. Finally, in the conclusion, the speaker states his or her hope for accomplishing the speech's purpose and thanks the audience for attending and listening to the speech.

Clearly Written Prose and Speeches

To achieve **clarity**, a writer or speaker must first define his or her purpose carefully. The speech should be organized logically, so that sentences make sense and follow each other in an understandable order. Sentences must also be constructed well, with carefully chosen words and structure. Organizing a speech in advance using an outline provides the writer or speaker with a blueprint, directing and focusing the composition to meet its intended purpose. Organized speeches enable audiences to comprehend and retain the presented information more easily. Humans naturally seek to impose order on the world by seeking patterns. Hence, when ideas in a speech are well-organized and adhere to a consistent pattern, the speaker communicates better with listeners and is more convincing. Speechwriters can use chronological patterns to organize events, sequential patterns to organize processes by their steps, and spatial patterns to help audiences visualize geographical locations and movements or physical scenarios. Also, comparison-contrast patterns give audiences insight about similarities and differences between and among topics, especially when listeners are more familiar with one than the other.

Evaluating Speeches for Concise Information

To convince or persuade listeners or reinforce a message, speeches must be succinct. Audiences can become confused by excessive anecdotes and details. If a speaker takes three minutes or more to get to the point, audience members' attention will start to fade and will only worsen when details deviate from the main subject. When answering a question, the asker and speaker may even forget the original question if the speaker takes too long. Speakers should practice not only rehearsing written speeches, but also developing skill for spontaneous question-and-answer sessions after speeches. Speakers should differentiate necessary from simply interesting information because audiences can become overwhelmed by too much information. Speakers should know what points they wish to make. They should not be afraid to pause before responding to questions, which indicates thoughtfulness and control rather than lack of knowledge. Restating questions increases comprehension and appropriate responses, and allows time to form answers mentally.

Organizational Patterns for Speeches

A speechwriter who uses an **advantages-disadvantages** pattern of organization presents the audience with the pros and cons of a topic. This aids writers in discussing two sides of an issue objectively without an argumentative position, enabling listeners to weigh both aspects. When a speechwriter uses a **cause-and-effect** pattern, it can help to persuade audiences to agree with an action or solution by showing significant relationships between factors. Writers may separate an outline into two main "cause" and "effect" sections or into separate sections for each cause, including the effect for each. Persuasive writing also benefits from **problem-solution** patterns: by establishing the existence of a problem, writers induce audiences to realize a need for change. By supplying a solution and supporting its superiority above other solutions, the writer convinces audiences of the value of that solution. When none of these patterns—or **chronological**, **sequential**, **spatial**, or **comparison-contrast** patterns—applies, speechwriters often use topical patterns. These organize information by various subtopics and types within the main topic or category.

EFFECTIVE SPEECH DELIVERY

Speakers should deliver speeches in a natural, conversational manner rather than being rigidly formal or theatrical. Effective delivery is also supported by confidence. Speakers should be direct, building audience rapport through personal connection and vivid imagery. Speakers should be mindful of the occasion, subject, and audience of their speeches and take care to use appropriate language. Good speakers learn vocal control, including volume, speed, pitch, use of pauses, tonal variety, correct pronunciation, and clear articulation. They can express enthusiasm and emphasize important points with their voices. Nonverbal behaviors, such as eye contact, facial expressions, gestures, good posture, and body movements clarify communication, stress important ideas, and influence perceptions that the speaker is trustworthy, competent, and credible. Nonverbal communications should seem as spontaneous and natural as vocal or verbal ones. Speakers should know their speeches well and practice frequently, taking care to avoid nervous or irrelevant movements such as tapping or pacing.

Chapter Quiz

1. Speeches should be delivered in which manner?

a. Flat and formal
b. Natural and conversational
c. Loud and theatrical
d. Stoic and academic

Chapter Quiz Answer Key

1. B: Speakers should deliver speeches in a natural, conversational manner rather than being rigidly formal or theatrical. Effective delivery is also supported by confidence. Speakers should be direct, building audience rapport through personal connection and vivid imagery. Speakers should be mindful of the occasion, subject, and audience of their speeches and take care to use appropriate language. Good speakers learn vocal control, including volume, speed, pitch, use of pauses, tonal variety, correct pronunciation, and clear articulation. They can express enthusiasm and emphasize important points with their voices. Nonverbal behaviors, such as eye contact, facial expressions, gestures, good posture, and body movements clarify communication, stress important ideas, and influence perceptions that the speaker is trustworthy, competent, and credible. Nonverbal communications should seem as spontaneous and natural as vocal or verbal ones. Speakers should know their speeches well and practice frequently, taking care to avoid nervous or irrelevant movements such as tapping or pacing.

Media Types

Media and Format Choices

Effective communication depends on choosing the correct method. Media and format choices are influenced by the target audience, the budget, and the needs of the audience.

Instructional Videos

Instructional videos have potential for excellent two-way communication because questions and feedback can be built in. Videos can be targeted to particular audiences, and they can be paused for discussion or replayed to reinforce concepts. Viewers can see processes, including "before," "during," and "after" phases. Videos are accessible because most communities have at least one DVD player or computer. Moreover, video players and computers are continually becoming less expensive to buy and use. Disadvantages include the necessity of editing software and equipment in some cases, as well as the need for support from other print materials. There is also danger of overuse, if other media or methods are more appropriate, and higher up-front costs. Producers of instructional videos must account for the costs of script development and hiring local performers as needed.

DVDs and CDs

Interactive DVDs and CDs, such as games, give viewers the opportunity to actively participate as they learn information. Additionally, videos are considered to be a professional method of sharing information. Compared to many other media formats, discs are comparatively inexpensive to make and are easy to transport due to their small size and weight. They are more resistant to damage and aging than older videotape technology, making them more durable. Some disadvantages include needing access to technology to play what is stored on the disc and access to certain software programs to add new content to a disc, especially if the producer wants to include video animation or audio commentary. Producers must also consider expenses concerning paid staff and production and labeling expenses. Content that would appear on DVDs and CDs can alternatively be shared through streaming services or digital files stored on a computer or other compatible device.

Television and Radio

Both television and radio are forms of mass media that reach many people. TV has the broadest reach and can market to the general public or be customized for target audiences, while radio only tends to reach specific target audiences. TV has the advantage of video plus audio, while radio broadcasts only feature audio. However, access to television programs is more expensive than access to radio broadcasts. A shared disadvantage is that TV and radio audiences can only interact directly during call-in programs. Additionally, programming times may be inconvenient, but tape, digital sound, and digital video recording (DVR) can remedy this. Many streaming services also provide access to these programs. Both television and radio are useful for communicating simple slogans and messages, and both can generate awareness, interest, and excitement.

Newspapers

Except for the occasional community columns, news releases, and letters to the editor, newspaper pages and features afford little opportunity for audience input or participation. However, they do reach and appeal to the general public. Cost is an advantage: hiring a PR writer and paying for a news advertisement costs much less than a radio or TV spot. Additionally, newspaper features are high-status, and audiences can reread and review them as often as they like. However, newspaper ads may have difficulty affecting the reader as deeply without audio or video, and they require a literate audience. Their publication is also subject to editors' whims and biases. Newspaper pieces combining advertising and editorial content—"advertorials"—provide inclusion of paid material, but are viewed as medium-status and cost more.

Websites, Blogs, Mobile Phones, and Text Messaging

Computer literacy is required for online material, but participation potential is high via websites, e-networking, and blogging. Mobile phones and text messaging are used for enormous direct, public, two-way and one-on-one communication, with timely information and reminders. Web media need a literate public and can be tailored for specific audiences. They afford global information, are accessible by increasingly technology-literate populations, and are high-status. Web media disadvantages include the necessity of computers and people to design, manage, and supply content, as well as to provide technical support. Mobile and text media are globally popular, but appeal especially to certain demographics like teens and young adults. They are increasingly available, especially in rural regions, and are decreasing in cost. Mobile and text media disadvantages include required brevity in texts and provider messaging charges. Links to related websites and pages within existing sites are also advantages of digital media.

Public Presentations and Slideshows

Public presentations have great potential for audience participation and can directly target various audiences. They can encourage the establishment of partnerships and groups, stimulate local ownership of issues and projects, and make information public. A drawback to public presentations is that they are limited to nights, weekends, or whenever audiences are available and do not always attract the intended audience.

Another method of presentation is to use **slideshows**. These presentations are best for sophisticated audiences like professionals, civil servants, and service organizations. Well-designed slideshows are good for stimulating audience interest, selling ideas, and marketing products. Also, they are accessible online as well as in-person so they can reach a broader audience. Slideshow disadvantages include the necessity of projectors and other equipment. They are also limited to communicating more general points, outlines, and summaries rather than conveying a multitude of information in more detail.

Posters and Brochures

Both **posters** and **brochures** can target audiences of the general public and more specific public sectors. Posters are better for communicating simple slogans and messages, while brochures can include more detail and are better for printing instructional information. Both can be inexpensive to produce, especially if printed only as needed and in-house. Posters can often be printed in-house without using outside printing companies. However, it is difficult to get feedback on both posters and brochures—unless they have been broadly tested, or if their publication is accompanied by workshops and other participatory events. A disadvantage of using posters is that they are designed to draw attention and communicate quickly, as they are mostly viewed in passing. This means that their messages must be simple and communicate efficiently. A disadvantage of using brochures is that they can only be distributed to a specific, limited group or area. Posters and brochures are also only understood when audiences are literate in both written language and visual elements.

Flyers and Fact Sheets

Flyers and fact sheets have one-way communication potential because readers cannot give feedback. Their target audiences are general. Some advantages of using this form of media include flexibility: people can distribute them at meetings or events, put them on car windshields in parking lots, leave them in stores or on bulletin boards at community agencies and schools, hand them out from booths and other displays, or mail them. When printed in black and white, they can be very inexpensive. They afford recipients the convenience of being able to review them at their leisure. Organizations and individuals can produce flyers and fact sheets in-house, or even at home with desktop publishing software. Disadvantages include their limitation to single facts or tips and specific information on specified topics.

Evaluating Media Information Sources

With the wealth of media in different formats available today, users are more likely to take media at face value. However, to understand the content of media, consumers must **critically evaluate each source**.

Users should ask themselves the following questions about media sources:

- Who is delivering this message and why?
- What methods do a media source's publishers employ to gain and maintain users' attention?
- Which points of view is the media source representing?
- What are the various ways this message could be interpreted?
- What information is missing from the message?
- Is the source scholarly, i.e., peer-reviewed?
- Does it include author names and their credentials as they relate to the topic?
- Who publishes it and why?
- Who is the target audience?
- Is the language technically specific or non-technical?
- Are sources cited, research claims documented, conclusions based on furnished evidence, and references provided?
- Is the publication current?

Other Considerations for the Validity of Sources

For books, consider whether information is **up-to-date** and whether **historical perspectives** apply. Content is more likely to be **scholarly** if publishers are universities, government, or professional organizations. Book reviews can also provide useful information. For articles, identify the author, publisher, frequency of the periodical's publication, and what kind of advertising, if any, is included. Looking for book reviews also informs users. For articles, look for biographical author information, publisher name, frequency of the periodical's publication, and whether advertising is included and, if so, whether it is for certain occupations or disciplines. For web pages, check their domain names, identify publishers or sponsors, look for the author or publisher's contact information, check dates of most recent page updates, be alert to biases, and verify the validity of the information on the webpage. The quality and accuracy of web pages located through search engines rather than library databases varies widely and requires careful user inspection. Web page recommendations from reliable sources like university faculties can help indicate quality and accuracy. Citations of websites by credible or scholarly sources also show reliability. Authors' names, relevant credentials, affiliations, and contact information support their authority. Site functionality, such as ease of navigation, ability to search, site maps, and indexes, is also a criterion to consider.

Persuasive Media

Advertising, public relations, and advocacy media all use **persuasion**. Advertisers use persuasion to sell goods and services. The public relations field uses persuasion to give good impressions of companies, governments, or organizations. Advocacy groups use persuasion to garner support or votes. Persuasion can come through commercials, public service announcements, speeches, websites, and newsletters, among other channels. Activists, lobbyists, government officials, and politicians use political rhetoric involving persuasive techniques. Basic techniques include using celebrity spokespersons, whom consumers admire or aspire to resemble, or conversely, "everyday people" (albeit often portrayed by actors) with whom consumers identify. Using expert testimonials lends credibility. Explicit claims of content, effectiveness, quality, and reliability—which often cannot be proven or disproven—are used to persuade. While news and advocacy messages mostly eschew humor for credibility's sake (except in political satire), advertising often persuades via humor, which gets consumer attention and associates its pleasure with advertised products and services. Qualifiers and other misleading terms, sometimes called "Weasel words," are often combined with exaggerated claims. Intensifiers, such as hyperboles, superlatives, repetitions, and sentimental appeals are also persuasive.

INTERMEDIATE TECHNIQUES

Dangerous propagandist Adolf Hitler said people suspect little lies more than big ones; hence the "Big Lie" is a persuasion method that cannot be identified without consumers' keen critical thinking. A related method is **charisma**, which can induce people to believe messages they would otherwise reject. **Euphemisms** substitute abstract, vague, or bland terms in place of more graphic, clear, and unpleasant ones. For example, the terms "layoffs" and "firing" are replaced by "downsizing," and "torture" is replaced with "intensive interrogation techniques." **Extrapolation** bases sweeping conclusions on small amounts of minor information to appeal to what consumers wish or hope. Flattery appeals to consumer self-esteem needs, such as L'Oréal's "You're worth it." Flattery is sometimes accomplished through contrast, like ads showing others' mistakes to make consumers feel superior and smarter. "Glittering generalities" refer to claims based on concepts such as beauty, love, health, democracy, freedom, and science. Persuaders use this tactic to gain consumer acceptance without consumers questioning what they mean. The opposite is name-calling to persuade consumers to reject someone or something.

American citizens love new ideas and technology. Persuaders exploit this by emphasizing the **newness** of products, services, and candidates. Conversely, they also use **nostalgia** to evoke consumers' happy memories, which they often remember more than unhappy ones. Citing "scientific evidence" is an intermediate version of the basic technique of expert testimonials. Consumers may accept this as proof, but some advertisers, politicians, and other persuaders may present inaccurate or misleading "evidence." Another intermediate technique is the "simple solution." Although the natures of people and life are complex, when consumers feel overwhelmed by complexity, persuaders exploit this by offering policies, products, or services they claim will solve complicated problems by simple means. Persuaders also use symbols, images, words, and names we associate with more general, emotional concepts like lifestyle, country, family, religion, and gender. While symbols have power, their significance also varies across individuals. For example, some consumers regard the Hummer SUV as a prestigious status symbol, while others regard it as environmentally harmful and irresponsible.

ADVANCED TECHNIQUES

Ad hominem, Latin for "against the man" attacks the person behind an idea rather than criticizing the idea itself. It operates by association: if a person is considered immoral or uneducated, then his or her ideas must be bad as well. **"Stacking the deck"** misleads by presenting only selected information that supports one position. **Apophasis**, or a false denial, allows the speaker or writer to indirectly bring attention to a flaw in an opponent's credibility. For example, a politician saying, "I won't mention my opponent's tax evasion issues" manages to mention them while seeming less accusatory. Persuaders may also use **majority belief**, making statements such as "Four out of five dentists recommend this brand" or "[insert number] people can't be wrong." In an intensified version, persuaders exploit group dynamics at rallies, speeches, and other live-audience events where people are vulnerable to surrounding crowd influences. **Scapegoating**, blaming one person or group for complex problems, is a form of the intermediate "simple solution" technique, a practice common in politics. **Timing** also persuades, like advertising flowers and candy in the weeks preceding Valentine's Day, ad campaigns preceding new technology rollouts, and politician speeches following big news events.

Visual Media

Some images have the power to communicate more information than an entire paragraph. Images can contain several elements and be interpreted different ways, making them an effective vessel for abstract and emotionally appealing ideas. Humans are also able to understand images before they fully acquire language, meaning that images can reach more people than language can at any time. Images are also more quickly comprehended than text, making them a highly efficient method of communication. People can remember or memorize images more easily than text, also. Historically, images have been used for propaganda and subliminal messaging. Images are also used by different companies as an effective technique to entice customers to buy their products. Though images do not always contain text, they can still convey explicit and implicit meanings. An image's explicit meaning would be the most recognizable shape or concept in the image. The implicit meaning may be obscured within the image through the use of negative space, background images, or out-of-focus shapes.

Interpreting and Evaluating Persuasive Media

Most messages can be interpreted in different ways. They can be interpreted explicitly, where the literal meaning of the words in the message creates the meaning of the message, and no context is considered. Alternatively, other contexts can be considered alongside the explicit meaning of the message. These create alternative, not clearly stated meanings called **implicit meanings**. Politics, current events, regional norms, and even emotions are examples of contexts that can add implicit meanings to a message. These implicit meanings can change the effect a message has on its recipient. Many products have slogans with both implicit and explicit meanings. These implicit meanings must be considered to fully interpret a message.

Messages come in different forms, and each form has a unique way of communicating both explicit and implicit meanings. Images can come with captions that communicate a message, but some images carry subliminal messages. This means that their implicit meaning is received by the viewer, but the viewer is not aware of it. The term **propaganda** describes messages that advocate for a specific opinion or way of thinking. Most propaganda is politically driven and has been used during historical periods, most notably World War II. Unlike messages with hidden or veiled implicit meanings, most propaganda aggressively communicates its entire meaning and is difficult to misinterpret. Documentaries are another prominent form of communication. Documentaries are informational videos that focus on a specific figure, subject, phenomenon, or time period. While documentaries are primarily fact based and contain excerpts from interviews and testimonials, documentaries feature a limited view of their subject and sometimes attempt to persuade viewers to take action or embrace their central message. While some documentaries communicate this clearly, some hide an implicit meaning through the way they present each piece of information.

Chapter Quiz

1. An *ad hominem* argument does which of the following?

a. Misleads by presenting only selected information that supports one position
b. Blames one group or person for complex problems
c. Attacks the person behind an idea rather than refuting the idea itself
d. Indirectly brings attention to a flaw in an opponent's credibility

2. An apophasis argument does which of the following?

a. Misleads by presenting only selected information that supports one position
b. Blames one group or person for complex problems
c. Attacks the person behind an idea rather than refuting the idea itself
d. Indirectly brings attention to a flaw in an opponent's credibility

Chapter Quiz Answer Key

1. C: *Ad hominem*, Latin for "against the man," attacks the person behind an idea rather than criticizing the idea itself. It operates by association: if a person is considered immoral or uneducated, then his or her ideas must be similarly flawed or meritless.

2. D: Apophasis, or a false denial, allows the speaker or writer to indirectly bring attention to a flaw in an opponent's credibility. For example, a politician saying, "I won't mention my opponent's tax evasion issues" manages to mention them while seeming less accusatory.

Developmental Literacy

Literacy

Literacy is commonly understood as the **ability to read and write**. UNESCO, the United Nations Educational, Scientific, and Cultural Organization, has further defined literacy as the "ability to identify, understand, interpret, create, communicate, compute, and use printed and written materials associated with varying contexts." Under the UNESCO definition, understanding cultural, political, and historical contexts of communities falls under the definition of literacy. While **reading literacy** may be gauged simply by the ability to read a newspaper, **writing literacy** includes spelling, grammar, and sentence structure. To be literate in a foreign language, one would also need to be able to understand a language by listening and be able to speak the language. Some argue that visual representation and numeracy should be included in the requirements one must meet to be considered literate. **Computer literacy** refers to one's ability to utilize the basic functions of computers and other technologies. Subsets of reading literacy include phonological awareness, decoding, comprehension, and vocabulary.

Phonological Awareness

A subskill of literacy, phonological awareness is the ability to perceive sound structures in a spoken word, such as syllables and the individual phonemes within syllables. **Phonemes** are the sounds represented by the letters in the alphabet. The ability to separate, blend, and manipulate sounds is critical to developing reading and spelling skills. Phonological awareness is concerned with not only syllables, but also **onset sounds** (the initial sound in a word, such as /k/ in 'cat') and **rime** (the sounds that follow the onset in a word, such as /at/ in 'cat'). Phonological awareness is an auditory skill that does not necessarily involve print. It should be developed before the student has learned letter to sound correspondences. A student's phonological awareness is an indicator of future reading success.

Review Video: Phonological and Phonemic Awareness, and Phonics
Visit mometrix.com/academy and enter code: 197017

Review Video: Components of Oral Language Development
Visit mometrix.com/academy and enter code: 480589

Communication Development Normally Occurring Within a Child's First Five Years of Life

Language and communication development depend strongly on the language a child develops within the first five years of life. During this time, three developmental periods are observed. At birth, the first period begins. This period is characterized by infant crying and gazing. Babies communicate their sensations and emotions through these behaviors, so they are expressive; however, they are not yet intentional. They indirectly indicate their needs through expressing how they feel, and when these needs are met, these communicative behaviors are reinforced. These expressions and reinforcement are the foundations for the later development of intentional communication. This becomes possible in the second developmental period, between 6 and 18 months. At this time, infants become able to coordinate their attention visually with other people relative to things and events, enabling purposeful communication with adults. During the third developmental period, from 18 months on, children come to use language as their main way of communicating and learning. Preschoolers can carry on conversations, exercise self-control through language use, and conduct verbal negotiations.

Milestones of Normal Language Development by the 2 Years Old

By the time most children reach the age of 2 years, they have acquired a vocabulary of about 150 to 300 words. They can name various familiar objects found in their environments. They are able to use at least two prepositions in their speech (e.g., *in*, *on*, and/or *under*). Two-year-olds typically combine the words they know into short sentences. These sentences tend to be mostly noun-verb or verb-noun combinations (e.g., "Daddy work," "Watch this"). They may also include verb-preposition combinations (e.g., "Go out," "Come in"). By the age of 2 years, children use pronouns, such as *I*, *me*, and *you*. They typically can use at least two such pronouns correctly. A normally developing 2-year-old will respond to some commands, directions, or questions, such as "Show me your eyes" or "Where are your ears?"

Salient General Aspects of Human Language Abilities from Before Birth to 5 Years of Age

Language and communication abilities are integral parts of human life that are central to learning, successful school performance, successful social interactions, and successful living. Human language ability begins before birth: the developing fetus can hear not only internal maternal sounds, but also the mother's voice, others' voices, and other sounds outside the womb. Humans have a natural sensitivity to human sounds and languages from before they are born until they are about 4½ years old. These years are critical for developing language and communication. Babies and young children are predisposed to greater sensitivity to human sounds than other sounds, orienting them toward the language spoken around them. Children absorb their environmental language completely, including vocal tones, syntax, usage, and emphasis. This linguistic absorption occurs very rapidly. Children's first 2½ years particularly involve amazing abilities to learn language, including grammatical expression.

6 Months, 12 Months, and 18 Months

Individual differences dictate a broad range of language development that is still normal. However, parents observing noticeably delayed language development in their children should consult professionals. Typically, babies respond to hearing their names by 6 months of age, turn their heads and eyes toward the sources of human voices they hear, and respond accordingly to friendly and angry tones of voice. By the age of 12 months, toddlers can usually understand and follow simple directions, especially when these are accompanied by physical and/or vocal cues. They can intentionally use one or more words with the correct meaning. By the age of 18 months, a normally developing child usually has acquired a vocabulary of roughly 5 to 20 words. Eighteen-month-old children use nouns in their speech most of the time. They are very likely to repeat certain words and/or phrases over and over. At this age, children typically are able to follow simple verbal commands without needing as many visual or auditory cues as at 12 months.

Three Years

By the time they are 3 years old, most normally developing children have acquired vocabularies of between 900 and 1,000 words. Typically, they correctly use the pronouns *I*, *me*, and *you*. They use more verbs more frequently. They apply past tenses to some verbs and plurals to some nouns. 3-year-olds usually can use at least three prepositions; the most common are *in*, *on*, and *under*. The normally developing 3-year-old knows the major body parts and can name them. 3-year-olds typically use 3-word sentences with ease. Normally, parents should find approximately 75 to 100 percent of what a 3-year-old says to be intelligible, while strangers should find between 50 and 75 percent of a 3-year-old's speech intelligible. Children this age comprehend most simple questions about their activities and environments and can answer questions about what they should do when they are thirsty, hungry, sleepy, hot, or cold. They can tell about their experiences in ways that adults can generally follow. By the age of 3 years, children should also be able to tell others their name, age, and sex.

Four Years

When normally developing children are 4 years old, most know the names of animals familiar to them. They can use at least four prepositions in their speech (e.g., *in*, *on*, *under*, *to*, *from*, etc.). They can name familiar objects in pictures, and they know and can identify one color or more. Usually, they are able to repeat four-syllable words they hear. They verbalize as they engage in their activities, which Vygotsky dubbed "private speech." Private speech helps young children think through what they are doing, solve problems, make decisions, and reinforce the correct sequences in multistep activities. When presented with contrasting items, 4-year-olds can understand comparative concepts like bigger and smaller. At this age, they are able to comply with simple commands without the target stimuli being in their sight (e.g., "Put those clothes in the hamper" [upstairs]). Four-year-old children will also frequently repeat speech sounds, syllables, words, and phrases, similar to 18-month-olds' repetitions but at higher linguistic and developmental levels.

Five Years

Once most children have reached the age of 5 years, their speech has expanded from the emphasis of younger children on nouns, verbs, and a few prepositions, and is now characterized by many more descriptive words, including adjectives and adverbs. Five-year-olds understand common antonyms, such as big/little, heavy/light, long/short, and hot/cold. They can now repeat longer sentences they hear, up to about 9 words. When given three consecutive, uninterrupted commands, the typical 5-year-old can follow these without forgetting one or two. At age 5, most children have learned simple concepts of time like today, yesterday, and tomorrow; day, morning, afternoon, and night; and before, after, and later. Five-year-olds typically speak in relatively long sentences and normally should be incorporating some compound sentences (with more than one independent clause) and complex sentences (with one or more independent and dependent clauses). Five-year-old children's speech is also grammatically correct most of the time.

Activities That Teach Phonological Awareness

Classroom activities that teach phonological awareness include language play and exposure to a variety of sounds and the contexts of sounds. Activities that teach phonological awareness include:

- Clapping to the sounds of individual words, names, or all words in a sentence
- Practicing saying blended phonemes
- Singing songs that involve phoneme replacement (e.g., The Name Game)
- Reading poems, songs, and nursery rhymes out loud
- Reading patterned and predictable texts out loud
- Listening to environmental sounds or following verbal directions
- Playing games with rhyming chants or fingerplays
- Reading alliterative texts out loud
- Grouping objects by beginning sounds
- Reordering words in a well-known sentence or making silly phrases by deleting words from a well-known sentence (perhaps from a favorite storybook)

Teaching of Reading Through Phonics

Phonics is the process of learning to read by learning how spoken language is represented by letters. Students learn to read phonetically by sounding out the **phonemes** in words and then blending them together to produce the correct sounds in words. In other words, the student connects speech sounds with letters or groups of letters and blends the sounds together to determine the pronunciation of an unknown word. Phonics is a method commonly used to teach **decoding and reading**, but it has been challenged by other methods, such as the whole language approach. Despite the complexity of pronunciation and combined sounds in the English language, phonics is a highly effective way to teach reading. Being able to read or pronounce a word does not mean the student comprehends the meaning of the word, but context aids comprehension. When phonics is used as a foundation for decoding, children eventually learn to recognize words automatically and advance to decoding multisyllable words with practice.

Alphabetic Principle and Alphabet Writing Systems

The **alphabetic principle** refers to the use of letters and combinations of letters to represent speech sounds. The way letters are combined and pronounced is guided by a system of rules that establishes relationships between written and spoken words and their letter symbols. Alphabet writing systems are common around the world. Some are **phonological** in that each letter stands for an individual sound and words are spelled just as they sound. However, keep in mind that there are other writing systems as well, such as the Chinese **logographic** system and the Japanese **syllabic** system.

Review Video: Print Awareness and Alphabet Knowledge
Visit mometrix.com/academy and enter code: 541069

Facts Children Should Know About Letters

To be appropriately prepared to learn to read and write, a child should learn:

- That each letter is **distinct** in appearance
- What **direction and shape** must be used to write each letter
- That each letter has a **name**, which can be associated with the shape of a letter
- That there are **26** letters in the English alphabet, and letters are grouped in a certain order
- That letters represent **sounds of speech**
- That **words** are composed of letters and have meaning
- That one must be able to **correspond** letters and sounds to read

Development of Language Skills

Children learn language through interacting with others, by experiencing language in daily and relevant context, and through understanding that speaking and listening are necessary for effective communication. Teachers can promote **language development** by intensifying the opportunities a child has to experience and understand language.

Teachers can assist language development by:

- Modeling enriched vocabulary and teaching new words
- Using questions and examples to extend a child's descriptive language skills
- Providing ample response time to encourage children to practice speech
- Asking for clarification to provide students with the opportunity to develop communication skills
- Promoting conversations among children
- Providing feedback to let children know they have been heard and understood, and providing further explanation when needed

Relationship Between Oral and Written Language Development

Oral and written language development occur simultaneously. The acquisition of skills in one area supports the acquisition of skills in the other. However, oral language is not a prerequisite to written language. An immature form of oral language development is babbling, and an immature form of written language development is scribbling. **Oral language development** does not occur naturally, but does occur in a social context. This means it is best to include children in conversations rather than simply talk at them. **Written language development** can occur without direct instruction. In fact, reading and writing do not necessarily need to be taught through formal lessons if the child is exposed to a print-rich environment. A teacher can assist a child's language development by building on what the child already knows, discussing relevant and meaningful events and experiences, teaching vocabulary and literacy skills, and providing opportunities to acquire more complex language.

Print-Rich Environment

A teacher can provide a **print-rich environment** in the classroom in a number of ways. These include:

- **Displaying** the following in the classroom:
  - Children's names in print or cursive
  - Children's written work
  - Newspapers and magazines
  - Instructional charts
  - Written schedules
  - Signs and labels
  - Printed songs, poems, and rhymes
- Using **graphic organizers** such as KWL charts or story road maps to:
  - Remind students about what was read and discussed
  - Expand on the lesson topic or theme
  - Show the relationships among books, ideas, and words
- Using **big books** to:
  - Point out features of print, such as specific letters and punctuation
  - Track print from right to left
  - Emphasize the concept of words and the fact that they are used to communicate

Benefits of Print and Book Awareness

Print and book awareness helps a child understand:

- That there is a **connection** between print and messages contained on signs, labels, and other print forms in the child's environment
- That reading and writing are ways to obtain information and communicate ideas
- That **print** written in English runs from left to right and from top to bottom
- That a book has **parts**, such as a title, a cover, a title page, and a table of contents
- That a book has an **author** and contains a **story**
- That **illustrations** can carry meaning
- That **letters and words** are different
- That **words and sentences** are separated by spaces and punctuation
- That different **text forms** are used for different functions

- That print represents **spoken language**
- How to **hold** a book

Decoding

Decoding is the method or strategy used to make sense of printed words and figure out how to correctly pronounce them. In order to **decode**, a student needs to know the relationships between letters and sounds, including letter patterns; that words are constructed from phonemes and phoneme blends; and that a printed word represents a word that can be spoken. This knowledge will help the student recognize familiar words and make informed guesses about the pronunciation of unfamiliar words. Decoding is not the same as comprehension. It does not require an understanding of the meaning of a word, only a knowledge of how to recognize and pronounce it. Decoding can also refer to the skills a student uses to determine the meaning of a **sentence**. These skills include applying knowledge of vocabulary, sentence structure, and context.

Role of Fluency in Literacy Development

Fluency is the goal of literacy development. It is the ability to read accurately and quickly. Evidence of fluency includes the ability to recognize words automatically and group words for comprehension. At this point, the student no longer needs to decode words except for complex, unfamiliar ones. He or she is able to move to the next level and understand the **meaning** of a text. The student should be able to self-check for comprehension and should feel comfortable expressing ideas in writing. Teachers can help students build fluency by continuing to provide:

- Reading experiences and discussions about text that gradually increase in level of difficulty
- Reading practice, both silently and out loud
- Word analysis practice
- Instruction on reading comprehension strategies
- Opportunities to express responses to readings through writing

Review Video: Fluency
Visit mometrix.com/academy and enter code: 531179

Role of Vocabulary in Literacy Development

When students do not know the meaning of words in a text, their comprehension is limited. As a result, the text becomes boring or confusing. The larger a student's **vocabulary** is, the better their reading comprehension will be. A larger vocabulary is also associated with an enhanced ability to **communicate** in speech and writing. It is the teacher's role to help students develop a good working vocabulary. Students learn most of the words they use and understand by listening to the world around them (adults, other students, media, etc.) They also learn from their reading experiences, which include being read to and reading independently. Carefully designed activities can also stimulate vocabulary growth, and should emphasize useful words that students see frequently, important words necessary for understanding text, and difficult words and phrases, such as idioms or words with more than one meaning.

Teaching Techniques Promoting Vocabulary Development

A student's **vocabulary** can be developed by:

- Calling upon a student's **prior knowledge** and making comparisons to that knowledge
- **Defining** a word and providing multiple examples of the use of the word in context
- Showing a student how to use **context clues** to discover the meaning of a word

- Providing instruction on **prefixes**, **roots**, and **suffixes** to help students break a word into its parts and decipher its meaning
- Showing students how to use a **dictionary and a thesaurus**
- Asking students to **practice** new vocabulary by using the words in their own writing
- Providing a **print-rich environment** with a word wall
- Studying a group of words related to a **single subject**, such as farm words, transportation words, etc. so that concept development is enhanced

Affixes, Prefixes, and Root Words

Affixes are syllables attached to the beginning or end of a word to make a derivative or inflectional form of a word. Both prefixes and suffixes are affixes. A **prefix** is a syllable that appears at the beginning of a word that creates a specific meaning in combination with the root or base word. For example, the prefix *mis* means wrong. When combined with the root word *spelling*, the word *misspelling* is created, which means wrong spelling. A **root word** is the base of a word to which affixes can be added. For example, the prefix *in-* or *pre-* can be added to the latin root word *vent* to create *invent* or *prevent*, respectively. The suffix *-er* can be added to the root word *manage* to create *manager*, which means one who manages. The suffix *-able*, meaning capable of, can be added to *manage* to create *managable*, which means capable of being managed.

Suffixes

A **suffix** is a syllable that appears at the end of a word that creates a specific meaning in combination with the root or base word. There are three types of suffixes:

- **Noun suffixes**—Noun suffixes can change a verb or adjective to a noun. They can denote the act of, state of, quality of, or result of something. For example, *-ment* added to *argue* becomes *argument*, which can be understood as the act the act of resulting state from arguing or the reasons given to prove an idea. Noun suffixes can also denote the doer, or one who acts. For example, *-eer* added to *auction* becomes *auctioneer*, meaning one who auctions. Other examples include *-hood*, *-ness*, *-tion*, *-ship*, and *-ism*.
- **Verb suffixes**—These change other words to verbs and denote to make or to perform the act of. For example, *-en* added to *soft* makes *soften*, which means to make soft. Other verb suffixes are *-ate* (perpetuate), *-fy* (dignify), and *-ize* (sterilize).
- **Adjectival suffixes**—These suffixes change other words to adjectives and include suffixes such as *-ful*, which means full of. When added to *care*, the word *careful* is formed, which means full of care. Other examples are *-ish* and *-less*.

Strategies to Improve Reading Comprehension

Teachers can model the strategies students can use on their own to better comprehend a text through a read-aloud. First, the teacher should do a walk-through of the story **illustrations** and ask, "What's happening here?" The teacher should then ask students to **predict** what the story will be about based on what they have seen. As the book is read, the teacher should ask open-ended questions such as, "Why do you think the character did this?" and "How do you think the character feels?" The teacher should also ask students if they can **relate** to the story or have background knowledge of something similar. After the reading, the teacher should ask the students to **retell** the story in their own words to check for comprehension. Possible methods of retelling include performing a puppet show or summarizing the story to a partner.

Review Video: The Link Between Grammar Skills and Reading Comprehension
Visit mometrix.com/academy and enter code: 411287

Role of Prior Knowledge in Determining Appropriate Literacy Education

Even preschool children have some literacy skills, and the extent and type of these skills have implications for instructional approaches. **Comprehension** results from relating two or more pieces of information. One piece comes from the text, and another piece might come from **prior knowledge** (something from a student's long-term memory). For a child, that prior knowledge comes from being read to at home; taking part in other literacy experiences, such as playing computer or word games; being exposed to a print-rich environment at home; and observing parents' reading habits. Children who have had **extensive literacy experience** are better prepared to further develop their literacy skills in school than children who have not been read to, have few books or magazines in their homes, are seldom exposed to high-level oral or written language activities, and seldom witness adults engaged in reading and writing. Children with a scant literacy background are at a disadvantage. The teacher must not make any assumptions about their prior knowledge, and should use intense, targeted instruction. Otherwise, the student may have trouble improving their reading comprehension.

CHAPTER QUIZ

1. Chinese uses which type of writing system?

a. Alphabetic
b. Syllabic
c. Logographic
d. Featural

2. Which of the following is an adjectival suffix?

a. *-ish*
b. *-eer*
c. *-ize*
d. *-fy*

3. Which of the following further defines literacy as the "ability to identify, understand, interpret, create, communicate, compute, and use printed and written materials associated with varying contexts"?

a. W.H.O.
b. N.A.E.D.U.
c. U.N.E.S.C.O.
d. D.O.E.

CHAPTER QUIZ ANSWER KEY

1. C: The alphabetic principle refers to the use of letters and combinations of letters to represent speech sounds. The way letters are combined and pronounced is guided by a system of rules that establishes relationships between written and spoken words and their letter symbols. Alphabet writing systems are common around the world. Some are phonological, meaning that each letter stands for an individual sound and words are spelled just as they sound. However, it is important to note that there are other writing systems as well, such as the Chinese logographic system and the Japanese syllabic system.

2. A: A suffix is a syllable that appears at the end of a word and creates a specific meaning in combination with the root or base word. There are three types of suffixes:

- Noun suffixes can change a verb or adjective to a noun. They can denote the act of, state of, quality of, or result of something. For example, *-ment* added to *argue* becomes *argument*, which can be understood as the resulting state from arguing or the reasons given to prove an idea. Noun suffixes can also denote the doer, or one who acts. For example, *-eer* added to *auction* becomes *auctioneer*, meaning one who auctions. Other examples include *-hood*, *-ness*, *-tion*, *-ship*, and *-ism*.
- Verb suffixes change other words to verbs and denote to make or to perform the act of. For example, *-en* added to *soft* makes *soften*, which means to make soft. Other verb suffixes are *-ate* (perpetuate), *-fy* (dignify), and *-ize* (sterilize).
- Adjectival suffixes change other words to adjectives and include suffixes such as *-ful*, which means full of. When added to *care*, the word *careful* is formed, which means full of care. Other examples are *-ish* and *-less*.

3. C: UNESCO, the United Nations Educational, Scientific, and Cultural Organization, has further defined literacy as the "ability to identify, understand, interpret, create, communicate, compute, and use printed and written materials associated with varying contexts." Under the UNESCO definition, understanding cultural, political, and historical contexts of communities falls under the definition of literacy.

English Language Learning

Theories of Language Development

Four theories of language development are:

- **Learning approach**—This theory assumes that language is first learned by imitating the speech of adults. It is then solidified in school through drills about the rules of language structures.
- **Linguistic approach**—Championed by Noam Chomsky in the 1950s, this theory proposes that the ability to use a language is innate. This is a biological approach rather than one based on cognition or social patterning.
- **Cognitive approach**—Developed in the 1970s and based on the work of Piaget, this theory states that children must develop appropriate cognitive skills before they can acquire language.
- **Sociocognitive approach**—In the 1970s, some researchers proposed that language development is a complex interaction of linguistic, social, and cognitive influences. This theory best explains the lack of language skills among children who are neglected, have uneducated parents, or live in poverty.

Classroom Practices Benefiting Second Language Acquisition

Since some students may have a limited understanding of English, a teacher should employ the following practices to promote second language acquisition:

- Make all instruction as **understandable** as possible and use simple and repeated terms.
- Relate instruction to the **cultures** of ESL children.
- Increase **interactive activities** and use gestures or nonverbal actions when modeling.
- Provide language and literacy development instruction in **all curriculum areas.**
- Establish **consistent routines** that help children connect words and events.
- Use a **schedule** so children know what will happen next and will not feel lost.
- Integrate ESL children into **group activities** with non-ESL children.
- Appoint bilingual students to act as **student translators.**
- Explain actions as activities happen so that a **word to action relationship** is established.
- Initiate opportunities for ESL children to **experiment** with and practice new language.
- Employ multisensory learning.

Teaching Strategies to Promote Listening Skills of ESL Students

Listening is a critical skill when learning a new language. Students spend a great deal more time listening than they do speaking, and far less time reading and writing than speaking. One way to encourage ESL students to listen is to talk about topics that are of **interest** to the ESL learner. Otherwise, students may tune out the speaker because they don't want to put in that much effort to learn about a topic they find boring. Another way to encourage ESL students to listen is to talk about content or give examples that are **easy** to understand or are **related** to a topic that is familiar to ESL students. Culturally relevant materials will be more interesting to ESL students, will make them feel more comfortable, and will contain vocabulary that they may already be familiar with.

Considerations Relevant to ESL Students Related to Learning by Listening

Listening is not a passive skill, but an **active** one. Therefore, a teacher needs to make the listening experience as rewarding as possible and provide as many auditory and visual clues as possible. Three ways that the teacher can make the listening experience rewarding for ESL students are:

- Avoid **colloquialisms** and **abbreviated or slang terms** that may be confusing to the ESL listener, unless there is enough time to define them and explain their use.
- Make the spoken English understandable by stopping to **clarify** points, **repeating** new or difficult words, and **defining** words that may not be known.
- Support the spoken word with as many **visuals** as possible. Pictures, diagrams, gestures, facial expressions, and body language can help the ESL learner correctly interpret the spoken language more easily and also leaves an image impression that helps them remember the words.

Top-Down and Bottom-Up Processing

ESL students need to be given opportunities to practice both top-down and bottom-up processing. If they are old enough to understand these concepts, they should be made aware that these are two processes that affect their listening comprehension. In **top-down processing**, the listener refers to **background and global knowledge** to figure out the meaning of a message. For example, when asking an ESL student to perform a task, the steps of the task should be explained and accompanied by a review of the vocabulary terms the student already understands so that the student feels comfortable tackling new steps and new words. The teacher should also allow students to ask questions to verify comprehension. In **bottom-up processing**, the listener figures out the meaning of a message by using "**data**" obtained from what is said. This data includes sounds (stress, rhythm, and intonation), words, and grammatical relationships. All data can be used to make conclusions or interpretations. For example, the listener can develop bottom-up skills by learning how to detect differences in intonation between statements and questions.

Listening Lessons

All students, but especially ESL students, can be taught **listening** through specific training. During listening lessons, the teacher should guide students through three steps:

- **Pre-listening activity**—This establishes the purpose of the lesson and engages students' background knowledge. This activity should ask students to think about and discuss something they already know about the topic. Alternatively, the teacher can provide background information.
- **The listening activity**—This requires the listener to obtain information and then immediately do something with that information. For example, the teacher can review the schedule for the day or the week. In this example, students are being given information about a routine they already know, and need to be able to identify names, tasks, and times.
- **Post-listening activity**—This is an evaluation process that allows students to judge how well they did with the listening task. Other language skills can be included in the activity. For example, this activity could involve asking questions about who will do what according to the classroom schedule (Who is the lunch monitor today?) and could also involve asking students to produce whole sentence replies.

Helping ESL Students Understand Subject Matter

Speaking

To help ESL students better understand subject matter, the following teaching strategies using spoken English can be used:

- **Read aloud** from a textbook, and then ask ESL students to **verbally summarize** what was read. The teacher should assist by providing new words as needed to give students the opportunity to practice vocabulary and speaking skills. The teacher should then read the passage again to students to verify accuracy and details.
- The teacher could ask ESL students to explain why the subject matter is important to them and where they see it fitting into their lives. This verbalization gives them speaking practice and helps them relate to the subject.
- Whenever small group activities are being conducted, ESL students can be placed with **English-speaking students**. It is best to keep the groups to two or three students so that the ESL student will be motivated by the need to be involved. English-speaking students should be encouraged to include ESL students in the group work.

Reading

There are supplemental printed materials that can be used to help ESL students understand subject matter. The following strategies can be used to help ESL students develop English reading skills.

- Make sure all ESL students have a **bilingual dictionary** to use. A thesaurus would also be helpful.
- Try to keep **content area books** written in the ESL students' native languages in the classroom. Students can use them side-by-side with English texts. Textbooks in other languages can be ordered from the school library or obtained from the classroom textbook publisher.
- If a student lacks confidence in his or her ability to read the textbook, the teacher can read a passage to the student and have him or her **verbally summarize** the passage. The teacher should take notes on what the student says and then read them back. These notes can be a substitute, short-form, in-their-own-words textbook that the student can understand.

General Teaching Strategies to Help ESL Students

Some strategies can help students develop more than one important skill. They may involve a combination of speaking, listening, and viewing. Others are mainly classroom management aids. General teaching strategies for ESL students include:

- **Partner** English-speaking students with ESL students as study buddies and ask the English-speaking students to share notes.
- Encourage ESL students to ask **questions** whenever they don't understand something. They should be aware that they don't have to be able to interpret every word of text to understand the concept.
- Dictate **key sentences** related to the content area being taught and ask ESL students to write them down. This gives them practice in listening and writing, and also helps them identify what is important.
- **Alternate** difficult and easy tasks so that ESL students can experience academic success.
- Ask ESL students to **label** objects associated with content areas, such as maps, diagrams, parts of a leaf, or parts of a sentence. This gives students writing and reading experience and helps them remember key vocabulary.

Chapter Quiz

1. Which theory of language development assumes that language is first learned by imitating the speech of adults?

a. Linguistic approach
b. Learning approach
c. Cognitive approach
d. Sociocognitive approach

Chapter Quiz Answer Key

1. B: Below are four theories of language development.

- Learning approach: This theory assumes that language is first learned by imitating the speech of adults. It is then solidified in school through drills about the rules of language structures.
- Linguistic approach: Championed by Noam Chomsky in the 1950s, this theory proposes that the ability to use language is innate. This is a biological approach rather than one based on cognition or social patterning.
- Cognitive approach: Developed in the 1970s and based on the work of Jean Piaget, this theory states that children must develop appropriate cognitive skills before they can acquire language.
- Socio-cognitive approach: In the 1970s, some researchers proposed that language development is a complex interaction of linguistic, social, and cognitive influences. This theory best explains the lack of language skills among children who are neglected, have uneducated parents, or live in poverty.

Promoting Student Achievement in Mathematics

Mathematics Pedagogy

Representations

Representations are the tools of symbols and materials. They are used to help students understand mathematics by giving them visual guides in their thinking. For example, the conventional symbols that indicate addition, subtraction, equality, and so on (into the higher realms of symbols used in geometry, algebra, and calculus) tell students, at a glance, the process that is being calculated. Materials that are used as representations are called **manipulatives**. These can be small plastic objects or pictures for the students to count, line up, or otherwise use to solve a problem. Representations make abstract concepts become concrete. They put mathematics into the students' hands as well as heads, and the result is improved learning. Using familiar manipulatives with new problems helps the student to make connections and feel more confident and capable of expanding their skills.

Concepts Taught in Kindergarten Before Introducing Numbers

In kindergarten, children can be prepared for the study of mathematics by practicing certain concepts such as:

- **position** – top, middle, bottom, above, below, before, after, between, under, inside, outside, left, and right
- **visual attributes** – same and different colors, shapes, and sizes; identifying items that are out-of-place or don't belong
- **sorting** – by size, color, type, or shape; identifying an equal number, more, or fewer of a given item
- **graphing** – the use of picture graphs and using data from graphs
- **patterns** – identifying, copying, extending, and making patterns; finding patterns that are different or alike, making predictions from patterns
- **measurements** – longer and shorter; how much they weigh, heavier and lighter; how much an item can hold

Problem-Solving Strategies for Mathematics and Steps for Solving Word Problems

For any problem, the following **strategies** can be used according to their appropriateness to the type of problem or calculation: i) Use manipulatives or act out the problem, ii) draw a picture, iii) look for a pattern, iv) guess and check, v) use logical reasoning, vi) make an organized list, vii) make a table, viii) solve a simpler problem, and ix) work backward.

In order to solve a word problem, the following steps can be used:

- Achieve an understanding of the problem by reading it carefully, finding and separating the information needed to solve the problem, and discerning the ultimate question in the problem.
- Make a plan as to what needs to be done to solve the problem.

- Solve the problem using the plan from step 2.
- Review the word problem to make sure that the answer is the correct solution to the problem and makes sense.

Building Number Sense Among Students

It is important to think **flexibly** to develop number sense. Therefore, it is imperative to impress upon students that there is more than one right way to solve a problem. Otherwise, students will try to learn only one method of computation, rather than think about what makes sense or contemplate the possibility of an easier way. Some strategies for helping students develop number sense include the following:

- Frequently asking students to make their calculations mentally and rely on their reasoning ability. Answers can be checked manually afterwards, if needed.
- Having a class discussion about solutions the students found using their minds only and comparing the different approaches to solving the problem. Have the students explain their reasoning in their own words.
- Modeling the different ideas by tracking them on the board as the discussion progresses.
- Presenting problems to the students that can have more than one answer.

Using Manipulative Materials in Mathematics Classrooms

As with all classroom supplies, the students must understand that there are rules for their use, including how to store the materials when they are not in use. In addition:

- The teacher should discuss with the students the purpose of the manipulatives and how they will help the students to learn.
- The students should understand that the manipulatives are intended for use with specific problems and activities; however, time for free exploration should be made available so students are less tempted to play when assigned specific tasks
- A chart posted in the classroom of the manipulatives with their names will help the students to gain familiarity with them and develop mathematical literacy skills.
- Loans of manipulatives for home use with a letter of explanation to the parents about the purpose and value of the manipulatives will encourage similar strategies with homework.

Connecting Math and Science to Real Life for Gifted Students

Since math and science are so often heavy in calculations and facts, students are usually not taught how these subjects relate to the real world. All students, especially gifted students, need to find meaning in an academic subject and understand how it **applies** in life. We may not appreciate enough that math and science are not like people whose opinions we can disagree with; they provide hard, objective, unchangeable facts. Teachers can show students the consequences of ignoring facts with examples like these: mathematicians and engineers advised not launching the Challenger space shuttle, but management overruled them, thereby leading to the deadly explosion. Pop singer Aaliyah died in a plane crash after pilot and crew ignored the mathematics indicating airplane overload and flew regardless. A mathematician proved racial bias in jury selection by calculating that the mathematical probability of fair selection was approximately 1 in 1,000,000,000,000,000.

Analyzing the Use of Appropriate Mathematical Concepts, Procedures, and Vocabulary when Evaluating Student Solutions

When evaluating student solutions, it is important to analyze the use of appropriate mathematical concepts, procedures, and vocabulary for a variety of reasons. First and foremost, we must be sure that we have provided adequate practice and instruction of **important concepts** before assessing them. Once we have established that instruction is sufficient, we must ensure that students are following the appropriate **procedures** when faced with various tasks and that those procedures are executed correctly. Finally, we must hold students accountable for using high-level **vocabulary** to ensure that students are able to read, understand, and communicate their mathematics thoughts at age- and grade-appropriate levels.

Correcting Student Errors

A student is asked to find the area of a rectangle measuring 8 feet by 4 feet. The student is able to break the rectangle into 32 squares but states that the area is 24 square feet. The student calculated the perimeter of the rectangle rather than the area. The perimeter of a rectangle is the sum of its sides. Here, the rectangle's sides measure 8 feet, 8 feet, 4 feet, and 4 feet, which total to 24 feet. To calculate area, the student must multiply the length by the width (8×4), which equals 32 square feet. To help the student correct his or her error, the teacher can explain that the student was on the right track when he or she broke the rectangle into 32 squares. Because area is the amount of unit squares that can be contained in a two-dimensional figure, the student could have also opted to simply count the unit squares he or she created, which would have also led him or her to the correct answer of 32 square feet.

Exploring Problem Structures with Unknowns in All Positions

It is important to provide students with the opportunity to explore and find solutions for **problem structures** to develop their higher-level thinking skills and problem-solving strategies. By exposing students to problems with unknowns in all positions, students are forced to not only memorize procedures but also to analyze the framework of a problem, make connections for relationships within the problem, and develop strategies for solving problems that may not follow specific rules or procedures. Problems that include put-together/take-apart scenarios are excellent problem structures for teachers to use in an effort to develop higher-level thinking skills. In addition, giving students the opportunity to use arrays to model their solutions provides teachers with a glimpse into the thought processes of each student's solution.

Unknown Addends

A teacher tells her students that she has five pieces of fruit in her refrigerator. Two are apples, and the rest are oranges. She asks the students how many oranges are in her refrigerator. In this type of problem, there is an **unknown addend**. When dealing with unknown addends and numbers up to 20 (typically in the elementary classroom), this type of problem is known as a put-together/take apart problem. Ideally, the teacher's goal is for the students to visualize this the scenario as $2 + ? = 5$. Depending on the students' approach (drawing a picture, subtracting, number facts, modeling, etc.), they may choose to put together or take apart the problem in a variety of ways. To analyze the students' process, the teacher should check that each student has developed a strategy that will result in correctly identifying the missing addend in a way that could be applied to other problems similar in nature, continually resulting in the correct answer.

Evaluating Validity of Mathematical Model or Argument when Analyzing a Solution

When assessing a student's **proficiency**, simply arriving at the correct answer does not validate true mastery of a mathematical concept. To determine that a student has truly mastered a skill or concept, that student must be able to explain or defend his or her **process** as well as the solution. By requiring a model or compelling students to defend their answers, teachers can truly assess the validity of each solution and determine whether or not each student has a true grasp of the concept being assessed. A teacher can be confident that a student has truly mastered a concept when that student can describe his or her process, explain the meaning behind his or her solution, and defend why that solution is logical and appropriate.

Analyzing Validity of a Student's Mathematical Process

A teacher is assessing a student's ability to multiply two-digit numbers. A student in the class arrives at the correct answer without using the traditional algorithm. In mathematics, there is often more than one way to arrive at the correct answer. The focus of the teacher should be to analyze the **validity** of the student's mathematical process to determine if it is a process that could be applied to other multiplication problems, which would result in the correct answer. If the student has modeled his or her thought process, or can argue that the inventive strategy is applicable across all multiplication problems, then that student should be considered to have mastered the skill of multiplication. However, if the student's argument or model is not applicable to other multiplication problems, that student should be provided with more instruction and opportunity for improvement.

Using Individual Student Mathematics Assessment Data to Guide Instructional Decisions and Differentiate Instruction

Teachers should constantly **assess** student learning. These assessments should be quick in nature and offer immediate feedback to both the teacher and student. Assessments such as quick "exit tickets" at the end of each lesson can tell a teacher whether or not students achieved the objective of the day. If the majority of the class achieved mastery, the teacher should look to modify and reteach that lesson to the students who did not achieve mastery. On the other hand, if the majority of the class did not achieve mastery, the teacher should reflect on the way in which the lesson was presented and try another whole-class approach before moving on. By monitoring student learning on a constant basis, teachers are able to improve their teaching skills as well as identify and differentiate for struggling learners more quickly and effectively.

Creating Structured Experiences for Groups According to Cognitive Complexity of Tasks

Depending on the complexity of the task, teachers should modify the **delivery** of instruction. For less complex tasks, the teacher may opt for **whole-group instruction**, in which the entire class is introduced to a new concept together. Whole-group instruction usually includes a connection to prior knowledge, direct instruction, and some form of media. For more complex tasks, the teacher may choose **small-group instruction**, where students are grouped based on ability levels. The more accelerated learners are given a quicker, more direct form of instruction, whereas the struggling learners work independently at a math center or station activity. After a rotation, the struggling learners are given a modified form of instruction by the teacher, which has been differentiated and allows for more gradual release based on individual needs and abilities.

Numbers

Classifications of Numbers

Numbers are the basic building blocks of mathematics. Specific features of numbers are identified by the following terms:

Integer – any positive or negative whole number, including zero. Integers do not include fractions $\left(\frac{1}{3}\right)$, decimals (0.56), or mixed numbers $\left(7\frac{3}{4}\right)$.

Prime number – any whole number greater than 1 that has only two factors, itself and 1; that is, a number that can be divided evenly only by 1 and itself.

Composite number – any whole number greater than 1 that has more than two different factors; in other words, any whole number that is not a prime number. For example: The composite number 8 has the factors of 1, 2, 4, and 8.

Even number – any integer that can be divided by 2 without leaving a remainder. For example: 2, 4, 6, 8, and so on.

Odd number – any integer that cannot be divided evenly by 2. For example: 3, 5, 7, 9, and so on.

Decimal number – any number that uses a decimal point to show the part of the number that is less than one. Example: 1.234.

Decimal point – a symbol used to separate the ones place from the tenths place in decimals or dollars from cents in currency.

Decimal place – the position of a number to the right of the decimal point. In the decimal 0.123, the 1 is in the first place to the right of the decimal point, indicating tenths; the 2 is in the second place, indicating hundredths; and the 3 is in the third place, indicating thousandths.

The **decimal**, or base 10, system is a number system that uses ten different digits (0, 1, 2, 3, 4, 5, 6, 7, 8, 9). An example of a number system that uses something other than ten digits is the **binary**, or base 2, number system, used by computers, which uses only the numbers 0 and 1. It is thought that the decimal system originated because people had only their 10 fingers for counting.

Rational numbers include all integers, decimals, and fractions. Any terminating or repeating decimal number is a rational number.

Irrational numbers cannot be written as fractions or decimals because the number of decimal places is infinite and there is no recurring pattern of digits within the number. For example, pi (π) begins with 3.141592 and continues without terminating or repeating, so pi is an irrational number.

Real numbers are the set of all rational and irrational numbers.

Review Video: Classification of Numbers
Visit mometrix.com/academy and enter code: 461071

Review Video: Prime and Composite Numbers
Visit mometrix.com/academy and enter code: 565581

THE NUMBER LINE

A number line is a graph to see the distance between numbers. Basically, this graph shows the relationship between numbers. So a number line may have a point for zero and may show negative numbers on the left side of the line. Any positive numbers are placed on the right side of the line. For example, consider the points labeled on the following number line:

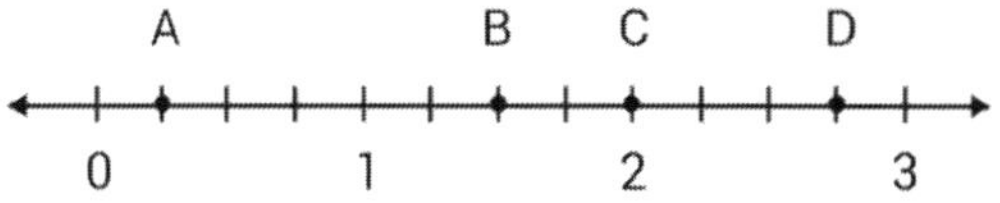

We can use the dashed lines on the number line to identify each point. Each dashed line between two whole numbers is $\frac{1}{4}$. The line halfway between two numbers is $\frac{1}{2}$.

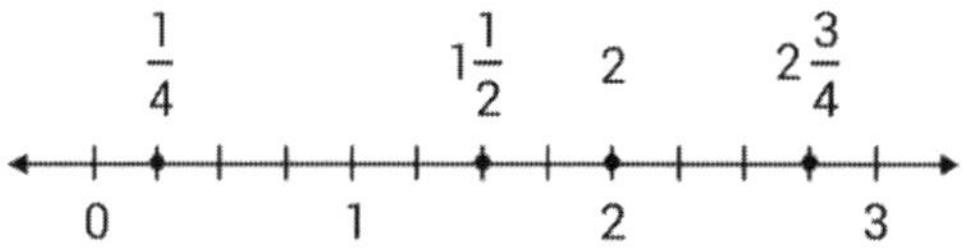

Review Video: The Number Line
Visit mometrix.com/academy and enter code: 816439

NUMBERS IN WORD FORM AND PLACE VALUE

When writing numbers out in word form or translating word form to numbers, it is essential to understand how a place value system works. In the decimal or base-10 system, each digit of a number represents how many of the corresponding place value—a specific factor of 10—are contained in the number being represented. To make reading numbers easier, every three digits to the left of the decimal place is preceded by a comma. The following table demonstrates some of the place values:

Power of 10	10^3	10^2	10^1	10^0	10^{-1}	10^{-2}	10^{-3}
Value	1,000	100	10	1	0.1	0.01	0.001
Place	thousands	hundreds	tens	ones	tenths	hundredths	thousandths

For example, consider the number 4,546.09, which can be separated into each place value like this:

4: thousands
5: hundreds
4: tens
6: ones
0: tenths
9: hundredths

This number in word form would be *four thousand five hundred forty-six and nine hundredths.*

Review Video: Place Value
Visit mometrix.com/academy and enter code: 205433

ABSOLUTE VALUE

A precursor to working with negative numbers is understanding what **absolute values** are. A number's absolute value is simply the distance away from zero a number is on the number line. The absolute value of a number is always positive and is written $|x|$. For example, the absolute value of 3, written as $|3|$, is 3 because the distance between 0 and 3 on a number line is three units. Likewise, the absolute value of –3, written as $|-3|$, is 3 because the distance between 0 and –3 on a number line is three units. So $|3| = |-3|$.

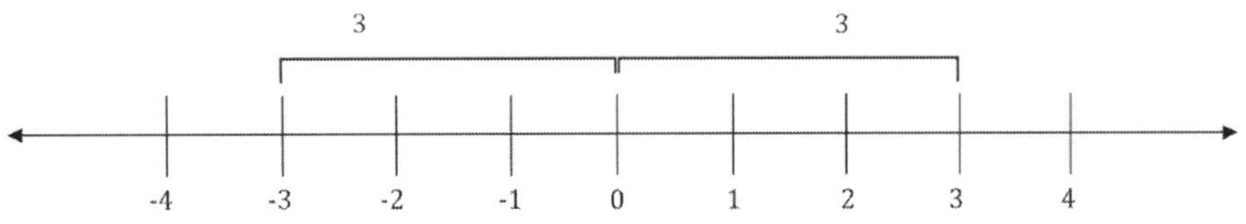

Review Video: Absolute Value
Visit mometrix.com/academy and enter code: 314669

PRACTICE

P1. Write the place value of each digit in 14,059.826

P2. Write out each of the following in words:

(a) 29
(b) 478
(c) 98,542
(d) 0.06
(e) 13.113

P3. Write each of the following in numbers:

(a) nine thousand four hundred thirty-five
(b) three hundred two thousand eight hundred seventy-six
(c) nine hundred one thousandths
(d) nineteen thousandths
(e) seven thousand one hundred forty-two and eighty-five hundredths

Practice Solutions

P1. The place value for each digit would be as follows:

Digit	Place Value
1	ten-thousands
4	thousands
0	hundreds
5	tens
9	ones
8	tenths
2	hundredths
6	thousandths

P2. Each written out in words would be:

(a) twenty-nine
(b) four hundred seventy-eight
(c) ninety-eight thousand five hundred forty-two
(d) six hundredths
(e) thirteen and one hundred thirteen thousandths

P3. Each in numeric form would be:

(a) 9,435
(b) 302876
(c) 0.901
(d) 0.019
(e) 7,142.85

Operations

Operations

An **operation** is simply a mathematical process that takes some value(s) as input(s) and produces an output. Elementary operations are often written in the following form: *value operation value*. For instance, in the expression $1 + 2$ the values are 1 and 2 and the operation is addition. Performing the operation gives the output of 3. In this way we can say that $1 + 2$ and 3 are equal, or $1 + 2 = 3$.

Addition

Addition increases the value of one quantity by the value of another quantity (both called **addends**). Example: $2 + 4 = 6$ or $8 + 9 = 17$. The result is called the **sum**. With addition, the order does not matter, $4 + 2 = 2 + 4$.

When adding signed numbers, if the signs are the same simply add the absolute values of the addends and apply the original sign to the sum. For example, $(+4) + (+8) = +12$ and $(-4) + (-8) = -12$. When the original signs are different, take the absolute values of the addends and subtract the smaller value from the larger value, then apply the original sign of the larger value to the difference. Example: $(+4) + (-8) = -4$ and $(-4) + (+8) = +4$.

Subtraction

Subtraction is the opposite operation to addition; it decreases the value of one quantity (the **minuend**) by the value of another quantity (the **subtrahend**). For example, $6 - 4 = 2$ or $17 - 8 = 9$. The result is called the **difference**. Note that with subtraction, the order does matter, $6 - 4 \neq 4 - 6$.

For subtracting signed numbers, change the sign of the subtrahend and then follow the same rules used for addition. Example: $(+4) - (+8) = (+4) + (-8) = -4$

Multiplication

Multiplication can be thought of as repeated addition. One number (the **multiplier**) indicates how many times to add the other number (the **multiplicand**) to itself. Example: $3 \times 2 = 2 + 2 + 2 = 6$. With multiplication, the order does not matter, $2 \times 3 = 3 \times 2$ or $3 + 3 = 2 + 2 + 2$, either way the result (the **product**) is the same.

If the signs are the same, the product is positive when multiplying signed numbers. Example: $(+4) \times (+8) = +32$ and $(-4) \times (-8) = +32$. If the signs are opposite, the product is negative. Example: $(+4) \times (-8) = -32$ and $(-4) \times (+8) = -32$. When more than two factors are multiplied together, the sign of the product is determined by how many negative factors are present. If there are an odd number of negative factors then the product is negative, whereas an even number of negative factors indicates a positive product. Example: $(+4) \times (-8) \times (-2) = +64$ and $(-4) \times (-8) \times (-2) = -64$.

Division

Division is the opposite operation to multiplication; one number (the **divisor**) tells us how many parts to divide the other number (the **dividend**) into. The result of division is called the **quotient**. Example: $20 \div 4 = 5$. If 20 is split into 4 equal parts, each part is 5. With division, the order of the numbers does matter, $20 \div 4 \neq 4 \div 20$.

The rules for dividing signed numbers are similar to multiplying signed numbers. If the dividend and divisor have the same sign, the quotient is positive. If the dividend and divisor have opposite signs, the quotient is negative. Example: $(-4) \div (+8) = -0.5$.

Review Video: Mathematical Operations
Visit mometrix.com/academy and enter code: 208095

Parentheses

Parentheses are used to designate which operations should be done first when there are multiple operations. Example: $4 - (2 + 1) = 1$; the parentheses tell us that we must add 2 and 1, and then subtract the sum from 4, rather than subtracting 2 from 4 and then adding 1 (this would give us an answer of 3).

Review Video: Mathematical Parentheses
Visit mometrix.com/academy and enter code: 978600

Exponents

An **exponent** is a superscript number placed next to another number at the top right. It indicates how many times the base number is to be multiplied by itself. Exponents provide a shorthand way to write what would be a longer mathematical expression, Example: $2^4 = 2 \times 2 \times 2 \times 2$. A number with an exponent of 2 is said to be "squared," while a number with an exponent of 3 is said to be "cubed." The value of a number raised to an exponent is called its power. So 8^4 is read as "8 to the 4th power," or "8 raised to the power of 4."

The properties of exponents are as follows:

Property	Description
$a^1 = a$	Any number to the power of 1 is equal to itself
$1^n = 1$	The number 1 raised to any power is equal to 1
$a^0 = 1$	Any number raised to the power of 0 is equal to 1
$a^n \times a^m = a^{n+m}$	Add exponents to multiply powers of the same base number
$a^n \div a^m = a^{n-m}$	Subtract exponents to divide powers of the same base number
$(a^n)^m = a^{n \times m}$	When a power is raised to a power, the exponents are multiplied
$(a \times b)^n = a^n \times b^n$ $(a \div b)^n = a^n \div b^n$	Multiplication and division operations inside parentheses can be raised to a power. This is the same as each term being raised to that power.
$a^{-n} = \frac{1}{a^n}$	A negative exponent is the same as the reciprocal of a positive exponent

Note that exponents do not have to be integers. Fractional or decimal exponents follow all the rules above as well. Example: $5^{\frac{1}{4}} \times 5^{\frac{3}{4}} = 5^{\frac{1}{4}+\frac{3}{4}} = 5^1 = 5$.

Review Video: Introduction to Exponents
Visit mometrix.com/academy and enter code: 600998

Review Video: Properties of Exponents
Visit mometrix.com/academy and enter code: 532558

Roots

A **root**, such as a square root, is another way of writing a fractional exponent. Instead of using a superscript, roots use the radical symbol ($\sqrt{\ }$) to indicate the operation. A radical will have a number underneath the bar, and may sometimes have a number in the upper left: $\sqrt[n]{a}$, read as "the nth root of a." The relationship between radical notation and exponent notation can be described by this equation:

$$\sqrt[n]{a} = a^{\frac{1}{n}}$$

The two special cases of $n = 2$ and $n = 3$ are called square roots and cube roots. If there is no number to the upper left, the radical is understood to be a square root ($n = 2$). Nearly all of the roots you encounter will be square roots. A square root is the same as a number raised to the one-half power. When we say that a is the square root of b ($a = \sqrt{b}$), we mean that a multiplied by itself equals b: ($a \times a = b$).

A **perfect square** is a number that has an integer for its square root. There are 10 perfect squares from 1 to 100: 1, 4, 9, 16, 25, 36, 49, 64, 81, 100 (the squares of integers 1 through 10).

Review Video: Roots
Visit mometrix.com/academy and enter code: 795655

Review Video: Square Root and Perfect Squares
Visit mometrix.com/academy and enter code: 648063

Order of Operations

The **order of operations** is a set of rules that dictates the order in which we must perform each operation in an expression so that we will evaluate it accurately. If we have an expression that includes multiple different operations, the order of operations tells us which operations to do first. The most common mnemonic for the order of operations is **PEMDAS**, or "Please Excuse My Dear Aunt Sally." PEMDAS stands for parentheses, exponents, multiplication, division, addition, and subtraction. It is important to understand that multiplication and division have equal precedence, as do addition and subtraction, so those pairs of operations are simply worked from left to right in order.

For example, evaluating the expression $5 + 20 \div 4 \times (2 + 3)^2 - 6$ using the correct order of operations would be done like this:

- **P:** Perform the operations inside the parentheses: $(2 + 3) = 5$
- **E:** Simplify the exponents: $(5)^2 = 5 \times 5 = 25$
  - The expression now looks like this: $5 + 20 \div 4 \times 25 - 6$
- **MD:** Perform multiplication and division from left to right: $20 \div 4 = 5$; then $5 \times 25 = 125$
  - The expression now looks like this: $5 + 125 - 6$
- **AS:** Perform addition and subtraction from left to right: $5 + 125 = 130$; then $130 - 6 = 124$

Review Video: Order of Operations
Visit mometrix.com/academy and enter code: 259675

SUBTRACTION WITH REGROUPING

A great way to make use of some of the features built into the decimal system would be regrouping when attempting longform subtraction operations. When subtracting within a place value, sometimes the minuend is smaller than the subtrahend, **regrouping** enables you to 'borrow' a unit from a place value to the left in order to get a positive difference. For example, consider subtracting 189 from 525 with regrouping.

Review Video: Subtracting Large Numbers
Visit mometrix.com/academy and enter code: 603350

First, set up the subtraction problem in vertical form:

$$\begin{array}{r} 525 \\ -\ 189 \\ \hline \end{array}$$

Notice that the numbers in the ones and tens columns of 525 are smaller than the numbers in the ones and tens columns of 189. This means you will need to use regrouping to perform subtraction:

$$\begin{array}{cccc} & 5 & 2 & 5 \\ - & 1 & 8 & 9 \\ \hline \end{array}$$

To subtract 9 from 5 in the ones column you will need to borrow from the 2 in the tens columns:

$$\begin{array}{cccc} & 5 & 1 & 15 \\ - & 1 & 8 & 9 \\ \hline & & & 6 \end{array}$$

Next, to subtract 8 from 1 in the tens column you will need to borrow from the 5 in the hundreds column:

$$\begin{array}{cccc} & 4 & 11 & 15 \\ - & 1 & 8 & 9 \\ \hline & & 3 & 6 \end{array}$$

Last, subtract the 1 from the 4 in the hundreds column:

$$\begin{array}{cccc} & 4 & 11 & 15 \\ - & 1 & 8 & 9 \\ \hline & 3 & 3 & 6 \end{array}$$

WORD PROBLEMS AND MATHEMATICAL SYMBOLS

When working on word problems, you must be able to translate verbal expressions or "math words" into math symbols. This chart contains several "math words" and their appropriate symbols:

Phrase	Symbol
equal, is, was, will be, has, costs, gets to, is the same as, becomes	$=$
times, of, multiplied by, product of, twice, doubles, halves, triples	$\times$
divided by, per, ratio of/to, out of	$\div$
plus, added to, sum, combined, and, more than, totals of	$+$
subtracted from, less than, decreased by, minus, difference between	$-$
what, how much, original value, how many, a number, a variable	x, n, etc.

Examples of Translated Mathematical Phrases

- The phrase four more than twice a number can be written algebraically as $2x + 4$.
- The phrase half a number decreased by six can be written algebraically as $\frac{1}{2}x - 6$.
- The phrase the sum of a number and the product of five and that number can be written algebraically as $x + 5x$.
- You may see a test question that says, "Olivia is constructing a bookcase from seven boards. Two of them are for vertical supports and five are for shelves. The height of the bookcase is twice the width of the bookcase. If the seven boards total 36 feet in length, what will be the height of Olivia's bookcase?" You would need to make a sketch and then create the equation to determine the width of the shelves. The height can be represented as double the width. (If x represents the width of the shelves in feet, then the height of the bookcase is $2x$. Since the seven boards total 36 feet, $2x + 2x + x + x + x + x + x = 36$ or $9x = 36$; $x = 4$. The height is twice the width, or 8 feet.)

Practice

P1. Demonstrate how to subtract 477 from 620 using regrouping.

P2. Simplify the following expressions with exponents:

(a) 37^0
(b) 1^{30}
(c) $2^3 \times 2^4 \times 2^x$
(d) $(3^x)^3$
(e) $(12 \div 3)^2$

Practice Solutions

P1. First, set up the subtraction problem in vertical form:

$$\begin{array}{cccc} & 6 & 2 & 0 \\ - & 4 & 7 & 7 \\ \hline \end{array}$$

To subtract 7 from 0 in the ones column you will need to borrow from the 2 in the tens column:

$$\begin{array}{cccc} & 6 & 1 & 10 \\ - & 4 & 7 & 7 \\ \hline & & & 3 \end{array}$$

Next, to subtract 7 from the 1 that's still in the tens column you will need to borrow from the 6 in the hundreds column:

$$\begin{array}{cccc} & 5 & 11 & 10 \\ - & 4 & 7 & 7 \\ \hline & & 4 & 3 \end{array}$$

Lastly, subtract 4 from the 5 remaining in the hundreds column:

$$\begin{array}{cccc} & 5 & 11 & 10 \\ - & 4 & 7 & 7 \\ \hline & 1 & 4 & 3 \end{array}$$

P2. Using the properties of exponents and the proper order of operations:

(a) Any number raised to the power of 0 is equal to 1: $37^0 = 1$
(b) The number 1 raised to any power is equal to 1: $1^{30} = 1$
(c) Add exponents to multiply powers of the same base: $2^3 \times 2^4 \times 2^x = 2^{(3+4+x)} = 2^{(7+x)}$
(d) When a power is raised to a power, the exponents are multiplied: $(3^x)^3 = 3^{3x}$
(e) Perform the operation inside the parentheses first: $(12 \div 3)^2 = 4^2 = 16$

Factoring

Factors and Greatest Common Factor

Factors are numbers that are multiplied together to obtain a **product**. For example, in the equation $2 \times 3 = 6$, the numbers 2 and 3 are factors. A **prime number** has only two factors (1 and itself), but other numbers can have many factors.

A **common factor** is a number that divides exactly into two or more other numbers. For example, the factors of 12 are 1, 2, 3, 4, 6, and 12, while the factors of 15 are 1, 3, 5, and 15. The common factors of 12 and 15 are 1 and 3.

A **prime factor** is also a prime number. Therefore, the prime factors of 12 are 2 and 3. For 15, the prime factors are 3 and 5.

The **greatest common factor** (**GCF**) is the largest number that is a factor of two or more numbers. For example, the factors of 15 are 1, 3, 5, and 15; the factors of 35 are 1, 5, 7, and 35. Therefore, the greatest common factor of 15 and 35 is 5.

Review Video: Factors
Visit mometrix.com/academy and enter code: 920086

Review Video: Prime Numbers and Factorization
Visit mometrix.com/academy and enter code: 760669

Review Video: Greatest Common Factor and Least Common Multiple
Visit mometrix.com/academy and enter code: 838699

Multiples and Least Common Multiple

Often listed out in multiplication tables, **multiples** are integer increments of a given factor. In other words, dividing a multiple by the factor will result in an integer. For example, the multiples of 7 include: $1 \times 7 = 7, 2 \times 7 = 14, 3 \times 7 = 21, 4 \times 7 = 28, 5 \times 7 = 35$. Dividing 7, 14, 21, 28, or 35 by 7 will result in the integers 1, 2, 3, 4, and 5, respectively.

The least common multiple (**LCM**) is the smallest number that is a multiple of two or more numbers. For example, the multiples of 3 include 3, 6, 9, 12, 15, etc.; the multiples of 5 include 5, 10, 15, 20, etc. Therefore, the least common multiple of 3 and 5 is 15.

Review Video: Multiples
Visit mometrix.com/academy and enter code: 626738

Rational Numbers

Fractions

A **fraction** is a number that is expressed as one integer written above another integer, with a dividing line between them $\left(\frac{x}{y}\right)$. It represents the **quotient** of the two numbers "x divided by y." It can also be thought of as x out of y equal parts.

The top number of a fraction is called the **numerator**, and it represents the number of parts under consideration. The 1 in $\frac{1}{4}$ means that 1 part out of the whole is being considered in the calculation. The bottom number of a fraction is called the **denominator**, and it represents the total number of equal parts. The 4 in $\frac{1}{4}$ means that the whole consists of 4 equal parts. A fraction cannot have a denominator of zero; this is referred to as "*undefined.*"

Fractions can be manipulated, without changing the value of the fraction, by multiplying or dividing (but not adding or subtracting) both the numerator and denominator by the same number. If you divide both numbers by a common factor, you are **reducing** or simplifying the fraction. Two fractions that have the same value but are expressed differently are known as **equivalent fractions**. For example, $\frac{2}{10}, \frac{3}{15}, \frac{4}{20}$, and $\frac{5}{25}$ are all equivalent fractions. They can also all be reduced or simplified to $\frac{1}{5}$.

When two fractions are manipulated so that they have the same denominator, this is known as finding a **common denominator**. The number chosen to be that common denominator should be the least common multiple of the two original denominators. Example: $\frac{3}{4}$ and $\frac{5}{6}$; the least common multiple of 4 and 6 is 12. Manipulating to achieve the common denominator: $\frac{3}{4} = \frac{9}{12}; \frac{5}{6} = \frac{10}{12}$.

Proper Fractions and Mixed Numbers

A fraction whose denominator is greater than its numerator is known as a **proper fraction**, while a fraction whose numerator is greater than its denominator is known as an **improper fraction**. Proper fractions have values *less than one* and improper fractions have values *greater than one.*

A **mixed number** is a number that contains both an integer and a fraction. Any improper fraction can be rewritten as a mixed number. Example: $\frac{8}{3} = \frac{6}{3} + \frac{2}{3} = 2 + \frac{2}{3} = 2\frac{2}{3}$. Similarly, any mixed number can be rewritten as an improper fraction. Example: $1\frac{3}{5} = 1 + \frac{3}{5} = \frac{5}{5} + \frac{3}{5} = \frac{8}{5}$.

Review Video: Improper Fractions and Mixed Numbers
Visit mometrix.com/academy and enter code: 211077

Review Video: Overview of Fractions
Visit mometrix.com/academy and enter code: 262335

Adding and Subtracting Fractions

If two fractions have a common denominator, they can be added or subtracted simply by adding or subtracting the two numerators and retaining the same denominator. If the two fractions do not already have the same denominator, one or both of them must be manipulated to achieve a common denominator before they can be added or subtracted. Example: $\frac{1}{2}+\frac{1}{4}=\frac{2}{4}+\frac{1}{4}=\frac{3}{4}$.

Review Video: Adding and Subtracting Fractions
Visit mometrix.com/academy and enter code: 378080

Multiplying Fractions

Two fractions can be multiplied by multiplying the two numerators to find the new numerator and the two denominators to find the new denominator. Example: $\frac{1}{3}\times\frac{2}{3}=\frac{1\times 2}{3\times 3}=\frac{2}{9}$.

Dividing Fractions

Two fractions can be divided by flipping the numerator and denominator of the second fraction and then proceeding as though it were a multiplication problem. Example: $\frac{2}{3}\div\frac{3}{4}=\frac{2}{3}\times\frac{4}{3}=\frac{8}{9}$.

Review Video: Multiplying and Dividing Fractions
Visit mometrix.com/academy and enter code: 473632

Multiplying a Mixed Number by a Whole Number or a Decimal

When multiplying a mixed number by something, it is usually best to convert it to an improper fraction first. Additionally, if the multiplicand is a decimal, it is most often simplest to convert it to a fraction. For instance, to multiply $4\frac{3}{8}$ by 3.5, begin by rewriting each quantity as a whole number plus a proper fraction. Remember, a mixed number is a fraction added to a whole number and a decimal is a representation of the sum of fractions, specifically tenths, hundredths, thousandths, and so on:

$$4\frac{3}{8}\times 3.5=\left(4+\frac{3}{8}\right)\times\left(3+\frac{1}{2}\right)$$

Next, the quantities being added need to be expressed with the same denominator. This is achieved by multiplying and dividing the whole number by the denominator of the fraction. Recall that a whole number is equivalent to that number divided by 1:

$$=\left(\frac{4}{1}\times\frac{8}{8}+\frac{3}{8}\right)\times\left(\frac{3}{1}\times\frac{2}{2}+\frac{1}{2}\right)$$

When multiplying fractions, remember to multiply the numerators and denominators separately:

$$=\left(\frac{4\times 8}{1\times 8}+\frac{3}{8}\right)\times\left(\frac{3\times 2}{1\times 2}+\frac{1}{2}\right)$$
$$=\left(\frac{32}{8}+\frac{3}{8}\right)\times\left(\frac{6}{2}+\frac{1}{2}\right)$$

Now that the fractions have the same denominators, they can be added:

$$=\frac{35}{8}\times\frac{7}{2}$$

Finally, perform the last multiplication and then simplify:

$$= \frac{35 \times 7}{8 \times 2} = \frac{245}{16} = \frac{240}{16} + \frac{5}{16} = 15\frac{5}{16}$$

Decimals

Decimals are one way to represent parts of a whole. Using the place value system, each digit to the right of a decimal point denotes the number of units of a corresponding *negative* power of ten. For example, consider the decimal 0.24. We can use a model to represent the decimal. Since a dime is worth one-tenth of a dollar and a penny is worth one-hundredth of a dollar, one possible model to represent this fraction is to have 2 dimes representing the 2 in the tenths place and 4 pennies representing the 4 in the hundredths place:

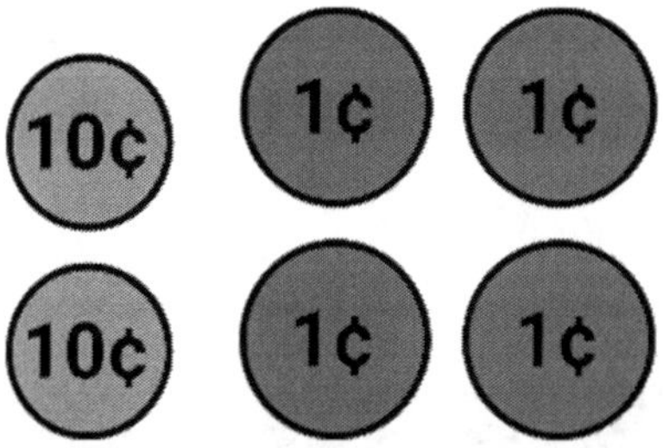

To write the decimal as a fraction, put the decimal in the numerator with 1 in the denominator. Multiply the numerator and denominator by tens until there are no more decimal places. Then simplify the fraction to lowest terms. For example, converting 0.24 to a fraction:

$$0.24 = \frac{0.24}{1} = \frac{0.24 \times 100}{1 \times 100} = \frac{24}{100} = \frac{6}{25}$$

Review Video: Decimals
Visit mometrix.com/academy and enter code: 837268

Operations with Decimals

Adding and Subtracting Decimals

When adding and subtracting decimals, the decimal points must always be aligned. Adding decimals is just like adding regular whole numbers. Example: $4.5 + 2.0 = 6.5$.

If the problem-solver does not properly align the decimal points, an incorrect answer of 4.7 may result. An easy way to add decimals is to align all of the decimal points in a vertical column visually. This will allow you to see exactly where the decimal should be placed in the final answer. Begin adding from right to left. Add each column in turn, making sure to carry the number to the left if a column adds up to more than 9. The same rules apply to the subtraction of decimals.

Review Video: Adding and Subtracting Decimals
Visit mometrix.com/academy and enter code: 381101

Multiplying Decimals

A simple multiplication problem has two components: a **multiplicand** and a **multiplier**. When multiplying decimals, work as though the numbers were whole rather than decimals. Once the final product is calculated, count the number of places to the right of the decimal in both the multiplicand and the multiplier. Then, count that number of places from the right of the product and place the decimal in that position.

For example, 12.3×2.56 has a total of three places to the right of the respective decimals. Multiply 123×256 to get 31,488. Now, beginning on the right, count three places to the left and insert the decimal. The final product will be 31.488.

Review Video: How to Multiply Decimals
Visit mometrix.com/academy and enter code: 731574

Dividing Decimals

Every division problem has a **divisor** and a **dividend**. The dividend is the number that is being divided. In the problem $14 \div 7$, 14 is the dividend and 7 is the divisor. In a division problem with decimals, the divisor must be converted into a whole number. Begin by moving the decimal in the divisor to the right until a whole number is created. Next, move the decimal in the dividend the same number of spaces to the right. For example, 4.9 into 24.5 would become 49 into 245. The decimal was moved one space to the right to create a whole number in the divisor, and then the same was done for the dividend. Once the whole numbers are created, the problem is carried out normally: $245 \div 49 = 5$.

Review Video: How to Divide Decimals
Visit mometrix.com/academy and enter code: 560690

Review Video: Dividing Decimals by Whole Numbers
Visit mometrix.com/academy and enter code: 535669

Percentages

Percentages can be thought of as fractions that are based on a whole of 100; that is, one whole is equal to 100%. The word **percent** means "per hundred." Percentage problems are often presented in three main ways:

- Find what percentage of some number another number is.
    - Example: What percentage of 40 is 8?
- Find what number is some percentage of a given number.
    - Example: What number is 20% of 40?
- Find what number another number is a given percentage of.
    - Example: What number is 8 20% of?

There are three components in each of these cases: a **whole** (W), a **part** (P), and a **percentage** (%). These are related by the equation: $P = W \times \%$. This can easily be rearranged into other forms that may suit different questions better: $\% = \frac{P}{W}$ and $W = \frac{P}{\%}$. Percentage problems are often also word problems. As such, a large part of solving them is figuring out which quantities are what. For example, consider the following word problem:

In a school cafeteria, 7 students choose pizza, 9 choose hamburgers, and 4 choose tacos. What percentage of student choose tacos?

To find the whole, you must first add all of the parts: $7 + 9 + 4 = 20$. The percentage can then be found by dividing the part by the whole $\left(\% = \frac{P}{W}\right)$: $\frac{4}{20} = \frac{20}{100} = 20\%$.

Review Video: Computation with Percentages
Visit mometrix.com/academy and enter code: 693099

Converting Between Percentages, Fractions, and Decimals

Converting decimals to percentages and percentages to decimals is as simple as moving the decimal point. To *convert from a decimal to a percentage*, move the decimal point **two places to the right**. To *convert from a percentage to a decimal*, move it **two places to the left**. It may be helpful to remember that the percentage number will always be larger than the equivalent decimal number. Example:

$$0.23 = 23\% \quad 5.34 = 534\% \quad 0.007 = 0.7\%$$
$$700\% = 7.00 \quad 86\% = 0.86 \quad 0.15\% = 0.0015$$

To convert a fraction to a decimal, simply divide the numerator by the denominator in the fraction. To convert a decimal to a fraction, put the decimal in the numerator with 1 in the denominator. Multiply the numerator and denominator by tens until there are no more decimal places. Then simplify the fraction to lowest terms. For example, converting 0.24 to a fraction:

$$0.24 = \frac{0.24}{1} = \frac{0.24 \times 100}{1 \times 100} = \frac{24}{100} = \frac{6}{25}$$

Fractions can be converted to a percentage by finding equivalent fractions with a denominator of 100. Example:

$$\frac{7}{10} = \frac{70}{100} = 70\% \quad \frac{1}{4} = \frac{25}{100} = 25\%$$

To convert a percentage to a fraction, divide the percentage number by 100 and reduce the fraction to its simplest possible terms. Example:

$$60\% = \frac{60}{100} = \frac{3}{5} \quad 96\% = \frac{96}{100} = \frac{24}{25}$$

Review Video: Converting Fractions to Percentages and Decimals
Visit mometrix.com/academy and enter code: 306233

Review Video: Converting Percentages to Decimals and Fractions
Visit mometrix.com/academy and enter code: 287297

Review Video: Converting Decimals to Fractions and Percentages
Visit mometrix.com/academy and enter code: 986765

Review Video: Converting Decimals, Improper Fractions, and Mixed Numbers
Visit mometrix.com/academy and enter code: 696924

Rational Numbers

The term **rational** means that the number can be expressed as a ratio or fraction. That is, a number, r, is rational if and only if it can be represented by a fraction $\frac{a}{b}$ where a and b are integers and b does not equal 0. The set of rational numbers includes integers and decimals. If there is no finite way to represent a value with a fraction of integers, then the number is **irrational**. Common examples of irrational numbers include: $\sqrt{5}$, $(1+\sqrt{2})$, and π.

Review Video: Rational and Irrational Numbers
Visit mometrix.com/academy and enter code: 280645

Practice

P1. What is 30% of 120?

P2. What is 150% of 20?

P3. What is 14.5% of 96?

P4. Simplify the following expressions:

(a) $\frac{2}{5} \div \frac{4}{7}$
(b) $\frac{7}{8} - \frac{8}{16}$
(c) $\frac{1}{2} + \left(3\left(\frac{3}{4}\right) - 2\right) + 4$
(d) $0.22 + 0.5 - (5.5 + 3.3 \div 3)$
(e) $\frac{3}{2} + (4(0.5) - 0.75) + 2$

P5. Convert the following to a fraction and to a decimal: **(a)** 15%; **(b)** 24.36%

P6. Convert the following to a decimal and to a percentage. **(a)** $\frac{4}{5}$; **(b)** $3\frac{2}{5}$

P7. A woman's age is thirteen more than half of 60. How old is the woman?

P8. A patient was given pain medicine at a dosage of 0.22 grams. The patient's dosage was then increased to 0.80 grams. By how much was the patient's dosage increased?

P9. At a hotel, $\frac{3}{4}$ of the 100 rooms are occupied today. Yesterday, $\frac{4}{5}$ of the 100 rooms were occupied. On which day were more of the rooms occupied and by how much more?

P10. At a school, 40% of the teachers teach English. If 20 teachers teach English, how many teachers work at the school?

P11. A patient was given blood pressure medicine at a dosage of 2 grams. The patient's dosage was then decreased to 0.45 grams. By how much was the patient's dosage decreased?

P12. Two weeks ago, $\frac{2}{3}$ of the 60 customers at a skate shop were male. Last week, $\frac{3}{6}$ of the 80 customers were male. During which week were there more male customers?

P13. Jane ate lunch at a local restaurant. She ordered a $4.99 appetizer, a $12.50 entrée, and a $1.25 soda. If she wants to tip her server 20%, how much money will she spend in all?

P14. According to a survey, about 82% of engineers were highly satisfied with their job. If 145 engineers were surveyed, how many reported that they were highly satisfied?

P15. A patient was given 40 mg of a certain medicine. Later, the patient's dosage was increased to 45 mg. What was the percent increase in his medication?

P16. Order the following rational numbers from least to greatest: 0.55, 17%, $\sqrt{25}$, $\frac{64}{4}$, $\frac{25}{50}$, 3.

P17. Order the following rational numbers from greatest to least: 0.3, 27%, $\sqrt{100}$, $\frac{72}{9}$, $\frac{1}{9}$, 4.5

P18. Perform the following multiplication. Write each answer as a mixed number.

(a) $\left(1\frac{11}{16}\right) \times 4$

(b) $\left(12\frac{1}{3}\right) \times 1.1$

(c) $3.71 \times \left(6\frac{1}{5}\right)$

P19. Suppose you are making doughnuts and you want to triple the recipe you have. If the following list is the original amounts for the ingredients, what would be the amounts for the tripled recipe?

$1\frac{3}{4}$	cup	Flour	$1\frac{1}{2}$	Tbsp	Butter
$1\frac{1}{4}$	tsp	Baking powder	2	large	Eggs
$\frac{3}{4}$	tsp	Salt	$\frac{3}{4}$	tsp	Vanilla extract
$\frac{3}{8}$	cup	Sugar	$\frac{3}{8}$	cup	Sour cream

Practice Solutions

P1. The word *of* indicates multiplication, so 30% of 120 is found by multiplying 120 by 30%. Change 30% to a decimal, then multiply: $120 \times 0.3 = 36$

P2. The word *of* indicates multiplication, so 150% of 20 is found by multiplying 20 by 150%. Change 150% to a decimal, then multiply: $20 \times 1.5 = 30$

P3. Change 14.5% to a decimal before multiplying. $0.145 \times 96 = 13.92$.

P4. Follow the order of operations and utilize properties of fractions to solve each:

(a) Rewrite the problem as a multiplication problem: $\frac{2}{5} \times \frac{7}{4} = \frac{2\times7}{5\times4} = \frac{14}{20}$. Make sure the fraction is reduced to lowest terms. Both 14 and 20 can be divided by 2.

$$\frac{14}{20} = \frac{14 \div 2}{20 \div 2} = \frac{7}{10}$$

(b) The denominators of $\frac{7}{8}$ and $\frac{8}{16}$ are 8 and 16, respectively. The lowest common denominator of 8 and 16 is 16 because 16 is the least common multiple of 8 and 16. Convert the first fraction to its equivalent with the newly found common denominator of 16: $\frac{7\times2}{8\times2} = \frac{14}{16}$. Now that the fractions have the same denominator, you can subtract them.

$$\frac{14}{16} - \frac{8}{16} = \frac{6}{16} = \frac{3}{8}$$

(c) When simplifying expressions, first perform operations within groups. Within the set of parentheses are multiplication and subtraction operations. Perform the multiplication first to get $\frac{1}{2} + \left(\frac{9}{4} - 2\right) + 4$. Then, subtract two to obtain $\frac{1}{2} + \frac{1}{4} + 4$. Finally, perform addition from left to right:

$$\frac{1}{2} + \frac{1}{4} + 4 = \frac{2}{4} + \frac{1}{4} + \frac{16}{4} = \frac{19}{4} = 4\frac{3}{4}$$

(d) First, evaluate the terms in the parentheses $(5.5 + 3.3 \div 3)$ using order of operations. $3.3 \div 3 = 1.1$, and $5.5 + 1.1 = 6.6$. Next, rewrite the problem: $0.22 + 0.5 - 6.6$. Finally, add and subtract from left to right: $0.22 + 0.5 = 0.72$; $0.72 - 6.6 = -5.88$. The answer is -5.88.

(e) First, simplify within the parentheses, then change the fraction to a decimal and perform addition from left to right:

$$\frac{3}{2} + (2 - 0.75) + 2 =$$

$$\frac{3}{2} + 1.25 + 2 =$$

$$1.5 + 1.25 + 2 = 4.75$$

P5. (a) 15% can be written as $\frac{15}{100}$. Both 15 and 100 can be divided by 5: $\frac{15 \div 5}{100 \div 5} = \frac{3}{20}$

When converting from a percentage to a decimal, drop the percent sign and move the decimal point two places to the left: $15\% = 0.15$

(b) 24.36% written as a fraction is $\frac{24.36}{100}$, or $\frac{2436}{10{,}000}$, which reduces to $\frac{609}{2500}$. 24.36% written as a decimal is 0.2436. Recall that dividing by 100 moves the decimal two places to the left.

P6. (a) Recall that in the decimal system the first decimal place is one tenth: $\frac{4 \times 2}{5 \times 2} = \frac{8}{10} = 0.8$

Percent means "per hundred." $\frac{4 \times 20}{5 \times 20} = \frac{80}{100} = 80\%$

(b) The mixed number $3\frac{2}{5}$ has a whole number and a fractional part. The fractional part $\frac{2}{5}$ can be written as a decimal by dividing 5 into 2, which gives 0.4. Adding the whole to the part gives 3.4.

To find the equivalent percentage, multiply the decimal by 100. $3.4(100) = 340\%$. Notice that this percentage is greater than 100%. This makes sense because the original mixed number $3\frac{2}{5}$ is greater than 1.

P7. "More than" indicates addition, and "of" indicates multiplication. The expression can be written as $\frac{1}{2}(60) + 13$. So, the woman's age is equal to $\frac{1}{2}(60) + 13 = 30 + 13 = 43$. The woman is 43 years old.

P8. The first step is to determine what operation (addition, subtraction, multiplication, or division) the problem requires. Notice the keywords and phrases "by how much" and "increased."

"Increased" means that you go from a smaller amount to a larger amount. This change can be found by subtracting the smaller amount from the larger amount: 0.80 grams– 0.22 grams = 0.58 grams.

Remember to line up the decimal when subtracting:

$$\begin{array}{r} 0.80 \\ -\ 0.22 \\ \hline 0.58 \end{array}$$

P9. First, find the number of rooms occupied each day. To do so, multiply the fraction of rooms occupied by the number of rooms available:

$$\text{Number occupied} = \text{Fraction occupied} \times \text{Total number}$$
$$\text{Number of rooms occupied today} = \frac{3}{4} \times 100 = 75$$
$$\text{Number of rooms occupied yesterday} = \frac{4}{5} \times 100 = 80$$

The difference in the number of rooms occupied is: $80 - 75 = 5$ rooms

P10. To answer this problem, first think about the number of teachers that work at the school. Will it be more or less than the number of teachers who work in a specific department such as English? More teachers work at the school, so the number you find to answer this question will be greater than 20.

40% of the teachers are English teachers. "Of" indicates multiplication, and words like "is" and "are" indicate equivalence. Translating the problem into a mathematical sentence gives $40\% \times t = 20$, where t represents the total number of teachers. Solving for t gives $t = \frac{20}{40\%} = \frac{20}{0.40} = 50$. Fifty teachers work at the school.

P11. The decrease is represented by the difference between the two amounts:

$$2 \text{ grams} - 0.45 \text{ grams} = 1.55 \text{ grams.}$$

Remember to line up the decimal point before subtracting.

$$\begin{array}{r} 2.00 \\ -\ 0.45 \\ \hline 1.55 \end{array}$$

P12. First, you need to find the number of male customers that were in the skate shop each week. You are given this amount in terms of fractions. To find the actual number of male customers, multiply the fraction of male customers by the number of customers in the store.

$$\text{Actual number of male customers} = \text{fraction of male customers} \times \text{total customers}$$
$$\text{Number of male customers two weeks ago} = \frac{2}{3} \times 60 = \frac{120}{3} = 40$$
$$\text{Number of male customers last week} = \frac{3}{6} \times 80 = \frac{1}{2} \times 80 = \frac{80}{2} = 40$$

The number of male customers was the same both weeks.

P13. To find total amount, first find the sum of the items she ordered from the menu and then add 20% of this sum to the total.

$$\$4.99 + \$12.50 + \$1.25 = \$18.74$$

$$\$18.74 \times 20\% = (0.20)(\$18.74) = \$3.748 \approx \$3.75$$

$$\text{Total} = \$18.74 + \$3.75 = \$22.49$$

P14. 82% of 145 is $0.82 \times 145 = 118.9$. Because you can't have 0.9 of a person, we must round up to say that 119 engineers reported that they were highly satisfied with their jobs.

P15. To find the percent increase, first compare the original and increased amounts. The original amount was 40 mg, and the increased amount is 45 mg, so the dosage of medication was increased by 5 mg ($45 - 40 = 5$). Note, however, that the question asks not by how much the dosage increased but by what percentage it increased.

$$\text{Percent increase} = \frac{\text{new amount} - \text{original amount}}{\text{original amount}} \times 100\%$$

$$= \frac{45\text{ mg} - 40\text{ mg}}{40\text{ mg}} \times 100\% = \frac{5}{40} \times 100\% = 0.125 \times 100\% = 12.5\%$$

P16. Recall that the term rational simply means that the number can be expressed as a ratio or fraction. Notice that each of the numbers in the problem can be written as a decimal or integer:

$$17\% = 0.17$$

$$\sqrt{25} = 5$$

$$\frac{64}{4} = 16$$

$$\frac{25}{50} = \frac{1}{2} = 0.5$$

So, the answer is $17\%, \frac{25}{50}, 0.55, 3, \sqrt{25}, \frac{64}{4}$.

P17. Converting all the numbers to integers and decimals makes it easier to compare the values:

$$27\% = 0.27$$

$$\sqrt{100} = 10$$

$$\frac{72}{9} = 8$$

$$\frac{1}{9} \approx 0.11$$

So, the answer is $\sqrt{100}, \frac{72}{9}, 4.5, 0.3, 27\%, \frac{1}{9}$.

Review Video: Ordering Rational Numbers
Visit mometrix.com/academy and enter code: 419578

P18. For each, convert improper fractions, adjust to a common denominator, perform the operations, and then simplify:

(a) Sometimes, you can skip converting the denominator and just distribute the multiplication.

$$\begin{aligned}\left(1\frac{11}{16}\right)\times 4 &= \left(1+\frac{11}{16}\right)\times 4\\ &= 1\times 4+\frac{11}{16}\times 4\\ &= 4+\frac{11}{16}\times\frac{4}{1}\\ &= 4+\frac{44}{16} = 4+\frac{11}{4} = 4+2\frac{3}{4} = 6\frac{3}{4}\end{aligned}$$

(b)

$$\begin{aligned}\left(12\frac{1}{3}\right)\times 1.1 &= \left(12+\frac{1}{3}\right)\times\left(1+\frac{1}{10}\right)\\ &= \left(\frac{12}{1}\times\frac{3}{3}+\frac{1}{3}\right)\times\left(\frac{10}{10}+\frac{1}{10}\right)\\ &= \left(\frac{36}{3}+\frac{1}{3}\right)\times\frac{11}{10}\\ &= \frac{37}{3}\times\frac{11}{10}\\ &= \frac{407}{30} = \frac{390}{30}+\frac{17}{30} = 13\frac{17}{30}\end{aligned}$$

(c)

$$\begin{aligned}3.71\times\left(6\frac{1}{5}\right) &= \left(3+\frac{71}{100}\right)\times\left(6+\frac{1}{5}\right)\\ &= \left(\frac{300}{100}+\frac{71}{100}\right)\times\left(\frac{6}{1}\times\frac{5}{5}+\frac{1}{5}\right)\\ &= \frac{371}{100}\times\left(\frac{30}{5}+\frac{1}{5}\right)\\ &= \frac{371}{100}\times\frac{31}{5}\\ &= \frac{11501}{500} = \frac{11500}{500}+\frac{1}{500} = 23\frac{1}{500}\end{aligned}$$

P19. Fortunately, some of the amounts are duplicated, so we do not need to convert every amount.

$$1\frac{3}{4} \times 3 = (1 \times 3) + \left(\frac{3}{4} \times 3\right) = 3 + \frac{9}{4} = 3 + 2\frac{1}{4} = 5\frac{1}{4}$$

$$1\frac{1}{4} \times 3 = (1 \times 3) + \left(\frac{1}{4} \times 3\right) = 3 + \frac{3}{4} = 3\frac{3}{4}$$

$$\frac{3}{4} \times 3 = \frac{3}{4} \times 3 = \frac{9}{4} = 2\frac{1}{4}$$

$$\frac{3}{8} \times 3 = \frac{3}{8} \times 3 = \frac{9}{8} = 1\frac{1}{8}$$

$$1\frac{1}{2} \times 3 = 1 \times 3 + \frac{1}{2} \times 3 = 3 + \frac{3}{2} = 3 + 1\frac{1}{2} = 4\frac{1}{2}$$

$$2 \times 3 = 6$$

So, the result for the triple recipe is:

$5\frac{1}{4}$	cup	Flour	$4\frac{1}{2}$	Tbsp	Butter
$3\frac{3}{4}$	tsp	Baking powder	6	large	Eggs
$2\frac{1}{4}$	tsp	Salt	$2\frac{1}{4}$	tsp	Vanilla extract
$1\frac{1}{8}$	cup	Sugar	$1\frac{1}{8}$	cup	Sour cream

Proportions and Ratios

Proportions

A proportion is a relationship between two quantities that dictates how one changes when the other changes. A **direct proportion** describes a relationship in which a quantity increases by a set amount for every increase in the other quantity, or decreases by that same amount for every decrease in the other quantity. Example: Assuming a constant driving speed, the time required for a car trip increases as the distance of the trip increases. The distance to be traveled and the time required to travel are directly proportional.

An **inverse proportion** is a relationship in which an increase in one quantity is accompanied by a decrease in the other, or vice versa. Example: the time required for a car trip decreases as the speed increases and increases as the speed decreases, so the time required is inversely proportional to the speed of the car.

Review Video: Proportions
Visit mometrix.com/academy and enter code: 505355

Ratios

A **ratio** is a comparison of two quantities in a particular order. Example: If there are 14 computers in a lab, and the class has 20 students, there is a student to computer ratio of 20 to 14, commonly written as $20:14$. Ratios are normally reduced to their smallest whole number representation, so $20:14$ would be reduced to $10:7$ by dividing both sides by 2.

Review Video: Ratios
Visit mometrix.com/academy and enter code: 996914

Constant of Proportionality

When two quantities have a proportional relationship, there exists a **constant of proportionality** between the quantities. The product of this constant and one of the quantities is equal to the other quantity. For example, if one lemon costs \$0.25, two lemons cost \$0.50, and three lemons cost \$0.75, there is a proportional relationship between the total cost of lemons and the number of lemons purchased. The constant of proportionality is the **unit price**, namely \$0.25/lemon. Notice that the total price of lemons, t, can be found by multiplying the unit price of lemons, p, and the number of lemons, n: $t = pn$.

Work/Unit Rate

Unit rate expresses a quantity of one thing in terms of one unit of another. For example, if you travel 30 miles every two hours, a unit rate expresses this comparison in terms of one hour: in one hour you travel 15 miles, so your unit rate is 15 miles per hour. Other examples are how much one ounce of food costs (price per ounce) or figuring out how much one egg costs out of the dozen (price per 1 egg, instead of price per 12 eggs). The denominator of a unit rate is always 1. Unit rates are used to compare different situations to solve problems. For example, to make sure you get the best deal when deciding which kind of soda to buy, you can find the unit rate of each. If soda #1 costs \$1.50 for a 1-liter bottle, and soda #2 costs \$2.75 for a 2-liter bottle, it would be a better deal to buy soda #2, because its unit rate is only \$1.375 per 1-liter, which is cheaper than soda #1. Unit rates can also help determine the length of time a given event will take. For example, if you can paint 2 rooms in 4.5 hours, you can determine how long it will take you to paint 5 rooms by solving for the unit rate per room and then multiplying that by 5.

Review Video: Rates and Unit Rates
Visit mometrix.com/academy and enter code: 185363

SLOPE

On a graph with two points, (x_1, y_1) and (x_2, y_2), the **slope** is found with the formula $m = \frac{y_2 - y_1}{x_2 - x_1}$; where $x_1 \neq x_2$ and m stands for slope. If the value of the slope is **positive**, the line has an *upward direction* from left to right. If the value of the slope is **negative**, the line has a *downward direction* from left to right. Consider the following example:

A new book goes on sale in bookstores and online stores. In the first month, 5,000 copies of the book are sold. Over time, the book continues to grow in popularity. The data for the number of copies sold is in the table below.

# of Months on Sale	1	2	3	4	5
# of Copies Sold (In Thousands)	5	10	15	20	25

So, the number of copies that are sold and the time that the book is on sale is a proportional relationship. In this example, an equation can be used to show the data: $y = 5x$, where x is the number of months that the book is on sale. Also, y is the number of copies sold. So, the slope of the corresponding line is $\frac{\text{rise}}{\text{run}} = \frac{5}{1} = 5$.

Review Video: Finding the Slope of a Line
Visit mometrix.com/academy and enter code: 766664

FINDING AN UNKNOWN IN EQUIVALENT EXPRESSIONS

It is often necessary to apply information given about a rate or proportion to a new scenario. For example, if you know that Jedha can run a marathon (26.2 miles) in 3 hours, how long would it take her to run 10 miles at the same pace? Start by setting up equivalent expressions:

$$\frac{26.2\text{ mi}}{3\text{ hr}} = \frac{10\text{ mi}}{x\text{ hr}}$$

Now, cross multiply and solve for x:

$$26.2x = 30$$
$$x = \frac{30}{26.2} = \frac{15}{13.1}$$
$$x \approx 1.15\text{ hrs } or \text{ 1 hr 9 min}$$

So, at this pace, Jedha could run 10 miles in about 1.15 hours or about 1 hour and 9 minutes.

Review Video: Cross Multiply Fractions
Visit mometrix.com/academy and enter code: 893904

Practice

P1. Solve the following for x.

(a) $\frac{45}{12} = \frac{15}{x}$

(b) $\frac{0.50}{2} = \frac{1.50}{x}$

(c) $\frac{40}{8} = \frac{x}{24}$

P2. At a school, for every 20 female students there are 15 male students. This same student ratio happens to exist at another school. If there are 100 female students at the second school, how many male students are there?

P3. In a hospital emergency room, there are 4 nurses for every 12 patients. What is the ratio of nurses to patients? If the nurse-to-patient ratio remains constant, how many nurses must be present to care for 24 patients?

P4. In a bank, the banker-to-customer ratio is 1: 2. If seven bankers are on duty, how many customers are currently in the bank?

P5. Janice made $40 during the first 5 hours she spent babysitting. She will continue to earn money at this rate until she finishes babysitting in 3 more hours. Find how much money Janice earns per hour and the total she earned babysitting.

P6. The McDonalds are taking a family road trip, driving 300 miles to their cabin. It took them 2 hours to drive the first 120 miles. They will drive at the same speed all the way to their cabin. Find the speed at which the McDonalds are driving and how much longer it will take them to get to their cabin.

P7. It takes Andy 10 minutes to read 6 pages of his book. He has already read 150 pages in his book that is 210 pages long. Find how long it takes Andy to read 1 page and also find how long it will take him to finish his book if he continues to read at the same speed.

Practice Solutions

P1. Cross multiply, then solve for x:

(a)

$$45x = 12 \times 15$$
$$45x = 180$$
$$x = \frac{180}{45} = 4$$

(b)

$$0.5x = 1.5 \times 2$$
$$0.5x = 3$$
$$x = \frac{3}{0.5} = 6$$

(c)

$$8x = 40 \times 24$$
$$8x = 960$$
$$x = \frac{960}{8} = 120$$

P2. One way to find the number of male students is to set up and solve a proportion.

$$\frac{\text{number of female students}}{\text{number of male students}} = \frac{20}{15} = \frac{100}{\text{number of male students}}$$

Represent the unknown number of male students as the variable x: $\frac{20}{15} = \frac{100}{x}$

Cross multiply and then solve for x:

$$20x = 15 \times 100$$
$$x = \frac{1500}{20}$$
$$x = 75$$

P3. The ratio of nurses to patients can be written as 4 to 12, 4: 12, or $\frac{4}{12}$. Because four and twelve have a common factor of four, the ratio should be reduced to 1: 3, which means that there is one nurse present for every three patients. If this ratio remains constant, there must be eight nurses present to care for 24 patients.

P4. Use proportional reasoning or set up a proportion to solve. Because there are twice as many customers as bankers, there must be fourteen customers when seven bankers are on duty. Setting up and solving a proportion gives the same result:

$$\frac{\text{number of bankers}}{\text{number of customers}} = \frac{1}{2} = \frac{7}{\text{number of customers}}$$

Represent the unknown number of customers as the variable x: $\frac{1}{2} = \frac{7}{x}$.

To solve for x, cross multiply: $1 \times x = 7 \times 2$, so $x = 14$.

P5. Janice earns \$8 per hour. This can be found by taking her initial amount earned, \$40, and dividing it by the number of hours worked, 5. Since $\frac{40}{5} = 8$, Janice makes \$8 in one hour. This can also be found by finding the unit rate, money earned per hour: $\frac{40}{5} = \frac{x}{1}$. Since cross multiplying yields $5x = 40$, and division by 5 shows that $x = 8$, Janice earns \$8 per hour.

Janice will earn \$64 babysitting in her 8 total hours (adding the first 5 hours to the remaining 3 gives the 8-hour total). Since Janice earns \$8 per hour and she worked 8 hours, $\frac{\$8}{\text{hr}} \times 8 \text{ hrs} = \$64$. This can also be found by setting up a proportion comparing money earned to babysitting hours. Since she earns \$40 for 5 hours and since the rate is constant, she will earn a proportional amount in 8 hours: $\frac{40}{5} = \frac{x}{8}$. Cross multiplying will yield $5x = 320$, and division by 5 shows that $x = 64$.

P6. The McDonalds are driving 60 miles per hour. This can be found by setting up a proportion to find the unit rate, the number of miles they drive per one hour: $\frac{120}{2} = \frac{x}{1}$. Cross multiplying yields $2x = 120$ and division by 2 shows that $x = 60$.

Since the McDonalds will drive this same speed for the remaining miles, it will take them another 3 hours to get to their cabin. This can be found by first finding how many miles the McDonalds have left to drive, which is $300 - 120 = 180$. The McDonalds are driving at 60 miles per hour, so a proportion can be set up to determine how many hours it will take them to drive 180 miles: $\frac{180}{x} = \frac{60}{1}$. Cross multiplying yields $60x = 180$, and division by 60 shows that $x = 3$. This can also be found by using the formula $D = r \times t$ (or distance = rate × time), where $180 = 60 \times t$, and division by 60 shows that $t = 3$.

P7. It takes Andy 10 minutes to read 6 pages, $\frac{10}{6} = 1\frac{2}{3}$ minutes, which is 1 minute and 40 seconds.

Next, determine how many pages Andy has left to read, $210 - 150 = 60$. Since it is now known that it takes him $1\frac{2}{3}$ minutes to read each page, that rate must be multiplied by however many pages he has left to read (60) to find the time he'll need: $60 \times 1\frac{2}{3} = 100$, so it will take him 100 minutes, or 1 hour and 40 minutes, to read the rest of his book.

Expressions

Terms and Coefficients

Mathematical expressions consist of a combination of one or more values arranged in terms that are added together. As such, an expression could be just a single number, including zero. A **variable term** is the product of a real number, also called a **coefficient**, and one or more variables, each of which may be raised to an exponent. Expressions may also include numbers without a variable, called **constants** or **constant terms**. The expression $6s^2$, for example, is a single term where the coefficient is the real number 6 and the variable term is s^2. Note that if a term is written as simply a variable to some exponent, like t^2, then the coefficient is 1, because $t^2 = 1t^2$.

Linear Expressions

A **single variable linear expression** is the sum of a single variable term, where the variable has no exponent, and a constant, which may be zero. For instance, the expression $2w + 7$ has $2w$ as the variable term and 7 as the constant term. It is important to realize that terms are separated by addition or subtraction. Since an expression is a sum of terms, expressions such as $5x - 3$ can be written as $5x + (-3)$ to emphasize that the constant term is negative. A real-world example of a single variable linear expression is the perimeter of a square, four times the side length, often expressed: $4s$.

In general, a **linear expression** is the sum of any number of variable terms so long as none of the variables have an exponent. For example, $3m + 8n - \frac{1}{4}p + 5.5q - 1$ is a linear expression, but $3y^3$ is not. In the same way, the expression for the perimeter of a general triangle, the sum of the side lengths $(a + b + c)$ is considered to be linear, but the expression for the area of a square, the side length squared $(s^2)$is not.

Equations

LINEAR EQUATIONS

Equations that can be written as $ax + b = 0$, where $a \neq 0$, are referred to as **one variable linear equations**. A solution to such an equation is called a **root**. In the case where we have the equation $5x + 10 = 0$, if we solve for x we get a solution of $x = -2$. In other words, the root of the equation is –2. This is found by first subtracting 10 from both sides, which gives $5x = -10$. Next, simply divide both sides by the coefficient of the variable, in this case 5, to get $x = -2$. This can be checked by plugging –2 back into the original equation $(5)(-2) + 10 = -10 + 10 = 0$.

The **solution set** is the set of all solutions of an equation. In our example, the solution set would simply be –2. If there were more solutions (there usually are in multivariable equations) then they would also be included in the solution set. When an equation has no true solutions, it is referred to as an **empty set**. Equations with identical solution sets are **equivalent equations**. An **identity** is a term whose value or determinant is equal to 1.

Linear equations can be written many ways. Below is a list of some forms linear equations can take:

- **Standard Form**: $Ax + By = C$; the slope is $\frac{-A}{B}$ and the y-intercept is $\frac{C}{B}$
- **Slope Intercept Form**: $y = mx + b$, where m is the slope and b is the y-intercept
- **Point-Slope Form**: $y - y_1 = m(x - x_1)$, where m is the slope and (x_1, y_1) is a point on the line
- **Two-Point Form**: $\frac{y-y_1}{x-x_1} = \frac{y_2-y_1}{x_2-x_1}$, where (x_1, y_1) and (x_2, y_2) are two points on the given line
- **Intercept Form**: $\frac{x}{x_1} + \frac{y}{y_1} = 1$, where $(x_1, 0)$ is the point at which a line intersects the x-axis, and $(0, y_1)$ is the point at which the same line intersects the y-axis

Review Video: Slope-Intercept and Point-Slope Forms
Visit mometrix.com/academy and enter code: 113216

Review Video: Linear Equations Basics
Visit mometrix.com/academy and enter code: 793005

SOLVING ONE-VARIABLE LINEAR EQUATIONS

Multiply all terms by the lowest common denominator to eliminate any fractions. Look for addition or subtraction to undo so you can isolate the variable on one side of the equal sign. Divide both sides by the coefficient of the variable. When you have a value for the variable, substitute this value into the original equation to make sure you have a true equation. Consider the following example:

Kim's savings are represented by the table below. Represent her savings, using an equation.

X (Months)	Y (Total Savings)
2	$1,300
5	$2,050
9	$3,050
11	$3,550
16	$4,800

The table shows a function with a constant rate of change, or slope, of 250. Given the points on the table, the slopes can be calculated as $\frac{(2{,}050-1300)}{(5-2)}$, $\frac{(3{,}050-2{,}050)}{(9-5)}$, $\frac{(3{,}550-3{,}050)}{(11-9)}$, and $\frac{(4{,}800-3{,}550)}{(16-11)}$, each of which equals 250. Thus, the table shows a constant rate of change, indicating a linear function. The slope-intercept form of a linear equation is written as $y = mx + b$, where m represents the slope and b represents the y-intercept. Substituting the slope into this form gives $y = 250x + b$. Substituting corresponding x- and y-values from any point into this equation will give the y-intercept, or b. Using the point, (2, 1,300), gives $1{,}300 = 250(2) + b$, which simplifies as $b = 800$. Thus, her savings may be represented by the equation, $y = 250x + 800$.

Rules for Manipulating Equations

Like Terms

Like terms are terms in an equation that have the same variable, regardless of whether or not they also have the same coefficient. This includes terms that *lack* a variable; all constants (i.e., numbers without variables) are considered like terms. If the equation involves terms with a variable raised to different powers, the like terms are those that have the variable raised to the same power.

For example, consider the equation $x^2 + 3x + 2 = 2x^2 + x - 7 + 2x$. In this equation, 2 and -7 are like terms; they are both constants. $3x$, x, and $2x$ are like terms, they all include the variable x raised to the first power. x^2 and $2x^2$ are like terms, they both include the variable x, raised to the second power. $2x$ and $2x^2$ are not like terms; although they both involve the variable x, the variable is not raised to the same power in both terms. The fact that they have the same coefficient, 2, is not relevant.

Review Video: Rules for Manipulating Equations
Visit mometrix.com/academy and enter code: 838871

Carrying Out the Same Operation on Both Sides of an Equation

When solving an equation, the general procedure is to carry out a series of operations on both sides of an equation, choosing operations that will tend to simplify the equation when doing so. The reason why the same operation must be carried out on both sides of the equation is because that leaves the meaning of the equation unchanged, and yields a result that is equivalent to the original equation. This would not be the case if we carried out an operation on one side of an equation and not the other. Consider what an equation means: it is a statement that two values or expressions are equal. If we carry out the same operation on both sides of the equation—add 3 to both sides, for example—then the two sides of the equation are changed in the same way, and so remain equal. If we do that to only one side of the equation—add 3 to one side but not the other—then that wouldn't be true; if we change one side of the equation but not the other then the two sides are no longer equal.

Advantage of Combining Like Terms

Combining like terms refers to adding or subtracting like terms—terms with the same variable—and therefore reducing sets of like terms to a single term. The main advantage of doing this is that it simplifies the equation. Often, combining like terms can be done as the first step in solving an equation, though it can also be done later, such as after distributing terms in a product.

For example, consider the equation $2(x + 3) + 3(2 + x + 3) = -4$. The 2 and the 3 in the second set of parentheses are like terms, and we can combine them, yielding $2(x + 3) + 3(x + 5) = -4$.

Now we can carry out the multiplications implied by the parentheses, distributing the outer 2 and 3 accordingly: $2x + 6 + 3x + 15 = -4$. The $2x$ and the $3x$ are like terms, and we can add them together: $5x + 6 + 15 = -4$. Now, the constants 6, 15, and –4 are also like terms, and we can combine them as well: subtracting 6 and 15 from both sides of the equation, we get $5x = -4 - 6 - 15$, or $5x = -25$, which simplifies further to $x = -5$.

Review Video: Solving Equations by Combining Like Terms
Visit mometrix.com/academy and enter code: 668506

Canceling Terms on Opposite Sides of an Equation

Two terms on opposite sides of an equation can be canceled if and only if they *exactly* match each other. They must have the same variable raised to the same power and the same coefficient. For example, in the equation $3x + 2x^2 + 6 = 2x^2 - 6$, $2x^2$ appears on both sides of the equation and can be canceled, leaving $3x + 6 = -6$. The 6 on each side of the equation *cannot* be canceled, because it is added on one side of the equation and subtracted on the other. While they cannot be canceled, however, the 6 and –6 are like terms and can be combined, yielding $3x = -12$, which simplifies further to $x = -4$.

It's also important to note that the terms to be canceled must be independent terms and cannot be part of a larger term. For example, consider the equation $2(x + 6) = 3(x + 4) + 1$. We cannot cancel the x's, because even though they match each other they are part of the larger terms $2(x + 6)$ and $3(x + 4)$. We must first distribute the 2 and 3, yielding $2x + 12 = 3x + 12 + 1$. Now we see that the terms with the x's do not match, but the 12s do, and can be canceled, leaving $2x = 3x + 1$, which simplifies to $x = -1$.

Process for Manipulating Equations

Isolating Variables

To **isolate a variable** means to manipulate the equation so that the variable appears by itself on one side of the equation, and does not appear at all on the other side. Generally, an equation or inequality is considered to be solved once the variable is isolated and the other side of the equation or inequality is simplified as much as possible. In the case of a two-variable equation or inequality, only one variable needs to be isolated; it will not usually be possible to simultaneously isolate both variables.

For a linear equation—an equation in which the variable only appears raised to the first power—isolating a variable can be done by first moving all the terms with the variable to one side of the equation and all other terms to the other side. (*Moving* a term really means adding the inverse of the term to both sides; when a term is *moved* to the other side of the equation its sign is flipped.) Then combine like terms on each side. Finally, divide both sides by the coefficient of the variable, if applicable. The steps need not necessarily be done in this order, but this order will always work.

Review Video: Solving One-Step Equations
Visit mometrix.com/academy and enter code: 777004

Equations with More Than One Solution

Some types of non-linear equations, such as equations involving squares of variables, may have more than one solution. For example, the equation $x^2 = 4$ has two solutions: 2 and –2. Equations with absolute values can also have multiple solutions: $|x| = 1$ has the solutions $x = 1$ and $x = -1$.

It is also possible for a linear equation to have more than one solution, but only if the equation is true regardless of the value of the variable. In this case, the equation is considered to have infinitely many solutions, because any possible value of the variable is a solution. We know a linear equation has infinitely many solutions if when we combine like terms the variables cancel, leaving a true statement. For example, consider the equation $2(3x + 5) = x + 5(x + 2)$. Distributing, we get $6x + 10 = x + 5x + 10$; combining like terms gives $6x + 10 = 6x + 10$, and the $6x$-terms cancel to leave $10 = 10$. This is clearly true, so the original equation is true for any value of x. We could also have canceled the 10s leaving $0 = 0$, but again this is clearly true—in general if both sides of the equation match exactly, it has infinitely many solutions.

Equations with No Solution

Some types of non-linear equations, such as equations involving squares of variables, may have no solution. For example, the equation $x^2 = -2$ has no solutions in the real numbers, because the square of any real number must be positive. Similarly, $|x| = -1$ has no solution, because the absolute value of a number is always positive.

It is also possible for an equation to have no solution even if does not involve any powers greater than one, absolute values, or other special functions. For example, the equation $2(x + 3) + x = 3x$ has no solution. We can see that if we try to solve it: first we distribute, leaving $2x + 6 + x = 3x$. But now if we try to combine all the terms with the variable, we find that they cancel: we have $3x$ on the left and $3x$ on the right, canceling to leave us with $6 = 0$. This is clearly false. In general, whenever the variable terms in an equation cancel leaving different constants on both sides, it means that the equation has no solution. (If we are left with the *same* constant on both sides, the equation has infinitely many solutions instead.)

Features of Equations That Require Special Treatment

Linear Equations

A linear equation is an equation in which variables only appear by themselves: not multiplied together, not with exponents other than one, and not inside absolute value signs or any other functions. For example, the equation $x + 1 - 3x = 5 - x$ is a linear equation; while x appears multiple times, it never appears with an exponent other than one, or inside any function. The two-variable equation $2x - 3y = 5 + 2x$ is also a linear equation. In contrast, the equation $x^2 - 5 = 3x$ is *not* a linear equation, because it involves the term x^2. $\sqrt{x} = 5$ is not a linear equation, because it involves a square root. $(x - 1)^2 = 4$ is not a linear equation because even though there's no exponent on the x directly, it appears as part of an expression that is squared. The two-variable equation $x + xy - y = 5$ is not a linear equation because it includes the term xy, where two variables are multiplied together.

Linear equations can always be solved (or shown to have no solution) by combining like terms and performing simple operations on both sides of the equation. Some non-linear equations can be solved by similar methods, but others may require more advanced methods of solution, if they can be solved analytically at all.

Solving Equations Involving Roots

In an equation involving roots, the first step is to isolate the term with the root, if possible, and then raise both sides of the equation to the appropriate power to eliminate it. Consider an example equation, $2\sqrt{x + 1} - 1 = 3$. In this case, begin by adding 1 to both sides, yielding $2\sqrt{x + 1} = 4$, and then dividing both sides by 2, yielding $\sqrt{x + 1} = 2$. Now square both sides, yielding $x + 1 = 4$. Finally, subtracting 1 from both sides yields $x = 3$.

Squaring both sides of an equation may, however, yield a spurious solution—a solution to the squared equation that is *not* a solution of the original equation. It's therefore necessary to plug the solution back into the original equation to make sure it works. In this case, it does: $2\sqrt{3+1}-1=2\sqrt{4}-1=2(2)-1=4-1=3$.

The same procedure applies for other roots as well. For example, given the equation $3+\sqrt[3]{2x}=5$, we can first subtract 3 from both sides, yielding $\sqrt[3]{2x}=2$ and isolating the root. Raising both sides to the third power yields $2x=2^3$; i.e., $2x=8$. We can now divide both sides by 2 to get $x=4$.

Review Video: Solving Equations Involving Roots
Visit mometrix.com/academy and enter code: 297670

Solving Equations with Exponents

To solve an equation involving an exponent, the first step is to isolate the variable with the exponent. We can then take the appropriate root of both sides to eliminate the exponent. For instance, for the equation $2x^3+17=5x^3-7$, we can subtract $5x^3$ from both sides to get $-3x^3+17=-7$, and then subtract 17 from both sides to get $-3x^3=-24$. Finally, we can divide both sides by -3 to get $x^3=8$. Finally, we can take the cube root of both sides to get $x=\sqrt[3]{8}=2$.

One important but often overlooked point is that equations with an exponent greater than 1 may have more than one answer. The solution to $x^2=9$ isn't simply $x=3$; it's $x=\pm 3$ (that is, $x=3$ or $x=-3$). For a slightly more complicated example, consider the equation $(x-1)^2-1=3$. Adding 1 to both sides yields $(x-1)^2=4$; taking the square root of both sides yields $x-1=2$. We can then add 1 to both sides to get $x=3$. However, there's a second solution. We also have the possibility that $x-1=-2$, in which case $x=-1$. Both $x=3$ and $x=-1$ are valid solutions, as can be verified by substituting them both into the original equation.

Review Video: Solving Equations with Exponents
Visit mometrix.com/academy and enter code: 514557

Solving Equations with Absolute Values

When solving an equation with an absolute value, the first step is to isolate the absolute value term. We then consider two possibilities: when the expression inside the absolute value is positive or when it is negative. In the former case, the expression in the absolute value equals the expression on the other side of the equation; in the latter, it equals the additive inverse of that expression—the expression times negative one. We consider each case separately and finally check for spurious solutions.

For instance, consider solving $|2x-1|+x=5$ for x. We can first isolate the absolute value by moving the x to the other side: $|2x-1|=-x+5$. Now, we have two possibilities. First, that $2x-1$ is positive, and hence $2x-1=-x+5$. Rearranging and combining like terms yields $3x=6$, and hence $x=2$. The other possibility is that $2x-1$ is negative, and hence $2x-1=-(-x+5)=x-5$. In this case, rearranging and combining like terms yields $x=-4$. Substituting $x=2$ and $x=-4$ back into the original equation, we see that they are both valid solutions.

Note that the absolute value of a sum or difference applies to the sum or difference as a whole, not to the individual terms; in general, $|2x-1|$ is not equal to $|2x+1|$ or to $|2x|-1$.

Spurious Solutions

A **spurious solution** may arise when we square both sides of an equation as a step in solving it or under certain other operations on the equation. It is a solution to the squared or otherwise modified equation that is *not* a solution of the original equation. To identify a spurious solution, it's useful when you solve an equation involving roots or absolute values to plug the solution back into the original equation to make sure it's valid.

Choosing Which Variable to Isolate in Two-Variable Equations

Similar to methods for a one-variable equation, solving a two-variable equation involves isolating a variable: manipulating the equation so that a variable appears by itself on one side of the equation, and not at all on the other side. However, in a two-variable equation, you will usually only be able to isolate one of the variables; the other variable may appear on the other side along with constant terms, or with exponents or other functions.

Often one variable will be much more easily isolated than the other, and therefore that's the variable you should choose. If one variable appears with various exponents, and the other is only raised to the first power, the latter variable is the one to isolate: given the equation $a^2 + 2b = a^3 + b + 3$, the b only appears to the first power, whereas a appears squared and cubed, so b is the variable that can be solved for: combining like terms and isolating the b on the left side of the equation, we get $b = a^3 - a^2 + 3$. If both variables are equally easy to isolate, then it's best to isolate the independent variable, if one is defined; if the two variables are x and y, the convention is that y is the independent variable.

Practice

P1. Seeing the equation $2x + 4 = 4x + 7$, a student divides the first terms on each side by 2, yielding $x + 4 = 2x + 7$, and then combines like terms to get $x = -3$. However, this is incorrect, as can be seen by substituting -3 into the original equation. Explain what is wrong with the student's reasoning.

P2. Describe the steps necessary to solve the equation $2x + 1 - x = 4 + 3x + 7$.

P3. Describe the steps necessary to solve the equation $2(x + 5) = 7(4 - x)$.

P4. Find all real solutions to the equation $1 - \sqrt{x} = 2$.

P5. Find all real solutions to the equation $|x + 1| = 2x + 5$.

P6. Solve for x: $-x + 2\sqrt{x + 5} + 1 = 3$.

P7. Ray earns $10 an hour at his job. Write an equation for his earnings as a function of time spent working. Determine how long Ray has to work in order to earn $360.

P8. Simplify the following: $3x + 2 + 2y = 5y - 7 + |2x - 1|$

Practice Solutions

P1. As stated, it's easy to verify that the student's solution is incorrect: $2(-3) + 4 = -2$ and $4(-3) + 7 = -5$; clearly $-2 \neq -5$. The mistake was in the first step, which illustrates a common type of error in solving equations. The student tried to simplify the two variable terms by dividing them by 2. However, it's not valid to multiply or divide only one term on each side of an equation by a number; when multiplying or dividing, the operation must be applied to *every* term in the equation. So, dividing by 2 would yield not $x + 4 = 2x + 7$, but $x + 2 = 2x + \frac{7}{2}$. While this is now valid, that fraction is inconvenient to work with, so this may not be the best first step in solving the equation. Rather, it may have been better to first combine like terms. Subtracting $4x$ from both sides yields $-2x + 4 = 7$; subtracting 4 from both sides yields $-2x = 3$; *now* we can divide both sides by –2 to get $x = -\frac{3}{2}$.

P2. Our ultimate goal is to isolate the variable, x. To that end we first move all the terms containing x to the left side of the equation, and all the constant terms to the right side. Note that when we move a term to the other side of the equation its sign changes. We are therefore now left with $2x - x - 3x = 4 + 7 - 1$.

Next, we combine the like terms on each side of the equation, adding and subtracting the terms as appropriate. This leaves us with $-2x = 10$.

At this point, we're almost done; all that remains is to divide both sides by -2 to leave the x by itself. We now have our solution, $x = -5$. We can verify that this is a correct solution by substituting it back into the original equation.

P3. Generally, in equations that have a sum or difference of terms multiplied by another value or expression, the first step is to multiply those terms, distributing as necessary: $2(x + 5) = 2(x) + 2(5) = 2x + 10$, and $7(4 - x) = 7(4) - 7(x) = 28 - 7x$. So, the equation becomes $2x + 10 = 28 - 7x$. We can now add $7x$ to both sides to eliminate the variable from the right-hand side: $9x + 10 = 28$. Similarly, we can subtract 10 from both sides to move all the constants to the right: $9x = 18$. Finally, we can divide both sides by 9, yielding the final answer, $x = 2$.

P4. It's not hard to isolate the root: subtract one from both sides, yielding $-\sqrt{x} = 1$. Finally, multiply both sides by –1, yielding $\sqrt{x} = -1$. Squaring both sides of the equation yields $x = 1$. However, if we plug this back into the original equation, we get $1 - \sqrt{1} = 2$, which is false. Therefore $x = 1$ is a spurious solution, and the equation has no real solutions.

P5. This equation has two possibilities: $x + 1 = 2x + 5$, which simplifies to $x = -4$; or $x + 1 = -(2x + 5) = -2x - 5$, which simplifies to $x = -2$. However, if we try substituting both values back into the original equation, we see that only $x = -2$ yields a true statement. $x = -4$ is a spurious solution; $x = -2$ is the only valid solution to the equation.

P6. Start by isolating the term with the root. We can do that by moving the $-x$ and the 1 to the other side, yielding $2\sqrt{x + 5} = 3 + x - 1$, or $2\sqrt{x + 5} = x + 2$. Dividing both sides of the equation by 2 would give us a fractional term that could be messy to deal with, so we won't do that for now. Instead, we square both sides of the equation; note that on the left-hand side the 2 is outside the square root sign, so we have to square it. As a result, we get $4(x + 5) = (x + 2)^2$. Expanding both sides gives us $4x + 20 = x^2 + 4x + 4$. In this case, we see that we have $4x$ on both sides, so we can cancel the $4x$ (which is what allows us to solve this equation despite the different powers of x). We now have $20 = x^2 + 4$, or $x^2 = 16$. Since the variable is raised to an even power, we need to take the positive and negative roots, so $x = \pm 4$: that is, $x = 4$ or $x = -4$. Substituting both values into the original equation, we see that $x = 4$ satisfies the equation but $x = -4$ does not; hence $x = -4$ is a spurious solution, and the only solution to the equation is $x = 4$.

P7. The number of dollars that Ray earns is dependent on the number of hours he works, so earnings will be represented by the dependent variable y and hours worked will be represented by the independent variable x. He earns 10 dollars per hour worked, so his earnings can be calculated as $y = 10x$. To calculate the number of hours Ray must work in order to earn \$360, plug in 360 for y and solve for x:

$$360 = 10x$$

$$x = \frac{360}{10} = 36$$

P8. To simplify this equation, we must isolate one of its variables on one side of the equation. In this case, the x appears under an absolute value sign, which makes it difficult to isolate. The y, on the other hand, only appears without an exponent—the equation is linear in y. We will therefore choose to isolate the y. The first step, then, is to move all the terms with y to the left side of the equation, which we can do by subtracting $5y$ from both sides:

$$3x + 2 - 3y = -7 + |2x - 1|$$

We can then move all the terms that do *not* include y to the right side of the equation, by subtracting $3x$ and 2 from both sides of the equation:

$$-3y = -3x - 9 + |2x - 1|$$

Finally, we can isolate the y by dividing both sides by -3.

$$y = x + 3 - \frac{1}{3}|2x - 1|$$

This is as far as we can simplify the equation; we cannot combine the terms inside and outside the absolute value sign. We can therefore consider the equation to be solved.

Inequalities

Working with Inequalities

Commonly in algebra and other upper-level fields of math you find yourself working with mathematical expressions that do not equal each other. The statement comparing such expressions with symbols such as $<$ (less than) or $>$ (greater than) is called an *inequality*. An example of an inequality is $7x > 5$. To solve for x, simply divide both sides by 7 and the solution is shown to be $x > \frac{5}{7}$. Graphs of the solution set of inequalities are represented on a number line. Open circles are used to show that an expression approaches a number but is never quite equal to that number.

Review Video: Solving Multi-Step Inequalities
Visit mometrix.com/academy and enter code: 347842

Review Video: Solving Inequalities Using All 4 Basic Operations
Visit mometrix.com/academy and enter code: 401111

Conditional inequalities are those with certain values for the variable that will make the condition true and other values for the variable where the condition will be false. **Absolute inequalities** can have any real number as the value for the variable to make the condition true, while there is no real number value for the variable that will make the condition false. Solving inequalities is done by following the same rules for solving equations with the exception that when multiplying or dividing by a negative number the direction of the inequality sign must be flipped or reversed. **Double inequalities** are situations where two inequality statements apply to the same variable expression. Example: $-c < ax + b < c$.

Review Video: Conditional and Absolute Inequalities
Visit mometrix.com/academy and enter code: 980164

Determining Solutions to Inequalities

To determine whether a coordinate is a solution of an inequality, you can substitute the values of the coordinate into the inequality, simplify, and check whether the resulting statement holds true. For instance, to determine whether $(-2,4)$ is a solution of the inequality $y \geq -2x + 3$, substitute the values into the inequality, $4 \geq -2(-2) + 3$. Simplify the right side of the inequality and the result is $4 \geq 7$, which is a false statement. Therefore, the coordinate is not a solution of the inequality. You can also use this method to determine which part of the graph of an inequality is shaded. The graph of $y \geq -2x + 3$ includes the solid line $y = -2x + 3$ and, since it excludes the point $(-2,4)$ to the left of the line, it is shaded to the right of the line.

Review Video: Graphing Linear Inequalities
Visit mometrix.com/academy and enter code: 439421

Flipping Inequality Signs

When given an inequality, we can always turn the entire inequality around, swapping the two sides of the inequality and changing the inequality sign. For instance, $x + 2 > 2x - 3$ is equivalent to $2x - 3 < x + 2$. Aside from that, normally the inequality does not change if we carry out the same operation on both sides of the inequality. There is, however, one principal exception: if we *multiply* or *divide* both sides of the inequality by a *negative number*, the inequality is flipped. For example, if we take the inequality $-2x < 6$ and divide both sides by –2, the inequality flips and we are left with

$x > -3$. This *only* applies to multiplication and division, and only with negative numbers. Multiplying or dividing both sides by a positive number, or adding or subtracting any number regardless of sign, does not flip the inequality. Another special case that flips the inequality sign is when reciprocals are used. For instance, $3 > 2$ but the relation of the reciprocals is $\frac{1}{2} < \frac{1}{3}$.

Compound Inequalities

A **compound inequality** is an equality that consists of two inequalities combined with *and* or *or*. The two components of a proper compound inequality must be of opposite type: that is, one must be greater than (or greater than or equal to), the other less than (or less than or equal to). For instance, "$x + 1 < 2$ or $x + 1 > 3$" is a compound inequality, as is "$2x \geq 4$ and $2x \leq 6$." An *and* inequality can be written more compactly by having one inequality on each side of the common part: "$2x \geq 1$ and $2x \leq 6$," can also be written as $1 \leq 2x \leq 6$.

In order for the compound inequality to be meaningful, the two parts of an *and* inequality must overlap; otherwise, no numbers satisfy the inequality. On the other hand, if the two parts of an *or* inequality overlap, then *all* numbers satisfy the inequality and as such the inequality is usually not meaningful.

Solving a compound inequality requires solving each part separately. For example, given the compound inequality "$x + 1 < 2$ or $x + 1 > 3$," the first inequality, $x + 1 < 2$, reduces to $x < 1$, and the second part, $x + 1 > 3$, reduces to $x > 2$, so the whole compound inequality can be written as "$x < 1$ or $x > 2$." Similarly, $1 \leq 2x \leq 6$ can be solved by dividing each term by 2, yielding $\frac{1}{2} \leq x \leq 3$.

Review Video: Compound Inequalities
Visit mometrix.com/academy and enter code: 786318

Solving Inequalities Involving Absolute Values

To solve an inequality involving an absolute value, first isolate the term with the absolute value. Then proceed to treat the two cases separately as with an absolute value equation, but flipping the inequality in the case where the expression in the absolute value is negative (since that essentially involves multiplying both sides by -1.) The two cases are then combined into a compound inequality; if the absolute value is on the greater side of the inequality, then it is an *or* compound inequality, if on the lesser side, then it's an *and*.

Consider the inequality $2 + |x - 1| \geq 3$. We can isolate the absolute value term by subtracting 2 from both sides: $|x - 1| \geq 1$. Now, we're left with the two cases $x - 1 \geq 1$ or $x - 1 \leq -1$: note that in the latter, negative case, the inequality is flipped. $x - 1 \geq 1$ reduces to $x \geq 2$, and $x - 1 \leq -1$ reduces to $x \leq 0$. Since in the inequality $|x - 1| \geq 1$ the absolute value is on the greater side, the two cases combine into an *or* compound inequality, so the final, solved inequality is "$x \leq 0$ or $x \geq 2$."

Review Video: Solving Absolute Value Inequalities
Visit mometrix.com/academy and enter code: 997008

Solving Inequalities Involving Square Roots

Solving an inequality with a square root involves two parts. First, we solve the inequality as if it were an equation, isolating the square root and then squaring both sides of the equation. Second, we restrict the solution to the set of values of x for which the value inside the square root sign is non-negative.

For example, in the inequality, $\sqrt{x-2}+1<5$, we can isolate the square root by subtracting 1 from both sides, yielding $\sqrt{x-2}<4$. Squaring both sides of the inequality yields $x-2<16$, so $x<18$. Since we can't take the square root of a negative number, we also require the part inside the square root to be non-negative. In this case, that means $x-2\geq 0$. Adding 2 to both sides of the inequality yields $x\geq 2$. Our final answer is a compound inequality combining the two simple inequalities: $x\geq 2$ and $x<18$, or $2\leq x<18$.

Note that we only get a compound inequality if the two simple inequalities are in opposite directions; otherwise, we take the one that is more restrictive.

The same technique can be used for other even roots, such as fourth roots. It is *not*, however, used for cube roots or other odd roots—negative numbers *do* have cube roots, so the condition that the quantity inside the root sign cannot be negative does not apply.

Review Video: Solving Inequalities Involving Square Roots
Visit mometrix.com/academy and enter code: 800288

Special Circumstances

Sometimes an inequality involving an absolute value or an even exponent is true for all values of x, and we don't need to do any further work to solve it. This is true if the inequality, once the absolute value or exponent term is isolated, says that term is greater than a negative number (or greater than or equal to zero). Since an absolute value or a number raised to an even exponent is *always* non-negative, this inequality is always true.

Graphical Solutions to Equations and Inequalities

When equations are shown graphically, they are usually shown on a **Cartesian coordinate plane**. The Cartesian coordinate plane consists of two number lines placed perpendicular to each other and intersecting at the zero point, also known as the origin. The horizontal number line is known as the x-axis, with positive values to the right of the origin, and negative values to the left of the origin. The vertical number line is known as the y-axis, with positive values above the origin, and negative values below the origin. Any point on the plane can be identified by an ordered pair in the form (x, y), called coordinates. The x-value of the coordinate is called the abscissa, and the y-value of the coordinate is called the ordinate. The two number lines divide the plane into **four quadrants**: I, II, III, and IV.

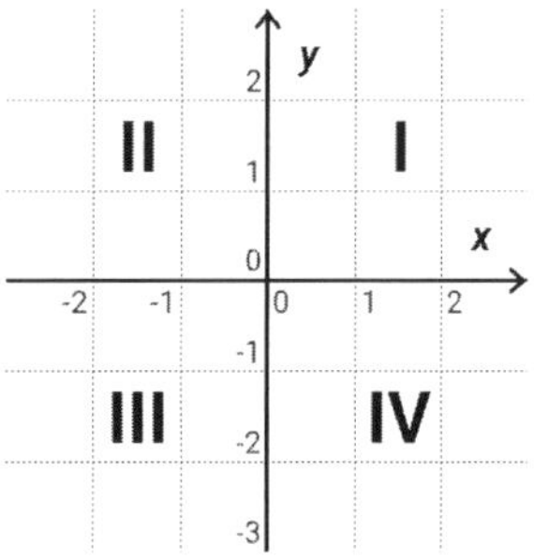

Note that in quadrant I $x>0$ and $y>0$, in quadrant II $x<0$ and $y>0$, in quadrant III $x<0$ and $y<0$, and in quadrant IV $x>0$ and $y<0$.

Recall that if the value of the slope of a line is positive, the line slopes upward from left to right. If the value of the slope is negative, the line slopes downward from left to right. If the y-coordinates are the same for two points on a line, the slope is 0 and the line is a **horizontal line**. If the x-

coordinates are the same for two points on a line, there is no slope and the line is a **vertical line**. Two or more lines that have equivalent slopes are **parallel lines**. **Perpendicular lines** have slopes that are negative reciprocals of each other, such as $\frac{a}{b}$ and $\frac{-b}{a}$.

Review Video: Cartesian Coordinate Plane and Graphing
Visit mometrix.com/academy and enter code: 115173

Graphing Simple Inequalities

To graph a simple inequality, we first mark on the number line the value that signifies the end point of the inequality. If the inequality is strict (involves a less than or greater than), we use a hollow circle; if it is not strict (less than or equal to or greater than or equal to), we use a solid circle. We then fill in the part of the number line that satisfies the inequality: to the left of the marked point for less than (or less than or equal to), to the right for greater than (or greater than or equal to).

For example, we would graph the inequality $x < 5$ by putting a hollow circle at 5 and filling in the part of the line to the left:

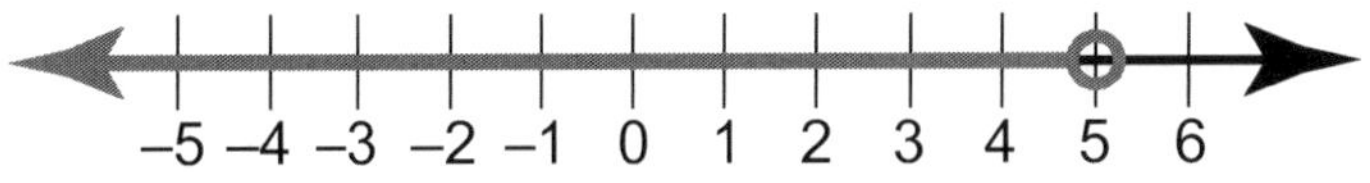

Graphing Compound Inequalities

To graph a compound inequality, we fill in both parts of the inequality for an *or* inequality, or the overlap between them for an *and* inequality. More specifically, we start by plotting the endpoints of each inequality on the number line. For an *or* inequality, we then fill in the appropriate side of the line for each inequality. Typically, the two component inequalities do not overlap, which means the shaded part is *outside* the two points. For an *and* inequality, we instead fill in the part of the line that meets both inequalities.

For the inequality "$x \leq -3$ or $x > 4$," we first put a solid circle at –3 and a hollow circle at 4. We then fill the parts of the line *outside* these circles:

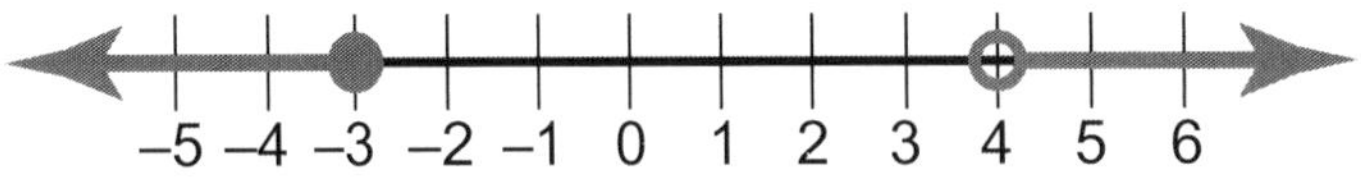

Graphing Inequalities Including Absolute Values

An inequality with an absolute value can be converted to a compound inequality. To graph the inequality, first convert it to a compound inequality, and then graph that normally. If the absolute value is on the greater side of the inequality, we end up with an *or* inequality; we plot the endpoints of the inequality on the number line and fill in the part of the line *outside* those points. If the absolute value is on the smaller side of the inequality, we end up with an *and* inequality; we plot the endpoints of the inequality on the number line and fill in the part of the line *between* those points.

For example, the inequality $|x + 1| \geq 4$ can be rewritten as $x \geq 3$ or $x \leq -5$. We place solid circles at the points 3 and -5 and fill in the part of the line *outside* them:

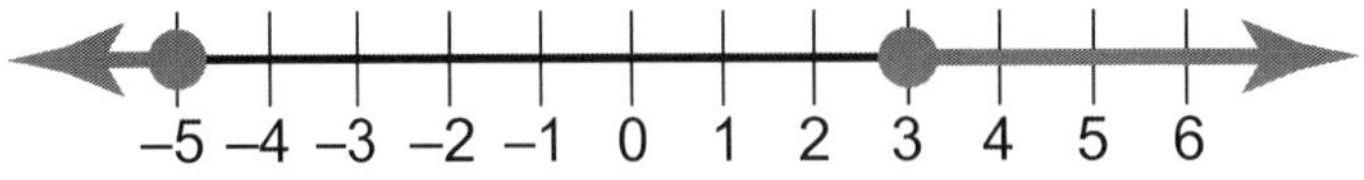

GRAPHING EQUATIONS IN TWO VARIABLES

One way of graphing an equation in two variables is to plot enough points to get an idea for its shape and then draw the appropriate curve through those points. A point can be plotted by substituting in a value for one variable and solving for the other. If the equation is linear, we only need two points and can then draw a straight line between them.

For example, consider the equation $y = 2x - 1$. This is a linear equation—both variables only appear raised to the first power—so we only need two points. When $x = 0$, $y = 2(0) - 1 = -1$. When $x = 2$, $y = 2(2) - 1 = 3$. We can therefore choose the points $(0, -1)$ and $(2, 3)$, and draw a line between them:

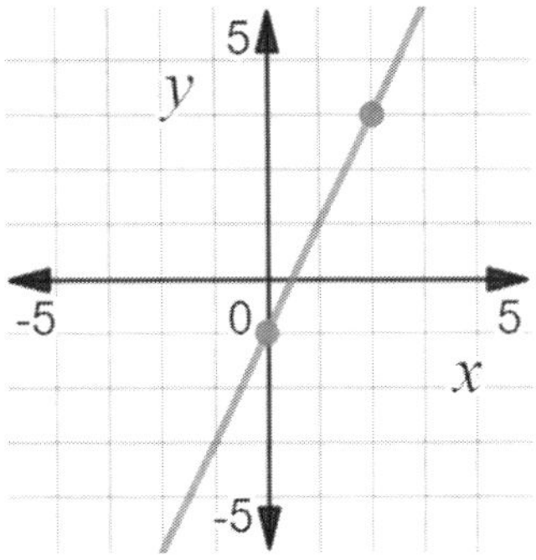

GRAPHING INEQUALITIES IN TWO VARIABLES

To graph an inequality in two variables, we first graph the border of the inequality. This means graphing the equation that we get if we replace the inequality sign with an equals sign. If the inequality is strict ($>$ or $<$), we graph the border with a dashed or dotted line; if it is not strict ($\geq$ or $\leq$), we use a solid line. We can then test any point not on the border to see if it satisfies the inequality. If it does, we shade in that side of the border; if not, we shade in the other side. As an example, consider $y > 2x + 2$. To graph this inequality, we first graph the border, $y = 2x + 2$. Since it is a strict inequality, we use a dashed line. Then, we choose a test point. This can be any point not on the border; in this case, we will choose the origin, (0,0). (This makes the calculation easy and is generally a good choice unless the border passes through the origin.) Putting this into the original inequality, we get $0 > 2(0) + 2$, i.e., $0 > 2$. This is *not* true, so we shade in the side of the border that does *not* include the point (0,0):

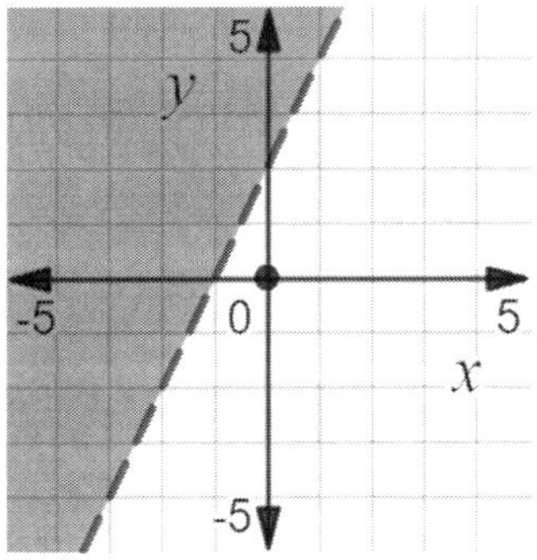

GRAPHING COMPOUND INEQUALITIES IN TWO VARIABLES

One way to graph a compound inequality in two variables is to first graph each of the component inequalities. For an *and* inequality, we then shade in only the parts where the two graphs overlap; for an *or* inequality, we shade in any region that pertains to either of the individual inequalities.

Consider the graph of "$y \geq x - 1$ and $y \leq -x$":

We first shade in the individual inequalities:

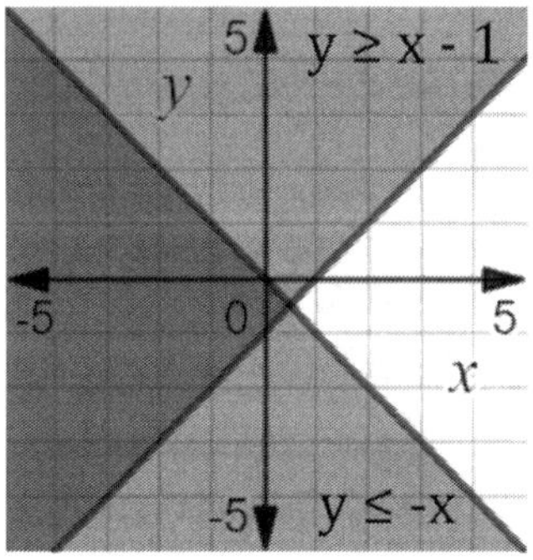

Now, since the compound inequality has an *and*, we only leave shaded the overlap—the part that pertains to *both* inequalities:

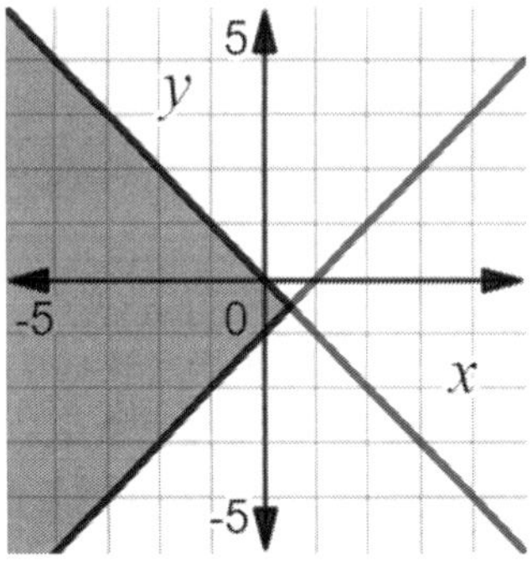

If instead the inequality had been "$y \geq x - 1$ or $y \leq -x$," our final graph would involve the *total* shaded area:

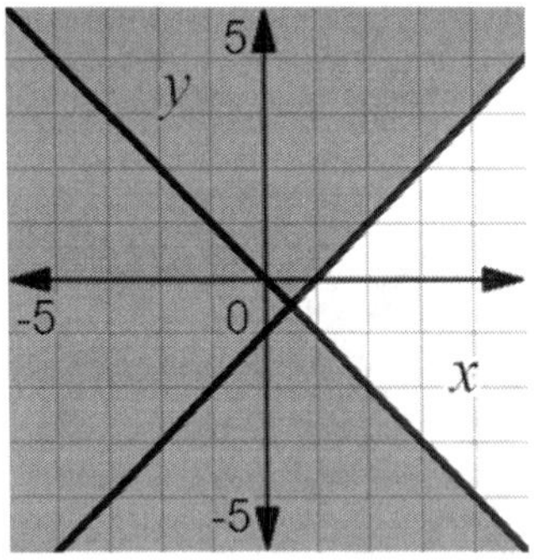

Review Video: Graphing Solutions to Inequalities
Visit mometrix.com/academy and enter code: 391281

Practice

P1. Analyze the following inequalities:

(a) $2 - |x + 1| < 3$

(b) $2(x - 1)^2 + 7 \leq 1$

P2. Graph the following on a number line:

(a) $x \geq 3$
(b) $-2 \leq x \leq 6$
(c) $|x| < 2$

Practice Solutions

P1. (a) Subtracting 2 from both sides yields $-|x + 1| < 1$; multiplying by -1 and flipping the inequality, since we're multiplying by a negative number, yields $|x + 1| > -1$. But since the absolute value cannot be negative, it's *always* greater than -1, so this inequality is true for all values of x.

(b) Subtracting 7 from both sides yields $2(x - 1)^2 \leq -6$; dividing by 2 yields $(x - 1)^2 \leq -3$. But $(x - 1)^2$ must be nonnegative, and hence cannot be less than or equal to -3; this inequality has no solution.

P2. (a) We would graph the inequality $x \geq 3$ by putting a solid circle at 3 and filling in the part of the line to the right:

(b) The inequality $-2 \leq x \leq 6$ is equivalent to "$x \geq -2$ and $x \leq 6$." To plot this compound inequality, we first put solid circles at -2 and 6, and then fill in the part of the line *between* these circles:

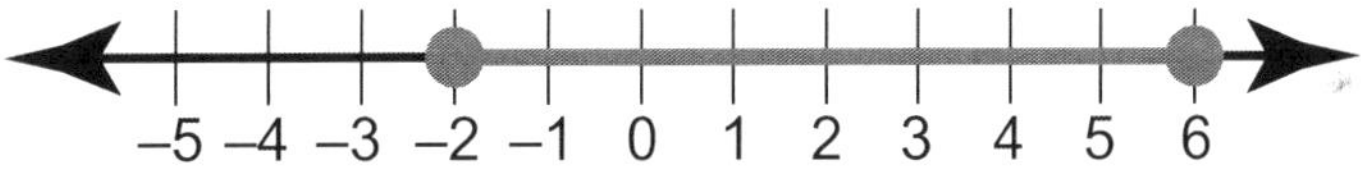

(c) The inequality $|x| < 2$ can be rewritten as "$x > -2$ and $x < 2$." We place hollow circles at the points -2 and 2 and fill in the part of the line between them:

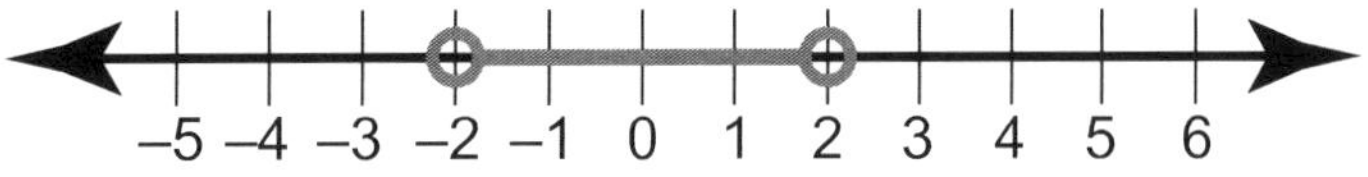

Systems of Equations

Solving Systems of Equations

A **system of equations** is a set of simultaneous equations that all use the same variables. A solution to a system of equations must be true for each equation in the system. **Consistent systems** are those with at least one solution. **Inconsistent systems** are systems of equations that have no solution.

Review Video: Solving Systems and Linear Equations
Visit mometrix.com/academy and enter code: 746745

Substitution

To solve a system of linear equations by **substitution**, start with the easier equation and solve for one of the variables. Express this variable in terms of the other variable. Substitute this expression in the other equation and solve for the other variable. The solution should be expressed in the form (x, y). Substitute the values into both of the original equations to check your answer. Consider the following system of equations:

$$x + 6y = 15$$
$$3x - 12y = 18$$

Solving the first equation for x: $x = 15 - 6y$

Substitute this value in place of x in the second equation, and solve for y:

$$\begin{aligned} 3(15 - 6y) - 12y &= 18 \\ 45 - 18y - 12y &= 18 \\ 30y &= 27 \\ y &= \frac{27}{30} = \frac{9}{10} = 0.9 \end{aligned}$$

Plug this value for y back into the first equation to solve for x:

$$x = 15 - 6(0.9) = 15 - 5.4 = 9.6$$

Check both equations if you have time:

$$\begin{aligned} 9.6 + 6(0.9) &= 15 \\ 9.6 + 5.4 &= 15 \\ 15 &= 15 \end{aligned} \qquad \begin{aligned} 3(9.6) - 12(0.9) &= 18 \\ 28.8 - 10.8 &= 18 \\ 18 &= 18 \end{aligned}$$

Therefore, the solution is (9.6,0.9).

Review Video: The Substitution Method
Visit mometrix.com/academy and enter code: 565151

Elimination

To solve a system of equations using **elimination**, begin by rewriting both equations in standard form $Ax + By = C$. Check to see if the coefficients of one pair of like variables add to zero. If not, multiply one or both of the equations by a non-zero number to make one set of like variables add to zero. Add the two equations to solve for one of the variables. Substitute this value into one of the original equations to solve for the other variable. Check your work by substituting into the other equation. Now, let's look at solving the following system using the elimination method:

$$5x + 6y = 4$$
$$x + 2y = 4$$

If we multiply the second equation by -3, we can eliminate the y-terms:

$$5x + 6y = 4$$
$$-3x - 6y = -12$$

Add the equations together and solve for x:

$$2x = -8$$
$$x = \frac{-8}{2} = -4$$

Plug the value for x back in to either of the original equations and solve for y:

$$-4 + 2y = 4$$
$$y = \frac{4+4}{2} = 4$$

Check both equations if you have time:

$$5(-4) + 6(4) = 4 \qquad -4 + 2(4) = 4$$
$$-20 + 24 = 4 \qquad -4 + 8 = 4$$
$$4 = 4 \qquad 4 = 4$$

Therefore, the solution is $(-4,4)$.

Review Video: The Elimination Method
Visit mometrix.com/academy and enter code: 449121

GRAPHICALLY

To solve a system of linear equations **graphically**, plot both equations on the same graph. The solution of the equations is the point where both lines cross. If the lines do not cross (are parallel), then there is **no solution**.

For example, consider the following system of equations:

$$y = 2x + 7$$
$$y = -x + 1$$

Since these equations are given in slope-intercept form, they are easy to graph; the y-intercepts of the lines are (0,7) and (0,1). The respective slopes are 2 and −1, thus the graphs look like this:

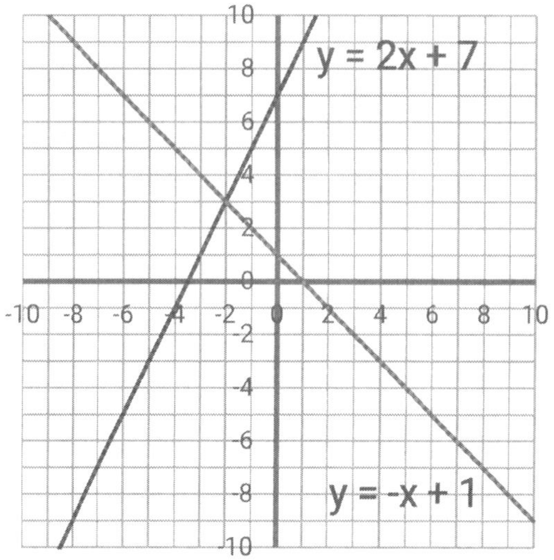

The two lines intersect at the point $(-2,3)$, thus this is the solution to the system of equations.

Solving a system graphically is generally only practical if both coordinates of the solution are integers; otherwise the intersection will lie between gridlines on the graph and the coordinates will be difficult or impossible to determine exactly. It also helps if, as in this example, the equations are in slope-intercept form or some other form that makes them easy to graph. Otherwise, another method of solution (by substitution or elimination) is likely to be more useful.

Review Video: Solving Systems by Graphing
Visit mometrix.com/academy and enter code: 634812

Solving Systems of Equations Using the Trace Feature

Using the trace feature on a calculator requires that you rewrite each equation, isolating the y-variable on one side of the equal sign. Enter both equations in the graphing calculator and plot the graphs simultaneously. Use the trace cursor to find where the two lines cross. Use the zoom feature if necessary to obtain more accurate results. Always check your answer by substituting into the original equations. The trace method is likely to be less accurate than other methods due to the resolution of graphing calculators but is a useful tool to provide an approximate answer.

Calculations Using Points

Sometimes you need to perform calculations using only points on a graph as input data. Using points, you can determine what the **midpoint** and **distance** are. If you know the equation for a line, you can calculate the distance between the line and the point.

To find the **midpoint** of two points (x_1, y_1) and (x_2, y_2), average the x-coordinates to get the x-coordinate of the midpoint, and average the y-coordinates to get the y-coordinate of the midpoint. The formula is: $\left(\frac{x_1+x_2}{2}, \frac{y_1+y_2}{2}\right)$.

The **distance** between two points is the same as the length of the hypotenuse of a right triangle with the two given points as endpoints, and the two sides of the right triangle parallel to the x-axis and y-axis, respectively. The length of the segment parallel to the x-axis is the difference between the x-coordinates of the two points. The length of the segment parallel to the y-axis is the difference between the y-coordinates of the two points. Use the Pythagorean theorem $a^2 + b^2 = c^2$ or $c = \sqrt{a^2 + b^2}$ to find the distance. The formula is $d = \sqrt{(x_2 - x_1)^2 + (y_2 - y_1)^2}$.

When a line is in the format $Ax + By + C = 0$, where A, B, and C are coefficients, you can use a point (x_1, y_1) not on the line and apply the formula $d = \frac{|Ax_1 + By_1 + C|}{\sqrt{A^2 + B^2}}$ to find the distance between the line and the point (x_1, y_1).

Review Video: Calculations Using Points on a Graph
Visit mometrix.com/academy and enter code: 883228

Practice

P1. Solve the following systems of equations:

(a)
$$3x + 4y = 9$$
$$-12x + 7y = 10$$

(b)
$$-3x + 2y = -1$$
$$4x - 5y = 6$$

P2. Find the distance and midpoint between points (2,4) and (8,6).

Practice Solutions

P1. (a) If we multiply the first equation by 4, we can eliminate the x-terms:

$$12x + 16y = 36$$
$$-12x + 7y = 10$$

Add the equations together and solve for y:

$$23y = 46$$
$$y = 2$$

Plug the value for y back in to either of the original equations and solve for x:

$$3x + 4(2) = 9$$
$$x = \frac{9 - 8}{3} = \frac{1}{3}$$

The solution is $\left(\frac{1}{3}, 2\right)$

(b) Solving the first equation for y:

$$-3x + 2y = -1$$
$$2y = 3x - 1$$
$$y = \frac{3x - 1}{2}$$

Substitute this expression in place of y in the second equation, and solve for x:

$$\begin{aligned} 4x - 5\left(\frac{3x-1}{2}\right) &= 6 \\ 4x - \frac{15x}{2} + \frac{5}{2} &= 6 \\ 8x - 15x + 5 &= 12 \\ -7x &= 7 \\ x &= -1 \end{aligned}$$

Plug the value for x back in to either of the original equations and solve for y:

$$\begin{aligned} -3(-1) + 2y &= -1 \\ 3 + 2y &= -1 \\ 2y &= -4 \\ y &= -2 \end{aligned}$$

The solution is $(-1, -2)$.

P2. Use the formulas for distance and midpoint:

$$\begin{aligned} \text{Distance} &= \sqrt{(x_2 - x_1)^2 + (y_2 - y_1)^2} \\ &= \sqrt{(8-2)^2 + (6-4)^2} \\ &= \sqrt{(6)^2 + (2)^2} \\ &= \sqrt{36 + 4} \\ &= \sqrt{40} \text{ or } 2\sqrt{10} \end{aligned}$$

$$\begin{aligned} \text{Midpoint} &= \left(\frac{x_1 + x_2}{2}, \frac{y_1 + y_2}{2}\right) \\ &= \left(\frac{2+8}{2}, \frac{4+6}{2}\right) \\ &= \left(\frac{10}{2}, \frac{10}{2}\right) \\ &= (5,5) \end{aligned}$$

Polynomial Algebra

Monomials and Polynomials

A **monomial** is a single constant, variable, or product of constants and variables, such as 7, x, $2x$, or x^3y. There will never be addition or subtraction symbols in a monomial. Like monomials have like variables, but they may have different coefficients. **Polynomials** are algebraic expressions that use addition and subtraction to combine two or more monomials. Two terms make a **binomial**, three terms make a **trinomial**, etc. The **degree of a monomial** is the sum of the exponents of the variables. The **degree of a polynomial** is the highest degree of any individual term.

> **Review Video: Polynomials**
> Visit mometrix.com/academy and enter code: 305005

Simplifying Polynomials

Simplifying polynomials requires combining like terms. The like terms in a polynomial expression are those that have the same variable raised to the same power. It is often helpful to connect the like terms with arrows or lines in order to separate them from the other monomials. Once you have determined the like terms, you can rearrange the polynomial by placing them together. Remember to include the sign that is in front of each term. Once the like terms are placed together, you can apply each operation and simplify. When adding and subtracting polynomials, only add and subtract the **coefficient**, or the number part; the variable and exponent stay the same.

> **Review Video: Adding and Subtracting Polynomials**
> Visit mometrix.com/academy and enter code: 124088

The FOIL Method

In general, multiplying polynomials is done by multiplying each term in one polynomial by each term in the other and adding the results. In the specific case for multiplying binomials, there is a useful acronym, FOIL, that can help you make sure to cover each combination of terms. The **FOIL method** for $(Ax + By)(Cx + Dy)$ would be:

F	Multiply the *first* terms of each binomial	$(\overset{first}{\overbrace{Ax}} + By)(\overset{first}{\overbrace{Cx}} + Dy)$	ACx^2
O	Multiply the *outer* terms	$(\overset{outer}{\overbrace{Ax}} + By)(Cx + \overset{outer}{\overbrace{Dy}})$	$ADxy$
I	Multiply the *inner* terms	$(Ax + \overset{inner}{\overbrace{By}})(\overset{inner}{\overbrace{Cx}} + Dy)$	$BCxy$
L	Multiply the *last* terms of each binomial	$(Ax + \overset{last}{\overbrace{By}})(Cx + \overset{last}{\overbrace{Dy}})$	BDy^2

Then, add up the result of each and combine like terms: $ACx^2 + (AD + BC)xy + BDy^2$.

For example, using the FOIL method on binomials $(x + 2)$ and $(x - 3)$:

$$\begin{aligned}
&\text{First:} && (\boxed{x} + 2)(\boxed{x} + (-3)) \rightarrow (x)(x) = x^2 \\
&\text{Outer:} && (\boxed{x} + 2)(x + \boxed{(-3)}) \rightarrow (x)(-3) = -3x \\
&\text{Inner:} && (x + \boxed{2})(\boxed{x} + (-3)) \rightarrow (2)(x) = 2x \\
&\text{Last:} && (x + \boxed{2})(x + \boxed{(-3)}) \rightarrow (2)(-3) = -6
\end{aligned}$$

This results in: $(x^2) + (-3x) + (2x) + (-6)$

Combine like terms: $x^2 + (-3 + 2)x + (-6) = x^2 - x - 6$

Review Video: Multiplying Terms Using the FOIL Method
Visit mometrix.com/academy and enter code: 854792

DIVIDING POLYNOMIALS

Use long division to divide a polynomial by either a monomial or another polynomial of equal or lesser degree.

When **dividing by a monomial**, divide each term of the polynomial by the monomial.

When **dividing by a polynomial**, begin by arranging the terms of each polynomial in order of one variable. You may arrange in ascending or descending order, but be consistent with both polynomials. To get the first term of the quotient, divide the first term of the dividend by the first term of the divisor. Multiply the first term of the quotient by the entire divisor and subtract that product from the dividend. Repeat for the second and successive terms until you either get a remainder of zero or a remainder whose degree is less than the degree of the divisor. If the quotient has a remainder, write the answer as a mixed expression in the form:

$$\text{quotient} + \frac{\text{remainder}}{\text{divisor}}$$

For example, we can evaluate the following expression in the same way as long division:

$$\frac{x^3 - 3x^2 - 2x + 5}{x - 5}$$

$$\begin{array}{r@{}l} & \quad x^2 \; + 2x \; + 8 \\ x - 5 \,\big) & \overline{\,x^3 \; - 3x^2 - 2x \; + 5} \\ & \underline{-(x^3 - 5x^2)} \\ & \qquad 2x^2 \; - 2x \\ & \qquad \underline{-(2x^2 - 10x)} \\ & \qquad\qquad 8x \; + 5 \\ & \qquad\qquad \underline{-(8x - 40)} \\ & \qquad\qquad\qquad 45 \end{array}$$

$$\frac{x^3 - 3x^2 - 2x + 5}{x - 5} = x^2 + 2x + 8 + \frac{45}{x - 5}$$

When **factoring** a polynomial, first check for a common monomial factor, that is, look to see if each coefficient has a common factor or if each term has an x in it. If the factor is a trinomial but not a perfect trinomial square, look for a factorable form, such as one of these:

$$x^2 + (a + b)x + ab = (x + a)(x + b)$$
$$(ac)x^2 + (ad + bc)x + bd = (ax + b)(cx + d)$$

For factors with four terms, look for groups to factor. Once you have found the factors, write the original polynomial as the product of all the factors. Make sure all of the polynomial factors are prime. Monomial factors may be *prime* or *composite*. Check your work by multiplying the factors to make sure you get the original polynomial.

Below are patterns of some special products to remember to help make factoring easier:

- Perfect trinomial squares: $x^2 + 2xy + y^2 = (x + y)^2$ or $x^2 - 2xy + y^2 = (x - y)^2$
- Difference between two squares: $x^2 - y^2 = (x + y)(x - y)$
- Sum of two cubes: $x^3 + y^3 = (x + y)(x^2 - xy + y^2)$
    - Note: the second factor is *not* the same as a perfect trinomial square, so do not try to factor it further.
- Difference between two cubes: $x^3 - y^3 = (x - y)(x^2 + xy + y^2)$
    - Again, the second factor is *not* the same as a perfect trinomial square.
- Perfect cubes: $x^3 + 3x^2y + 3xy^2 + y^3 = (x + y)^3$ and $x^3 - 3x^2y + 3xy^2 - y^3 = (x - y)^3$

RATIONAL EXPRESSIONS

Rational expressions are fractions with polynomials in both the numerator and the denominator; the value of the polynomial in the denominator cannot be equal to zero. Be sure to keep track of values that make the denominator of the original expression zero as the final result inherits the same restrictions. For example, a denominator of $x - 3$ indicates that the expression is not defined when $x = 3$ and, as such, regardless of any operations done to the expression, it remains undefined there.

To **add or subtract** rational expressions, first find the common denominator, then rewrite each fraction as an equivalent fraction with the common denominator. Finally, add or subtract the numerators to get the numerator of the answer, and keep the common denominator as the denominator of the answer.

When **multiplying** rational expressions, factor each polynomial and cancel like factors (a factor which appears in both the numerator and the denominator). Then, multiply all remaining factors in the numerator to get the numerator of the product, and multiply the remaining factors in the denominator to get the denominator of the product. Remember: cancel entire factors, not individual terms.

To **divide** rational expressions, take the reciprocal of the divisor (the rational expression you are dividing by) and multiply by the dividend.

Review Video: Rational Expressions
Visit mometrix.com/academy and enter code: 415183

SIMPLIFYING RATIONAL EXPRESSIONS

To simplify a rational expression, factor the numerator and denominator completely. Factors that are the same and appear in the numerator and denominator have a ratio of 1. For example, look at the following expression:

$$\frac{x - 1}{1 - x^2}$$

The denominator, $(1 - x^2)$, is a difference of squares. It can be factored as $(1 - x)(1 + x)$. The factor $1 - x$ and the numerator $x - 1$ are opposites and have a ratio of –1. Rewrite the numerator as $-1(1 - x)$. So, the rational expression can be simplified as follows:

$$\frac{x-1}{1-x^2} = \frac{-1(1-x)}{(1-x)(1+x)} = \frac{-1}{1+x}$$

Note that since the original expression is only defined for $x \neq \{-1, 1\}$, the simplified expression has the same restrictions.

Review Video: Reducing Rational Expressions
Visit mometrix.com/academy and enter code: 788868

Practice

P1. Expand the following polynomials:

(a) $(x + 3)(x - 7)(2x)$

(b) $(x + 2)^2(x - 2)^2$

(c) $(x^2 + 5x + 5)(3x - 1)$

P2. Evaluate the following rational expressions:

(a) $\frac{x^3-2x^2-5x+6}{3x+6}$

(b) $\frac{x^2+4x+4}{4-x^2}$

Practice Solutions

P1. (a) Apply the FOIL method and the distributive property of multiplication:

$$\begin{aligned}(x+3)(x-7)(2x) &= (x^2 - 7x + 3x - 21)(2x)\\ &= (x^2 - 4x - 21)(2x)\\ &= 2x^3 - 8x^2 - 42x\end{aligned}$$

(b) Note the difference of squares form:

$$\begin{aligned}(x+2)^2(x-2)^2 &= (x+2)(x+2)(x-2)(x-2)\\ &= [(x+2)(x-2)][(x+2)(x-2)]\\ &= (x^2-4)(x^2-4)\\ &= x^4 - 8x^2 + 16\end{aligned}$$

(c) Multiply each pair of monomials and combine like terms:

$$\begin{aligned}(x^2+5x+5)(3x-1) &= 3x^3 + 15x^2 + 15x - x^2 - 5x - 5\\ &= 3x^3 + 14x^2 + 10x - 5\end{aligned}$$

P2. (a) Rather than trying to factor the third-degree polynomial, we can use long division:

$$\frac{x^3 - 2x^2 - 5x + 6}{3x + 6} = \frac{x^3 - 2x^2 - 5x + 6}{3(x + 2)}$$

$$\begin{array}{r|rrrr}
 & x^2 & -4x & +3 & \\
\hline
x + 2 & x^3 & -2x^2 & -5x & +6 \\
 & x^3 & +2x^2 & & \\
\hline
 & & -4x^2 & -5x & \\
 & & -4x^2 & -8x & \\
\hline
 & & & 3x & +6 \\
 & & & 3x & +6 \\
\hline
 & & & & 0
\end{array}$$

$$\frac{x^3 - 2x^2 - 5x + 6}{3(x + 2)} = \frac{x^2 - 4x + 3}{3}$$

Note that since the original expression is only defined for $x \neq \{-2\}$, the simplified expression has the same restrictions.

(b) The denominator, $(4 - x^2)$, is a difference of squares. It can be factored as $(2 - x)(2 + x)$. The numerator, $(x^2 + 4x + 4)$, is a perfect square. It can be factored as $(x + 2)(x + 2)$. So, the rational expression can be simplified as follows:

$$\frac{x^2 + 4x + 4}{4 - x^2} = \frac{(x + 2)(x + 2)}{(2 - x)(2 + x)} = \frac{(x + 2)}{(2 - x)}$$

Note that since the original expression is only defined for $x \neq \{-2, 2\}$, the simplified expression has the same restrictions.

Quadratics

Solving Quadratic Equations

Quadratic equations are a special set of trinomials of the form $y = ax^2 + bx + c$ that occur commonly in math and real-world applications. The **roots** of a quadratic equation are the solutions that satisfy the equation when $y = 0$; in other words, where the graph touches the x-axis. There are several ways to determine these solutions including using the quadratic formula, factoring, completing the square, and graphing the function.

Review Video: Quadratic Equations Overview
Visit mometrix.com/academy and enter code: 476276

Review Video: Solutions of a Quadratic Equation on a Graph
Visit mometrix.com/academy and enter code: 328231

Quadratic Formula

The **quadratic formula** is used to solve quadratic equations when other methods are more difficult. To use the quadratic formula to solve a quadratic equation, begin by rewriting the equation in standard form $ax^2 + bx + c = 0$, where a, b, and c are coefficients. Once you have identified the values of the coefficients, substitute those values into the quadratic formula

$$x = \frac{-b \pm \sqrt{b^2 - 4ac}}{2a}$$

Evaluate the equation and simplify the expression. Again, check each root by substituting into the original equation. In the quadratic formula, the portion of the formula under the radical $(b^2 - 4ac)$ is called the **discriminant**. If the discriminant is zero, there is only one root: $-\frac{b}{2a}$. If the discriminant is positive, there are two different real roots. If the discriminant is negative, there are no real roots; you will instead find complex roots. Often these solutions don't make sense in context and are ignored.

Review Video: Using the Quadratic Formula
Visit mometrix.com/academy and enter code: 163102

Factoring

To solve a quadratic equation by factoring, begin by rewriting the equation in standard form, $x^2 + bx + c = 0$. Remember that the goal of factoring is to find numbers f and g such that $(x + f)(x + g) = x^2 + (f + g)x + fg$, in other words $(f + g) = b$ and $fg = c$. This can be a really useful method when b and c are integers. Determine the factors of c and look for pairs that could sum to b.

For example, consider finding the roots of $x^2 + 6x - 16 = 0$. The factors of -16 include, -4 and 4, -8 and 2, -2 and 8, -1 and 16, and 1 and -16. The factors that sum to 6 are -2 and 8. Write these factors as the product of two binomials, $0 = (x - 2)(x + 8)$. Finally, since these binomials multiply together to equal zero, set them each equal to zero and solve each for x. This results in $x - 2 = 0$, which simplifies to $x = 2$ and $x + 8 = 0$, which simplifies to $x = -8$. Therefore, the roots of the equation are 2 and -8.

Review Video: Factoring Quadratic Equations
Visit mometrix.com/academy and enter code: 336566

COMPLETING THE SQUARE

One way to find the roots of a quadratic equation is to find a way to manipulate it such that it follows the form of a perfect square $(x^2 + 2px + p^2)$ by adding and subtracting a constant. This process is called **completing the square**. In other words, if you are given a quadratic that is not a perfect square, $x^2 + bx + c = 0$, you can find a constant d that could be added in to make it a perfect square:

$$x^2 + bx + c + (d - d) = 0; \{\text{Let } b = 2p \text{ and } c + d = p^2\}$$

then:

$$x^2 + 2px + p^2 - d = 0 \text{ and } d = \frac{b^2}{4} - c$$

Once you have completed the square you can find the roots of the resulting equation:

$$\begin{aligned} x^2 + 2px + p^2 - d &= 0 \\ (x + p)^2 &= d \\ x + p &= \pm\sqrt{d} \\ x &= -p \pm \sqrt{d} \end{aligned}$$

It is worth noting that substituting the original expressions into this solution gives the same result as the quadratic formula where $a = 1$:

$$x = -p \pm \sqrt{d} = -\frac{b}{2} \pm \sqrt{\frac{b^2}{4} - c} = -\frac{b}{2} \pm \frac{\sqrt{b^2 - 4c}}{2} = \frac{-b \pm \sqrt{b^2 - 4c}}{2}$$

Completing the square can be seen as arranging block representations of each of the terms to be as close to a square as possible and then filling in the gaps. For example, consider the quadratic expression $x^2 + 6x + 2$:

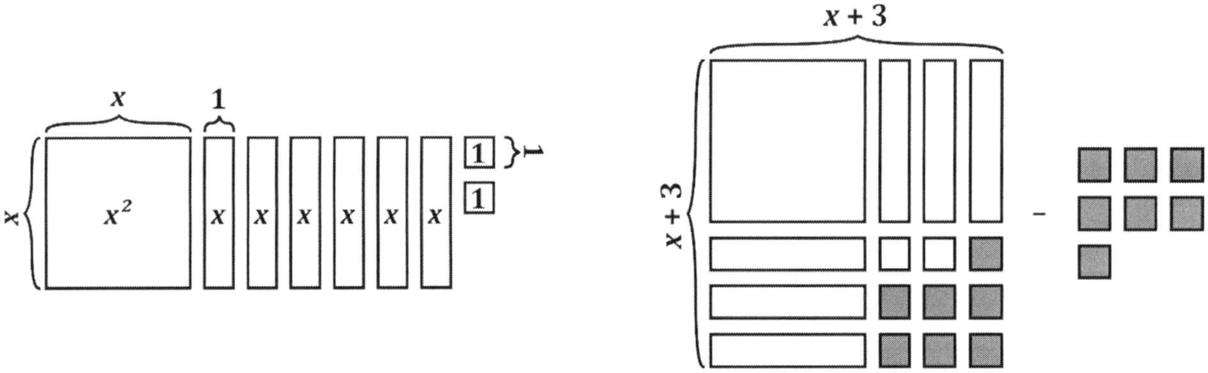

$$x^2 + 6x + 2 \quad = \quad (x + 3)^2 - 7$$

Review Video: Completing the Square
Visit mometrix.com/academy and enter code: 982479

Using Given Roots to Find Quadratic Equation

One way to find the roots of a quadratic equation is to factor the equation and use the **zero product property**, setting each factor of the equation equal to zero to find the corresponding root. We can use this technique in reverse to find an equation given its roots. Each root corresponds to a linear equation which in turn corresponds to a factor of the quadratic equation.

For example, we can find a quadratic equation whose roots are $x = 2$ and $x = -1$. The root $x = 2$ corresponds to the equation $x - 2 = 0$, and the root $x = -1$ corresponds to the equation $x + 1 = 0$.

These two equations correspond to the factors $(x - 2)$ and $(x + 1)$, from which we can derive the equation $(x - 2)(x + 1) = 0$, or $x^2 - x - 2 = 0$.

Any integer multiple of this entire equation will also yield the same roots, as the integer will simply cancel out when the equation is factored. For example, $2x^2 - 2x - 4 = 0$ factors as $2(x - 2)(x + 1) = 0$.

Solving a System of Equations Consisting of a Linear Equation and a Quadratic Equation

Algebraically

Generally, the simplest way to solve a system of equations consisting of a linear equation and a quadratic equation algebraically is through the method of substitution. One possible strategy is to solve the linear equation for y and then substitute that expression into the quadratic equation. After expansion and combining like terms, this will result in a new quadratic equation for x, which, like all quadratic equations, may have zero, one, or two solutions. Plugging each solution for x back into one of the original equations will then produce the corresponding value of y.

For example, consider the following system of equations:

$$\begin{gathered} x + y = 1 \\ y = (x + 3)^2 - 2 \end{gathered}$$

We can solve the linear equation for y to yield $y = -x + 1$. Substituting this expression into the quadratic equation produces $-x + 1 = (x + 3)^2 - 2$. We can simplify this equation:

$$\begin{aligned} -x + 1 &= (x + 3)^2 - 2 \\ -x + 1 &= x^2 + 6x + 9 - 2 \\ -x + 1 &= x^2 + 6x + 7 \\ 0 &= x^2 + 7x + 6 \end{aligned}$$

This quadratic equation can be factored as $(x + 1)(x + 6) = 0$. It therefore has two solutions: $x_1 = -1$ and $x_2 = -6$. Plugging each of these back into the original linear equation yields $y_1 = -x_1 + 1 = -(-1) + 1 = 2$ and $y_2 = -x_2 + 1 = -(-6) + 1 = 7$. Thus, this system of equations has two solutions, $(-1,2)$ and $(-6,7)$.

It may help to check your work by putting each x- and y-value back into the original equations and verifying that they do provide a solution.

Graphically

To solve a system of equations consisting of a linear equation and a quadratic equation graphically, plot both equations on the same graph. The linear equation will, of course, produce a straight line, while the quadratic equation will produce a parabola. These two graphs will intersect at zero, one, or two points; each point of intersection is a solution of the system.

For example, consider the following system of equations:

$$y = -2x + 2$$
$$y = -2x^2 + 4x + 2$$

The linear equation describes a line with a y-intercept of $(0,2)$ and a slope of -2.

To graph the quadratic equation, we can first find the vertex of the parabola: the x-coordinate of the vertex is $h = -\frac{b}{2a} = -\frac{4}{2(-2)} = 1$, and the y-coordinate is $k = -2(1)^2 + 4(1) + 2 = 4$. Thus, the vertex lies at $(1,4)$. To get a feel for the rest of the parabola, we can plug in a few more values of x to find more points; by putting in $x = 2$ and $x = 3$ in the quadratic equation, we find that the points $(2,2)$ and $(3,-4)$ lie on the parabola; by symmetry, so must $(0,2)$ and $(-1,-4)$. We can now plot both equations:

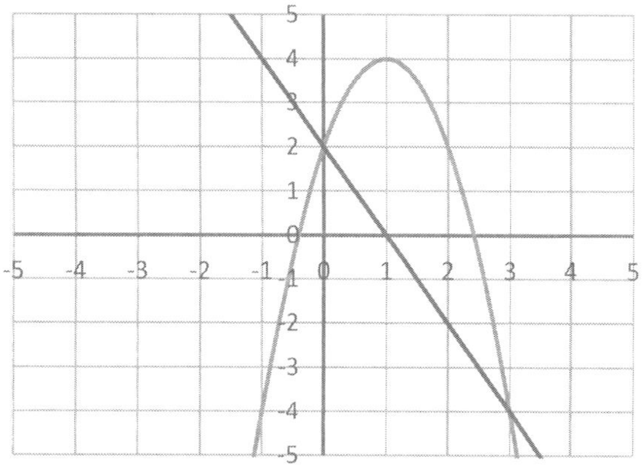

These two curves intersect at the points $(0,2)$ and $(3,-4)$, thus these are the solutions of the equation.

Review Video: Solving a System of Equations Consisting of a Linear Equation and Quadratic Equations
Visit mometrix.com/academy and enter code: 194870

Review Video: Parabolas
Visit mometrix.com/academy and enter code: 129187

Review Video: Vertex of a Parabola
Visit mometrix.com/academy and enter code: 272300

PRACTICE

P1. Find the roots of $y = 2x^2 + 8x + 4$.

P2. Find a quadratic equation with roots $x = 4$ and $x = -6$.

PRACTICE SOLUTIONS

P1. First, substitute 0 in for y in the quadratic equation: $0 = 2x^2 + 8x + 4$.

Next, try to factor the quadratic equation. Since $a \neq 1$, list the factors of ac, or 8:

$$(1,8), (-1,-8), (2,4), (-2,-4)$$

Look for the factors of ac that add up to b, or 8. Since none do, the equation cannot be factored with whole numbers. Substitute the values of a, b, and c into the quadratic formula, $x = \frac{-b \pm \sqrt{b^2-4ac}}{2a}$:

$$x = \frac{-8 \pm \sqrt{8^2 - 4(2)(4)}}{2(2)}$$

Use the order of operations to simplify:

$$x = \frac{-8 \pm \sqrt{64 - 32}}{4}$$
$$x = \frac{-8 \pm \sqrt{32}}{4}$$

Reduce and simplify:

$$x = \frac{-8 \pm \sqrt{(16)(2)}}{4}$$
$$x = \frac{-8 \pm 4\sqrt{2}}{4}$$
$$x = -2 \pm \sqrt{2}$$
$$x = \left(-2 + \sqrt{2}\right) \text{ and } \left(-2 - \sqrt{2}\right)$$

P2. The root $x = 4$ corresponds to the equation $x - 4 = 0$, and the root $x = -6$ corresponds to the equation $x + 6 = 0$. These two equations correspond to the factors $(x - 4)$ and $(x + 6)$, from which we can derive the equation $(x - 4)(x + 6) = 0$, or $x^2 + 2x - 24 = 0$.

Basic Functions

Function and Relation

When expressing functional relationships, the **variables** x and y are typically used. These values are often written as the **coordinates** (x, y). The x-value is the independent variable and the y-value is the dependent variable. A **relation** is a set of data in which there is not a unique y-value for each x-value in the dataset. This means that there can be two of the same x-values assigned to different y-values. A relation is simply a relationship between the x- and y-values in each coordinate but does not apply to the relationship between the values of x and y in the data set. A **function** is a relation where one quantity depends on the other. For example, the amount of money that you make depends on the number of hours that you work. In a function, each x-value in the data set has one unique y-value because the y-value depends on the x-value.

Functions

A function has exactly one value of **output variable** (dependent variable) for each value of the **input variable** (independent variable). The set of all values for the input variable (here assumed to be x) is the domain of the function, and the set of all corresponding values of the output variable (here assumed to be y) is the range of the function. When looking at a graph of an equation, the easiest way to determine if the equation is a function or not is to conduct the vertical line test. If a vertical line drawn through any value of x crosses the graph in more than one place, the equation is not a function.

Determining a Function

You can determine whether an equation is a **function** by substituting different values into the equation for x. You can display and organize these numbers in a data table. A **data table** contains the values for x and y, which you can also list as coordinates. In order for a function to exist, the table cannot contain any repeating x-values that correspond with different y-values. If each x-coordinate has a unique y-coordinate, the table contains a function. However, there can be repeating y-values that correspond with different x-values. An example of this is when the function contains an exponent. Example: if $x^2 = y$, $2^2 = 4$, and $(-2)^2 = 4$.

Review Video: Definition of a Function
Visit mometrix.com/academy and enter code: 784611

Finding the Domain and Range of a Function

The **domain** of a function $f(x)$ is the set of all input values for which the function is defined. The **range** of a function $f(x)$ is the set of all possible output values of the function—that is, of every possible value of $f(x)$, for any value of x in the function's domain. For a function expressed in a table, every input-output pair is given explicitly. To find the domain, we just list all the x-values and to find the range, we just list all the values of $f(x)$. Consider the following example:

x	−1	4	2	1	0	3	8	6
$f(x)$	3	0	3	−1	−1	2	4	6

In this case, the domain would be $\{-1, 4, 2, 1, 0, 3, 8, 6\}$ or, putting them in ascending order, $\{-1, 0, 1, 2, 3, 4, 6, 8\}$. (Putting the values in ascending order isn't strictly necessary, but generally makes the set easier to read.) The range would be $\{3, 0, 3, -1, -1, 2, 4, 6\}$. Note that some of these values appear more than once. This is entirely permissible for a function; while each value of x must be matched to a unique value of $f(x)$, the converse is not true. We don't need to list each value more than once, so eliminating duplicates, the range is $\{3, 0, -1, 2, 4, 6\}$, or, putting them in ascending order, $\{-1, 0, 2, 3, 4, 6\}$.

Note that by definition of a function, no input value can be matched to more than one output value. It is good to double-check to make sure that the data given follows this and is therefore actually a function.

Review Video: Domain and Range
Visit mometrix.com/academy and enter code: 778133

Review Video: Domain and Range of Quadratic Functions
Visit mometrix.com/academy and enter code: 331768

Writing a Function Rule Using a Table

If given a set of data, place the corresponding x- and y-values into a table and analyze the relationship between them. Consider what you can do to each x-value to obtain the corresponding y-value. Try adding or subtracting different numbers to and from x and then try multiplying or dividing different numbers to and from x. If none of these **operations** give you the y-value, try combining the operations. Once you find a rule that works for one pair, make sure to try it with each additional set of ordered pairs in the table. If the same operation or combination of operations satisfies each set of coordinates, then the table contains a function. The rule is then used to write the equation of the function in "$y = f(x)$" form.

Direct and Inverse Variations of Variables

Variables that vary directly are those that either both increase at the same rate or both decrease at the same rate. For example, in the functions $y = kx$ or $y = kx^n$, where k and n are positive, the value of y increases as the value of x increases and decreases as the value of x decreases.

Variables that vary inversely are those where one increases while the other decreases. For example, in the functions $y = \frac{k}{x}$ or $y = \frac{k}{x^n}$ where k and n are positive, the value of y increases as the value of x decreases and decreases as the value of x increases.

In both cases, k is the constant of variation.

Properties of Functions

There are many different ways to classify functions based on their structure or behavior. Important features of functions include:

- **End behavior**: the behavior of the function at extreme values ($f(x)$ as $x \to \pm\infty$)
- **y-intercept**: the value of the function at $f(0)$
- **Roots**: the values of x where the function equals zero ($f(x) = 0$)
- **Extrema**: minimum or maximum values of the function or where the function changes direction ($f(x) \geq k$ or $f(x) \leq k$)

Classification of Functions

An **invertible function** is defined as a function, $f(x)$, for which there is another function, $f^{-1}(x)$, such that $f^{-1}(f(x)) = x$. For example, if $f(x) = 3x - 2$ the inverse function, $f^{-1}(x)$, can be found:

$$x = 3(f^{-1}(x)) - 2$$
$$\frac{x+2}{3} = f^{-1}(x)$$

$$f^{-1}(f(x)) = \frac{3x - 2 + 2}{3} = \frac{3x}{3} = x$$

Note that $f^{-1}(x)$ is a valid function over all values of x.

In a **one-to-one function**, each value of x has exactly one value for y on the coordinate plane (this is the definition of a function) and each value of y has exactly one value for x. While the vertical line test will determine if a graph is that of a function, the horizontal line test will determine if a function is a one-to-one function. If a horizontal line drawn at any value of y intersects the graph in more than one place, the graph is not that of a one-to-one function. Do not make the mistake of using the horizontal line test exclusively in determining if a graph is that of a one-to-one function. A one-to-one function must pass both the vertical line test and the horizontal line test. As such, one-to-one functions are invertible functions.

A **many-to-one function** is a function whereby the relation is a function, but the inverse of the function is not a function. In other words, each element in the domain is mapped to one and only one element in the range. However, one or more elements in the range may be mapped to the same element in the domain. A graph of a many-to-one function would pass the vertical line test, but not the horizontal line test. This is why many-to-one functions are not invertible.

A **monotone function** is a function whose graph either constantly increases or constantly decreases. Examples include the functions $f(x) = x$, $f(x) = -x$, or $f(x) = x^3$.

An **even function** has a graph that is symmetric with respect to the y-axis and satisfies the equation $f(x) = f(-x)$. Examples include the functions $f(x) = x^2$ and $f(x) = ax^n$, where a is any real number and n is a positive even integer.

An **odd function** has a graph that is symmetric with respect to the origin and satisfies the equation $f(x) = -f(-x)$. Examples include the functions $f(x) = x^3$ and $f(x) = ax^n$, where a is any real number and n is a positive odd integer.

Review Video: Even and Odd Functions
Visit mometrix.com/academy and enter code: 278985

Constant functions are given by the equation $f(x) = b$, where b is a real number. There is no independent variable present in the equation, so the function has a constant value for all x. The graph of a constant function is a horizontal line of slope 0 that is positioned b units from the x-axis. If b is positive, the line is above the x-axis; if b is negative, the line is below the x-axis.

Identity functions are identified by the equation $f(x) = x$, where every value of the function is equal to its corresponding value of x. The only zero is the point (0,0). The graph is a line with a slope of 1.

In **linear functions**, the value of the function changes in direct proportion to x. The rate of change, represented by the slope on its graph, is constant throughout. The standard form of a linear equation is $ax + cy = d$, where a, c, and d are real numbers. As a function, this equation is commonly in the form $y = mx + b$ or $f(x) = mx + b$ where $m = -\frac{a}{c}$ and $b = \frac{d}{c}$. This is known as the slope-intercept form, because the coefficients give the slope of the graphed function (m) and its y-intercept (b). Solve the equation $mx + b = 0$ for x to get $x = -\frac{b}{m}$, which is the only zero of the function. The domain and range are both the set of all real numbers.

Review Video: Linear Functions
Visit mometrix.com/academy and enter code: 699478

Algebraic functions are those that exclusively use polynomials and roots. These would include polynomial functions, rational functions, square root functions, and all combinations of these functions, such as polynomials as the radicand. These combinations may be joined by addition, subtraction, multiplication, or division, but may not include variables as exponents.

Review Video: Common Functions
Visit mometrix.com/academy and enter code: 629798

Absolute Value Functions

An **absolute value function** is in the format $f(x) = |ax + b|$. Like other functions, the domain is the set of all real numbers. However, because absolute value indicates positive numbers, the range is limited to positive real numbers. To find the zero of an absolute value function, set the portion inside the absolute value sign equal to zero and solve for x. An absolute value function is also known as a piecewise function because it must be solved in pieces—one for if the value inside the absolute value sign is positive, and one for if the value is negative. The function can be expressed as:

$$f(x) = \begin{cases} ax + b \text{ if } ax + b \geq 0 \\ -(ax + b) \text{ if } ax + b < 0 \end{cases}$$

This will allow for an accurate statement of the range. The graph of an example absolute value function, $f(x) = |2x - 1|$, is below:

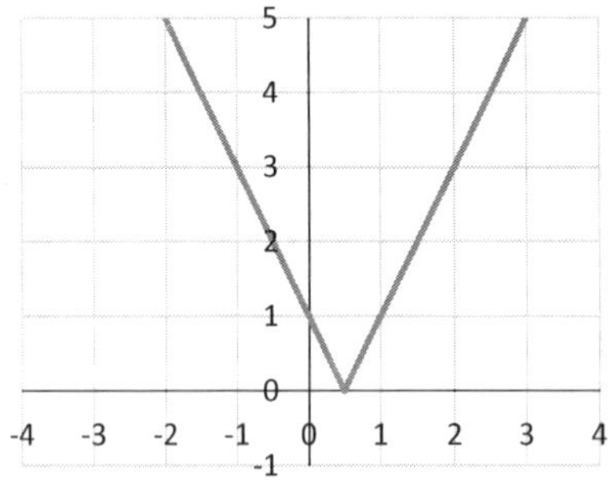

Piecewise Functions

A **piecewise function** is a function that has different definitions on two or more different intervals. The following, for instance, is one example of a piecewise-defined function:

$$f(x) = \begin{cases} x^2, & x < 0 \\ x, & 0 \leq x \leq 2 \\ (x-2)^2, & x > 2 \end{cases}$$

To graph this function, you would simply graph each part separately in the appropriate domain. The final graph would look like this:

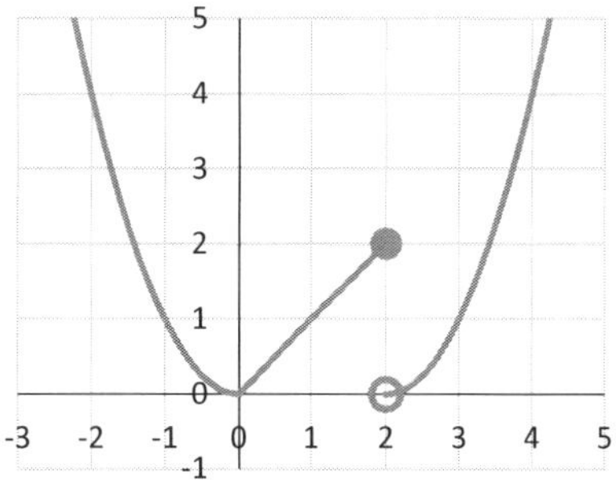

Note the filled and hollow dots at the discontinuity at $x = 2$. This is important to show which side of the graph that point corresponds to. Because $f(x) = x$ on the closed interval $0 \leq x \leq 2$, $f(2) = 2$. The point $(2, 2)$ is therefore marked with a filled circle, and the point (2,0), which is the endpoint of the rightmost $(x - 2)^2$ part of the graph but *not actually part of the function*, is marked with a hollow dot to indicate this.

Review Video: Piecewise Functions
Visit mometrix.com/academy and enter code: 707921

Quadratic Functions

A **quadratic function** is a function in the form $y = ax^2 + bx + c$, where a does not equal 0. While a linear function forms a line, a quadratic function forms a **parabola**, which is a u-shaped figure that either opens upward or downward. A parabola that opens upward is said to be a **positive quadratic function,** and a parabola that opens downward is said to be a **negative quadratic function**. The shape of a parabola can differ, depending on the values of a, b, and c. All parabolas contain a **vertex**, which is the highest possible point, the **maximum**, or the lowest possible point, the **minimum**. This is the point where the graph begins moving in the opposite direction. A quadratic function can have zero, one, or two solutions, and therefore zero, one, or two x-intercepts. Recall that the x-intercepts are referred to as the zeros, or roots, of a function. A quadratic function will have only one y-intercept. Understanding the basic components of a quadratic function can give you an idea of the shape of its graph.

Example graph of a positive quadratic function, $x^2 + 2x - 3$:

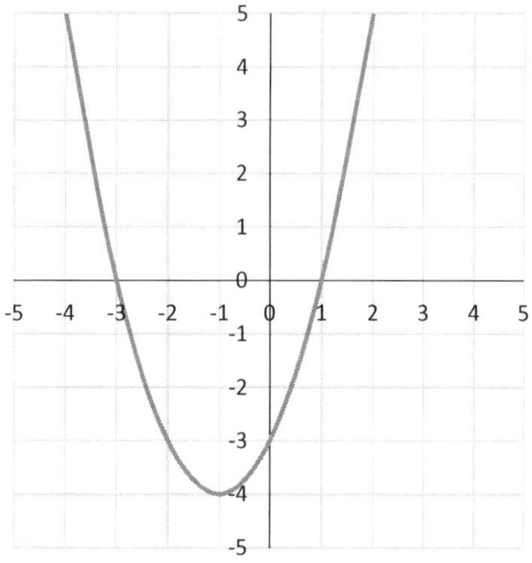

Polynomial Functions

A **polynomial function** is a function with multiple terms and multiple powers of x, such as:

$$f(x) = a_n x^n + a_{n-1}x^{n-1} + a_{n-2}x^{n-2} + \cdots + a_1 x + a_0$$

where n is a non-negative integer that is the highest exponent in the polynomial and $a_n \neq 0$. The domain of a polynomial function is the set of all real numbers. If the greatest exponent in the polynomial is even, the polynomial is said to be of even degree and the range is the set of real numbers that satisfy the function. If the greatest exponent in the polynomial is odd, the polynomial is said to be odd and the range, like the domain, is the set of all real numbers.

Rational Functions

A **rational function** is a function that can be constructed as a ratio of two polynomial expressions: $f(x) = \frac{p(x)}{q(x)}$, where $p(x)$ and $q(x)$ are both polynomial expressions and $q(x) \neq 0$. The domain is the set of all real numbers, except any values for which $q(x) = 0$. The range is the set of real numbers that satisfies the function when the domain is applied. When you graph a rational function, you will have vertical asymptotes wherever $q(x) = 0$. If the polynomial in the numerator is of lesser degree than the polynomial in the denominator, the x-axis will also be a horizontal asymptote. If the numerator and denominator have equal degrees, there will be a horizontal asymptote not on the x-axis. If the degree of the numerator is exactly one greater than the degree of the denominator, the graph will have an oblique, or diagonal, asymptote. The asymptote will be along the line $y = \frac{p_n}{q_{n-1}}x + \frac{p_{n-1}}{q_{n-1}}$, where p_n and q_{n-1} are the coefficients of the highest degree terms in their respective polynomials.

Square Root Functions

A **square root function** is a function that contains a radical and is in the format $f(x) = \sqrt{ax + b}$. The domain is the set of all real numbers that yields a positive radicand or a radicand equal to zero. Because square root values are assumed to be positive unless otherwise identified, the range is all real numbers from zero to infinity. To find the zero of a square root function, set the radicand equal to zero and solve for x. The graph of a square root function is always to the right of the zero and always above the x-axis.

Example graph of a square root function, $f(x) = \sqrt{2x + 1}$:

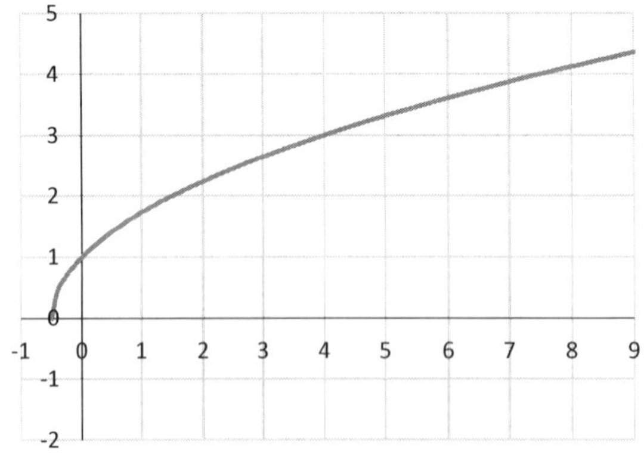

Practice

P1. Martin needs a 20% medicine solution. The pharmacy has a 5% solution and a 30% solution. He needs 50 mL of the solution. If the pharmacist must mix the two solutions, how many milliliters of 5% solution and 30% solution should be used?

P2. Describe two different strategies for solving the following problem:

Kevin can mow the yard in 4 hours. Mandy can mow the same yard in 5 hours. If they work together, how long will it take them to mow the yard?

P3. A car, traveling at 65 miles per hour, leaves Flagstaff and heads east on I-40. Another car, traveling at 75 miles per hour, leaves Flagstaff 2 hours later, from the same starting point and also heads east on I-40. Determine how many hours it will take the second car to catch the first car by:

(a) Using a table.

(b) Using algebra.

Practice Solutions

P1. To solve this problem, a table may be created to represent the variables, percentages, and total amount of solution. Such a table is shown below:

	mL solution	% medicine	Total mL medicine
5% solution	x	0.05	$0.05x$
30% solution	y	0.30	$0.30y$
Mixture	$x + y = 50$	0.20	$(0.20)(50) = 10$

The variable x may be rewritten as $50 - y$, so the equation $0.05(50 - y) + 0.30y = 10$ may be written and solved for y. Doing so gives $y = 30$. So, 30 mL of 30% solution are needed. Solving the equation $x = 50 - y$ for x shows that 20 mL of 5% solution are needed.

P2. Two possible strategies both involve the use of rational equations to solve. The first strategy involves representing the fractional part of the yard mowed by each person in one hour and setting this sum equal to the ratio of 1 to the total time needed. The appropriate equation is $\frac{1}{4} + \frac{1}{5} = \frac{1}{t}$, which simplifies as $\frac{9}{20} = \frac{1}{t}$, and finally as $t = \frac{20}{9}$. So, the time it will take them to mow the yard, when working together, is a little more than 2.2 hours.

A second strategy involves representing the time needed for each person as two fractions and setting the sum equal to 1 (representing 1 yard). The appropriate equation is $\frac{t}{4} + \frac{t}{5} = 1$, which simplifies as $\frac{9t}{20} = 1$, and finally as $t = \frac{20}{9}$. This strategy also shows the total time to be a little more than 2.2 hours.

P3. (a) One strategy might involve creating a table of values for the number of hours and distances for each car. The table may be examined to find the same distance traveled and the corresponding number of hours taken. Such a table is shown below:

Car A		Car B	
x (hours)	y (distance)	x (hours)	y (distance)
0	0	0	
1	65	1	
2	130	2	0
3	195	3	75
4	260	4	150
5	325	5	225
6	390	6	300
7	455	7	375
8	520	8	450
9	585	9	525
10	650	10	600
11	715	11	675
12	780	12	750
13	845	13	825
14	910	14	900
15	975	15	975

The table shows that after 15 hours, the distance traveled is the same. Thus, the second car catches up with the first car after a distance of 975 miles and 15 hours.

(b) A second strategy might involve setting up and solving an algebraic equation. This situation may be modeled as $65x = 75(x - 2)$. This equation sets the distances traveled by each car equal to one another. Solving for x gives $x = 15$. Thus, once again, the second car will catch up with the first car after 15 hours.

Advanced Functions

Step Functions

The double brackets indicate a step function. For a step function, the value inside the double brackets is rounded down to the nearest integer. The graph of the function $f_0(x) = [\![x]\!]$ appears on the left graph. In comparison $f(x) = 2\left[\!\left[\frac{1}{3}(x-1)\right]\!\right]$ is on the right graph. The coefficient of 2 shows that it's stretched vertically by a factor of 2 (so there's a vertical distance of 2 units between successive "steps"). The coefficient of $\frac{1}{3}$ in front of the x shows that it's stretched horizontally by a factor of 3 (so each "step" is three units long), and the $x - 1$ shows that it's displaced one unit to the right.

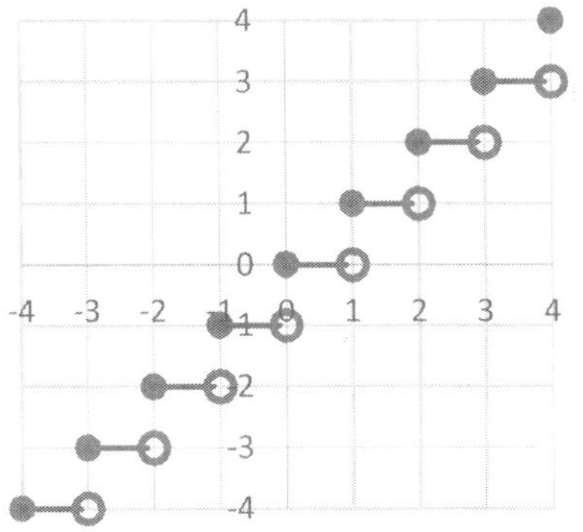

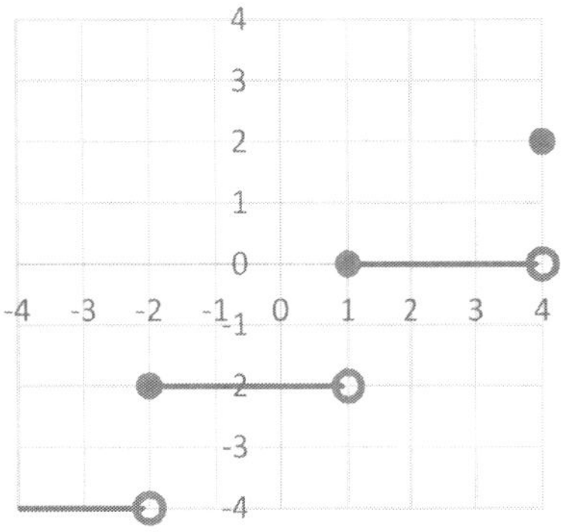

Transcendental Functions

Transcendental functions are all functions that are non-algebraic. Any function that includes logarithms, trigonometric functions, variables as exponents, or any combination that includes any of these is not algebraic in nature, even if the function includes polynomials or roots.

Review Video: Common Functions
Visit mometrix.com/academy and enter code: 629798

Exponential Functions

Exponential functions are equations that have the format $y = b^x$, where base $b > 0$ and $b \neq 1$. The exponential function can also be written $f(x) = b^x$. Recall the properties of exponents, like the product of terms with the same base is equal to the base raised to the sum of the exponents ($a^x \times a^y = a^{x+y}$) and a term with an exponent that is raised to an exponent is equal to the base of the original term raised to the product of the exponents: $((a^x)^y = a^{xy})$. The graph of an example exponential function, $f(x) = 2^x$, is below:

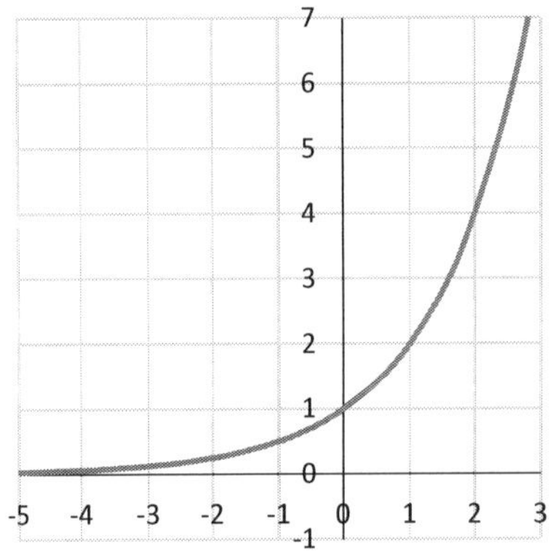

Note in the graph that the y-value approaches zero to the left and infinity to the right. One of the key features of an exponential function is that there will be one end that goes off to infinity and another that asymptotically approaches a lower bound. Common forms of exponential functions include:

Geometric sequences: $a_n = a_1 \times r^{n-1}$, where a_n is the value of the nth term, a_1 is the initial value, r is the common ratio, and n is the number of terms. Note that $a_1 \times r^{1-1} = a_1 \times r^0 = a_1 \times 1 = a_1$.

Population growth: $f(t) = ae^{rt}$, where $f(t)$ is the population at time $t \geq 0$, a is the initial population, e is the mathematical constant known as Euler's number, and r is the growth rate.

Review Video: Population Growth
Visit mometrix.com/academy and enter code: 109278

Compound interest: $f(t) = P\left(1 + \frac{r}{n}\right)^{nt}$, where $f(t)$ is the account value at a certain number of time periods $t \geq 0$, P is the initial principal balance, r is the interest rate, and n is the number of times the interest is applied per time period.

Review Video: Interest Functions
Visit mometrix.com/academy and enter code: 559176

General exponential growth or decay: $f(t) = a(1 + r)^t$, where $f(t)$ is the future count, a is the current or initial count, r is the growth or decay rate, and t is the time.

For example, suppose the initial population of a town was 1,200 people. The annual population growth is 5%. The current population is 2,400. To find out how much time has passed since the town was founded, we can use the following function:

$$2{,}400 = 1{,}200e^{0.05t}.$$

The general form for population growth may be represented as $f(t) = ae^{rt}$, where $f(t)$ represents the current population, a represents the initial population, r represents the growth rate, and t represents the time. Thus, substituting the initial population, current population, and rate into this form gives the equation above.

The number of years that have passed were found by first dividing both sides of the equation by 1,200. Doing so gives $2 = e^{0.05t}$. Taking the natural logarithm of both sides gives $\ln(2) = ln(e^{0.05t})$. Applying the power property of logarithms, the equation may be rewritten as $\ln(2) = 0.05t \times \ln(e)$, which simplifies as $\ln(2) = 0.05t$. Dividing both sides of this equation by 0.05 gives $t \approx 13.86$. Thus, approximately 13.86 years passed.

Logarithmic Functions

Logarithmic functions are equations that have the format $y = \log_b x$ or $f(x) = \log_b x$. The base b may be any number except one; however, the most common bases for logarithms are base 10 and base e. The log base e is the natural logarithm, or ln, expressed by the function $f(x) = \ln x$.

Any logarithm that does not have an assigned value of b is assumed to be base 10: $\log x = \log_{10} x$. Exponential functions and logarithmic functions are related in that one is the inverse of the other. If $f(x) = b^x$, then $f^{-1}(x) = \log_b x$. This can perhaps be expressed more clearly by the two equations: $y = b^x$ and $x = \log_b y$.

The following properties apply to logarithmic expressions:

Property	Description
$\log_b 1 = 0$	The log of 1 is equal to 0 for any base
$\log_b b = 1$	The log of the base is equal to 1
$\log_b b^p = p$	The log of the base raised to a power is equal to that power
$\log_b MN = \log_b M + \log_b N$	The log of a product is the sum of the log of each factor
$\log_b \frac{M}{N} = \log_b M - \log_b N$	The log of a quotient is equal to the log of the dividend minus the log of the divisor
$\log_b M^p = p \log_b M$	The log of a value raised to a power is equal to the power times the log of the value

The graph of an example logarithmic function, $f(x) = \log_2(x + 2)$, is below:

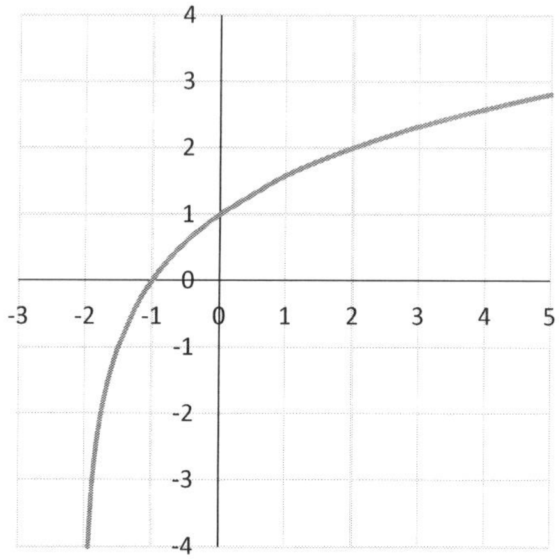

Review Video: Logarithmic Function
Visit mometrix.com/academy and enter code: 658985

Trigonometric Functions

Trigonometric functions are periodic, meaning that they repeat the same form over and over. The basic trigonometric functions are sine (abbreviated 'sin'), cosine (abbreviated 'cos'), and tangent (abbreviated 'tan'). The simplest way to think of them is as describing the ratio of the side lengths of a right triangle in relation to the angles of the triangle.

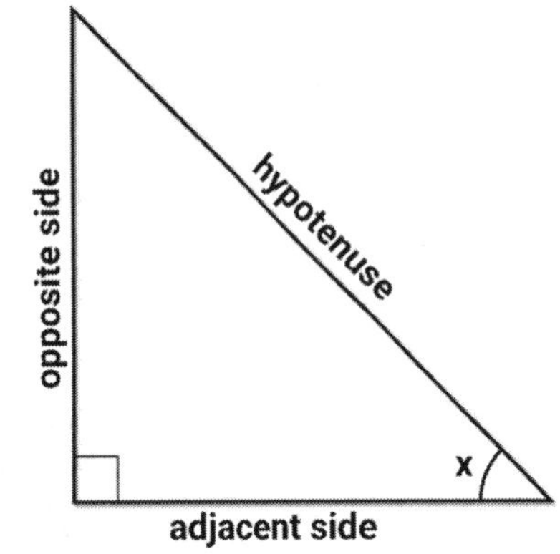

$$\sin x = \frac{\text{opposite side}}{\text{hypotenuse}}$$
$$\cos x = \frac{\text{adjacent side}}{\text{hypotenuse}}$$
$$\tan x = \frac{\text{opposite side}}{\text{adjacent side}}$$

Using sine as an example, trigonometric functions take the form $f(x) = A\sin(Bx + C) + D$, where the **amplitude** is simply equal to A. The **period** is the distance between successive peaks or troughs, essentially the length of the repeated pattern. In this form, the period is equal to $\frac{2\pi}{B}$. As for C, this is the **phase shift** or the horizontal shift of the function. The last term, D, is the vertical shift and determines the **midline** as $y = D$.

For instance, consider the function $f(x) = 2 + \frac{3}{2}\sin\left(\pi x + \frac{\pi}{2}\right)$. Here, $A = \frac{3}{2}$, $B = \pi$, $C = \frac{\pi}{2}$, and $D = 2$, so the midline is at $y = 2$, the amplitude is $\frac{3}{2}$, and the period is $\frac{2\pi}{\pi} = 2$. To graph this function, we center the sine wave on the midline and extend it to a height above and below the midline equal to the amplitude—so this graph would have a minimum value of $2 - \frac{3}{2} = \frac{1}{2}$ and a maximum of $2 + \frac{3}{2} = \frac{7}{2}$. So, the function would be graphed as follows:

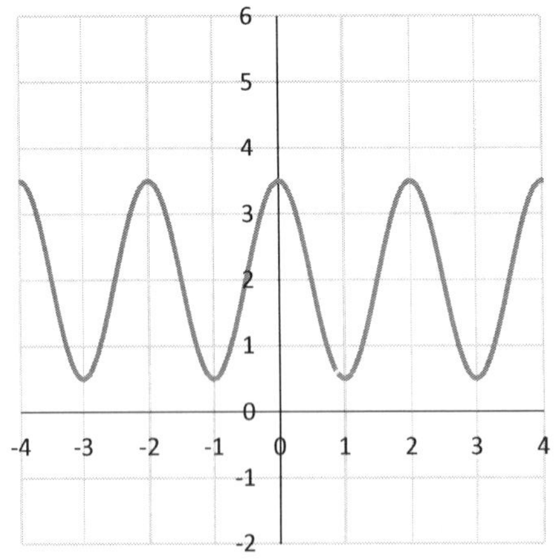

Manipulation of Functions

Translation occurs when values are added to or subtracted from the x- or y-values. If a constant is added to the y-portion of each point, the graph shifts up. If a constant is subtracted from the y-portion of each point, the graph shifts down. This is represented by the expression $f(x) \pm k$, where k is a constant. If a constant is added to the x-portion of each point, the graph shifts left. If a constant is subtracted from the x-portion of each point, the graph shifts right. This is represented by the expression $f(x \pm k)$, where k is a constant.

Stretching, compression, and reflection occur when different parts of a function are multiplied by different groups of constants. If the function as a whole is multiplied by a real number constant greater than 1, $(k \times f(x))$, the graph is stretched vertically. If k in the previous equation is greater than zero but less than 1, the graph is compressed vertically. If k is less than zero, the graph is reflected about the x-axis, in addition to being either stretched or compressed vertically if k is less than or greater than –1, respectively. If instead, just the x-term is multiplied by a constant greater than 1 $(f(k \times x))$, the graph is compressed horizontally. If k in the previous equation is greater than zero but less than 1, the graph is stretched horizontally. If k is less than zero, the graph is reflected about the y-axis, in addition to being either stretched or compressed horizontally if k is greater than or less than –1, respectively.

Review Video: Manipulation of Functions
Visit mometrix.com/academy and enter code: 669117

Algebraic Theorems

According to the **fundamental theorem of algebra**, every non-constant, single-variable polynomial has exactly as many roots as the polynomial's highest exponent. For example, if x^4 is the largest exponent of a term, the polynomial will have exactly 4 roots. However, some of these roots may have multiplicity or be complex numbers. For instance, in the polynomial function $f(x) = x^4 - 4x + 3$, the only real root is 1, though it has multiplicity of 2 – that is, it occurs twice. The other two roots, $(-1 - i\sqrt{2})$ and $(-1 + i\sqrt{2})$, are complex, consisting of both real and non-real components.

The **remainder theorem** is useful for determining the remainder when a polynomial is divided by a binomial. The remainder theorem states that if a polynomial function $f(x)$ is divided by a binomial $x - a$, where a is a real number, the remainder of the division will be the value of $f(a)$. If $f(a) = 0$, then a is a root of the polynomial.

The **factor theorem** is related to the remainder theorem and states that if $f(a) = 0$ then $(x\text{–} a)$ is a factor of the function.

According to the **rational root theorem,** any rational root of a polynomial function $f(x) = a_n x^n + a_{n-1}x^{n-1} + \cdots + a_1 x + a_0$ with integer coefficients will, when reduced to its lowest terms, be a positive or negative fraction such that the numerator is a factor of a_0 and the denominator is a factor of a_n. For instance, if the polynomial function $f(x) = x^3 + 3x^2 - 4$ has any rational roots, the numerators of those roots can only be factors of 4 (1, 2, 4), and the denominators can only be factors of 1 (1). The function in this example has roots of 1 (or $\frac{1}{1}$) and –2 (or $\frac{-2}{1}$).

Applying the Basic Operations to Functions

For each of the basic operations, we will use these functions as examples: $f(x) = x^2$ and $g(x) = x$.

To find the sum of two functions f and g, assuming the domains are compatible, simply add the two functions together: $(f + g)(x) = f(x) + g(x) = x^2 + x$.

To find the difference of two functions f and g, assuming the domains are compatible, simply subtract the second function from the first: $(f - g)(x) = f(x) - g(x) = x^2 - x$.

To find the product of two functions f and g, assuming the domains are compatible, multiply the two functions together: $(f \times g)(x) = f(x) \times g(x) = x^2 \times x = x^3$.

To find the quotient of two functions f and g, assuming the domains are compatible, divide the first function by the second: $\frac{f}{g}(x) = \frac{f(x)}{g(x)} = \frac{x^2}{x} = x\,; x \neq 0$.

The example given in each case is fairly simple, but on a given problem, if you are looking only for the value of the sum, difference, product, or quotient of two functions at a particular x-value, it may be simpler to solve the functions individually and then perform the given operation using those values.

The composite of two functions f and g, written as $(f \circ g)(x)$ simply means that the output of the second function is used as the input of the first. This can also be written as $f\big(g(x)\big)$. In general, this can be solved by substituting $g(x)$ for all instances of x in $f(x)$ and simplifying. Using the example functions $f(x) = x^2 - x + 2$ and $g(x) = x + 1$, we can find that $(f \circ g)(x)$ or $f\big(g(x)\big)$ is equal to $f(x + 1) = (x + 1)^2 - (x + 1) + 2$, which simplifies to $x^2 + x + 2$.

It is important to note that $(f \circ g)(x)$ is not necessarily the same as $(g \circ f)(x)$. The process is not always commutative like addition or multiplication expressions. It *can* be commutative, but most often this is not the case.

Practice

P1. A professor wishes to invest $20,000 in a CD that compounds annually. The annual interest rate at his bank is 1.9%. How many years will it take for his account to reach $50,000?

P2. Suppose a new strain of bacteria shows a daily growth rate of 10%. The current count for the new bacteria strain is 100. How many days will pass before the count reaches 1 million bacteria?

P3. Each of the following functions cross the x- and y-axes at the same points. Identify the most likely function type of each graph

(a)

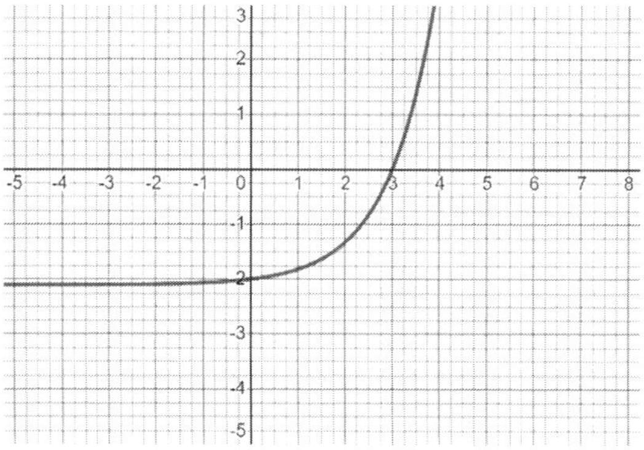

(b)

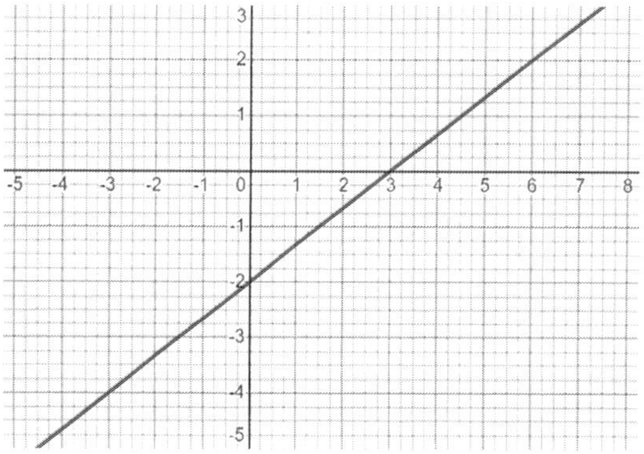

(c)

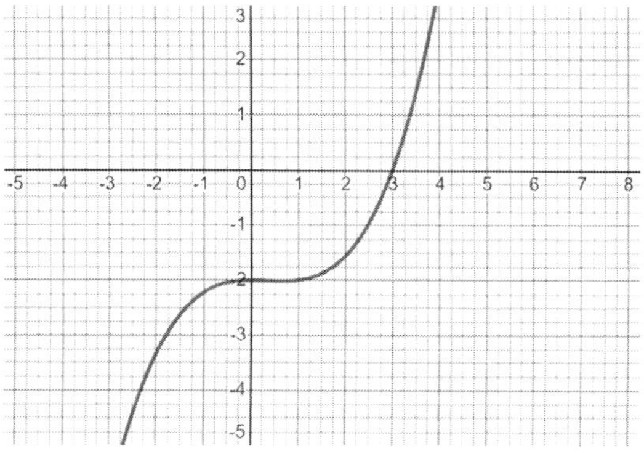

(d)

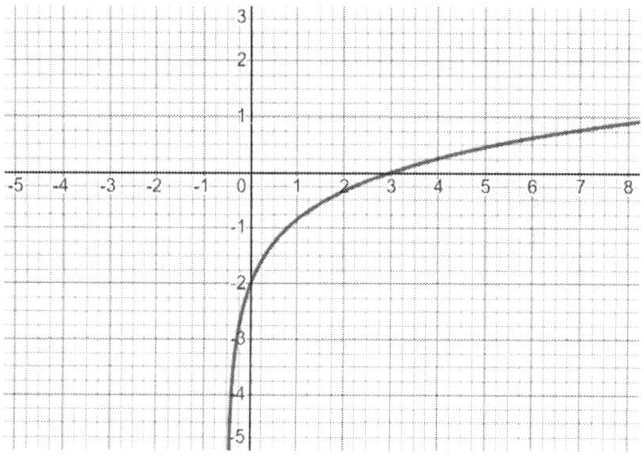

P4. Given the functions $f(x) = -3x + 3$, $g(x) = e^x + 3$, and $h(x) = x^2 - 2x + 1$, perform the following operations and write out the resulting function:

(a) Shift $g(x)$ 4 units to the left and 1 unit up, then compress the new function by a factor of $\frac{1}{2}$

(b) $\frac{f(x)}{h(x)}$

(c) $h(g(x))$

(d) $\frac{f(x)+h(x)}{x-1}$

Practice Solutions

P1. In order to solve this problem, the compound interest formula should be evaluated for a future value of \$50,000, principal of \$20,000, rate of 0.019, and number of years of t. The exponential equation may then be solved by taking the logarithm of both sides. The process is shown below:

$$50{,}000 = 20{,}000\left(1 + \frac{0.019}{1}\right)^t$$

Dividing both sides of the equation by 20,000 gives $2.5 = 1.019^t$. Taking the logarithm of both sides gives $\log(2.5) = t\log(1.019)$. Dividing both sides of this equation by $\log(1.019)$ gives $t \approx 48.68$. Thus, after approximately 49 years, the professor's account will reach \$50,000.

P2. The problem may be solved by writing and solving an exponential growth function, in the form, $f(x) = a(1+r)^x$, where $f(x)$ represents the future count, a represents the current count, r represents the growth rate, and x represents the time. Once the function is evaluated for a future count of 1,000,000, a current count of 100, and a growth rate of 0.10, the exponential equation may be solved by taking the logarithm of both sides.

The problem may be modeled with the equation $1{,}000{,}000 = 100 \times (1.10)^x$. Dividing both sides of the equation by 100 gives $10{,}000 = 1.10^x$. Taking the logarithm of both sides gives $\log(10{,}000) = x\log(1.10)$. Dividing both sides of this equation by $\log(1.10)$ gives $x \approx 96.6$. Thus, after approximately 97 days, the bacteria count will reach 1 million.

P3. (a) Exponential function—positive, increasing slope.

(b) Linear function—positive, continuous slope.

(c) Polynomial function (odd degree)—positive, changing slope. Note that the graph goes off to infinity in opposite quadrants I and III, thus it is an odd degree.

(d) Logarithmic function—positive, decreasing slope.

P4. (a) Shifting $g(x)$ to the left 4 units is the same as $g(x+4)$ and shifting the function up one unit is $g(x)+1$. Combining these and multiplying by $\frac{1}{2}$ results in the following:

$$\begin{aligned}\frac{1}{2}(g(x+4)+1) &= \frac{1}{2}\big((e^{x+4}+3)+1\big)\\ &= \frac{e^{x+4}}{2}+2\end{aligned}$$

(b) Factor $h(x)$, noting that it is a perfect square, and be sure to note the constraint on x due to the original denominator of the rational expression:

$$\frac{f(x)}{h(x)} = \frac{-3x+3}{x^2-2x+1} = \frac{-3(x-1)}{(x-1)(x-1)} = \frac{-3}{(x-1)};\, x \neq 1$$

(c) Evaluate the composition as follows:

$$\begin{aligned}h\big(g(x)\big) &= (e^x+3)^2 - 2(e^x+3)+1\\ &= (e^x)^2 + 6e^x + 9 - 2e^x - 6 + 1\\ &= e^{2x} + 4e^x + 4\\ &= (e^x+2)^2\end{aligned}$$

(d) Note the constraint on x due to the original denominator of the rational expression:

$$\begin{aligned}\frac{f(x)+h(x)}{x-1} &= \frac{(-3x+3)+(x^2-2x+1)}{x-1}\\ &= \frac{-3(x-1)+(x-1)(x-1)}{x-1}\\ &= -3+(x-1)\\ &= x-4;\, x \neq 1\end{aligned}$$

Measurement Principles

Precision, Accuracy, and Error

Precision: How reliable and repeatable a measurement is. The more consistent the data is with repeated testing, the more precise it is. For example, hitting a target consistently in the same spot, which may or may not be the center of the target, is precision.

Accuracy: How close the data is to the correct data. For example, hitting a target consistently in the center area of the target, whether or not the hits are all in the same spot, is accuracy.

Note: it is possible for data to be precise without being accurate. If a scale is off balance, the data will be precise, but will not be accurate. For data to have precision and accuracy, it must be repeatable and correct.

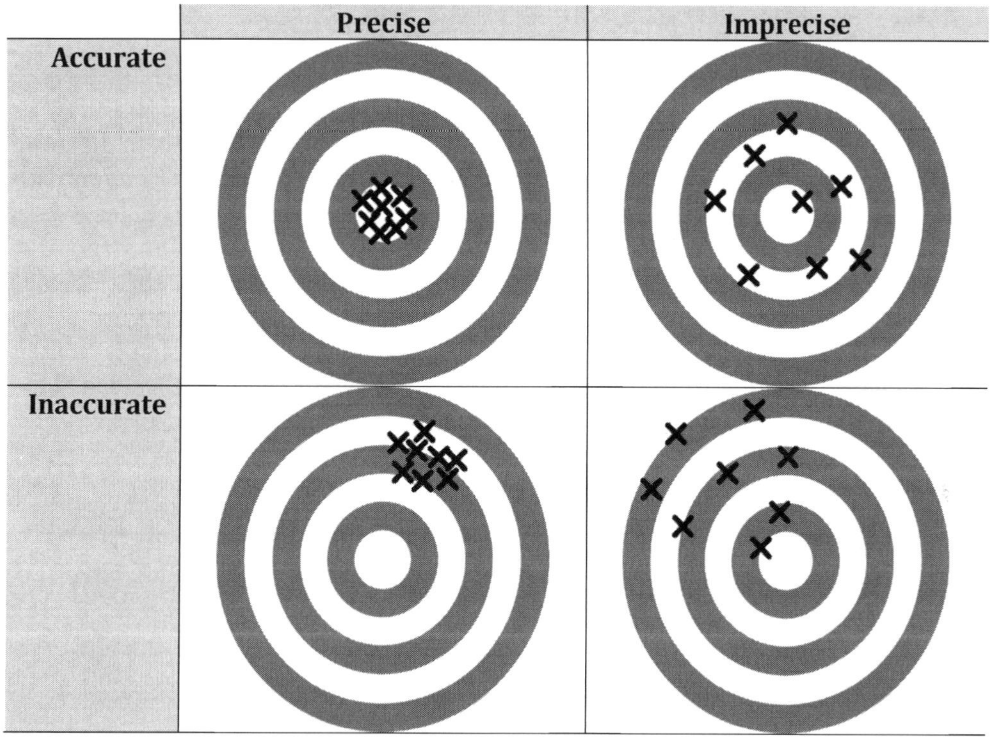

Approximate error: The amount of error in a physical measurement. Approximate error is often reported as the measurement, followed by the $\pm$ symbol and the amount of the approximate error.

Maximum possible error: Half the magnitude of the smallest unit used in the measurement. For example, if the unit of measurement is 1 centimeter, the maximum possible error is $\frac{1}{2}$ cm, written as ± 0.5 cm following the measurement. It is important to apply significant figures in reporting maximum possible error. Do not make the answer appear more accurate than the least accurate of your measurements.

Review Video: Precision, Accuracy, and Error
Visit mometrix.com/academy and enter code: 520377

Rounding and Estimation

Rounding is reducing the digits in a number while still trying to keep the value similar. The result will be less accurate but in a simpler form and easier to use. Whole numbers can be rounded to the nearest ten, hundred, or thousand.

When you are asked to estimate the solution to a problem, you will need to provide only an approximate figure or **estimation** for your answer. In this situation, you will need to round each number in the calculation to the level indicated (nearest hundred, nearest thousand, etc.) or to a level that makes sense for the numbers involved. When estimating a sum **all numbers must be rounded to the same level**. You cannot round one number to the nearest thousand while rounding another to the nearest hundred.

Review Video: Rounding and Estimation
Visit mometrix.com/academy and enter code: 126243

Scientific Notation

Scientific notation is a way of writing large numbers in a shorter form. The form $a \times 10^n$ is used in scientific notation, where a is greater than or equal to 1 but less than 10, and n is the number of places the decimal must move to get from the original number to a. Example: The number 230,400,000 is cumbersome to write. To write the value in scientific notation, place a decimal point between the first and second numbers, and include all digits through the last non-zero digit ($a = 2.304$). To find the appropriate power of 10, count the number of places the decimal point had to move ($n = 8$). The number is positive if the decimal moved to the left, and negative if it moved to the right. We can then write 230,400,000 as 2.304×10^8. If we look instead at the number 0.00002304, we have the same value for a, but this time the decimal moved 5 places to the right ($n = -5$). Thus, 0.00002304 can be written as 2.304×10^{-5}. Using this notation makes it simple to compare very large or very small numbers. By comparing exponents, it is easy to see that 3.28×10^4 is smaller than 1.51×10^5, because 4 is less than 5.

Review Video: Scientific Notation
Visit mometrix.com/academy and enter code: 976454

Practice

P1. Round each number to the indicated degree:

(a) Round to the nearest ten: 11; 47; 118

(b) Round to the nearest hundred: 78; 980; 248

(c) Round each number to the nearest thousand: 302; 1,274; 3,756

P2. Estimate the sum of 345,932 and 96,369 by rounding each number to the nearest ten thousand.

P3. A runner's heart beats 422 times over the course of six minutes. About how many times did the runner's heart beat during each minute?

Practice Solutions

P1. (a) When rounding to the nearest ten, anything ending in 5 or greater rounds up. So, 11 rounds to 10, 47 rounds to 50, and 118 rounds to 120.

(b) When rounding to the nearest hundred, anything ending in 50 or greater rounds up. So, 78 rounds to 100, 980 rounds to 1000, and 248 rounds to 200.

(c) When rounding to the nearest thousand, anything ending in 500 or greater rounds up. So, 302 rounds to 0, 1,274 rounds to 1,000, and 3,756 rounds to 4,000.

P2. Start by rounding each number to the nearest ten thousand: 345,932 becomes 350,000, and 96,369 becomes 100,000. Then, add the rounded numbers: $350{,}000 + 100{,}000 = 450{,}000$. So, the answer is approximately 450,000. The exact answer would be $345{,}932 + 96{,}369 = 442{,}301$. So, the estimate of 450,000 is a similar value to the exact answer.

P3. "About how many" indicates that you need to estimate the solution. In this case, look at the numbers you are given. 422 can be rounded down to 420, which is easily divisible by 6. A good estimate is $420 \div 6 = 70$ beats per minute. More accurately, the patient's heart rate was just over 70 beats per minute since his heart actually beat a little more than 420 times in six minutes.

Units of Measurement

Metric Measurement Prefixes

Giga-	One billion	1 *giga*watt is one billion watts
Mega-	One million	1 *mega*hertz is one million hertz
Kilo-	One thousand	1 *kilo*gram is one thousand grams
Deci-	One-tenth	1 *deci*meter is one-tenth of a meter
Centi-	One-hundredth	1 *centi*meter is one-hundredth of a meter
Milli-	One-thousandth	1 *milli*liter is one-thousandth of a liter
Micro-	One-millionth	1 *micro*gram is one-millionth of a gram

Review Video: Metric System Conversion - How the Metric System Works
Visit mometrix.com/academy and enter code: 163709

Measurement Conversion

When converting between units, the goal is to maintain the same meaning but change the way it is displayed. In order to go from a larger unit to a smaller unit, multiply the number of the known amount by the equivalent amount. When going from a smaller unit to a larger unit, divide the number of the known amount by the equivalent amount.

For complicated conversions, it may be helpful to set up conversion fractions. In these fractions, one fraction is the **conversion factor**. The other fraction has the unknown amount in the numerator. So, the known value is placed in the denominator. Sometimes, the second fraction has the known value from the problem in the numerator and the unknown in the denominator. Multiply the two fractions to get the converted measurement. Note that since the numerator and the denominator of the factor are equivalent, the value of the fraction is 1. That is why we can say that the result in the new units is equal to the result in the old units even though they have different numbers.

It can often be necessary to chain known conversion factors together. As an example, consider converting 512 square inches to square meters. We know that there are 2.54 centimeters in an inch and 100 centimeters in a meter, and we know we will need to square each of these factors to achieve the conversion we are looking for.

$$\frac{512\text{ in}^2}{1} \times \left(\frac{2.54\text{ cm}}{1\text{ in}}\right)^2 \times \left(\frac{1\text{ m}}{100\text{ cm}}\right)^2 = \frac{512\text{ }\cancel{\text{in}^2}}{1} \times \left(\frac{6.4516\text{ }\cancel{\text{cm}^2}}{1\text{ }\cancel{\text{in}^2}}\right) \times \left(\frac{1\text{ m}^2}{10{,}000\text{ }\cancel{\text{cm}^2}}\right) = 0.330\text{ m}^2$$

Review Video: Measurement Conversions
Visit mometrix.com/academy and enter code: 316703

Common Units and Equivalents

Metric Equivalents

1000 μg (microgram)	1 mg
1000 mg (milligram)	1 g
1000 g (gram)	1 kg
1000 kg (kilogram)	1 metric ton
1000 mL (milliliter)	1 L
1000 μm (micrometer)	1 mm
1000 mm (millimeter)	1 m
100 cm (centimeter)	1 m
1000 m (meter)	1 km

Distance and Area Measurement

Unit	Abbreviation	US equivalent	Metric equivalent
Inch	in	1 inch	2.54 centimeters
Foot	ft	12 inches	0.305 meters
Yard	yd	3 feet	0.914 meters
Mile	mi	5280 feet	1.609 kilometers
Acre	ac	4840 square yards	0.405 hectares
Square Mile	sq. mi. or $mi.^2$	640 acres	2.590 square kilometers

Capacity Measurements

Unit	Abbreviation	US equivalent	Metric equivalent
Fluid Ounce	fl oz	8 fluid drams	29.573 milliliters
Cup	c	8 fluid ounces	0.237 liter
Pint	pt.	16 fluid ounces	0.473 liter
Quart	qt.	2 pints	0.946 liter
Gallon	gal.	4 quarts	3.785 liters
Teaspoon	t or tsp.	1 fluid dram	5 milliliters
Tablespoon	T or tbsp.	4 fluid drams	15 or 16 milliliters
Cubic Centimeter	cc or cm^3	0.271 drams	1 milliliter

Weight Measurements

Unit	Abbreviation	US equivalent	Metric equivalent
Ounce	oz	16 drams	28.35 grams
Pound	lb	16 ounces	453.6 grams
Ton	tn.	2,000 pounds	907.2 kilograms

Volume and Weight Measurement Clarifications

Always be careful when using ounces and fluid ounces. They are not equivalent.

1 pint = 16 fluid ounces	1 fluid ounce ≠ 1 ounce
1 pound = 16 ounces	1 pint ≠ 1 pound

Having one pint of something does not mean you have one pound of it. In the same way, just because something weighs one pound does not mean that its volume is one pint.

In the United States, the word "ton" by itself refers to a short ton or a net ton. Do not confuse this with a long ton (also called a gross ton) or a metric ton (also spelled *tonne*), which have different measurement equivalents.

$$1 \text{ US ton} = 2000 \text{ pounds} \qquad \neq \qquad 1 \text{ metric ton} = 1000 \text{ kilograms}$$

Practice

P1. Perform the following conversions:

(a) 1.4 meters to centimeters

(b) 218 centimeters to meters

(c) 42 inches to feet

(d) 15 kilograms to pounds

(e) 80 ounces to pounds

(f) 2 miles to kilometers

(g) 5 feet to centimeters

(h) 15.14 liters to gallons

(i) 8 quarts to liters

(j) 13.2 pounds to grams

Practice Solutions

P1. (a) $\frac{100 \text{ cm}}{1 \text{ m}} = \frac{x \text{ cm}}{1.4 \text{ m}}$ Cross multiply to get $x = 140$

(b) $\frac{100 \text{ cm}}{1 \text{ m}} = \frac{218 \text{ cm}}{x \text{ m}}$ Cross multiply to get $100x = 218$, or $x = 2.18$

(c) $\frac{12 \text{ in}}{1 \text{ ft}} = \frac{42 \text{ in}}{x \text{ ft}}$ Cross multiply to get $12x = 42$, or $x = 3.5$

(d) $15 \text{ kilograms} \times \frac{2.2 \text{ pounds}}{1 \text{ kilogram}} = 33 \text{ pounds}$

(e) $80 \text{ ounces} \times \frac{1 \text{ pound}}{16 \text{ ounces}} = 5 \text{ pounds}$

(f) $2 \text{ miles} \times \frac{1.609 \text{ kilometers}}{1 \text{ mile}} = 3.218 \text{ kilometers}$

(g) $5 \text{ feet} \times \frac{12 \text{ inches}}{1 \text{ foot}} \times \frac{2.54 \text{ centimeters}}{1 \text{ inch}} = 152.4 \text{ centimeters}$

(h) $15.14 \text{ liters} \times \frac{1 \text{ gallon}}{3.785 \text{ liters}} = 4 \text{ gallons}$

(i) $8 \text{ quarts } \times \frac{1 \text{ gallon}}{4 \text{ quarts}} \times \frac{3.785 \text{ liters}}{1 \text{ gallon}} = 7.57 \text{ liters}$

(j) $13.2 \text{ pounds } \times \frac{1 \text{ kilogram}}{2.2 \text{ pounds}} \times \frac{1{,}000 \text{ grams}}{1 \text{ kilogram}} = 6{,}000 \text{ grams}$

Lines and Planes

Points and Lines

A **point** is a fixed location in space, has no size or dimensions, and is commonly represented by a dot. A **line** is a set of points that extends infinitely in two opposite directions. It has length, but no width or depth. A line can be defined by any two distinct points that it contains. A **line segment** is a portion of a line that has definite endpoints. A **ray** is a portion of a line that extends from a single point on that line in one direction along the line. It has a definite beginning, but no ending.

Interactions between Lines

Intersecting lines are lines that have exactly one point in common. **Concurrent lines** are multiple lines that intersect at a single point. **Perpendicular lines** are lines that intersect at right angles. They are represented by the symbol ⊥. The shortest distance from a line to a point not on the line is a perpendicular segment from the point to the line. **Parallel lines** are lines in the same plane that have no points in common and never meet. It is possible for lines to be in different planes, have no points in common, and never meet, but they are not parallel because they are in different planes.

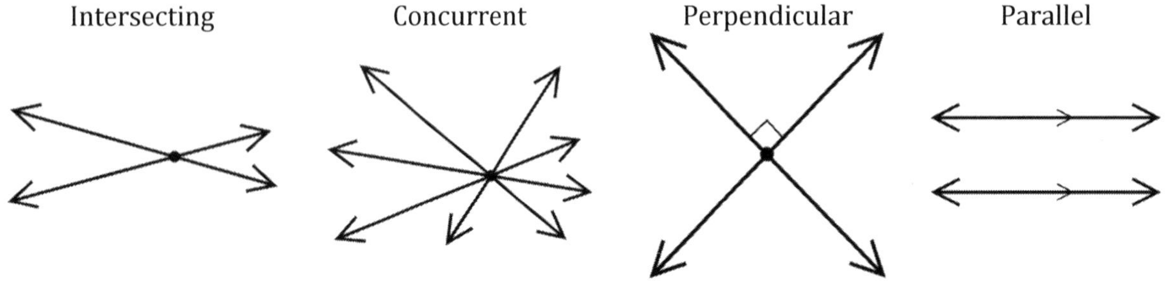

Review Video: Parallel and Perpendicular Lines
Visit mometrix.com/academy and enter code: 815923

A **transversal** is a line that intersects at least two other lines, which may or may not be parallel to one another. A transversal that intersects parallel lines is a common occurrence in geometry. A **bisector** is a line or line segment that divides another line segment into two equal lengths. A **perpendicular bisector** of a line segment is composed of points that are equidistant from the endpoints of the segment it is dividing.

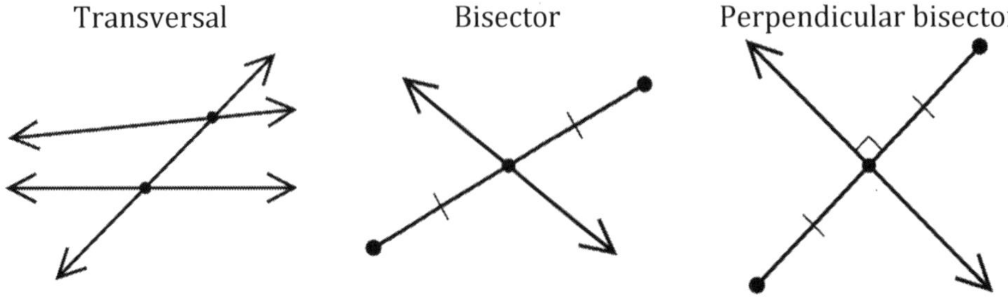

The **projection of a point on a line** is the point at which a perpendicular line drawn from the given point to the given line intersects the line. This is also the shortest distance from the given point to the line. The **projection of a segment on a line** is a segment whose endpoints are the points formed when perpendicular lines are drawn from the endpoints of the given segment to the given line. This is similar to the length a diagonal line appears to be when viewed from above.

Projection of a point on a line

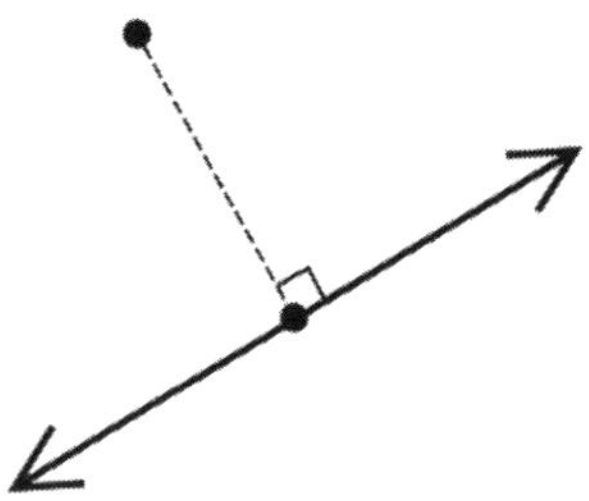

Projection of a segment on a line

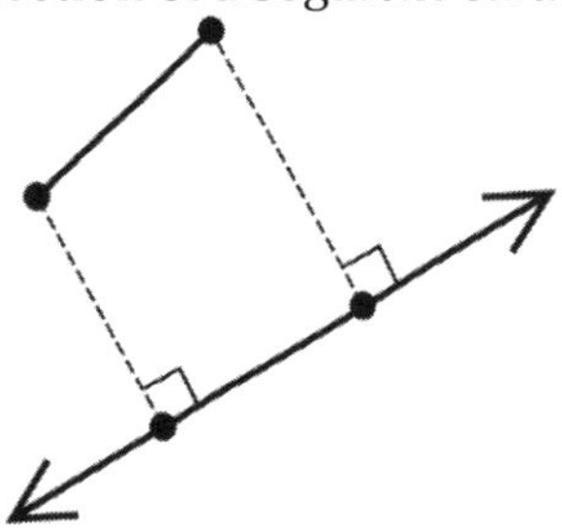

PLANES

A **plane** is a two-dimensional flat surface defined by three non-collinear points. A plane extends an infinite distance in all directions in those two dimensions. It contains an infinite number of points, parallel lines and segments, intersecting lines and segments, as well as parallel or intersecting rays. A plane will never contain a three-dimensional figure or skew lines, which are lines that don't intersect and are not parallel. Two given planes are either parallel or they intersect at a line. A plane may intersect a circular conic surface to form **conic sections**, such as a parabola, hyperbola, circle or ellipse.

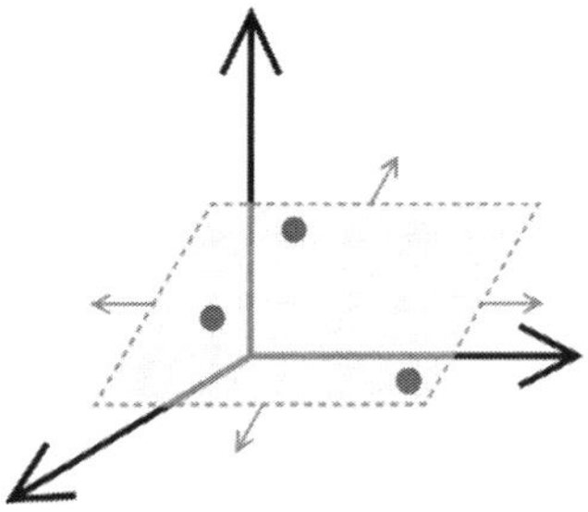

Review Video: Lines and Planes
Visit mometrix.com/academy and enter code: 554267

Angles

Angles and Vertices

An **angle** is formed when two lines or line segments meet at a common point. It may be a common starting point for a pair of segments or rays, or it may be the intersection of lines. Angles are represented by the symbol ∠.

The **vertex** is the point at which two segments or rays meet to form an angle. If the angle is formed by intersecting rays, lines, and/or line segments, the vertex is the point at which four angles are formed. The pairs of angles opposite one another are called vertical angles, and their measures are equal.

- An **acute** angle is an angle with a degree measure less than 90°.
- A **right** angle is an angle with a degree measure of exactly 90°.
- An **obtuse** angle is an angle with a degree measure greater than 90° but less than 180°.
- A **straight angle** is an angle with a degree measure of exactly 180°. This is also a semicircle.
- A **reflex angle** is an angle with a degree measure greater than 180° but less than 360°.

A **full angle** is an angle with a degree measure of exactly 360°. This is also a circle.

Review Video: Angles
Visit mometrix.com/academy and enter code: 264624

Relationships Between Angles

Two angles whose sum is exactly 90° are said to be **complementary**. The two angles may or may not be adjacent. In a right triangle, the two acute angles are complementary.

Two angles whose sum is exactly 180° are said to be **supplementary**. The two angles may or may not be adjacent. Two intersecting lines always form two pairs of supplementary angles. Adjacent supplementary angles will always form a straight line.

Two angles that have the same vertex and share a side are said to be **adjacent**. Vertical angles are not adjacent because they share a vertex but no common side.

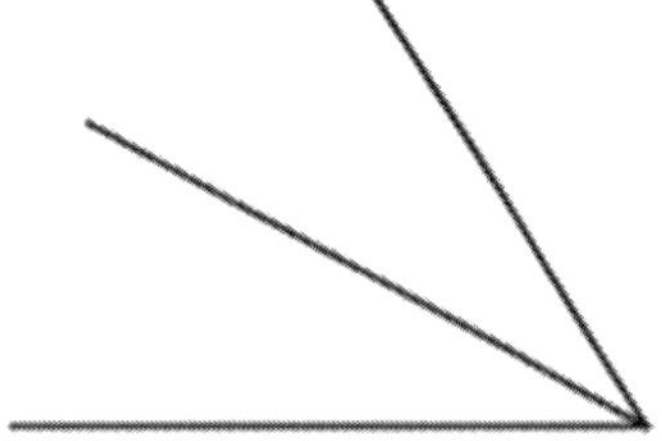

Adjacent
Share vertex and side

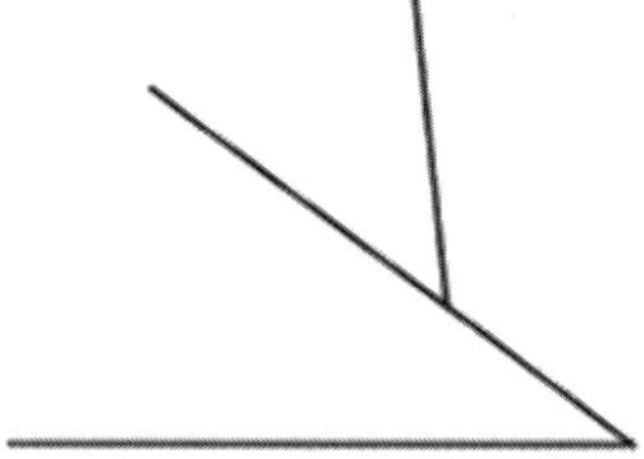

Not adjacent
Share part of a side, but not vertex

When two parallel lines are cut by a transversal, the angles that are between the two parallel lines are **interior angles**. In the diagram below, angles 3, 4, 5, and 6 are interior angles.

When two parallel lines are cut by a transversal, the angles that are outside the parallel lines are **exterior angles**. In the diagram below, angles 1, 2, 7, and 8 are exterior angles.

When two parallel lines are cut by a transversal, the angles that are in the same position relative to the transversal and a parallel line are **corresponding angles**. The diagram below has four pairs of corresponding angles: angles 1 and 5, angles 2 and 6, angles 3 and 7, and angles 4 and 8. Corresponding angles formed by parallel lines are congruent.

When two parallel lines are cut by a transversal, the two interior angles that are on opposite sides of the transversal are called **alternate interior angles**. In the diagram below, there are two pairs of alternate interior angles: angles 3 and 6, and angles 4 and 5. Alternate interior angles formed by parallel lines are congruent.

When two parallel lines are cut by a transversal, the two exterior angles that are on opposite sides of the transversal are called **alternate exterior angles**.

In the diagram below, there are two pairs of alternate exterior angles: angles 1 and 8, and angles 2 and 7. Alternate exterior angles formed by parallel lines are congruent.

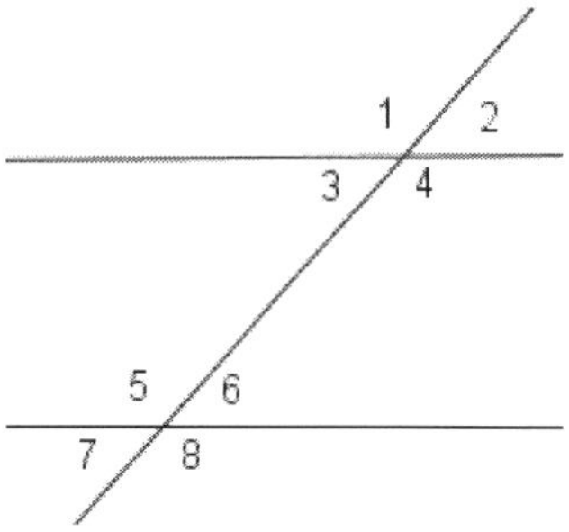

When two lines intersect, four angles are formed. The non-adjacent angles at this vertex are called vertical angles. Vertical angles are congruent. In the diagram, $\angle ABD \cong \angle CBE$ and $\angle ABC \cong \angle DBE$. The other pairs of angles, $(\angle ABC, \angle CBE)$ and $(\angle ABD, \angle DBE)$, are supplementary, meaning the pairs sum to 180°.

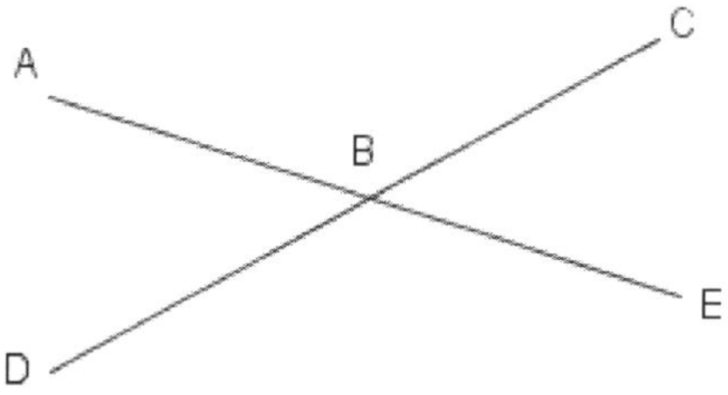

Practice

P1. Find the measure of angles $\angle a$, $\angle b$, and $\angle c$ based on the figure with two parallel lines, two perpendicular lines and one transversal:

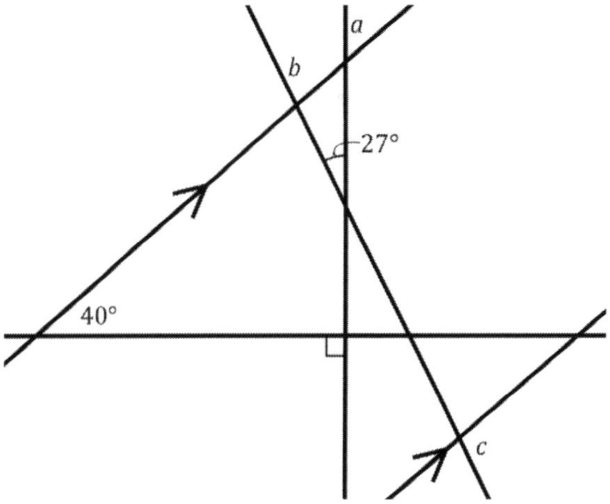

Practice Solutions

P1. (a) The vertical angle paired with $\angle a$ is part of a right triangle with the 40° angle. Thus the measure can be found:

$$90° = 40° + a$$
$$a = 50°$$

(b) The triangle formed by the supplementary angle to $\angle b$ is part of a triangle with the vertical angle paired with $\angle a$ and the given angle of 27°. Since $\angle a = 50°$:

$$180° = (180° - b) + 50° + 27°$$
$$103° = 180° - b$$
$$-77° = -b$$
$$77° = b$$

(c) As they are part of a transversal crossing parallel lines, angles $\angle b$ and $\angle c$ are supplementary. Thus $\angle c = 103°$.

Transformations

ROTATION

A **rotation** is a transformation that turns a figure around a point called the **center of rotation**, which can lie anywhere in the plane. If a line is drawn from a point on a figure to the center of rotation, and another line is drawn from the center to the rotated image of that point, the angle between the two lines is the **angle of rotation**. The vertex of the angle of rotation is the center of rotation.

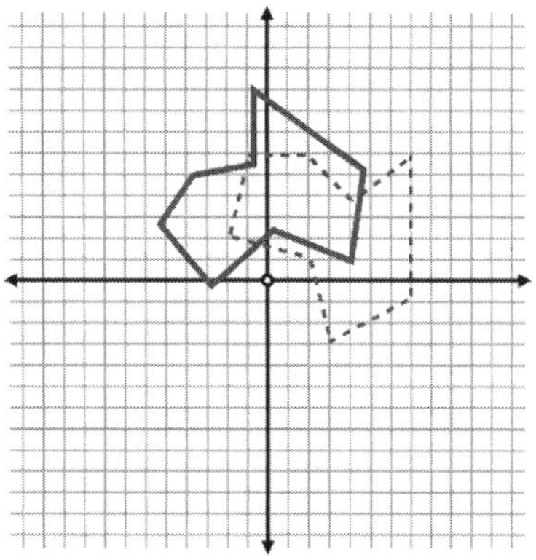

Review Video: Rotation
Visit mometrix.com/academy and enter code: 602600

TRANSLATION AND DILATION

A **translation** is a transformation which slides a figure from one position in the plane to another position in the plane. The original figure and the translated figure have the same size, shape, and orientation. A **dilation** is a transformation which proportionally stretches or shrinks a figure by a **scale factor**. The dilated image is the same shape and orientation as the original image but a different size. A polygon and its dilated image are similar.

Translation

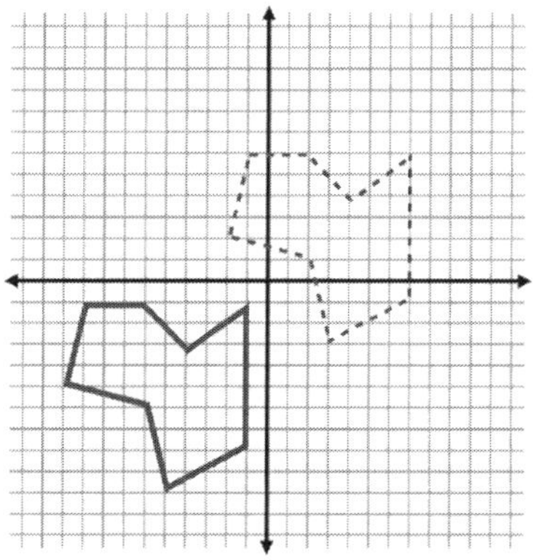

Dilation

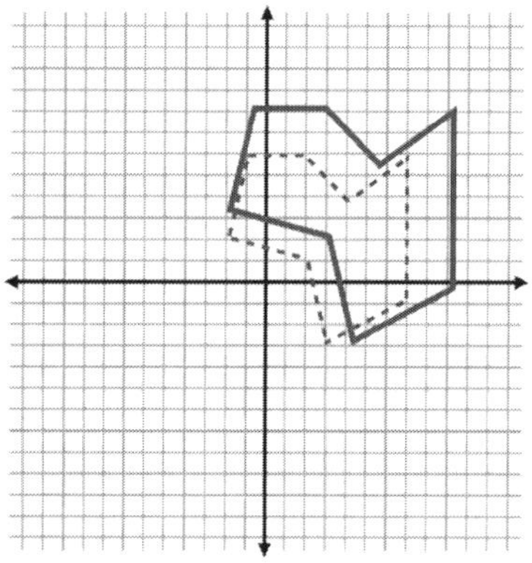

Review Video: Translation
Visit mometrix.com/academy and enter code: 718628

Review Video: Dilation
Visit mometrix.com/academy and enter code: 471630

A **reflection of a figure over a line** (a "flip") creates a congruent image that is the same distance from the line as the original figure but on the opposite side. The **line of reflection** is the perpendicular bisector of any line segment drawn from a point on the original figure to its reflected image (unless the point and its reflected image happen to be the same point, which happens when a figure is reflected over one of its own sides). A **reflection of a figure over a point** (an inversion) in two dimensions is the same as the rotation of the figure 180° about that point. The image of the figure is congruent to the original figure. The **point of reflection** is the midpoint of a line segment which connects a point in the figure to its image (unless the point and its reflected image happen to be the same point, which happens when a figure is reflected in one of its own points).

Reflection of a figure over a line

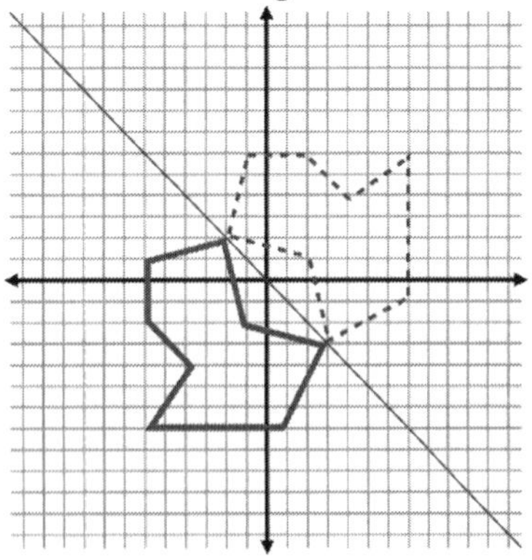

Reflection of a figure over a point

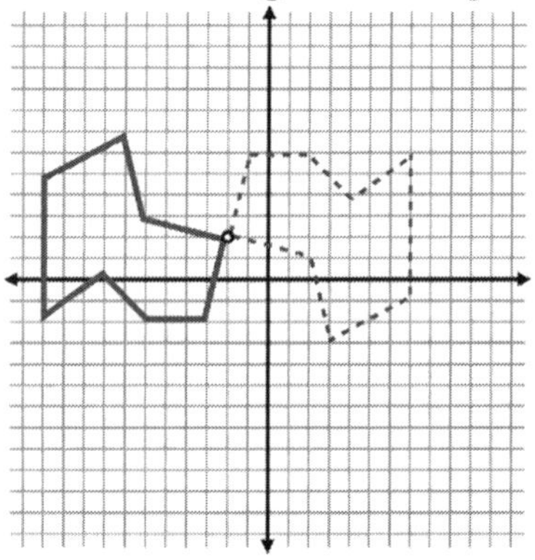

Review Video: Reflection
Visit mometrix.com/academy and enter code: 955068

PRACTICE

P1. Use the coordinate plane to reflect the figure below across the y-axis.

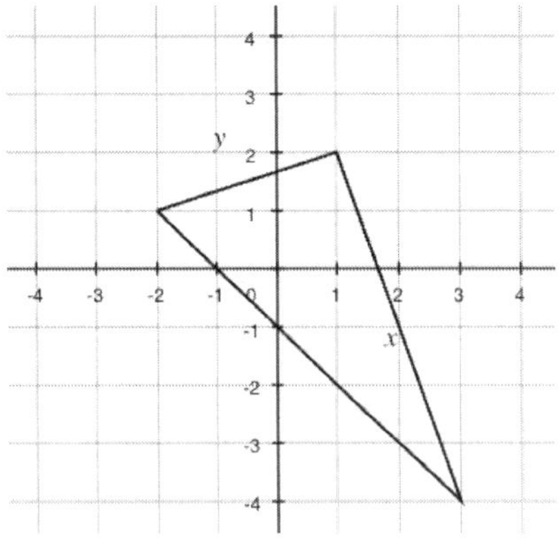

P2. Use the coordinate plane to enlarge the figure below by a factor of 2.

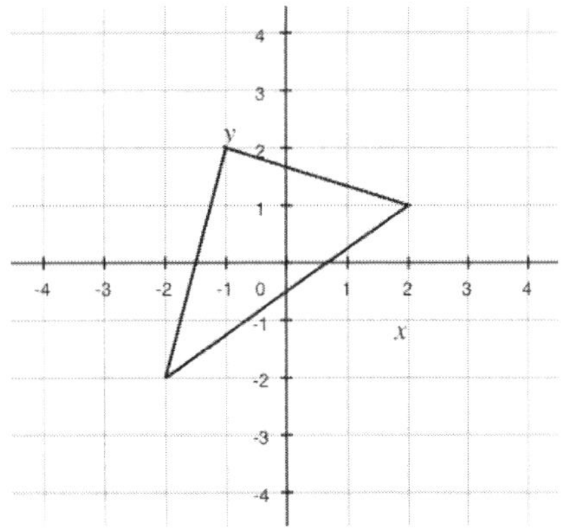

Practice Solutions

P1. To reflect the image across the y-axis, replace each x-coordinate of the points that are the vertex of the triangle, x, with its negative, $-x$.

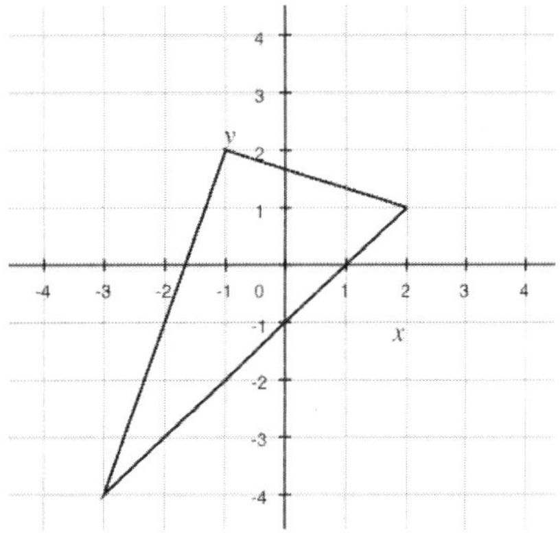

P2. An enlargement can be found by multiplying each coordinate of the coordinate pairs located at the triangle's vertices by 2. The original coordinates were $(-1, 2)$, $(2, 1)$, $(-2, -2)$, so the new coordinates are $(-2, 4)$, $(4, 2)$, $(-4, -4)$:

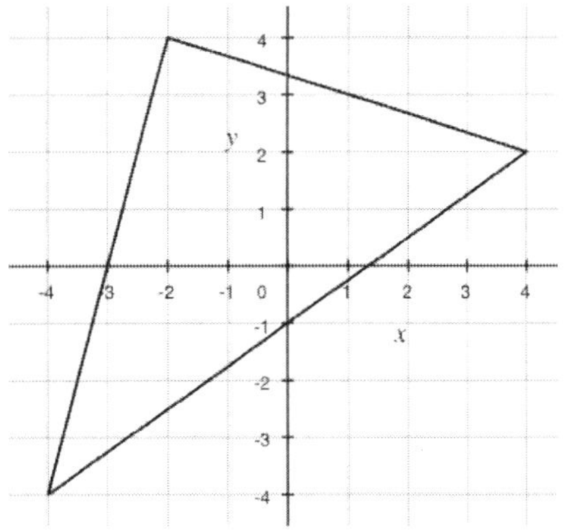

Two-Dimensional Shapes

POLYGONS

A **polygon** is a closed, two-dimensional figure with three or more straight line segments called **sides**. The point at which two sides of a polygon intersect is called the **vertex**. In a polygon, the number of sides is always equal to the number of vertices. A polygon with all sides congruent and all angles equal is called a **regular polygon**. Common polygons are:

$$\begin{aligned} \text{Triangle} &= 3 \text{ sides} \\ \text{Quadrilateral} &= 4 \text{ sides} \\ \text{Pentagon} &= 5 \text{ sides} \\ \text{Hexagon} &= 6 \text{ sides} \\ \text{Heptagon} &= 7 \text{ sides} \\ \text{Octagon} &= 8 \text{ sides} \\ \text{Nonagon} &= 9 \text{ sides} \\ \text{Decagon} &= 10 \text{ sides} \\ \text{Dodecagon} &= 12 \text{ sides} \end{aligned}$$

More generally, an n-gon is a polygon that has n angles and n sides.

Review Video: Intro to Polygons
Visit mometrix.com/academy and enter code: 271869

Review Video: Sum of Interior Angles
Visit mometrix.com/academy and enter code: 984991

The sum of the interior angles of an n-sided polygon is $(n - 2) \times 180°$. For example, in a triangle $n = 3$. So the sum of the interior angles is $(3 - 2) \times 180° = 180°$. In a quadrilateral, $n = 4$, and the sum of the angles is $(4 - 2) \times 180° = 360°$.

Review Video: Sum of Interior Angles
Visit mometrix.com/academy and enter code: 984991

APOTHEM AND RADIUS

A line segment from the center of a polygon that is perpendicular to a side of the polygon is called the **apothem**. A line segment from the center of a polygon to a vertex of the polygon is called a **radius**. In a regular polygon, the apothem can be used to find the area of the polygon using the formula $A = \frac{1}{2}ap$, where a is the apothem, and p is the perimeter.

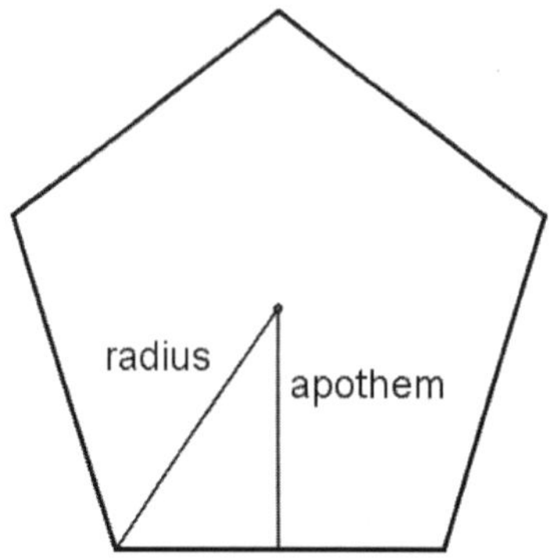

A **diagonal** is a line segment that joins two non-adjacent vertices of a polygon. The number of diagonals a polygon has can be found by using the formula:

$$\text{number of diagonals} = \frac{n(n-3)}{2}$$

Note that n is the number of sides in the polygon. This formula works for all polygons, not just regular polygons.

Convex and Concave Polygons

A **convex polygon** is a polygon whose diagonals all lie within the interior of the polygon. A **concave polygon** is a polygon with a least one diagonal that is outside the polygon. In the diagram below, quadrilateral $ABCD$ is concave because diagonal $\overline{AC}$ lies outside the polygon and quadrilateral $EFGH$ is convex because both diagonals lie inside the polygon.

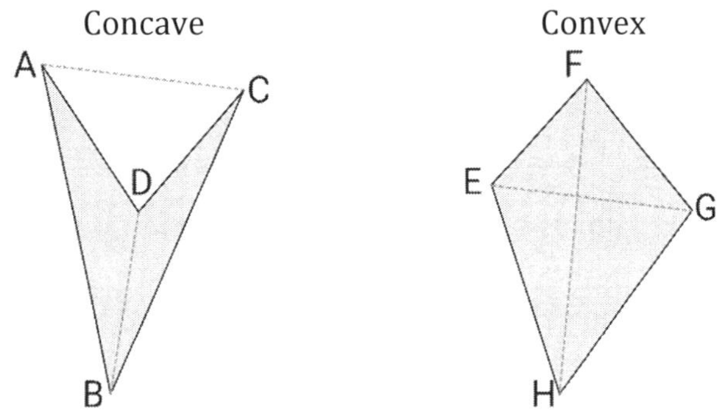

Congruence and Similarity

Congruent figures are geometric figures that have the same size and shape. All corresponding angles are equal, and all corresponding sides are equal. Congruence is indicated by the symbol $\cong$.

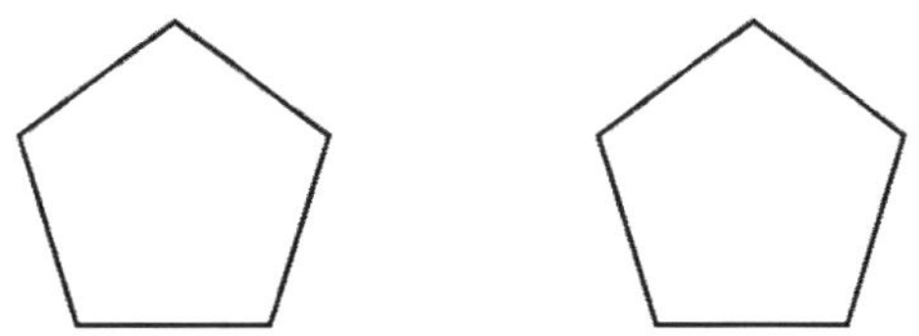

Congruent polygons

Similar figures are geometric figures that have the same shape, but do not necessarily have the same size. All corresponding angles are equal, and all corresponding sides are proportional, but they do not have to be equal. It is indicated by the symbol ~.

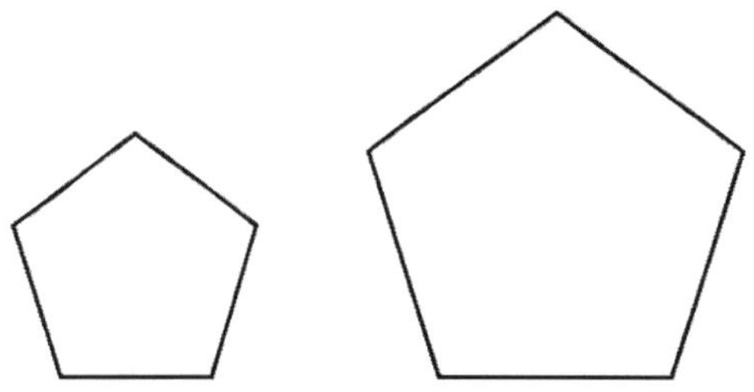

Similar polygons

Note that all congruent figures are also similar, but not all similar figures are congruent.

Review Video: What is a Congruent Shape?
Visit mometrix.com/academy and enter code: 492281

LINE OF SYMMETRY

A line that divides a figure or object into congruent parts is called a **line of symmetry**. An object may have no lines of symmetry, one line of symmetry, or multiple (i.e., more than one) lines of symmetry.

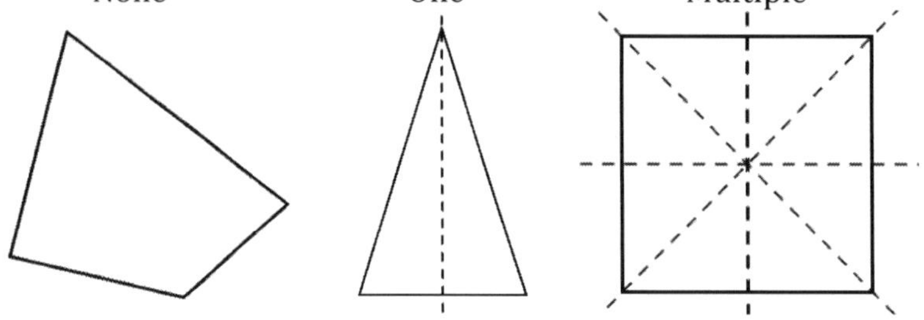

Review Video: Symmetry
Visit mometrix.com/academy and enter code: 528106

TRIANGLES

A triangle is a three-sided figure with the sum of its interior angles being 180°. The **perimeter of any triangle** is found by summing the three side lengths; $P = a + b + c$. For an equilateral triangle, this is the same as $P = 3a$, where a is any side length, since all three sides are the same length.

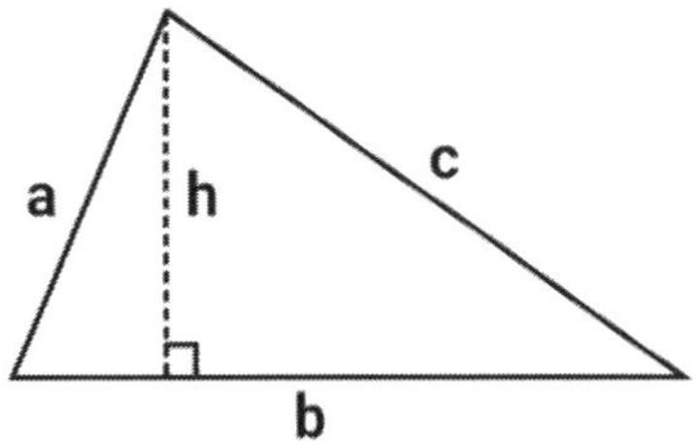

Review Video: Proof that a Triangle is 180 Degrees
Visit mometrix.com/academy and enter code: 687591

Review Video: Area and Perimeter of a Triangle
Visit mometrix.com/academy and enter code: 853779

The **area of any triangle** can be found by taking half the product of one side length referred to as the base, often given the variable b and the perpendicular distance from that side to the opposite vertex called the altitude or height and given the variable h. In equation form that is $A = \frac{1}{2}bh$. Another formula that works for any triangle is $A = \sqrt{s(s-a)(s-b)(s-c)}$, where s is the semiperimeter: $\frac{a+b+c}{2}$, and a, b, and c are the lengths of the three sides. Special cases include isosceles triangles, $A = \frac{1}{2}b\sqrt{a^2 - \frac{b^2}{4}}$, where b is the unique side and a is the length of one of the two congruent sides, and equilateral triangles, $A = \frac{\sqrt{3}}{4}a^2$, where a is the length of a side.

Review Video: Area of Any Triangle
Visit mometrix.com/academy and enter code: 138510

PARTS OF A TRIANGLE

An **altitude** of a triangle is a line segment drawn from one vertex perpendicular to the opposite side. In the diagram that follows, $\overline{BE}$, $\overline{AD}$, and $\overline{CF}$ are altitudes. The length of an altitude is also called the height of the triangle. The three altitudes in a triangle are always concurrent. The point of concurrency of the altitudes of a triangle, O, is called the **orthocenter**. Note that in an obtuse triangle, the orthocenter will be outside the triangle, and in a right triangle, the orthocenter is the vertex of the right angle.

A **median** of a triangle is a line segment drawn from one vertex to the midpoint of the opposite side. In the diagram that follows, $\overline{BH}$, $\overline{AG}$, and $\overline{CI}$ are medians. This is not the same as the altitude, except the altitude to the base of an isosceles triangle and all three altitudes of an equilateral triangle. The point of concurrency of the medians of a triangle, T, is called the **centroid**. This is the same point as the orthocenter only in an equilateral triangle. Unlike the orthocenter, the centroid is always inside the triangle. The centroid can also be considered the exact center of the triangle. Any shape triangle can be perfectly balanced on a tip placed at the centroid. The centroid is also the point that is two-thirds the distance from the vertex to the opposite side.

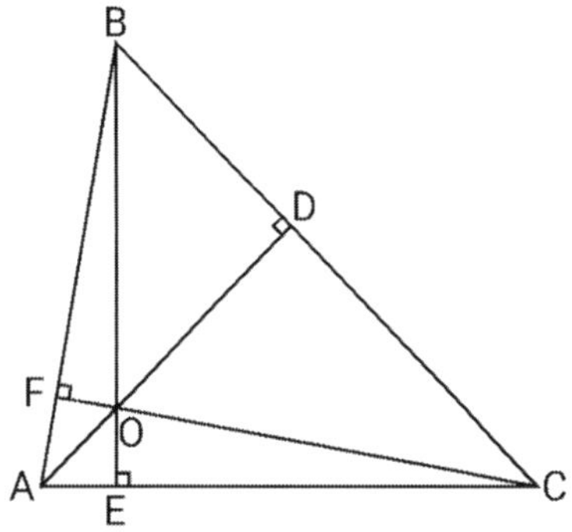

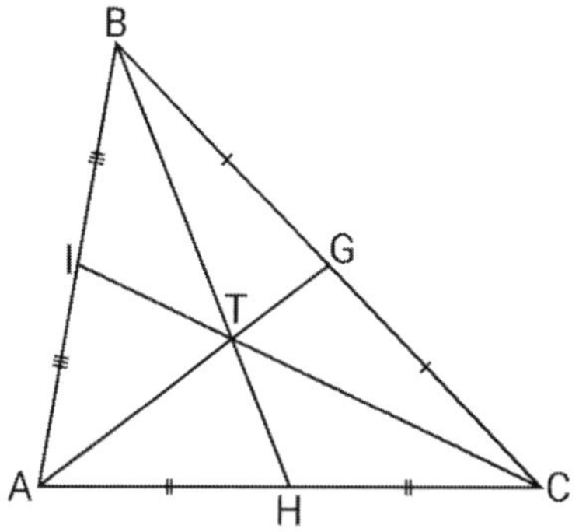

Review Video: Centroid, Incenter, Circumcenter, and Orthocenter
Visit mometrix.com/academy and enter code: 598260

QUADRILATERALS

A **quadrilateral** is a closed two-dimensional geometric figure that has four straight sides. The sum of the interior angles of any quadrilateral is 360°.

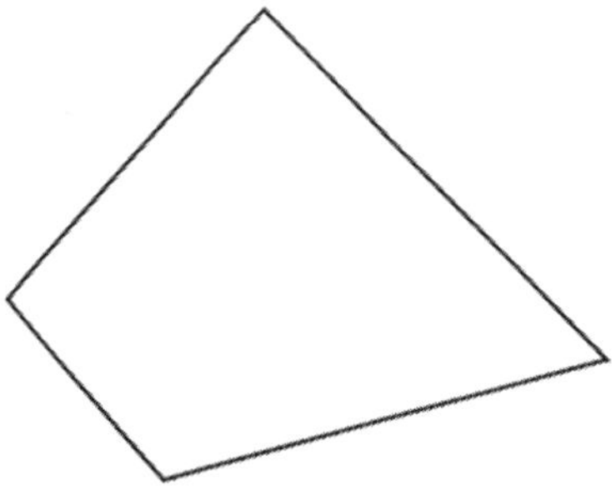

Review Video: Diagonals of Parallelograms, Rectangles, and Rhombi
Visit mometrix.com/academy and enter code: 320040

KITE

A **kite** is a quadrilateral with two pairs of adjacent sides that are congruent. A result of this is perpendicular diagonals. A kite can be concave or convex and has one line of symmetry.

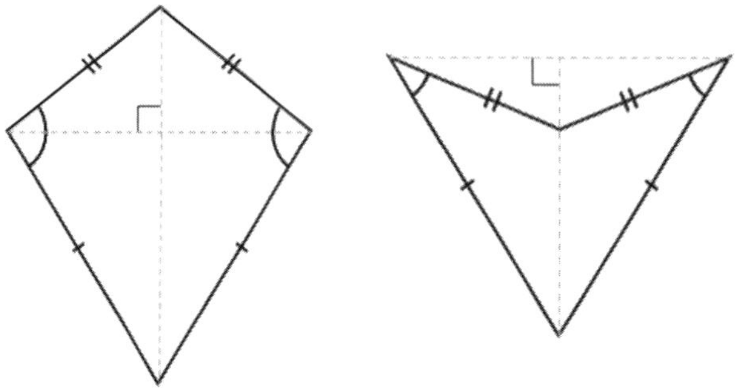

TRAPEZOID

Trapezoid: A trapezoid is defined as a quadrilateral that has at least one pair of parallel sides. There are no rules for the second pair of sides. So, there are no rules for the diagonals and no lines of symmetry for a trapezoid.

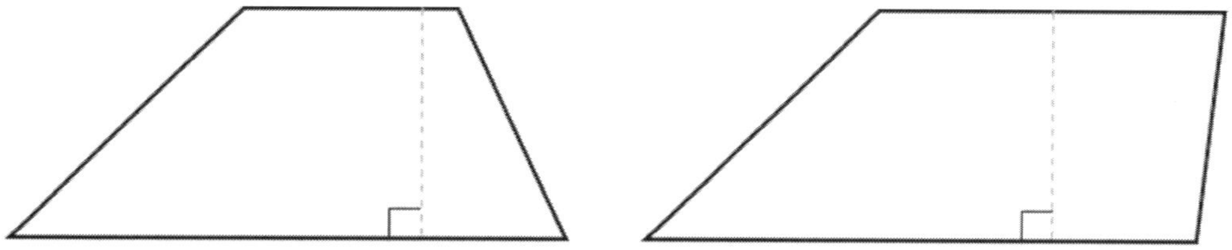

The **area of a trapezoid** is found by the formula $A = \frac{1}{2}h(b_1 + b_2)$, where h is the height (segment joining and perpendicular to the parallel bases), and b_1 and b_2 are the two parallel sides (bases). Do not use one of the other two sides as the height unless that side is also perpendicular to the parallel bases.

The **perimeter of a trapezoid** is found by the formula $P = a + b_1 + c + b_2$, where a, b_1, c, and b_2 are the four sides of the trapezoid.

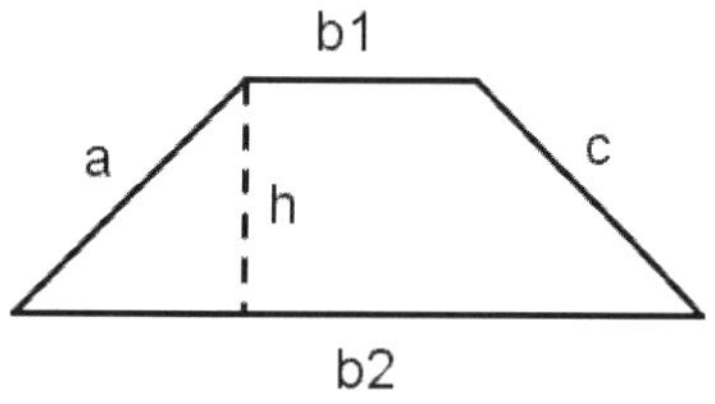

Review Video: Area and Perimeter of a Trapezoid
Visit mometrix.com/academy and enter code: 587523

Isosceles trapezoid: A trapezoid with equal base angles. This gives rise to other properties including: the two nonparallel sides have the same length, the two non-base angles are also equal, and there is one line of symmetry through the midpoints of the parallel sides.

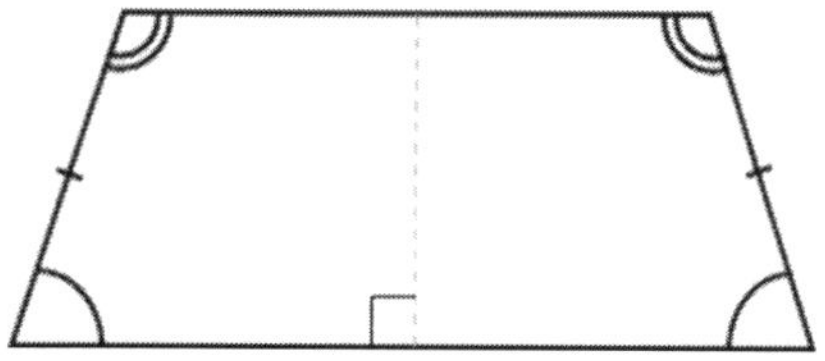

PARALLELOGRAM

A **parallelogram** is a quadrilateral that has two pairs of opposite parallel sides. As such it is a special type of trapezoid. The sides that are parallel are also congruent. The opposite interior angles are always congruent, and the consecutive interior angles are supplementary. The diagonals of a parallelogram divide each other. Each diagonal divides the parallelogram into two congruent triangles. A parallelogram has no line of symmetry, but does have 180-degree rotational symmetry about the midpoint.

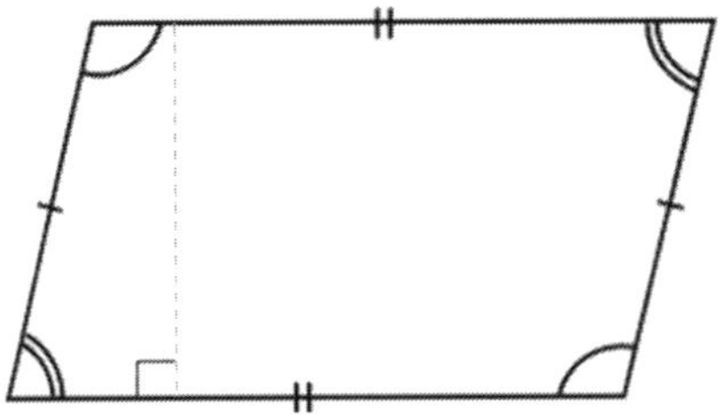

The **area of a parallelogram** is found by the formula $A = bh$, where b is the length of the base, and h is the height. Note that the base and height correspond to the length and width in a rectangle, so this formula would apply to rectangles as well. Do not confuse the height of a parallelogram with the length of the second side. The two are only the same measure in the case of a rectangle.

The **perimeter of a parallelogram** is found by the formula $P = 2a + 2b$ or $P = 2(a + b)$, where a and b are the lengths of the two sides.

Review Video: How to Find the Area and Perimeter of a Parallelogram
Visit mometrix.com/academy and enter code: 718313

Rectangle

A **rectangle** is a quadrilateral with four right angles. All rectangles are parallelograms and trapezoids, but not all parallelograms or trapezoids are rectangles. The diagonals of a rectangle are congruent. Rectangles have two lines of symmetry (through each pair of opposing midpoints) and 180-degree rotational symmetry about the midpoint.

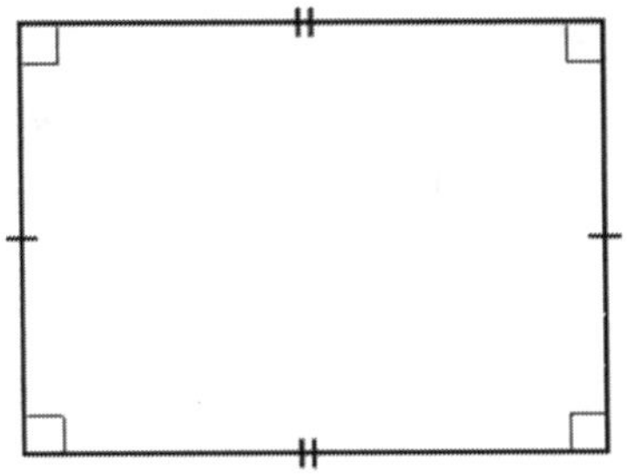

The **area of a rectangle** is found by the formula $A = lw$, where A is the area of the rectangle, l is the length (usually considered to be the longer side) and w is the width (usually considered to be the shorter side). The numbers for l and w are interchangeable.

The **perimeter of a rectangle** is found by the formula $P = 2l + 2w$ or $P = 2(l + w)$, where l is the length, and w is the width. It may be easier to add the length and width first and then double the result, as in the second formula.

Rhombus

A **rhombus** is a quadrilateral with four congruent sides. All rhombuses are parallelograms and kites; thus, they inherit all the properties of both types of quadrilaterals. The diagonals of a rhombus are perpendicular to each other. Rhombi have two lines of symmetry (along each of the diagonals) and 180° rotational symmetry. The **area of a rhombus** is half the product of the diagonals: $A = \frac{d_1 d_2}{2}$ and the perimeter of a rhombus is: $P = 2\sqrt{(d_1)^2 + (d_2)^2}$.

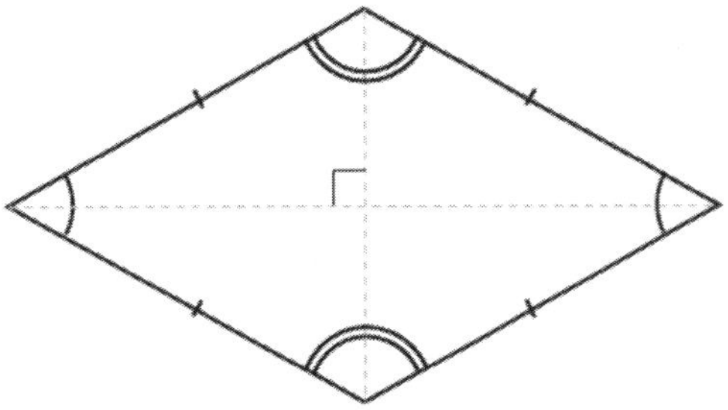

SQUARE

A **square** is a quadrilateral with four right angles and four congruent sides. Squares satisfy the criteria of all other types of quadrilaterals. The diagonals of a square are congruent and perpendicular to each other. Squares have four lines of symmetry (through each pair of opposing midpoints and along each of the diagonals) as well as 90° rotational symmetry about the midpoint.

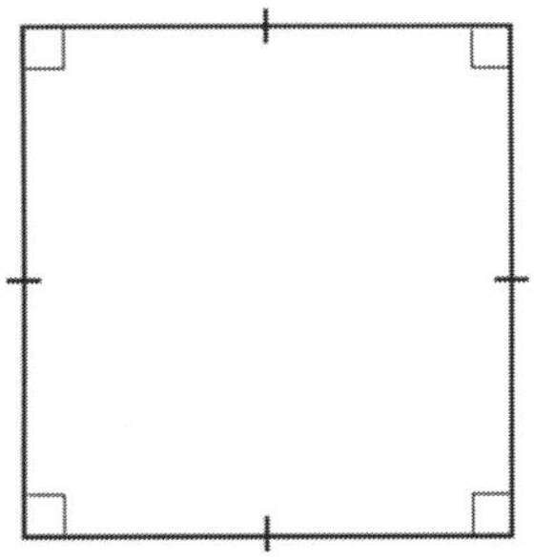

The **area of a square** is found by using the formula $A = s^2$, where s is the length of one side. The **perimeter of a square** is found by using the formula $P = 4s$, where s is the length of one side. Because all four sides are equal in a square, it is faster to multiply the length of one side by 4 than to add the same number four times. You could use the formulas for rectangles and get the same answer.

HIERARCHY OF QUADRILATERALS

The hierarchy of quadrilaterals is as follows:

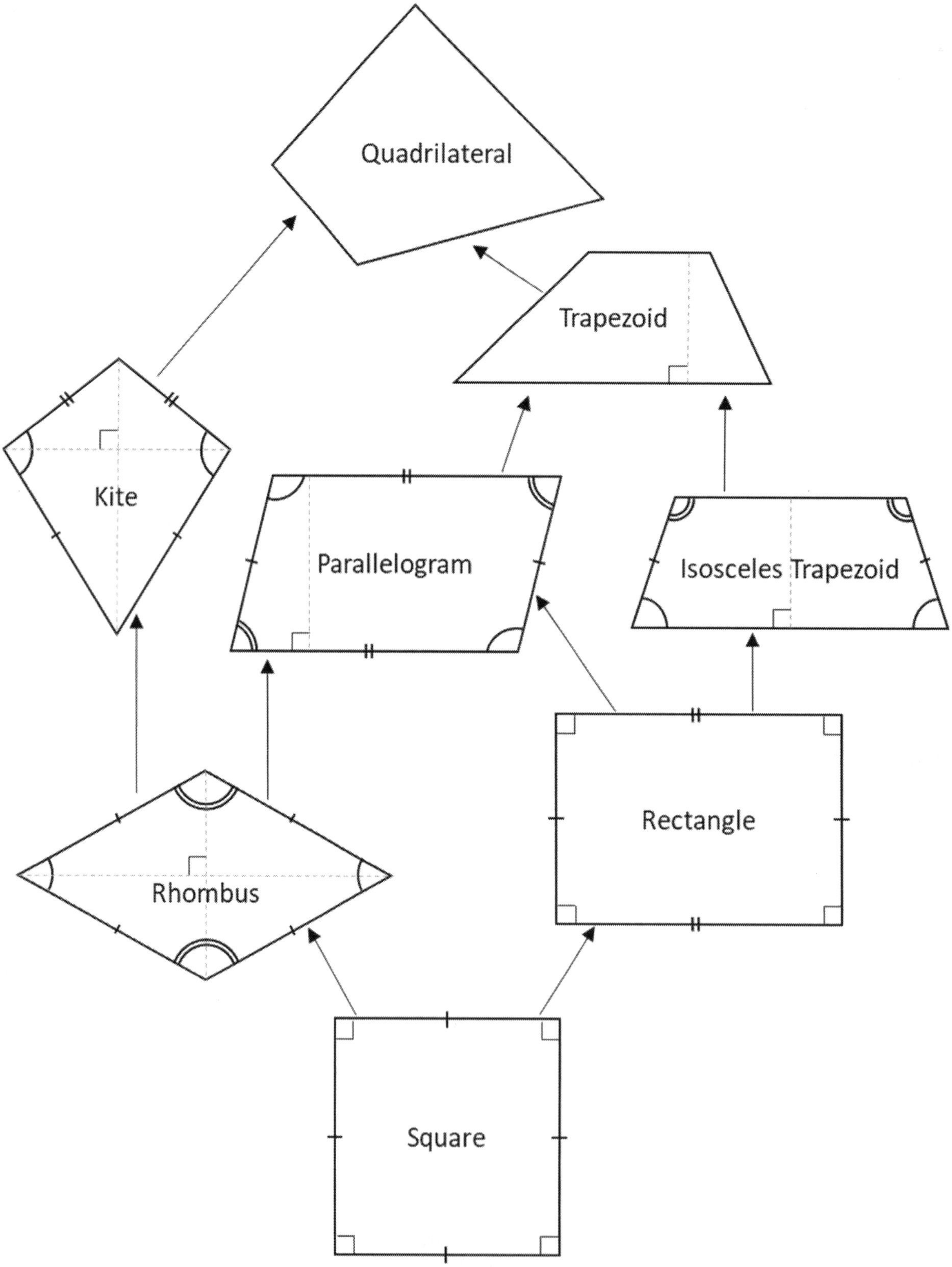

CIRCLES

The **center** of a circle is the single point from which every point on the circle is **equidistant**. The **radius** is a line segment that joins the center of the circle and any one point on the circle. All radii of a circle are equal. Circles that have the same center but not the same length of radii are **concentric**. The **diameter** is a line segment that passes through the center of the circle and has both endpoints on the circle. The length of the diameter is exactly twice the length of the radius. Point O in the diagram below is the center of the circle, segments $\overline{OX}$, $\overline{OY}$, and $\overline{OZ}$ are radii; and segment $\overline{XZ}$ is a diameter.

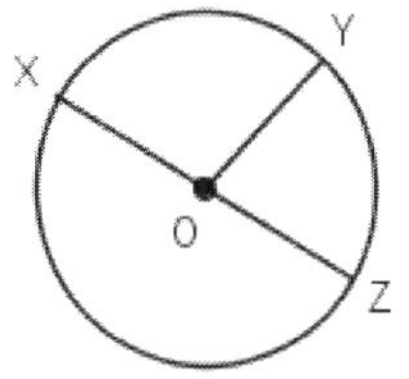

Review Video: Points of a Circle
Visit mometrix.com/academy and enter code: 420746

Review Video: The Diameter, Radius, and Circumference of Circles
Visit mometrix.com/academy and enter code: 448988

The **area of a circle** is found by the formula $A = \pi r^2$, where r is the length of the radius. If the diameter of the circle is given, remember to divide it in half to get the length of the radius before proceeding.

The **circumference** of a circle is found by the formula $C = 2\pi r$, where r is the radius. Again, remember to convert the diameter if you are given that measure rather than the radius.

Review Video: Area and Circumference of a Circle
Visit mometrix.com/academy and enter code: 243015

INSCRIBED AND CIRCUMSCRIBED FIGURES

These terms can both be used to describe a given arrangement of figures, depending on perspective. If each of the vertices of figure A lie on figure B, then it can be said that figure A is **inscribed** in figure B, but it can also be said that figure B is **circumscribed** about figure A. The following table and examples help to illustrate the concept. Note that the figures cannot both be circles, as they would be completely overlapping and neither would be inscribed or circumscribed.

Given	Description	Equivalent Description	Figures
Each of the sides of a pentagon is tangent to a circle	The circle is inscribed in the pentagon	The pentagon is circumscribed about the circle	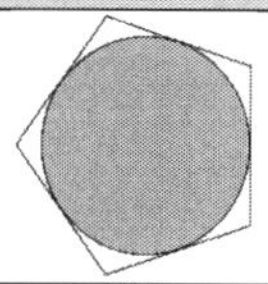
Each of the vertices of a pentagon lie on a circle	The pentagon is inscribed in the circle	The circle is circumscribed about the pentagon	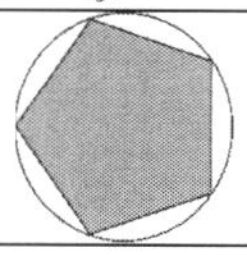

PRACTICE

P1. Find the area and perimeter of the following quadrilaterals:

(a) A square with side length 2.5 cm.

(b) A parallelogram with height 3 m, base 4 m, and other side 6 m.

(c) A rhombus with diagonals 15 in and 20 in.

P2. Calculate the area of a triangle with side lengths of 7 ft, 8 ft, and 9 ft.

P3. Square $ABCD$ is inscribed in a circle with radius 20 m. What is the area of the part of the circle outside of the square?

PRACTICE SOLUTIONS

P1. (a) $A = s^2 = (2.5\text{ cm})^2 = 6.25\text{ cm}^2; P = 4s = 4 \times 2.5\text{ cm} = 10\text{ cm}$

(b) $A = bh = (3\text{ m})(4\text{ m}) = 12\text{ m}^2; P = 2a + 2b = 2 \times 6\text{ m} + 2 \times 4\text{ m} = 20\text{ m}$

(c) $A = \frac{d_1 d_2}{2} = \frac{(15\text{ in})(20\text{ in})}{2} = 150\text{ in}^2;$
$P = 2\sqrt{(d_1)^2 + (d_2)^2} = 2\sqrt{(15\text{ in})^2 + (20\text{ in})^2} = 2\sqrt{625\text{ in}^2} = 50\text{ in}$

P2. Given only side lengths, we can use the semi perimeter to the find the area based on the formula, $A = \sqrt{s(s-a)(s-b)(s-c)}$, where s is the semiperimeter, $\frac{a+b+c}{2} = \frac{7+8+9}{2} = 12$ ft:

$$\begin{aligned} A &= \sqrt{12(12-7)(12-8)(12-9)} \\ &= \sqrt{(12)(5)(4)(3)} \\ &= 12\sqrt{5}\text{ ft}^2 \end{aligned}$$

P3. Begin by drawing a diagram of the situation, where we want to find the shaded area:

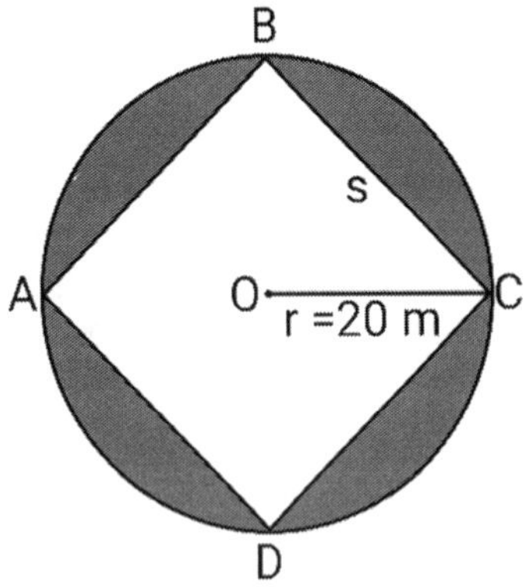

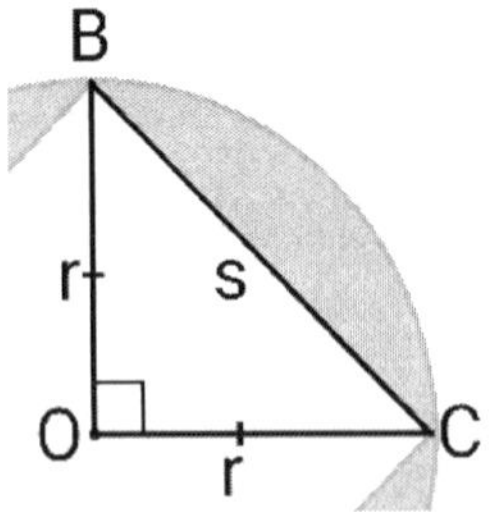

The area of the square is s^2, so the area we want to find is: $\pi r^2 - s^2$. Since the inscribed figure is a square, the triangle BCO is a 45-45-90 right triangle. Now we can find $s^2 = r^2 + r^2 = 2r^2$. So the shaded area is:

$$\begin{aligned} A &= \pi r^2 - s^2 \\ &= \pi r^2 - 2r^2 \\ &= (\pi - 2)r^2 \\ &= (\pi - 2) \times 400 \\ &\approx 456.6 \text{ m}^2 \end{aligned}$$

Three-Dimensional Shapes

SOLIDS

The **surface area of a solid object** is the area of all sides or exterior surfaces. For objects such as prisms and pyramids, a further distinction is made between base surface area (B) and lateral surface area (LA). For a prism, the total surface area (SA) is $SA = LA + 2B$. For a pyramid or cone, the total surface area is $SA = LA + B$.

The **surface area of a sphere** can be found by the formula $A = 4\pi r^2$, where r is the radius. The volume is given by the formula $V = \frac{4}{3}\pi r^3$, where r is the radius. Both quantities are generally given in terms of π.

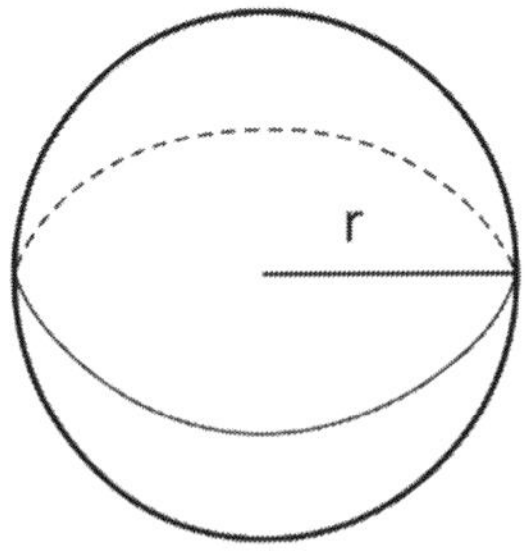

Review Video: Volume and Surface Area of a Sphere
Visit mometrix.com/academy and enter code: 786928

The **volume of any prism** is found by the formula $V = Bh$, where B is the area of the base, and h is the height (perpendicular distance between the bases). The surface area of any prism is the sum of the areas of both bases and all sides. It can be calculated as $SA = 2B + Ph$, where P is the perimeter of the base.

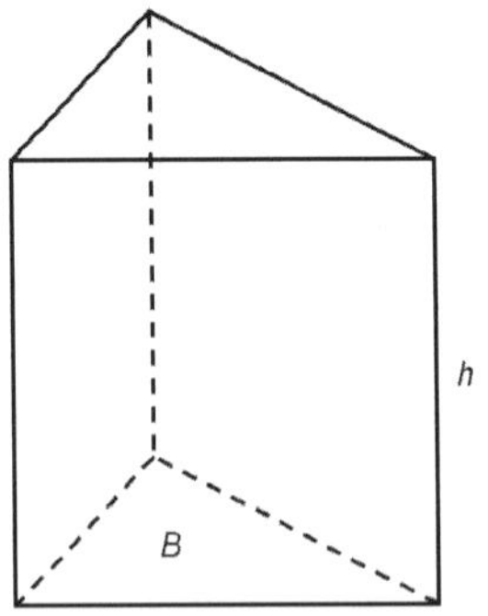

Review Video: Volume and Surface Area of a Prism
Visit mometrix.com/academy and enter code: 420158

For a **rectangular prism**, the volume can be found by the formula $V = lwh$, where V is the volume, l is the length, w is the width, and h is the height. The surface area can be calculated as $SA = 2lw + 2hl + 2wh$ or $SA = 2(lw + hl + wh)$.

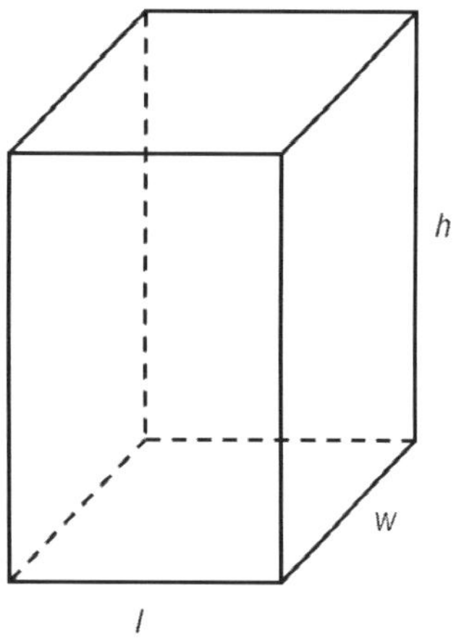

Review Video: Volume and Surface Area of a Rectangular Prism
Visit mometrix.com/academy and enter code: 282814

The **volume of a cube** can be found by the formula $V = s^3$, where s is the length of a side. The surface area of a cube is calculated as $SA = 6s^2$, where SA is the total surface area and s is the length of a side. These formulas are the same as the ones used for the volume and surface area of a rectangular prism, but simplified since all three quantities (length, width, and height) are the same.

Review Video: Volume and Surface Area of a Cube
Visit mometrix.com/academy and enter code: 664455

The **volume of a cylinder** can be calculated by the formula $V = \pi r^2 h$, where r is the radius, and h is the height. The surface area of a cylinder can be found by the formula $SA = 2\pi r^2 + 2\pi rh$. The first term is the base area multiplied by two, and the second term is the perimeter of the base multiplied by the height.

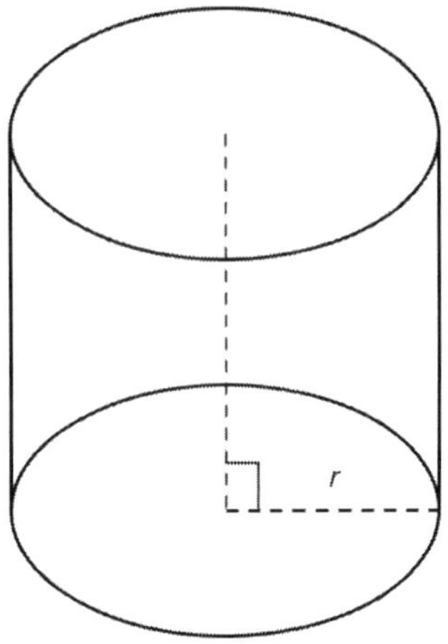

Review Video: Finding the Volume and Surface Area of a Right Circular Cylinder
Visit mometrix.com/academy and enter code: 226463

The **volume of a pyramid** is found by the formula $V = \frac{1}{3}Bh$, where B is the area of the base, and h is the height (perpendicular distance from the vertex to the base). Notice this formula is the same as $\frac{1}{3}$ times the volume of a prism. Like a prism, the base of a pyramid can be any shape.

Finding the **surface area of a pyramid** is not as simple as the other shapes we've looked at thus far. If the pyramid is a right pyramid, meaning the base is a regular polygon and the vertex is directly over the center of that polygon, the surface area can be calculated as $SA = B + \frac{1}{2}Ph_s$, where P is the perimeter of the base, and h_s is the slant height (distance from the vertex to the midpoint of one side of the base). If the pyramid is irregular, the area of each triangle side must be calculated individually and then summed, along with the base.

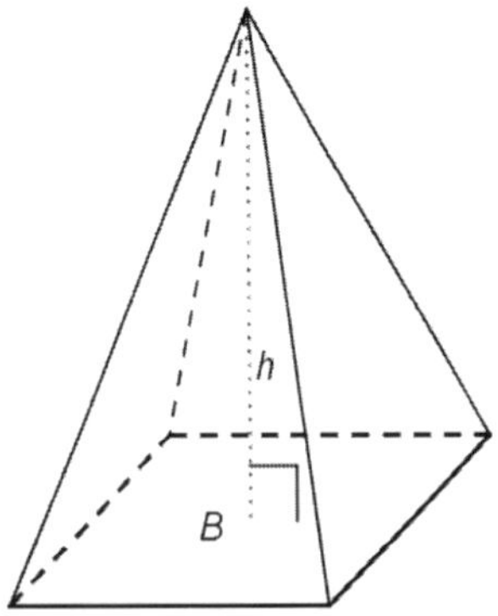

Review Video: Finding the Volume and Surface Area of a Pyramid
Visit mometrix.com/academy and enter code: 621932

The **volume of a cone** is found by the formula $V = \frac{1}{3}\pi r^2 h$, where r is the radius, and h is the height. Notice this is the same as $\frac{1}{3}$ times the volume of a cylinder. The surface area can be calculated as $SA = \pi r^2 + \pi r s$, where s is the slant height. The slant height can be calculated using the Pythagorean theorem to be $\sqrt{r^2 + h^2}$, so the surface area formula can also be written as $SA = \pi r^2 + \pi r\sqrt{r^2 + h^2}$.

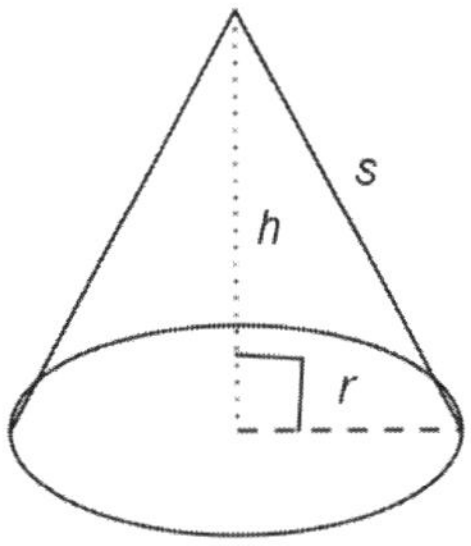

Review Video: Volume and Surface Area of a Right Circular Cone
Visit mometrix.com/academy and enter code: 573574

Practice

P1. Find the surface area and volume of the following solids:

(a) A cylinder with radius 5 m and height 0.5 m.

(b) A trapezoidal prism with base area of 254 mm^2, base perimeter 74 mm, and height 10 mm.

(c) A half sphere (radius 5 yds) on the base of an inverted cone with the same radius and a height of 7 yds.

Practice Solutions

P1. (a) $SA = 2\pi r^2 + 2\pi rh = 2\pi(5\text{ m})^2 + 2\pi(5\text{ m})(0.5\text{ m}) = 55\pi\text{ m}^2 \approx 172.79\text{ m}^2$;
$V = \pi r^2 h = \pi(5\text{ m})^2(0.5\text{ m}) = 12.5\pi\text{ m}^3 \approx 39.27\text{ m}^3$

(b) $SA = 2B + Ph = 2(254\text{ mm}^2) + (74\text{ mm})(10\text{ mm}) = 1{,}248\text{ mm}^2$;
$V = Bh = (254\text{ mm}^2)(10\text{ mm}) = 2{,}540\text{ mm}^3$

(c) We can find s, the slant height using the Pythagorean theorem, and since this solid is made of parts of simple solids, we can combine the formulas to find surface area and volume:

$$s = \sqrt{r^2 + h^2} = \sqrt{(5\text{ yd})^2 + (7\text{ yd})^2} = \sqrt{74}\text{ yd}$$

$$\begin{aligned} SA_{Total} &= \frac{(SA_{sphere})}{2} + SA_{cone} - SA_{base} \\ &= \frac{4\pi r^2}{2} + (\pi rs + \pi r^2) - \pi r^2 \\ &= 2\pi(5\text{ yd})^2 + \pi(5\text{ yd})(\sqrt{74}\text{ yd}) \\ &= 5\pi(10 + \sqrt{74})\text{ yd}^2 \\ &\approx 292.20\text{ yd}^2 \end{aligned}$$

$$\begin{aligned} V_{Total} &= \frac{(V_{sphere})}{2} + V_{cone} \\ &= \frac{\frac{4}{3}\pi r^3}{2} + \frac{1}{3}\pi r^2 h \\ &= \frac{2}{3}\pi(5\text{ yd})^3 + \frac{1}{3}\pi(5\text{ yd})^2(7\text{ yd}) \\ &= \frac{5^2 \times \pi}{3}(10 + 7)\text{ yd}^3 \\ &\approx 445.06\text{ yd}^3 \end{aligned}$$

Triangle Classification and Properties

Classifications of Triangles

A **scalene triangle** is a triangle with no congruent sides. A scalene triangle will also have three angles of different measures. The angle with the largest measure is opposite the longest side, and the angle with the smallest measure is opposite the shortest side. An **acute triangle** is a triangle whose three angles are all less than 90°. If two of the angles are equal, the acute triangle is also an **isosceles triangle**. An isosceles triangle will also have two congruent angles opposite the two congruent sides. If the three angles are all equal, the acute triangle is also an **equilateral triangle**. An equilateral triangle will also have three congruent angles, each 60°. All equilateral triangles are also acute triangles. An **obtuse triangle** is a triangle with exactly one angle greater than 90°. The other two angles may or may not be equal. If the two remaining angles are equal, the obtuse triangle is also an isosceles triangle. A **right triangle** is a triangle with exactly one angle equal to 90°. All right triangles follow the Pythagorean theorem. A right triangle can never be acute or obtuse.

The table below illustrates how each descriptor places a different restriction on the triangle:

Angles / Sides	**Acute:** All angles < 90°	**Obtuse:** One angle > 90°	**Right:** One angle = 90°
Scalene: No equal side lengths	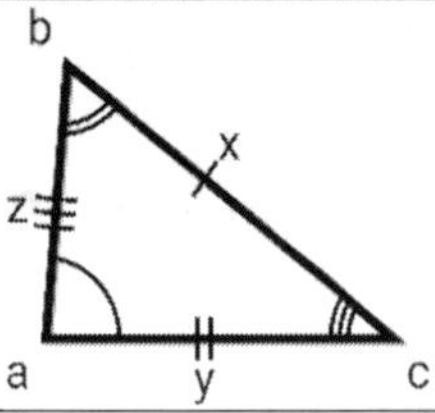 $90° > \angle a > \angle b > \angle c$ $x > y > z$	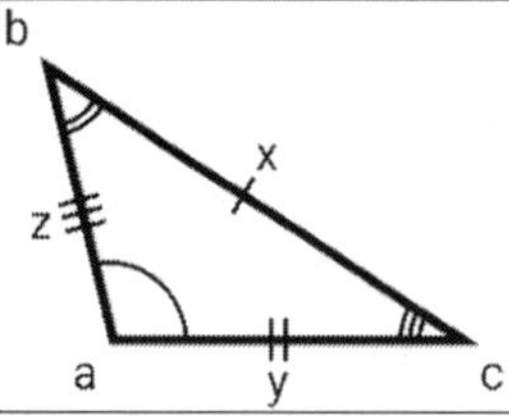 $\angle a > 90° > \angle b > \angle c$ $x > y > z$	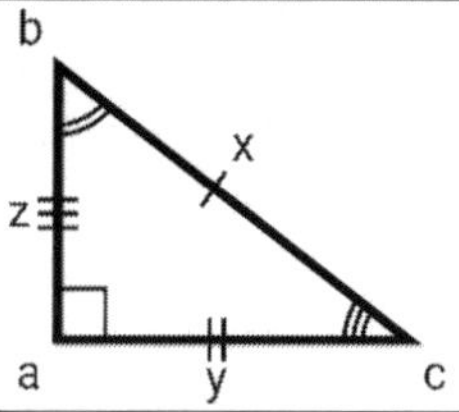 $90° = \angle a > \angle b > \angle c$ $x > y > z$
Isosceles: Two equal side lengths	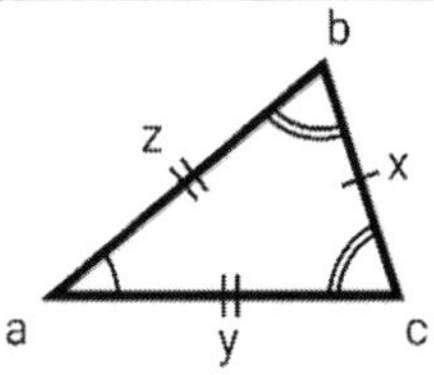 $90° > \angle a, \angle b, or\ \angle c$ $\angle b = \angle c, \quad y = z$	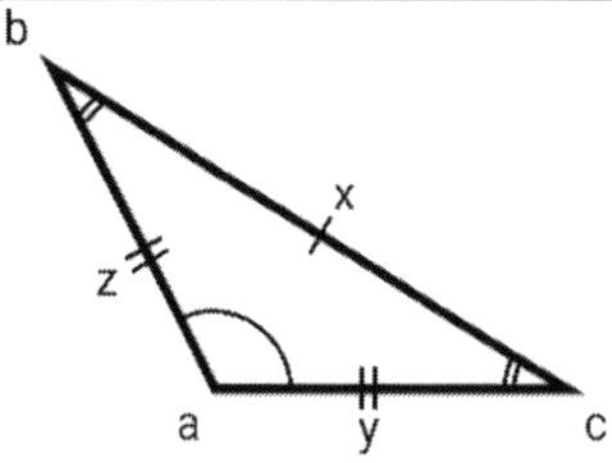 $\angle a > 90° > \angle b = \angle c$ $x > y = z$	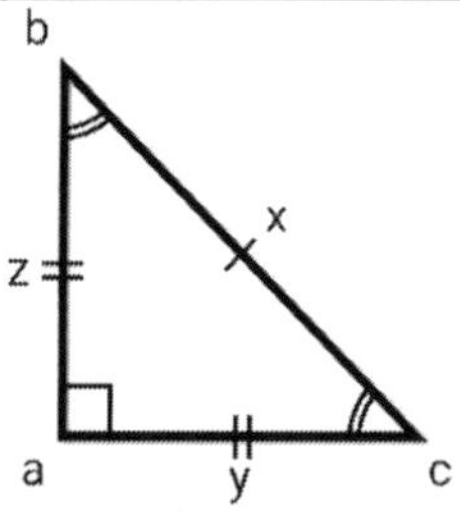 $\angle a = 90°$ $\angle b = \angle c = 45°$ $x > y = z$
Equilateral: Three equal side lengths	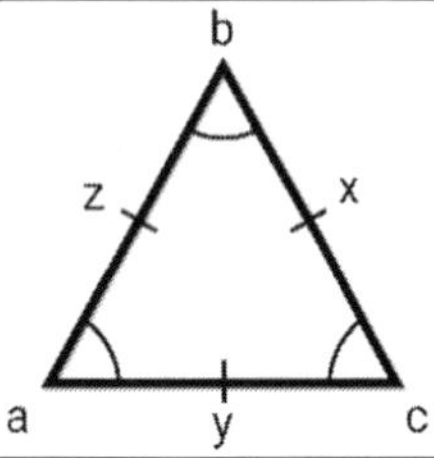 $60° = \angle a = \angle b = \angle c$ $x = y = z$		

Review Video: Introduction to Types of Triangles
Visit mometrix.com/academy and enter code: 511711

Similarity and Congruence Rules

Similar triangles are triangles whose corresponding angles are equal and whose corresponding sides are proportional. Represented by AAA. Similar triangles whose corresponding sides are congruent are also congruent triangles.

Triangles can be shown to be **congruent** in 5 ways:

- **SSS**: Three sides of one triangle are congruent to the three corresponding sides of the second triangle.
- **SAS**: Two sides and the included angle (the angle formed by those two sides) of one triangle are congruent to the corresponding two sides and included angle of the second triangle.
- **ASA**: Two angles and the included side (the side that joins the two angles) of one triangle are congruent to the corresponding two angles and included side of the second triangle.

- **AAS**: Two angles and a non-included side of one triangle are congruent to the corresponding two angles and non-included side of the second triangle.
- **HL**: The hypotenuse and leg of one right triangle are congruent to the corresponding hypotenuse and leg of the second right triangle.

Review Video: Similar Triangles
Visit mometrix.com/academy and enter code: 398538

General Rules for Triangles

The **triangle inequality theorem** states that the sum of the measures of any two sides of a triangle is always greater than the measure of the third side. If the sum of the measures of two sides were equal to the third side, a triangle would be impossible because the two sides would lie flat across the third side and there would be no vertex. If the sum of the measures of two of the sides was less than the third side, a closed figure would be impossible because the two shortest sides would never meet. In other words, for a triangle with sides lengths A, B, and C: $A + B > C$, $B + C > A$, and $A + C > B$.

The sum of the measures of the interior angles of a triangle is always 180°. Therefore, a triangle can never have more than one angle greater than or equal to 90°.

In any triangle, the angles opposite congruent sides are congruent, and the sides opposite congruent angles are congruent. The largest angle is always opposite the longest side, and the smallest angle is always opposite the shortest side.

The line segment that joins the midpoints of any two sides of a triangle is always parallel to the third side and exactly half the length of the third side.

Review Video: General Rules (Triangle Inequality Theorem)
Visit mometrix.com/academy and enter code: 166488

PRACTICE

P1. Given the following pairs of triangles, determine whether they are similar, congruent, or neither (note that the figures are not drawn to scale):

(a).

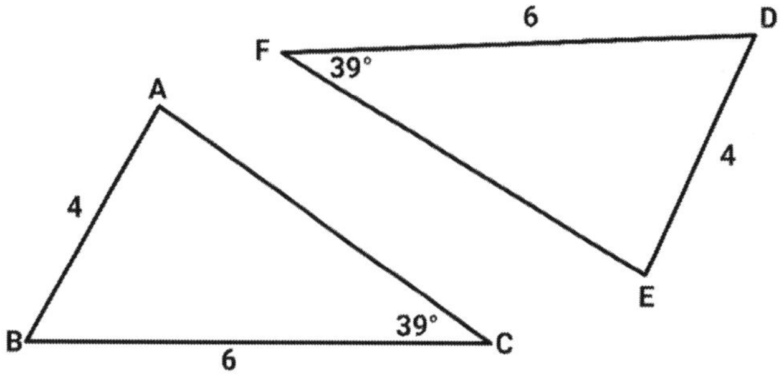

(b).

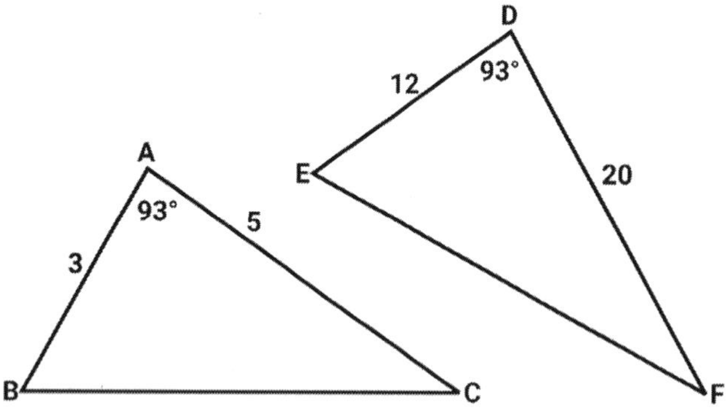

(c).

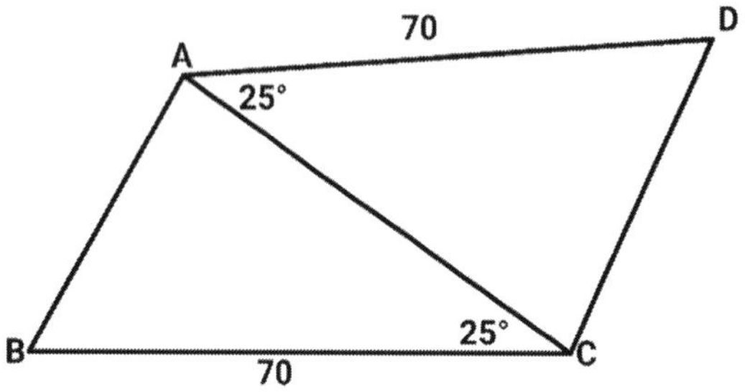

PRACTICE SOLUTIONS

P1. (a). Neither: We are given that two sides lengths and an angle are equal, however, the angle given is not between the given side lengths. That means there are two possible triangles that could satisfy the given measurements. Thus, we cannot be certain of congruence:

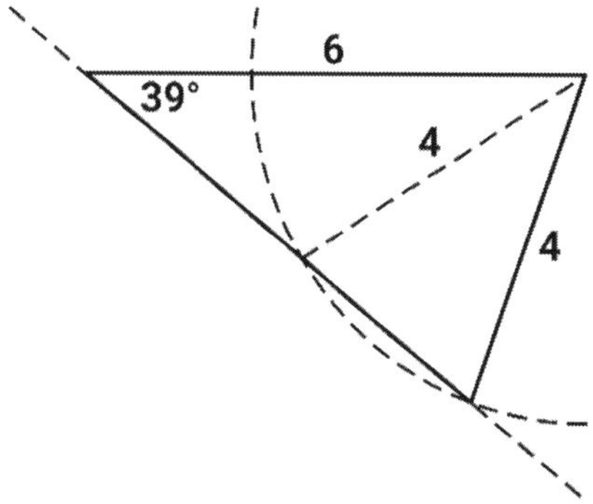

(b) Similar: Since we are given a side-angle-side of each triangle and the side lengths given are scaled evenly $\left(\frac{3}{5} \times \frac{4}{4} = \frac{12}{20}\right)$ and the angles are equal. Thus, $\Delta ABC \sim \Delta DEF$. If the side lengths were equal, then they would be congruent.

(c) Congruent: Even though we aren't given a measurement for the shared side of the figure, since it is shared it is equal. So, this is a case of SAS. Thus, $\Delta ABC \cong \Delta CDA$.

Introductory Trigonometry

Pythagorean Theorem

The side of a triangle opposite the right angle is called the **hypotenuse**. The other two sides are called the legs. The Pythagorean theorem states a relationship among the legs and hypotenuse of a right triangle: ($a^2 + b^2 = c^2$), where a and b are the lengths of the legs of a right triangle, and c is the length of the hypotenuse. Note that this formula will only work with right triangles.

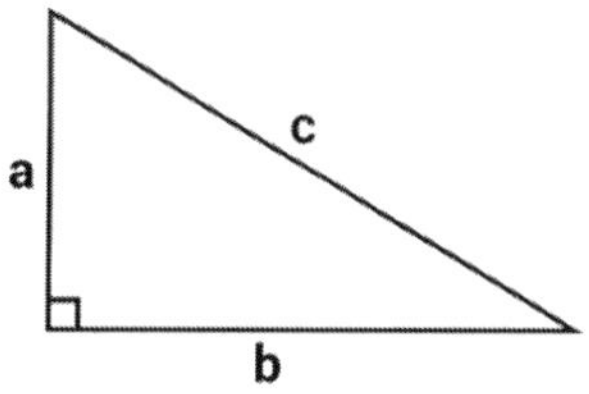

Review Video: Pythagorean Theorem
Visit mometrix.com/academy and enter code: 906576

Trigonometric Formulas

In the diagram below, angle C is the right angle, and side c is the hypotenuse. Side a is the side opposite to angle A and side b is the side opposite to angle B. Using ratios of side lengths as a means to calculate the sine, cosine, and tangent of an acute angle only works for right triangles.

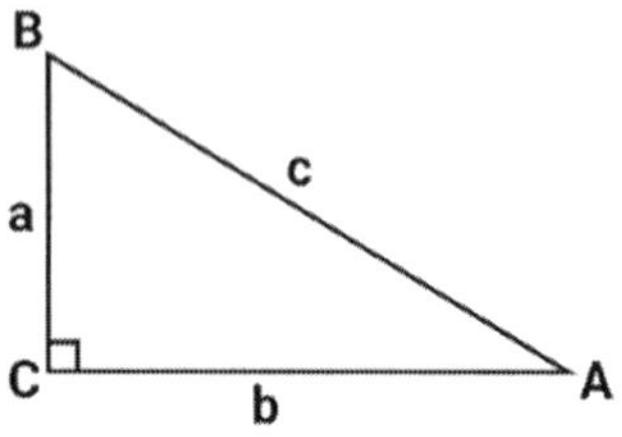

$$\sin A = \frac{\text{opposite side}}{\text{hypotenuse}} = \frac{a}{c} \qquad \csc A = \frac{1}{\sin A} = \frac{\text{hypotenuse}}{\text{opposite side}} = \frac{c}{a}$$

$$\cos A = \frac{\text{adjacent side}}{\text{hypotenuse}} = \frac{b}{c} \qquad \sec A = \frac{1}{\cos A} = \frac{\text{hypotenuse}}{\text{adjacent side}} = \frac{c}{b}$$

$$\tan A = \frac{\text{opposite side}}{\text{adjacent side}} = \frac{a}{b} \qquad \cot A = \frac{1}{\tan A} = \frac{\text{adjacent side}}{\text{opposite side}} = \frac{b}{a}$$

Laws of Sines and Cosines

The **law of sines** states that $\frac{\sin A}{a} = \frac{\sin B}{b} = \frac{\sin C}{c}$, where A, B, and C are the angles of a triangle, and a, b, and c are the sides opposite their respective angles. This formula will work with all triangles, not just right triangles.

The **law of cosines** is given by the formula $c^2 = a^2 + b^2 - 2ab(\cos C)$, where a, b, and c are the sides of a triangle, and C is the angle opposite side c. This is a generalized form of the Pythagorean theorem that can be used on any triangle.

Review Video: Law of Sines
Visit mometrix.com/academy and enter code: 206844

Review Video: Law of Cosines
Visit mometrix.com/academy and enter code: 158911

PRACTICE

P1. Calculate the following values based on triangle MNO:

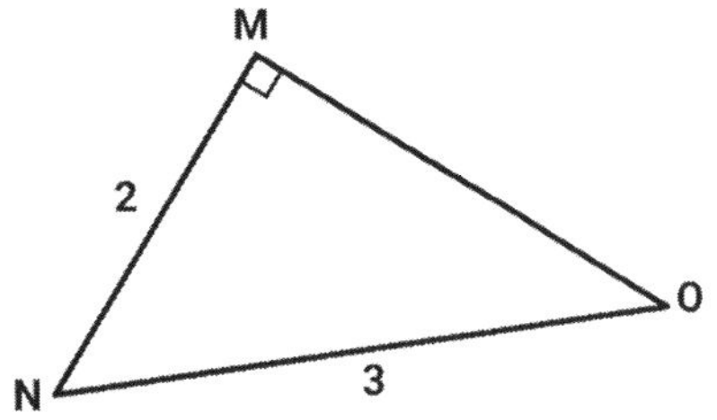

(a) length of $\overline{MO}$

(b) $\sin(\angle NOM)$

(c) area of the triangle, if the units of the measurements are in miles

PRACTICE SOLUTIONS

P1. (a) Since triangle MNO is a right triangle, we can use the simple form of Pythagoras theorem to find the missing side length:

$$\left(\overline{MO}\right)^2 + 2^2 = 3^2$$
$$\left(\overline{MO}\right)^2 = 9 - 4$$
$$\overline{MO} = \sqrt{5}$$

(b) Recall that sine of an angle in a right triangle is the ratio of the opposite side to the hypotenuse. So, $\sin(\angle NOM) = \frac{2}{3}$

(c) Since triangle MNO is a right triangle, we can use either of the legs as the height and the other as the base in the simple formula for the area of a triangle:

$$\begin{aligned} A &= \frac{bh}{2} \\ &= \frac{(2\text{ mi})(\sqrt{5}\text{ mi})}{2} \\ &= \sqrt{5}\text{ mi}^2 \end{aligned}$$

Circle Properties

ARCS

An **arc** is a portion of a circle. Specifically, an arc is the set of points between and including two points on a circle. An arc does not contain any points inside the circle. When a segment is drawn from the endpoints of an arc to the center of the circle, a sector is formed. A **minor arc** is an arc that has a measure less than 180°. A **major arc** is an arc that has a measure of at least 180°. Every minor arc has a corresponding major arc that can be found by subtracting the measure of the minor arc from 360°. A **semicircle** is an arc whose endpoints are the endpoints of the diameter of a circle. A semicircle is exactly half of a circle.

Arc length is the length of that portion of the circumference between two points on the circle. The formula for arc length is $s = \frac{\pi r\theta}{180^{\circ}}$, where s is the arc length, r is the length of the radius, and θ is the angular measure of the arc in degrees, or $s = r\theta$, where θ is the angular measure of the arc in radians (2π radians $=$ 360 degrees).

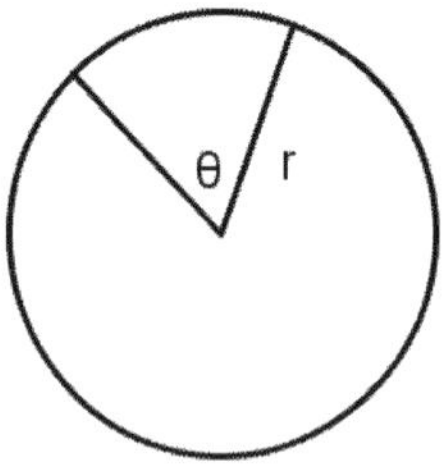

ANGLES OF CIRCLES

A **central angle** is an angle whose vertex is the center of a circle and whose legs intercept an arc of the circle. The measure of a central angle is equal to the measure of the minor arc it intercepts.

An **inscribed angle** is an angle whose vertex lies on a circle and whose legs contain chords of that circle. The portion of the circle intercepted by the legs of the angle is called the intercepted arc. The measure of the intercepted arc is exactly twice the measure of the inscribed angle. In the following diagram, angle ABC is an inscribed angle. $\widehat{AC} = 2(\text{m}\angle ABC)$.

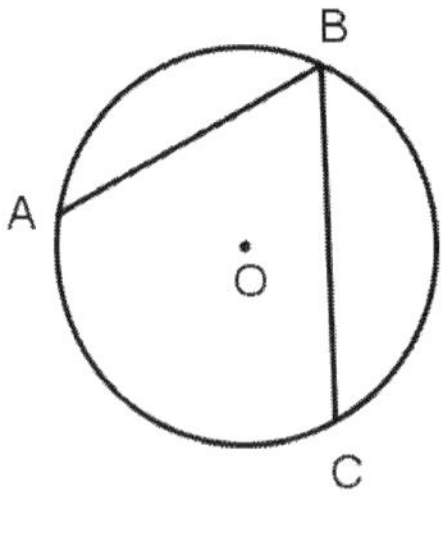

Any angle inscribed in a semicircle is a right angle. The intercepted arc is 180°, making the inscribed angle half that, or 90°. In the diagram below, angle ABC is inscribed in semicircle ABC, making angle ABC equal to 90°.

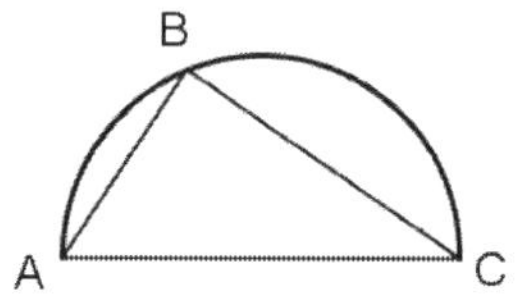

Review Video: Arcs and Angles of Circles
Visit mometrix.com/academy and enter code: 652838

SECANTS, CHORDS, AND TANGENTS

A **secant** is a line that intersects a circle in two points. The segment of a secant line that is contained within the circle is called a **chord**. Two secants may intersect inside the circle, on the circle, or outside the circle. When the two secants intersect on the circle, an inscribed angle is formed. When two secants intersect inside a circle, the measure of each of two vertical angles is equal to half the sum of the two intercepted arcs. Consider the following diagram where $\text{m}\angle AEB = \frac{1}{2}(\widehat{AB} + \widehat{CD})$ and $\text{m}\angle BEC = \frac{1}{2}(\widehat{BC} + \widehat{AD})$.

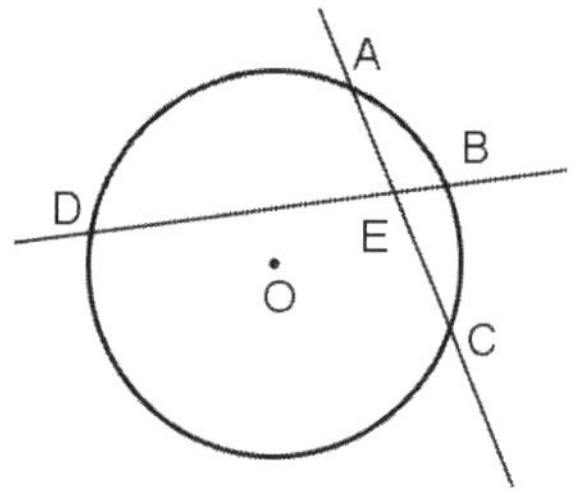

When two secants intersect outside a circle, the measure of the angle formed is equal to half the difference of the two arcs that lie between the two secants. In the diagram below, $\text{m}\angle AEB = \frac{1}{2}(\widehat{AB} - \widehat{CD})$.

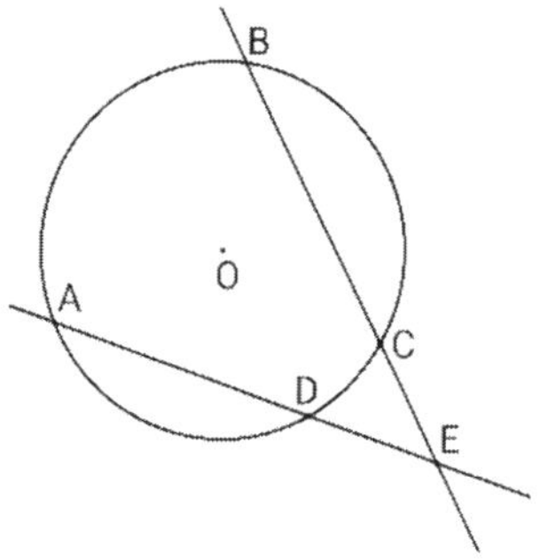

A **tangent** is a line in the same plane as a circle that touches the circle in exactly one point. The point at which a tangent touches a circle is called the **point of tangency**. While a line segment can be tangent to a circle as part of a line that is tangent, it is improper to say a tangent can be simply a line segment that touches the circle in exactly one point.

In the diagram below, $\overleftrightarrow{EB}$ is a secant and contains chord $\overline{EB}$, and $\overleftrightarrow{CD}$ is tangent to circle A. Notice that $\overline{FB}$ is not tangent to the circle. $\overline{FB}$ is a line segment that touches the circle in exactly one point, but if the segment were extended, it would touch the circle in a second point. In the diagram below, point B is the point of tangency.

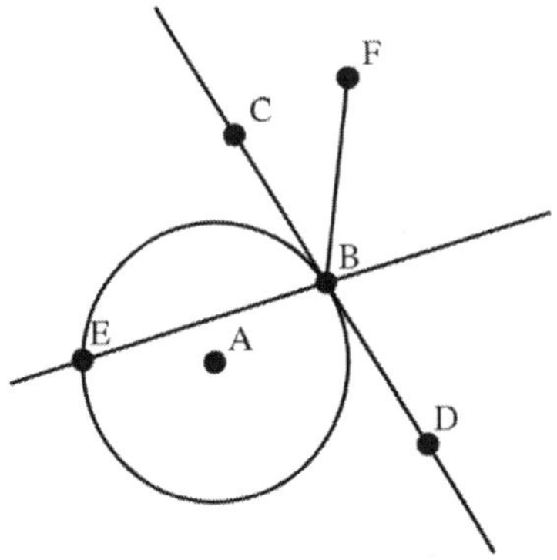

Review Video: Secants, Chords, and Tangents
Visit mometrix.com/academy and enter code: 258360

Review Video: Tangent Lines of a Circle
Visit mometrix.com/academy and enter code: 780167

Sectors

A **sector** is the portion of a circle formed by two radii and their intercepted arc. While the arc length is exclusively the points that are also on the circumference of the circle, the sector is the entire area bounded by the arc and the two radii.

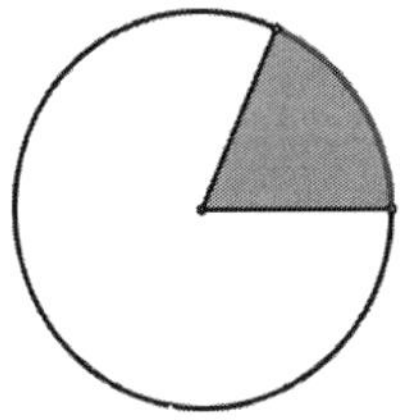

The **area of a sector** of a circle is found by the formula, $A = \frac{\theta r^2}{2}$, where A is the area, θ is the measure of the central angle in radians, and r is the radius. To find the area with the central angle in degrees, use the formula, $A = \frac{\theta \pi r^2}{360}$, where θ is the measure of the central angle and r is the radius.

PRACTICE

P1. Given that $\angle DEB = 80°$ and $\widehat{BC} = 90°$, determine the following values based on the figure:

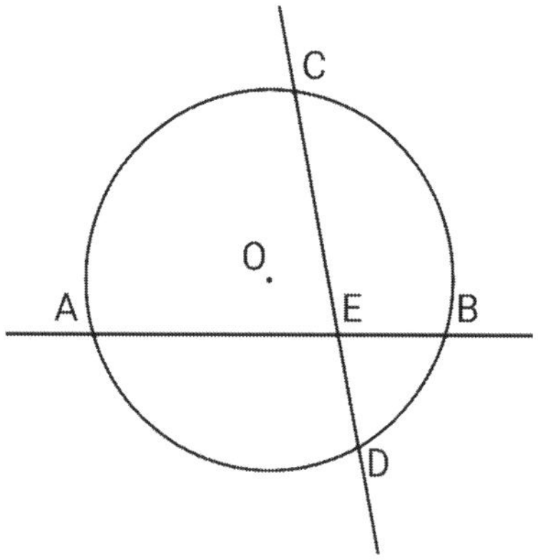

(a) $\widehat{AD}$

(b) $\widehat{DB} + \widehat{CA}$

P2. Given that $\angle OCB = 50°$, $\overleftrightarrow{EF}$ is tangent to the circle at B, and $\overline{CB} = 6$ km, determine the following values based on the figure:

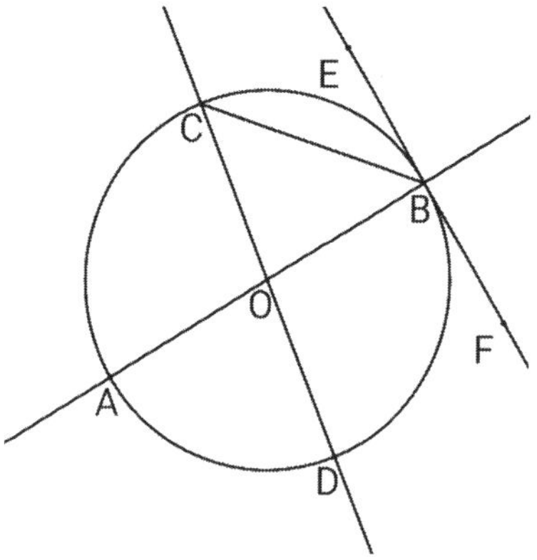

(a) The angle made between $\overleftrightarrow{CD}$ and a line tangent to the circle at A.

(b) The area of the sector of the circle between C and B.

PRACTICE SOLUTIONS

P1. (a). Recall that when two secants intersect inside of a circle, the measure of each of two vertical angles is equal to half the sum of the two intercepted arcs. Also, since $\angle DEB$ and $\angle CEB$ are supplementary, the measure of $\angle CEB = 180° - 80° = 100°$. In other words:

$$\angle CEB = \frac{1}{2}\left(\widehat{BC} + \widehat{AD}\right)$$
$$100° = \frac{1}{2}\left(90° + \widehat{AD}\right)$$
$$200° = 90° + \widehat{AD}$$
$$110° = \widehat{AD}$$

(b) Note that the whole circle is divided into four arcs. Thus,

$$\widehat{AD} + \widehat{DB} + \widehat{BC} + \widehat{CA} = 360°$$
$$110° + \widehat{DB} + 90° + \widehat{CA} = 360°$$
$$\widehat{DB} + \widehat{CA} = 160°$$

P2. (a) A line tangent to the circle at A creates a right triangle with one vertex at O, one at A, and the final vertex where $\overleftrightarrow{CD}$ intersects the tangent line, let us call that point G.

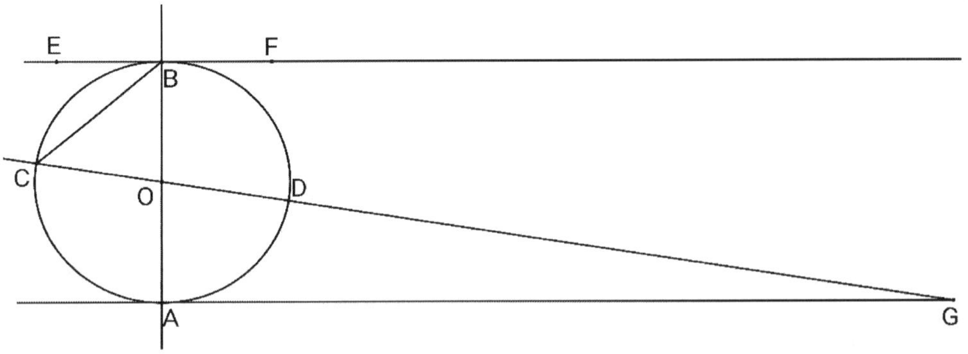

Since AB is a diameter, the line tangent at A is perpendicular to AB, so $\angle OAG = 90°$. The triangle COB has two legs that are the radius of the circle and so must be isosceles. So, $50° \times 2 + \angle COB = 180°$, which means that $\angle COB$ and the vertical angle $\angle GOA$ both equal 80°. Knowing this we can find $\angle AGO$:

$$80° + 90° + \angle AGO = 180°$$
$$\angle AGO = 10°$$

(b) We know $\angle OCB = 50°$ and that triangle COB is isosceles with two legs equal to the radius, so a perpendicular bisector of the triangle as shown will create a right triangle:

Recall that the cosine of an angle in a right triangle is the ratio of the adjacent side to the hypotenuse. Thus, we can find r:

$$\cos 50° = \frac{3}{r}$$
$$r = \frac{3}{\cos 50°}$$

As noted in part (a), $\angle COB = 80°$, so the area of the sector is:

$$
\begin{aligned}
A &= \frac{\theta \pi r^2}{360°} \\
&= \frac{80° \pi \left(\frac{3}{\cos 50°}\right)^2}{360°} \\
&= \frac{2\pi \left(\frac{9}{\cos^2 50°}\right)}{9} \\
&= \frac{2\pi}{\cos^2 50°} \approx 15.2 \text{ km}^2
\end{aligned}
$$

Conic Sections

Conic Sections

Conic sections are a family of shapes that can be thought of as cross sections of a pair of infinite right cones stacked vertex to vertex. This is easiest to see with a visual representation:

A three-dimensional look at representative conic sections. (Note that a hyperbola intersects both cones.)

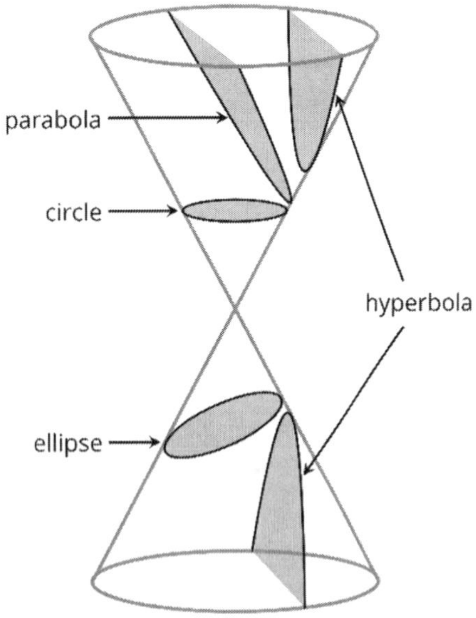

A side-on look at representative conic sections. (Note that the parabola is parallel to the slant of the cones.)

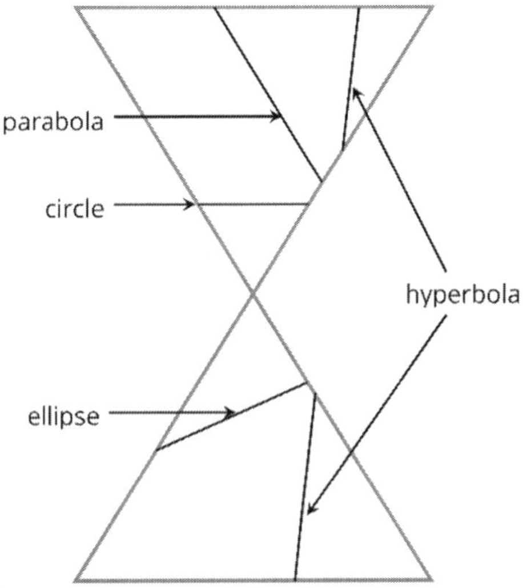

In short, a circle is a horizontal cross section, a parabola is a cross section parallel to the slant of the cone, an ellipse is a cross section at an angle *less than* the slant of the cone, and a hyperbola is a cross section at an angle *greater than* the slant of the cone.

Ellipse

An **ellipse** is the set of all points in a plane whose total distance from two fixed points called the **foci** (singular: focus) is constant, and whose center is the midpoint between the foci.

The standard equation of an ellipse that is taller than it is wide is $\frac{(x-h)^2}{a^2} + \frac{(y-k)^2}{b^2} = 1$, where a and b are coefficients. The center is the point (h, k) and the foci are the points $(h, k + c)$ and $(h, k - c)$, where $c^2 = a^2 - b^2$ and $a^2 > b^2$.

The major axis has length $2a$, and the minor axis has length $2b$.

Eccentricity (e) is a measure of how elongated an ellipse is, and is the ratio of the distance between the foci to the length of the major axis. Eccentricity will have a value between 0 and 1. The closer to 1 the eccentricity is, the closer the ellipse is to being a circle. The formula for eccentricity is $e = \frac{c}{a}$.

Review Video: Ellipse
Visit mometrix.com/academy and enter code: 703899

PARABOLA

A **parabola** is the set of all points in a plane that are equidistant from a fixed line, called the **directrix**, and a fixed point not on the line, called the **focus**. The **axis** is the line perpendicular to the directrix that passes through the focus.

For parabolas that open up or down, the standard equation is $(x-h)^2 = 4c(y-k)$, where h, c, and k are coefficients. If c is positive, the parabola opens up. If c is negative, the parabola opens down. The vertex is the point (h,k). The directrix is the line having the equation $y = -c + k$, and the focus is the point $(h, c + k)$.

For parabolas that open left or right, the standard equation is $(y-k)^2 = 4c(x-h)$, where k, c, and h are coefficients. If c is positive, the parabola opens to the right. If c is negative, the parabola opens to the left. The vertex is the point (h,k). The directrix is the line having the equation $x = -c + h$, and the focus is the point $(c + h, k)$.

Review Video: Parabolas
Visit mometrix.com/academy and enter code: 129187

HYPERBOLA

A **hyperbola** is the set of all points in a plane, whose distance from two fixed points, called foci, has a constant difference.

The standard equation of a horizontal hyperbola is $\frac{(x-h)^2}{a^2} - \frac{(y-k)^2}{b^2} = 1$, where a, b, h, and k are real numbers. The center is the point (h,k), the vertices are the points $(h+a,k)$ and $(h-a,k)$, and the foci are the points that every point on one of the parabolic curves is equidistant from. The foci are found using the formulas $(h+c,k)$ and $(h-c,k)$, where $c^2 = a^2 + b^2$. The asymptotes are two lines the graph of the hyperbola approaches but never reaches, and are given by the equations $y = \left(\frac{b}{a}\right)(x-h) + k$ and $y = -\left(\frac{b}{a}\right)(x-h) + k$.

The standard equation of a vertical hyperbola is $\frac{(y-k)^2}{a^2} - \frac{(x-h)^2}{b^2} = 1$, where a, b, k, and h are real numbers. The center is the point (h,k), the vertices are the points $(h, k+a)$ and $(h, k-a)$, and the foci are the points that every point on one of the hyperbolic curves is equidistant from and are found using the formulas $(h, k+c)$ and $(h, k-c)$, where $c^2 = a^2 + b^2$. The asymptotes are two lines the graph of the hyperbola approaches but never reaches, and are given by the equations $y = \left(\frac{a}{b}\right)(x-h) + k$ and $y = -\left(\frac{a}{b}\right)(x-h) + k$.

Review Video: Hyperbolas
Visit mometrix.com/academy and enter code: 509429

Probability

Probability

Probability is the likelihood of a certain outcome occurring for a given event. An **event** is any situation that produces a result. It could be something as simple as flipping a coin or as complex as launching a rocket. Determining the probability of an outcome for an event can be equally simple or complex. As such, there are specific terms used in the study of probability that need to be understood:

- **Compound event**—an event that involves two or more independent events (rolling a pair of dice and taking the sum)
- **Desired outcome** (or success)—an outcome that meets a particular set of criteria (a roll of 1 or 2 if we are looking for numbers less than 3)
- **Independent events**—two or more events whose outcomes do not affect one another (two coins tossed at the same time)
- **Dependent events**—two or more events whose outcomes affect one another (two cards drawn consecutively from the same deck)
- **Certain outcome**—probability of outcome is 100% or 1
- **Impossible outcome**—probability of outcome is 0% or 0
- **Mutually exclusive outcomes**—two or more outcomes whose criteria cannot all be satisfied in a single event (a coin coming up heads and tails on the same toss)
- **Random variable**—refers to all possible outcomes of a single event which may be discrete or continuous.

Review Video: Intro to Probability
Visit mometrix.com/academy and enter code: 212374

Theoretical and Experimental Probability

Theoretical probability can usually be determined without actually performing the event. The likelihood of an outcome occurring, or the probability of an outcome occurring, is given by the formula:

$$P(A) = \frac{\text{Number of acceptable outcomes}}{\text{Number of possible outcomes}}$$

Note that $P(A)$ is the probability of an outcome A occurring, and each outcome is just as likely to occur as any other outcome. If each outcome has the same probability of occurring as every other possible outcome, the outcomes are said to be equally likely to occur. The total number of acceptable outcomes must be less than or equal to the total number of possible outcomes. If the two are equal, then the outcome is certain to occur and the probability is 1. If the number of acceptable outcomes is zero, then the outcome is impossible and the probability is 0. For example, if there are 20 marbles in a bag and 5 are red, then the theoretical probability of randomly selecting a red marble is 5 out of 20, $\left(\frac{5}{20} = \frac{1}{4}, 0.25, \text{or } 25\%\right)$.

If the theoretical probability is unknown or too complicated to calculate, it can be estimated by an experimental probability. **Experimental probability**, also called empirical probability, is an estimate of the likelihood of a certain outcome based on repeated experiments or collected data. In other words, while theoretical probability is based on what *should* happen, experimental probability is based on what *has* happened. Experimental probability is calculated in the same way as theoretical probability, except that actual outcomes are used instead of possible outcomes. The more experiments performed or datapoints gathered, the better the estimate should be.

Theoretical and experimental probability do not always line up with one another. Theoretical probability says that out of 20 coin-tosses, 10 should be heads. However, if we were actually to toss 20 coins, we might record just 5 heads. This doesn't mean that our theoretical probability is incorrect; it just means that this particular experiment had results that were different from what was predicted. A practical application of empirical probability is the insurance industry. There are no set functions that define lifespan, health, or safety. Insurance companies look at factors from hundreds of thousands of individuals to find patterns that they then use to set the formulas for insurance premiums.

Review Video: Empirical Probability
Visit mometrix.com/academy and enter code: 513468

Objective and Subjective Probability

Objective probability is based on mathematical formulas and documented evidence. Examples of objective probability include raffles or lottery drawings where there is a pre-determined number of possible outcomes and a predetermined number of outcomes that correspond to an event. Other cases of objective probability include probabilities of rolling dice, flipping coins, or drawing cards. Most gambling games are based on objective probability.

In contrast, **subjective probability** is based on personal or professional feelings and judgments. Often, there is a lot of guesswork following extensive research. Areas where subjective probability is applicable include sales trends and business expenses. Attractions set admission prices based on subjective probabilities of attendance based on varying admission rates in an effort to maximize their profit.

Sample Space

The total set of all possible results of a test or experiment is called a **sample space**, or sometimes a universal sample space. The sample space, represented by one of the variables S, Ω, or U (for universal sample space) has individual elements called outcomes. Other terms for outcome that may be used interchangeably include elementary outcome, simple event, or sample point. The number of outcomes in a given sample space could be infinite or finite, and some tests may yield multiple unique sample sets. For example, tests conducted by drawing playing cards from a standard deck would have one sample space of the card values, another sample space of the card suits, and a third sample space of suit-denomination combinations. For most tests, the sample spaces considered will be finite.

An **event**, represented by the variable E, is a portion of a sample space. It may be one outcome or a group of outcomes from the same sample space. If an event occurs, then the test or experiment will generate an outcome that satisfies the requirement of that event. For example, given a standard deck of 52 playing cards as the sample space, and defining the event as the collection of face cards, then the event will occur if the card drawn is a J, Q, or K. If any other card is drawn, the event is said to have not occurred.

For every sample space, each possible outcome has a specific likelihood, or probability, that it will occur. The probability measure, also called the **distribution**, is a function that assigns a real number probability, from zero to one, to each outcome. For a probability measure to be accurate, every outcome must have a real number probability measure that is greater than or equal to zero and less than or equal to one. Also, the probability measure of the sample space must equal one, and the probability measure of the union of multiple outcomes must equal the sum of the individual probability measures.

Probabilities of events are expressed as real numbers from zero to one. They give a numerical value to the chance that a particular event will occur. The probability of an event occurring is the sum of the probabilities of the individual elements of that event. For example, in a standard deck of 52 playing cards as the sample space and the collection of face cards as the event, the probability of drawing a specific face card is $\frac{1}{52} = 0.019$, but the probability of drawing any one of the twelve face cards is $12(0.019) = 0.228$. Note that rounding of numbers can generate different results. If you multiplied 12 by the fraction $\frac{1}{52}$ before converting to a decimal, you would get the answer $\frac{12}{52} = 0.231$.

Tree Diagram

For a simple sample space, possible outcomes may be determined by using a **tree diagram** or an organized chart. In either case, you can easily draw or list out the possible outcomes. For example, to determine all the possible ways three objects can be ordered, you can draw a tree diagram:

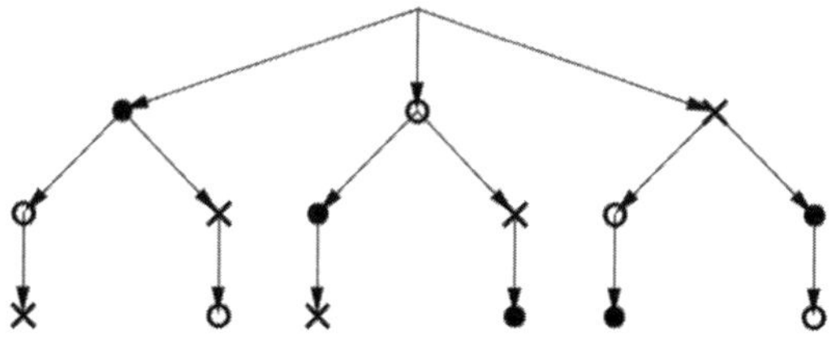

Review Video: Tree Diagrams
Visit mometrix.com/academy and enter code: 829158

You can also make a chart to list all the possibilities:

First object	Second object	Third object
●	x	o
●	o	x
0	●	x
o	x	●
x	●	o
x	o	●

Either way, you can easily see there are six possible ways the three objects can be ordered.

If two events have no outcomes in common, they are said to be **mutually exclusive**. For example, in a standard deck of 52 playing cards, the event of all card suits is mutually exclusive to the event of all card values. If two events have no bearing on each other so that one event occurring has no influence on the probability of another event occurring, the two events are said to be independent. For example, rolling a standard six-sided die multiple times does not change that probability that a particular number will be rolled from one roll to the next. If the outcome of one event does affect the probability of the second event, the two events are said to be dependent. For example, if cards are drawn from a deck, the probability of drawing an ace after an ace has been drawn is different than the probability of drawing an ace if no ace (or no other card, for that matter) has been drawn.

In probability, the **odds in favor of an event** are the number of times the event will occur compared to the number of times the event will not occur. To calculate the odds in favor of an event, use the formula $\frac{P(A)}{1-P(A)}$, where $P(A)$ is the probability that the event will occur. Many times, odds in favor is given as a ratio in the form $\frac{a}{b}$ or $a:b$, where a is the probability of the event occurring and b is the complement of the event, the probability of the event not occurring. If the odds in favor are given as 2:5, that means that you can expect the event to occur two times for every 5 times that it does not occur. In other words, the probability that the event will occur is $\frac{2}{2+5} = \frac{2}{7}$.

In probability, the **odds against an event** are the number of times the event will not occur compared to the number of times the event will occur. To calculate the odds against an event, use the formula $\frac{1-P(A)}{P(A)}$, where $P(A)$ is the probability that the event will occur. Many times, odds against is given as a ratio in the form $\frac{b}{a}$ or $b:a$, where b is the probability the event will not occur (the complement of the event) and a is the probability the event will occur. If the odds against an event are given as 3:1, that means that you can expect the event to not occur 3 times for every one time it does occur. In other words, 3 out of every 4 trials will fail.

Permutations and Combinations

When trying to calculate the probability of an event using the $\frac{\text{desired outcomes}}{\text{total outcomes}}$ formula, you may frequently find that there are too many outcomes to individually count them. **Permutation** and **combination formulas** offer a shortcut to counting outcomes. A permutation is an arrangement of a specific number of a set of objects in a specific order. The number of **permutations** of r items given a set of n items can be calculated as ${}_nP_r = \frac{n!}{(n-r)!}$. Combinations are similar to permutations, except there are no restrictions regarding the order of the elements. While ABC is considered a different permutation than BCA, ABC and BCA are considered the same combination. The number of **combinations** of r items given a set of n items can be calculated as ${}_nC_r = \frac{n!}{r!(n-r)!}$ or ${}_nC_r = \frac{{}_nP_r}{r!}$.

Suppose you want to calculate how many different 5-card hands can be drawn from a deck of 52 cards. This is a combination since the order of the cards in a hand does not matter. There are 52 cards available, and 5 to be selected. Thus, the number of different hands is ${}_{52}C_5 = \frac{52!}{5! \times 47!} =$ 2,598,960.

Review Video: Probability - Permutation and Combination
Visit mometrix.com/academy and enter code: 907664

Union and Intersection of Two Sets of Outcomes

If A and B are each a set of elements or outcomes from an experiment, then the **union** (symbol $\cup$) of the two sets is the set of elements found in set A or set B. For example, if $A = \{2, 3, 4\}$ and $B = \{3, 4, 5\}$, $A \cup B = \{2, 3, 4, 5\}$. Note that the outcomes 3 and 4 appear only once in the union. For statistical events, the union is equivalent to "or"; $P(A \cup B)$ is the same thing as $P(A \text{ or } B)$. The **intersection** (symbol $\cap$) of two sets is the set of outcomes common to both sets. For the above sets

A and B, $A \cap B = \{3, 4\}$. For statistical events, the intersection is equivalent to "and"; $P(A \cap B)$ is the same thing as $P(A \text{ and } B)$. It is important to note that union and intersection operations commute. That is:

$$A \cup B = B \cup A \text{ and } A \cap B = B \cap A$$

Complement of an Event

Sometimes it may be easier to calculate the possibility of something not happening, or the **complement of an event**. Represented by the symbol $\bar{A}$, the complement of A is the probability that event A does not happen. When you know the probability of event A occurring, you can use the formula $P(\bar{A}) = 1 - P(A)$, where $P(\bar{A})$ is the probability of event A not occurring, and $P(A)$ is the probability of event A occurring.

Addition Rule

The **addition rule** for probability is used for finding the probability of a compound event. Use the formula $P(A \cup B) = P(A) + P(B) - P(A \cap B)$, where $P(A \cap B)$ is the probability of both events occurring to find the probability of a compound event. The probability of both events occurring at the same time must be subtracted to eliminate any overlap in the first two probabilities.

Conditional Probability

Given two events A and B, the **conditional probability** $P(A|B)$ is the probability that event A will occur, given that event B has occurred. The conditional probability cannot be calculated simply from $P(A)$ and $P(B)$; these probabilities alone do not give sufficient information to determine the conditional probability. It can, however, be determined if you are also given the probability of the intersection of events A and B, $P(A \cap B)$, the probability that events A and B both occur. Specifically, $P(A|B) = \frac{P(A \cap B)}{P(B)}$. For instance, suppose you have a jar containing two red marbles and two blue marbles, and you draw two marbles at random. Consider event A being the event that the first marble drawn is red, and event B being the event that the second marble drawn is blue. If we want to find the probability that B occurs given that A occurred, $P(B|A)$, then we can compute it using the fact that $P(A)$ is $\frac{1}{2}$, and $P(A \cap B)$ is $\frac{1}{3}$. (The latter may not be obvious, but may be determined by finding the product of $\frac{1}{2}$ and $\frac{2}{3}$). Therefore $P(B|A) = \frac{P(A \cap B)}{P(A)} = \frac{1/3}{1/2} = \frac{2}{3}$.

Conditional Probability in Everyday Situations

Conditional probability often arises in everyday situations in, for example, estimating the risk or benefit of certain activities. The conditional probability of having a heart attack given that you exercise daily may be smaller than the overall probability of having a heart attack. The conditional probability of having lung cancer given that you are a smoker is larger than the overall probability of having lung cancer. Note that changing the order of the conditional probability changes the meaning: the conditional probability of having lung cancer given that you are a smoker is a very different thing from the probability of being a smoker given that you have lung cancer. In an extreme case, suppose that a certain rare disease is caused only by eating a certain food, but even then, it is unlikely. Then the conditional probability of having that disease given that you eat the dangerous food is nonzero but low, but the conditional probability of having eaten that food given that you have the disease is 100%!

Review Video: Conditional Probability
Visit mometrix.com/academy and enter code: 397924

INDEPENDENCE

The conditional probability $P(A|B)$ is the probability that event A will occur given that event B occurs. If the two events are independent, we do not expect that whether or not event B occurs should have any effect on whether or not event A occurs. In other words, we expect $P(A|B) = P(A)$.

This can be proven using the usual equations for conditional probability and the joint probability of independent events. The conditional probability $P(A|B) = \frac{P(A \cap B)}{P(B)}$. If A and B are independent, then $P(A \cap B) = P(A)P(B)$. So $P(A|B) = \frac{P(A)P(B)}{P(B)} = P(A)$. By similar reasoning, if A and B are independent then $P(B|A) = P(B)$.

TWO-WAY FREQUENCY TABLES

If we have a two-way frequency table, it is generally a straightforward matter to read off the probabilities of any two events A and B, as well as the joint probability of both events occurring, $P(A \cap B)$. We can then find the conditional probability $P(A|B)$ by calculating $P(A|B) = \frac{P(A \cap B)}{P(B)}$. We could also check whether or not events are independent by verifying whether $P(A)P(B) = P(A \cap B)$.

For example, a certain store's recent T-shirt sales:

	Small	Medium	Large	Total
Blue	25	40	35	100
White	27	25	22	74
Black	8	23	15	46
Total	60	88	72	220

Suppose we want to find the conditional probability that a customer buys a black shirt (event A), given that the shirt he buys is size small (event B). From the table, the probability $P(B)$ that a customer buys a small shirt is $\frac{60}{220} = \frac{3}{11}$. The probability $P(A \cap B)$ that he buys a small, black shirt is $\frac{8}{220} = \frac{2}{55}$. The conditional probability $P(A|B)$ that he buys a black shirt, given that he buys a small shirt, is therefore $P(A|B) = \frac{2/55}{3/11} = \frac{2}{15}$.

Similarly, if we want to check whether the event a customer buys a blue shirt, A, is independent of the event that a customer buys a medium shirt, B. From the table, $P(A) = \frac{100}{220} = \frac{5}{11}$ and $P(B) = \frac{88}{220} = \frac{4}{10}$. Also, $P(A \cap B) = \frac{40}{220} = \frac{2}{11}$. Since $\left(\frac{5}{11}\right)\left(\frac{4}{10}\right) = \frac{20}{110} = \frac{2}{11}$, $P(A)P(B) = P(A \cap B)$ and these two events are indeed independent.

MULTIPLICATION RULE

The **multiplication rule** can be used to find the probability of two independent events occurring using the formula $P(A \cap B) = P(A) \times P(B)$, where $P(A \cap B)$ is the probability of two independent events occurring, $P(A)$ is the probability of the first event occurring, and $P(B)$ is the probability of the second event occurring.

The multiplication rule can also be used to find the probability of two dependent events occurring using the formula $P(A \cap B) = P(A) \times P(B|A)$, where $P(A \cap B)$ is the probability of two dependent events occurring and $P(B|A)$ is the probability of the second event occurring after the first event has already occurred.

Use a **combination of the multiplication** rule and the rule of complements to find the probability that at least one outcome of the element will occur. This is given by the general formula $P(\text{at least one event occurring}) = 1 - P(\text{no outcomes occurring})$. For example, to find the probability that at least one even number will show when a pair of dice is rolled, find the probability that two odd numbers will be rolled (no even numbers) and subtract from one. You can always use a tree diagram or make a chart to list the possible outcomes when the sample space is small, such as in the dice-rolling example, but in most cases it will be much faster to use the multiplication and complement formulas.

Review Video: Multiplication Rule
Visit mometrix.com/academy and enter code: 782598

EXPECTED VALUE

Expected value is a method of determining the expected outcome in a random situation. It is a sum of the weighted probabilities of the possible outcomes. Multiply the probability of an event occurring by the weight assigned to that probability (such as the amount of money won or lost). A practical application of the expected value is to determine whether a game of chance is really fair. If the sum of the weighted probabilities is equal to zero, the game is generally considered fair because the player has a fair chance to at least break even. If the expected value is less than zero, then players are expected to lose more than they win. For example, a lottery drawing might allow the player to choose any three-digit number, 000–999. The probability of choosing the winning number is 1:1000. If it costs \$1 to play, and a winning number receives \$500, the expected value is $\left(-\$1 \times \frac{999}{1{,}000}\right) + \left(\$499 \times \frac{1}{1{,}000}\right) = -\$0.50$. You can expect to lose on average 50 cents for every dollar you spend.

Review Video: Expected Value
Visit mometrix.com/academy and enter code: 643554

EXPECTED VALUE AND SIMULATORS

A die roll simulator will show the results of n rolls of a die. The result of each die roll may be recorded. For example, suppose a die is rolled 100 times. All results may be recorded. The numbers of 1s, 2s, 3s, 4s, 5s, and 6s, may be counted. The experimental probability of rolling each number will equal the ratio of the frequency of the rolled number to the total number of rolls. As the number of rolls increases, or approaches infinity, the experimental probability will approach the theoretical probability of $\frac{1}{6}$. Thus, the expected value for the roll of a die is shown to be $\left(1 \times \frac{1}{6}\right) + \left(2 \times \frac{1}{6}\right) + \left(3 \times \frac{1}{6}\right) + \left(4 \times \frac{1}{6}\right) + \left(5 \times \frac{1}{6}\right) + \left(6 \times \frac{1}{6}\right)$, or 3.5.

PRACTICE

P1. Determine the theoretical probability of the following events:

(a) Rolling an even number on a regular 6-sided die.

(b) Not getting a red ball when selecting one from a bag of 3 red balls, 4 black balls, and 2 green balls.

(c) Rolling a standard die and then selecting a card from a standard deck that is less than the value rolled.

P2. There is a game of chance involving a standard deck of cards that has been shuffled and then laid on a table. The player wins $10 if they can turn over 2 cards of matching color (black or red), $50 for 2 cards with matching value (A-K), and $100 for 2 cards with both matching color and value. What is the expected value of playing this game?

P3. Today, there were two food options for lunch at a local college cafeteria. Given the following survey data, what is the probability that a junior selected at random from the sample had a sandwich?

	Freshman	Sophomore	Junior	Senior
Salad	15	12	27	36
Sandwich	24	40	43	35
Nothing	42	23	23	30

PRACTICE SOLUTIONS

P1. (a). The values on the faces of a regular die are 1, 2, 3, 4, 5, and 6. Since three of these are even numbers (2, 4, 6), The probability of rolling an even number is $\frac{3}{6} = \frac{1}{2} = 0.5 = 50\%$.

(b) The bag contains a total of 9 balls, 6 of which are not red, so the probability of selecting one non-red ball would be $\frac{6}{9} = \frac{2}{3} \cong 0.667 \cong 66.7\%$.

(c) In this scenario, we need to determine how many cards could satisfy the condition for each possible value of the die roll. If a one is rolled, there is no way to achieve the desired outcome, since no cards in a standard deck are less than 1. If a two is rolled, then any of the four aces would achieve the desired result. If a three is rolled, then either an ace or a two would satisfy the condition, and so on. Note that any value on the die is equally likely to occur, meaning that the probability of each roll is $\frac{1}{6}$. Putting all this in a table can help:

Roll	Cards < Roll	Probability of Card	Probability of Event
1	-	$\frac{0}{52} = 0$	$\frac{1}{6} \times 0 = 0$
2	1	$\frac{4}{52} = \frac{1}{13}$	$\frac{1}{6} \times \frac{1}{13} = \frac{1}{78}$
3	1,2	$\frac{8}{52} = \frac{2}{13}$	$\frac{1}{6} \times \frac{2}{13} = \frac{2}{78}$
4	1,2,3	$\frac{12}{52} = \frac{3}{13}$	$\frac{1}{6} \times \frac{3}{13} = \frac{3}{78}$
5	1,2,3,4	$\frac{16}{52} = \frac{4}{13}$	$\frac{1}{6} \times \frac{4}{13} = \frac{4}{78}$
6	1,2,3,4,5	$\frac{20}{52} = \frac{5}{13}$	$\frac{1}{6} \times \frac{5}{13} = \frac{5}{78}$

Assuming that each value of the die is equally likely, then the probability of selecting a card less than the value of the die is the sum of the probabilities of each way to achieve the desired outcome: $\frac{0+1+2+3+4+5}{78} = \frac{15}{78} = \frac{5}{26} \cong 0.192 \cong 19.2\%$.

P2. First, determine the probability of each way of winning. In each case, the first card simply determines which of the remaining 51 cards in the deck correspond to a win. For the color of the cards to match, there are 25 cards remaining in the deck that match the color of the first, but one of the 25 also matches the value, so only 24 are left in this category. For the value of the cards to match, there are 3 cards remaining in the deck that match the value of the first, but one of the three also matches the color, so only 2 are left in this category. There is only one card in the deck that will match both the color and value. Finally, there are 24 cards left that don't match at all.

Now we can find the expected value of playing the game, where we multiply the value of each event by the probability it will occur and sum over all of them:

$$\$10 \times \frac{24}{51} = \$4.71$$
$$\$50 \times \frac{2}{51} = \$1.96$$
$$\$100 \times \frac{1}{51} = \$1.96$$
$$\$0 \times \frac{24}{51} = \$0$$
$$\$4.71 + \$1.96 + \$1.96 = \$8.63$$

This game therefore has an expected value of $8.63 each time you play, which means if the cost to play is less than $8.63 then you would, on average, *gain* money. However, if the cost to play is more than $8.63, then you would, on average, *lose* money.

P3. With two-way tables it is often most helpful to start by totaling the rows and columns:

	Freshman	Sophomore	Junior	Senior	Total
Salad	15	12	27	36	90
Sandwich	24	40	43	35	142
Nothing	42	23	23	30	118
Total	81	75	93	101	350

Since the question is focused on juniors, we can focus on that column. There was a total of 93 juniors surveyed and 43 of them had a sandwich for lunch. Thus, the probability that a junior selected at random had a sandwich would be $\frac{43}{93} \cong 0.462 \cong 46.2\%$.

Statistics

Statistics

Statistics is the branch of mathematics that deals with collecting, recording, interpreting, illustrating, and analyzing large amounts of **data**. The following terms are often used in the discussion of data and **statistics**:

- **Data** – the collective name for pieces of information (singular is datum)
- **Quantitative data** – measurements (such as length, mass, and speed) that provide information about quantities in numbers
- **Qualitative data** – information (such as colors, scents, tastes, and shapes) that cannot be measured using numbers
- **Discrete data** – information that can be expressed only by a specific value, such as whole or half numbers. (e.g., since people can be counted only in whole numbers, a population count would be discrete data.)
- **Continuous data** – information (such as time and temperature) that can be expressed by any value within a given range
- **Primary data** – information that has been collected directly from a survey, investigation, or experiment, such as a questionnaire or the recording of daily temperatures. (Primary data that has not yet been organized or analyzed is called **raw data**.)
- **Secondary data** – information that has been collected, sorted, and processed by the researcher
- **Ordinal data** – information that can be placed in numerical order, such as age or weight
- **Nominal data** – information that *cannot* be placed in numerical order, such as names or places

Data Collection

Population

In statistics, the **population** is the entire collection of people, plants, etc., that data can be collected from. For example, a study to determine how well students in local schools perform on a standardized test would have a population of all the students enrolled in those schools, although a study may include just a small sample of students from each school. A **parameter** is a numerical value that gives information about the population, such as the mean, median, mode, or standard deviation. Remember that the symbol for the mean of a population is μ and the symbol for the standard deviation of a population is σ.

Sample

A **sample** is a portion of the entire population. Whereas a parameter helped describe the population, a **statistic** is a numerical value that gives information about the sample, such as mean, median, mode, or standard deviation. Keep in mind that the symbols for mean and standard deviation are different when they are referring to a sample rather than the entire population. For a sample, the symbol for mean is $\bar{x}$ and the symbol for standard deviation is s. The mean and standard deviation of a sample may or may not be identical to that of the entire population due to a sample only being a subset of the population. However, if the sample is random and large enough, statistically significant values can be attained. Samples are generally used when the population is too large to justify including every element or when acquiring data for the entire population is impossible.

Inferential Statistics

Inferential statistics is the branch of statistics that uses samples to make predictions about an entire population. This type of statistic is often seen in political polls, where a sample of the population is questioned about a particular topic or politician to gain an understanding of the attitudes of the entire population of the country. Often, exit polls are conducted on election days using this method. Inferential statistics can have a large margin of error if you do not have a valid sample.

Sampling Distribution

Statistical values calculated from various samples of the same size make up the **sampling distribution**. For example, if several samples of identical size are randomly selected from a large population and then the mean of each sample is calculated, the distribution of values of the means would be a sampling distribution.

The **sampling distribution of the mean** is the distribution of the sample mean, $\bar{x}$, derived from random samples of a given size. It has three important characteristics. First, the mean of the sampling distribution of the mean is equal to the mean of the population that was sampled. Second, assuming the standard deviation is non-zero, the standard deviation of the sampling distribution of the mean equals the standard deviation of the sampled population divided by the square root of the sample size. This is sometimes called the standard error. Finally, as the sample size gets larger, the sampling distribution of the mean gets closer to a normal distribution via the central limit theorem.

Survey Study

A **survey study** is a method of gathering information from a small group in an attempt to gain enough information to make accurate general assumptions about the population. Once a survey study is completed, the results are then put into a summary report.

Survey studies are generally in the format of surveys, interviews, or questionnaires as part of an effort to find opinions of a particular group or to find facts about a group.

It is important to note that the findings from a survey study are only as accurate as the sample chosen from the population.

Correlational Studies

Correlational studies seek to determine how much one variable is affected by changes in a second variable. For example, correlational studies may look for a relationship between the amount of time a student spends studying for a test and the grade that student earned on the test or between student scores on college admissions tests and student grades in college.

It is important to note that correlational studies cannot show a cause and effect, but rather can show only that two variables are or are not potentially correlated.

Experimental Studies

Experimental studies take correlational studies one step farther, in that they attempt to prove or disprove a cause-and-effect relationship. These studies are performed by conducting a series of experiments to test the hypothesis. For a study to be scientifically accurate, it must have both an experimental group that receives the specified treatment and a control group that does not get the treatment. This is the type of study pharmaceutical companies do as part of drug trials for new medications. Experimental studies are only valid when the proper scientific method has been followed. In other words, the experiment must be well-planned and executed without bias in the testing process, all subjects must be selected at random, and the process of determining which subject is in which of the two groups must also be completely random.

Observational Studies

Observational studies are the opposite of experimental studies. In observational studies, the tester cannot change or in any way control all of the variables in the test. For example, a study to determine which gender does better in math classes in school is strictly observational. You cannot change a person's gender, and you cannot change the subject being studied. The big downfall of observational studies is that you have no way of proving a cause-and-effect relationship because you cannot control outside influences. Events outside of school can influence a student's performance in school, and observational studies cannot take that into consideration.

Random Samples

For most studies, a **random sample** is necessary to produce valid results. Random samples should not have any particular influence to cause sampled subjects to behave one way or another. The goal is for the random sample to be a **representative sample**, or a sample whose characteristics give an accurate picture of the characteristics of the entire population. To accomplish this, you must make sure you have a proper **sample size**, or an appropriate number of elements in the sample.

Biases

In statistical studies, biases must be avoided. **Bias** is an error that causes the study to favor one set of results over another. For example, if a survey to determine how the country views the president's job performance only speaks to registered voters in the president's party, the results will be skewed because a disproportionately large number of responders would tend to show approval, while a disproportionately large number of people in the opposite party would tend to express disapproval. **Extraneous variables** are, as the name implies, outside influences that can affect the outcome of a study. They are not always avoidable but could trigger bias in the result.

Statistical Analysis

Measures of Central Tendency

A **measure of central tendency** is a statistical value that gives a reasonable estimate for the center of a group of data. There are several different ways of describing the measure of central tendency. Each one has a unique way it is calculated, and each one gives a slightly different perspective on the data set. Whenever you give a measure of central tendency, always make sure the units are the same. If the data has different units, such as hours, minutes, and seconds, convert all the data to the same unit, and use the same unit in the measure of central tendency. If no units are given in the data, do not give units for the measure of central tendency.

Mean

The **statistical mean** of a group of data is the same as the arithmetic average of that group. To find the mean of a set of data, first convert each value to the same units, if necessary. Then find the sum of all the values, and count the total number of data values, making sure you take into consideration each individual value. If a value appears more than once, count it more than once. Divide the sum of the values by the total number of values and apply the units, if any. Note that the mean does not have to be one of the data values in the set, and may not divide evenly.

$$\text{mean} = \frac{\text{sum of the data values}}{\text{quantity of data values}}$$

For instance, the mean of the data set {88, 72, 61, 90, 97, 68, 88, 79, 86, 93, 97, 71, 80, 84, 89} would be the sum of the fifteen numbers divided by 15:

$$\frac{88 + 72 + 61 + 90 + 97 + 68 + 88 + 79 + 86 + 93 + 97 + 71 + 80 + 84 + 88}{15} = \frac{1242}{15} = 82.8$$

While the mean is relatively easy to calculate and averages are understood by most people, the mean can be very misleading if it is used as the sole measure of central tendency. If the data set has outliers (data values that are unusually high or unusually low compared to the rest of the data values), the mean can be very distorted, especially if the data set has a small number of values. If unusually high values are countered with unusually low values, the mean is not affected as much. For example, if five of twenty students in a class get a 100 on a test, but the other 15 students have an average of 60 on the same test, the class average would appear as 70. Whenever the mean is skewed by outliers, it is always a good idea to include the median as an alternate measure of central tendency.

A **weighted mean**, or weighted average, is a mean that uses "weighted" values. The formula is weighted mean $= \frac{w_1x_1+w_2x_2+w_3x_3...+w_nx_n}{w_1+w_2+w_3+\cdots+w_n}$. Weighted values, such as $w_1, w_2, w_3, \ldots w_n$ are assigned to each member of the set $x_1, x_2, x_3, \ldots x_n$. When calculating the weighted mean, make sure a weight value for each member of the set is used.

Review Video: All About Averages
Visit mometrix.com/academy and enter code: 176521

Median

The **statistical median** is the value in the middle of the set of data. To find the median, list all data values in order from smallest to largest or from largest to smallest. Any value that is repeated in the set must be listed the number of times it appears. If there are an odd number of data values, the median is the value in the middle of the list. If there is an even number of data values, the median is the arithmetic mean of the two middle values.

For example, the median of the data set {88, 72, 61, 90, 97, 68, 88, 79, 86, 93, 97, 71, 80, 84, 88} is 86 since the ordered set is {61, 68, 71, 72, 79, 80, 84, **86**, 88, 88, 88, 90, 93, 97, 97}.

The big disadvantage of using the median as a measure of central tendency is that is relies solely on a value's relative size as compared to the other values in the set. When the individual values in a set of data are evenly dispersed, the median can be an accurate tool. However, if there is a group of rather large values or a group of rather small values that are not offset by a different group of values, the information that can be inferred from the median may not be accurate because the distribution of values is skewed.

Mode

The **statistical mode** is the data value that occurs the greatest number of times in the data set. It is possible to have exactly one mode, more than one mode, or no mode. To find the mode of a set of data, arrange the data like you do to find the median (all values in order, listing all multiples of data values). Count the number of times each value appears in the data set. If all values appear an equal number of times, there is no mode. If one value appears more than any other value, that value is the mode. If two or more values appear the same number of times, but there are other values that appear fewer times and no values that appear more times, all of those values are the modes.

For example, the mode of the data set {**88**, 72, 61, 90, 97, 68, **88**, 79, 86, 93, 97, 71, 80, 84, **88**} is 88.

The main disadvantage of the mode is that the values of the other data in the set have no bearing on the mode. The mode may be the largest value, the smallest value, or a value anywhere in between in the set. The mode only tells which value or values, if any, occurred the greatest number of times. It does not give any suggestions about the remaining values in the set.

Review Video: Mean, Median, and Mode
Visit mometrix.com/academy and enter code: 286207

Dispersion

A **measure of dispersion** is a single value that helps to "interpret" the measure of central tendency by providing more information about how the data values in the set are distributed about the measure of central tendency. The measure of dispersion helps to eliminate or reduce the disadvantages of using the mean, median, or mode as a single measure of central tendency, and give a more accurate picture of the dataset as a whole. To have a measure of dispersion, you must know or calculate the range, standard deviation, or variance of the data set.

Range

The **range** of a set of data is the difference between the greatest and lowest values of the data in the set. To calculate the range, you must first make sure the units for all data values are the same, and then identify the greatest and lowest values. If there are multiple data values that are equal for the highest or lowest, just use one of the values in the formula. Write the answer with the same units as the data values you used to do the calculations.

Review Video: Statistical Range
Visit mometrix.com/academy and enter code: 778541

Sample Standard Deviation

Standard deviation is a measure of dispersion that compares all the data values in the set to the mean of the set to give a more accurate picture. To find the **standard deviation of a sample**, use the formula

$$s = \sqrt{\frac{\sum_{i=1}^{n}(x_i - \bar{x})^2}{n-1}}$$

Note that s is the standard deviation of a sample, x_i represents the individual values in the data set, $\bar{x}$ is the mean of the data values in the set, and n is the number of data values in the set. The higher the value of the standard deviation is, the greater the variance of the data values from the mean. The units associated with the standard deviation are the same as the units of the data values.

Review Video: Standard Deviation
Visit mometrix.com/academy and enter code: 419469

Sample Variance

The **variance of a sample** is the square of the sample standard deviation (denoted s^2). While the mean of a set of data gives the average of the set and gives information about where a specific data value lies in relation to the average, the variance of the sample gives information about the degree to which the data values are spread out and tells you how close an individual value is to the average compared to the other values. The units associated with variance are the same as the units of the data values squared.

Percentile

Percentiles and quartiles are other methods of describing data within a set. **Percentiles** tell what percentage of the data in the set fall below a specific point. For example, achievement test scores are often given in percentiles. A score at the 80th percentile is one which is equal to or higher than 80 percent of the scores in the set. In other words, 80 percent of the scores were lower than that score.

Quartiles are percentile groups that make up quarter sections of the data set. The first quartile is the 25th percentile. The second quartile is the 50th percentile; this is also the median of the dataset. The third quartile is the 75th percentile.

Skewness

Skewness is a way to describe the symmetry or asymmetry of the distribution of values in a dataset. If the distribution of values is symmetrical, there is no skew. In general the closer the mean of a data set is to the median of the data set, the less skew there is. Generally, if the mean is to the right of the median, the data set is *positively skewed*, or right-skewed, and if the mean is to the left of the median, the data set is *negatively skewed*, or left-skewed. However, this rule of thumb is not infallible. When the data values are graphed on a curve, a set with no skew will be a perfect bell curve.

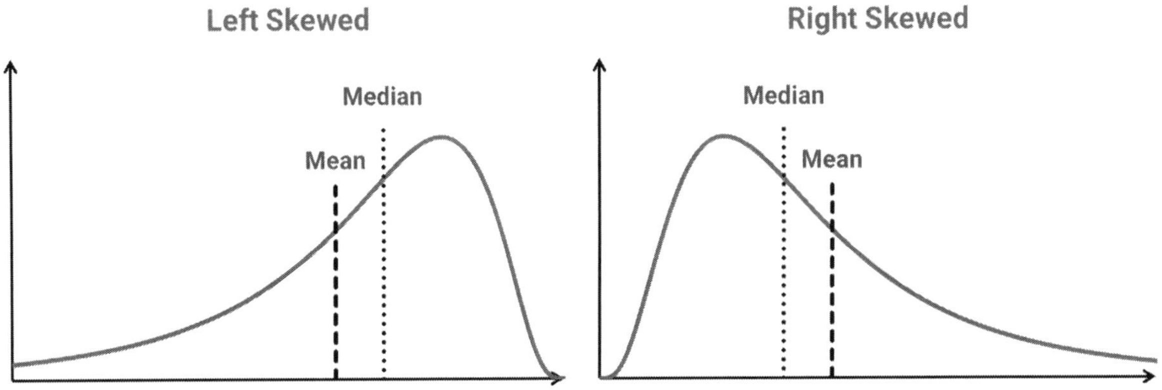

To estimate skew, use the formula:

$$\text{skew} = \frac{\sqrt{n(n-1)}}{n-2}\left(\frac{\frac{1}{n}\sum_{i=1}^{n}(x_i-\bar{x})^3}{\left(\frac{1}{n}\sum_{i=1}^{n}(x_i-\bar{x})^2\right)^{\frac{3}{2}}}\right)$$

Note that n is the datapoints in the set, x_i is the ith value in the set, and $\bar{x}$ is the mean of the set.

Review Video: Skew
Visit mometrix.com/academy and enter code: 661486

Unimodal vs. Bimodal

If a distribution has a single peak, it would be considered **unimodal**. If it has two discernible peaks it would be considered **bimodal**. Bimodal distributions may be an indication that the set of data being considered is actually the combination of two sets of data with significant differences. A **uniform distribution** is a distribution in which there is *no distinct peak or variation* in the data. No values or ranges are particularly more common than any other values or ranges.

Outlier

An outlier is an extremely high or extremely low value in the data set. It may be the result of measurement error, in which case, the outlier is not a valid member of the data set. However, it may also be a valid member of the distribution. Unless a measurement error is identified, the experimenter cannot know for certain if an outlier is or is not a member of the distribution. There are arbitrary methods that can be employed to designate an extreme value as an outlier. One method designates an outlier (or possible outlier) to be any value less than $Q_1 - 1.5(IQR)$ or any value greater than $Q_3 + 1.5(IQR)$.

Data Analysis

Simple Regression

In statistics, **simple regression** is using an equation to represent a relation between independent and dependent variables. The independent variable is also referred to as the explanatory variable or the predictor and is generally represented by the variable x in the equation. The dependent variable, usually represented by the variable y, is also referred to as the response variable. The equation may be any type of function – linear, quadratic, exponential, etc. The best way to handle this task is to use the regression feature of your graphing calculator. This will easily give you the curve of best fit and provide you with the coefficients and other information you need to derive an equation.

Line of Best Fit

In a scatter plot, the **line of best fit** is the line that best shows the trends of the data. The line of best fit is given by the equation $\hat{y} = ax + b$, where a and b are the regression coefficients. The regression coefficient a is also the slope of the line of best fit, and b is also the y-coordinate of the point at which the line of best fit crosses the y-axis. Not every point on the scatter plot will be on the line of best fit. The differences between the y-values of the points in the scatter plot and the corresponding y-values according to the equation of the line of best fit are the residuals. The line of best fit is also called the least-squares regression line because it is also the line that has the lowest sum of the squares of the residuals.

Correlation Coefficient

The **correlation coefficient** is the numerical value that indicates how strong the relationship is between the two variables of a linear regression equation. A correlation coefficient of −1 is a perfect negative correlation. A correlation coefficient of +1 is a perfect positive correlation. Correlation coefficients close to −1 or +1 are very strong correlations. A correlation coefficient equal to zero indicates there is no correlation between the two variables. This test is a good indicator of whether or not the equation for the line of best fit is accurate. The formula for the correlation coefficient is

$$r = \frac{\sum_{i=1}^{n}(x_i - \bar{x})(y_i - \bar{y})}{\sqrt{\sum_{i=1}^{n}(x_i - \bar{x})^2}\sqrt{\sum_{i=1}^{n}(y_i - \bar{y})^2}}$$

where r is the correlation coefficient, n is the number of data values in the set, (x_i, y_i) is a point in the set, and $\bar{x}$ and $\bar{y}$ are the means.

Z-Score

A **z-score** is an indication of how many standard deviations a given value falls from the sample mean. To calculate a z-score, use the formula:

$$\frac{x - \bar{x}}{\sigma}$$

In this formula x is the data value, $\bar{x}$ is the mean of the sample data, and σ is the standard deviation of the population. If the z-score is positive, the data value lies above the mean. If the z-score is negative, the data value falls below the mean. These scores are useful in interpreting data such as standardized test scores, where every piece of data in the set has been counted, rather than just a small random sample. In cases where standard deviations are calculated from a random sample of the set, the z-scores will not be as accurate.

Central Limit Theorem

According to the **central limit theorem**, regardless of what the original distribution of a sample is, the distribution of the means tends to get closer and closer to a normal distribution as the sample size gets larger and larger (this is necessary because the sample is becoming more all-encompassing of the elements of the population). As the sample size gets larger, the distribution of the sample mean will approach a normal distribution with a mean of the population mean and a variance of the population variance divided by the sample size.

PRACTICE

P1. Suppose the class average on a final exam is 87, with a standard deviation of 2 points. Find the z-score of a student that got an 82.

P2. Given the following graph, determine the range of patient ages:

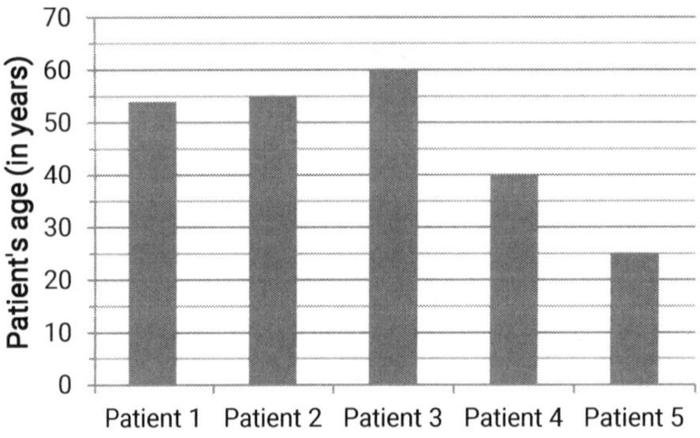

P3. Calculate the sample variance for the dataset $\{10, 13, 12, 5, 8, 18\}$

PRACTICE SOLUTIONS

P1. Using the formula for z-score: $z = \frac{82-87}{2} = -2.5$

P2. Patient 1 is 54 years old; Patient 2 is 55 years old; Patient 3 is 60 years old; Patient 4 is 40 years old; and Patient 5 is 25 years old. The range of patient ages is the age of the oldest patient minus the age of the youngest patient. In other words, $60 - 25 = 35$. The range of ages is 35 years.

P3. To find the variance, first find the mean:

$$\frac{10 + 13 + 12 + 5 + 8 + 18}{6} = \frac{66}{6} = 11$$

Now, apply the formula for sample variance:

$$\begin{aligned} s^2 &= \frac{\sum_{i=1}^{n}(x_i - \bar{x})^2}{n-1} = \frac{\sum_{i=1}^{6}(x_i - 11)^2}{6-1} \\ &= \frac{(10-11)^2 + (13-11)^2 + (12-11)^2 + (5-11)^2 + (8-11)^2 + (18-11)^2}{5} \\ &= \frac{(-1)^2 + 2^2 + 1^2 + (-6)^2 + (-3)^2 + 7^2}{5} \\ &= \frac{1 + 4 + 1 + 36 + 9 + 49}{5} \\ &= \frac{100}{5} = 20 \end{aligned}$$

Displaying Information

Frequency Tables

Frequency tables show how frequently each unique value appears in a set. A **relative frequency table** is one that shows the proportions of each unique value compared to the entire set. Relative frequencies are given as percentages; however, the total percent for a relative frequency table will not necessarily equal 100 percent due to rounding. An example of a frequency table with relative frequencies is below.

Favorite Color	Frequency	Relative Frequency
Blue	4	13%
Red	7	22%
Green	3	9%
Purple	6	19%
Cyan	12	38%

Review Video: Data Interpretation of Graphs
Visit mometrix.com/academy and enter code: 200439

Circle Graphs

Circle graphs, also known as *pie charts*, provide a visual depiction of the relationship of each type of data compared to the whole set of data. The circle graph is divided into sections by drawing radii to create central angles whose percentage of the circle is equal to the individual data's percentage of the whole set. Each 1% of data is equal to 3.6° in the circle graph. Therefore, data represented by a 90° section of the circle graph makes up 25% of the whole. When complete, a circle graph often looks like a pie cut into uneven wedges. The pie chart below shows the data from the frequency table referenced earlier where people were asked their favorite color.

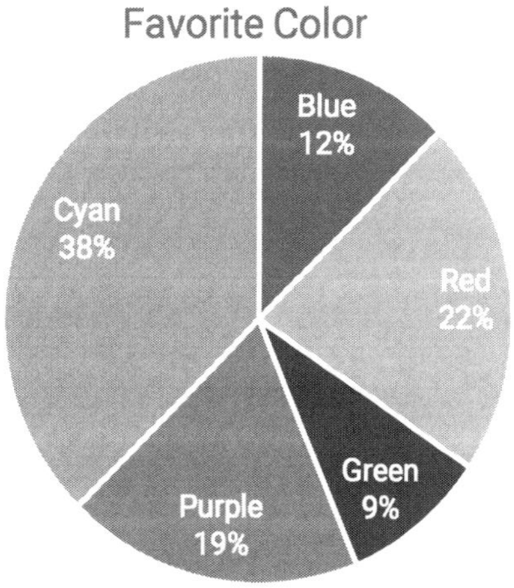

Pictographs

A **pictograph** is a graph, generally in the horizontal orientation, that uses pictures or symbols to represent the data. Each pictograph must have a key that defines the picture or symbol and gives the quantity each picture or symbol represents. Pictures or symbols on a pictograph are not always shown as whole elements. In this case, the fraction of the picture or symbol shown represents the same fraction of the quantity a whole picture or symbol stands for. For example, a row with $3\frac{1}{2}$ ears of corn, where each ear of corn represents 100 stalks of corn in a field, would equal $3\frac{1}{2} \times 100 = 350$ stalks of corn in the field.

Review Video: Pictographs
Visit mometrix.com/academy and enter code: 147860

LINE GRAPHS

Line graphs have one or more lines of varying styles (solid or broken) to show the different values for a set of data. The individual data are represented as ordered pairs, much like on a Cartesian plane. In this case, the x- and y-axes are defined in terms of their units, such as dollars or time. The individual plotted points are joined by line segments to show whether the value of the data is increasing (line sloping upward), decreasing (line sloping downward), or staying the same (horizontal line). Multiple sets of data can be graphed on the same line graph to give an easy visual comparison. An example of this would be graphing achievement test scores for different groups of students over the same time period to see which group had the greatest increase or decrease in performance from year to year (as shown below).

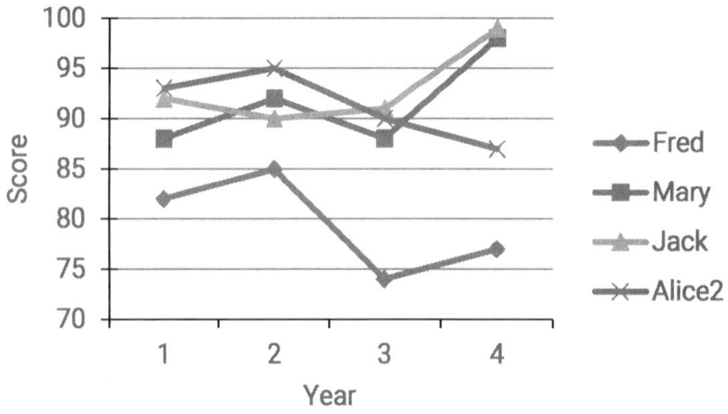

Review Video: How to Create a Line Graph
Visit mometrix.com/academy and enter code: 480147

LINE PLOTS

A **line plot**, also known as a *dot plot*, has plotted points that are not connected by line segments. In this graph, the horizontal axis lists the different possible values for the data, and the vertical axis lists the number of times the individual value occurs. A single dot is graphed for each value to show the number of times it occurs. This graph is more closely related to a bar graph than a line graph. Do not connect the dots in a line plot or it will misrepresent the data.

Review Video: Line Plot
Visit mometrix.com/academy and enter code: 754610

STEM AND LEAF PLOTS

A **stem and leaf plot** is useful for depicting groups of data that fall into a range of values. Each piece of data is separated into two parts: the first, or left, part is called the stem; the second, or right, part is called the leaf. Each stem is listed in a column from smallest to largest. Each leaf that has the common stem is listed in that stem's row from smallest to largest. For example, in a set of two-digit numbers, the digit in the tens place is the stem, and the digit in the ones place is the leaf. With a stem and leaf plot, you can easily see which subset of numbers (10s, 20s, 30s, etc.) is the largest. This information is also readily available by looking at a histogram, but a stem and leaf plot also allows you to look closer and see exactly which values fall in that range. Using a sample set of test scores (82, 88, 92, 93, 85, 90, 92, 95, 74, 88, 90, 91, 78, 87, 98, 99), we can assemble a stem and leaf plot like the one below.

Test Scores

7	4	8							
8	2	5	7	8	8				
9	0	0	1	2	2	3	5	8	9

Review Video: Stem and Leaf Plots
Visit mometrix.com/academy and enter code: 302339

Bar Graphs

A **bar graph** is one of the few graphs that can be drawn correctly in two different configurations – both horizontally and vertically. A bar graph is similar to a line plot in the way the data is organized on the graph. Both axes must have their categories defined for the graph to be useful. Rather than placing a single dot to mark the point of the data's value, a bar, or thick line, is drawn from zero to the exact value of the data, whether it is a number, percentage, or other numerical value. Longer bar lengths correspond to greater data values. To read a bar graph, read the labels for the axes to find the units being reported. Then, look where the bars end in relation to the scale given on the corresponding axis and determine the associated value.

The bar chart below represents the responses from our favorite-color survey.

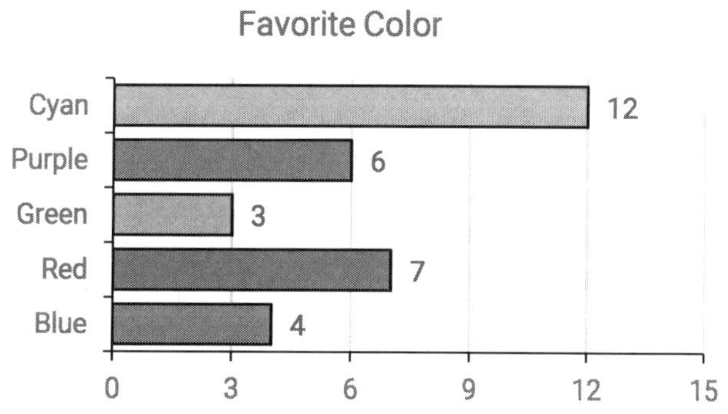

Histograms

At first glance, a **histogram** looks like a vertical bar graph. The difference is that a bar graph has a separate bar for each piece of data and a histogram has one continuous bar for each *range* of data. For example, a histogram may have one bar for the range 0–9, one bar for 10–19, etc. While a bar graph has numerical values on one axis, a histogram has numerical values on both axes. Each range is of equal size, and they are ordered left to right from lowest to highest. The height of each column on a histogram represents the number of data values within that range. Like a stem and leaf plot, a histogram makes it easy to glance at the graph and quickly determine which range has the greatest quantity of values. A simple example of a histogram is below.

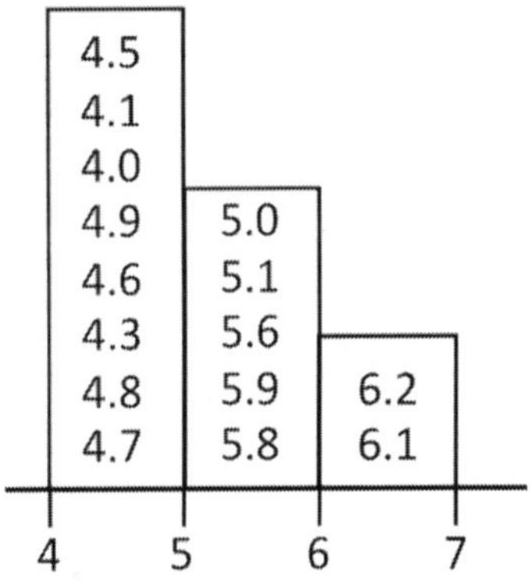

BIVARIATE DATA

Bivariate data is simply data from two different variables. (The prefix *bi-* means *two.*) In a *scatter plot*, each value in the set of data is plotted on a grid similar to a Cartesian plane, where each axis represents one of the two variables. By looking at the pattern formed by the points on the grid, you can often determine whether or not there is a relationship between the two variables, and what that relationship is, if it exists. The variables may be directly proportionate, inversely proportionate, or show no proportion at all. It may also be possible to determine if the data is linear, and if so, to find an equation to relate the two variables. The following scatter plot shows the relationship between preference for brand "A" and the age of the consumers surveyed.

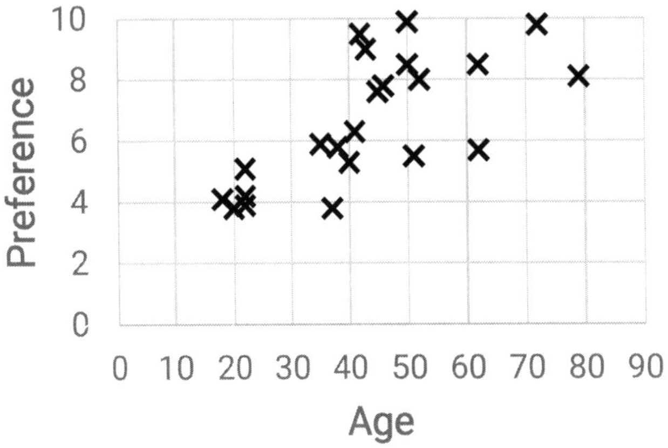

Scatter Plots

Scatter plots are also useful in determining the type of function represented by the data and finding the simple regression. Linear scatter plots may be positive or negative. Nonlinear scatter plots are generally exponential or quadratic. Below are some common types of scatter plots:

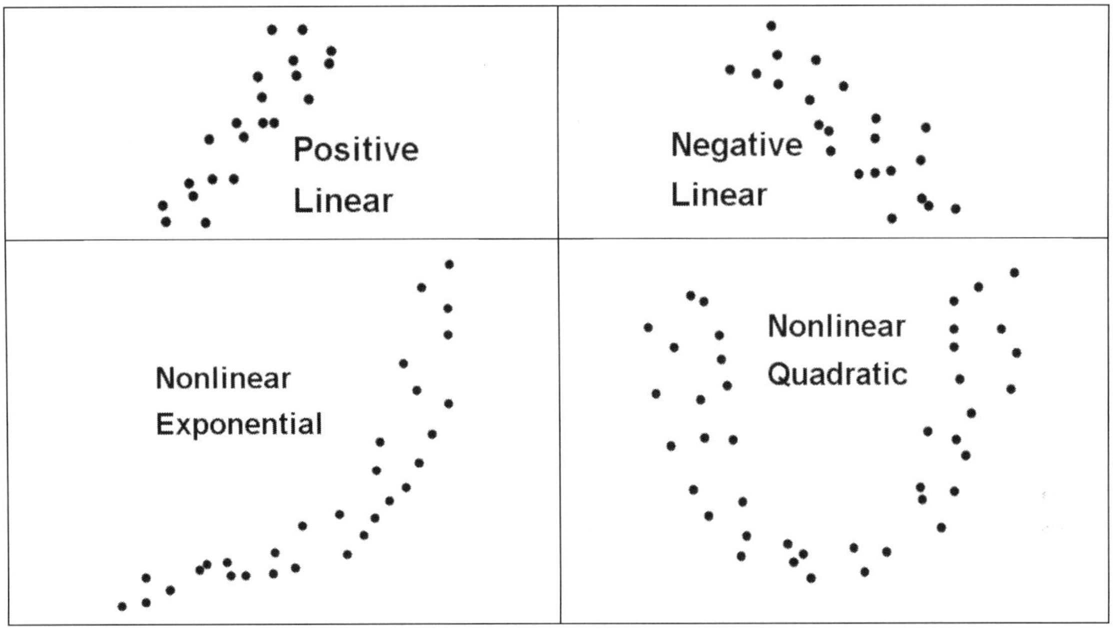

Review Video: What is a Scatter Plot?
Visit mometrix.com/academy and enter code: 596526

5-Number Summary

The **5-number summary** of a set of data gives a very informative picture of the set. The five numbers in the summary include the minimum value, maximum value, and the three quartiles. This information gives the reader the range and median of the set, as well as an indication of how the data is spread about the median.

Box and Whisker Plots

A **box-and-whiskers plot** is a graphical representation of the 5-number summary. To draw a box-and-whiskers plot, plot the points of the 5-number summary on a number line. Draw a box whose ends are through the points for the first and third quartiles. Draw a vertical line in the box through the median to divide the box in half. Draw a line segment from the first quartile point to the minimum value, and from the third quartile point to the maximum value.

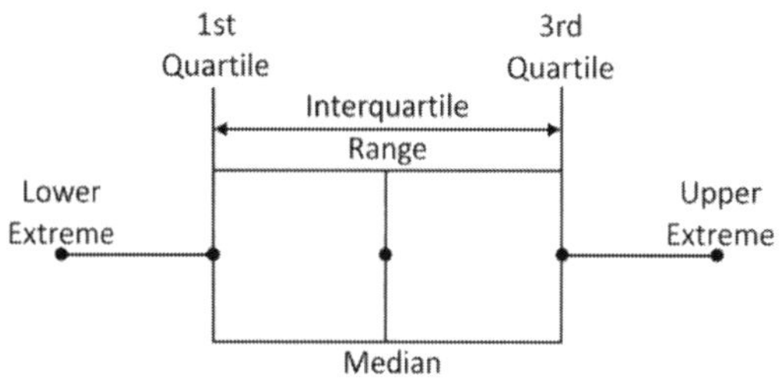

Review Video: Box and Whisker Plots
Visit mometrix.com/academy and enter code: 810817

68-95-99.7 Rule

The **68–95–99.7 rule** describes how a normal distribution of data should appear when compared to the mean. This is also a description of a normal bell curve. According to this rule, 68 percent of the data values in a normally distributed set should fall within one standard deviation of the mean (34 percent above and 34 percent below the mean), 95 percent of the data values should fall within two standard deviations of the mean (47.5 percent above and 47.5 percent below the mean), and 99.7 percent of the data values should fall within three standard deviations of the mean, again, equally distributed on either side of the mean. This means that only 0.3 percent of all data values should fall more than three standard deviations from the mean. On the graph below, the normal curve is centered on the y-axis. The x-axis labels are how many standard deviations away from the center you are. Therefore, it is easy to see how the 68-95-99.7 rule can apply.

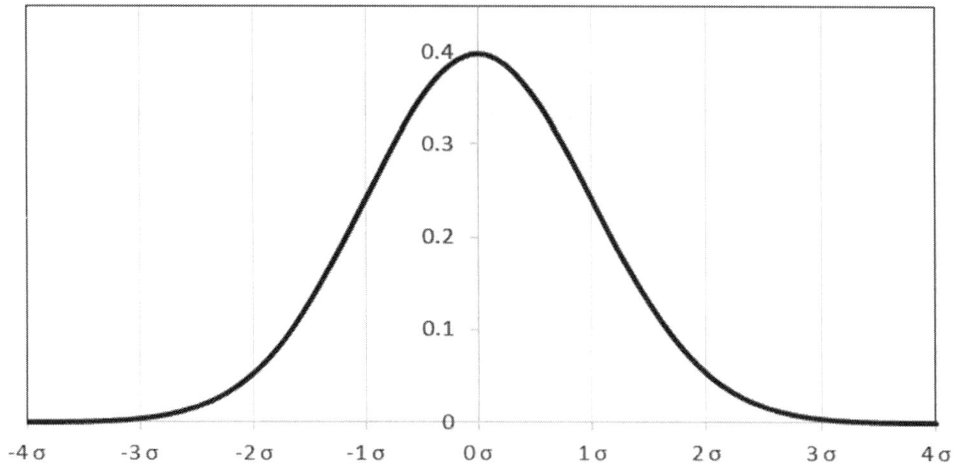

Foundations and Professional Roles and Responsibilities

Foundations and Professional Responsibilities

Individuals with Disabilities Education Act

The Individuals with Disabilities Education Act (**IDEA**) includes six major principles that focus on students' rights and the responsibilities public schools have for educating children with **disabilities**. One of the main principles of the IDEA law is to provide a **free and appropriate public education (FAPE)** suited to the individual needs of a child with a disability. This requires schools to provide special education and related services to students identified as having disabilities. Another purpose of IDEA is to require schools to provide an appropriate **evaluation** of a child with a suspected disability and an **Individualized Education Program (IEP)** for a child with a disability who qualifies under IDEA. Students with IEPs are guaranteed **least restrictive environment (LRE)**, or a guarantee that they are educated in the general education classroom as much as possible. IDEA also ensures **parent participation**, providing a role for parents as equal participants and decision makers. Lastly, **procedural safeguards** also serve to protect parents' rights to advocate for their children with disabilities.

People Protected by Parts B and C of IDEA Law

Early intervention services are provided to children with special needs from birth to age three under **IDEA Part C**. Children from birth to age 3 who are identified as having disabilities and qualify under IDEA receive **Individualized Family Service Plans (IFSPs)**.

Special education and related services are provided to children with disabilities from ages 3 to 21 under **IDEA Part B**. Children ages 3 to 21 who are identified as having disabilities and qualify under IDEA receive educational documents, called **Individualized Education Programs (IEPs)**.

Individualized Education Programs vs. Individualized Family Service Plans

IFSPs and IEPs are both educational documents provided under IDEA to service the rights of children with disabilities and their families. The major differences between IEPs and IFSPs, aside from the ages they service, is that **IFSPs** cover **broader services** for children with disabilities and their families. IFSP services are often provided in the children's homes. **IEPs** focus on special education and related services within the children's **school settings**.

Purpose of IEPs and Function of the PLOPs

An IEP is a written statement for a child with a disability. Its primary purposes are to establish **measurable annual goals** and to list the **services** needed to help the child with a disability meet the annual goals.

The IDEA law mandates that a statement of the child's academic achievement and functional performance be included within the IEP. This statement is called **Present Levels of Performance (PLOPs)**. It provides a snapshot of the student's current performance in school. Present Levels of Performance should also report how a student's disability is affecting, or not affecting, progress in school.

The IDEA law mandates that an **Annual Goals section** be provided within the IEP. Annual goals outline what a student is expected to learn within a 12-month period. These goals are influenced by the student's PLOPs and are developed using objective, measurable data based on the student's previous academic performance.

Review Video: 504 Plans and IEPs
Visit mometrix.com/academy and enter code: 881103

Child Find Law

Child Find is part of the Individuals with Disabilities Education Act (IDEA) and states that schools are legally required to find children who have **disabilities** and need **special education** or other services. According to the **Child Find law**, all school districts must have processes for identifying students who need special education and related services. Children with disabilities from birth to age 21, children who are homeschooled, and children in private schools are all covered by the Child Find law. Infants and toddlers can be identified and provided with services so that parents have the right tools in place to meet their children's needs before they enter grade school. The Child Find law does not mean that public schools need to agree to evaluate students when evaluations are requested. Schools may still refuse evaluation if school professionals do not suspect the children of having disabilities.

Steps to Implementing IEPs

The five most important steps in the **Individualized Education Program (IEP)** process are the identification via "Child Find" or the referral for special education services, evaluation, determination of eligibility, the first IEP meeting at which the IEP is written, and the ongoing provision of services during which progress is measured and reported. The referral can be initiated by a teacher, a special team in the school district, the student's parent, or another professional. The evaluation provides a snapshot of a student's background history, strengths, weaknesses, and academic, behavioral, or social needs. An IEP team of professionals as well as the student's parent(s)/guardian(s) uses the evaluation and any other reports regarding a student's progress to determine if the student is eligible for special education services. Once a student has been found eligible for special education, the first IEP meeting is held during which an IEP is written by a special education teacher or other specialist familiar with the student. The IEP meeting, either initial or annual, is held before the new IEP is implemented. Once the IEP meeting has occurred, services will be provided as detailed in the written IEP, during which the student's progress will continually be measured and reported. The IEP team includes the student, parent(s)/guardian(s), special education teacher, general education teacher, school psychologist, school administrator, appropriate related service professionals, and any other professionals or members that can comment on the student's strengths.

Manifestation Determination

Manifestation determination is a process defined by the Individuals with Disabilities Education Act (IDEA). The **manifestation determination process** is put into effect when a student receiving special education needs to be removed from the educational setting due to a suspension, expulsion or alternative placement. Manifestation determination is the process that determines if the **disciplinary action** resulted from a **manifestation of the student's disability**. This is important because if the action was a manifestation of the disability, the outcome of the disciplinary action may change. During the initial part of this process, relevant data is collected about the student and the circumstances of the offending behavior. The student's Individualized Education Program team determines whether or not the student's behavior was related to the disability. If they determine that the behavior was not related to the disability, the disciplinary action is carried out. If the behavior is determined to be related to the disability, the student is placed back into the original educational setting.

Provision of Title III of the Americans with Disabilities Act

Title III of ADA prohibits the discrimination of people with disabilities in **public accommodations**. Title III seeks to level the playing field of access for people with disabilities participating in public activities. Businesses open to the public, such as schools, restaurants, movie theaters, day care facilities, recreation facilities, doctor's offices, and restaurants, are required to comply with **ADA standards**. Additionally, commercial facilities, such as privately-owned businesses, factories, warehouses, and office buildings, are required to provide access per ADA standards. Title III of ADA outlines the general requirements of the **reasonable modifications** that businesses must provide. Title III also provides detailed, specific requirements for reasonable modifications within businesses and requires new construction and building alterations to abide by ADA regulations. Title III also outlines rules regarding **enforcement of ADA regulations**, such as the consequences for a person or persons participating in discrimination of a person with a disability. Title III provides for **certification of state laws or local building codes**. This means that a state's Assistant Attorney General may issue certification to a place of public accommodation or commercial facility that meets or exceeds the minimum requirements of Title III.

Larry P. v. Riles

The *Larry P. v. Riles* (1977) court case examined possible **cultural discrimination** of African-American students. The court case questioned whether an intelligence quotient (IQ) test was an accurate measurement of a student's true intelligence. The case argued that there was a disproportionate number of African-American students identified as needing special education services (EMR program services). The court plaintiff Larry P. argued that IQ tests were **biased** against African-American students, which resulted in their placements in limiting educational settings. The defendant Riles argued that the prevalence of African-American students in the EMR classes was due to genetics and social and environmental factors. The court ultimately ruled that the IQ tests were discriminatory and resulted in the disproportionate placement of African-American students in the EMR setting. It was determined that these particular assessments were **culturally biased**, and the students' performances would be more accurately measured using adaptive behavior assessments, diagnostic tests, observations, and other assessments.

Diana v. State Board of Education

Diana v. State Board of Education (1970) is a court case that examined the case of a student who was placed in special education after results of the Stanford Binet Intelligence test indicated she had a mild case of "mental retardation." This class-action lawsuit was developed on behalf of nine **Mexican-American children**, arguing that IQ scores were not an adequate measurement to determine special education placement in the EMR setting. The case argued that Mexican-American children might be at a disadvantage because the IQ tests were written and administered in English. This might possibly constitute **discrimination**. The plaintiffs in the case argued that IQ scores were not a valid measurement because the children might have been unable to comprehend the test written in English. In the conclusive results of this case, the court ordered children to be tested in their primary language, if it was not English. As a result of this case, IQ tests were no longer used as the sole assessments for determining **special education placement**. There was also increased focus on **cultural and linguistic diversity** in students.

Winkelman v. Parma City Board of Education

This court case began as an argument against a **free and appropriate public education** as required by the Individuals with Disabilities Education Act (IDEA). The parents of Jacob Winkelman believed their son was not provided with a FAPE in his special education setting in Parma City Schools. The disagreement became about whether or not children can be **represented by their parents** per IDEA law in federal court. The U.S Court of Appeals for the Sixth Circuit argued that IDEA protected the rights of the children and not the parents. In the end, the District Court ruled that parents could represent their children within disputes over a free and appropriate public education as constituted by IDEA. Ultimately, this settled the question of whether or not **parents have rights under IDEA**, in addition to their children. The court case determined that parents play a significant role in the education of their children on Individualized Education Programs (IEPs) and are IEP team members. Therefore, parents are entitled to litigate *pro se* for their children.

Honig v. Doe

Honig v. Doe (1998) was a Supreme Court case examining the violation of the **Education for All Handicapped Children Act** (EAHCA, an earlier version of the Individuals with Disabilities Education Act) against the California School Board. The offense occurred when a child was suspended for a violent behavior outburst that was related to his disability. The court case centered on two plaintiffs. Both were diagnosed with an Emotional Disturbance and qualified for special education under EAHCA. Following the violent incident, the school suspended the students and recommended them for expulsion. The plaintiff's case argued that the suspension/expulsion went against the **stay-put provision of EAHCA**, which states that children with disabilities must remain in their current educational placements during review proceedings unless otherwise agreed upon by both parents and educational representatives. The defendant argued that the violence of the situation marked an exception to the law. The court determined that schools are able to justify the placement removal of a student when maintaining a **safe learning environment** outweighs a student's right to a free and appropriate public education.

Pennsylvania Association for Retarded Children v. Commonwealth of Pennsylvania

The Commonwealth of Pennsylvania was accused by the Pennsylvania Association for Retarded Children (PARC 1971), now known as the Arc of Pennsylvania, of denying a **free and appropriate public education** to students with disabilities. The Commonwealth of Pennsylvania was accused of refusing to educate students who had not met the "mental age of 5." The groups argued before the District Court of the Eastern District of Pennsylvania. This case was significant because PARC was one of the first institutions in the country to challenge the **placement of students with special needs**. The plaintiffs argued that all children should and would benefit from some sort of educational instruction and training. Ultimately, this was the beginning of instituting the state requirement of a free and appropriate public education (**FAPE**) for all children in public education from ages 6–21. The Commonwealth of Pennsylvania was tasked with providing a FAPE and sufficient education and training for all eligible children receiving special education. They could no longer deny students based on their mental ages. This triggered other state institutions to make similar decisions and led to the creation of similar federal policies in the **Education for All Handicapped Children Act** (1974).

1990 Amendments to the IDEA

The **Individuals with Disabilities Education Act (IDEA)** replaced the Education for All Handicapped Children Act in 1990. IDEA amendments changed the **age range** for children to receive special education services to ages 3–21. IDEA also changed the language of the law, changing the focus onto the **individuals with disabilities** rather than the **handicapped children**. Therefore, the focus shifted from the conditions or disabilities to the individual children and their needs. IDEA amendments also **categorized** different disabilities. IDEA 1997 increased the emphasis on the individualized education plans for students with disabilities and increased parents' roles in the educational decision-making processes for their children with disabilities. Part B of the 1997 amendment provided services to children ages 3–5, mandating that their learning needs be outlined in **Individualized Education Programs** or **Individualized Family Service Plans**. Part C of IDEA provided **financial assistance** to the families of infants and toddlers with disabilities. Part C states that educational agencies must provide **early intervention services** that focus on children's developmental and medical needs, as well as the needs of their families. Part C also gives states the option to provide services to children who are at risk for developmental disabilities.

Effect of the Individuals with Disabilities Education Improvement Act of 2004 on IDEA

In 2004, the Individuals with Disabilities Education Act implemented the **Individuals with Disabilities Education Improvement Act**. IDEA was reauthorized to better meet the needs of children in special education programs and children with special needs. As a result of these changes:

- Special educators are required to achieve **Highly Qualified Teacher status** and be **certified in special education**.
- Individualized Education Programs must contain measurable **annual goals** and descriptions of how progress toward the goals will be **measured and reported**.
- Schools or agencies must provide science or research-based **interventions** as part of the evaluation process to determine if children have specific learning disabilities. This may be done in addition to assessments that measure achievement or intelligence.

The changes made to require science or research-based interventions resulted in many districts implementing **Response to Intervention procedures**. These procedures meet the IDEA 2004 requirement of providing interventions in addition to achievement reports or intelligence tests on the Individualized Education Programs for children with disabilities.

Development of Educational Laws Like Goals 2000 and No Child Left Behind

President Bill Clinton signed the **National Educational Goals Act**, also known as Goals 2000, into effect in the 1990s to trigger standardized educational reform. The act focused on **outcomes-based education** and was intended to be completed by the year 2000. The goals of this act included ensuring that children are ready to learn by the time they start school, increasing high school graduation rates, demonstration of competency by students in grades 4, 8, and 12 in core content areas, and positioning the United States as first in the world in mathematics and science achievement. Goals 2000 was withdrawn when President George W. Bush implemented the **No Child Left Behind Act (NCLB)** in 2001. NCLB also supported standards-based reform, and it mandated that states develop more **skills-based assessments**. The act emphasized state testing, annual academic progress, report cards, and increased teacher qualification standards. It also outlined changes in state funding. NCLB required schools to meet **Adequate Yearly Progress (AYP)**. AYP was measured by results of achievement tests taken by students in each school district, and consequences were implemented for school districts that missed AYP during consecutive years.

Every Student Succeeds Act of 2015

NCLB was replaced in 2015 by the Every Student Succeeds Act (**ESSA**). ESSA built upon the foundations of NCLB and emphasized **equal opportunity** for students. ESSA currently serves as the main K–12 educational law in the United States. ESSA affects students in public education, including students with disabilities. The purpose of ESSA is to provide a **quality education** for all students. It also aims to address the achievement of **disadvantaged students**, including students living in poverty, minority groups, students receiving special education services, and students with limited

English language skills. ESSA determined that states may decide educational plans as long as they follow the government's framework. ESSA also allows states to develop their own educational standards and mandates that the curriculum focus on preparing students for post-secondary educations or careers. The act requires students to be tested annually in math and reading during grades 3–8 and once in high school. Students must also be tested in science once in elementary school, middle school, and high school. **School accountability** was also mandated by ESSA. The act requires states to have plans in place for any schools that are underperforming.

ESL Rights for Students and Parents

As public schools experience an influx of English as a Second Language (ESL) students, knowledge of their **rights** becomes increasingly important. The **Every Student Succeeds Act (ESSA)** of 2015 addresses funding discrepancies for ESL students and families. ESSA allocates funds to schools and districts where low-income families comprise 40% or more of the enrollment. This is intended to assist with ESL students who are underperforming or at risk for underperforming. ESSA also provides funding for ESL students to become English proficient and find academic success. However, in order for schools and districts to receive this funding, they must avoid discrimination, track ESL student progress, assess ESL student English proficiency, and notify parents of their children's ESL status. Avoiding discrimination includes preventing the over-identification of ESL students for special education services. The referral and evaluation process must be carried out with caution to ensure that students' perceived disabilities are actual deficits and not related to their English language learning abilities.

Rehabilitation Act of 1973

The Rehabilitation Act of 1973 was the law that preceded IDEA 1975. The Rehab Act serves to protect the rights of people with disabilities in several ways.

- It protects people with disabilities against discrimination relating to **employment**.
- It provides students with disabilities equal access to the **general education curriculum** (Section 504).

Americans with Disabilities Act of 1990 (ADA)

The Americans with Disabilities Act (1990) also protects the rights of people with disabilities.

- The ADA provides **equal employment** for people with disabilities. This means employers must provide reasonable accommodations for people with disabilities in their job and work environments.
- It provides **access** for people with disabilities to both public and private places open to the public (i.e. access ramps and automatic doors).
- It provides **telecommunications access** to people with disabilities. This ensures people with hearing and speech disabilities can communicate over the telephone and Internet.

Elementary and Secondary Education Act (ESEA)

The Elementary and Secondary Education Act (ESEA) also protects the rights of people with disabilities.

- Passed by President Johnson in 1965, ESEA was part of the president's "War on Poverty." The law sought to allow **equal access to a quality education**.
- ESEA extended more funding to secondary and primary schools and emphasized high **standards and accountability**.
- This law was authorized as **No Child Left Behind** (2001) under President Bush, then reauthorized as the **Every Student Succeeds Act** (ESSA) under President Obama.

Section 504

A Section 504 Plan comes from the civil rights law, Section 504 of the Rehabilitation Act of 1973, and protects the rights of individuals with disabilities. A 504 Plan is a formal plan or blueprint for how the school will provide services to a student with a disability. This essentially removes barriers for individuals with disabilities by ensuring that **appropriate services** are provided to meet their special needs. A 504 Plan includes:

- **Accommodations**: A 504 Plan includes accommodations a student with a disability may need to be successful in a regular education classroom. For example, a student with ADHD may need to sit near the front of the room to limit distractions.
- **Related Services**: A 504 Plan includes related services, such as speech therapy or occupational therapy, a student may need to be successful in the general education classroom.
- **Modifications**: Although it is rare for a 504 Plan to include modifications, sometimes they are included. Modifications change what the student is expected to do, such as being given fewer homework assignments.

504 Plans vs. Individualized Education Programs

- A 504 Plan and an Individualized Education Program are similar in that they serve as a blueprint for a student with a disability. However, a 504 Plan serves as a blueprint for how the student will have **access to school**, whereas the IEP serves as a blueprint for a student's **special education experience**.
- A 504 Plan helps level the playing field for a student with a disability by providing services and changes to the **learning environment**. An IEP provides individualized special education and related services to meet the **unique needs of a student with a disability**. Both IEPs and 504 Plans are provided at no cost to parents.
- The 504 Plan was established under the **Rehabilitation Act of 1973** as a civil rights law. The Individualized Education Program was established under the **Individuals with Disabilities Education Act** (1975 and amended in 2004).
- Unlike an IEP, a 504 Plan does **not** have to be a planned, written document. An IEP is a **planned, written document** that includes unique annual learning goals and describes related services for the student with a disability.

Informed Parental Consent

The Individuals with Disabilities Education Act (IDEA) requires that parents be **informed** before a student is evaluated for special education services. IDEA mandates that a school district receive **parental consent** to initiate an evaluation of a student for special education services. Consent means the school district has fully informed the parent of their intentions or potential reasons for evaluation of the student. Legally, the request must be written in the parent's native language. This consent does not mean the parent gives consent for a student's placement in special education. In order for a student to be initially placed in special education or receive special education services, parental consent must be given for this issue separately. At any time, parents can withdraw consent for special education placement or special education services. Schools are able to file **due process** if they disagree with the parental withdrawal of consent. Parents also have a right to consent to parts of a student's Individualized Education Program (IEP), but not necessarily all of the IEP. Once parental consent is granted for all parts of the IEP, it can be implemented.

Tiers of the Response to Intervention Model

- **Tier 1: High Quality Classroom Instruction, Screening, and Group Interventions**: In Tier 1, all students are screened using universal screening and/or the results of statewide assessments. Students identified as at risk receive supplemental instruction. Students who make adequate progress are returned to their regular instruction. Students who do not make adequate progress move to Tier 2.
- **Tier 2: Targeted Interventions**: These interventions are designed to improve the progress of the students who did not make adequate progress in Tier 1. Targeted instruction is usually in the areas of reading and math and does not last longer than one grading period.
- **Tier 3: Intensive Interventions and Comprehensive Evaluation**: Students who are not successful in Tier 2 move on to Tier 3. They receive intensive interventions that target their specific deficits. Students who do not meet progress goals during intensive interventions are referred to receive comprehensive evaluations and are considered to be eligible for special education under IDEA.

Stakeholders in Special Education

Stakeholders that play roles in educating students with disabilities include the students, parents, general educators, administrators, and community members. Students should receive an educational **curriculum** based on strict standards, such as the Common Core Content Standards. This ensures that they receive good educational foundations from which to grow and expand upon during their school careers. Parents, legal guardians, and sometimes agencies act in the best interests of their children. If they do not think the Individualized Education Programs suit the needs of their children, they can request **due process hearings** in court. FAPE and LRE ensure that students are educated alongside peers in general education classrooms by general educators. General educators collaborate with special educators to create **successful inclusion classrooms**. When inclusion is done successfully, the students with disabilities meet their IEP goals.

Information to Be Evaluated During Multi-Factored Evaluations or Evaluation Team Reports

Multi-Factored Evaluations are processes required by the Individuals with Disabilities Education Act to determine if a student is eligible for special education. When a student is suspected of having a disability, the parent or school district can initiate the evaluation process. **Student information** that is evaluated in a Multi-Factored Evaluation includes background information, health information, vision testing, hearing testing, social and emotional development, general intelligence, past and current academic performance, communication needs, gross and fine motor abilities, results of aptitude or achievement tests, academic skills, and current progress toward Individualized Education Program (IEP) goals. Progress reporting on IEP goals is only appropriate during an annual MFE when a student has already qualified for special education services. The purpose of an MFE is to provide **comprehensive information** about a student for professionals working with the student. An MFE also helps determine what academic or behavioral **goals** or related services might be appropriate for a student with disabilities.

Free and Appropriate Public Education Components

The Individuals with Disabilities Education Act (IDEA) defines free and appropriate public education (FAPE) as an educational right for children with disabilities in the United States. FAPE stands for:

- **Free**: All students found eligible for special education services must receive free services, expensed to the public instead of the parents.
- **Appropriate**: Students are eligible for educations that are appropriate for their specific needs, as stated in their Individualized Education Programs (IEPs).
- **Public**: Students with disabilities have the right to be educated in public schools.
- **Education**: An education must be provided to any school-aged child with a disability. Education and services are defined in a student's IEP.

Ideally, FAPE components are put in place in order to guarantee the best education possible that also suits the individual needs of a student with a disability. FAPE should take place in the least restrictive environment, or the environment with the fewest barriers to learning for the individual student with a disability.

Multi-Factored Evaluation or Evaluation Team Report

A Multi-Factored Evaluation (**MFE**), sometimes referred to as an Evaluation Team Report (**ETR**), serves as a snapshot of a child's abilities, strengths, and weaknesses. An MFE is conducted to determine a student's eligibility for special education. Once a student with a disability qualifies for special education, an MFE is conducted at least every three years after the initial MFE date. MFEs are conducted for students ages 3 to 21 who are on IEPs. The purpose of the MFE is to influence a student's **Individualized Education Program**. An MFE reports on a student's **current abilities** and how the disability may affect **educational performance**. MFEs can also determine if a student qualifies for related services, such as occupational therapy or speech-language therapy. An MFE can be requested by a parent or school district when a child is suspected of having a disability. The school district typically has 30 days or less to respond to a parental request to evaluate a student, giving consent or refusal for an evaluation. While initial MFEs are conducted as a means to determine special education qualification, annual MFEs are conducted to address any changes in the needs or services of a student already receiving special education services.

Least Restrictive Environments to Deliver Special Education Services

Special education services are delivered to students that qualify with a **disability** defined by the Individuals with Disabilities Education Act (IDEA). IDEA law also requires that students who qualify for special education must receive special education services in **least restrictive environments** that provide the fewest barriers to their learning. A student's most appropriate instructional setting is written out in the **Individualized Education Program (IEP)**. Some special education instructional settings include:

- no instructional setting
- mainstream setting
- resource room
- self-contained classroom
- homebound instruction

With **no instructional setting**, students participate in the general education curriculum but may receive related services, such as speech-language therapy or occupational therapy. In the **mainstream setting**, students are instructed in the general education classroom for most or part of the day and provided with special education supports, accommodations, modifications, and related services. A **resource room** is an environment where students receive remedial instruction when they cannot participate in the general curriculum for one or more subject areas. A **self-contained classroom** is a setting for students who need special education and related services for more than 50% of the day. **Homebound instruction** is for students who are homebound or hospital bound for more than four consecutive weeks.

Purpose of Special Education

Special education is specially designed instruction delivered to meet the individual needs of children with disabilities. Special education includes a free and appropriate education in the least restrictive environment. In the past, a special education model might consist of a self-contained classroom of students with special needs whose needs were addressed in that setting. Today, students who qualify for special education must receive instruction in **free and appropriate settings**. This means they receive special education services in settings that provide the **fewest barriers** to their learning. The most appropriate setting varies, depending on the student and the disability. The purpose of special education is to ensure that the unique needs of children with disabilities are addressed. In the public school setting, the Individuals with Disabilities Education Act mandates that students with disabilities receive free and appropriate public educations. The goal of special education is to create **fair environments** for students with special needs to learn. Ideally, the settings should enable students to learn to their fullest potential.

Due Process Rights Available to Parents and Legal Guardians

When parents or legal guardians and school districts cannot agree on components of a student with a disability's Individualized Education Program (IEP), parents and legal guardians have a right to **due process**. Due process is a legal right under the Individuals with Disabilities Education Act (IDEA) that usually involves the school district violating a legal rule. Examples of these violations include a school district not running an IEP meeting, failing to conduct a tri-annual evaluation, or failing to implement a student's IEP. Disputes often involve a student's instructional placement, appropriate accommodations or modifications, related services, or changes to IEPs. School districts' due process policies vary depending on the district. IDEA, however, mandates that a **due process legal form** be completed by the parent or legal guardian in order to move forward. This form must be completed within two years of a dispute. **Mediation**, or the process of coming to an agreement before filing due process, can be a solution to the dispute. IEP meetings, even when it is not time for an annual review, are also appropriate options for resolving a dispute before filing due process.

Purpose of Mediation in Lieu of a Parent or Legal Guardian Filing for Due Process

Mediation is a process used to address a dispute prior to a parent or legal guardian filing for due process. The purpose of mediation is to **resolve a dispute** between the parent or legal guardian of a student with a disability and the school district. Disputes occur when the parent or legal guardian does not agree with an IEP component, such as what related services are provided or the way a student's IEP is being implemented. Mediation is not a parent or legal guardian's legal right, but school districts often support mediation to offset a **due process filing**. Mediation involves the attempt to resolve a dispute and includes a meeting between the parent or legal guardian, school district member, and a neutral third party, such as a mediator provided by the state. States have lists of **mediators** available for these situations. Agreements that come out of the mediation process are put into writing and, if appropriate, put into a student's IEP. Disagreements can continue to be mediated, or the decision may be made to file due process. Prior to mediation, parents or legal guardians and school districts have the option of holding IEP meetings (outside of annual meetings) to resolve disputes.

Maintaining Confidentiality and Privacy of Student Records

Similar to the Health Insurance Portability and Accountability Act of 1966 (HIPAA), **FERPA** is a law that protects privacy. However, FERPA is specific to the privacy of students. The FERPA law applies to any school or agency that receives funds from the U.S. Department of Education. This ensures that schools or agencies cannot share any confidential information about a student without a parent or student's written consent. **Student educational records** can be defined as records, files, documents, or other materials which contain a student's personal information. **Individualized Education Programs (IEPs)** and **Evaluation Team Reports (ETRs)** are examples of private documents under the FERPA law. The responsibility of a school covered by FERPA is to maintain confidentiality and privacy. The members of an IEP team, such as special educators, related service professionals, general educators, or other professionals, cannot share any identifying, private information about a student. Information addressing the needs of individual students found on an IEP, Evaluation Team Report, or other identifying document must remain confidential unless express written consent is given by the parent or legal guardian.

Pre-Referral/Referral Process for Identifying and Placing a Student with a Disability

The purpose of a pre-referral process for a child with a suspected disability is to attempt **reasonable modifications and accommodations** before the child is referred for special education services. Schools often have **pre-referral teams** whose purpose is to identify the strengths and needs of a child, put reasonable strategies into action, and evaluate the results of this pre-referral intervention. If the results do not show any change, another intervention can be attempted, or the student can be referred for a special education evaluation.

If a child is suspected of having a disability and did not succeed with pre-referral interventions, the school or parent can request an **evaluation**. During the evaluation process, the school compiles information to see if the student needs special education or related services. This information is used to determine if the student's disability is affecting school performance and if the student qualifies for special education. The evaluation lists and examines the student's strengths, weaknesses, and development and determines what supports the student needs in order to learn. An evaluation must be completed before special education services can be provided.

Role of a School Psychologist in Special Education

School psychologists are certified members of school teams that **support the needs of students and teachers**. They help students with overall academic, social, behavioral, and emotional success. School psychologists are trained in data collection and analysis, assessments, progress monitoring, risk factors, consultation and collaboration, and special education services. In special education, school psychologists may work directly with students and collaborate with teachers, administrators, parents, and other professionals working with particular students. They may also be involved in counseling students' parents, the Response to Intervention process, and performing initial evaluations of students who are referred for special education services. School psychologists also work to improve academic achievement, promote positive behavior and health by implementing school-wide programs, support learning needs of diverse learners, maintain safe school environments, and strengthen and maintain good school-parent relationships.

Overrepresentation of Students from Diverse Backgrounds

Disproportionate representation occurs when there is not an equal representation of students from different **cultural and linguistic backgrounds** identified for special education services. Students from different cultural and linguistic groups should be identified for special education services in similar proportions. This ensures that no one group is **overrepresented** and

overidentified as having special needs due to their cultural or linguistic differences. Disproportionality can occur based on a child's sex, language proficiency, receipt of free and reduced lunch, or race and ethnicity. Historically, most disproportionality has been a civil rights issue and due to a child's cultural or linguistic background. Recently, the focus has been on the disproportional number of students who spend time in special education classrooms instead of being educated alongside regularly educated peers.

The referral process, **Response to Intervention (RTI)**, provides safeguards against disproportionality. The RTI process requires instruction and intervention catered to the unique, specific needs of the individual student. The purpose of RTI is not the identification of a disability or entitlement to services. Instead, it focuses on data used to make educational decisions about individuals, classrooms, schools, or districts. Models like RTI address disproportionate representation, but they are not perfect.

Chapter Quiz

1. Which of the following states that school districts must have processes for identifying students who need special education and related services?

a. Rehabilitation Act
b. Every Student Succeeds Act
c. Elementary and Secondary Education Act
d. Child Find law

2. Which section of the Americans with Disabilities Act prohibits discrimination against people with disabilities in public accommodations?

a. Title III
b. Title IV
c. Title IX
d. Title XI

3. Which of the following cases determined that parents are entitled to litigate *pro se* for their children?

a. *Larry P. v. Riles*
b. *Honig v. Doe*
c. *Winkelman v. Parma City School District*
d. *Diana v. State Board of Education*

4. Which of the following presidents signed the Educate America Act?

a. George W. Bush
b. Barack Obama
c. Bill Clinton
d. Jimmy Carter

5. Which of the following is a formal plan or blueprint for how a school will provide services to a student with a disability?

a. 808 Plan
b. 504 Plan
c. 409 Plan
d. 911 Plan

6. Which tier of the Response to Intervention model utilizes group interventions?

a. Tier 1
b. Tier 2
c. Tier 3
d. Tier 4

7. One of the main principles of the IDEA is to provide a FAPE. What does FAPE stand for?

a. Fair Accessible Private Environment
b. Free and Appropriate Public Education
c. Fair and Accepting Public Environment
d. Free Accessible Private Education

8. The 1990 Amendment to the IDEA changed the age range for children to receive special education services to:

a. 5-25
b. 6-21
c. 5-18
d. 3-21

Chapter Quiz Answer Key

1. D: According to the Child Find law, all school districts must have processes for identifying students who need special education and related services. Children with disabilities (from birth to age 21), children who are homeschooled, and children in private schools are all covered by the Child Find law.

2. A: Title III of the Americans with Disabilities Act (ADA) prohibits discrimination against people with disabilities in public accommodations. Title III seeks to level the playing field of access for people with disabilities participating in public activities. Businesses open to the public, such as schools, restaurants, movie theaters, day care facilities, recreation facilities, doctor's offices, and restaurants, are required to comply with ADA standards. Additionally, commercial facilities, such as privately owned businesses, factories, warehouses, and office buildings, are required to provide access per ADA standards.

3. C: In *Winkelman v. Parma City School District,* the parents of Jacob Winkelman believed their son was not provided with a free and appropriate public education (FAPE) in his special education setting in Parma City Schools. The court case determined that parents play a significant role in the education of their children in Individualized Education Programs (IEPs) and are IEP team members. Therefore, parents are entitled to litigate *pro se* for their children.

4. C: President Bill Clinton signed the Educate America Act, also known as Goals 2000, into effect in the 1990s to trigger standardized educational reform. The act focused on outcomes-based education and was intended to be completed by the year 2000.

5. B: A Section 504 Plan comes from Section 504 of the Rehabilitation Act of 1973 (a civil rights law) and protects the rights of individuals with disabilities. A 504 Plan is a formal plan or blueprint for how the school will provide services to a student with a disability. This essentially removes barriers for individuals with disabilities by ensuring that appropriate services are provided to meet their special needs.

6. A: The tiers of the Response to Intervention model are:

- Tier 1: High-quality classroom instruction, screening, and group interventions. In Tier 1, all students are screened using universal screening and/or the results of statewide assessments. Students identified as at risk receive supplemental instruction. Students who make adequate progress are returned to their regular instruction. Students who do not make adequate progress move to Tier 2.
- Tier 2: Targeted interventions. These interventions are designed to improve the progress of the students who did not make adequate progress in Tier 1. Targeted instruction is usually in the areas of reading and math and does not last longer than one grading period.

- Tier 3: Intensive interventions and comprehensive evaluation. Students who are not successful in Tier 2 move on to Tier 3. They receive intensive interventions that target their specific deficits. Students who do not meet progress goals during intensive interventions are referred to receive comprehensive evaluations and are considered to be eligible for special education under the IDEA.

7. B: The Individuals with Disabilities Education Act (IDEA) includes six major principles that focus on students' rights and the responsibilities public schools have for educating children with disabilities. One of the main principles of the IDEA law is to provide a free and appropriate public education (FAPE) suited to the individual needs of a child with a disability.

8. D: The Individuals with Disabilities Education Act (IDEA) replaced the Education for All Handicapped Children Act in 1990. IDEA amendments changed the age range for children to receive special education services to ages 3–21. The IDEA also changed the language of the law, changing the focus to the individuals with disabilities rather than the "handicap[s]" of children. The focus shifted from the conditions or disabilities to the individual children and their needs.

Collaborating with the Learning Community

Collaborating with IEP Team Members

It is important for Individualized Education Program (IEP) team members to **collaborate** with each other in order to certify that students are receiving educational plans that are suitable to their needs in the least restrictive environments. **IEP team members** include special education teachers, general education teachers, parents or legal guardians, students, school district representatives, and others knowledgeable about the students' performances. Each member brings a valuable piece of information about the students for instructional planning and IEP planning meetings. It is important for special educators to establish good relationships and collaborate with the students and parents or legal guardians in order to gauge the students' strengths and weaknesses. Collaboration is essential between the general and special educators in order to ensure that students' IEP goals and needs are being met in the appropriate settings. Collaboration with district team members or others like school psychologists is helpful for gaining insight on special education procedures or assessment results.

Communicating with Related Service Members Across All Special Education Settings

In order to provide the best educations possible for students with disabilities, it is important for special educators and related service members to **communicate** effectively. Communication is important due to the degree of collaboration required between the special educators and the related service members. Related service members are often Individualized Education Program (IEP) team members and help students meet their IEP goals and objectives. **Related service members**, like speech pathologists and occupational therapists, also work on a consultation basis with special educators. They may also consult with general education teachers to ensure that students receive required related services in the general education or inclusive classroom settings. Special educators and related service members must collaborate in order to ensure the needs of the students are met, especially when IEP goals or objectives are out of the scope of the special educators' knowledge bases. For example, a speech pathologist might help a teacher address a student's fluency goal.

Communicating with Parents of Students with Disabilities

It is good practice to communicate with parents outside of progress reporting times and Individualized Education Program meetings. This is especially important for students with **communication deficits** who may not be able to communicate with their parents or legal guardians. Communication also helps prevent potential crises or problem behaviors and alerts parents or legal guardians before any major issues arise. Special educators should find methods of communication that work best for parents or legal guardians, such as phone calls, emails, or writing in daily communication logs. Email is beneficial for creating paper trails, especially for any discussions about educating students. However, email lacks tone and body language and can sometimes be misunderstood. Phone calls fulfill an immediate need to speak with a parent or legal guardian. However, there are no paper trails with phone calls, and they can also lead to misunderstanding. Phone calls may be time consuming, but they can be conducted on special occasions or when behavioral issues need to be discussed. Written communication logs are useful for writing brief summaries about students' days. With any mode of communication, it is essential to **document** what is communicated between the parents or legal guardians and the educators.

Roles of Parents/Legal Guardians and the School District During Evaluation

If parents or legal guardians suspect their children have disabilities, they can request that the school districts **evaluate** the children for special education. A parent or legal guardian can send a

written evaluation request to the child's school, principal, and the school district's director or director of special education services. In some states, parents and legal guardians may be required to sign a school district form requesting the evaluation. Parents should follow up on the request and/or set a timeframe for the school district to respond. The school district may choose to implement the **Response to Intervention (RTI) pre-referral process**. RTI is a process by which the school gives the student special academic support before determining whether or not to move forward with the evaluation process. Not all states or school districts have the same method for applying RTI. Under IDEA, the timeframe for completion of RTI is 60 days. However, some states can set their own timelines. RTI should not be the only means by which the school district collects data on the student and should be part of a comprehensive evaluation conducted by the student's school.

Speech Language Pathologist

Speech language pathologists (**SLPs**) provide interventions for children with communication disorders. They can assist, evaluate, prevent, and diagnose a variety of **speech issues**, from fluency to voice disorders. Before children reach grade school age, it is important that they receive early interventions for suspected communication disorders. SLPs are helpful with targeting speech or language issues, identifying at-risk students, or providing interventions for children and adults. SLPs also play a role in helping children develop good reading and writing skills, especially when deficits are evident. SLPs work collaboratively with special educators to deliver **interventions** to children with speech and language disorders in grade school. In schools, SLPs play a role in prevention, assessment, intervention, program design, data collection and analysis, and Individualized Education Program compliance. SLPs work with special educators, parents, students, reading specialists, occupational therapists, school psychologists, and others in order to provide effective services to students who require them.

Occupational Therapist

Students with special needs may need **occupational therapy services**. The number of services students receive is defined on their Individualized Education Programs (IEPs). **Occupational therapists (OTs)** may help students on IEPs refine their fine motor skills, improve sensory processing deficits, improve visual skills, and improve self-care skills. OTs can also assist with behavior management, social skills, and improving attention and focus. When a student is identified as possibly needing occupational therapy, the OT spends time observing the student in a variety of settings where the skill or skill deficit will be demonstrated. Prior to the student's IEP meeting, the OT typically meets with the student's teachers, parents, and other professionals in order to discuss observations, assessment results, and determinations. **Determinations** are then put into the IEP and implemented as related services. Fine motor skill instruction begins with the OT instructing the student on a particular skill. OTs can set up regimens for teachers and parents to generalize using the fine motor skills in the classroom and home environments.

Reasonable Accommodations for Students

According to the Americans with Disabilities Act, a **reasonable accommodation** is a change to workplace conditions, equipment, or environment that allow an individual to effectively perform a job. Title I under ADA requires businesses with more than 15 employees to abide by certain regulations, ensuring that their needs are reasonably met. Any change to the work environment or the way a job is performed that gives a person with a disability access to **equal employment** is considered a reasonable accommodation. Reasonable accommodations fall into **three categories**: changes to a job application process, changes to the work environment or to the way a job is usually done, and changes that enable employee access to equal benefits and privileges that employees without disabilities receive. These effectively level the playing field for people with disabilities to receive the same benefits as their peers. It also allows for the fewest barriers to success in the workplace. Many communities have resources available to help people with disabilities find jobs. They also have resources that help employers make their workplaces accessible for people with disabilities.

PARAPROFESSIONAL

The U.S. Department of Education requires paraprofessionals to have high school diplomas or equivalent under Title I law. Paraprofessionals (paras), sometimes called **paraeducators**, assist classroom teachers with classroom activities and help students with special needs. In a special education setting, a para works with a certified teacher to help deliver **instruction** and help students meet **Individualized Education Program goals and objectives**. Paras are not responsible for teaching new skills or introducing new goals and objectives to students. In this respect, special educators generally work alongside the paras and students to introduce new skills, goals, or objectives. At times, paras may be responsible for helping students maintain behavior plans, working with students who may be aggressive or violent, and providing physical assistance if necessary. Training is usually provided by the school district for situations when physical assistance is a possible necessity. Paras can also help take notes on students' progress toward meeting their goals or objectives. They can also discuss how students are progressing with behavior plans.

Chapter Quiz

1. Which of the following laws require paraprofessionals to have a high school diploma or practical equivalent?

a. Title I
b. Title III
c. Title V
d. Title IX

2. Which of the following is NOT within the scope of a reasonable accommodation?

a. Changes to a job application process
b. Changes to create new jobs
c. Changes to the work environment or to the way a job is usually done
d. Changes that enable employee access to benefits and privileges equal to those received by employees without disabilities

Chapter Quiz Answer Key

1. A: The US Department of Education requires paraprofessionals to have high school diplomas or equivalent under Title I law. Paraprofessionals (paras), sometimes called paraeducators, assist classroom teachers with classroom activities and help students with special needs.

2. B: Any change to the work environment or the way a job is performed that gives a person with a disability access to equal employment is considered a reasonable accommodation. Reasonable accommodations fall into three categories: changes to a job application process, changes to the work environment or to the way a job is usually done, and changes that enable employee access to benefits and privileges equal to those received by employees without disabilities. These changes effectively level the playing field for people with disabilities to receive the same benefits as their peers.

Behavioral and Crisis Support

Behavior Issues of Students and Intervention Strategies

Behavior issues occur with students with and without disabilities. However, they may occur more frequently or to a higher degree for some students with disabilities. Behavior issues are often a **manifestation** of a child's disability. For example, students with attention-deficit/hyperactivity disorder may present with attention and focus issues and impulsivity. **Common behavior issues** include the following:

- Emotional outbursts
- Inattention and inability to focus
- Impulsivity
- Aggression
- Abusive language
- Oppositional defiance
- Lying or stealing
- Threatening adults or peers

Other behavior issues may include inappropriate sexual behavior, inability to control sexual behavior, self-harm, or self-harm attempts. Behavior issues can be **avoided** or **remediated** with classroom management skills like setting clear and consistent classroom goals, setting time limits, and providing visuals to assist with transitions or concepts. When a student is in an aggressive state, it is important for the teacher to remain calm, provide choices for the student, and restate the consequences of any aggressive outbursts.

Review Video: Student Behavior Management Approaches
Visit mometrix.com/academy and enter code: 843846

Review Video: Promoting Appropriate Behavior
Visit mometrix.com/academy and enter code: 321015

Managing Students with Emotional Disorders

Managing a classroom of students with emotional disorders can be challenging and unpredictable. Students with emotional disorders have Individualized Education Program (IEP) goals that focus on **controlling** or **monitoring** their daily behavior choices. However, this does not always mean they will engage in meeting these goals. It is important for educators to know how to **manage** issues that students with emotional disorders may bring to the classroom. When creating resources and lesson plans, an educator should do the following:

- Establish a **safety plan**, which includes knowing how to implement a **crisis prevention plan**.
- Maintain an environment that reduces **stimulation** and provides **visual cues** for expected behavior.
- Implement **intervention-based strategies** for managing student behavior.
- Collect and use **data** to identify triggers, track behaviors, and recognize strategies that produce positive outcomes.
- Practice open **communication** about classroom expectations to students, parents, and other teachers.

Special education teachers can be helpful in implementing these guidelines, especially when students with emotional disorders are in inclusive settings.

Concept of Antecedents, Behavior, and Consequences as Stimuli Used in Behavior Analysis

Antecedents and consequences play a role in behavioral analysis, which is important for evaluating the behaviors of students. The purpose of behavior analysis is to gather information about a specific behavior demonstrated by a student. **Antecedents** are the actions or events that occur before the behavior occurs. It is important to recognize antecedents for behaviors to better understand under what circumstances the behavior is occurring. The **behavior** is the undesirable action that occurs as a result of the antecedent. **Consequences** are what happens immediately after the behavior occurs. These can be natural or enforced. A student might desire a certain consequence when engaging in the behavior. Understanding the relationships between antecedents, behavior, and consequences allows a professional to determine how to minimize or eliminate the behavior. In some circumstances, antecedents and consequences can be manipulated, changed, or removed in order to avoid reinforcing the undesired behavior.

Behavior Rating Scale Assessments

Behavior rating scales address the needs of students with emotional disorders who are referred to special education. Problems with behavior are often the reason a student has been referred for special education. These scales are used in determining a student's **eligibility** for special education, and in addressing **undesirable behaviors** demonstrated by students already in special education for reasons other than behavior problems. They are similar to adaptive behavior scales in that teachers or other professionals can administer the scales with little training as long as they are familiar with the students. Behavior rating scales help measure the frequency and intensity of the behaviors for a particular student often by assigning numbered ratings. They serve as a starting point for learning more about a student's behavior so that behavior interventions and management can take place. These scales are **norm-referenced**, so the outcomes of the behavior rating scales are compared to the behaviors of others.

Negative and Positive Reinforcement Related to Applied Behavior Analysis

Part of applied behavior analysis (ABA) is applying negative and positive reinforcement strategies, which are forms of conditioning strategies. In behavioral conditioning, the term **reinforcement** refers to trying to increase the frequency of a desired behavior, whereas the term **punishment** refers to trying to decrease the frequency of an undesired behavior. Similarly, when discussing behavioral conditioning methods, the word **positive** refers to the *addition* of a stimulus, whereas the word **negative** refers to the *removal* of a stimulus. These four terms tend to be confused, but are very specifically used to denote particular types of behavioral conditioning.

Positive reinforcement works by providing a desired **reward** for a desired behavior. For example, parents may give a child an allowance (the positive reinforcement) for doing chores (the behavior). In contrast, **negative reinforcement** removes an aversive stimulus to encourage a desired behavior. An example of this might be that a parent rewards a child's behavior by taking away some of his chores. Negative reinforcement is different from a punishment because the goal of punishment is to *discourage* an unwanted behavior while the goal of negative reinforcement is to *encourage* a desirable behavior. Although it is not commonly discussed, positive and negative stimuli may be used at the same in conditioning to effect a greater change.

Term:	**Example:**
Positive Reinforcement	A teacher *gives* the high-scorers on a test a sticker.
Negative Reinforcement	A teacher *takes away* an assignment if the class performs well on a test.
Positive Punishment	A police officer *gives* a driver a speeding ticket.

Term:	Example:
Negative Punishment	A parent grounds a student, *taking away* video games for two weeks.
Combination Reinforcement	A physical education teacher *replaces* a workout with a game because the class was well-behaved.
Combination Punishment	A student gets low grades and is required to complete extra school work (positive) and is not allowed to participate in sports for a week (negative).

Developing Positive Behavioral Interventions and Supports

Positive behavioral intervention and support (**PBIS**) plans can be implemented in classrooms or schoolwide to encourage specific, positive outcomes in groups of students with and without disabilities. A PBIS plan, such as an anti-bullying campaign, is put in place to encourage **good behavior** and **school safety** and to remove **environmental triggers** of undesirable behavior. The goal of a PBIS plan is for students to learn appropriate behavior just as they would learn an academic subject. Effective PBIS plans are based on research and analysis of data collected on targeted, large-scale behaviors. As with any behavioral plan, the success of PBIS plans is determined by monitoring student progress. PBIS plans should change if they do not work or if they stop working.

Developing a Functional Behavior Assessment

A functional behavior assessment (**FBA**) is a formal process used to examine student behavior. The goal of an FBA is to identify what is causing a specific behavior and evaluate how the behavior is affecting the student's educational performance. Once these factors are determined, the FBA is useful in implementing **interventions** for the behavior. When an FBA is developed, a student's behavior must be specifically defined; then the teacher or other professional devises a plan for collecting data on the behavior. These points of data are helpful in determining possible causes of the behavior, such as environmental triggers. The teacher or other professional can then implement the most appropriate plan for addressing the student's behavior. Often, this means implementing a **behavior intervention plan**, which includes introducing the student to actions or processes that are incompatible with the problem behavior. It is important to monitor the plan to ensure its effectiveness or remediate certain steps.

Crises and Crisis Prevention and Management Plans

Crises

A **crisis** is generally defined as a situation that is so emotionally impactful that an individual is not able to cope with the situation by normal means and is at risk of harming themselves or others. Crises can arise from either developmental changes that happen throughout life, such as going through puberty or graduating from school, or they can be situational and arise at any time. Examples of situational crises include sickness, losses, family deaths, and any other kind of unpredictable situation that comes up throughout life. Students with disabilities often have particular difficulty coping with stressful life situations and may need the help of a **crisis prevention plan** as a result. Crisis prevention and management goals generally focus on coping mechanisms and healthy anticipation of unavoidable situations to help the individual understand and safely navigate their way through a crisis.

Crisis Prevention Plans

Crisis prevention plans essentially serve to help with early identification of a crisis and to provide the necessary support to help the individual through a crisis to an effective resolution. These plans are often put together with the help of various members of an individual's support team, taking into account past behaviors, health, and other factors of his or her life. Some organizations, such as the Crisis Prevention Institute (CPI), specialize in crisis prevention and intervention training for professionals. Crisis prevention plans should take into account principles of least restrictive environment (LRE) to support individuals in their normal environments, while also removing or being aware of any known **behavioral triggers** that may be problematic. In the event that the individual in crisis becomes physically violent or harmful to themselves, stronger emergent response may be warranted. The ultimate goal is to keep the individual and others safe until his or her emotional state has been normalized. There is no specific duration of time for a crisis, but any intervention should be treated as short-term to prevent restricting the individual's rights through unnecessary intervention. It is important to provide the individual with clear structures and expectations to help understand direct consequences for undesired choices prior to entering a crisis. Crisis prevention plans should also provide clear processes that professionals and family members can use when students do enter a crisis in order to de-escalate the situations.

Review Video: Crisis Management and Prevention
Visit mometrix.com/academy and enter code: 351872

Developing Behavior Intervention Plans

A behavior intervention plan (BIP) is based on a **functional behavior assessment (FBA)**. The purpose of the BIP is to teach the student actions, behaviors, or processes that are incompatible with the problem behavior. The BIP may be included in an Individualized Education Program or 504 Plan, or components of the BIP may be written out as IEP goals. Once an FBA is conducted, a BIP is put in place that describes the target behavior, lists factors that trigger the behavior, and lists any interventions that help the student avoid the behavior. The interventions include problem-solving skills for the student to use instead of demonstrating the target behavior. If the interventions fail to target the problem behavior or are no longer effective for targeting the behavior, then the FBA must be revisited and a new BIP developed.

Positive Classroom Discipline Strategies

A core element of effective classroom management, positive classroom discipline is a means of holding students accountable for their actions and it starts with establishing clear and consistent **consequences** for poor choices. Students learn to predict consequences and self-correct their behaviors. It is helpful to give students **reminders** about behavior and rules instead of immediately resorting to consequences. **Pre-reminders** about expectations can be given before starting a lesson. **Nonverbal reminders** such as looks, touches, silence, or removal are possible ways to discourage students from engaging in poor choices. Removal as a consequence involves sending the student out of the classroom either to protect the other students from harm or to prevent a student from impeding the course of instruction. Removal laws vary between states and local districts, but removal is generally mandatory whenever a student is being violent. **Spoken reminders** can be used to further encourage self-management skills and should be used as precursors for reminding students about expectations instead of delivering immediate consequences.

Promoting Appropriate Behavior in Inclusive Learning Environments

Effective classrooms have good management strategies in place that promote good learning environments and minimize disruptions. Teachers with effective classroom management strategies demonstrate good leadership and organization skills. They also promote positive classroom experiences, establish clear expectations for behavior, and reinforce positive behaviors. In **inclusive learning environments**, it is important for teachers to keep all students on track with their learning. When it comes to students with disabilities, planning classroom management strategies presents different challenges. Effective teachers understand how students' special needs come into play with expected classroom behaviors. General and special educators can demonstrate effective classroom management strategies by figuring out what is causing students to act out or misbehave. They should collaborate with other professionals and students' parents to ensure the success of students with special needs in their classrooms. Lastly, effective classroom management includes setting goals for inclusive classrooms to achieve. Clear goals help establish good rapport with students with special needs because they know what is expected of them.

Supporting Mental Health Issues

Students with disabilities may also have mental health issues. These students may not necessarily be diagnosed with emotional disturbances, as mental health issues can occur concurrently with other disabilities. Students' mental health symptoms may fluctuate on an hourly, daily, or weekly basis. Intervention techniques and supports must be determined by the individual needs of each student. General and special educators across all special education settings can **support** these students by learning how to **recognize mental health issues** in schools. Teachers can use observations and research-based strategies for identifying issues. Training in working with students who have certain mental health disorders may also be useful. Occasionally, training in crisis prevention plans is required of teachers working with students who may become aggressive due to their disorders.

Working with Students with Physical Disabilities

Students with physical disabilities should be included in **general education classrooms** with accommodations if their disabilities do not coexist with other disabilities, such as learning disabilities. IDEA states that students must be assigned to a classroom that conforms with the student's least restrictive environment, which generally means the general education classroom, unless appropriate accommodations cannot be made. If sufficient accommodations or modifications may are not able to be made within the general education, a student may be placed in a more specialized environment that provides for his or her particular needs. In any of these settings, it is essential for educators to practice **instructional strategies** that facilitate the learning processes and accommodate the needs of students with physical disabilities. Classrooms should be arranged so they can be **navigated** easily by everyone. This includes giving students using wheelchairs adequate aisle space and work space. **Partner work** is helpful for students with physical disabilities, who may struggle with handwriting or using keyboards. Partners can assist these students with skills like note-taking, which may be difficult for students with physical disabilities. Additionally, assignments can include **accommodations** or **modifications** to meet the specific needs of students with physical disabilities. For example, text-to-speech software can be provided for students who struggle with using regular keyboards.

Chapter Quiz

1. Which of the following is NOT a helpful response when a student is in an aggressive state?

a. Remaining calm
b. Isolating the student
c. Providing choices for the student
d. Restating the consequences of any aggressive outbursts

2. Which of the following refers to the actions or events that occur before an undesirable behavior?

a. Precedents
b. Antecedents
c. Auras
d. Manifestations

3. Providing a desired reward for a desired behavior is known as:

a. Negative reinforcement
b. Positive reinforcement
c. Negative punishment
d. Positive punishment

4. When the outcomes of behavior rating scales for a student are compared to the behaviors of others, this is called:

a. Norm-referencing
b. Peer-measuring
c. Weight-averaging
d. Primarily distributing

Chapter Quiz Answer Key

1. B: Behavior issues can be avoided or remediated with classroom management skills, like setting clear and consistent classroom goals, setting time limits, and providing visuals to assist with transitions or concepts. When a student is in an aggressive state, it is important for the teacher to remain calm, provide choices for the student, and restate the consequences of any aggressive outbursts.

2. B: Antecedents are the actions or events that occur before a behavior occurs. It is important to recognize antecedents for a behavior to better understand under what circumstances the behavior is occurring. The behavior is the undesirable action that occurs as a result of the antecedent. Consequences are what happen immediately after the behavior occurs.

3. B: Positive reinforcement works by providing a desired reward for a desired behavior. Reinforcing the desired behavior when it is exhibited increases the likelihood that the behavior will occur in the future. For example, parents may give a child an allowance for doing chores, and the allowance is the positive reinforcement for the behavior (the chores).

4. A: Behavior rating scales help rate the frequency and intensity of the behaviors for a particular student. Behavior frequency and intensity are often rated with numbered rating scales. They serve as starting points for learning more about a student's behavior so that behavior interventions and management can take place. These scales are norm-referenced, so the outcomes of the behavior rating scales are compared to the behaviors of others.

TExES Practice Test

Want to take this practice test in an online interactive format?
Check out the bonus page, which includes interactive practice questions and much more: **mometrix.com/bonus948/texesspedec12**

SCAN HERE

1. Jessica is a six-year-old kindergarten student. Which description may indicate typical language development?

a. She speaks in sentences of five to six words.
b. She has a vocabulary of 500 words.
c. She holds up her fingers to tell her age.
d. She uses phrases such as "me want"

2. Which of these social and emotional behaviors may be atypical of a third grader?

a. Complaining about friendships and others not sharing
b. Struggling to pay attention to teachers' directions
c. Having a tantrum due to a change in routine
d. Attempting to express feelings with words

3. Of the following criteria for defining intellectual disabilities, which was NOT used before 1961?

a. IQ score
b. Social incompetence
c. Impaired adaptive behavior
d. Essentially incurable

4. Josh is a fourth-grade student with a specific learning disability in reading fluency. What would be the best strategy to motivate Josh to make improvements with his reading?

a. Giving him extra reading practice for homework
b. Letting him skip some of his reading homework
c. Allowing him to pick what story he would like to read
d. Contacting his parents when he does not want to read

5. According to the Individuals with Disabilities Education Act (IDEA), which condition could fall under the umbrella term of *specific learning disability*?

a. Speech or language impairment
b. Auditory processing disorder
c. Attention deficit disorder
d. Bipolar disorder

6. Chris is a sixth grader who receives services as a student with autism spectrum disorder. Which would be the best response when he shows frustration in the classroom?

a. Giving him a sensory break
b. Talking to him in the hallway about what is bothering him
c. Asking him to try a new activity
d. Allowing him to skip the next lesson

7. Which disorder is not listed under the Individuals with Disabilities Education Act's (IDEA's) definition of the speech or language impairment category?

a. Stuttering
b. Impaired articulation
c. Voice Impairment
d. Dysgraphia

8. It is important to teach life skills to developmentally delayed students to prepare them for life after school. Which of the following skills sets should these students be taught?

a. Count money, plan meals, grocery shop, recognize safety concerns
b. Count money, order delivery meals, dating skills, how to drive
c. How to drive, style and hygiene tips, social strategies, dating skills
d. Stock market investment, hairdressing, house painting, pet care

9. Introducing each of the stages of career development for students with disabilities should be determined *most* by which of the following?

a. The student's developmental level
b. The student's grade level in school
c. The student's level of experience
d. The student's chronological age

10. A student is taking a reading test in which several words have been replaced with blanks. Below each blank is a series of three possible answers. The student chooses the right answer from each set. The student is taking:

a. A Cloze test, which is a type of Maze test.
b. A Maze test, which is a type of Cloze test.
c. A multiple-choice quiz.
d. A vocabulary test incorporating a type of multiple-choice quiz.

11. You want to interpret the results of a student's responses on the WISC-IV. Which of the following is correct regarding the FSIQ?

a. The FSIQ is the average of all of the subtest scores.
b. The FSIQ is the sum of the test's four index scores.
c. The FSIQ is a separate score unrelated to subtests.
d. The FSIQ is a measure not used by Wechsler tests.

12. Jack is a student who is being evaluated for special education services. He has been determined to have an orthopedic impairment and specific learning disability. Why might he not be eligible for the multiple disabilities category according to the Individuals with Disabilities Education Act (IDEA)?

a. Orthopedic impairment and specific learning disability have their own categories.
b. Autism spectrum disorders must be one of the disabilities in the multiple disability category.
c. The combination of these two disabilities does not increase needs beyond the individual disability categories.
d. Students with an orthopedic impairment are not eligible for the multiple disability category.

13. Cory is a fifth-grade student who suffers from attention deficit hyperactivity disorder (ADHD). Which of the following has an increased chance of co-occurring in addition to ADHD?

a. Learning disability
b. Speech impairment
c. Depression
d. Anxiety

14. African American students receive a higher percentage of special education services when compared to their peers of other racial or ethnic backgrounds. Which strategy can be MOST productive in applying this information?

a. Identifying African American students starting at an early age
b. Ignoring this information
c. Trying to maintain more of a balance in identification based on race
d. Being cautious about the evaluation process

15. Emily is a seven-year-old who has been a victim of severe neglect and is being evaluated for special education services as a student with an emotional disturbance. What is the primary reason for choosing this category as a result of the neglect?

a. Emotional disturbance tends to include behaviors exhibited over a long period of time.
b. Emotional disturbance tends to involve unhappiness or depression.
c. Emotional disturbance tends to include a pervasive mood.
d. Emotional disturbance tends to incorporate physical symptoms.

16. What is NOT an environmental factor that could lead to positive student development?

a. Relationships with teachers
b. Structure in daily routine
c. Getting enough sleep
d. Having intelligent parents

17. What would be the best example of negative social influence?

a. Conformity
b. Independence
c. Compliance
d. Individualism

18. What would be an example of effective feedback in a lesson plan for a third-grade class?

a. Selectively choosing students to call on
b. Immediately calling on a student after asking a question
c. Reinforcing student behavior
d. Providing corrective feedback the next day

19. What is a poor example of how to establish a positive class environment?

a. Incorporating cooperative learning activities
b. Discussing individual differences
c. Establishing consequences
d. Correcting misbehavior

20. When co-teaching a high school science class with a general education teacher, which assessment choice would be best to incorporate into the lesson plan?

a. Having each student take the same test
b. Giving each student an individualized test
c. Having two groups of assessments
d. Not assessing the students

21. What would be the best warm-up for a lesson on adding and subtracting fractions?

a. Multiplying and dividing fractions
b. Adding and subtracting fractions
c. Multiplying and dividing whole numbers
d. Adding and subtracting whole numbers

22. Of the following, which is the best example of a learning objective in a lesson plan?

a. John will demonstrate that he is able to read and comprehend at his grade level.
b. John will score at least 80% on all specified reading comprehension tests by June 1.
c. John will be able to read all grade-level materials, demonstrating 100% comprehension.
d. John will complete the assigned activity for reading and comprehending grade-level materials.

23. When lesson planning for a life skills class for students with severe needs, which element is MOST important to include?

a. Objectives
b. Warmup
c. Direct instruction
d. Practical application

24. What would be the MOST appropriately challenging learning objective for a small-group writing intervention pullout group at the second-grade level?

a. Students will be able to write a five-sentence paragraph with 80 percent accuracy by the end of the writing unit.
b. Students will be able to write one sentence with 80 percent accuracy by the end of the writing unit.
c. Students will be able to write a three-paragraph story with 80 percent accuracy by the end of the writing unit.
d. Students will be able to write a letter with 80 percent accuracy by the end of the writing unit.

25. What is an example of a learning objective that is NOT measurable?

a. Students will be able to sound out each letter in the alphabet in six weeks.
b. Students will be able to understand 20 percent of the English language in six months.
c. Students will be able to complete half of their reading packets in one week.
d. Students will be able to read a chapter of a novel in one day.

26. When writing learning objectives, the acronym "SMART" is often used. What do the letters in "SMART" stand for?

a. Systematic, measurable, attainable, reasonable, targeted
b. Specific, measurable, attainable, relevant, time-bound
c. Systematic, measurable, attainable, reasonable, tested
d. Specific, measurable, attainable, reasonable, time-bound

27. Which technique would be MOST appropriate for a student with a specific learning disability in reading to access the curriculum?

a. Modifications
b. Assistive technology
c. Accommodations
d. Adaptations

28. What is an example of a modification of the curriculum?

a. Access to textbooks with larger print
b. Access to a computer to type assignments
c. Access to manipulatives
d. Access to alternative books

29. Kevin is an eighth grader with behavioral challenges, which makes it difficult for him to stay in the classroom. What would be the best strategy to ensure that he is able to access the general education curriculum?

a. Allowing him to complete less work than the other students
b. Having him complete his work outside of the classroom
c. Requiring that he complete only the work he does in the classroom
d. Allowing him to stay in the classroom without completing work and just listening to instruction

30. Which strategy would promote the safest learning environment in a sixth-grade science class with students with varying disabilities?

a. Displaying lab supplies at the front of the classroom
b. Displaying lab supplies at the back of the classroom
c. Locking lab supplies in a closet in the classroom
d. Locking lab supplies in a closet in a separate room

31. Paul is a fourth-grade student who uses a wheelchair. Which situation would provide the greatest challenge in his ability to maneuver around the classroom?

a. Rows of desks facing the front of the classroom
b. Clusters of desks throughout the classroom
c. Desks in a circle in the middle of the classroom
d. Desks randomly spread throughout the classroom

32. Ms. Jones is a special education resource teacher who specializes in small-group reading lessons. Which poster may NOT be a good idea to display for the students to see?

a. A list of sight words
b. A list of letter sounds
c. A list of letters
d. A list of popular sentences

33. When managing student behavior, what is always the number one priority for teachers?

a. Ensuring students have access to the curriculum
b. Ensuring students are making progress with their behavior goals
c. Ensuring each student in the classroom is safe
d. Ensuring each student has a behavior plan

34. When reviewing rules and expectations in a kindergarten class, which technique would be MOST effective in ensuring the students understand?

a. Having the rules listed in the classroom
b. Modeling proper following of the rules
c. Reading a list of rules orally
d. Playing a video with a song that contains the rules

35. Which consequence would be the MOST inappropriate for a third-grade student with behavioral issues?

a. Having him or her stay in during recess
b. Having him or her go to a time-out area during class
c. Having him or her fill out a points sheet when he or she displays poor behavior
d. Having him or her skip the fun activity at the end of the day

36. What is NOT a productive way to promote a safe classroom environment?

a. Consistent routines
b. Clean and orderly classrooms
c. Giving students choices
d. Giving students control

37. Jacob is a first-grade student who receives services as a student with autism spectrum disorders and struggles with changes in routines. What would be the best strategy to provide a supportive classroom environment?

a. The use of a visual schedule
b. Daily check-ins
c. Having the student access a paraprofessional
d. The use of a behavior plan

38. What would be the MOST effective instructional strategy in teaching a reading lesson to students with dyslexia?

a. Using a whole-word approach
b. Using multisensory strategies
c. Using modeling
d. Using graphic organizers

39. Cooperative learning is an important strategy for students with autism. What may be a reason to hesitate to implement this strategy in a general education classroom with students with autism?

a. General education students may not be accepting of students with autism.
b. Students with autism may not learn as much through this strategy.
c. Students with autism may struggle to understand concepts initially.
d. Cooperative learning may negatively affect the confidence of a student with autism.

40. When teaching a small group of students with varying reading levels, what is the best strategy to ensure they are appropriately challenged?

a. Have the students read the same story, and give them comprehension questions at their ability levels.
b. Have the students read the same story, and have the more advanced students read aloud.
c. Have the students read different stories and work independently on their own questions.
d. Have the students read different stories, and have each student read their story aloud.

41. Patrick is a third-grade student with Individual Education Program goals in math problem-solving and math calculations. What is the best instructional strategy to ensure success when working with him in a one-to-one pullout group?

a. Reviewing the material from his math class
b. Working on his homework for that day
c. Working on math facts with flash cards
d. Using a program separate from the math class

42. When working with a small group of students that struggle with study skills, which instructional strategy would be the MOST effective?

a. Group discussion
b. Independent practice
c. Portfolio development
d. Cooperative learning

43. Bobby is a fifth-grade student who struggles with reading comprehension and writing. When working on social studies with the entire class, what is an instructional strategy that would be the least effective for Bobby's ability to learn the subject matter?

a. Grouping the students based on their abilities
b. Including hands-on activities
c. Offering choices for learning
d. Using technology

44. Peter is a second-grade student with a specific learning disability in the area of writing and struggles to remember how to write his name. Which strategy would be best in helping him maintain that skill?

a. Asking him to practice writing his name for 30 minutes each day during a pullout group
b. Asking his teachers to help him practice writing his name throughout each day
c. Providing incentives and rewards each time he writes his name correctly
d. Giving him some extra writing materials to practice at home

45. When working with eighth-grade students on reading comprehension, what is the best strategy in ensuring that they are able to generalize these concepts across each of their classes?

a. Teaching them how to memorize certain parts of the text
b. Teaching them how to search for important information
c. Teaching them how to skim through the text
d. Teaching them how to reread passages

46. Sam is a third-grade student who struggles with writing. In diagnosing which part of the writing process he struggles most with, where would it be best to start?

a. Planning
b. Spelling
c. Mechanics
d. Semantics

47. Flash cards can be a useful math intervention for students who struggle with math fact calculations. When may the use of flash cards be inappropriate for students to practice?

a. When memorizing division facts
b. When students pass their math fact quizzes
c. When students are too young to read
d. When reviewing already known facts

48. Students with learning disabilities in the area of reading fluency often benefit from systematic reading instruction that helps them read at their own pace. Which is NOT a component of this kind of instruction?

a. Phonemic awareness practice
b. Sight word practice
c. Vocabulary practice
d. Reading comprehension practice

49. When selecting a functional curriculum for a high school class focusing on independent living skills, what would be the MOST essential to include in the curriculum?

a. Cooking
b. Laundry
c. Personal hygiene
d. Shopping

50. What would be the MOST beneficial in supplementing the daily math curriculum of a tenth-grade student with Down syndrome who is working on functional skills?

a. Including addition fact worksheets
b. Including time-telling worksheets
c. Including measuring worksheets
d. Including order-of-operations worksheets

51. Which scenario would least likely be considered assistive technology?

a. Computers for students to type
b. Pencil grip to improve handwriting
c. Switch toys to participate in leisure activities
d. Calculators to use in math class

52. Richard is a sophomore in high school who is nonverbal. Which assistive technology devices would be MOST beneficial in allowing him to communicate effectively?

a. Audio players
b. FM listening systems
c. Schedule boards
d. Graphic organizers

53. Joy is a high school student who has a postsecondary transition goal of attending college. Which strategy can be MOST effective in supporting this goal?

a. Providing flyers for her from colleges
b. Researching entrance requirements for a college
c. Contacting jobs for her to shadow
d. Providing instruction at the college level

54. Billy is a ninth-grade student with an other health impairment with a transition goal of working in construction. How could this transition goal be implemented in the general education classroom?

a. Billy's math teacher teaches him about how to measure objects.
b. Billy's case manager teaches him about how to apply for construction jobs.
c. Billy's English teacher teaches him about how to read textbooks.
d. Billy's history teacher teaches him about famous construction workers.

55. For students with independent living skills goals in accessing daily community programs, which technique is MOST beneficial?

a. Teaching them how to use the bus system
b. Teaching them how to communicate with the people in charge of the programs
c. Teaching them how to make purchases at the store
d. Teaching them how to access their cell phones

56. Which intervention strategy would be MOST effective for a high school student with a specific learning disability who is at-risk of failing classes and not graduating high school?

a. Speaking to the teachers of the classes he or she is failing and ask them to help
b. Speaking to the school counselor and ensuring the student passes
c. Speaking to the student's parents and coming up with a plan for the student to graduate
d. Speaking to the student and asking him or her to complete his or her work

57. Dante is a seventh-grade student who seems to have given up on schoolwork and always talks about dropping out when he is old enough. Which strategy would be the least likely to succeed in helping Dante get on the right track and care more about school?

a. Amending his Individualized Education Program (IEP) to include a goal that focuses on graduating
b. Speaking to the counselors about activities he could get involved in at school
c. Checking in with him each day to see how he is doing
d. Lightening the load of the work he has to complete

58. Developmental assessments can be useful tools in the identification of students with disabilities. Which component would MOST likely be incorporated into this kind of assessment?

a. Identifying sight words
b. Identifying letter sounds
c. Identifying math facts
d. Identifying colors

59. One of the most effective ways to assess student growth or identify areas of weakness is to use a screening such as the Iowa Test of Basic Skills. What is the advantage of using a screening like this?

a. To get results quickly to identify next steps
b. To determine eligibility for special education
c. To compare with peers in the class
d. To measure a student's intelligence

60. Intelligence quotients (IQ) tests can help determine whether or not students have learning issues connected with intellectual ability. What could be a disadvantage of this kind of test?

a. These tests cannot identify gifted students.
b. These tests cannot reveal student strengths.
c. These tests cannot measure certain skills.
d. These tests cannot identify future success.

61. Academic achievement tests can be beneficial in evaluating students with academic struggles for special education and typically include subtests in many areas. Which subtest would not be included in one of these achievement tests?

a. Spelling
b. Numerical operations
c. Essay composition
d. Reasoning

62. Adaptive behavior scales are assessments that are often used for students diagnosed with intellectual disabilities. Which area would not typically be assessed in one of these scales?

a. Cognition
b. Communication
c. Motor skills
d. Social skills

63. Behavior rating scales can be used to evaluate or assess student behavior. Which of the following best describes the goal of a behavior rating scale?

a. To determine what the target behaviors are
b. To determine anchor points for the students
c. To determine the frequency of the behavior
d. To determine discipline for the student

64. One of the most important assessment tools for students with specific learning disabilities is a curriculum-based measure. Which of the following describes the MOST effective use of this kind of measure?

a. To determine whether or not a student is keeping up with his or her peers
b. To determine whether or not a student is making progress on his or her Individualized Education Program (IEP) goals
c. To determine whether or not a student is learning the curriculum
d. To determine whether or not a student in earning sufficient grades

65. Standardized tests can be a valuable assessment tool in evaluating students who receive special education services. When would standardized tests be inappropriate to use for data in measuring student growth or progress?

a. When evaluating students who take alternate assessments
b. When evaluating students new to the school
c. When evaluating students who have frequent absences
d. When evaluating students with accommodations

66. Which would be the most appropriate time to use a diagnostic assessment?

a. To develop instruction
b. To learn what the students already know
c. To understand if the outcomes have been reached
d. To measure a student against a previous performance

67. Joseph is a fourth grader who receives special education services as a student with an other health impairment due to his attention deficit hyperactivity disorder. Which formative assessment would be MOST appropriate when starting a new lesson?

a. Giving him a math test to complete at the end of the unit
b. Giving him a fact test to complete before the unit
c. Monitoring his progress throughout the unit
d. Monitoring his behavior during the test

68. When working with a group of high school students on executive functioning skills, which is the best example of a summative assessment?

a. End-of-unit test
b. End-of-unit essay
c. End-of-unit presentation
d. End-of-unit performance task

69. Maria is a seventh-grade student with a specific learning disability in math and has failed three tests in a row in her general education math class. Which strategy would be least likely to help Maria improve her test scores in the future?

a. Asking her questions about the content
b. Discuss study habits she may have
c. Ask the counselors about changing classes
d. Updating the accommodations in her Individualized Education Program

70. Phillip is a third-grade student who has been struggling with reading fluency. The team has decided to evaluate Phillip for special education services and is considering the specific learning disability category. Which statement is true about this evaluation?

a. The team must have documentation of interventions that were implemented.
b. The team must administer an achievement test.
c. The team must administer an IQ test.
d. The team must consider state or local measures.

71. Which would be the best interpretation of a student who performs well on tests, and standardized assessments, but generally has low scores for smaller assessments such as classwork and homework?

a. The tests and standardized assessments are poorly constructed.
b. The student does not give his or her best effort on classwork and homework.
c. The standardized test was not age appropriate for the student.
d. The standardized tests are a better indicator than the other assessments.

72. Jacob is a ninth grader who receives special education services as a student with an emotional disturbance. In looking at the behavior rating scales that were given to his teachers and parents, the results were much different at home than they were at school. What is MOST likely the reason for this variance?

a. Jacob only exhibits certain behaviors at school.
b. Jacob's parents do not want the school to know his behaviors at home.
c. Jacob's teachers all see different behaviors at school.
d. Jacob's teachers and parents have different interpretations of the questions.

73. Which would be the best use for the results of a student's curriculum-based assessment?

a. To determine which grade level a student performs at
b. To determine a student's percentage in a class
c. To incorporate into an Individualized Education Program (IEP) to show progress
d. To incorporate in a student's school file

74. Sandi is a ninth-grade student being evaluated for special education services due to her failing grades in multiple classes. Her assessment results reveal that she scored in the average range on her IQ test and in the low range on her achievement test. What is MOST likely the reason for this?

a. Sandi has a high amount of potential but has made little progress.
b. Sandi has a low amount of potential but has made a lot of progress.
c. Sandi has a high amount of potential and has made a lot of progress.
d. Sandi has a low amount of potential and has made little progress.

75. The Individuals with Disabilities Education Act (IDEA) states that students must receive a Free and Appropriate Public Education (FAPE). What is not included in FAPE?

a. Students will be provided with an Individualized Education Program (IEP).
b. Students will be educated under public supervision.
c. Students will receive the best services possible.
d. Students will receive services unique to their needs.

76. What would be the MOST appropriate least restrictive environment (LRE) for a fourth-grade student with a specific learning disability in reading fluency?

a. General education classes all day
b. General education classes most of the day with a small group pullout
c. Special education classes most of the day with one general education class
d. Special education classes all day

77. Freddy is a sixth-grade student who is struggling with his math class. Freddy's math teacher has provided some remediation to his work, but he is still struggling. What would be the MOST appropriate next step?

a. Evaluate Freddy for special education
b. Continue providing remediation
c. Attempt more intensive interventions
d. Remove the remediation and collect data

78. After a parent requests a special education evaluation for his or her child, what would be the next step in the process?

a. Obtain consent and start the evaluation
b. Continue to provide responses to interventions (RTIs) until the team determines a need
c. Discuss some strategies the parent can use with his or her child at home instead
d. Ask the student's teachers whether or not they think an evaluation is warranted

79. Which federal safeguard is not protected according to Individuals with Disabilities Education Act (IDEA)?

a. Schools must provide guardians with their rights in writing.
b. Schools must provide notice before changing special education services.
c. Schools must provide opportunities for guardian input in Individualized Education Program (IEP) meetings.
d. Schools must provide the services that a guardian requests.

80. What is true of due process complaints of stakeholders who do not agree with the services being provided by the school?

a. A complaint must be filed within one year of the action.
b. A decision cannot be challenged if they lose.
c. Stakeholders must provide evidence at the hearing.
d. The school may have to pay the legal fees.

81. Of the following criteria for defining intellectual disabilities, which one was widely used only from 1961 on?

a. Mental deficiency/incomplete development
b. Originates during the developmental period
c. Associated with impaired adaptive behavior
d. A condition manifested at maturity

82. What is true of an elementary school student's progress on his or her annual Individualized Education Program (IEP) goals, according to Individuals with Disabilities Education Act (IDEA)?

a. Parents are updated on progress once a year at the IEP meeting.
b. Parents are updated on progress weekly.
c. Parents are updated on progress each quarter.
d. Parents are updated at the beginning and end of the school year.

83. What was NOT one of the major changes that occurred in the 2004 Individuals with Disabilities Education Act (IDEA)?

a. Transition goals must be written starting at the age of 16.
b. Special education teachers must be highly qualified.
c. Alternative assessments are included in state accountability.
d. Early intervention included systems for students zero to three and three to five.

84. What role does section 504 of the Rehabilitation Act of 1973 play in the identification of students for special education services?

a. Students who are determined ineligible for special education services receive a 504 plan.
b. Students that have a 504 plan can be evaluated for special education services.
c. Students who receive special education services cannot also have a 504 plan.
d. Students who are determined ineligible for a 504 plan cannot receive special education services.

85. What is NOT typically a responsibility of the special education teacher?

a. Managing paraprofessionals
b. Scheduling Individualized Education Program (IEP) meetings
c. Developing student class schedules
d. Supporting general education teachers

86. When working as a case manager for students with Individualized Education Programs (IEPs), which role must be taken on as part of that duty?

a. Ensuring students on the caseload do not fail.
b. Ensuring students on the caseload attend class.
c. Ensuring students on the caseload meet IEP goals.
d. Ensuring students on the caseload access accommodations.

87. The school psychologist can be a crucial member of the Individualized Education Program team. Which responsibility does the psychologist typically hold?

a. Administering IQ tests
b. Administering achievement tests
c. Administering progress monitoring probes
d. Administering transition planning inventories

88. A classroom includes one student with visual impairment, two students with hearing impairments, three students with Down syndrome, and four with other intellectual disabilities. In addition to special education teachers, which of the following other professionals are most likely to be included in delivering special education services (excluding testing) to this group?

a. Physical therapist, occupational therapist, behavior specialist
b. Physical therapist, speech-language pathologist, orientation & mobility specialist, behavior specialist
c. Orientation and mobility specialist, physical therapist, school psychologist, audiologist
d. Audiologist, speech-language pathologist, orientation & mobility specialist, occupational therapist

89. When collaborating with general education teachers, there may be disagreements that arise. What would be the MOST productive way to handle a disagreement about a student's accommodations?

a. Hold an Individualized Education Plan (IEP) meeting to address the change that needs to be made.
b. Hold a meeting with the student and the general education teacher.
c. Hold a meeting with the school principal.
d. Hold a meeting with the student's parents.

90. Miguel is a second grader with a specific learning disability that began exhibiting some behaviors that have never arisen before. What would be the best strategy in communicating these issues to Miguel's parents?

a. Calling the parents immediately to try and resolve the issue
b. Waiting a week or two to see if the behavior improves
c. Setting up a meeting for the parents to come in and discuss it
d. Holding an Individualized Education Program (IEP) meeting to gather the entire team

91. When holding an Individualized Education Program (IEP) meeting with stakeholders, which method would be least effective in establishing rapport?

a. Facilitated meetings
b. Slide show meetings
c. Student-led meetings
d. Scripted meetings

92. Edgar is a seventh-grade student with an other health impairment (OHI) who is new to your caseload. Which strategy would be MOST effective in eliminating any kind of bias toward him?

a. Reviewing his Individualized Education Program (IEP) to ensure his needs are understood
b. Meeting with him to know more about his background
c. Calling his parents to introduce yourself
d. Reviewing his educational record from his previous school

93. What is the best example of an implicit bias that may negatively affect a relationship with a particular group of students?

a. Over-identifying certain students for special education services because of race
b. Over-teaching certain concepts to students because of gender
c. Under-teaching certain students because of a disability
d. Under-identifying certain students for special education services because of socioeconomic status

94. Jack is a fourth-grade student who is being assessed for an other health impairment due to a diagnosis of attention deficit hyperactivity disorder, which affects his executive functioning abilities. Which assessment would MOST likely be included in this evaluation?

a. Behavior Rating Inventory
b. Cognitive Assessment System
c. Adaptive Behavior Inventory
d. Test of Problem-Solving

95. What is the greatest advantage to working with students in a small group rather than one on one?

a. Students can learn by copying each other.
b. Students are more likely to pay attention.
c. Students can improve social communication.
d. Students are less likely to exhibit negative behavior.

96. When working with a general education math teacher, which instructional strategy would be the best in allowing a student with a visual impairment access to the curriculum?

a. Modified assignment length
b. An audio version of the textbook
c. Preferential seating close to the board
d. Extended time on tests

97. Brian is a fourth-grade student who is being reevaluated for special education services as a student with a visual impairment. Which circumstances would be MOST likely to determine Brian eligible for services?

a. An existing vision and hearing loss that affects his educational performance
b. Visual field restriction that is 30 degrees
c. Visual acuity of 20/70 after correction
d. Visual impairment that started after the age of three

98. Jasmine is a first-grade student with an emotional disturbance who is observed to assess her behavioral patterns. Which method of recording her behavior would likely be the MOST effective?

a. Discretely recording her behavior at random times in different classes
b. Recording her behavior at the same time and class each week
c. Asking Jasmine to help record her behavior
d. Having her teacher record each of her behaviors throughout the day

99. Which would most likely be considered a disadvantage of an inclusion program?

a. Students cannot meet their Individualized Education Program (IEP) goals in an inclusion classroom.
b. The expectations are high in an inclusion classroom.
c. There is more staff collaboration in an inclusion classroom.
d. Students may act out more in an inclusion classroom.

100. Albert is a senior in high school with a specific learning disability in the area of reading comprehension. What would be the greatest benefit to Albert completing one of his English classes online?

a. The teacher does not have to be involved as much.
b. He can complete the work at his own pace.
c. There is less work to complete than in the classroom.
d. He will be more likely to pass the class.

Answer Key and Explanations

1. A: By the age of six, typical language development will include speaking in sentences of about five or six words. By this age, children tend to have a vocabulary of 2,000 or more words, so answer choice B is incorrect. Children at age six are also expected to communicate their age orally rather than with their fingers, so answer choice C is incorrect. They also no longer say simple phrases such as "me want," which eliminates answer choice D.

2. C: Although tantrums are expected of younger children, a tantrum isn't typical in a third grader. Typical development in third graders includes complaining or telling on their peers, so answer A is incorrect. It is also typical for a third grader to struggle to pay attention, so answer B is incorrect. Attempting to express feelings with words is typical for a third-grade student, so answer D is incorrect.

3. A: An IQ score one or more standard deviations below the mean, or a score of 85 or lower, is a criterion used in the definition by Heber of the American Association on Mental Deficiency (American Association on Intellectual disabilities) in 1961. Definitions widely used prior to 1961 did not include this criterion. Therefore option A is correct.

Social incompetence was included as one of six criteria for the definition of intellectual disabilities by Edgar A. Doll in 1941. (Doll developed the Vineland Social Maturity Scale, now the Vineland Adaptive Behavior Scales.) Therefore option B is incorrect.

Impaired adaptive behavior was cited in 1937 by Tredgold of Great Britain: "...the individual is incapable of adapting himself to the normal environment..." Therefore option C is incorrect.

Being essentially incurable is another one of Doll's 1941 six criteria for the definition of intellectual disabilities. Therefore option D is incorrect.

4. C: Allowing him to choose what he wants to read will increase the chances that he enjoys the text and therefore improves his reading ability. Answer A is incorrect because giving him extra homework may make him dislike reading even more. Answers B and D may be helpful but ultimately will not improve his reading because he will not get the practice or enjoy the reading.

5. B: Specific learning disability is a disorder that affects a person's ability to listen, think, speak, read, write, spell, or do math. Auditory processing disorder affects a person's ability to listen. Answer A is incorrect because speech or language impairment is its own category of disability. Answers C and D are incorrect because each of these falls under other disability categories and not specific learning disability.

6. A: Students with autism will frequently have sensory needs, such as becoming easily overstimulated. Giving them a break to return to a lower-level of stimulation can be beneficial and help the student to self-regulate his or her behavior. According to the Individuals with Disabilities Education Act (IDEA), autism is a developmental disability that may impact verbal and nonverbal communication, including social interactions, so answer B may not be the best option. Answer C is incorrect because changes in routine can also affect students with autism. Answer D may be effective but would not be the best practice as he may miss important practice.

7. D: Speech or language impairment, according to the IDEA, is a communication disorder that adversely affects a child's educational performance. Dysgraphia is a learning disorder, so answer D is not listed under IDEA's definition of speech or language impairment. Answers A, B, and C are all incorrect because each of these disorders are listed as examples under the speech or language impairment disability category under IDEA's definition.

8. A: Count money, plan meals, grocery shop, recognize safety concerns. These are among the most basic life skills developmentally delayed students must master. Other life skills include specific occupational skills, home maintenance, clothes selection and care, food preparation and personal hygiene.

9. A: With students who have disabilities, the time to introduce each career development stage depends more on the individual student's developmental level, which often is not commensurate with the student's grade level (B) or chronological age (D) in some or all domains. While the student's experiential level (C) is important for selecting instructional materials and methods, the developmental level has more impact on whether a student will be able to learn the skills acquired in each stage.

10. B: A Maze test, which is a type of Cloze test. A Cloze test offers a text with key words blanked out and the student must determine the most likely words based upon context and his vocabulary. A Maze test offers a number of possible answers and the student must read very carefully in order to make the correct selection.

11. B: The FSIQ stands for Full Scale IQ. It is the sum of the test's four index scores: the Verbal Comprehension Index (VCI), from the Similarities, Comprehension, and Vocabulary subtests; the Perceptual Reasoning Index (PRI), using the Matrix Reasoning, Picture Concepts, and Block Design subtests; the Working Memory Index (WMI), from the Letter-Number Sequencing and Digit Span subtests; and the Processing Speed Index (PSI), from the Coding and Symbol Search subtests. FSIQ gives a global IQ score. It is not the average of all subtest scores (A) or a separate unrelated score (C). Wechsler's tests do use FSIQ (D).

12. C: According to the IDEA, the multiple disabilities category is for students who are affected by multiple disabilities in which the combination of those disabilities severely affects their educational needs beyond what can be accommodated by one of the qualifying categories. Answer A is incorrect because although they do have their own category, they can still be considered for multiple disabilities. Answer B is incorrect because autism is not required for the multiple disabilities category. Answer D is incorrect because students with an orthopedic impairment can be eligible for multiple disabilities.

13. A: Students with ADHD have a higher chance of having a learning disability than those without it. Although students with ADHD can be affected by other disabilities as well, students with learning disabilities who have ADHD are the most common. Students with ADHD tend to have their ability to learn affected and therefore struggle to learn or fall behind. They may also suffer from speech impairments, depression, and anxiety, but those do not tend to be as frequent as learning disabilities, so answers B, C, and D are incorrect.

14. D: Overall, African American students have a higher likelihood of having a disability than others. It is important to not over or under-identify students simply because of their race, and we must be cautious of need rather than race. Answer A is incorrect because it is important to identify every student at an early age and not just a specific race. Answer B is incorrect because this can be important information to analyze. Answer C is incorrect because balancing out those who receive services based on race can lead to some students not receiving the services they need.

15. A: Victims of neglect tend to suffer from emotional disturbances long after the abuse. These behaviors tend to occur over a long period of time and have an impact on a student's educational performance. Answers B, C, and D are incorrect because although these reasons are certainly concerning, the behavior exhibited comes as a result of the severe neglect over a long period of time. Unhappiness, depression, pervasive moods, and physical symptoms by themselves do not necessarily identify a student eligible for an emotional disturbance unless they are displayed over a long period of time.

16. D: Environmental factors that lead to positive development include the influences from the outside world that shape who we are or who we become. Having intelligent parents is a biological factor that may shape who we are. Answers A, B, and C are incorrect because each of these involve environmental factors and influences that come from the outside world. Although they may each have a positive impact, they would be considered environmental factors.

17. A: Social influences are everywhere around us, from the people we talk with, to social media, to entertainment. Conformity means changing one's behavior to be more like the norm. This can have negative effects. Changing to be like everyone else may mean that a person has changed a part of who he or she is just to fit in. Answers B, C, and D are incorrect because these all tend to be positive effects of social influence. Independence and individualism are the result of thinking for oneself. Compliance is the result of following the rules or guidelines.

18. C: One of the characteristics of an effective lesson plan is positive feedback. Reinforcing student behavior is one of the most effective ways to praise students and provide this positive feedback. Answer A is incorrect because selectively calling on students may create an imbalance of who gets called on. Answer B is incorrect because it is best to give students some time to think before asking a question. Answer D is incorrect because feedback should be provided immediately so they can make corrections.

19. B: To create a positive class environment, it is important that everyone in the class feels welcome, safe, and wanted. Discussing individual differences may exclude students or make them feel uncomfortable, which would not establish a positive environment for that student. Answer A is incorrect because cooperative learning activities are a great way to establish a positive environment by having students interact. Answers C and D are incorrect because it is important to set ground rules so students understand the expectations.

20. C: One of the most important components of the lesson plan is the assessment, and it must be a true evaluation of student growth and knowledge. Having one set of assessments for students in the general education population and one set of accommodated assessments is the best practice. Answer A is incorrect because students with Individualized Education Programs may need an accommodated test. Answer B is incorrect because it is inefficient to create an assessment for each student. Answer D is incorrect because it is important to assess the students to see their progress and growth.

21. D: When lesson planning, a warm-up is beneficial in that it provides students an opportunity to practice some of the skills they are going to learn in that lesson, which is connected to previous knowledge. To learn how to add and subtract fractions, it would be beneficial to practice adding and subtracting whole numbers. Answers A and B are incorrect because these would be more advanced than the lesson they will be learning. Answer C may be a good warm-up, but it is best practice for the warmup to relate directly to the lesson, so answer D is the best option.

22. B: This objective specifies what John should be able to do through the lesson; it is measurable by specifying a minimum score on all appropriate assessments indicated in the lesson plan; and it specifies by what time he should have achieved this. (A) does not specify how to measure or assess John's reading ability or comprehension, or any time frame. (C) not only fails to specify these things, but moreover is unrealistic in dictating 100%. (D) not only fails to specify measurability; it moreover states only what activity John will complete, but not what he should learn and be able to do through completing it.

23. D: For students who are learning about life skills, the practical application portion of the lesson is most important for them to practice their skills. Answer A is incorrect because although it is important for them to know the objective, the application tends to be more productive and memorable. Answer B is incorrect because a warm-up may not be practical for a group of severe needs students. Answer C is incorrect because life skills are often easier learned by doing rather than lectures.

24. A: Although each student has different strengths, the most appropriately challenging learning objective for second graders would be learning to write a paragraph. Appropriately challenging learning objectives must be something the students can attain over the course of a unit but also challenges them and is not too easy. Answers C and D are incorrect because they would most likely be too challenging for a second-grade student. Answer B is incorrect because this may be too easy.

25. B: For learning objectives to be measurable, they must be written in a way that can be quantifiably described. Answer B isn't measurable because it is impossible to determine what 20 percent of the English language is and cannot be quantified. Answers A, C, and D are incorrect because they are all measurable. There are 26 letters in the alphabet, so answer a can be quantified. Half of a reading packet and one chapter are also quantities.

26. B: When writing learning objectives, it is important that they are specific to the needs of the student, measurable or quantifiable, appropriately attainable for the group of students, relevant to the current topic or lesson, and include a timeframe for the student to achieve the goal. Answers A, C, and D are incorrect because they are each missing some of these SMART components.

27. C: A student with a specific learning disability in reading would likely use accommodations to access the curriculum. Accommodations allow the students to access the same content as their peers with a change in presentation, timing, setting, scheduling, or formatting. This may include oral presentation of the text or extended time to read assignments. Answers A and D are incorrect because modifications and adaptations adjust the assignment and change what a student is taught. Assistive technology may be helpful in helping some students access the curriculum, but a student with a learning disability wouldn't typically access this.

28. D: Modifications of the curriculum alter the curriculum that is being taught, and these students are expected to complete assessments different than that of their peers. Access to alternative books changes what the student is learning and therefore would change the expectations for the assignment. Answers A, B, and C are all accommodations that allow students to access the same curriculum as their peers with alterations to how the material is presented. Textbooks with large print, computers for typing, and manipulatives are all accommodations to allow students to access the curriculum.

29. A: Although each student is different and may require different levels of support, modifying the curriculum to allow the student to complete less work still allows the student to access the curriculum. Answer B is incorrect because completing work outside of the classroom does not allow him access to the teacher for instruction. Answers C and D are incorrect because just being in the classroom and not completing work does not allow a student to demonstrate knowledge of the curriculum.

30. C: To organize the classroom in the safest way possible, it is best to keep items like lab supplies hidden from the students. This way, students are not tempted to play with the lab supplies when they are not allowed to. Answers A and B are incorrect because having the supplies displayed can be dangerous for impulsive students or those with behavior problems. Answer D is incorrect because, although it is a good idea to have the supplies locked away, it is best practice to have them in a more accessible location.

31. D: When organizing the classroom to meet the needs with accessibility concerns such as wheelchairs, it is always important to consider the path in and out of the classroom. If the desks are spread randomly throughout the class, it may be difficult for a student to maneuver in and out. Answers A, B, and C are incorrect because each of these provides organization and gives Paul and the other students an easy path.

32. B: When organizing the classroom, it is important to consider what is displayed and how it will benefit the students. When teaching students to read, it may not be beneficial to have a list of letter sounds because that is what students are going to be practicing each day. Having a list of sight words, letters, and popular sentences will help the students but will not simply give them the answers. It may be a better idea to teach the students a pattern or another way to memorize the letter sounds rather than having them displayed.

33. C: When teaching students with behavioral concerns, the safety of each student in the classroom is always the top priority. It is imperative that behavioral issues are addressed right away and that actions are taken to ensure safety. Answers A and B are important because students need access to the curriculum and do make progress, but these answers are incorrect. Answer D is incorrect because behavior plans are not necessary for every student.

34. B: For kindergarten students who may be new to the school environment, it is important to model the behavior so they can see exactly what it looks like and know what to expect. Answer A is incorrect because students of this age may not be able to read yet, so having the rules posted wouldn't help. Answer C is incorrect because simply reading the rules wouldn't be the best way for every student to understand. Answer D may be beneficial eventually, but modeling the behaviors initially is likely the most effective way to start.

35. A: Although each of these could be beneficial consequences for a third-grade student, having him or her skip recess may be the most inappropriate. Students with behavior needs often need sensory stimulation, which recess provides. It is also likely this student's favorite part of the day, and behavior may escalate if he or she has to skip it. Answer B could be an effective strategy in changing his or her behavior quickly. Answer C is beneficial in that a point sheet keeps him or her on top of his or her own behavior. Answer D may not be the best option, but having a student skip a fun activity at the end of the day gives him or her something to work toward.

36. D: Although letting students feel involved and part of decisions that are made in the classroom is important, the teacher must always maintain control for the classroom to be safe. Giving students control of the classroom can be unsafe for the rest of the students. Answers A, B, and C are all incorrect because having routines, clean classrooms, and providing choices for students are all ways to promote safety in the classroom.

37. A: Visual schedules can provide students who struggle with routines support in understanding what the expectations are and will be. Seeing what the expectations are help eliminate negative behavior and promote and safe and supportive classrooms. Although daily check-ins, using a paraprofessional, and behavior plans can all be beneficial, the best support for a student who struggles with routines is a visual schedule.

38. B: Multisensory strategies, including the use of touch in manipulating letters or tapping the letters with their fingers, can be effective strategies for students with dyslexia. This sensory approach allows them to break down words and memorize them in different ways. Answer A is incorrect because the whole-word approach does not tend to be as effective for students with dyslexia. Answer C is incorrect because modeling may not be appropriate as the students need to use the strategies themselves. Answer D is incorrect because graphic organizers may be advanced for teaching reading.

39. C: Students with autism often have difficulty with changes in routine and the environment. It may be difficult for them to adjust to a new kind of learning strategy that may affect what they are able to learn. Answer A is incorrect because although not all students are accepting, it is important for students with autism to attempt to engage with everyone. Answer B is incorrect because these students can still learn as much as their peers once they are able to adjust to the new environment. Answer D is incorrect because this kind of learning should actually improve confidence over time.

40. C: When working with students with varying levels in the area of reading, it is important to challenge each student appropriately while also making good use of the time. Having the students work independently on their own stories and questions accomplishes both of these. Answer A is incorrect because some of the students may not be appropriately challenged if they all read the same story. Answer B is incorrect because the students who struggle more may not get enough practice. Answer D is incorrect because this may not be the most appropriate use of time.

41. D: For Patrick to make gains in math problem-solving and math calculations, he will likely need a spiraling curriculum, which is one that is constantly reviewing concepts that he has already learned to give him more practice. Patrick may need to relearn or have more practice with different topics to learn in a different way. Answer A is incorrect because simply reviewing material he does not understand likely will not help him. Answer B is incorrect because he likely will struggle with the homework if he did not understand the concepts from class. Answer C is incorrect because he will not get his problem-solving practice if it is just math facts.

42. A: When teaching students about study skills and how to use them, it is important to assist them in developing some methods that will work for them. Answer B is incorrect because independent practice would be difficult for students who are struggling to come up with ideas. Answer C is incorrect because developing a portfolio likely would be too much of a task to take on. Answer D is incorrect because although it may be beneficial, having the whole-group discussion is likely more valuable with the teacher's input.

43. A: Although grouping the students based on their abilities may be the easiest method to teach, it will likely single some students out. It could also make it more difficult for the students to learn if they are all struggling with the content. Answer B is incorrect because having more hands-on learning activities could make it easier for Bobby to learn. Answer C is incorrect because having choices and including each student in the selection process will likely make them more eager to learn. Answer D is incorrect because the use of technology, such as computers, may make the learning easier and more effective.

44. B: The best way for students to maintain a skill that they struggle to work on is to continue to work on that skill across subjects and at different times throughout the day. Answer A is incorrect because just having him work on it once a day will likely not give him enough opportunities to practice it no matter how long he practices it. Answer C is incorrect because although these incentives may work at first, it is likely not going to help him long term in remembering to write his name. Answer D is incorrect because having him complete extra homework will likely make him resent writing and not want to do it.

45. B: Although each of these can be helpful in improving reading comprehension abilities, being able to search for important information can help in any subject manner. Answer A is incorrect because students who struggle with reading comprehension will also likely struggle to memorize. Answer C is incorrect because skimming through the text can be valuable but likely will not help comprehension. Answer D is incorrect because although rereading passages can be helpful, it is more important to seek valuable information.

46. A: In trying to discover where a student is struggling with writing, it is best to determine whether or not they are able to develop their own ideas. If students cannot come up with thoughts, they will be unable to write. Answer B is incorrect because spelling will be lacking if a student cannot come up with an idea. Answer C is incorrect because the mechanics will also struggle without being able to develop thoughts. Answer D is incorrect because semantics can also be affected by a lack of planning.

47. D: If students have already memorized the facts on flash cards, it may be considered a waste of time to continue to review them over and over again. Answer A is incorrect because flash cards can be great to help memorize division facts. Answer B is incorrect because flash cards can still be used with problems students struggled with even if they passed a test. Answer C is incorrect because even if students are too young to read, they can still practice math facts.

48. C: Although learning new vocabulary is important, students who struggle with reading fluency tend to learn more about how to read words as opposed to what those words may mean. Answer A is incorrect because learning the letter sounds is crucial to developing fluency. Answer B is incorrect because sight words are important to memorize when improving fluency. Answer D is incorrect because comprehension is always an important component of reading even if fluency is the primary target.

49. C: When selecting a curriculum for functional skills, it is important to focus on tasks that will occur the most often. Personal hygiene is a skill that people do every single day and is a crucial skill to work on. Answer A is incorrect because although cooking is important, personal hygiene is more useful and vital. Answer B is incorrect because laundry is something that should be learned after personal hygiene skills have been mastered. Answer D is incorrect because people must be able to care for themselves and their bodies before they can go out shopping in the community.

50. B: To supplement the curriculum for someone with Down syndrome, it is best to focus on skills that a student is likely to use for the rest of his or her life. Answer A is incorrect because although addition facts are important, being able to tell time is a skill that will need to be used every day. Answer C is incorrect because measuring is not a skill that a student with Down syndrome will use regularly. Answer D is incorrect because using order of operations is a complex skill that is not functional.

51. D: Although calculators are considered technology, they are universally used by each student in the class so would not be considered assistive technology. Answer A is incorrect because the use of a computer to type can be considered assistive technology for a student who struggles to hand write. Answer B is incorrect because a pencil grip is also considered assistive technology for those who struggle to hold a pencil. Answer C is incorrect because switch toys can be assistive to those with physical disabilities.

52. C: Schedule boards and communication boards allow people to communicate what their daily schedule is going to be and anything else they may need to communicate. Answer A is incorrect because audio players are for students who struggle with reading. Answer B is incorrect because listening systems are to help in reading a text. Answer D is incorrect because graphic organizers tend to be for those students who struggle with executive functioning.

53. B: Although each of these strategies may be effective and important, helping a student who plans to attend college research the entrance requirements is the most effective initially. This way, she knows what she needs to do to go to the college of her choice. Answer A is incorrect because she may not read or understand the flyers. Answer C is incorrect because the goal is focused on colleges and not jobs. Answer D is incorrect because she may not be ready for receiving college-level instruction.

54. A: To best support Billy and his goal of becoming a construction worker, it is best to provide him with opportunities that allow him to gain the experience he will get in the profession. Teaching him about measuring objects directly relates to working in construction. Answer B is incorrect because the question asked is about general education, not special education. Answer C is incorrect because reading textbooks does not directly apply to working in construction. Answer D is incorrect because knowing famous construction workers will not help him prepare to work in construction.

55. A: For students who are going to be accessing services after high school, it is important that they practice independence in being able to use the bus system. This is something that they will be able to remember so they can access it every day. Answer B is incorrect because although communicating is important, they will first need to know how to get to the program every day. Answer C is incorrect because making purchases does not directly relate to this goal. Answer D is incorrect because although using a cell phone is important, knowing how to access the transportation is more difficult of a task to master.

56. C: Although each of these strategies can be effective in some capacity, it is most important to develop a plan that the student's parents and students are all aware of. This way, there is a tangible path to graduate that does not necessarily rely solely on the student. Answer A is incorrect because it is not the responsibility of the teachers to ensure the student passes. Answer B is incorrect because the school counselor may be able to help, but it is up to the student to complete the work. Answer D is incorrect because the student will not likely want to complete work if he or she is struggling to pass classes.

57. A: Although adding a goal to his IEP may be helpful in getting his teachers to focus on Dante graduating, it likely will not have much of an impact on what he does. Answer B is incorrect because it may be a good idea to get him involved with some activities and friends outside of school. Answer C is incorrect because a daily check-in will likely make him feel needed and welcome. Answer D is incorrect because lightening his load may encourage him to do the work and pass the classes.

58. B: Developmental assessments tend to be used at the preschool or kindergarten level to identify students that may have a developmental disability. Identifying letter sounds would be a major component of this and an indicator of what a student can do. Answer A is incorrect because this is a skill that would likely come along a little later. Answer C is incorrect because math facts would also be worked on in a later grade. Answer D is incorrect because identifying colors does not necessarily provide academic insight into what a student is capable of doing.

59. A: These types of screening assessments are used to quickly determine whether or not students are making the progress they are expected to make and whether or not a more in-depth test needs to be administered. Answer B is incorrect because this kind of screening assessment does not provide enough information to determine eligibility. Answer C is incorrect because although this kind of information may compare a student with peers, that is not the end goal. Answer D is incorrect because a simple screening will not measure a student's intelligence.

60. C: Although IQ tests can be beneficial for a number of reasons, they are limited in that they only measure certain subjects and skills. Because of this, they must be taken as part of a body of evidence that incorporates other tests and skills. Answer A is incorrect because IQ tests are one of the most popular ways to identify gifted students. Answer B is incorrect because these tests are designed to measure specific strengths and weaknesses. Answer D is incorrect because IQ tests often identify future student success in the areas tested.

61. D: Although reasoning can be an important skill to assess, this would typically be associated with an IQ test rather than an academic achievement test. Answer A is incorrect because spelling is one of the subtests commonly found in an achievement test. Answer B is incorrect because numerical operations are found in most every achievement test. Answer C is incorrect because an essay composition portion of the test is common for older students taking achievement tests.

62. A: Adaptive behavior scales are designed to assess how well students do with daily and basic living skills. Cognition is not something that would be assessed by one of these kinds of assessments. Answer B is incorrect because communicating with others is an important skill for students to possess after school ends. Answer C is incorrect because motor skills must be evaluated to determine what support a student may need. Answer D is incorrect because social skills are important to have in the community when working with others.

63. C: Behavior rating scales can have a number of uses, but ultimately the main goal is to quantify student behaviors to understand why they are happening. Answer A is incorrect because determining target behaviors is one of the first steps in assessing a student's behavior but is a starting point and not the end goal. Answer B is incorrect because anchor points for a student's behavior are used to guide the rating scale. Answer D is incorrect because behavior rating scales are not designed to discipline the students.

64. B: Curriculum-based measures are designed to be quick assessments to determine whether or not students are making sufficient progress on their IEP goals. Answer A is incorrect because a standardized test would be the best assessment measure to compare students with their peers. Answer C is incorrect because classroom grades would decide whether or not students are learning the curriculum. Answer D is incorrect because report cards would determine whether or not a student is earning sufficient grades.

65. A: Students who are eligible to take alternate assessment due to the impact of their disability will likely not take the same standardized tests as their peers. These students will likely struggle with the standardized test, and the alternate assessment will provide more valuable information. Answer B is incorrect because students new to the school can still take standardized tests as they are the same for every grade level. Answer C is incorrect because although students with absences may struggle more with the test, it is still valuable in determining what they know. Answer D is incorrect because students with accommodations can access those for standardized tests.

66. B: Diagnostic assessments are used to get an idea of what the student's strengths and weaknesses are even before the instruction begins. Answer A is incorrect because a formative assessment would be used to develop instruction. Answer C is incorrect because this would be completed after the instruction has been given. Answer D is incorrect because a diagnostic assessment is completed before any kind of instruction so there would not be a previous performance to compare with.

67. C: Formative assessments are used to monitor the students during instruction to provide feedback. This way, the teacher can make changes to the lesson plans as necessary or fill holes in the gaps of student knowledge. Answer A is incorrect because a test at the end of the unit would be considered a summative assessment. Answer B is incorrect because a test before the unit would be considered a diagnostic assessment. Answer D is incorrect because monitoring his behavior during tests would be completed after the unit rather than throughout it.

68. D: When assessing students at the end of a unit who are working on executive functioning skills, it is best to see what they are able to do. A performance task allows them to complete a task that demonstrates their knowledge of executive functioning. Answer A is incorrect because a test doesn't show that they can complete a certain task. Answer B is incorrect because an essay would not show that they can perform certain skills they may have learned. Answer C is incorrect because presenting information does not necessarily mean that they have learned to complete something on their own.

69. A: Reviewing the content with her if she is already struggling with the material may prove to be ineffective to a student with a learning disability. There is likely a reason she is struggling with these tests. Answer B is incorrect because it is possible that Maria does not know how to study for a math test. Answer C is incorrect because changing classes would likely improve her grade if she were to move to a lower class. Answer D is incorrect because she may need to access accommodations that weren't previously in her Individualized Education Program.

70. A: To consider a student eligible for special education services as a student with a specific learning disability, there must be documentation of interventions that have been attempted to show the student is not achieving growth. Answer B is incorrect because although an achievement test might be helpful, it is not mandatory. Answer C is incorrect because IQ tests do not typically show academic performance. Answer D is incorrect because these data aren't necessary in the process but can be useful.

71. B: Although standardized tests are merely the result of one assessment, they tend to be a good indication of students' academic performance capabilities. Statewide tests are usually well constructed as the tests are analyzed and refined for significance over time. It is likely that the student is not giving as much effort in other areas if the results were significantly higher. Oftentimes, lower performance on homework and classwork is a result of boredom or distractions and the teacher should respond by investigating what the source of the low scores is. It is also unreasonable to assume that the standardized test is not age appropriate when other students are performing as expected on the test.

72. D: Although Jacob may or may not exhibit the same behaviors at home as he does at school, it is likely that the interpretation of the questions is different for parents and teachers. Because the setting is different, it is expected that the behavior may look different to different people. Answer A is incorrect because although the behaviors may not be the same all the time, Jacob is likely to exhibit similar behaviors at home and school. Answer B is incorrect because it is not likely that a parent would answer questions with incorrect answers. Answer C is incorrect because most likely Jacob's teachers each see similar behaviors.

73. C: Curriculum-based assessments can be valuable tools in monitoring a student's progress compared with what his or her IEP goals are. These are typically quick assessments that give the teacher data right away. Answer A is incorrect because curriculum-based assessments typically compare students to their own growth rather than determine grade level. Answer B is incorrect because curriculum-based assessments are separate from classroom grades. Answer D is incorrect because it would likely not end up in a student's school file.

74. A: Typically, IQ tests show what a student's potential outcomes for academic achievement can be, whereas an achievement test shows how much progress a student has made and what he or she is currently capable of doing. Answer B is incorrect because low potential would mean she had a lower IQ score. Answer C is incorrect because a lot of progress would mean that she had a higher achievement score. Answer D is incorrect because low potential would mean lower IQ scores.

75. C: Although schools will do their best in ensuring that students receive the best services possible, there is nothing in FAPE that says this must be done, and it is at the discretion of the schools. Answer A is incorrect because students who receive FAPE also will be provided with an IEP that meets their needs. Answer B is incorrect because FAPE states that students who receive FAPE are entitled to public school supervision. Answer D is incorrect because FAPE states that students receive services according to their unique needs.

76. B: The purpose of the LRE is to ensure that students who receive special education services are in the general education setting as often as possible while still receiving the support they need. Answer A is incorrect because a student with a disability in reading fluency will need individualized instruction in that area. Answer C is incorrect because students with learning disabilities typically spend most of the day in the general education setting so they have access to their peers. Answer D is incorrect because special education classes all day would provide a restrictive environment.

77. C: Before being referred for special education services, the team must provide intensive interventions to see how Freddy responds to those. Answer A is incorrect because the team must provide more support before evaluating for special education. Answer B is incorrect because continuing to provide the remediation likely will not work as there have been no improvements. Answer D is incorrect because removing the remediation would likely cause Freddy to struggle more.

78. A: According to the Individuals with Disabilities Education Act (IDEA), any time a parent formally requests a special education evaluation, the team must obtain consent and conduct the evaluation. Answer B is incorrect because an evaluation must be conducted whether the school believes it is needed or not. Answer C is incorrect because although it may be helpful to discuss strategies with the parent, this would need to be done in addition to the evaluation. Answer D is incorrect because the evaluation must be conducted even if the teachers do not think it is warranted.

79. D: Although parent input is valuable in the special education process, the school does not necessarily have to provide all of the services that a guardian requests. Answer A is incorrect because guardians must be provided a list of their rights. Answer B is incorrect because guardians must be contacted or provided consent before any of the changes to a student's services can be made. Answer C is incorrect because the input of guardians must be included at an IEP meeting.

80. D: In due process complaints, the school may be responsible for the legal fees of the stakeholder if the court decides they win the case. Answer A is incorrect because a complaint must be filed within two years of the action, not one. Answer B is incorrect because a decision can be challenged by the stakeholder if they lose the case. Answer C is incorrect because stakeholders can provide evidence, but it is not required.

81. B: James M. Baldwin used the term "mental deficiency" in 1901 and, in 1937, Tredgold referred to "a state of incomplete mental development." Therefore option A is incorrect.

The criterion that intellectual disabilities originates during the developmental period, defined as from birth to age 16, was used by Heber for the AAMD's 1961 definition. It does not appear in earlier definitions. Therefore option B is correct.

The association of intellectual disabilities with impaired adaptive behavior appears as early as 1937: In Tredgold's definition he states "...that the individual is incapable of adapting himself to the normal environment of his fellows..." Therefore option C is incorrect.

Contrary to Heber's 1961 AAMD definition, which states that intellectual disabilities originates in the developmental period, defined as from birth to age sixteen, or Grossman's 1973 AAMD definition, which extends the developmental period to age eighteen, Edgar A. Doll's 1941 definition includes as one of his six criteria that intellectual disabilities "obtains at maturity." Therefore option D is incorrect.

82. C: Parents at the elementary school level must be updated on their child's progress on the IEP goals each quarter with report cards. Answer A is incorrect because parents must be notified more frequently than once a year on the progress their child is making. Answer B is incorrect because weekly progress reports would be too frequent and not always provide the best data. Answer D is incorrect because being updated just at the beginning and end of the year is not sufficient enough.

83. D: The 1997 version of IDEA stated that there were two systems for early intervention. This was changed in 2004 to include just one system for all students from birth to age five. Answer A is incorrect because the 2004 version of the act established that students must have transition goals. Answer B is incorrect because the act also establishes that teachers must be considered highly qualified. Answer C is incorrect because alternative assessments started to be included in state accountability systems in 2004.

84. B: Students who are receiving accommodations through their 504 plan can be evaluated for special education services if their 504 accommodations are not meeting their educational needs. Answer A is incorrect because students who do not qualify for special education do not necessarily qualify for 504 accommodations. Answer C is incorrect because it is possible for students to have both a 504 plan and an Individual Education Plan. Answer D is incorrect because students can be evaluated for special education services even if they do not qualify for a 504 plan.

85. C: Typically, the special education teacher will collaborate with school counselors and administrators about what the best placement for students may be, but they aren't solely responsible for coming up with the class schedule. Answer A is incorrect because managing paraprofessionals is an important task for the special education teacher. Answer B is incorrect because scheduling IEP meetings with the parent is also an important task. Answer D is incorrect because it is important for the special education teacher to help support the general education teacher about ways to help students with IEPs.

86. D: It is the responsibility of the special education case manager to ensure that each student on his or her caseload is accessing accommodations and that general education teachers know how to implement them. Answer A is incorrect because it is not the responsibility of the case manager to make sure students do not fail. Answer B is incorrect because it is also not the responsibility of the case manager to make sure students are attending school. Answer C is incorrect because although the case manager will track the progress of students on their IEP goals, it is not their job to make sure they meet the goal.

87. A: School psychologists are trained to administer IQ tests to students. Although it is possible for the special education teacher to assist in this process, IQ tests are typically administered by the psychologist. Answer B is incorrect because achievement tests are most often administered by the special education teacher. Answer C is incorrect because progress monitoring is completed by the special education case manager. Answer D is incorrect because transition planning inventories are also administered by the special education teacher.

88. D: The audiologist is likely to deliver services to the hearing-impaired students. The SLP is likely to deliver services to both the students with hearing impairments and those with Down syndrome. The O&M specialist is likely to serve the visually impaired student. The OT is likely to serve the intellectually disabled and/or any students with poor fine motor control, common in this population. The PT [(A), (B), and (C)] would serve students with poor gross motor control, not identified here. Excluding testing as specified, the school psychologist and behavior specialist [(A), (B), and (C)] are less likely to serve this group as no emotional, social, or behavioral problems are identified.

89. B: It is important to get feedback from both the general education teacher and the student to try and understand what the student needs and how to proceed. This way, everyone is on the same page, and the best decision can be made. Answer A is incorrect because it is probably best to see if the issue can be resolved before an IEP meeting is called. Answer C is incorrect because a meeting with the principal likely will not solve the issue. Answer D is incorrect because although the input from the parents may be valuable, meeting with the teacher and student likely will resolve the issue more efficiently as they are the parties involved.

90. C: It is likely best to try and have this conversation in person with the parents as there may be something going on at home or elsewhere. Answer A is incorrect because calling the parents immediately may catch them off guard and they may think their son is in trouble. Answer B is incorrect because it is possible the behavior continues to worsen, and more issues arise if no action is taken. Answer D is incorrect because an IEP meeting likely isn't warranted until more information is discussed with the parents and student to see what might be going on.

91. D: If the IEP meeting is already scripted, it does not provide each of the stakeholders with an opportunity to provide input and share their side of the story. Answer A is incorrect because facilitated meetings are a great way to make everyone feel included and have a say. Answer B is incorrect because a slide show presentation can be more entertaining than simply reading from the IEP. Answer C is incorrect because a student-led meeting heavily includes the student and allows him or her to truly be the center of the meeting.

92. B: Meeting the student to get to know more about him and his background will provide more information so you have a better idea of how to meet his needs. Answer A is incorrect because simply reading his IEP will not give you as much personal information about who he is as a person. Answer C is incorrect because calling his parents might be helpful, but it is important to have a relationship with the student. Answer D is incorrect because knowing his history also will not help you with personal information.

93. C: Although each of these biases have the potential to cause negative relationships with groups of students and their families, not teaching students because of their disabilities can cause the most harm. Answer A is incorrect because over-identifying students because of their race is not the best practice but may not necessarily cause a negative relationship with the students simply because of this. Answer B is incorrect because over-teaching can sometimes show that a teacher cares and wants students to learn. Answer D is incorrect because although it may not be best practice to under-identify students because of socioeconomic status, it is likely that this scenario is rare.

94. A: The Behavior Rating Inventory test is used to identify behaviors that affect a student's performance in the classroom and includes executive functioning. Answer B is incorrect because the Cognitive Assessment System is a test that emphasizes cognition and a student's ability to use acquired knowledge. Answer C is incorrect because the Adaptive Behavior Inventory is used to identify which independent living skills a student may struggle with. Answer D is incorrect because the Test of Problem-Solving is used to assess students with communication needs.

95. C: Although each of these may be advantages, having students work together in small groups allows students to communicate with each other and work on social skills they would not get in a one-on-one situation. Answer A is incorrect because students will often copy what another student is saying rather than critically thinking for themselves. Answer B is incorrect because students may actually pay attention less when it is not their turn. Answer D is incorrect because students may be more likely to exhibit negative behavior when there are other students to talk to.

96. B: For a class such as math, which tends to be book heavy and involves a lot of the work using the textbook, the most beneficial strategy to use for this student would be an audio version of the textbook. This way, the student can listen to the problems instead of reading them. Answer A is incorrect because although a modified assignment length may be helpful, it may not be necessary if the student is completing the entire assignment. Answer C is incorrect because although preferential seating might be helpful, it likely will not have as much of an impact as having access to the audio book. Answer D is incorrect because although having extended time may also help, it may or may not be accessed based on the needs of the student.

97. C: To be eligible for special education services as a student with a visual impairment, one of the criteria is having a visual acuity of no better than 20/70 after correction in the better eye. Answer A is incorrect because, if a student has a vision and hearing loss that affects educational performance, he or she will instead be eligible for the deaf-blindness category. Answer B is incorrect because one of the criteria that would determine a student eligible is a field restriction of 20 degrees or less. Answer D is incorrect because a visual impairment that started after birth will be less likely to affect a student than an impairment from birth.

98. A: To assess Jasmine's behavioral patterns, it is best to record her behavior during random times when she may or may not know she is being observed. This will provide a true indication of her behavior and give results from different parts of her day and in different classes. Answer B is incorrect because if her behavior is recorded at the same time, she will catch on and change her behavior. Answer C is incorrect because although having her help may be beneficial, it may not always provide the most reliable results. Answer D is incorrect because it would be a difficult task for her teacher to record everything and some behavior might be missed.

99. D: Students who are placed in a general education setting with more students may have a high chance of exhibiting negative behaviors. This is especially the case for students who are new to the classroom and have a history of outbursts. Answer A is incorrect because students in an inclusion setting can still meet their IEP goals as they are being instructed in a general education setting. Answer B is incorrect because although the expectations may be higher than a special education classroom, it is a positive that the students are challenged. Answer C is incorrect because the more the staff talk and collaborate on the students, the more progress the students are likely to make.

100. B: One of the major advantages for students to complete an online class is that they can work at their own pace. A student like Albert, who struggles with reading comprehension, may have a hard time keeping up with the work in his regular class. Answer A is incorrect because even though the class is online, there is still a teacher involved to help facilitate and answer questions. Answer C is incorrect because there is not likely to be less work involved, although he can complete the work at his own pace. Answer D is incorrect because he will still have to do the work to pass the class, so he likely will have the same chance of passing.

How to Overcome Test Anxiety

Just the thought of taking a test is enough to make most people a little nervous. A test is an important event that can have a long-term impact on your future, so it's important to take it seriously and it's natural to feel anxious about performing well. But just because anxiety is normal, that doesn't mean that it's helpful in test taking, or that you should simply accept it as part of your life. Anxiety can have a variety of effects. These effects can be mild, like making you feel slightly nervous, or severe, like blocking your ability to focus or remember even a simple detail.

If you experience test anxiety—whether severe or mild—it's important to know how to beat it. To discover this, first you need to understand what causes test anxiety.

Causes of Test Anxiety

While we often think of anxiety as an uncontrollable emotional state, it can actually be caused by simple, practical things. One of the most common causes of test anxiety is that a person does not feel adequately prepared for their test. This feeling can be the result of many different issues such as poor study habits or lack of organization, but the most common culprit is time management. Starting to study too late, failing to organize your study time to cover all of the material, or being distracted while you study will mean that you're not well prepared for the test. This may lead to cramming the night before, which will cause you to be physically and mentally exhausted for the test. Poor time management also contributes to feelings of stress, fear, and hopelessness as you realize you are not well prepared but don't know what to do about it.

Other times, test anxiety is not related to your preparation for the test but comes from unresolved fear. This may be a past failure on a test, or poor performance on tests in general. It may come from comparing yourself to others who seem to be performing better or from the stress of living up to expectations. Anxiety may be driven by fears of the future—how failure on this test would affect your educational and career goals. These fears are often completely irrational, but they can still negatively impact your test performance.

Elements of Test Anxiety

As mentioned earlier, test anxiety is considered to be an emotional state, but it has physical and mental components as well. Sometimes you may not even realize that you are suffering from test anxiety until you notice the physical symptoms. These can include trembling hands, rapid heartbeat, sweating, nausea, and tense muscles. Extreme anxiety may lead to fainting or vomiting. Obviously, any of these symptoms can have a negative impact on testing. It is important to recognize them as soon as they begin to occur so that you can address the problem before it damages your performance.

The mental components of test anxiety include trouble focusing and inability to remember learned information. During a test, your mind is on high alert, which can help you recall information and stay focused for an extended period of time. However, anxiety interferes with your mind's natural processes, causing you to blank out, even on the questions you know well. The strain of testing during anxiety makes it difficult to stay focused, especially on a test that may take several hours. Extreme anxiety can take a huge mental toll, making it difficult not only to recall test information but even to understand the test questions or pull your thoughts together.

Effects of Test Anxiety

Test anxiety is like a disease—if left untreated, it will get progressively worse. Anxiety leads to poor performance, and this reinforces the feelings of fear and failure, which in turn lead to poor performances on subsequent tests. It can grow from a mild nervousness to a crippling condition. If allowed to progress, test anxiety can have a big impact on your schooling, and consequently on your future.

Test anxiety can spread to other parts of your life. Anxiety on tests can become anxiety in any stressful situation, and blanking on a test can turn into panicking in a job situation. But fortunately, you don't have to let anxiety rule your testing and determine your grades. There are a number of relatively simple steps you can take to move past anxiety and function normally on a test and in the rest of life.

Physical Steps for Beating Test Anxiety

While test anxiety is a serious problem, the good news is that it can be overcome. It doesn't have to control your ability to think and remember information. While it may take time, you can begin taking steps today to beat anxiety.

Just as your first hint that you may be struggling with anxiety comes from the physical symptoms, the first step to treating it is also physical. Rest is crucial for having a clear, strong mind. If you are tired, it is much easier to give in to anxiety. But if you establish good sleep habits, your body and mind will be ready to perform optimally, without the strain of exhaustion. Additionally, sleeping well helps you to retain information better, so you're more likely to recall the answers when you see the test questions.

Getting good sleep means more than going to bed on time. It's important to allow your brain time to relax. Take study breaks from time to time so it doesn't get overworked, and don't study right before bed. Take time to rest your mind before trying to rest your body, or you may find it difficult to fall asleep.

Along with sleep, other aspects of physical health are important in preparing for a test. Good nutrition is vital for good brain function. Sugary foods and drinks may give a burst of energy but this burst is followed by a crash, both physically and emotionally. Instead, fuel your body with protein and vitamin-rich foods.

Also, drink plenty of water. Dehydration can lead to headaches and exhaustion, especially if your brain is already under stress from the rigors of the test. Particularly if your test is a long one, drink water during the breaks. And if possible, take an energy-boosting snack to eat between sections.

Along with sleep and diet, a third important part of physical health is exercise. Maintaining a steady workout schedule is helpful, but even taking 5-minute study breaks to walk can help get your blood pumping faster and clear your head. Exercise also releases endorphins, which contribute to a positive feeling and can help combat test anxiety.

When you nurture your physical health, you are also contributing to your mental health. If your body is healthy, your mind is much more likely to be healthy as well. So take time to rest, nourish your body with healthy food and water, and get moving as much as possible. Taking these physical steps will make you stronger and more able to take the mental steps necessary to overcome test anxiety.

Mental Steps for Beating Test Anxiety

Working on the mental side of test anxiety can be more challenging, but as with the physical side, there are clear steps you can take to overcome it. As mentioned earlier, test anxiety often stems from lack of preparation, so the obvious solution is to prepare for the test. Effective studying may be the most important weapon you have for beating test anxiety, but you can and should employ several other mental tools to combat fear.

First, boost your confidence by reminding yourself of past success—tests or projects that you aced. If you're putting as much effort into preparing for this test as you did for those, there's no reason you should expect to fail here. Work hard to prepare; then trust your preparation.

Second, surround yourself with encouraging people. It can be helpful to find a study group, but be sure that the people you're around will encourage a positive attitude. If you spend time with others who are anxious or cynical, this will only contribute to your own anxiety. Look for others who are motivated to study hard from a desire to succeed, not from a fear of failure.

Third, reward yourself. A test is physically and mentally tiring, even without anxiety, and it can be helpful to have something to look forward to. Plan an activity following the test, regardless of the outcome, such as going to a movie or getting ice cream.

When you are taking the test, if you find yourself beginning to feel anxious, remind yourself that you know the material. Visualize successfully completing the test. Then take a few deep, relaxing breaths and return to it. Work through the questions carefully but with confidence, knowing that you are capable of succeeding.

Developing a healthy mental approach to test taking will also aid in other areas of life. Test anxiety affects more than just the actual test—it can be damaging to your mental health and even contribute to depression. It's important to beat test anxiety before it becomes a problem for more than testing.

Study Strategy

Being prepared for the test is necessary to combat anxiety, but what does being prepared look like? You may study for hours on end and still not feel prepared. What you need is a strategy for test prep. The next few pages outline our recommended steps to help you plan out and conquer the challenge of preparation.

Step 1: Scope Out the Test

Learn everything you can about the format (multiple choice, essay, etc.) and what will be on the test. Gather any study materials, course outlines, or sample exams that may be available. Not only will this help you to prepare, but knowing what to expect can help to alleviate test anxiety.

Step 2: Map Out the Material

Look through the textbook or study guide and make note of how many chapters or sections it has. Then divide these over the time you have. For example, if a book has 15 chapters and you have five days to study, you need to cover three chapters each day. Even better, if you have the time, leave an extra day at the end for overall review after you have gone through the material in depth.

If time is limited, you may need to prioritize the material. Look through it and make note of which sections you think you already have a good grasp on, and which need review. While you are studying, skim quickly through the familiar sections and take more time on the challenging parts.

Write out your plan so you don't get lost as you go. Having a written plan also helps you feel more in control of the study, so anxiety is less likely to arise from feeling overwhelmed at the amount to cover.

Step 3: Gather Your Tools

Decide what study method works best for you. Do you prefer to highlight in the book as you study and then go back over the highlighted portions? Or do you type out notes of the important information? Or is it helpful to make flashcards that you can carry with you? Assemble the pens, index cards, highlighters, post-it notes, and any other materials you may need so you won't be distracted by getting up to find things while you study.

If you're having a hard time retaining the information or organizing your notes, experiment with different methods. For example, try color-coding by subject with colored pens, highlighters, or post-it notes. If you learn better by hearing, try recording yourself reading your notes so you can listen while in the car, working out, or simply sitting at your desk. Ask a friend to quiz you from your flashcards, or try teaching someone the material to solidify it in your mind.

Step 4: Create Your Environment

It's important to avoid distractions while you study. This includes both the obvious distractions like visitors and the subtle distractions like an uncomfortable chair (or a too-comfortable couch that makes you want to fall asleep). Set up the best study environment possible: good lighting and a comfortable work area. If background music helps you focus, you may want to turn it on, but otherwise keep the room quiet. If you are using a computer to take notes, be sure you don't have any other windows open, especially applications like social media, games, or anything else that could distract you. Silence your phone and turn off notifications. Be sure to keep water close by so you stay hydrated while you study (but avoid unhealthy drinks and snacks).

Also, take into account the best time of day to study. Are you freshest first thing in the morning? Try to set aside some time then to work through the material. Is your mind clearer in the afternoon or evening? Schedule your study session then. Another method is to study at the same time of day that you will take the test, so that your brain gets used to working on the material at that time and will be ready to focus at test time.

Step 5: Study!

Once you have done all the study preparation, it's time to settle into the actual studying. Sit down, take a few moments to settle your mind so you can focus, and begin to follow your study plan. Don't give in to distractions or let yourself procrastinate. This is your time to prepare so you'll be ready to fearlessly approach the test. Make the most of the time and stay focused.

Of course, you don't want to burn out. If you study too long you may find that you're not retaining the information very well. Take regular study breaks. For example, taking five minutes out of every hour to walk briskly, breathing deeply and swinging your arms, can help your mind stay fresh.

As you get to the end of each chapter or section, it's a good idea to do a quick review. Remind yourself of what you learned and work on any difficult parts. When you feel that you've mastered the material, move on to the next part. At the end of your study session, briefly skim through your notes again.

But while review is helpful, cramming last minute is NOT. If at all possible, work ahead so that you won't need to fit all your study into the last day. Cramming overloads your brain with more information than it can process and retain, and your tired mind may struggle to recall even previously learned information when it is overwhelmed with last-minute study. Also, the urgent nature of cramming and the stress placed on your brain contribute to anxiety. You'll be more likely to go to the test feeling unprepared and having trouble thinking clearly.

So don't cram, and don't stay up late before the test, even just to review your notes at a leisurely pace. Your brain needs rest more than it needs to go over the information again. In fact, plan to finish your studies by noon or early afternoon the day before the test. Give your brain the rest of the day to relax or focus on other things, and get a good night's sleep. Then you will be fresh for the test and better able to recall what you've studied.

Step 6: Take a Practice Test

Many courses offer sample tests, either online or in the study materials. This is an excellent resource to check whether you have mastered the material, as well as to prepare for the test format and environment.

Check the test format ahead of time: the number of questions, the type (multiple choice, free response, etc.), and the time limit. Then create a plan for working through them. For example, if you have 30 minutes to take a 60-question test, your limit is 30 seconds per question. Spend less time on the questions you know well so that you can take more time on the difficult ones.

If you have time to take several practice tests, take the first one open book, with no time limit. Work through the questions at your own pace and make sure you fully understand them. Gradually work up to taking a test under test conditions: sit at a desk with all study materials put away and set a timer. Pace yourself to make sure you finish the test with time to spare and go back to check your answers if you have time.

After each test, check your answers. On the questions you missed, be sure you understand why you missed them. Did you misread the question (tests can use tricky wording)? Did you forget the information? Or was it something you hadn't learned? Go back and study any shaky areas that the practice tests reveal.

Taking these tests not only helps with your grade, but also aids in combating test anxiety. If you're already used to the test conditions, you're less likely to worry about it, and working through tests until you're scoring well gives you a confidence boost. Go through the practice tests until you feel comfortable, and then you can go into the test knowing that you're ready for it.

Test Tips

On test day, you should be confident, knowing that you've prepared well and are ready to answer the questions. But aside from preparation, there are several test day strategies you can employ to maximize your performance.

First, as stated before, get a good night's sleep the night before the test (and for several nights before that, if possible). Go into the test with a fresh, alert mind rather than staying up late to study.

Try not to change too much about your normal routine on the day of the test. It's important to eat a nutritious breakfast, but if you normally don't eat breakfast at all, consider eating just a protein bar. If you're a coffee drinker, go ahead and have your normal coffee. Just make sure you time it so that the caffeine doesn't wear off right in the middle of your test. Avoid sugary beverages, and drink enough water to stay hydrated but not so much that you need a restroom break 10 minutes into the test. If your test isn't first thing in the morning, consider going for a walk or doing a light workout before the test to get your blood flowing.

Allow yourself enough time to get ready, and leave for the test with plenty of time to spare so you won't have the anxiety of scrambling to arrive in time. Another reason to be early is to select a good seat. It's helpful to sit away from doors and windows, which can be distracting. Find a good seat, get out your supplies, and settle your mind before the test begins.

When the test begins, start by going over the instructions carefully, even if you already know what to expect. Make sure you avoid any careless mistakes by following the directions.

Then begin working through the questions, pacing yourself as you've practiced. If you're not sure on an answer, don't spend too much time on it, and don't let it shake your confidence. Either skip it and come back later, or eliminate as many wrong answers as possible and guess among the remaining ones. Don't dwell on these questions as you continue—put them out of your mind and focus on what lies ahead.

Be sure to read all of the answer choices, even if you're sure the first one is the right answer. Sometimes you'll find a better one if you keep reading. But don't second-guess yourself if you do immediately know the answer. Your gut instinct is usually right. Don't let test anxiety rob you of the information you know.

If you have time at the end of the test (and if the test format allows), go back and review your answers. Be cautious about changing any, since your first instinct tends to be correct, but make sure you didn't misread any of the questions or accidentally mark the wrong answer choice. Look over any you skipped and make an educated guess.

At the end, leave the test feeling confident. You've done your best, so don't waste time worrying about your performance or wishing you could change anything. Instead, celebrate the successful completion of this test. And finally, use this test to learn how to deal with anxiety even better next time.

Review Video: Test Anxiety
Visit mometrix.com/academy and enter code: 100340

Important Qualification

Not all anxiety is created equal. If your test anxiety is causing major issues in your life beyond the classroom or testing center, or if you are experiencing troubling physical symptoms related to your anxiety, it may be a sign of a serious physiological or psychological condition. If this sounds like your situation, we strongly encourage you to seek professional help.

Tell Us Your Story

We at Mometrix would like to extend our heartfelt thanks to you for letting us be a part of your journey. It is an honor to serve people from all walks of life, people like you, who are committed to building the best future they can for themselves.

We know that each person's situation is unique. But we also know that, whether you are a young student or a mother of four, you care about working to make your own life and the lives of those around you better.

That's why we want to hear your story.

We want to know why you're taking this test. We want to know about the trials you've gone through to get here. And we want to know about the successes you've experienced after taking and passing your test.

In addition to your story, which can be an inspiration both to us and to others, we value your feedback. We want to know both what you loved about our book and what you think we can improve on.

SCAN HERE

The team at Mometrix would be absolutely thrilled to hear from you! So please, send us an email at tellusyourstory@mometrix.com or visit us at mometrix.com/tellusyourstory.php and let's stay in touch.

Additional Bonus Material

Due to our efforts to try to keep this book to a manageable length, we've created a link that will give you access to all of your additional bonus material:

mometrix.com/bonus948/texesspedec12